Eastern and Western Traditions

THE COMPLETE WORKS OF SANGHARAKSHITA include all his previously published work, as well as talks, seminars, and writings published here for the first time. The collection represents the definitive edition of his life's work as Buddhist writer and teacher. For further details, including the contents of each volume, please turn to the 'Guide' on pp.765–73.

FOUNDATION

INDIA

THE WEST

COMMENTARY

MEMOIRS

POETRY AND THE ARTS

COMPLETE WORKS 13 **THE WEST**

Sangharakshita

Eastern and Western Traditions

EDITED BY VIDYADEVI

Windhorse Publications
17e Sturton Street
Cambridge
CB1 2SN
UK

info@windhorsepublications.com
www.windhorsepublications.com

Cover design by Dhammarati
Cover images: Back flap: Sangharakshita at Stonehenge, 1964, courtesy of Clear Vision Trust; front: *Satan Watching the Caresses of Adam and Eve* (Illustration to Milton's *Paradise Lost*), William Blake, 1808. Public domain.

Typesetting and layout by Ruth Rudd
Printed by Bell & Bain Ltd, Glasgow

British Library Cataloguing in Publication Data:
A catalogue record for this book is available from the British Library.

ISBN 978-1-911407-35-5 (hardback)
ISBN 978-1-911407-36-2 (paperback)

CONTENTS

LIST OF ILLUSTRATIONS

FOREWORD

In the 1960s westerners were particularly attracted to, indeed fascinated by, Zen, Tibetan Buddhism, and Tantra, with first Zen and then Tibetan teachers arriving in the West. In this exotic atmosphere, Sangharakshita gave the lectures from which the first three books in the volume originate, seeking to express the 'essence' of Zen, and we can say no less the 'essence' of Tibetan Buddhism and the 'essence' of the Tantra. However, even if many westerners were attracted to these Buddhist traditions, like it or not they were also the inheritors of two thousand years of Christianity. The English academic whose work impelled Sangharakshita to write *The FWBO and 'Protestant Buddhism': An Affirmation and a Protest* argued that the FWBO (the Friends of the Western Buddhist Order, later the Triratna Buddhist Community) founded by Sangharakshita had much in common with the Protestantism that grew out of the Reformation of the seventeenth century, in its reaction to the Church as embodied in Catholicism. This Sangharakshita vigorously denies – the 'protest' – while taking the opportunity to lay out no less vigorously a number of the principles and practices upon which the FWBO was in fact based – the 'affirmation'. A work of a very different nature, *From Genesis to the Diamond Sūtra*, while indicating some of the harm Sangharakshita regards Christianity as having done and making it clear why he finds himself unable to believe in or accept orthodox Christian doctrine, also expresses the author's wish to write about what he has personally appreciated of the influence of Christianity (which of course also has its origins in the East) on western culture.

Turning now to the first of the books in the volume, as a look at the chapter headings for *Tibetan Buddhism: an Introduction* demonstrates, in these lectures Sangharakshita surveyed his subject from several angles – historical, doctrinal, ecclesiastical, and symbolic – as well as introducing some of the Tantric practices which form the foundation of Buddhism in Tibet, using information gleaned and insights arising not only from his reading but also from his meetings with Tibetan lamas in Kalimpong in the 1950s and early 1960s, as recounted in *Precious Teachers* (*Complete Works*, Vol. 22) and elsewhere. However, it is the last chapter entitled 'The Future of Tibetan Buddhism' which may be of particular interest. At the beginning of this chapter, Sangharakshita asks whether Tibetan Buddhism has any future and gives the perhaps shocking answer: 'As far as we can see, it has no future.' If this prognosis seems unduly pessimistic, I invite you to turn to this chapter and read Sangharakshita's reasoning. He goes on to argue that perhaps in the future Buddhism will be stronger in the West than in the East, whilst at the same time asserting that 'it is important for us in the West to study, to practise, and if possible to preserve Tibetan Buddhism'. He expresses the view that westerners are interested in essence, not trappings, and that this applies to all the forms of Buddhism with which westerners have begun to become acquainted. Then he comes to the second fundamental question of this chapter, and, in a way, of this series of lectures: 'The main question we need to ask ourselves is: what can we learn from [Tibetan Buddhism]?' Not only, he argues, can one tradition be the key to understanding the whole Buddhist tradition, 'but we can also learn things which we may not learn from any other form of Buddhism, because Tibetan Buddhism is in many respects unique'. What we can learn from Tibetan Buddhism includes how to achieve a harmonious synthesis – described as 'rich and magnificent' – of all the different elements in the total Buddhist tradition. Sangharakshita's writings over more than seven decades, as well as the principles underpinning the Buddhist movement he founded in 1967, demonstrate how important he saw this synthesis as being.

Although originating in India, Tantric Buddhism was preserved for us most of all in Tibet, but *Creative Symbols of Tantric Buddhism* is a rather different book from the introduction to Tibetan Buddhism just discussed. Its purpose is well set out by Sangharakshita in his introduction: 'Tantric Buddhism is concerned not with theories or speculations, not with formal religiosity or external piety, but with the direct experience, in the depths of one's being, of what one truly and essentially is.' As he goes on to suggest, the more receptivity to the resonances of the words we can bring to our reading of the chapters in this book, and the more we can see in our mind's eye the pictures they conjure up, the more alive the symbols will become. This is because 'symbols ... are full of energy, and give birth to life, spiritual life, in us. They are by their very nature creative. The creative symbols of Tantric Buddhism are not just of historical interest.' This is important, indeed of the essence not just of the Tantra but of Buddhism itself, because 'the progressive transformation of psycho-spiritual energy is the central business of the spiritual life'. In order to benefit from Sangharakshita's survey of some of the symbols found in the Tantra we will not necessarily need to undertake the actual Tantric practices and rituals, although some of them are described, thanks to the *translation* of their meaning which Sangharakshita provides. For example, he explains the cremation ground as a willingness to enter into a 'crucial situation' which can be transformative for us, while the chapter on offerings and self-sacrifice introduces the topic of devotion and gratitude, as a counter to the common instinct these days to want to pull down, denigrate, and deflate. Furthermore, the element of animism found in Tantric Buddhism is taken as an encouragement to enter into relationship with the universe – 'If you want to love it, you have to see it as personal' – and this seems particularly important in these days of possibly impending ecological disaster.

In 1973, out of the many lecture series he had given in the preceding several years, Sangharakshita chose for his first book published under the auspices of the FWBO his 1965 series *The Essence of Zen*. This must partly have been because Zen was popular in the West, but the series also gave him the opportunity to do further important translation work from East to West. For instance, in the first of the five short chapters which make up this book, he addresses what he identifies as the three most common current western misunderstandings of Zen: firstly, considering that it is just intellectual, secondly, divorcing Zen from Buddhism, and thirdly, mistaking the finger for the moon, which is to say taking particular methods and teachings as ends in themselves rather than as so many pointers to the experience of Enlightenment.

In the spirit of the harmonious synthesis of all the different elements in the total Buddhist tradition which as we have seen he so admired in Tibetan Buddhism, he informed his listeners, and then through this book his readers, that 'despite the apparent differences, even mutual opposition (of different Buddhist schools), we should study and learn to appreciate them all, thus making ourselves acquainted, as far as possible, with the whole vast range of Buddhist thought and practice. Only in this way will it be possible for us to obtain a balanced picture of Buddhism. Otherwise, we might commit the mistake of identifying Buddhism with one or another of its expressions, maintaining that this, and this alone, was the true embodiment of the Buddha's teaching. Such a course would be unfortunate.'

It would be unfortunate not least because we would miss out on some of the particular features of the Zen schools of Buddhism which Sangharakshita draws out in *The Essence of Zen*. In particular he emphasizes that Zen is essentially concerned with the transmission of the living spirit of Buddhism which is made possible through the high level of spiritual communication existing between master and disciple, usually within the context of meditation and study. In his preface Sangharakshita informs us that it is very doubtful whether he would have ventured to speak on this subject at all if it were not for his regular contact, over several years whilst living in Kalimpong, with Mr Chen, an advanced practitioner both of Tantric Buddhism and of Chan (the Chinese form of Zen). At the time Mr Chen refused to act as a guru and accepted no disciples, but nevertheless Sangharakshita was subsequently to name him as one of his eight principal teachers.

Towards the end of *The Essence of Zen*, Sangharakshita asks us to take these five short lectures as a direct pointing to our mind: 'Take it as a talk about direct pointing to the mind, and you will miss the whole point.... What I have said should be taken ... as being itself a direct pointing to the mind.' So, when you read these chapters, see if you can hear Sangharakshita speaking. As Sangharakshita writes in his preface, he resisted the temptation to recast the talks in more literary form, writing that 'in the following pages I am still just talking.... I wonder if you can hear me?' Can you hear the mystery beyond the words, just as Mahākāśyapa understood when the Buddha held up a golden flower? As Sangharakshita says as he concludes these talks: 'Zen is simply a voice crying "Wake up! Wake up!"'

In 1991, in an English university journal, appeared an article entitled 'Protestant Buddhism? The Cultural Translation of Buddhism in England'. As Sangharakshita writes in his introduction to the fourth book to be found in this volume, *The FWBO and 'Protestant Buddhism': an Affirmation and a Protest,* the information given about the FWBO in his article by the young academic Philip Mellor was either so simplistic and selective as to give a quite misleading impression or simply erroneous. With Sangharakshita's encouragement Dharmachari Kulananda sent to the journal a response correcting a number of factual errors, but this was published alongside an immediate rebuttal from Mellor, who argued that Kulananda's response only showed that the FWBO 'appears hesitant to respond constructively to academic analyses stressing its relationship with contemporary trends in western modernity'. At this, Sangharakshita himself put pen to paper, producing a detailed critical commentary of Mellor's article, correcting facts and no less importantly challenging the reliability of his academic analysis.

Sangharakshita's motivation to write a reply was not primarily to clear up misunderstandings in academia – which to judge from Mellor's response to Kulananda might have proved impossible – and nor was it only to protect the reputation of the FWBO. His main concern was that western Buddhism as a whole should not take a 'Protestant' course, which would in effect make it into a 'secular humanism', reducing the Dharma to something purely rational and excluding any imaginative element. Since the publication of this book, on several occasions he has told his disciples that he regards this as one of his most important works, for the reason just given and also because he wanted to demonstrate to western Buddhists in general and his disciples in particular the need to answer critics intelligently and effectively. This was important because Mellor's article is not simply about misrepresentation but also about misunderstanding, and if Mellor can have these misunderstandings, or others like them, presumably so can others, whether academics or not.

As Nagabodhi wrote in his introduction to the original publication in 1992, 'It has to be said that this book is not for the squeamish.... Sangharakshita's concern is with the deeper issues, but if Mellor's treatment of his theme has dictated that an "adversarial" approach is the only way to join in, then so be it.' We should not underestimate the extent of Mellor's adversarial approach, even though he presents his argument with references supposedly demonstrating academic objectivity. As along with Sangharakshita we go through Mellor's text, he uncovers non sequiturs and misquotations, finds Mellor attributing to the FWBO views the exact opposite of those it actually holds and has always held, demonstrates Mellor's specious logic, and indeed finds that his misrepresentation is 'breathtaking' and 'cavalier'. Worst of all, perhaps, there seems to be a hidden agenda. (You will need to read the book to find out what this may be!)

Sangharakshita's polemical response reflects the fact that Mellor's article was itself a polemic, i.e. a strong attack on the then FWBO (now Triratna Buddhist Community). In this polemic – as often elsewhere in his writing – Sangharakshita often uses references from literature including the Bible, both Old and New Testament. This comes naturally and easily to him though the contemporary reader may well miss the references. (In the *Complete Works* the editors have where possible provided those references in endnotes.) A striking example is the thrice repeated refrain, 'But Mellor says ... and Mellor has a PhD in the problems of theory and method in the study of contemporary religion.' This ironic repetition, which some readers at first may feel is overdone, is inspired by Shakespeare's Mark Anthony in *Julius Caesar,* thrice repeating his response to Brutus, with increasing irony, for Brutus has just murdered the emperor and claims to have done so for good reason: 'For Brutus is an honourable man....'

However, we must not forget that *The FWBO and 'Protestant Buddhism'* is an Affirmation as well as a Protest. As Sangharakshita says in his introduction, he wanted to take advantage of an opportunity to clarify his position on certain topics. In response to the proposition that the FWBO represents a 'Protestant Buddhism', although the FWBO's critique of 'mainstream Christianity' represented by the Catholic Church is acknowledged, we also find a critique of 'liberal Protestantism's personalist understanding of religious significance', thereby distancing the FWBO from the very view which Mellor has attributed to it, the argument central to Mellor's thesis being that the FWBO embraces 'individual rather than collective values'. Sangharakshita's understanding of the relation between individual and collective values has a number of dimensions, and the opportunity to appreciate this is one of the several reasons why this book will repay careful study. For example, he argues in several places that moral decisions are indeed best left to individuals, but importantly only in the sense of the 'individual-in-relation-to-Buddhahood'.

Another reason this book is worth studying is that we find here important presentations of the Dharma and Sangharakshita's distinctive approach to it. Amongst the topics covered are a number of aspects of sexual ethics – the sexual relationship itself, abortion, homosexuality, and celibacy or chastity – and also the individual in relation to family, charismatic authority, and the thinking regarding the giving of Pāli and Sanskrit names to members of the Western Buddhist Order. Sangharakshita's response to Mellor also gives him an opportunity to explore what modernism is and is not in respect of contemporary Buddhism and to reject the belief that the new is by definition better than the old, especially as that belief finds expression in the sphere of religion. The work also includes a critical discussion of the scientific approach to Buddhism, and a useful and important exegesis in its own right of the role and radical nature of tradition.

As Sangharakshita writes in his preface to *From Genesis to the Diamond Sūtra: a Western Buddhist's encounters with Chrisitianity*, it had been his intention to write a full-length comparative study of Buddhism and Christianity. Having been unable to carry out this plan he decided in 2004, with the help of his friend Nityabandhu as amanuensis, to produce a work that would be largely autobiographical while also exploring some aspects of Christianity that were of interest to him: 'I wanted to take stock of my attitude to Christianity as it had impinged on my life and thought in the last eighty years.' Although, as he says, he wrote this book for his own satisfaction, he wanted also to share his experience with western Buddhists who, like him, had grown up within a Christian culture, as well as with Christians who might be interested in how he, as a western Buddhist, viewed their religion. By Christianity – which here he sometimes refers to as 'mainstream Christianity' – and 'the Church' he particularly means Roman Catholicism, this being the form of Christianity that has played a dominant part in the political and economic life of Western Europe until relatively recently, that is to say until the Reformation of the sixteenth century. This sets the scene for the fifth book in our volume. The book as a whole weaves together autobiographical material with reflections on Christianity from a western Buddhist perspective, and there is much of autobiographical interest here, especially the first chapter, entitled 'Early Memories', and the sixth chapter, 'Christian Ethics', and accounts of meetings and friendships with Christians at different times in his life.

While we are told, in no uncertain terms, what Sangharakshita does *not* believe – see for example the fourth chapter, 'The Apostles' Creed' – he finds much to appreciate, such as in Chapter 2, 'The Bible as Literature', Chapter 7, 'Saints and Mystics', and Chapter 9, the story of the monk Barlaam and the priest Josaphat – which, as he explains, includes a Christianized version of episodes from the life of the Buddha which found its way into Shakespeare's *The Merchant of Venice*. No less appreciative are Sangharakshita's recollections of visits to art galleries over many decades, with sometimes detailed descriptions of works of art depicting Christian mythology still vividly present to him in his mind's eye (all from memory, his sight having failed). To take but one example, reflecting in Chapter 8 ('Jesus') on Leonardo da Vinci's depiction of the Last Supper, which he visited in the refectory of Santa Maria delle Grazie, Milan, he writes, 'I find it difficult to believe that Leonardo drew the head from a model, however much he might have idealized the features. Leonardo must have sought – and found – that beauty and celestial grace in the depths of his own soul.' When I read this, I was reminded of Sangharakshita's discussion of the nature of symbolism in his introduction to *Creative Symbols of Tantric Buddhism*. A symbol, he informs us, is illuminated by some other, higher dimension of reality. We have to be receptive to the symbol: 'the symbolism is in the eye of the beholder'. It is only a symbol to the extent that you respond to it, feel for it. If the Buddha image were really a symbol for us, it would move us powerfully, and rouse and harness all our energies. So, reading the five books in this volume in this spirit, may our energies be aroused, so that the Dharma may flourish throughout the world, both East and West.

Mahamati
Great Malvern
July 2018

Tibetan Buddhism

AN INTRODUCTION

1
HOW BUDDHISM CAME TO TIBET

This is a story of special interest because of its sheer improbability. It is quite remarkable that Buddhism should have come from India to Tibet at all. We are accustomed to thinking of Tibet as a Buddhist country, perhaps *the* Buddhist country. But it wasn't always such. Before it actually happened, the chances that Buddhism might ever be transplanted from India to the Land of Snows must have appeared pretty remote.

India and Tibet may be very close as the crow flies, but they are in fact worlds apart. Between them there is a tremendous barrier: the Himalayas. This colossal mountain range extends roughly 2,000 miles, dividing India, on the southern side, from Tibet in the north. The two countries are therefore virtually cut off from each other. They are also divided climatically. India's climate is subtropical, characterized by blazing hot sunshine, torrential monsoon rains, and periods of drought. Tibet, on the other hand, at 12,000 feet above sea level, has clear skies, a bracing atmosphere, and temperatures that are often well below freezing point.

With different climates we find different ways of life. India was, and still is, a predominantly agricultural country. The land has been cultivated for centuries, and its people enjoy a settled, placid existence in thousands of little villages. But in Tibet the economy is mainly pastoral. People keep great flocks of sheep and herds of yaks, and follow a nomadic way of life, wandering all over the vast open spaces, living in tents and on horseback. Indians and Tibetans also belong to quite different ethnic groups. India is inhabited by a mixture of the predominantly Aryan peoples of the north and the Dravidians of the south, while the Tibetans belong to a sub-group of the Mongolian peoples which also includes the Burmese and the Newars of Nepal.

All these factors are reflected in the marked differences of temperament that exist between Indians and Tibetans. At the risk of over-generalizing, I would say that Indians tend to be rather mystical, in the broadest sense of the term. They are very aware of the presence of a higher spiritual world or transcendental dimension. If you happen to meet someone in India, say on a bus or train or simply walking along the road, you can very quickly strike up a conversation about things of a religious or mystical nature. This is the sort of language Indians understand, the sort of outlook they accept and, in a sense, take for granted. Where practical matters are concerned, they can sometimes be rather vague and uncomprehending, but speak to them in terms of ultimate reality and they will know at once what you are talking about.

The Tibetan character is quite different. In the West we like to think of Tibetans as mysterious, exotic, other-worldly people. We imagine that when they are not levitating or flying through the air they are busy opening their third eye. But in reality they are not like this at all. From my experience of living among the Tibetans of Kalimpong, I would say that there are no people on Earth more practical. They are hard-headed businessmen; even the monks know how to handle complex business transactions. And when it comes to practical tasks, even if they have not done something before they will study it, find out all about it, and puzzle out the secret of how to do it. Tibetans coming to India often make good motor mechanics; in fact they take well to anything of a mechanical nature. Whereas Indians can be rather mystical, with their heads in the clouds (the Sikhs are an exception to this), Tibetans tend to be very practical, with their feet firmly on the ground. Tibetans also have this practical, down-to-earth approach when it comes to the religious life, as we shall see in subsequent chapters.

Then again Indians, especially Hindus, are generally peaceable people. As individuals, at least, they don't like getting into a fight. In India a dispute in the street usually remains verbal. The disputants may scream at each other, they may dance around each other in a rage, and perhaps even go so far as to pull one another's hair, but they are very unlikely to come to blows. Tibetans, on the other hand, tend to be warlike and aggressive, even swashbuckling. In Kalimpong some of the refugees used to strut around as though they had conquered the place. Many of them wore short swords, and they would swagger along the road, shouldering any Indians who happened to get in their way roughly aside, sometimes sending them flying. People learned to be wary of the Tibetans, especially of the Khampas of eastern Tibet.

I used to teach English to Tibetan students in Kalimpong, and I sometimes gave them an exercise in which they had to complete a sentence like 'I ... my brother,' filling in the blank with a suitable verb. In nine cases out of ten they would come up with 'I *killed* my brother.' A Nepalese friend of mine, who was the police surgeon and worked in the local hospital, told me that every week he had to deal with at least two cases of stabbing from within the Tibetan community, which at that time numbered about 2,000. Occasionally the stabbings were fatal.

In my experience Tibetan Buddhists are thus quite a fierce people, quite rough at the edges, so to speak. Indians are rather more gentle and refined. Even those leading a materially simple rural existence are often more truly cultured than many westerners. Tibetans, by comparison, I found to be on the whole rather unpolished, though members of the Lhasa aristocracy could be very sophisticated indeed.

When Indian Buddhism came to Tibet, it therefore encountered a completely different culture and way of life. Of course, when the Buddha gained Enlightenment, he went beyond all distinctions of race and nationality. What he had reached, what he had realized, was something purely spiritual, something transcendental. Historically speaking, however, Buddhism is a product of markedly Indian origin, reflecting Indian modes of thought, Indian cultural attitudes and assumptions. For instance, when we read Indian Buddhist texts, especially the great Mahāyāna *sūtras*, we encounter the characteristically Indian tendency to exaggerate. If a story is being told, say about a woman who had so many children, the story might begin by saying that she had a dozen children; but then, not content to leave it at that, the author will go on to say that she had twenty children, or even fifty or a hundred. This kind of exaggeration is typically Indian.

In view of the vast differences between the Indian and Tibetan people, and the fact that after fifteen hundred years in India Buddhism possessed many typically Indian characteristics, one might have thought that Indian Buddhism was the last religion the Tibetans would choose to adopt. But, strange as it may seem, they did choose it. It took them, however, a very long time, a fact which is not always appreciated. It was not that one day someone went from India to Tibet and preached Buddhism, and then a few years later the Tibetans were all Buddhists. The Tibetans, especially the Tibetan nobles, put up considerable resistance, and the establishment of Buddhism as the religion of Tibet was a long and sometimes difficult process.

Perhaps we in the West can derive some comfort from this. We might think that things here are moving pretty slowly. Buddhism has been known in the West for about a century, yet we do not seem to have got very far with it. But in the case of Tibet it took very much longer. In fact the mere introduction of Buddhism into Tibet took approximately 500 years – much longer than it took, for example, to introduce Christianity into Britain. The 500-year period in question, from the seventh to the eleventh centuries CE, was a time of constant political upheaval. This was no coincidence, much of the upheaval being directly connected with the introduction of Buddhism.

In the East at that time – as in the West – the predominant form of government was absolute monarchy. (Throughout the East, wherever Buddhism spread, it did so under the patronage of powerful kings.) This is true of India, where Buddhism was given a great impetus by the emperor Aśoka, it is true of China and Japan, and it is also true of Tibet. The introduction of Buddhism into Tibet was associated particularly with four *dharmarājas*, or religious kings, and with the Buddhist monks and scholars, both Indian and Tibetan, with whom these kings collaborated. The first three of these kings ruled over the whole of Tibet, and the fourth was a king of western Tibet after the country had split up into a number of independent states.

The first religious king of Tibet was Songtsen Gampo, who ruled in the seventh century, and seems to have been a remarkable man. His earliest achievement consisted in continuing the political and administrative reforms initiated by his father. Until that time, Tibet had been split into a number of different feudal principalities, but Songtsen Gampo – and his father before him – gradually brought them all together, centralizing the administration and establishing Tibet as a single political unit with a military power that was greatly feared by all her neighbours.

This was itself a great achievement, but it was not enough for Songtsen Gampo. At that time Tibet was surrounded by a number of highly civilized states: Khotan to the north-west; Kashmir (then an independent kingdom) to the west; Nepal to the south-west (and beyond Nepal, of course, India); and the great empire of China, then under the Tang emperors, to the East. All these states were Buddhist in those days, and all of them had attained a very high level of civilization and culture. Songtsen Gampo could not help noticing this. He saw that although Tibet was politically united and in military terms a force to be reckoned with, where civilization and culture were concerned she very much lagged behind all her neighbours.

So Songtsen Gampo embarked on a programme of social reform and cultural development. First he redistributed the land that was in the possession of the nobles and great landowners, to give the common people a bigger and better share. At the same time he encouraged agriculture, trying to persuade the wandering nomadic tribes to settle down and cultivate the soil. He introduced weaving, masonry, and carpentry. He also decided to prohibit blood sports, a step which hints at the beginnings of his sympathy with Buddhism. Another old custom he prohibited was that of face-painting. Apparently Tibetans, men and women alike, had a custom of painting their faces bright red, but Songsten Gampo outlawed this, thinking it rather uncivilized.

In the course of his travels and military campaigns Songtsen Gampo had observed that the culture of the surrounding countries was very closely linked with Buddhism, and this led him to decide that Buddhism should be introduced in Tibet. He was supported in this mission by his two principal wives, the daughter of the king of Nepal, and the daughter of the emperor of China. What might have happened if the king's wives had followed religions other than Buddhism is an open question, but fortunately both were devout Buddhists. In Tibetan art they are often depicted on either side of Songtsen Gampo.

For his Nepalese wife, Songtsen Gampo built the Jokhang, literally 'Lord's House', in Lhasa. European writers often call it the 'Cathedral of Lhasa'. It is the oldest religious building in the Tibetan capital, and the one the Tibetans consider the most sacred. For his Chinese wife he built a smaller temple known as the Ramoche. In these temples were installed images of Akṣobhya and Śākyamuni brought from their respective countries by his wives. The temples were desecrated and demolished by the Chinese during the Cultural Revolution. Devout Tibetans later surreptitiously removed the battered heads of these two great images, which had been there for thirteen centuries, and brought them to India, where they presented them to the Dalai Lama. They were made of a sort of painted stucco, quite easily damaged, and I remember that many Indians were deeply affected by the photographs of them in the newspapers.

During the course of his reign, Songtsen Gampo built many other temples, the first Buddhist temples to be built in Tibet. He also sent a group of young Tibetans to study Buddhism in Kashmir, which in those days had a reputation for Buddhist learning. But such were the rigours of the climate (Kashmir being decidedly hot compared to Tibet, even though it is cool compared to the rest of India) that only one of the party survived to return to Tibet. This was the celebrated Thönmi Sambhota, who invented the Tibetan alphabet in around 632 CE. Before that time the Tibetans had no script and therefore, of course, no literature. Thönmi Sambhota devised the Tibetan alphabet on the basis of one of the Indian scripts, probably the Sharada script, with which he had become familiar during his sojourn in Kashmir, and the first Tibetan translations of Indian Buddhist scriptures began to be made. According to tradition, the very first text to be translated was the *Maṇi Kabum*. *Maṇi* here refers to the *oṃ maṇi padme hūṃ* mantra, and *kabum* means 100,000 words, the text being a sort of encyclopedia about the mantra – how it originated, what it means, how it should be recited, and so on. Paper and ink for printing were also introduced from China at this time, as well as painting and sculpture.

Thus Songtsen Gampo practically created Tibetan culture, at least in its rudimentary form. Furthermore, he caused a new code of civil law to be drafted, and he ensured that the ethical precepts of Buddhism were widely taught throughout his domain. But as yet there were no Buddhist monks or monasteries in Tibet. In fact, Songtsen Gampo's interest in Buddhism appears to have been more cultural than religious. This was inevitable, given the state of Tibet in those days. The spiritual life can develop only when a certain standard of culture – in the sense not of material improvement but of the refinement of one's whole way of life – has been attained. But, even with this very important reservation, Songtsen Gampo's work remains of the first importance. He laid the foundations of the Tibetan nation, of its culture and literature, and of Tibetan Buddhism itself – surely a very considerable achievement for one man. The Tibetans show their gratitude to Songtsen Gampo even to this day by regarding him as a manifestation of the great Bodhisattva of Compassion, Avalokiteśvara (the Dalai Lama being another, later, one).

Songtsen Gampo's work did not come to an end when he died. More and more texts were translated from Indian languages into Tibetan. Monks started coming from neighbouring countries, including refugees from Khotan, where Buddhists were being persecuted, and even put to the sword, by the Muslim hordes that were beginning to sweep across Central Asia. At the same time, there was growing opposition to Buddhism in Tibet itself amongst the followers of the indigenous religion, Bön. This opposition stemmed mainly from noble families who resented the growing power and prestige of the Buddhist monarchy, and also the Bön priests who no doubt felt that their livelihood was under threat.

The second religious king of Tibet, Trisong Detsen, lived in the eighth century. He was an ardent supporter of Buddhism, but during the earlier part of his reign he was greatly hampered by the hostility of the followers of Bön. He invited to Tibet the Indian scholar and teacher Śāntarakṣita, best known nowadays as the author of a great work of Mahāyāna Buddhist philosophy called the *Tattvasaṃgraha*. But unfortunately Śāntarakṣita's mission was not very successful. He visited several places, he spoke on Buddhism, he gave a number of lectures, but then apparently an epidemic broke out all over the country. This gave the Bönists the opportunity they had been waiting for. They said, 'You see what happens. In comes this Indian Buddhist teacher, and there is an epidemic! The demons are angry.' Śāntarakṣita could find no answer for this, and knew another approach was needed. He advised the king to invite to Tibet the great Indian master Padmasambhava, who was then living at Nalanda University near Bodh Gaya.

Padmasambhava is one of the most remarkable figures in the entire history of Buddhism. Not only was he a great scholar and an accomplished debater and philosopher; he was also a formidable yogi, a great meditator, and a mystic. He was a great master of the occult sciences, and according to tradition he was also a magician to be reckoned with. He spent only eighteen months in Tibet, but during that time he brought the Bön 'demons' under control. Tradition tells us that he incorporated the lot of them, willy-nilly, into the Tantric Buddhist pantheon, converting them into guardian deities of the Buddhist faith.

We should not dismiss stories of this kind as mere legendary accretions to the historical facts. The story has a profound psychological and spiritual significance. After all, what is Bön? What does it represent? Broadly speaking, it is the indigenous shamanistic religion of Tibet, and like all forms of shamanism it is very closely connected with the psyche of the people practising it. One may go so far as to say that the Bön deities or 'demons' are in a sense archetypes of the Tibetan collective unconscious. Thus their hostility to Buddhism, in the traditional account, can be said to represent the unconscious resistance of the Tibetan psyche to the higher and more spiritual ideals of Buddhism. The Tibetans could not take them in all at once. The Tibetan mind was, after all, very different from the Indian mind. It therefore put up resistance, and this is symbolized on the archetypal level by the resistance and hostility of the Bön deities who created the epidemic.

Śāntarakṣita was a very great man, but he had his limitations. As a scholar, a philosopher, he could appeal to the conscious mind of the Tibetans, but he did not have the resources to overcome their unconscious resistance to Buddhist ideals. Padmasambhava, on the other hand, was not just a great scholar, not just an eminent philosopher; he was also a yogi and mystic, which meant that he could break through to a deeper level and make contact with the forces operating within the Tibetan collective unconscious. He was able to incorporate the Bön deities and the forces they represented into the framework of Buddhism, and even to use the energy contained in these archetypes in the interests of the spiritual life.

The Bön demons having been 'converted', Padmasambhava and Śāntarakṣita together founded the first monastery in Tibet, Samye, in 779 CE. Built after the model of the famous Odantapuri Monastery in India, Samye was completed in the year 787 CE. Much of it was recently destroyed by the Chinese, but a film of it made by the Indian representative in Lhasa before the desecration shows that it was a very beautiful place, reminiscent of what the great ancient Indian monastic universities must have looked like in their heyday. Śāntarakṣita and Padmasambhava also ordained seven Tibetans as monks, thus founding the Tibetan monastic sangha.

Padmasambhava left a permanent mark on Tibetan Buddhism, through the sheer force of his personality. Although he only stayed in Tibet for about eighteen months, the Tibetan accounts of his visit usually make out that it lasted for thirty-five years, presumably because he created such an impact in those eighteen months that it was as though he had been there for thirty-five years. He is traditionally regarded as the founder of the Nyingma school, but he is greatly revered by the followers of all sects and schools of Tibetan Buddhism. If you go into practically any Tibetan Buddhist temple you will see an image or picture of the great guru Padmasambhava.

It is a very distinctive image, so much so that one can readily believe it represents him as he appeared in life, because the details are always the same. He is a tall well-built Indian, in the prime of life, with the faintly Mongoloid features characteristic of the people of East Bengal. He has a drooping moustache and a little beard, and a hint of ferocity in his expression. He is dressed in princely robes and wears a lotus cap with a vulture's feather on the top. Sometimes he carries a skull-cup filled with blood, sometimes a dagger, and sometimes the *dorje*, the diamond-thunderbolt. In the crook of his arm is a staff surmounted by three skulls (the *khaṭvāṅga*). The images convey an impression of a remarkable figure, a supremely lively, virile, active, and powerful person. You can't mistake Padmasambhava for anyone else.

Another highly significant event during Trisong Detsen's reign was what western scholars usually call the 'Council of Lhasa', although it was in fact more of a debate than a council, and it took place at Samye. The debate was between Kamalaśīla, one of Śāntarakṣita's Indian disciples, and a Chinese monk who had turned up in Tibet and was preaching Chan (the Chinese forerunner of Japanese Zen) to the disapproval of some Tibetan Buddhists. So in 792 CE a discussion was arranged between Kamalaśīla and the Chan monk. We still have detailed records of this event,[1] and the chief point of contention, apparently, was over the question of whether Enlightenment came gradually, little by little, or occurred all at once, in a great rush. Following the general Indian tradition, the Indian scholar held that it came gradually, step by step, by following the Eightfold Path, practising the ten *pāramitās*, and so on; while the Chinese monk argued that it happened all at once. The debate was adjudicated by King Trisong Detsen, and he decided in favour of Kamalaśīla. However, those who have studied the records believe that the Chinese Chan master did pretty well too. Looking at it quite objectively and impartially, one might say that the point at issue between them is really a distinction without a difference. One does not attain Enlightenment either slowly or quickly; ultimately the question of time does not come into it at all. But the king said that Kamalaśīla had won, and that was that.

Trisong Detsen further decreed that from then on Tibetan Buddhists should follow the Sarvāstivāda school (one of the main Hīnayāna schools) with respect to *vinaya* or religious discipline, the Mādhyamaka and Yogācāra schools of the Mahāyāna for their philosophy and metaphysics, and the Tantra, the Vajrayāna, as far as meditation was concerned. In this way a synthesis of the three *yānas* was established. These three aspects of practice were also conceived of as constituting successive stages of the spiritual path. First you follow Sarvāstivāda discipline, then you study Mādhyamaka and Yogācāra philosophy, and then you practise Tantric meditation; in this way your spiritual life is complete. Thus the reign of Trisong Detsen saw three main developments: interest in Buddhism shifted from the cultural to the religious; the monastic order was established; and the *triyāna* character of Tibetan Buddhism was determined.

The third religious king of Tibet was Ralpacan, who reigned in the ninth century. He was an even more ardent Buddhist than Trisong Detsen, and did a great deal for the propagation of Buddhism. He established more temples and monasteries, he encouraged Buddhist arts and crafts, and perhaps most important of all, he set up a permanent commission for the translation of the scriptures. This meant that you could not just learn Sanskrit if you felt like it and translate a Buddhist text into Tibetan; you had to get permission from this commission, which laid down rules of translation. It compiled a glossary (which still exists) of Buddhist terms in Sanskrit and Tibetan, and in this way the translation of Buddhist scriptures into Tibetan was made regular and uniform.[2] For example, the commission decided that the Sanskrit word 'Dharma' was to be translated *chos*, and nobody was allowed to translate it any other way. This decision meant that the Tibetans did not come up against the sort of obstacle which English-speaking students of Buddhism have to deal with. When you read *chos* in a Tibetan text you know that it means 'Dharma'; but in English translations Dharma is sometimes translated as 'Law', sometimes as 'Doctrine', sometimes as 'Truth', sometimes as 'Norm'. Beginners hardly know where they are, because the same word is rendered in so many different ways by different translators. By compiling a glossary which everyone had to follow, the Tibetan commission prevented this sort of confusion, thus making way for the effective study of Buddhism.

Unfortunately, in the midst of these advances, King Ralpacan was assassinated as a result of a Bön conspiracy, and was succeeded, in 836 CE, by his brother Langdarma, who was completely opposed to Buddhism. A period of persecution ensued. Buddhist temples and monasteries were demolished, monks were killed or driven out, scriptures were destroyed, and the result was that Buddhism practically perished in Tibet, especially in central Tibet, for nearly two centuries. Only a few faithful followers kept the flame of the Dharma alive in those dark days.

It was a time of great political upheaval, and eventually the country broke up into a number of different states. It was also a period of religious confusion. Hindu Tantric teachers infiltrated Tibet from Kashmir with some very questionable practices that began to give the Tantra a bad name. Even Buddhism itself, as much of it as had survived in Tibet, became more and more debased and corrupt, and this was a source of serious concern to a number of earnest Buddhists. When things quietened down a little they decided, under the protection of the fourth religious king, Yeshe-Ö, to invite to Tibet the great teacher Atīśa from Vikramaśīla, another of the great monastic universities of north-eastern India.

Yeshe-Ö was king of western Tibet in the eleventh century. Buddhism had fared rather better here during the period of persecution, and Yeshe-Ö did much, within the boundaries of his own kingdom, to revive and propagate it. He even took the step of becoming a monk himself. His fortunes then took an even more dramatic turn. Towards the end of his life he went on an expedition to collect from his subjects the huge quantity of gold needed to fetch Atīśa from India. But in the course of his journey he was captured by a neighbouring Muslim king who gave him an ultimatum. He should either become a Muslim or be ransomed for his own weight in gold.

It was, of course, out of the question for Yeshe-Ö to become a Muslim. But where was the ransom to come from? The king's nephew was very devoted to him and resolved to collect as much gold as he possibly could, but even in a gold-bearing country like Tibet it's not easy to collect the weight of a man in gold. Over the months, over the years, he gradually amassed a large quantity. But when he finally visited the king in the dungeon where he had been kept all those years, he found that he had only enough gold to weigh against his uncle's body, not against his head as well. So he said 'What shall I do? Shall I make a last effort to get more gold?' But the king said, 'I'm a very old man, and I have not yet had the opportunity to sacrifice my life for the Dharma. Don't bother about me any more. Don't give the gold to my captors. Use it instead to bring Atīśa to Tibet.' So it was what was done, and when the Muslim king realized that no gold was going to be forthcoming, Yeshe-Ö was murdered.

So Atīśa, the greatest Buddhist teacher in India at that time, came to Tibet, and stayed there for twelve years, until his death. He worked hard and accomplished a great deal. He reformed the monastic discipline, he purified the practice of the Tantra, he laid the foundations for the Kadam school, and he wrote a number of works for the spiritual guidance of the Tibetans. Largely as a result of Atīśa's influence, there ensued a tremendous revival of Buddhism in Tibet. Before the end of the eleventh century Marpa and Milarepa had initiated the Kagyu lineage, and Könchok Gyalpo had founded the Sakya school. After so many struggles, ups and downs, reverses and successes, Buddhism was at last (by the time of the Norman conquest in England) finally established in Tibet. From then onwards it was never seriously challenged as the dominant religion until the invasion in the 1950s by communist China.

2
THE SCHOOLS OF TIBETAN BUDDHISM

Tibetan Buddhism is divided, broadly speaking, into four major schools, but as the term 'school' could be misleading we need to be clear about what it means in this context. I have chosen to use the word 'school' in preference to 'sect', which has a rather negative connotation. We might equally speak of the four major 'traditions' of Tibetan Buddhism. None of these English words, however, is completely satisfactory. We usually think of the sects or schools of any religion as being mutually exclusive in membership and doctrine; if you belong to one, you cannot belong to another, and what one of them teaches may even contradict the teaching of another. But it is not like that in Buddhism, not in Tibetan Buddhism, nor in Indian Buddhism, which provided the pattern for the Tibetan tradition.

To trace the rise and fall, the development and the flowering, of the different schools of the Indian Buddhist tradition is very difficult. The lines of transmission continually overlap and flow into one another, so that you can never identify any particular school very clearly or definitively. It keeps shading off into another school – or even into several. In the western religious context we are accustomed to sharp divisions. If we look at the history of the Christian churches down the centuries, we can say quite definitely that someone was either, say, Roman Catholic or Methodist or Baptist. These are all clear-cut divisions. But Indian Buddhism is not sectarian. Schools exist, but they are not very sharply defined, so that in the case of certain great teachers, they cannot be definitely identified with one particular school more than with another. There is a dispute, for example, as to whether Maitreyanātha, the great author of the Five Treatises, was a Mādhyamika or a Yogācārin. It is very difficult to say, because his works strike such a beautiful balance between these two viewpoints.

Tibetan Buddhism follows this Indian non-sectarian pattern. So if we ask ourselves what is meant by a 'school' of Tibetan Buddhism, all we can say is that it is a particular lineage of teachers and disciples. A certain teacher teaches Buddhism to his disciples, they teach their disciples, and so on. This succession from master to pupils, who become masters in their turn and teach their own pupils, is what we call the school. The line of transmission may have its own angle on the Dharma, it may stress a particular aspect of the doctrine or a particular practice, but the emphasis is no more than an emphasis. Rarely, if ever, is it exclusive.

Sometimes a certain line of teachers and pupils may be associated with a particular monastery. This is usually quite fortuitous; the teacher happens to live in a certain monastery to which his disciples come, and when the original teacher dies his pupils stay on and teach there. Thus the monastery comes to be associated with a certain line of transmission and may become the 'headquarters' of that school.

Sometimes too a certain school, or line of teachers, may be associated with a particular group of texts. The Buddhist scriptures are voluminous, and it is not easy – indeed not possible – for one person to study them all even in a cursory manner. We therefore find in the history of Buddhism a sort of division of labour whereby a particular line of teachers and disciples concentrates on the study, the explication, and even the propagation, of a specific group of texts. Again, this is one of the ways in which a school arises. It is as if a particular group of Christians were to take up, say, the study of St John's Gospel and were to concentrate on studying, teaching, and writing commentaries only on that text, thus becoming a school of teachers and pupils devoted exclusively to it – though without detriment to their respect for the rest of the Bible. This has never happened in the case of Christianity, but it is the sort of thing that happens very often in Buddhism. Chinese Buddhist schools, especially, tend to be associated with a particular scriptural text or group of texts; the Tiantai school, for instance, concentrates on the *Saddharma Puṇḍarīka*, the '*Sūtra* of the White Lotus of the Good Law'.

Then again, schools sometimes arise because a certain line of teachers and pupils is associated with a particular type of spiritual practice, especially a particular type of meditation. The teacher has practised a certain kind of meditation, he teaches it to his pupils, and in this way a line is established which may become the nucleus of a school.

The birth of a school may involve several such factors combined together. Over time, each school assumes a more and more distinctive character, but without ever becoming exclusive. In keeping with the tolerant spirit of Buddhism, no school of Tibetan Buddhism claims to teach the one true version of the Dharma. Differences are recognized, they are not glossed over, but no school would go so far as to maintain that it had a monopoly of Buddhist truth.

In chronological order, the four major schools of Tibetan Buddhism are: the Nyingma school, the Kagyu school, the Sakya school, and the Gelug school. The first three are known as the old schools, and the Gelug is called the new school. Sometimes the first three are called the unreformed schools and the Gelug the reformed school, but some Tibetan Buddhists contend that this distinction is not quite fair. I once discussed this with a very eminent Nyingma lama. I asked him, 'What is the basis for this classification? How is it that you and the Kagyupas and Sakyapas are called unreformed whereas the Gelugpas are known as reformed?' (The suffix *-pa* means simply 'man' or 'person'.) He just smiled and said, 'We didn't need to be reformed.'

Western scholars tend to regard the three old schools as unreformed much as they regard the Roman Catholic Church as unreformed compared to the Protestant churches, but this analogy is not very helpful. In fact, the major difference between them is that the three old schools are of directly Indian origin, having been founded either by Indians or by Tibetans who had studied in India. But the Gelug school, the new school, is indigenous in the sense that Tsongkhapa, its founder, never went outside Tibet. The school which he founded is of purely Tibetan origin.

Before we look at the four schools individually, we should note some of their common characteristics. Firstly, the Buddhism of all these schools is *triyāna* in character. To understand this term, one needs to understand something of the history of Indian Buddhism. Buddhism lasted for about 1,500 years in India, from about 500 BCE to 1000 CE, and passed through three clearly marked stages during each of which particular aspects were predominant.

The first stage, which lasted for some 500 years, was marked by a predominantly ethical and psychological emphasis in the way the Dharma was expounded. There was a great deal of close study and analysis of the mind, especially in connection with meditation and higher states of consciousness. There was also a strong emphasis on ethical discipline and monastic rules. This first stage in the development of Indian Buddhism is therefore often described as the ethico-psychological phase.

The second stage developed and emphasized two additional elements: the metaphysical and the devotional. There was no rejection of the ethical and psychological, but while that tradition was continued, the nature of reality was explored more deeply in conceptual terms. At the same time much more stress was placed on the importance of the devotional element in Buddhism, the importance of the worship of the Buddhas and bodhisattvas and of the emotions of reverence, love, and respect. This metaphysical-devotional phase in the development of Indian Buddhism also lasted about 500 years.

During the third stage, from approximately 500 CE to 1000 CE, the ethico-psychological and the metaphysical-devotional traditions were continued, but the emphasis again shifted. It came to be placed more and more on the performance of ritual acts and procedures with certain archetypal meanings and values, and also on what we can only describe as 'esoteric meditation'. This is not ordinary concentration of mind, but advanced meditation which may be practised only under the personal guidance of a guru after the proper initiation or empowerment, about which more is said in Chapter 7.

In traditional Buddhist language each of these three stages of development is called a *yāna*, which means 'path' or 'way', and is also sometimes translated as 'vehicle', in the sense of a vehicle for spiritual practice and progress. So the Sanskrit term *triyāna* refers to these three phases of Indian Buddhism: the Hīnayāna or 'Little Way' (the ethico-psychological), the Mahāyāna or 'Great Way' (the metaphysical-devotional), and the Vajrayāna or 'Adamantine Way' (the ritualistic-yogic). From the time of Trisong Detsen the Buddhism of all schools was of this *triyāna* character.

So although Tibetan Buddhism is described as a branch of the Mahāyāna, this is not really accurate. All its schools follow the Hīnayāna in respect both of monastic discipline and organization, as well as all the basic teachings such as the Four Noble Truths, the Noble Eightfold Path, and the twelve links of conditioned co-production. All these teachings in Tibetan Buddhism are derived from the first, or Hīnayāna, phase of Indian Buddhism, especially in its Sarvāstivādin form. As regards philosophy, all Tibetan schools follow the Mahāyāna, especially the two great traditions of Indian Buddhist thought, the Mādhyamaka, the teaching of the middle way between extremes, and the Yogācāra, the teaching of yoga (in the sense of meditation). Also from the Mahāyāna comes Tibetan Buddhism's overall spiritual ideal, that of the bodhisattva. And its ritual and its esoteric meditation are taken from the Vajrayāna or Tantra. In this way, all the schools of Tibetan Buddhism are composite in character.

Furthermore, Tibetan Buddhism regards the three *yānas* not just as three successive stages in the historical development of Buddhism, but as constituting successive stages of the spiritual path for each individual Buddhist. This idea is especially associated with Atīśa, who went from India to Tibet and taught there in the eleventh century. Though a late development in Indian Buddhism, it plays a prominent part in the structure of all schools of Tibetan Buddhism.

Hence we cannot distinguish schools of Tibetan Buddhism as being either Tantric or non-Tantric, as some early western writers on Tibetan Buddhism tried to do. All schools accept this threefold structure both in terms of the historical development of Buddhism and within the spiritual life of the individual. All accept all three *yānas*, and all regard the Tantra as the highest flowering, the culmination, of Buddhism. In the West the Tantra has been widely misunderstood and is often thought rather shocking. But for Tibetan Buddhists the Tantra represents the highest and most sacred stage in the development of Buddhism.

The second characteristic common to all Tibetan Buddhist schools is that they accept the same scriptures as their canonical basis – though, as we shall see, the Nyingmapas have certain extra texts. These scriptures comprise the Kangyur, which is in 100, or in some editions 108, xylograph volumes, and the Tengyur, which is in 225 volumes. The Kangyur comprises translations into Tibetan of the *sūtras* and tantras, in other words all those works which are traditionally believed to be the utterance of the Buddha himself or of one of his Enlightened disciples speaking under his inspiration and guidance. These include texts such as the Perfection of Wisdom literature, the *Saddharma Puṇḍarīka*, and the *Laṅkāvatāra*, in Tibetan translation. The Tengyur consists of translations of commentaries and other expository works by the great Indian Buddhist sages and philosophers – Nāgārjuna, Dharmakīrti, Dignāga, and others.

A volume of one of these texts consists, like all Tibetan books, of oblong pages of tough hand-made paper, usually made from bamboo and very thick and crisp; they make quite a sound as you turn them over. The pages are stacked between wooden covers, not bound together but loose, and you just turn them over one by one as you read them. They are quite massive, so that to speak of a 'small Tibetan library' would be something of a contradiction in terms. Usually libraries contain hundreds of these enormous and heavy volumes. Once when I was studying a Tibetan painting of the wheel of life, I noticed that the realm which we would call hell – that is, the realm of torment and punishment – showed people being crushed by these enormous volumes of the sacred texts. (When I asked a Tibetan friend what this meant, he said that these were people who had not shown respect for the scriptures.)

The third common characteristic of all schools is that those of their followers who happen to be monks all follow the same *vinaya*, the same pattern of monastic life and observance. Thus the four schools have a lot in common; in fact, the similarities are greater than the differences. Nevertheless differences do exist, each school having distinctive features which are of great significance.

THE NYINGMA SCHOOL

The name Nyingma means 'old school', and it is so called because it follows the old translations of the tantras, those which were made before the time of King Ralpacan. It's rather as though there were in this country a Christian church which insisted on following only the Authorized Version of the Bible, ignoring the Revised Version and other modern translations.

The Nyingmapas regard the great Indian teacher Padmasambhava, the Lotus-Born One, as their founder, and such is their respect for him and devotion to him that they sometimes refer to him as the second Buddha. According to the Nyingma tradition, Padmasambhava has eight principal forms in which he manifests in eight different regions of the world, and Śākyamuni, the historical Buddha, is regarded as being simply one of these.

You can see this emphasis in Nyingma temples. These are usually three-storeyed. As you enter, you find on the ground floor an enormous image, usually many times larger than life, of the great guru Padmasambhava. He is dressed in royal robes with the lotus cap, seated with the *khaṭvāṅga* in the crook of his arm, a skull-cup containing blood or nectar in one hand, and a *vajra* or diamond-thunderbolt in the other, and with his characteristic 'wrathfully smiling' expression. Usually images of his two consorts, the Indian princess Mandāravā and the Tibetan yoginī Yeshe Tsogyal, are placed on either side of him. All around there are different frescoes and images, and you generally find Gautama the Buddha in a corner somewhere, a very minor figure in this pantheon. For the Nyingmapas, Padmasambhava is everything. He has become the embodiment of the ideal of Buddhahood, more so than even Śākyamuni himself.

By all the accounts that have come down to us, Padmasambhava was a many-sided character. He was a brilliant scholar and dialectician, and often worsted the Brahmin scholars in debate. He was a respected sage and teacher, a prolific author, and also a renowned yogi and ascetic, spending much of his time in meditation. Furthermore he was a magician. According to legend he could perform all sorts of wonderful feats. He was, it would seem, one of the greatest masters of the occult that the world has ever seen. And according to some accounts he was also an accomplished dancer. In Tibet he is always referred to as Guru Rimpoche, which means 'the greatly precious teacher', rather than as Padmasambhava, it being considered disrespectful to use someone's personal name.

The Nyingma tradition reflects the many-sidedness of its legendary founder, and in my own opinion, after considerable contact with this school, I would say that it is the richest form of Tibetan Buddhism. It is therefore very difficult to generalize about it. Nyingma teaching of course accepts the *triyāna* framework, but it is a distinctive feature of this tradition that it subdivides the three *yānas* into nine, a division which is the basis of that system of practice.

First in this enumeration is the *śrāvakayāna*, the path of the disciple. *Śrāvaka* or disciple here means someone who does not find out the Truth by himself but hears it from an Enlightened teacher, a Buddha, and then directs his efforts towards his own individual emancipation. So while he (or she) makes a genuine effort to attain liberation from *saṃsāra*, that effort is made solely for his own benefit, no thought being given to the spiritual welfare of others.

Secondly, there is the *yāna* of the *pratyekabuddha*. *Pratyeka* means private or solitary, so the *pratyekabuddha* is one who finds out the Truth by his own efforts. He has no teacher, but also no disciples because he does not care to pass on what he has discovered, being concerned only with his own spiritual emancipation. The *pratyekabuddha*, like the *śrāvaka*, is a kind of spiritual individualist.

The third *yāna* is the *bodhisattvayāna*. The bodhisattva has a teacher and also aspires to have disciples, because the aim of the bodhisattva is to gain Enlightenment not just for his or her own sake but for the benefit of all living beings. He makes the effort to develop spiritually so that he can help and guide other beings; and he does this by practising the six (or ten) *pāramitās* or perfect virtues. Thus the *bodhisattvayāna* is the path of unmitigated spiritual altruism.

Fourthly, there is the *kriyāyoga tantrayāna*. *Kriyā* literally means 'ritual', and this *yāna* involves a certain amount of external symbolical ritual together with repetition of the mantra and visualization of a particular Buddha (this is described in more detail in Chapter 7). Fifthly, there is the *ubhayayoga tantrayāna*. *Ubhaya* means 'both sides' or 'equally', so this is the *yāna* in which ritual and meditation are practised equally. The sixth *yāna* is called the *yoga tantrayāna* and comprises various practices for developing the union of wisdom and compassion, so that neither exceeds the other. These second three *yānas* are collectively called the 'Exoteric Tantra' or the Mantrayāna.

The last three *yānas* of the Nyingmapas' ninefold scheme comprise the Vajrayāna proper, the Esoteric or 'Inner' Tantra. The seventh is the *mahāyogayāna*, consisting mainly of the practices known as the 'growing' yoga and the 'perfect' yoga (which will be explained later). The eighth is the *anuyogayāna*, which comprises all meditation exercises connected with the control of the breath, the nervous system and psychic centres, and sexual energy. Its aim is the sublimation of all the different gross and subtle forces of the personality of the individual in the direction of Enlightenment. Ninthly, there is the *atiyogayāna*. This is the direct practice and realization of the highest truth without any intermediaries at all, and corresponds very roughly to Chan or Zen in the fullest sense. There are several different traditions of *atiyogayāna* practice, the most important being *dzogchen* or the 'Great Perfection'. The Nyingmapas maintain special monasteries for this practice.

The way in which the three *yānas* are divided into nine is very significant. The first two *yānas* are seen as Hīnayāna, the third comprises the Mahāyāna, and the remaining six cover the Vajrayāna. This reflects the emphasis of the Nyingma school which, while it accepts the *triyāna*, in practice depends almost entirely on the Vajrayāna or Tantra. Generalizing broadly, when you get a Tantric initiation in the Nyingma tradition, they start off by giving you the Three Refuges and the Five Precepts, and this represents your practice of the Hīnayāna. Next you take the bodhisattva vow, which represents your practice of the Mahāyāna. All this usually only takes a few minutes, and then the rest of the initiation is concerned entirely with the Vajrayāna. The whole emphasis of Nyingma practice is on the Vajrayāna; the Hīnayāna and Mahāyāna are studied and practised to a much lesser degree.

The Nyingmapas accept the same scriptures as the other schools, the Kangyur and the Tengyur, but they also have a collection of what they call the Nyingma tantras. These consist of about 300 Tantric texts which the other schools regard as uncanonical, as not really given out by the Buddha. Western scholars used to think that these were forgeries, that they had been written by Tibetans, and that there were no Sanskrit originals as alleged. But Sanskrit originals of some of the Nyingma tantras have been discovered quite recently in Nepal, so it would seem that at least some of them are genuinely canonical.

The Nyingmapas also have a collection of sixty-four volumes of texts known as the *rinchen terma*, which they consider extremely important. These are the so-called 'concealed scriptures' – *rinchen* meaning a 'great treasure', and *terma* 'what is taken out'. According to legend they were written by Padmasambhava during his visit to Tibet. But then – so the legend goes – he realized that the Tibetans were not ready for these particular teachings, so he hid them in different spots, in caves and under stones, and they are supposed to have been discovered gradually over the centuries. Not surprisingly, Western scholars tend to regard these texts as being simply forgeries. However, the *rinchen terma* contains some very important material which we cannot so easily dismiss. For instance, one of these taken-out texts is the *Bardo Thödol* or *Tibetan Book of the Dead*, a very sublime and important document indeed. It is certainly not the work of an ordinary forger. The author of it would have to have been a very great spiritual teacher, whether Padmasambhava himself or not.

During my stay in Kalimpong I knew many followers of the Nyingma school, including great lamas, ordinary monks, and lay people. They used to come to my own monastery, and we would cooperate over Buddhist meetings and celebrations. In this way I got to know many of them quite well. And I observed that they all placed a very definite emphasis on the practice of meditation, in a way that the Gelugpas didn't. The Gelugpas are very devoted to debate. A couple of monks will get together and, surrounded by an audience, have a sort of dialectical discussion. This is all rigidly prescribed by tradition. The questions and answers are all out of their books of logic and philosophy, and are accompanied by appropriate dramatic gestures. They spend hours or even days practising these debates, and are examined for their proficiency. But the Nyingmapas – with whom the Gelugpas maintain a certain friendly rivalry – profess to regard all this as rather childish, and say that one should spend more time in meditation.

I also noticed that Nyingma lamas tended to be very spontaneous. If you ask a Gelug lama a question, nine times out of ten he will refer you to the appropriate page in Tsongkhapa's writings. He will tend to answer by the book, to stick to tradition rather strictly. The Nyingmapas are also very learned, though without pedantry, but if you ask *them* a question they are likely to answer directly, out of their own experience. Some of the Nyingma lamas I knew were entirely guided by what came to them in their meditation. If they were meditating in the morning and it came to them that they should go and see someone, or hold a big puja – well, as soon as they came out of their meditation they would do it. They were guided by their inner inspiration and tended to speak and act out of this inspiration – something the Gelugpas might have regarded as being rather presumptuous.

One of my own Nyingma teachers, Kachu Rimpoche, was staying with me once in Kalimpong. One morning at breakfast he said to me, 'What do you think I saw in my meditation this morning? I saw a great banner of victory on the roof of your monastery. We must get one put up.' For the next week we were busy buying cloth of various colours in the bazaar and ordering the necessary wooden base from a carpenter, and at the end of the week we were able to hoist the banner of victory up onto the roof. It was six feet high, with flounces of coloured silk surmounted by a golden *dharmacakra*. And it was put there simply because the Rimpoche had seen it in his meditation. Subsequently he told me that every morning he'd see in his meditation who would be coming to see him later that day.

He was a remarkable person. Another story about him was told to me by a Buddhist nun, a Frenchwoman who lived in Kalimpong. She had had a number of teachers, and tended to go from one to another, always dissatisfied because they didn't teach her enough or not quickly enough. She was a bit of a handful, to put it mildly. She had a doctorate in philosophy from the Sorbonne and was rather intellectual and difficult to please. On one occasion she had just finished with her latest teacher, and was wandering in the wilds of Sikkim, where she happened to meet Kachu Rimpoche. She was on the look-out for a new teacher, so she entered very eagerly into conversation. She told him what meditation practice she had been doing, and when he asked her how often she had been doing it, she said, 'Oh, every day.' Then he said 'You are not speaking the truth – you haven't done it for six months.' She told me that when he said this she almost jumped out of her skin, because it was true. Being annoyed with her previous teacher, she had not done that meditation for six months.

Of course, she asked to become Kachu Rimpoche's disciple on the spot – though eventually she became disgruntled with him as well, having found him sprinkling all the sacred images in the shrine-room of Pemayangse Monastery with whisky. There is of course nothing wrong with this. The Nyingmapas have occasion in their rituals to use liquor in a skull-cup, or in a little silver dish; it represents *amṛta* or immortality, and in the course of the ritual they take a single drop in the palm of the hand and drink it. But to her this was all wrong, so off she went. But for a time she was very taken by Kachu Rimpoche.

On another occasion, Kachu Rimpoche and I were having lunch with an American couple who had come to study the mysteries of Tibetan Buddhism in Kalimpong. At one point the young man said to me laughingly, 'You know the old story about people levitating. Ask the lama if he has ever seen anyone do it.' He meant this as a joke, but the lama replied very seriously, 'Oh yes, I've seen people do this in Tibet; in fact I can do it a little myself.' When he heard this, the young American almost fell off his chair. In the course of the conversation with this young couple, I noticed that Kachu Rimpoche at times answered their questions before I had had time to translate, even though some of the questions were quite complex. Later on, I questioned him a little more closely on the subject of levitation, and he told me that he couldn't just levitate on the spot. He had to isolate himself for about six months in a secluded cave or jungle somewhere in order to develop the requisite state of mind.[3]

These stories illustrate the nature of the Nyingma lama and the general nature of the Nyingma tradition. The Nyingmapas are often more spontaneous and lively than other lamas. They are also much less organized, especially compared to the Gelugpas. Traditionally the Gelugpas have tended to think in terms of enormous monasteries in Lhasa from which directives would go flying to all the subordinate monasteries. The Nyingmapas tended to be much more on their own, with individual lamas having their own circles of monk and lay disciples. They are also less exclusively monastic. Some of the greatest Nyingma lamas are not monks at all. Another of my own teachers, Dudjom Rimpoche, one of the most famous Nyingma lamas, was a layman with a family.[4]

THE KAGYU SCHOOL

Ka means simply 'speech', and *gyu* is 'tradition', so the name means the school of the oral tradition or oral lineage. The Kagyupas place very little emphasis on scriptural study. They attach much more importance to what they call 'ear-whispered instructions', instructions that the guru gives directly to the disciple and which may in fact never have been written down. The Kagyu school traces its lineage back to the eleventh century, to the great Indian – or rather Bhutanese – teacher Marpa, who had studied in India under Naropa.

The most famous figure of this school is Milarepa. His name means simply 'Mila who wears cotton cloth', and he is surely one of the most vivid and interesting characters in the history of Buddhism, indeed in the whole history of religion. Apparently his father died when he was quite small, and his aunt and uncle robbed him and his widowed mother of their inheritance so that they were left penniless. Milarepa's mother wanted revenge, and encouraged her son to learn black magic. He studied and practised sorcery for many years, and eventually wreaked a terrible vengeance on his relations. But afterwards he was overcome with remorse, because many lives had been lost as a result of his practices.

Eventually he came to the feet of the great guru Marpa, who saw at once that Milarepa was an immensely gifted person, a spiritual genius. But he also saw that he had done a great deal of harm and had to be purified. Marpa was nothing if not a spiritual disciplinarian, and he put Milarepa through such difficult trials that Milarepa was reduced to despair and even wanted to commit suicide. But he was encouraged and helped by Marpa's wife (apparently without her husband's knowledge) and eventually, after many struggles, he was initiated and sent to meditate in the solitude of the high mountains.

If we look at the life of Milarepa thereafter – he lived to be quite an old man – its most prominent feature is his sheer uncompromisingness. He never did things by halves, never made concessions, never gave way even by a fraction. For instance there are all sorts of things which a monk is allowed to possess, but Milarepa would have none of them. He did not wear any robes, just his piece of cotton cloth. At one time he had an earthenware bowl in which he used to boil the nettles he gathered for his meal, but one day the bowl broke and then he truly had nothing.[5]

Another story relates how once Milarepa was asleep in his cave. It was a cold winter's night, and he had no clothes. There was no blanket in the cave, no fire, no food: nothing. In the middle of the night he was woken up by the sound of someone moving about in the cave, and realized that it was a robber. Milarepa was quite amused by this, and called out, 'I don't know how you'll find anything by night, I couldn't find anything by day.' Tibetans – even robbers apparently – have a great sense of humour, so the robber laughed and went away.[6]

Milarepa is traditionally said to have been the greatest yogi in Tibet. There was no spiritual practice, no form of meditation, no attainment of which he was not the master. He was also a remarkable teacher, besides being Tibet's greatest poet. The best-known collection of his poetry is the *Mila Grubum*, the 100,000 songs of Milarepa (there are not literally 100,000; in Tibetan the title really means 'the collected songs'). These poems are not only of profound spiritual import, but often quite wonderful as poetry.[7]

The Kagyu school, following in the footsteps of Milarepa, stresses the actual practice of Buddhism much more than study of the theory, and until the Chinese occupation there were many Kagyu hermits living in remote, inaccessible places in Tibet. Kagyu practices consist mainly of the six Dharmas or Yogas of Naropa.[8] The first of these is the generating of psychic or internal heat. It was his mastery of this that enabled Milarepa to live amidst the snow and ice of the high mountain ranges clad in only a single cotton garment. In modern times one finds Kagyu lamas wearing their single piece of cotton cloth – which is *all* they are supposed to wear if they are practising the yoga of psychic heat – over their thick woollen robes. This suggests that things are not quite what they were in Milarepa's day.

The second of the six Dharmas of Naropa is the realizing of the illusory nature of personality, of one's own individual being. The third is the practice of realizing that the whole of existence is like a dream. Fourthly, there is the comprehending of the clear light of the Void. The fifth Dharma is gaining Enlightenment in the after-death state, a practice which is connected with the teaching of the *Tibetan Book of the Dead*. And the sixth Dharma or Yoga of Naropa is the transference of consciousness, not just into other forms of life but into higher states of being.

These six Dharmas involve many complex yogic practices and exercises. However, the highest of the Kagyu practices is the *mahāmudrā* or 'great symbol', which corresponds to the *atiyoga* or 'supreme yoga' of the Nyingmapas as well as approximating in some ways to Chan or Zen in the very highest sense.

THE SAKYA SCHOOL

This term *sakya* has nothing to do with the Indian word *śākya*, the name of the tribe to which the Buddha belonged. In Tibetan, *sakya* means 'tawny earth', in the sense of fallow or unploughed land, and it is the name of the principal monastery of this school, which was situated in a place known as 'the region of tawny earth'. The school was begun in 1073 CE by the great teacher Drokmi, who had studied in India for a number of years under many spiritual masters. However, Drokmi's disciple Könchok Gyalpo is usually regarded as the founder of the school, and he was not a monk but a layman. Though the early heads of the school were married, subsequently it became the custom for them to be monks and to be succeeded by a nephew who was also a monk. Thus when the head of the Sakya school dies, his brother's or his sister's son will succeed, and when *he* dies, the succession will revert to *his* nephew. In this way the succession goes backwards and forwards between two collateral family branches.

The Sakyapas are especially distinguished for their scholarship. The greatest of their scholars, perhaps the greatest of all Tibetan scholars, was the celebrated Butön, who lived in the fourteenth century. He it was who was responsible for the compilation of the Kangyur and the Tengyur, and his collection of the Buddhist texts into these two great editions is accepted as standard and authoritative by all schools of Tibetan Buddhism. He also wrote an important history of Buddhism, covering Buddhism in India as well as in Tibet.[9] Another great historian, Tāranātha, belonged to an offshoot of the Sakya tradition.

Historically there is a close connection between the Sakyapas and the Mongols, as it was the Sakyapas who converted this rather warlike people to Buddhism. Out of gratitude for the teaching they had received, the Mongols supported the Sakyapas politically to such an extent that the supreme abbot of the Sakya school ruled practically the whole of Tibet for a period of about eighty years, spanning the second half of the thirteenth century and the first half of the fourteenth. They can thus be said to have paved the way for the later rule of the Dalai Lamas.

In connection with this there is an interesting story about Pakpa, who consolidated the political power of the Sakyapas in Tibet in the thirteenth century. This celebrated Sakya leader was the guru of the even more famous Kublai Khan, who at that time ruled not only China, but also the whole of Central Asia and even parts of the West. Kublai Khan was apparently very grateful for the spiritual instruction and inspiration that Pakpa had given him, and very devoted to the Sakya school. One day he proposed to Pakpa that he should make a law compelling all the people of Tibet to give up the other traditions and follow only the teaching of the Sakya school. Such was Kublai Khan's enthusiasm.

Now one might have expected Pakpa to have been overjoyed at this development. One might have thought that he would have agreed at once with Kublai Khan's proposal and even have urged him to punish those who refused to conform. After all, such has been the pattern of religious history in the West. But Pakpa did not agree. On the contrary, he dissuaded Kublai Khan from making such a law. Such a law, he said, would not be in accordance with the Dharma. In effect Pakpa was saying that the other Buddhists of Tibet, the non-Sakyapas, should be free to follow whatever school they wished. There must be no compulsion, no coercion. This is, in fact, the Buddhist tradition, and it is very much the attitude of Tibetan Buddhists. They are very devoted to their own form of Buddhism; they believe in it, and follow it wholeheartedly. But at the same time they respect other traditions. Rarely is there any attempt to coerce anybody into a particular school. This is indeed the attitude of Buddhists throughout the East. They are generally very tolerant, whether towards other forms of Buddhism or other religions.

THE GELUG SCHOOL

The Gelugpas are, literally, 'the virtuous ones'. Not that the followers of the other schools were not virtuous, but the Gelugpas specialized, as it were, in virtue; it was their strong point. The Gelug school was founded by Tsongkhapa in the fourteenth century, and is the school to which the Dalai Lamas especially belong, as we shall see in Chapter 3.

This fourth and latest of the great schools of Tibetan Buddhism cannot be understood apart from the character and career of its founder Tsongkhapa, who is undoubtedly one of the greatest figures in Tibetan Buddhism. He embodies the characteristic spiritual or religious genius of the Tibetan people. He is known primarily as the reformer of Buddhism in Tibet, as he swept away many abuses. He was also a great organizer; he unified the monastic sangha to a considerable extent and imposed a consistent discipline. And he is renowned as a scholar-saint of the highest distinction. Saints are often not scholars, and only too often scholars are by no means saints. But Tsongkhapa was that rather rare combination, a man of saintly life and at the same time a scholar, and both almost to perfection.

Tsongkhapa's life is very well documented, the Tibetans having always been very historically-minded. Here they differ from the ancient Indians. Sanskrit literature is one of the richest in the world, including drama, poetry, and fiction, but it can boast just one historical work.[10] The Tibetans, on the other hand, produced many histories of India, of Tibet, and of Buddhism, as well as innumerable biographies, mainly of saints and religious people, which are often sound critical works, not just hagiography. Hence we know that Tsongkhapa was born in the year 1357 CE, the fourth son of his parents, and that, like many other famous and illustrious men, he came from a very poor family. He was born in Tsongkha – literally 'onion valley' – in the province of Amdo in north-eastern Tibet; the famous Kumbum Monastery, the monastery of the 100,000 Buddha images, was later built over the place of his birth.

Tsongkhapa therefore means 'the man from the onion valley'. This again reflects the Tibetan notion that it is disrespectful to refer to people by their personal names. For any respectable, especially religious person, they coin some sort of title. This happened to me when I arrived in Kalimpong. Most Tibetans there never knew that my name was Sangharakshita because nobody ever used it. During the first few years they called me Imji Gelong, which means 'the English monk'; and when I had been there a few years they called me Imji Gelong Geshe Rimpoche. Tsongkhapa's monastic name, given to him on his ordination, was Sumatikīrti which is a Sanskrit name meaning one who is praised, or is praiseworthy, on account of superior intelligence – a very appropriate name for Tsongkhapa. The Tibetans also refer to him as Jetsun Tsongkhapa – Jetsun meaning 'the venerable one' – or as Je Rimpoche, which means 'the greatly precious ruler', the spiritual sovereign as it were.

He seems to have been precocious, not to say a prodigy; his religious education began at the age of three, when he received various initiations and started practising meditation, and he became a *śrāmaṇera*, a novice monk, at the age of seven. According to the Vinaya Piṭaka, the 'Book of the Discipline', you can be ordained if you are old enough to earn your living by scaring crows away from the crops (a very important occupation in an agricultural country), and in the East this is usually understood to be when you are about seven.[11] So Tsongkhapa was ordained at the earliest possible opportunity; this is not unusual even today in Buddhist countries. Indeed, there are records in the Buddhist scriptures of little boys of seven, eight, and nine attaining arhantship or Enlightenment. This only goes to show what one can do and how far one can get if one only starts early enough, before one has been corrupted by what Thomas Traherne, the seventeenth-century English poet and mystic, calls 'the dirty devices of this world'.[12]

At sixteen Tsongkhapa was sent to study at a number of famous monasteries in central Tibet. For a number of years he moved from one great teacher to another, in this way systematically covering the whole field of Buddhist studies. He studied the voluminous Tibetan scriptures and also the translations of works by the great Indian Buddhist sages and philosophers, which are even more voluminous. In particular he studied logic – in later life he was very strong on logic – as well as mathematics and the Indo-Tibetan Ayurvedic tradition of medical science. In addition to this, of course, he studied and practised the teachings of all three *yānas* of Buddhism.

Thus in his own teaching work, Tsongkhapa had a rich source of material to draw upon. By his time Buddhism had been firmly established in Tibet for several hundred years, and practically everything of importance had been translated and could be studied. Tsongkhapa was therefore able to take quite an encyclopedic approach. He immersed himself in all the existing traditions, took the best of them, and codified and systematized these in a manner which is still of the utmost importance for the study of Tibetan Buddhism.

At the age of twenty-five he received his full ordination as a Buddhist monk. This 'higher ordination', as it is also called, is available to monks at twenty, but as he was busy with his studies he deferred it until he was twenty-five. After that he was fully occupied both with continuing his studies and with teaching; and the remaining thirty or so years of his life were passed in this way. In the course of these years he gathered many disciples who, on account of their devotion and dedication to the Dharma and the purity and holiness of their lives, gradually became known as the Gelugpas, meaning 'the virtuous ones'. They were so called because, following Tsongkhapa's example, they insisted on a stricter observance of the Vinaya than was customary at that time, including a total prohibition of marriage and of alcohol.

In the West the Gelugpas are often known as the Yellow Hats, in contradistinction to members of the older schools who are known as the Red Hats and to some of the Kagyu offshoots who are called the White Hats or Black Hats. This distinction relates to certain Tantric ceremonies, at least with regard to the Yellow Hats and the Red Hats. At the time of Tantric initiation, the officiating lama or guru puts on a cap – yellow in the case of the Gelugpas, red in the case of the Nyingmapas – and this has a definite significance. The cap is put on at those moments in the ceremony when the lama is identifying himself mentally, through meditation, with the Buddha or bodhisattva whose initiation he is giving.

So when an acolyte hands the yellow cap – or the red cap, as the case may be – to the guru, this is a very solemn moment. The cap is usually handed over ceremoniously on a piece of silk or a cushion. When the guru puts it on, you know that he is at that moment identifying himself in his meditation with the Buddha or bodhisattva whose initiation he is about to give. The recipient of the initiation therefore feels that he is receiving it from the Buddha or bodhisattva himself, through the guru. After that moment has passed, the hat is solemnly taken off and given back to the acolyte, to be folded up and put away. Up to the time of Tsongkhapa all the lamas, following the Indian tradition, used to have red caps for this purpose. Tsongkhapa wanted to make a visible distinction between his followers and those of the existing schools, so he changed the colour of the hat used in these ceremonies from red to yellow.

In the course of Tsongkhapa's lifetime his disciples founded in or near Lhasa, the capital of Tibet, three great Gelug monasteries: Ganden, Sera, and Drepung. These have survived to the present day, although they have been seriously damaged by the Chinese. Before the Chinese occupation Ganden and Sera each housed about 5,000 monks, and Drepung was even bigger, with over 7,000. They were almost like monastic towns or even cities.

Tsongkhapa was a prolific author; the standard collected edition of his writings fills sixteen massive Tibetan volumes. His two principal works are the *Lamrim Chenmo* and the *Ngakrim Chenmo*. *Lamrim* literally means 'stages of the path' (*chenmo* means 'great'); the work is a survey of the whole spiritual path according to the Mahāyāna tradition, discussing in detail the practice of the *pāramitās* and so on, citing innumerable Buddhist scriptures. The *Ngakrim* is a similar account of the Tantric Path, that is, the Vajrayāna. These two comprehensive and highly systematic works are the basis of Gelug studies.[13] Tsongkhapa also wrote a shortened version of the *Lamrim* for those of lesser intelligence, and this is the one which even the monks usually study, the longer version being extremely difficult, abstruse, and technical. Besides these, he composed some commentaries on scriptures, and a number of rather beautiful minor works.

Tsongkhapa died in the year 1419, by which time the Gelug order and the movement which it represented was well established, with a firm footing in the religious life of Tibet. Thereafter the anniversary of his death was observed every year – not just by the Gelugpas but by all schools – with a great festival of lights. As the evening draws in and it begins to get dark, people put rows of tiny oil or butter lamps round every house, monastery, and temple, in the windows, along the parapets, on the flat roofs, on the window sills. Hundreds or even thousands of these lamps can be seen all over the town, presenting a beautiful sight.

On account of the force of his personality, his vast scholarship and organizational ability, and his spiritual genius, Tsongkhapa left a permanent imprint on Tibetan Buddhism. But even more than this, in the estimation of the Tibetan people, especially the Gelugpas, Tsongkhapa is above all a bodhisattva. He is traditionally regarded as a manifestation of the bodhisattva Mañjuśrī, the Bodhisattva of Wisdom, who is associated in particular with the Perfection of Wisdom teachings. Tibetan paintings or images representing Tsongkhapa therefore show him with the attributes and insignia of Mañjuśrī. He is depicted as a rather typical Tibetan scholar-saint, seated in his monastic robes and wearing his tall yellow cap, but growing out of his shoulders, as it were, rather like two little wings, are lotus flowers. On one lotus is the flaming sword of Mañjuśrī, the sword which cuts asunder the bonds of ignorance, and on the other is the book of the Perfection of Wisdom scriptures. This indicates that Tsongkhapa is regarded as a manifestation on the earthly plane of Mañjuśrī, the great archetype of spiritual wisdom.

3
THE 'REINCARNATIONS' OF THE DALAI LAMA

Even if they know nothing else about Buddhism, people in the West have all heard of the Dalai Lama. His role and significance, however, are often greatly misunderstood. In fact, this misunderstanding prevails not just in Western countries. I remember when the Chinese first invaded Tibet, and again at the time of the Lhasa uprising in 1959, the newspapers in India, where I was then living, contained all sorts of rather grotesque references to the Dalai Lama which showed quite clearly that they had no idea of his status or function. Some reporters, for instance, would describe him as 'the living Buddha', which of course he is not. Other headlines said something like 'Priest-king flees to India'. Some newspapers went so far as to refer to the Dalai Lama as the Buddhist pope, the Potala as the Buddhist Vatican, and the leading incarnate lamas as the Buddhist princes of the Church, thus showing that they really did not have the faintest idea of who or what the Dalai Lama really is.

We cannot understand the Dalai Lama, his nature and functions, apart from the general background of Tibetan Buddhism, and especially the background of the Gelug school. This is the school with which he is personally affiliated, though he is revered by Tibetans of all schools.

The Gelugpas continued to flourish after Tsongkhapa's death. Skipping a generation or two, we find that the third abbot of Ganden (one of the three monasteries founded in the Jetsun's lifetime) was a nephew of Tsongkhapa called Gendun Drup. He founded the famous monastery of Tashi Lhunpo in Shigatse, and installed his own personal teacher as its abbot. Gendun Drup was popularly regarded as the reincarnation of the second abbot of Ganden (Tsongkhapa himself being regarded as Ganden's first abbot), and it is from this time that the idea of what scholars – using a Mongolian term – call Khubilghanic succession, that is to say succession by reincarnation, originates.

At this early stage, there were only two lines of Khubilghanic succession within the Gelugpa: firstly, the line of successive reincarnations of Tsongkhapa's nephew, the third abbot of Ganden; and secondly, those of his teacher, the first abbot of Tashi Lhunpo. These two lines subsequently became known as those of the Dalai Lama and the Panchen Lama respectively. The Dalai Lamas are the descendants – in the sense of continued reincarnations – of the third abbot of Ganden, whereas the Panchen Lamas are the reincarnations of the first abbot of Tashi Lhunpo. The present Dalai Lama is the fourteenth of his line of Khubilghanic succession, and the late Panchen Lama was the tenth of his particular line.[14]

Though this Khubilghanic succession is peculiar to Tibetan Buddhism, it does not represent anything radically new in Buddhism. It is simply a new application of an old principle, one that permeates practically all aspects and schools of Buddhism: the principle of the bodhisattva ideal. The bodhisattva ideal, a Mahāyāna conception, embodies the Buddhist spiritual ideal in its loftiest form. It is the ideal of Enlightenment not just for one's own sake but for the benefit of all – the ideal not of individual, but, in a sense, of 'collective' or even cosmic salvation.

Although the bodhisattva ideal is open to a number of abstruse, metaphysical constructions, it can also be expressed in comparatively simple terms. It needs to be understood in the context of the Buddhist view of karma and rebirth – the idea that people do not live just once on this Earth but undergo a succession of lives according to the law of karma, the law of cause and effect working on the psychological and ethical plane. Rebirth, according to Buddhist teaching, takes place on account of the residue of craving, aversion, and ignorance in the individual stream of consciousness (popularly known as the 'soul') at the time of death. In other words, if you have died with your passions unexhausted, if there is something for which you still crave, something to which you are still attached – whether family, or riches, or fame, or even study, even Buddhism itself, perhaps – then you will have to come back.

You will be drawn back by the power of your craving, by the power of your desire, your attachment, into a new body, a 'reincarnation'.

This process is depicted by the Tibetan wheel of life. In the hub there are three animals – a cock, a snake, and a pig – representing the three mental poisons of craving, aversion, and ignorance which set the whole process going. In the second circle are the upward and the downward paths of ethical and unethical conduct. The third circle shows the six spheres of conditioned existence (including the human realm) into which one can be reborn. The outermost circle consists of the twelve links of the chain of conditioned co-production in accordance with which the whole process takes place. This is standard Buddhist teaching. The wheel of birth and death and rebirth revolves on account of the three poisons of craving, aversion, and ignorance.[15]

However, in the course of spiritual practice, one is able gradually to eliminate these three poisons. Craving and aversion become less pronounced, ignorance is dispelled, and in the end there is in one's mind or consciousness only a state of peace, of love, of wisdom. One is no longer bound to the wheel, one no longer has to be reborn. So at death, when the consciousness flashes out of the physical body, there is nothing to draw it back. It remains on the higher, transcendental plane of existence, in the state of undisturbed Enlightenment.

But – and this is a very important but – according to the Mahāyāna, at this point two possibilities, two paths, disclose themselves. Having reached this point one can just remain there and allow oneself to simply 'disappear' into Nirvāṇa, to vanish from the ken of the world. On the other hand one can turn back. One can decide, quite voluntarily, to be reborn – not because there is any residue of karma left unaccounted for, but out of compassion, in order to continue to help other living beings in the world using the knowledge and spiritual experience one has gained.

This moment of choice is described in the legend of the great bodhisattva Avalokiteśvara. It is said that originally, many thousands of years ago, he was a great yogi who had, for most of his life, practised meditation in a cave in the Himalayas. Eventually the time came when he found himself on the verge of Enlightenment, the very brink of Nirvāṇa. He ascended from one stage of higher consciousness to another, going further and further away from the world, experiencing all sorts of archetypal and paradisal realms, seeing all sorts of glorious forms and figures. At last even these faded away and he came to the shore of a great ocean of light. He could see, he could hear, nothing but this ocean of light, and with the most profound joy he knew that at last he was returning to his source. He was going to 'merge' with reality itself. With a great sigh of relief, he started to let go, to allow himself to slip into that great ocean.

But at that very moment he heard a sound, coming as though from a great distance, from far below. At first he did not know what it was, but it arrested his attention and he listened. He became aware of not just one sound but many sounds, many voices, and they were all crying out, wailing, weeping, lamenting, grieving. As he listened the sound became louder and louder until at last he turned away from the great ocean of light, and looked down (hence his name, Avalokiteśvara, which means 'the lord who looks down'). He looked down into the depths, right down to this world itself, and he saw so many people, so many millions of living beings, suffering in various ways due to their ignorance and their lack of spiritual instruction. And the thought came to him: 'How can I leave these beings? How can I allow myself to merge into this ocean of light, just saving myself, when there are in the world below so many beings who need my help and guidance?' So he turned back. He not only looked down; he went down, he went back into the world.

The first path, that of allowing oneself to merge into Nirvāṇa, is considered – at least by the Mahāyāna – to be the path of the *arhant*, the one who desires individual salvation. The second path, that chosen by Avalokiteśvara, is the path of the bodhisattva, the one who desires not just his (or her) own emancipation but also the liberation and Enlightenment of all living beings whatsoever, and who is not satisfied until he can gather them all into his arms and carry them to Buddhahood, to a sort of cosmic Enlightenment. The path of the bodhisattva is traditionally regarded as a separate and higher path from that of the *arhant*. However, in a sense the path of the bodhisattva includes and contains that of the *arhant*, inasmuch as one must have the capacity to gain liberation for oneself if one's renunciation of that individual liberation is to have any significance. Otherwise the bodhisattva path may be not so much a spiritual ideal as a mere rationalization of one's attachment to the world.

Tibetan Buddhists take the bodhisattva ideal very seriously. For them it is a real, living thing. Marco Pallis called it 'the presiding idea of Tibetan Buddhism',[16] and if we do not understand it we have probably not understood Tibetan Buddhism. The Tibetans believe that there are people, currently living in the world, who have made this great sacrifice, people who have literally turned their backs upon Nirvāṇa and returned to the world to help in the higher evolution of the human race towards Enlightenment. For Tibetans the bodhisattva ideal is not just a beautiful myth, it is not – as I have found it described by a Roman Catholic writer – just a spiritual pipe-dream (in contrast, the implication being, to the historical reality of the crucified Christ). Tibetans regard the bodhisattvas as being very much with us, as being part of what we might call the 'spiritual economy' of the world; and they believe very strongly that some of these bodhisattvas can be identified. And the bodhisattvas they identify include the Dalai Lamas and the Panchen Lamas.

The Dalai Lama is regarded as a manifestation of Avalokiteśvara, the Bodhisattva of Compassion, while the Panchen Lama is believed to be a manifestation of Amitābha, the Buddha of Infinite Light. But if one is supposed to be a Buddha and the other a bodhisattva, what sort of distinction (one might wonder) is being made here? In this context, the difference between a Buddha and a bodhisattva is the distinction between the static and the dynamic aspects of the same spiritual reality. The Buddha represents the static aspect of Enlightenment, not in the sense of standing still *in* time but standing outside time altogether. The bodhisattva represents that same eternal transcendental experience in its dynamic aspect, in other words, in the process of realization within historical time.

Technically a Buddha could be seen as superior to a bodhisattva, for which reason some western scholars have assumed that the Panchen Lama must occupy a higher position than the Dalai Lama, that the Dalai Lama may be the temporal ruler of Tibet, but the Panchen Lama must be the spiritual head. This sounds logical, but it is not the case. In the eyes of the Tibetans, the Dalai Lama is all in all – he is the temporal ruler, *de jure* if not *de facto*, and he is also the spiritual head of Tibet. The Panchen Lama is in comparison a rather shadowy figure.

Tibetans in Kalimpong always had on their shrines a large framed photograph of the Dalai Lama; very rarely would there be one of the Panchen Lama. So when in the winter of 1956 the Dalai Lama and the Panchen Lama were officially welcomed at Siliguri airport and (through the machinations of the Chinese, who were semi-sponsoring the Panchen Lama) the two of them were provided with thrones of the same height, the Tibetans were highly indignant.

From their earliest years the Dalai Lamas are given a very careful training in all departments of Buddhist thought and Buddhist life. They learn to meditate and they undertake a difficult course of study and practice. So by the time a Dalai Lama reaches his majority he is usually very well-informed about all aspects of Buddhist tradition, both theoretical and practical. At the same time, despite his great learning, despite his immense authority and prestige, the Dalai Lama is never regarded as any kind of supreme doctrinal authority. He is not responsible for laying down how Tibetan Buddhists should practise Buddhism, nor even how Gelug Buddhists should practise. If anyone has this function it is a comparatively subordinate figure, the Ti Rimpoche, who is the abbot of the Ganden Monastery. Thus the Dalai Lama's position in Tibetan Buddhism is in no way analogous to that of the pope in the Roman Catholic Church. The pope defines morals and dogma, but the Dalai Lama does no such thing.

The Third, Fifth, and Thirteenth Dalai Lamas are of special historical importance. The Third Dalai Lama lived in the sixteenth century, roughly contemporary with England's Queen Elizabeth I, and it was he who finally converted the Mongols. They had originally been converted – as we saw in the previous chapter – by Pakpa, the Sakya hierarch, but subsequently fell away from Buddhism after the collapse of their empire in China. The Third Dalai Lama was responsible for bringing them back into the fold of Buddhism, and thereafter they became staunch followers of the Gelug school. Indeed, learned as the Gelugpas are, the Mongolians came to surpass them in learning. They are formidable scholars. I once travelled with a Mongolian lama, and whenever we stopped, out would come a book. He'd put a silk cloth across his knees, open the book, and start studying. Day and night he never did anything else. He was indefatigable.

It was the Third Dalai Lama who first received the title of Dalai Lama from Altan Khan, the ruler of the Mongols, and it was then bestowed posthumously on his predecessors. The word *dalai* is Mongolian, and means 'great like the ocean', so *dalai lama* means 'the lama, or teacher, who is great like the ocean'. This is the title used when they are speaking to westerners, but amongst themselves Tibetans usually refer to the Dalai Lama either as *galwa rimpoche*, which means 'precious ruler', or *yeshe norbu*, which means 'jewel of knowledge'.

The Fifth Dalai Lama, known as the 'Great Fifth', lived in the seventeenth century. He was a very learned man, a great scholar and author.

Although he was the leading representative of the Gelug school, he was very sympathetic to the Nyingma school and wrote several books on the Nyingma tradition. In addition to writing a great deal on purely religious subjects, he wrote on history, grammar, poetry, and astrology. He was a great statesman and administrator, and with the support of the Mongols he took over the temporal rule of Tibet. He also started building the Potala, the famous seat of the Dalai Lamas in Lhasa, named after Avalokiteśvara's legendary abode in South India.

So it is from the days of the Great Fifth that Tibet became what we in the West call a theocracy, a sort of religious state. We tend to think of the Dalai Lamas and the theocracy of Tibet as something fixed and established for all time, as being typically Tibetan, but in fact it is a comparatively recent development. Tibet has been a theocracy for only 300 out of the 1,300 years of Tibetan Buddhist history.

The Thirteenth Dalai Lama ruled in the twentieth century, and it was he who reasserted Tibet's independence from China after the collapse of the Manchu dynasty. He also tightened up the training of monks. When on the occasion of the Younghusband expedition to Lhasa[17] the Thirteenth Dalai Lama took refuge in Mongolia, in the course of his discussions with Mongolian lamas he found, rather to his consternation (so Dhardo Rimpoche, one of my Tibetan teachers, told me), that they were referring to texts which he had never studied. On his return to Lhasa he therefore reorganized the curriculum of studies for monks.

As for the present Dalai Lama, he was discovered and identified in 1935. Having fled from Tibet after the Lhasa uprising of 1959, he now lives in exile in Dharamsala in northern India. There have been prophecies to the effect that he will be the last of the line, and many Tibetans believe this. However, nobody can say with any certainty what the future holds.

The tragic story of Tibet in recent years has highlighted what the Dalai Lama means to the Tibetans. To begin with, he is regarded as the temporal ruler of the Tibetan people, and as such he is the focal point of the national consciousness. Both for Tibetans in Tibet who do not accept the Chinese rule, and for those in exile in India and elsewhere, he is the symbol, even the incarnation, of the Tibetan national spirit. But his significance is by no means confined to that.

Above all, the Dalai Lama is for the Tibetans a bodhisattva living in their midst. Whatever *we* might think, the Tibetans take this quite literally, just as the pious Catholic regards the pope as infallible. The Dalai Lama is not just a very good man, not just the ruler of the country, not just an eminent teacher or a great spiritual figure. He is for the Tibetans quite literally Avalokiteśvara, manifest in the world. They feel that through him the whole of Tibet, the whole of their tradition, the whole of their life, is in contact with the archetypal world, in contact with the transcendental. This is why he is the focal point of so much spiritual emotion, so much devotion. I have met hundreds if not thousands of Tibetans of all shades of opinion, all social classes, all degrees of education, but there was never any doubt about their absolute devotion to the person of the Dalai Lama – a devotion based on the firm belief that he was quite literally a bodhisattva, one who had earned the freedom of Nirvāṇa but who had voluntarily elected to remain behind in the world to help them.

4
MONKS AND LAITY IN BUDDHIST TIBET

All Buddhists 'go for Refuge' to the 'Three Jewels', the three most precious values for the sake of which everything else in the spiritual life exists. The Three Jewels are the Buddha (the ideal of Enlightenment), the Dharma (his teaching), and the Sangha (the spiritual community of his followers). In this chapter we shall be looking at the third of these refuges, the Sangha.

The Sangha exists at three different levels. The Āryasaṅgha or 'noble sangha' – the spiritual élite, one might say – consists of those who have gained at least a degree of spiritual insight. They are Enlightened, or well on the way to the goal of Enlightenment. Then there is the sangha as it exists at the level of formal monastic life, the order of *bhikṣus* and *bhikṣuṇīs* – monks and nuns – who have in a sense separated themselves from the world and who devote all their time and energy to the religious life. Thirdly, there is the *Mahāsaṅgha*, which includes all those who, whatever their degree of spiritual attainment and regardless of whether they are monks, nuns, or lay people, have committed themselves, at least to some extent, to following the path, practising the Dharma, and realizing the ideal of Buddhahood.

Within the sangha as it exists – or existed – in Tibet, there are different kinds of monks and teachers, and one may easily get confused about the role and status of each. This chapter describes the various categories of monks and lay followers, how they live and practise, the relations between them, and the great bodhisattva ideal that inspires and unites them. Much of what pertains to the monks and lay people of Tibet is also true of other Buddhist countries, but Tibetan Buddhism has many unique features and its monks and laity therefore have certain distinctive characteristics.

Tibetan monks belong to the Sarvāstivāda *nikāya* or branch of the sangha, one of the four *nikāyas* into which the early Indian monastic sangha split up. At the time of the Buddha's death, the monastic order consisted simply of those of his followers who had given up worldly life to devote themselves to meditation and spiritual practice. There were a number of rules, but on the whole they led a fairly free and easy existence, not unlike that of the modern Hindu sadhu. As time went on the order became more organized, more rules were introduced, and inevitably some differences of opinion occurred. About a hundred years after the Buddha's death the monastic order split into two: the more progressive Mahāsāṃghikas or 'Great Assemblists' and the more conservative Sthaviras, or 'elders'. According to some scholars, the Mahāsāṃghikas may have contributed to the rise of the Mahāyāna.

Over the next two centuries the Sthaviras themselves split, giving rise to the Pudgalavādins or 'Personalists' and the Sarvāstivādins or 'Pan-realists'. All four *nikāyas* transmitted essentially the same *vinaya*, or code of monastic discipline. They eventually subdivided further to make up the eighteen classical schools of Early Buddhism which collectively came to be known as the Hīnayāna.[18] Nowadays only two traditions of monastic ordination remain: that of the Sthaviras in their Theravāda form, concentrated in Sri Lanka, Myanmar (Burma), and Thailand; and the Sarvāstivādin lineage, found mainly in Tibet, China, Mongolia, and Vietnam. As we saw in Chapter 1, when King Trisong Detsen in the eighth century decided that Tibetan Buddhism should be a *triyāna* system, he decreed that it should follow the Sarvāstivāda in *vinaya*, the Mādhyamaka and Yogācāra in philosophy, and the Tantra in meditation. Since that time Tibetan monks have followed a Tibetan translation of the Sarvāstivādin *vinaya*.

There are six grades of Tibetan monk. The first grade is that of the *genye*. There are two kinds of *genye*. The first is that of the lay person who observes the five *śīlas* or moral precepts; this corresponds to the Indian *upāsaka* or lay Buddhist. The other kind of *genye* is a sort of probationer who lives in a monastery, serves the monks, and observes ten ethical precepts. It is this second kind of *genye* that constitutes the first grade of Tibetan monk.

The second grade is that of the *getsul*, corresponding to the Indian *śrāmaṇera*. A *getsul* is a novice monk who is studying to become fully ordained and who observes thirty-six precepts. Ordination as a *getsul* or *śrāmaṇera* cannot be given before the age of seven or eight (in Tibet reckoned from the inferred date of conception).

Thirdly the *gelong*, the fully ordained monk, corresponds to the Indian *bhikṣu* (Pāli *bhikkhu*). One cannot be ordained as a *gelong* before one's twentieth year, and often one waits until later than this, as did Tsongkhapa who was twenty-five when he took his higher ordination. The Tibetan *gelong* observes 150 ethical precepts, divided into seven categories, as well as various rules of monastic etiquette. The first category is the most important, containing as it does the four precepts which prohibit sexual intercourse, theft, the deliberate taking of life, and making false claims regarding one's spiritual attainments.

The fourth grade of monk is the *geshe*. This term is sometimes translated as 'doctor of Buddhist divinity' – I even saw this once on the visiting card of an English-speaking Tibetan *geshe*. But the *geshe* is better described as the 'learned monk'. There are five chief subjects of study for the *geshe*, to which he devotes many years of his life. First he studies the *vinaya*, or monastic discipline. There is a great deal of literature on this subject, some of it rather abstruse. Over the centuries a few simple monastic rules grew into a vast, complex, quasi-legal system; sometimes special 'monk-lawyers' are needed to unravel it before a monk can tell whether or not he has committed an offence.

The *geshe*'s second subject of study is the Abhidharma, a vast body of essentially scholastic Buddhist literature which includes the detailed analysis of mental states into their constituent functions. Thirdly the *geshe* studies the Prajñāpāramitā or Perfection of Wisdom scriptures, the most important group of Mahāyāna *sūtras*. Ideally the *geshe* studies all these *sūtras* – there are about thirty-five of them plus commentaries. Of these the *Vajracchedikā* or *Diamond Sūtra* is particularly popular in Tibet, and is recited on every possible occasion. The fourth area of study is Mādhyamaka philosophy, the teaching of the doctrine of the Middle Way. This highly metaphysical and dialectical tradition, based on the Prajñāpāramitā scriptures, was founded by the great Indian Buddhist thinker Nāgārjuna early in the Christian era.

Finally the *geshe* studies logic. Before it was wiped out by Islam, Indian Buddhism had a very rich tradition in this field, and many Indian Buddhist treatises on logic, by masters such as Dignāga and Dharmakīrti, have been translated into Tibetan. Tibet, and especially the Gelug school, kept up the tradition of the study of logic more than other parts of the Buddhist world, certainly compared to China or Japan where they preferred a more direct, intuitive approach.

Some scholars are of the opinion that the Indian and Tibetan Buddhist logicians eventually got rather far away from the spiritual teachings of the Buddha, but the Tibetans would argue that it is all part of the bodhisattva ideal. The bodhisattva aspires to bring everyone on to the path and enable them to mature spiritually, and this is not easy. You have to be able to discuss and debate with people – and how can you do this without rational argument? Logic – along with rhetoric, arts and crafts, and even poetry and dance – is part of the equipment, as it were, by which the bodhisattva leads all beings on the path to Enlightenment.

It usually takes not less than twelve years, sometimes much longer, to master these five subjects and complete the *geshe* course. The system of study is largely tutorial, either by individual tuition or in the context of very small classes. Examinations are held yearly, and are entirely oral; there is no written work. On the appointed day the individual candidate comes into the examination hall where, sitting round in a great circle, are hundreds of *geshes* who have already passed the course. One after another, they fire questions on any of the five subjects. The individual candidate sits in the middle, perhaps quaking a little, and waits for the first question. From the right there will perhaps come a very technical question about the *vinaya*, which you have to answer at once. No sooner have you answered it than there comes from behind you a question about logic. You answer *that*, and before you have recovered yourself someone asks a question on the Perfection of Wisdom. The questions get more and more difficult; the *geshes* are trying to catch you out the whole time. The examination goes on for several hours, with questions being fired from all sides.

Even the Dalai Lama has to undergo this gruelling experience. Tibetan friends who were present on the occasion once described to me the current Dalai Lama's *geshe* examination. Apparently there was one terrible instant when it seemed he was not going to be able to answer the question. But suddenly recovering himself, he came out with the answer with a terrific roar. Everyone was delighted. After all, he *was* the Dalai Lama. He was given a second class pass, which shows the system is quite fair and impartial. (There are four grades of pass, and a first is virtually unheard of.) If you fail the yearly examination, as often happens, you simply carry on studying and try again next time. You can take as long as you like, there being no fixed time limit by which you must complete the course. You present yourself when you feel ready. Obviously, you have to start quite young if you want to get anywhere by middle life.

The whole process of this viva voce examination is strictly stylized: there are certain ritual gestures that have to be observed in the asking and answering of questions. When you put your question you might thrust out your forefinger and fix your opponent with your eye, and if he cannot reply you might make a gesture of triumph. If he can get back at you, he does so with another gesture. It is very animated and dramatic to watch, even if one cannot quite follow the more abstruse exchanges. This type of formalized debate is very popular with the Gelugpas – they spend hours at it. If you go to a monastery you will often find in the courtyard under the trees groups of young monks practising their debating skills. Even when they are engaged in some other business, one of them may suddenly turn to another and fire at him a question about logic, or about the Perfection of Wisdom, so that they are kept on their toes all the time.

The *geshe* course, although very comprehensive, is concerned only with Hīnayāna and Mahāyāna subjects. The fifth kind of Tibetan monk, however, is one who is proficient in both the theory and the practice of the tantras. This is the *lama gyupa*, which means literally 'the lama in the lineage', that is to say a lama in the guru-disciple tradition of the Tantra. According to the Gelug system, it is only after passing out as a *geshe* that you go on to take up the full Tantric course. They insist that you should embark upon the study and practice of the Tantra, the Vajrayāna, only after thorough study of the Hīnayāna and the Mahāyāna. The other schools are not so strict and tend to allow people to study the Tantra directly, with little or no acquaintance with the Hīnayāna and Mahāyāna.

The three great monasteries around Lhasa – Ganden, Drepung, and Sera – were used for the *geshe* course. For Tantric study and practice there were two colleges in Lhasa, which you could join only after having completed the *geshe* degree. The discipline in these colleges was extremely rigorous. For example, while in the big monasteries you might have your own room, in the colleges you would sleep side by side with only a thin blanket over two or three people. A strict routine was followed, starting very early in the morning – a routine of study, meditation, discussion, and practice of all kinds. My teacher and friend Dhardo Rimpoche joined one of the Tantric colleges after passing out as a *geshe* from Drepung, but he was only able to remain there for a year because his health broke down under the austere way of life. Apparently this happened quite often.

The *lama gyupas*, those who have completed the Tantric course, are very highly honoured by both lay people and other monks. When the refugees started pouring out of Tibet, especially after the 1959 Lhasa uprising, there were many monks among them, and I remember that Dhardo Rimpoche was particularly anxious about the fate of the *lama gyupas*. I asked him why this was, and he explained that what the *geshes* had studied could be found in books, so that even if the *geshes* did not survive, the books were available and one could read them. But what the *lama gyupas* had learned had been transmitted to them orally. The teachings were not recorded in books but in the spiritual experiences of the *lama gyupas*, and thus were not so easily preserved. If the *lama gyupas* were not able to pass on the oral traditions to other people, they would be lost for ever.

The sixth grade of Tibetan Buddhist monk is the *khenpo*, a term usually translated as 'abbot'. It corresponds to the Indian *upādhyāya* or 'preceptor', in other words the one who gives ordination. The *khenpo* is head of the monastery. If the monastery has a number of constituent colleges, as at Drepung and Sera, then each college would have its own abbot, with a sort of grand abbot over them. A *khenpo* is traditionally appointed by the Dalai Lama on the recommendation of the monastery council. It is a fairly democratic system. When a *khenpo* dies, the council or governing body of the monastery selects someone from among the *geshes* and *lama gyupas* of the monastery – or perhaps from another monastery – to be the new *khenpo*, and the Dalai Lama confirms this. He very rarely refuses to confirm someone recommended by the council, though he has the power to do so. Under the *khenpo* there are lay administrators, responsible for the upkeep of the monastery, and various monastic functionaries in charge of things like discipline and ceremonies.

One question remains: where do the incarnate lamas come in? The answer is quite simple. The incarnate lamas, as such, do not come in at all. These six grades of monkhood are achieved either by ordination, or by passing an examination, or by appointment. Incarnate lamas belong to a quite different category. They are not made, they are born. The Dalai Lama, for example, is not elected to that position, and he does not pass an examination to become Dalai Lama. He is not even necessarily the most learned monk. He is simply someone who is recognized as the reincarnation of the previous Dalai Lama. In the same way, all incarnate lamas or *nirmāṇakāyas* – *tulkus*, as the Tibetans call them – are people who are recognized from birth, or from shortly after birth, as being the reincarnations of their predecessors. So the classification of Tibetan monks does not include a separate category of incarnate lama.

Normally, however, especially in the case of the Gelugpas, the incarnate lamas still progress through all six stages. After their discovery or identification, they are ordained as *genyes*, then when they are seven or eight as *getsuls* and when they are about twenty as *gelongs*. Long before that they will have started on their *geshe* course, often when they are about eight. Starting so early, they also finish early, and sometimes pass out as *geshes*, with flying colours in some cases, by their mid-twenties. Other monks usually start later and take much longer, but the incarnate lamas seem to go through the process much more quickly. Usually they then become abbot of their predecessor's monastery. And as they are reincarnations of the most distinguished abbots, so they may be regarded as being in a sense a subdivision of the *khenpos*.

Many western writers use the word 'lama' indiscriminately to mean a Tibetan monk, but it translates the Sanskrit word *uttama* meaning 'superior', in the sense of the spiritual superior, the teacher, the guru. Tibetan Buddhism places great importance on the figure of the lama. Indeed, it goes so far as to consider the lama as a fourth Jewel of Buddhism. Like Buddhists of all traditions, Tibetan Buddhists recite 'to the Buddha for refuge I go, to the Dharma for refuge I go, to the Sangha for refuge I go,' expressing their commitment to the realization of these three highest values. But before that, Tibetans say, 'To the Lama (or Guru) for refuge I go'. They do so because according to the Tibetan tradition you do not even know the Buddha, Dharma, or Sangha except through the lama, the spiritual master or teacher.

Strictly speaking only the *lama gyupas* and the *khenpos* are lamas, who may or may not be *tulkus*. In Tibet, monks are usually referred to collectively as *trapas*, literally 'students', because they go on studying all their lives. Whether they are fifteen or fifty, they have an outlook on life which is very much that of the student, of someone who is interested in study, in knowledge, and is not at all concerned with getting on in the world.

Another term you often hear is *rimpoche*, which is really a mode of address. It translates the Sanskrit *mahāratna*, and means 'great precious one' or 'great jewel'. It is used in speaking to, or about, monks of grades four to six, that is to say, the *geshe*, the *lama gyupa*, and the abbot. Incarnate lamas are also addressed as Rimpoche, and occasionally the word is used in addressing very old or very learned and pious monks, even if they are not technically *geshes*, just to pay respect to their advanced age or great learning.

Monks of all grades nearly always live in *gompas* or monasteries (*gompa* meaning literally 'a place for meditation'). Usually they are registered at a particular monastery, so that they officially belong there and cannot be absent without permission. There are proctors who go round every night making sure every monk is in his cell. They carry great iron-bound staves and bang them on the ground as they go along, to let you know they are coming. You must not be outside the monastery gate after that hour, otherwise you are hauled up in front of the abbot next morning. Monks are allowed to visit their old home and family very rarely, perhaps only once every year or two.

So how do the monks spend their time? Firstly, in every monastery, large or small, there are what we might call liturgical services, at least two or three daily, in the course of which there is a lot of chanting, accompanied by blowing of horns, banging of drums, and clashing of cymbals. It all creates a very powerful effect. Several times a day you sit for an hour or two at a time chanting the words of the sacred scriptures, perhaps the *Diamond Sūtra* or the *Heart Sūtra*, or invocations to the lamas, or praises of the Buddha, or summaries of the doctrine.

Then to the tremendous sound made by the booming of the great trumpets, the rattling of hand drums, and the higher register of clarinets when Buddhas and bodhisattvas are being invoked, are added the extraordinarily deep bass voices of the monks. I once heard the Dalai Lama chanting in the Japanese Buddhist temple in Bombay, and his voice filled the whole place with perhaps the deepest human sound I have ever heard. He was only in his mid-twenties at the time, but his voice was so deep that when he chanted the mantras the whole place seemed to tremble, and people told me afterwards that they felt shivers going up and down their spines.

So imagine the effect when there is not just one person doing this, but a great throng of monks. Imagine, in the semi-darkness of a great hall, with massive Buddha-images at one end and *thangkas* (painted scrolls) on the walls, with incense burning and butter-lamps flickering, that along with the sound of musical instruments there are hundreds or even thousands of voices all chanting together in these very deep tones, sending a wave of sound rolling from every corner of the congregation. There is nothing quite like it for sheer volume and depth and intensity of sound. Just imagine participating two, three, four, perhaps even five times a day in this sort of liturgical meditation. You are swept along on a wave of sound. You hardly need to meditate; you just let yourself go. You may not be a very holy monk, you may not be a very bright *geshe*, you may not know your logic or your *vinaya* very well, but when you participate in this kind of service several times a day, it cannot fail to have an effect.

At other times, the monks may be chatting with friends, reading and studying in their cells, painting pictures, splitting wood in the monastery yard, ploughing or reaping in the monastery fields, or carrying great buckets of water up hundreds of stone steps. But whatever you are doing, when the trumpet sounds you drop everything and go into the shrine-room. When you do this week after week, month after month, year after year, until a point comes when you do not remember the time when you were not a monk, then obviously it all sinks in, it has its effect. Perhaps a third of the time in many monasteries is given over to these great chanting services, and all the monks – whether they are great spiritual masters, or cooks or carpenters – take part in them.

If they are intellectually inclined, the monks spend the rest of their time studying. They read the scriptures, go to their teachers for explanations, discuss among themselves, and practise formal debate. They also meditate, they teach if they are qualified to do so, and some of them follow various professions. In Tibet the doctors were mostly monks. There was a special medical college in Lhasa for training monk-physicians, who followed a mixture of the Indian and Chinese medical systems, including acupuncture.

In addition, they may be artists; most *thangkas* or painted scrolls were painted by monks. They may be carpenters, making the monastic furniture, or tailors, making not only the monks' robes but garments for lay people too. In this way they can earn a little money on the side; the Tibetans consider this quite acceptable. Of course the vast army of monks has to be fed, so there are also monk cooks and chefs preparing meals for hundreds or even thousands of monks every day. I remember once in Kalimpong a new restaurant opened, serving Tibetan, Chinese, and Indian food, and everybody started going there. I asked someone why it was so popular, and I was told that among the refugees recently arrived from Tibet were some of the best cooks from Drepung Monastery, and that they had taken on the running of this restaurant. Thus they were able to provide for themselves even though they were refugees.

Tibetan monks wear dark maroon robes, and these are the same regardless of rank or school (though the Nyingmapas' robes are of a slightly brighter and lighter shade). The three yellow robes of Indian tradition are also incorporated into the dress of the Tibetan monastic orders, though they are usually kept for ceremonial use only.

Thus far I have mentioned only monks. What about Tibetan Buddhist nuns? There are no fully ordained nuns, no *bhikṣuṇīs*, in Tibet, and there never have been. This ordination was not introduced into Tibet, apparently because there were never enough Indian *bhikṣuṇīs* in Tibet to form the necessary quorum. The nuns in Tibet are technically either *genyemas*, female probationers, or *getsulmas*, female novices, and there are not very many of them. In Kalimpong I met hundreds of Tibetan refugee monks but only a handful of nuns.

Tibetan nuns might live in a nunnery or *ani gompa* but there were also two other kinds of nun. First there were those from well-to-do families who lived at home rather than going into a convent. The family would set aside a special set of rooms, even a little cottage in the grounds of their property, for the daughter or sister or mother who had become a nun. Often a learned monk would visit regularly to teach her, but although she had her own establishment – her own kitchen, her own shrine – technically she was still living at home under the guardianship of her family. Owing to the rather unsettled social and political conditions that prevailed in Tibet for many centuries, often it was not safe for such women to live in any other way.

Then there were a number of wandering mendicant nuns, who may or may not have taken monastic ordination. Some of these were a bit rough and ready, but others were very pious, spiritual people, rather like the Indian female sadhus. There were also a few female hermits – nuns or lay women – who lived quite alone regardless of dangers, in the forest or in mountain caves, simply meditating like Milarepa. There was also one female incarnate lama, the famous Dorje Phagmo, who was the abbess of a monastery of 500 monks. Tibet was probably the only part of the Buddhist world where this could happen. Unfortunately the current Dorje Phagmo eventually defected to Beijing and was last heard of broadcasting communist propaganda on the radio.[19]

Lay Buddhists are numerous in Tibet, and often are no less sincere in their spiritual life than the monks and nuns. The strict lay followers observe the five *śīlas* or precepts; but most lay Buddhists are 'one *śīla upāsakas*' – they take only the first precept, which is to refrain from taking life. This is not because they consider the other precepts unimportant, but because in their view it is a great sin to take precepts and then break them. They therefore prefer to take only those which they are quite sure they will be able to observe. A few just take the three Refuges.

In my experience Tibetan lay people are extremely generous, in particular giving a great deal both in money and in kind for the support of their religion. In my early days in Kalimpong one of the Tibetans who studied English with me was a merchant from Kham in eastern Tibet, and he told me that people there usually gave one third of their income for the support, in one way or another, of Buddhism. They would divide their income into three equal portions. One third went on domestic and business expenditure, another third went on pleasure, that is to say picnicking, gambling, horse racing – the Tibetans are very fond of these things – and the rest was used for donations to monasteries, offerings to monks, ordering new images or paintings, after-death ceremonies, and so on.

Most Tibetan lay people, like the monks, regularly recite mantras. They have nearly all been initiated into a meditation on a Buddha or bodhisattva, and they recite their mantras whenever they can. They may chant as they are walking along the road, or, when the day's work is done, a woman might sit on her doorstep quietly reciting mantras to herself. You can tell as you pass that they are quite absorbed. They do not do it mechanically; there is a great deal of religious feeling involved.

Every Tibetan Buddhist home has (or at least had) a domestic shrine with an image of the Buddha or one of the bodhisattvas. This shrine, which occupies the place of honour in the sitting room where visitors are entertained and guests put up for the night, is the focal point for the entire household.

Pilgrimage is another important part of Tibetan lay Buddhist life. There is still a great deal of the nomad in the Tibetans. They love to wander, to go on long journeys all over Tibet – even, in the past, all over India – visiting the shrines and holy places. They would also sometimes go into retreat and meditate. A man might entrust his family and business to his wife and spend three months in retreat, meditating and reciting mantras. Lay women are also very active in religious life, and are very much in evidence at all religious functions, celebrations, pujas, and so on. Often women take the initiative, having their own religious organizations, their own processions, their own meetings, even their own publications.

Tibetan Buddhists attach great importance to what we would call precedence – social, ecclesiastical, and spiritual. This is strictly observed on all formal religious occasions. Its importance for Tibetan Buddhists consists in the fact that it reflects the important principle of spiritual hierarchy. Inasmuch as the Dharma is a path there must be different stages on that path, different grades of attainment and realization. People can therefore be regarded as forming a hierarchy along these lines, and everything which they do, and which is done in connection with them, should reflect this hierarchy of stages of attainment. The Tibetans are therefore very particular about things to which we in the West would attach relatively little importance. For example, if you attend a religious ceremony in a Tibetan temple or monastery, you will notice that all the seats are graded. Towards the altar the seats are very high, perhaps six feet off the ground, like thrones; then they gradually become lower until you are perhaps just sitting on an ordinary mat. This is not done in accordance with any aesthetic principle, but with strict ideas of precedence and hierarchy. You can quickly tell how highly or otherwise the Tibetans esteem you according to the number of inches from the ground you are requested to sit.

Whenever I arranged Tibetan ceremonies at my vihara in Kalimpong I had to be very careful – especially when I invited certain high-ranking incarnate lamas – to make sure that everyone got the right kind of cushion, the right number of stripes of brocade, and so on. Protocol was really carried to a fine art. Even the tea cups, when tea was served ceremonially, would be graded from simple china cups, through more elaborate cups with lids and stands, right up to beautiful jade cups on silver stands. Eventually you might find yourself being served tea in an ancient jade cup on a solid silver stand, with a gold decorated lid topped by a magnificent jewel. Then you would know you had really arrived.

In accordance with this idea of precedence, the monks, and to a lesser extent the nuns, are – or were – treated with much reverence and devotion in Tibet. At the same time, the connections between monks and laity were very close. Every family had someone in robes, a son or brother who was a monk, so it was as though they had their own representative in the monastery. If another member of the family wanted to become a monk he would usually go to the same monastery, so that his uncle or brother could teach him. As well as this sort of link between the monks and laity, there is also the economic dependence of the monks on the laity, though this is perhaps less than it is for the monks of South-east Asia where it is seen as a disgrace for a monk to work, or even to do anything with his hands. It is not like that in Tibet, as we have seen.

The laity are for the most part dependent on the monks for spiritual guidance and advice. They often go to the *gompas* to visit and consult the monks, to attend pujas, to participate in processions, or to listen to lectures; and they often invite the monks to their homes. The monks are free to go out during the day, and can even get leave of absence for a few days or weeks to go to a lay person's house to teach, conduct services, and so on. Thus there is a constant coming and going between the houses of the lay people and the monasteries. The spiritual connection is much closer than in Theravādin countries, where the monks tend to be divided from the lay people rather sharply. The Theravādin view is that whereas the monk aims for Enlightenment, the lay person can aim only for a good rebirth, and this tends to produce a division, even a dichotomy, between the monks and the laity. But in Tibetan Buddhism all alike can aim for Enlightenment. Whether monk or lay, all Tibetan Buddhists accept the bodhisattva ideal. They all believe they should aspire to gain Enlightenment for the sake of all living beings. Serious Tibetan Buddhists, both monks and lay people, in fact take the bodhisattva ordination and the bodhisattva vow – the vow to strive for Enlightenment not just for one's own sake but for the sake of all sentient beings.

Along with this vow, they may undertake to observe the bodhisattva precepts, of which there are eighteen major and forty-six minor ones in the Tibetan tradition.[20] These constitute a common factor in the spiritual life of monks and lay people in Buddhist Tibet. Indeed, we may say that the bodhisattva precepts have helped to mould the whole character of Tibetan Buddhism. The first major bodhisattva precept is very simple (simple to understand, that is, not easy to practise). It is to undertake not to praise oneself or disparage others. In one way or another we do this all the time, either individually or collectively; we always want to exalt ourselves and deprecate others. Thus we extol our own country at the expense of other countries, our own religion at the expense of other religions, or just ourselves at the expense of other people. So this first precept is about trying not to do this – and in fact Tibetans are very unwilling to criticize. It is particularly unthinkable for them to criticize someone else's religion.

Another of the major precepts is a warning not to instruct in the doctrine of *śūnyatā*, emptiness, anyone who is not prepared for it. Teaching must be adjusted to the psychological and spiritual needs of the person concerned. There is also a precept that enjoins us not to disparage the Hīnayāna. It may not be as fully developed as the Mahāyāna, but it is an indispensable stepping-stone. You might as well say that the lower rungs of a ladder are less important than the higher rungs. Another precept consists in the determination not to give up the *bodhicitta*, the will to Enlightenment for the benefit of all. However difficult things may be, however impossible other people may be, you must never give up the aspiration that one day they too will realize Enlightenment, will come to Buddhahood.

One of the minor offences for one who has taken the bodhisattva vow is not showing respect for those who are one's seniors in bodhisattva ordination. Another is to despise evildoers because you think they are less virtuous than you. They may be, but that is no reason to look down on them. It is also an offence to laugh heedlessly. This does not mean that you should not laugh, but if you are a bodhisattva, or aspirant bodhisattva, you should not do so mindlessly, without awareness. Another precept is that if someone in your vicinity is angry, you should try to pacify their anger. According to the Mahāyāna, anger is the worst of all mental states, so that if there is even a hint of it in our surroundings we should try to reduce it. Another offence is to neglect the sick – a very practical down-to-earth precept – and it is also an offence not to work for one's own circle of disciples and students.

These precepts illustrate the spirit of Tibetan Buddhism, the common ideal of monks and lay people alike. Whatever their differences in life-style, type of ordination, or level of spiritual attainment, the unifying factor of all Tibetan Buddhists is their reverence and devotion to the bodhisattva ideal, the ideal of Enlightenment for the benefit of all.

5
SYMBOLS OF TIBETAN BUDDHIST ART

We have seen that Tibetan Buddhism is a direct continuation of Indian Buddhism, that it is almost as if Indian Buddhism died in India only to be reborn on the soil of Tibet. Likewise, Tibetan Buddhist art is largely a continuation of the Indian Buddhist artistic tradition, particularly that of the Pala dynasty of eastern India in the eighth to twelfth centuries CE. Tibetan Buddhism continued that artistic tradition especially in its iconography, that is, in the depiction of images of Buddhas, bodhisattvas, *ḍākinīs*, and so on. There is also some influence from Nepalese Buddhist art, but that tradition had itself been deeply influenced by the Pala tradition.

Chinese influence on Tibetan art is very secondary, and shows up mainly in matters of detail. For instance, if we look at *thangkas*, painted scrolls, we see that the iconography of the figures – their colours, the ritual implements they bear, their expressions and gestures, insignia and emblems – is all strictly determined by the Indian iconographical tradition. But when it comes to little details like the way in which the artist painted mountains, flowers, clouds, streams, or waterfalls, these reflect a definitely Chinese artistic tradition. We find a charming contrast between the Indian tradition, reflected in the iconography, and the Chinese influence, reflected in the natural objects – perhaps especially the clouds which are often very beautiful, with an effect of movement and iridescence which it takes a great deal of skill to capture. This Chinese influence is naturally more pronounced in the art of the areas of eastern Tibet adjacent to China itself. In the decorative arts also, the Tibetan tradition incorporates many Chinese motifs, such as the phoenix and the dragon. These symbolize, respectively, the yin and yang forces in the universe, and they are represented in Tibetan art as in Chinese art. Whether woven into carpets or carved into the woodwork of shrines, the Tibetan phoenix and dragon are exact replicas of their Chinese prototypes.

If we look more closely at the Indian and Chinese elements in Tibetan Buddhist art, we find that the specifically religious component of the art is Indian, whereas the secular component tends to be Chinese. Often these two aspects exist separately, side by side, but the best examples of Tibetan art display a perfect blending of the two. At its most perfect, Tibetan art is neither Indian nor Chinese, nor even both together, but uniquely and characteristically Tibetan. At the same time, however, the original Tibetan contribution is rather meagre. Tibetan Buddhist art draws its religious inspiration from India and its secular or more aesthetic inspiration from China, and although it fuses them into something distinctive and incomparable, it draws very little from purely indigenous sources.

This lack of originality brings us to perhaps the most important characteristic of Tibetan art. We speak of Tibetan *Buddhist* art, but strictly speaking this is a tautology. All Tibetan art is entirely Buddhist, or entirely religious; there is no secular art, or at least none worth mentioning. This is in accordance with the general pattern of Tibetan life, at least as it was before being disrupted by the Chinese occupation. The whole scheme of Tibetan life was based on certain traditional values, spiritual values, which had been handed down by way of a succession of teachers and disciples through the ages. All aspects of Tibetan life, therefore, inasmuch as they are related to these values in one way or another, also provide means of access to them. This applies to all areas of Tibetan life: economics, government, and administration, and even social customs and manners, as we saw with the idea of precedence in Chapter 4.

Because these aspects of life are closely interwoven with spiritual ideals, it is not surprising that Tibetan art and literature should be mainly religious. Apart from the Gesar epic, the Tibetans' only secular poetry, so far as I am aware, is a little book of love poems attributed to none other than the Sixth Dalai Lama.[21] Otherwise, their poetry is entirely religious. Similarly, there is no secular painting or sculpture. Where religious art does depict secular life, it is only in little details, for instance in some of the illustrations on the Tibetan wheel of life. Music, dance, and drama are entirely religious, apart from a little folk music and folk dancing. Even many of the applied arts such as woodcarving and metalwork are basically religious.

It is largely because its main function is religious that Tibetan Buddhist art is not very original in the modern sense. It doesn't even try to be original. A Tibetan Buddhist artist would in fact regard striving for originality as an aberration. He would be highly unlikely to decide spontaneously to paint his own idea of, say, the Buddha Amitābha. Instead, he will just sit in his studio or workshop until someone comes and orders a *thangka* of that particular Buddha.

If you do go along to order a picture, you don't get down to business straight away. That is not the way things are done. Polite enquiries about each other's health must be exchanged, and tea must be offered and drunk. Only then will the purpose of your visit be broached. The first question to be settled will be the rather prosaic one of the size of the *thangka* you want. The next question, usually, is whether you want gold to be used and, if so, how much – gold being charged for separately. When all this has been settled, you can get down to discussing the deity you would like to have depicted. If it is a well-known figure like Amitābha, the artist will know the iconography off by heart. Otherwise, if it is a more obscure figure, he will rummage in a drawer containing wood-block prints of a variety of figures – Buddhas and bodhisattvas, *ḍākinīs*, *dharmapālas*, and so on. Eventually he will pull one out and ask, 'Is this the one you want?' If it is, then after your departure he will transfer the outline on to the rectangle of silk on which he will paint it.

In other words, the picture is executed according to the traditional iconography. The artist does not depict Amitābha according to his own ideas. Such things as proportion and colour, posture, and insignia, are all determined by tradition. There is some scope for originality, but it is very limited, on the whole being confined to the more secular and Chinese-influenced details, such as landscape, and to the offerings that are being made to the deity. A great deal of originality sometimes goes into these things. The better artists will, of course, produce finer works of art, but they still work within the tradition and will never try to paint the Buddha as they think he looked or ought to look.

The purpose of Tibetan religious art is not to give expression to the artist's own attitude or mentality. All the different forms of Tibetan art have one aim, which is to put the viewer, the individual Buddhist, in touch with what the Tibetan tradition calls the 'One Mind', the absolute consciousness, the *dharmakāya*, or reality. If that is not possible, at the very least it aims to put the individual in touch with a higher, wider, and more comprehensive level of being and consciousness. Tibetan art does this with the help of symbols.

We can define a symbol as 'that which by custom or convention represents something else'. In other words, it has a meaning beyond itself, represents something other than itself. But in the context of Tibetan art a symbol is much more than this. It is not like the symbols of mathematics, not like, for instance, the letter x which represents the unknown quantity. A true symbol can be defined as an object or a phenomenon on a lower order of existence which stands for, represents, or takes the place of, a corresponding object on a higher order of existence. This definition of a symbol is based on the conception of a hierarchically ordered system of reality. For example, in some traditions the sun is regarded as a symbol of God, or, as in Plato's thought, a symbol of the Good.[22] This is because the sun – the source of heat and light and therefore life – occupies a position in the physical world analogous to that of 'God' on the spiritual plane. The sun is a symbol not just in the sense of representing God, but in the sense that on its own level – the level of the physical world – the sun directly corresponds to that higher reality which is called God on the spiritual level. The same reality is being looked at from two different points of view, or within two different contexts.

The symbols of Tibetan Buddhist art are of this order. They are symbols by virtue of their place in a system of correspondences, based on a hierarchy of spiritual values in the universe as a whole. Though they themselves are material or mundane, they remind us of the existence of a higher order of being, and in a sense they even put us in touch with that higher order and enable us to communicate with and experience it. Symbols in this sense pervade all four of the principal categories of Tibetan art: architecture, paintings and iconography, ritual objects, and decorative arts. Here we will look in more detail at the first two of these.

One of the few indigenous Tibetan contributions to Buddhist art is its architecture. And one of the best-known and most wonderful examples of this is the Potala, the palace or monastery or temple – really all three combined – of the Dalai Lama in Lhasa. This was originally a secular building, a sort of castle of the Tibetan kings, but it was transformed by the Great Fifth Dalai Lama into something much more characteristically Tibetan. The Tibetan style of architecture was, of course, determined to a great extent by the climate. In Tibet one needs protection from the terrific winds and extreme cold. It was also influenced by the available materials; there is plenty of stone and rock for building purposes, but very little wood, Tibet being largely non-forested.

These two constraints determine some of the most distinctive features of Tibetan religious architecture. We find enormously thick walls, perhaps ten or fifteen feet thick, like European castle walls, to keep out the cold and frost and damp. Usually the lines are very simple, the basic pattern being of vertical walls that slope slightly inwards, and flat roofs. The most characteristic of all religious buildings, the monasteries or *gompas*, are very often situated high in the mountains, sometimes on crags or spurs of rock. A *gompa* rises out of the rock as if it were a natural growth of the mountain, as if it had grown straight out of the living rock. This is true above all of the Potala, but also of many temples and monasteries in Tibet. From a distance, they seem to be continuations of the mountains themselves.

This feature of Tibetan architecture is brought out in a number of paintings by Lama Govinda, who was not only a great writer on Buddhism but also a skilled artist. Many of his paintings depict these magnificent, rather barren and rocky Tibetan landscapes, with *gompas* – at heights many thousands of feet above sea level – 'growing' out of the mountains.[23] This style of architecture seems to possess its own symbolic significance, acting as a reminder that the spiritual life is not 'stuck on to' the secular life. No, the one grows naturally out of the other as its culmination and perfection. Lama Govinda's paintings convey this impression very strongly indeed, but even in ordinary photographs of the great monastic shrines of Tibet one can see how their lines continue the lines of the mountains. This type of architecture is specifically Tibetan, owing nothing to India or China.

Another architectural feature of the Tibetan landscape is one of the most important and most ubiquitous of all Buddhist symbols: the stupa (*chorten* in Tibetan). This was originally a sort of funerary mound, a great heap of earth which enshrined the ashes of some great teacher or hero, a Buddha or *arhant*, or a universal king. The stupa is very prominent in Indian Buddhist art and architecture, but the Tibetans adapted it in their own way, as did the Buddhists of other countries. There are many different kinds of stupa in Tibet, but their basic structure is quite simple.

Essentially a stupa is made up of geometrical forms that symbolize the five elements: earth, water, fire, air, and space or ether (*ākāśa*). The earth element is symbolized by a cube. Just as a cube is very stable and can't easily be pushed over, so earth represents stability. It is the grossest of the elements, the heaviest, and so its representation, the cube, is the first element in the stupa. If you want to build a stupa you start by laying down a cube as the base.

On top of that is placed a sphere – or, more often, a hemisphere – which symbolizes water. The sphere is the least stable solid figure: just a touch and it will move. It is therefore an appropriate symbol for water, because unlike earth water always moves. It flows, it is unstable. On top of the sphere or hemisphere comes a cone. This represents fire – a cone is almost the shape of a flame – and it points upwards just as a flame points upwards as it burns.

Balanced on the point of the cone is a sort of bowl or saucer (which also looks like a crescent if depicted two-dimensionally). This symbolizes air, and is the inverted bowl of the sky or firmament. In the crescent or bowl is a flame tapering to a point, and this point, this position without magnitude, represents the so-called sixth element, consciousness. It is represented in this way because a point has no dimensions, just as consciousness itself, unlike the other elements, has no dimensions. Consciousness is that which 'contains' them all without itself being contained by anything. It is symbolized by that point, which indicates a transition from the physical or material plane to another dimension, that of mind or consciousness.[24]

But why is this particular architectural form, the stupa, built up from symbols representing the five elements? Why should a *chorten*, a funerary monument, incorporate these symbols? The reason is related to the very fact that it is a funerary monument, built over the ashes of a dead person or in memory of them. The stupa is made up of the symbols of the elements because at the time of death the physical body, in fact the whole psychophysical being, is resolved back into the elements from which it came.

At death, the solid parts of the body revert to earth. The fluid parts – blood and the rest – revert to water. The vital heat in the body returns to fire, being absorbed into the total heat and warmth of the universe. The air which fills our lungs is just exhaled into the atmosphere. When our physical body ceases to exist, the space it occupies merges into the great space. Finally, our mind also, when the bonds of the ego are dissolved – which is a sort of spiritual death – becomes non-different from absolute mind or absolute consciousness. This arrangement of the elements in the symbol of the stupa forms the basis of the six element meditation, a traditional Buddhist practice designed to deepen one's insight into the constituents of the body and their dissolution at death.[25]

Another architectural symbol is the three-storeyed temple. Many Tibetan temples are built with three storeys, which represent the three levels of existence, one of many ways in which existence can be divided, and one of the most ancient. The three levels are the mundane level, the archetypal level, and the absolute level. One finds enshrined on each storey an image of the Buddha, and these images represent the three *kāyas* of the Buddha. *Kāya* literally means 'body', but it is to be understood here more in the sense of personality. The three *kāyas* are the *nirmāṇakāya*, the created body; the *sambhogakāya*, the body of mutual enjoyment or glorious body; and the *dharmakāya*, the body of reality. These three aspects represent the Buddha-nature itself as perceived at different levels of existence. When one perceives the Buddha-nature, the Buddha-being if you like, on the level of mundane historical reality, then one sees the historical Buddha. Going higher, one reaches the archetypal level, where one sees the same reality more closely, more truly, as the *sambhogakāya* Buddha, a sort of archetypal form. And if one goes higher still, then one sees the inner essence of those Buddha-bodies, the *dharmakāya*, or reality itself, without any form.

Thus we find, on these three different levels, images of the Buddha representing the three *kāyas*. For instance, on the ground floor of the temple we find an image of Śākyamuni, the human historical Buddha: Gautama the Buddha, the Indian prince who lived around 500 BCE and became Enlightened under the bodhi tree at the age of thirty-five.

There he is, wearing his monk's robe, with his begging-bowl, and so on; and the walls of the ground-floor temple are covered with frescoes depicting incidents from his life. They show him sitting under the bodhi tree, resisting Māra the Evil One; giving his first teaching; and passing away under the twin *sāl* trees. There are also very often stories from the *Jātakas*, the legends of his previous lives on the historical – or at least on the material – plane. All this represents the *nirmāṇakāya*. Or, as we saw in Chapter 2, in a Nyingma temple we might well find at this level an image of Padmasambhava, the 'second Buddha'.

But when we climb up to the middle floor it is rather different. Here we are in a different world, on a higher plane, and we find an archetypal Buddha enthroned. He wears not the ordinary monastic robe but princely garments of flowing, flowered silks, together with jewellery of various kinds. He is quite a different kind of figure, resplendent, archetypal, and glorified. On the walls we see nothing historical or human. We find, for example, mandalas, circles containing the principal archetypal Buddha forms. On this storey we find ourselves in the archetypal plane, above and beyond the human, historical world.

Then, climbing to the top storey, we find what is called the Ādibuddha, the primeval Buddha, the Buddha from the beginning, the Absolute Buddha. He is not represented wearing monastic robes, or even princely garments. He is represented without any clothes at all, and he may be blue, or black, or white, or dark brown; but in any case he is completely naked, because here all veils, all vestures, have been removed. This is the level as it were of reality itself. Very often the Ādibuddha figure is in the *yab-yum* position, that is to say the male Buddha is depicted in sexual union with his female counterpart, symbolizing the fusion in the Enlightened mind of Wisdom, represented by the female, and Compassion, represented by the male. One finds these only at the top level because such *yab-yum* figures are regarded in Tibetan Buddhism as pertaining not to any lower mundane level, but to the highest and most spiritual level of all, the level of absolute reality. Then on the walls, ideally, according to the best traditions, you find nothing: no form, no figure, not even a leaf or a flower. Apart from the Ādibuddha figure the room is completely bare.

In this way the architecture of the temple itself, including all its images, paintings, and decorations, symbolizes concretely these different levels of existence which one must ascend, from the historical reality at the bottom, through the archetypal or celestial reality, towards the ultimate, the absolute reality.

PAINTINGS AND ICONOGRAPHY

Another of the few indigenous contributions to Tibetan art is the remarkable colour sense of the Tibetans, as seen especially in their *thangka* paintings. The atmosphere of Tibet is remarkably clear, because at 12,000 feet or more above sea level the air becomes much thinner and more free of impurities. On emerging from the passes from India to Tibet, you find yourself in a completely clear, almost crystalline, atmosphere. If you are high enough up, you can see for scores, perhaps even hundreds, of miles. When everything is so transparent, so translucent and sparkling, then the sky is really blue. In the West we seldom see a really blue sky because we usually look at it as though through a sort of fog. But in the heights of Tibet, above the level of smog and dirt and dust, you see how blue the sky can really be. And this is how the Tibetans see colours: they see a blue sky which is really blue, red rocks which are really red.

Lama Govinda once told me how astonished he was to open his eyes on a clear bright morning in Tibet and see rocks and mountains all around him which were so richly and brilliantly red that he couldn't believe his eyes. He even thought it was some sort of hallucination. But Tibet is really like that. When you look at the waters of a lake, they are a deep, vivid turquoise. When you look at the hundreds of miles of landscape, you see rich browns merging into beautiful purples. All around you are glowing colours.

It is because of this that the Tibetans have such a highly developed sensitivity to colour, and their art, particularly their *thangka* painting, reflects this. The best *thangkas*, those painted in the pure orthodox tradition, contain only organic and mineral pigments. Tibetan artists traditionally do not use prepared colours. They take earth, vegetable products, and semi-precious stones, and grind them and mix them for use as paints. Some, I am afraid, who have come into contact with western civilization, are beginning to use ready-made paints, but the old artists, the traditional ones, still employ these natural colours. This helps them to create brilliant and really jewel-like effects. The best *thangkas* are remarkable for the sheer dazzling brilliance of their colouring. At the same time there is nothing loud or harsh about them, nothing that shrieks at you. The colours are brilliant, but at the same time soft and gentle: they seem natural and real.

The fact that the *thangkas* are so vividly coloured is connected with the purpose for which the paintings are intended. They are not just beautiful decorations to hang in your shrine; they are aids to visualization. They are painted in accordance with a particular tradition, which derives ultimately from somebody's meditation. Long ago, usually, a great mystic or yogi would have seen in his meditation a sort of divine vision, and described it to his disciples. He might have written about it, or even, if he was an artist himself, have painted or drawn it. Anybody else who wants to meditate upon that form or figure, that aspect of reality, does so by means of a drawing or a painting deriving from the tradition which goes back to the original experience. (The actual process of visualization in meditation is described in more detail in Chapters 6 and 7.)

The vivid colours in which the *thangkas* are painted are themselves an important aspect of the symbolism of Tibetan art. The colour of a visualized form is often an important key to its significance. If you know what colour a Buddha or bodhisattva is, then you already have some idea of his or her general spiritual significance. There are five basic colours in Tibetan iconography. Firstly there is red, a very deep, brilliant, rich vivid red. In the Tibetan Buddhist tradition, especially the Tantric tradition, red is the colour of love and compassion. If you see a red deity, a red Buddha or bodhisattva, or a red *ḍākinī*, then you can be sure that the figure represents the Buddha-nature under the aspect of love or compassion. In the Tibetan tradition green is the colour of peace, calm, and tranquillity, and salvation from fear and danger of every kind. If you are rather anxious, if you worry a lot, then you should surround yourself with green; it will have a pacifying effect. Yellow – brilliant, vivid yellow – is the colour of growth, of prosperity and riches, even worldly riches, and of beauty and maturation. It is of course the colour of sunlight, the light which brings everything organic to a state of maturity. All this is represented by yellow in Tibetan iconography. Then there are two shades of blue, light and dark, both of which represent knowledge, that is, knowledge of the Truth, of the undifferentiated Absolute, knowledge of *śūnyatā*. This is represented by blue, the colour of the unclouded sky.

In addition to these colours, we also find black and white. As in many other traditions, white represents purity. It also represents primordial being, the absolute reality that transcends time. Black, or very dark blue, symbolizes death and destruction, but in a very positive sense. A dark blue or black figure, usually with a wrathful expression, represents Enlightenment under the aspect of the destruction of spiritual ignorance.

Thus in Tibetan Buddhist art we can tell the general nature of a deity, whether Buddha or bodhisattva, from the colour. If the deity is green, we'll know that it is connected with peace. If it is connected with love it will be red, if with purification white – or sometimes very pale blue – and so on. For instance, Green Tārā, a female Buddha form much loved by the Tibetans, is that form of Tārā which is concerned with pacification, and salvation from danger. Similarly the red Kurukullā, a rather extraordinary female Buddha figure, being bright red represents the love aspect, the passion aspect even, of the Enlightened mind.

The black or dark blue or brown figures are sometimes referred to by western writers as demons or devils. Laurence Waddell, an early writer on Tibetan Buddhism, who was very well informed but didn't have much understanding, often used this sort of nomenclature, referring to the 'Buddha fiendesses' and the 'Buddha demonesses', but this gives quite the wrong impression.[26] These figures are not demons or fiends or anything like that. They in fact belong to the highest level of all, the Buddha level, but as seen under the aspect of the destruction of spiritual ignorance. Sometimes they are very fierce indeed. Often they have thick dark strong bodies, wear garlands of skulls and elephant hides and tiger skins, and have long teeth or tusks and three or more eyes. They are very wrathful, they trample upon enemies, and have an aureole of flames. Though they look very fearsome, they are not demons and have nothing to do with hell in the western sense. They symbolize those aspects of Enlightenment which burn up, overcome, and destroy ignorance in all its forms.

The point is that ignorance is so strong, so powerful, that the beautiful peaceful figures are unable to cope with it. They have to assume these terrible, wrathful forms in order to make some impression, at least, on the forces of ignorance, which otherwise don't take any notice of them. There are many legends to this effect, describing how a Buddha or bodhisattva closed his eyes in meditation and out of his forehead emerged a great beam of light at the end of which appeared a terrifying monster, a wrathful figure brandishing a club and roaring 'I want your blood.' Apparently this is sometimes the only way in which the Enlightened mind can operate in this deluded world. When one confronts and surveys the world, one can feel every sympathy with this sort of approach. Perhaps it isn't the peaceful, meek and mild Buddhas and bodhisattvas who are going to get anything done, but the more wrathful and terrifying ones.

However, one must always remember that this is not ordinary anger but what the Tantric tradition calls 'the Great Anger' or 'the Great Wrath'. Great, *mahā*, here means 'purified by *śūnyatā*', because it has passed through the fires of the Absolute. It is not an anger based on ignorance or on the ego; on the contrary, it is based on pure compassion, pure love. When ignorance and hatred encounter that love, they can experience it only as wrath or anger. This is the basis of this sort of symbolism in Tibetan Buddhism, especially in the Tantra.

There are, of course, also many peaceful symbolic forms in Tibetan iconography. One of the best-known and most popular is the eleven-headed and thousand-armed Avalokiteśvara (Chenrezig in Tibetan), the Bodhisattva of Compassion. This particular form represents absolute compassion, operating simultaneously in all directions and in all possible ways. The thousand arms represent the innumerable expedients of compassion, to help and save living beings, and it is significant that in each hand there is an eye, which means that even in the remotest operations of compassion there is awareness, or wisdom. There is a saying that it takes all the wisdom of the wise to undo the harm done by the merely good. The activity of compassion is not a sort of do-gooding, divorced from awareness or wisdom. Avalokiteśvara's eleven heads represent the eleven directions: north, south, east, west, the intermediate points, the zenith, the nadir, and the middle.

One of the most beautiful peaceful figures in Tibetan Buddhism is Green Tārā. As we have seen, her colour represents peace and salvation. Her left hand holds a lotus which has three blue blossoms – one quite open, one half open, and one just a bud. These represent the Buddhas of the three periods of time. It is as though Tārā manifests herself as these three Buddhas. The Buddha of the past is fully opened – he's gone, as it were, he has reached perfection. The Buddha of the present is half open, because his dispensation, his teaching, is still in force. The bud represents the Buddha of the future, who is yet to come. Green Tārā wears a tiara of five skulls or sometimes five jewels, representing the five wisdoms. She has two feet – which may not sound worth mentioning, but Tibetan Buddhist figures sometimes have ten feet, or sixteen, or more. One of her feet is in the lotus posture, which means that she is always in meditation. But the other is just hanging down, suggesting that she is ready to step out into the world.

We have only touched on a few of the symbols of Tibetan Buddhist art, but we can perhaps imagine the effect they have on the minds of people who are in touch with them all the time. In the West we suffer from a dearth of symbols. Often the nearest we get to a symbol is a Christmas tree. But the Tibetan Buddhist is, or was, surrounded by symbols. Wherever you looked, there would be a stupa, or a three-storey temple, or a *thangka*, or someone twirling a prayer wheel or telling their beads. Even Tibetan social customs and etiquette – the way people eat and drink and receive friends and visitors – have a symbolic value which helps to keep them in touch with that which is beyond the symbols, but to which the symbols point – higher levels of being and consciousness and reality.

Not all Tibetans understand the meanings of their symbols, but at least they have a sense of something greater, nobler, more spiritual, lying above and beyond and, at the same time, affecting them. Tibetan Buddhist art and its symbolism is therefore an important and vital aspect of Tibetan Buddhism. Our own lives in the West would be richer, and certainly more interesting, if they incorporated more symbolism of a spiritual nature. If we could follow the Tibetans' example and bring that about, perhaps we would be less estranged, less alienated, from reality.

6

THE FOUR FOUNDATION YOGAS

In Tibetan Buddhism, as in all Buddhist traditions, meditation lies at the heart of the spiritual life. Meditation has been part of Buddhism from the very beginning, going right back to the Buddha's own teachings. For example, the last three stages of the Noble Eightfold Path – Perfect Effort, Perfect Awareness, and Perfect *Samādhi* – are all concerned in one way or another with meditation. *Samādhi* or meditation is also the fifth of the six *pāramitās* or perfections, which, according to the Mahāyāna, form the path of the bodhisattva. Not all schools of Buddhism have meditation as their main focus – it is Chan or Zen which specializes in it, while other schools may concentrate more on ethics or metaphysics – but for all schools meditation is a fundamental practice.

The details of the meditation experience differ greatly from one person to another depending on temperament, as well as on the kind of meditation one is doing, so it is not easy to generalize. But, very broadly, there are five successive stages of meditation, regardless of the Buddhist tradition we follow or the specific meditative path we pursue. These stages are not sharply demarcated from each other but, like the colours of the rainbow, fade into one another by imperceptible degrees.

The first stage can be described as withdrawal of the mind from the senses. Finding a quiet and secluded place, sitting still and closing our eyes, we gradually withdraw our awareness from the input of our physical senses until the mind is poised, as it were, in itself. But this is only the beginning of meditation.

The second stage is traditionally called the suppression of the five hindrances, the five kinds of negative emotional state which undermine our meditation and need to be dealt with if we are to make further progress. The first hindrance is 'craving for sensuous experience'. You may for a while shut out the external world – you are not looking at anything or listening to anything – but as you sit there, concentrated, a sort of tremor may arise in your mind, based on a recollection of a previous experience, and that will lead your mind almost insensibly back towards the original sense object. Along with that will come a desire for the experience of that sense object. This hindrance has deep roots that reach to the very depths of the unconscious mind. The second hindrance is hatred or ill will or antagonism of any kind – irritation, indignation, and so on. Then there is 'sloth and torpor', physical sluggishness and psychological inertia, a sort of stagnation. Fourthly, there is restlessness and anxiety, or 'worry and flurry': a nagging sense of insecurity that won't let you settle down. The final hindrance is 'doubt and indecision'. This is not doubt in the sense of not being absolutely sure; as a hindrance, doubt is an unwillingness to commit oneself without being absolutely sure. So this stage of meditation consists in freeing oneself temporarily – under the special conditions of the meditation practice – from these five hindrances.[27]

The third stage consists in elimination of discursive thought. Often people think that meditation is about getting rid of thought, and in a sense this is true, but with the proviso that you do not just eliminate thoughts or try not to have them. You just forget about thinking altogether, by taking a particular object of concentration and focusing all your attention on it. For example, in doing the Mindfulness of Breathing practice you concentrate on the breath, ignoring discursive thoughts and paying attention to the breath. You will then find – or rather won't 'find' because you won't even notice – that the thoughts are no longer there.

At first you may have to hang on to your concentration object, the breath, for dear life, vaguely conscious of a swarm of thoughts swirling all around you. But gradually you can relax your grip. Becoming more and more absorbed in the breath, you feel, rather than see, the wandering thoughts subside. They become faint and indistinct, and eventually die away altogether. But you are not thinking about the fact that you are not thinking. As soon as it occurs to you to think 'Oh look!

I'm not thinking about anything,' your concentration slips and you have to start again. But when we eliminate discursive thought, the result is not a blank unconsciousness. We enter not a psychological vacuum, but a positive state of awareness in which the true nature of the mind, in its fullness and purity, begins to be revealed.

This brings us to the fourth stage of meditation: the development of higher states of awareness, new levels of consciousness. This experience comes naturally, almost of its own accord, as you become more and more absorbed in the object of concentration. Eventually you become as it were unified with it. You are not concentrating on anything in particular; you are just concentrated. Along with this comes an experience of increasing purity, peace, and bliss. You may have a sensation of being carried out of yourself, of being swept away. Sometimes, when this happens, it is a little frightening. It feels as if you are being borne along by a rushing river, and you don't know where it will take you. But if you resist giving in to the fear, the experience eventually passes away. We need to have faith in the nature of the experience, to surrender ourselves to it and let it carry us wheresoever it will.

The fifth and final stage is the arising of Insight, of direct knowledge of ultimate reality. This represents a suffusion of our whole being with reality in such a way that it is transformed and transfigured. At this point there is a qualitative change in our meditation experience: we start seeing into the heart of things, seeing things as they really are, more clearly than we had ever seen them in our lives before. It was said of the early nineteenth-century actor, Charles Kean, that to see him act was like reading Shakespeare by flashes of lightning.[28] It is a little like that. At first we see just by flashes which for an instant illuminate the whole intellectual or spiritual landscape. Eventually the experience becomes more stable, the flashes last longer, and we start to take in more and more of the spiritual vista being revealed. It is as though a continuous beam of light gradually dawns, which we never again altogether lose. In this way, in the course of years or decades of practice, Enlightenment is attained.

These stages are common to all kinds of meditation practice, but there are many variations and the Tibetan tradition of course has its own particular approach. In Tibetan Buddhism meditation is mainly Tantric. We have seen in Chapters 1 and 2 that Tibetan Buddhism is *triyāna* in character, and that it derives its meditation from the Vajrayāna, which specializes in esoteric meditation and symbolic ritual. There are many methods of Tantric practice; indeed, the Tantra contains a bewildering profusion of material. However, we can distinguish between the foundation yogas, which are the preliminary practices, and Tantric meditation proper.

THE FOUR FOUNDATION YOGAS

The four foundation yogas or *mūla yogas* form the basis of Tibetan spiritual practice, and some acquaintance with them is crucial to an understanding of the spiritual life of Tibet. However much we may know about the Dalai Lama, or about Mahāyāna philosophy, if we have not caught the feeling of these practices then really we know nothing at all, spiritually speaking, about Tibetan Buddhism. The *mūla yogas* underpin as it were the whole vast fabric, the whole superstructure, of Tibetan religious life.

Mūla is a Sanskrit word, meaning literally root, or foundation. Just as if a tree's roots don't go deeply into the ground the tree will topple over when the wind blows, in the same way if the *mūla yogas* are weak, then the spiritual life which grows from those roots is weak and may also collapse. The four foundation yogas are therefore prefatory to the whole system of Vajrayāna meditation and religious observance. Tibetan Buddhism emphasizes that there is no success on the Tantric path if the four *mūla yogas* are neglected. You must practise them before you can think of embarking on the Vajrayāna.

In the West people are always looking for short cuts, and as soon as the Vajrayāna (or Zen for that matter) is mentioned, their ears prick up and they think: 'Here is a quick and easy path which circumvents all that meditation, asceticism, and study.' The truth is that the Tantra is a short path only if one practises it long enough, and an easy path only if one practises it hard enough. Tibetans often spend many years working on these foundation yogas, especially when they go into a 'long retreat' which traditionally lasts for a period of three years, three months, three weeks, three days, three hours, and three minutes. Most of us probably wouldn't get very far just sitting in a semi-darkened room and meditating indefinitely. After an hour or so we would be restlessly pacing up and down, wondering what to do next. But when the Tibetans go into this sort of retreat, they really get on with their practice, and in particular they get on with the four *mūla yogas*. I have met Tibetan monks who said that it was remarkable how quickly the time seemed to pass. The days, weeks, and months just slipped by because they were fully engaged in these practices. The more time they spent on them, the more deeply they went into them, the more interesting and fascinating they found them. Tibetan Buddhists, in short, are prepared to practise hard and to practise long.

In the West, unfortunately, we tend to be less patient. We want Enlightenment not at the end of twenty years' practice, but right here and now. And in a sense we are right to do so. But we can only get it here and now if we make a hundred per cent effort – which the very nature of our minds keeps us from doing. We tend to expect quick results from our spiritual life, neglecting the preliminaries. But these, if mastered, constitute half the battle. One could go so far as to say that if you prepare for meditation properly then you are already meditating. The end or aim of the spiritual life cannot be sharply separated from the means. Indeed, as Mahatma Gandhi once remarked, the end is the extreme of the means.[29] If you devote yourself wholeheartedly to the means, then, almost without noticing, you gain the end. If you peg away at the preliminaries of the spiritual life, you will find yourself in due course deep in the heart of the essentials; but if you neglect the basics and try to leap ahead then you may not find yourself anywhere at all.

The word *yoga* literally means simply that which unites or joins. It is etymologically connected with the English word 'yoke'. In the West, yoga usually refers to a system of exercises. In Hinduism, it means any practice which unites one with Truth or Reality or God or, as in the more philosophical Advaita Vedanta, unites the lower self with the higher self by the recognition of their underlying non-duality.

But in the context of Tantric Buddhism the word yoga has a different meaning again. It refers especially to the union – both in the Enlightened mind and at all stages of the spiritual path – of wisdom and compassion, of supreme awareness of reality and universal loving-kindness. It can also mean the union of the experience of emptiness, *śūnyatā*, and great bliss, *mahāsukha*. The Tantric tradition describes this kind of union by the term *yuganaddha*, usually translated as 'two-in-oneness' – the two-in-oneness of wisdom and compassion, or of emptiness and bliss. We could also speak of the two-in-oneness of *saṃsāra* and *nirvāṇa*, or of the Buddha and the bodhisattva. This state of non-duality, this experience of unity in difference and difference in unity, is the highest goal of Tantric practice, and the *mūla yogas* are so called because they are practices which initiate the process of integration of one part of our nature with another. At the highest level this process culminates in the state of perfect integration of wisdom and compassion, of emptiness and bliss, which is Enlightenment itself.

The four foundation yogas therefore form the entrance to the Vajrayāna, or the Tantra, which, as we saw in Chapter 2, is the last of the three stages of development of Buddhism in India. The spiritual practices, the rites, the ceremonies, the meditation, and the symbolism of Tibetan Buddhism mostly come from the Vajrayāna. Although it incorporates all three *yānas*, in practice Tibetan Buddhism often starts straight away with the Vajrayāna, beginning with the four foundation yogas. This does not mean that the spiritual practices of the Hīnayāna and the Mahāyāna are neglected, for the most important of these practices are incorporated into the *mūla yogas* themselves.

The *mūla yogas* are practised in much the same way in all Tibetan Buddhist schools, though sometimes the order of practice is different and details may vary. The following summary accords mainly with the Nyingma tradition, the one with which I have had the closest personal connection.

THE GOING FOR REFUGE AND PROSTRATION PRACTICE

The *mūla yogas* begin where the whole Buddhist path begins, with Going for Refuge to the Three Jewels: the Buddha, the Dharma, and the Sangha. Going for Refuge is common to all schools of Buddhism, but the ceremony of Going for Refuge – 'taking the refuges' as it is often called – is not always taken very seriously. In India, for instance, the organizers of Buddhist public meetings sometimes insist that everybody recites the Refuges and Precepts even though the audience is mainly non-Buddhist and the meeting is itself political rather than religious. Such recitation has no real significance and in fact represents an abuse of tradition. In the Tantric Buddhism of Tibet, by contrast, Going for Refuge is not only taken very seriously, but is treated as an important spiritual practice in its own right. It is in this way that it figures in the *mūla yogas*.

The Going for Refuge and Prostration practice consists of three main elements: prostration, recitation, and visualization, corresponding to body, speech, and mind. In this way the whole being, the whole personality, is involved. This is characteristic of all Tantric practices. It is not enough just to do something mentally; you have to do it verbally and physically as well. In the case of the Buddha himself, these three modes of functioning correspond to the three *kāyas*. What in us are body, speech, and mind, are in an Enlightened being *nirmāṇakāya, sambhogakāya*, and *dharmakāya* respectively. (More is said about this in Chapter 7.)

The mental element of the first *mūla yoga* is the visualization of what is called the Refuge Tree. You start by sitting for meditation with your eyes closed. You see in your mind's eye a blue sky-like background, and against it, growing out of the water – or perhaps the mud – an enormous lotus-flower, in fact a whole lotus plant, as big as a great tree, with a thick central stem and four branches rising out of the stem in the four cardinal directions. At the top of each of these, there blooms an enormous lotus flower. These lotuses can be any colour you like, but they must be enormous, and together they form a sort of mandala. When you have this great plant with its five blossoms firmly in your mind, and can see it quite clearly, then you direct your attention to the central lotus. You see layers upon layers of petals folded back, and right in the centre, sitting on the calyx of the central lotus, you visualize the founder of the particular Tantric tradition within which you are practising. For the Nyingmapas this is Padmasambhava, for the Gelugpas Tsongkhapa, and so on. You imagine this figure as clearly as possible, firmly seated in the middle of the central lotus, and you think of him as being the embodiment of all the Buddhas, the embodiment of your highest ideal in all its possible manifestations. All spiritual perfections, all qualities of Enlightenment, are concentrated in that one figure.

In the next stage you go a little further. You notice that the lotus has many tiers of petals, and underneath the central figure you visualize – sitting in rows on the tiers of petals – other lamas or gurus of the lineage, including your personal teacher and other masters from whom you have received instruction. Even lower down (still on the central lotus) you visualize the various Tantric deities – Buddhas and bodhisattvas, both peaceful and wrathful – and underneath them the *ḍākinīs* and the *dharmapālas*. These figures represent the three Refuges under their more Tantric or esoteric aspect. The guru is the esoteric counterpart of the Buddha; the deities, archetypal symbols of spiritual experiences, are the esoteric aspects of the Dharma; and the *ḍākas, ḍākinīs*, and *dharmapālas*, the beings (or spiritual forces) in whose company one follows the path, represent the esoteric sangha.

On the lotus blossom in front, the southern one, sits Śākyamuni, the human historical Buddha, along with other historical Buddhas, usually the Buddha of the past, Dīpaṅkara, to the left and the Buddha of the future, Maitreya, to the right. On the lotus to the left (as you look at the tree) are the bodhisattvas, usually the eight or ten principal ones including such figures as Avalokiteśvara and Mañjuśrī. They represent the sangha, the spiritual community, of the Mahāyāna. On the lotus to the north, behind the central lotus, you see a pile of sacred scriptures representing the Dharma. To the right, on the eastern lotus, you see the assembly of *arhants* – those who are said to have gained liberation for themselves alone – who constitute the Hīnayāna sangha. They include great Enlightened disciples of the Buddha such as Śāriputra and Maudgalyāyana.

These images make up the main features of the Refuge Tree. The whole tree has to be visualized quite clearly and vividly before you begin the rest of the practice. You build up this mental picture, at the same time trying to develop a feeling of devotion for all these great spiritual figures and archetypal forms. Tibetans themselves are of course familiar with the appearance of the Refuge Tree from *thangkas*. So many figures are involved that the painting of even one such *thangka* may keep an artist busy for months on end, so *thangkas* of the Refuge Tree are not easy to come by. One was given to me once, but within a week it had gone. Tomo Geshe Rimpoche, who was a friend of mine, not only saw and admired it but remarked, rather thoughtfully, that he had no such *thangka* in his monastery in Ghoom, so that I had no alternative but to present it to him.[30]

The verbal element of this *mūla yoga* consists in reciting aloud a series of verses expressive of one's Going for Refuge. One takes refuge in the founder of the tradition – Padmasambhava in the case of the Nyingma school – as the embodiment of all the Refuges.

Finally, there is the physical element of the Going for Refuge, as represented by the prostration. The body occupies an important place in the Vajrayāna as compared with the scant regard for it of the Hīnayāna. Of course all forms of Buddhism recognize that one cannot gain Enlightenment unless one has a human body, but despite this the body is often disparaged. Sometimes it is referred to as an animated corpse, or a bucket of filth that you carry around with you; all sorts of picturesque expressions of that kind are used. But in the Vajrayāna it is considered a great mistake to speak in dispraise of the human body, because it is the vehicle for emancipation and can become the body of a Buddha. Indeed, it is only through this physical body that one can gain Enlightenment. It is therefore viewed as rare and precious, something to be prized, and spiritual practice is seen as meaningless if the body does not play a part.

Religion must therefore be not just mental and verbal, but physical as well, and Tibetan spiritual life involves a great deal of bodily exertion. This is not just to keep you warm when there is snow outside your monastery. It is because the Tibetans believe that if the body is not involved, you are not seriously practising. This is why we find Tibetans doing things like prostrating themselves all the way from Lhasa to Bodh Gaya, a distance of five or six hundred miles. We might think this is crazy, but the Tibetans take it very seriously and they greatly respect people who do this sort of thing. In the same spirit, in the first *mūla yoga* you don't just visualize the Refuge Tree and repeat the formula of Going for Refuge; you also fling yourself down in a full-length prostration in front of the imagined Refuge Tree with all its lamas and deities and so on. In India abbreviated prostrations are more common, but the Tibetans prostrate fully and rather dramatically, flat on their faces with their arms shooting out in front of them.

Having started by sitting and building up the visualization, you hold the completed mental image of the Refuge Tree while you rise from your seat, start reciting the Going for Refuge verses, and do the prostrations. In this way, the three elements of the practice – visualization, recitation, and prostration – come to be done simultaneously, which is quite an exercise in concentration and mindfulness. Body, speech, and mind cooperate: you keep the visualized Refuge Tree steady in your mind, repeat the verses, *and* fling yourself down. You also have to count your prostrations – which are traditionally done in multiples of 108 – either on your *mālā* or by moving one of a pile of little stones every time you get up. The effect of all this is impossible to describe; you have to do it to know what it feels like. What one can certainly say is that it is good physical exercise. The Tibetans believe that it's a certain cure for tuberculosis, provided you do it long and energetically enough.

According to tradition you do 100,000 prostrations. This takes about three months if you do it full-time, but if you do just a few hundred a day it takes nearly a year to complete. The important thing is to do as many as possible. You can in fact take up other Vajrayāna practices before you have finished the preliminary practices, so that you are adding to your total of prostrations while at the same time embarking on a meditation on Tārā or Mañjuśrī, or even on a more advanced practice. This may be a concession to the corruptions of modern times, but it is what the Tibetans themselves do.

The Going for Refuge and Prostration practice represents the 'Hīnayāna' component of the four *mūla yogas*, though this component is transformed by the general Vajrayāna context within which it takes place. Indeed, Tibetan Buddhism regards the whole of the Hīnayāna, or what we may call Basic Buddhism, as being summed up in the Going for Refuge to the Buddha, Dharma, and Sangha.

THE DEVELOPMENT OF THE *BODHICITTA*

The second *mūla yoga* is the arising of the *bodhicitta*, the will or urge towards Enlightenment for the benefit of all living beings. To bring this about, we need firstly to develop love and compassion for all beings. This aspiration of course reverberates throughout the whole of Buddhism, but here as elsewhere the Tibetans add their own particular flavour, their own particular colouring. They suggest that one should regard all living beings as if they were one's own parents. Like most Buddhists, the Tibetans believe in rebirth, and they take this to its logical conclusion. (Tibetan Buddhists are rather fond of carrying things to their logical conclusions, so far as Buddhism is concerned.) They believe that we have each lived on this Earth thousands or even millions of times, and that therefore, if we look far enough back, it is practically certain that everybody we meet has at some time, ten or a hundred or a thousand lifetimes ago, been our mother or our father. It's as though we have not just one set of parents, but millions of them.

To us in the West, even if we are Buddhists, and even if we accept – with more or less reservation – the idea of rebirth, it is not really part of our being. But in the case of the Tibetans it is in their bones and their blood, as it were, and they feel it very strongly. They actually believe that every single person they meet has been, at some time in the remote past, related to them as their mother or father, and therefore that they should be kind and affectionate towards them and treat them well. The Tantric tradition emphasizes that inasmuch as you have this degree of love and compassion for all sentient beings, you should naturally resolve to deliver them from suffering.

The Tibetans illustrate the point in the following way. Happening to walk through the bazaar, you notice that in one corner a disturbance of some kind is going on. Quite a crowd has gathered, and in the middle of the crowd someone is being kicked and beaten. Out of curiosity you draw near, and see that it is a woman – an old woman – who is being assaulted. Feeling somewhat concerned, and thinking that perhaps someone should intervene, you elbow your way through the crowd and discover, to your horror and astonishment, that it is your own mother who is lying there on the ground with blood streaming from her head. At once your attitude of impersonal civic concern is transformed into one of intense love and compassion and you rush forward to help, for the person who is suffering is near and dear to you.

The spiritual masters of Tibet say that if you can see each suffering being as your own mother or father, or as someone else who is near and dear to you, then compassion will well up in your heart – otherwise not. This is why they emphasize the idea. We see so much suffering in the world. We read in the newspapers of people being killed in accidents or disasters, or being slaughtered in their thousands in war, but so often we just turn to the next page and read the sports results. We think nothing of such horrors, because no one near and dear to us is involved. But if we feel as if all living beings are deeply and intimately related to us, if we act as though all beings are in fact our own reincarnated mothers and fathers, then compassion arises. Seeing all the suffering beings around us in this light, we will feel a tremendous urge to deliver them, to lead them on the path to Buddhahood. Moved in this way, we will resolve that through our practice of the Vajrayāna we will gain Enlightenment for the benefit of all living beings. In this way we are led to take the bodhisattva vow.

The second *mūla yoga* consists in the repetition of a formula expressing this vow, this determination to gain Enlightenment not just for the sake of one's own emancipation, but for the welfare of the whole world of sentient beings. And it is to be recited 100,000 times. It is a characteristic feature of the Vajrayāna that you do a practice 100,000 times. This is because it needs to penetrate into the unconscious mind. It is no use just repeating something once and then thinking we have understood it and can put it aside. It is all too easy to say, 'I vow to gain Enlightenment for the sake of all sentient beings,' and think we have taken the bodhisattva vow. But just *saying* the words may have made no impression whatsoever, not even a scratch on the surface of our mind. Hence the Vajrayāna exhorts us to go on repeating it, a thousand or ten thousand or a hundred thousand times. Maybe when we have done it a hundred thousand times, the meaning will begin to percolate below the level of the conscious mind and permeate the unconscious mind, which is what really matters.

Furthermore, between one's sessions of practice one should reflect that with every incoming breath the sins of all beings, all their weaknesses and imperfections, are entering one's body and are being absorbed into, and annihilated by, the will to Enlightenment one has developed. Then one should imagine that with every outgoing breath, one's own good qualities, such as they are, are falling upon others like moonlight, and conferring happiness upon them. In other words one should feel that one's influence upon others is beneficent and positive, like moonlight. The comparison recalls Indian tradition, because in India, after the heat of the day, the moonlight is cool and soothing. If you practise the *mūla yogas* you have to ask yourself whether this is the kind of effect you have on others, and whether your friends would compare you with moonlight.

Besides doing this practice one should also cultivate the *brahma vihāras*, the four sublime states of love, compassion, sympathetic joy, and equanimity.[31] These practices are common to both the Hīnayāna and the Mahāyāna; however, in general this *mūla yoga*, the development of the *bodhicitta*, represents the Mahāyāna component of the four foundation yogas.

THE MEDITATION AND MANTRA RECITATION OF VAJRASATTVA

The third *mūla yoga* is purely Tantric, with no real counterpart in the Hīnayāna or Mahāyāna. It is undertaken for what the tradition calls 'purification of sins', and the Vajrayāna attaches great importance to this. While its conception of sin is very different from that of Christianity, it recognizes that our minds are obscured by all sorts of things that we would rather forget about. If we are to get anywhere with our spiritual practice, however, we cannot forget about them; we have to drag them all out into the light of day, into the light of the Buddha, and resolve them. We have to recognize them clearly and face up to them before they can be purified. The Vajrasattva yoga, as it is also called, is undertaken for this purpose.

Vajrasattva's name means 'the Diamond (or Adamantine) Being'. Though a Buddha, he is represented iconographically in the form of a bodhisattva, that is to say, as a young man wearing princely garments, jewellery, and other ornaments. Sometimes he is called the sixth Buddha, the esoteric or hidden Buddha. The Tantric tradition speaks of a sixth Buddha much as we might speak of a sixth dimension. It implies something mysterious, a sort of 'x-factor' which we do not really apprehend. Vajrasattva is the sixth Buddha in relation to the scheme of the five Buddhas, who are the transcendental counterparts of the five *skandhas*, the five constituents of conditioned existence.

In Buddhism the whole of existence is viewed as having two aspects: that which is conditioned, called *saṃsāra* (i.e. all that is depicted in the Tibetan wheel of life) and that which is unconditioned, called Nirvāṇa. Conditioned existence, the whole mundane universe both material and mental, consists of the five *skandhas*: form, feeling, perception, volition, and consciousness. On the Unconditioned or transcendental plane there is a corresponding division into the five archetypal Buddhas, often depicted in a mandala with one in the centre and one at each of the four cardinal points. The usual arrangement is to have the white Buddha, Vairocana, in the centre; then to the north the green Amoghasiddhi, to the south the yellow Ratnasambhava, to the west the red Amitābha, and to the east the dark blue Akṣobhya (though he is sometimes in the centre, with Vairocana to the east). The central Buddha is a synthesis of the other four, which represent special aspects of the main figure. Vajrasattva is the esoteric aspect of the central or fifth Buddha. We can imagine him as being behind the central Buddha in a different dimension, as it were, 'outside' the plane on which the five Buddhas are differentiated.

One of the fundamental principles of the Tantra, and of Tibetan Buddhism generally, is that all the Buddhas, bodhisattvas, *ḍākas, ḍākinīs, dharmapālas*, and so on are to be found within one's own mind. If you penetrate right into the depths of your mind, beyond your ordinary conscious mind into something far greater, far higher and wider, then you encounter these forms and figures. And if you go deep enough into your own mind, beyond all thoughts, words, and deeds, even beyond all the other Buddhas and bodhisattvas, you encounter the fundamental intrinsic purity of Vajrasattva. He symbolizes the primeval, original purity of one's own mind, its transcendental purity beyond space and beyond time. In other words, Vajrasattva represents the truth that whatever you might have done on the phenomenal plane, whatever sins you might have committed, however low you might have sunk on the scale of being and consciousness, in the depths of your being you are pure. Your true nature remains untouched and unsullied. Obviously this can be misunderstood. The fact that your basic mind remains pure does not mean that it doesn't matter what you do. It matters very much, because it is only if you behave ethically and develop Insight that you can realize the primordial purity of your own mind that is symbolized by Vajrasattva.

The purpose of the Vajrasattva practice is therefore to reintegrate us with our own innate purity, to purify us of our sins by the recognition that underneath the sins the immaculate purity of our own mind has never been tainted. Above and beyond all Buddhas and bodhisattvas, above and beyond all worlds and universes, all thoughts and ideas, even all realizations and experiences, outside time altogether, our own mind remains absolutely pure. We acknowledge our sins as sins on their own level, but we purify ourselves by realizing that in the depths of our being we have never sinned. This is the essence of the practice.

The practice begins with another visualization. You visualize Vajrasattva immediately above your head. He is a brilliant white, like sunlit snow, and is sometimes without either garments or ornaments, sometimes clad in silks and jewels. He is youthful – the texts say sixteen years of age, which is supposed to be the ideal age so far as beauty is concerned – and he is smiling. You then visualize the *bīja* or seed syllable *hūṃ*, blue in colour, at the centre of his heart. This is surrounded by the circle of letters of the hundred syllable mantra of Vajrasattva. The letters stand upright, rather like the stones at Stonehenge, all white and emitting light.

A stream of milk-like nectar then descends from the seed syllable in the heart of Vajrasattva, as well as from the surrounding letters of the mantra. Descending into you through the top of your head, it goes right through your body, washing away all sins. You both visualize and experience this. With practice you can actually feel a sensation of coolness flowing down into the whole body and permeating it. Eventually your body becomes like a crystal vase filled with curds – the traditional comparison – and you feel cleansed and purified. You feel transparent like crystal, or even like pure light. (In fact, all visualization exercises have this kind of psychological effect.)

These are the main features of the visualization. Having done it, you then recite the hundred syllable mantra as many times as you can at one sitting, the aim being eventually to recite it 100,000 times. The mantra itself expresses the idea of reintegration with one's intrinsically pure Vajrasattva nature. At the end of the practice the visualized Vajrasattva is dissolved back into the void, into *śūnyatā*, which is the usual procedure at the end of any visualization exercise.

THE OFFERING OF THE MANDALA

The word mandala – literally 'circle' – has several meanings. In this context it means a symbolic representation of the entire universe according to ancient Indian cosmological tradition. The practice consists in offering this mandala, offering the cosmos as it were, to the three Jewels – the Buddha, the Dharma, and the Sangha – in both their exoteric and esoteric aspects. These are visualized more or less as in the Going for Refuge and Prostration practice except that here there is no tree. One then performs a special Tantric version of the devotional practice known as the Sevenfold Puja, after which one builds up and offers the mandala as a symbol of the universe.

This symbolic representation of the universe is made up of thirty-seven parts, representing prominent features of the universe as well as its most precious contents, including Mount Meru (the central mountain), the four major and eight minor continents, the 'seven precious things', and so on. The traditional practice is to construct it by heaping up grains of rice on a circular copper base and adding rings of copper or silver until one has built up a conical structure with several tiers. The various heaps of rice, around the foundation and at higher levels, represent different elements of the physical universe and one bears these in mind and repeats their names while building up the model. There are several ways of offering the mandala. Usually one lifts it up in one's hands, at the same time reciting various mantras and verses expressive of one's offering of the entire universe to the Three Jewels.

The meaning of the practice relates back to the second *mūla yoga*, whose aim is the development of the wish to gain Enlightenment for the sake of all beings. In order to do this, one needs an enormous accumulation of 'merit' or *puṇya*, in other words, good qualities and auspicious spiritual attributes. It is axiomatic for Buddhism that merit is gained by *dāna*, by giving. This is the basic, cardinal virtue. It is one of the most wonderful features of life in Buddhist countries that people are so generous, readily sharing with you whatever they have. If you visit someone's home, you will be offered at least a cup of tea, perhaps a whole meal, or a small gift. Similarly, you yourself must not go to see someone empty handed. So if it is meritorious just to offer a cup of tea or a little money, or to give one's time or energy, or even to offer a monastery or a temple, how much more meritorious it would be to offer the whole universe! If you offered absolutely everything, you would gain incalculable merit.

The problem is that we don't have at our disposal as much as we would like to offer, and many of us are quite poor. But Buddhism teaches that it is the intention that counts. The mental offering is in fact the real offering (with the proviso that one's offering is more likely to be real if it is accompanied by a physical act of giving). You offer this symbolic representation of the whole universe in all its aspects, with all its treasures, and at the same time try to develop the attitude that if everything was yours you really would offer it all to the Buddha, the Dharma, and the Sangha.

This must not become a mere formality. While offering the mandala, you should genuinely feel that you are offering up absolutely everything, that even if you became the richest person in the world you would devote it all to Buddhism. If you became master of the universe, you really could think of nothing better to do with it than to offer it to the Three Jewels. Some Buddhist kings actually used to offer their kingdom to the Buddha in a rather spectacular way (though sometimes they took it back again the next day). The offering of the mandala signifies the will to give, the will to surrender. It is the longest of the *mūla yogas* to complete, but the whole procedure should be done, as one would expect, 100,000 times.

Together, these four foundation yogas form the basis of Tibetan spiritual practice. They are regarded as preparatory to the practice of the Vajrayāna, of Tantric Buddhism as a whole, but it is also said that if any one of them – especially the Vajrasattva yoga – is practised sufficiently thoroughly, frequently, and sincerely, it will bring one very close indeed to Enlightenment.

7
TANTRIC INITIATION

It is clear from the details of the *mūla yogas* that Vajrayāna methods of meditation differ in many respects from those of Early Buddhism and the Mahāyāna. However, Tantric meditation is not defined by its practices. Its essential feature is that it is practised by the *sādhaka*, the practitioner, after initiation by a guru. This does not just mean being taught the method of meditation, although in a sense that is an initiation. The Sanskrit term for a Tantric initiation is *abhiṣeka*, the dictionary meaning of which is 'a sprinkling'. It is true that in the course of the initiation the person being initiated is sometimes ceremonially sprinkled with water. But this is just an aspect of the ritual: it does not tell us anything about the essential meaning of the initiation. The word the Tibetans use for *abhiṣeka* is *wongkur* (*wong* for short), and it gives us more of a clue as to what Tantric initiation really implies. *Wong* means 'power', 'energy', or 'spiritual potency', and *kur* means 'transmission' or 'bestowal'. So *wongkur* – transmission of power – renders the inner meaning of the word *abhiṣeka* rather than its dictionary definition. A Tantric initiation is essentially a transmission of spiritual power from the guru to the disciple. This is symbolized by the sprinkling of water, and very often embodied in a mantra, a sacred syllable or phrase to be repeated over and over again, which is given at the time of initiation.

On the other hand, we may prefer to think of *wongkur* in terms of the *activation* of power. The guru does not so much literally give some of his own power to the disciple as activate by his spiritual presence the latent spiritual forces of the disciple. But it must be said that in the course of a Tantric initiation many people do experience an actual transmission of power. They do not feel that something is being activated within them, but rather that something is passing into them from the guru, piercing them like a spiritual electric shock. Anyone who has experienced spiritual healing should be able to understand the sort of thing that is going on here. Not that Tantric initiation is in any way akin to spiritual healing; but just as a health-giving, positive force manifestly passes from the healer to the patient, so, on a much higher level, a kind of charge of spiritual energy passes from the guru to the disciple.

It is evident from this that Tantric meditation cannot be practised without a guru; this would be a contradiction in terms. If one practises an allegedly Tantric meditation without having been appropriately initiated by a guru, then it becomes a Mahāyāna meditation. On the other hand, if what is technically a Mahāyāna type of meditation is practised after initiation by a guru, it becomes a Tantric practice. We cannot categorize specific meditation practices as either Tantric or non-Tantric; the distinction depends entirely on whether you practise them after having been initiated, in the Tantric sense, by a guru. If you practise a meditation technique on your own, even though a book may label it Tantric, it is not a Tantric practice at all. So while there are in Tibetan Buddhism a number of meditation practices which are never (or never should be) practised without initiation, and might be described as Tantric meditation proper, they are 'Tantric' not on account of what you do in the course of them, but on account of the fact that you are initiated into them by a Tantric guru.

Broadly speaking there are four different '*wongs*' or Tantric initiations in the Vajrayāna. First there is the *kalaśa abhiṣeka* or 'jar initiation', so called because in ancient India a jar was used in the course of this initiation (which consists of six minor initiations). Second is the *guhya abhiṣeka*, the 'secret – or esoteric – initiation'. This is so called because it includes, among other things, the practice of various esoteric methods of control of the breath and of the nervous energy. The third initiation is called the *jñāna-prajñā abhiṣeka*, which means 'the knowledge of *prajñā*'. *Prajñā* generally means 'wisdom', but in the Vajrayāna every term has a rather different meaning from its Mahāyāna definition. In this context *prajñā* means the female partner in the practice, also called the *ḍākinī*. This can be understood literally to mean a person with whom one performs various practices belonging to this level of Tantric meditation experience. Transposed into a lower key, so to speak, it can also be understood as representing what we may call the unrealized 'feminine' side of one's own nature in the case of a man, or the 'masculine' side in the case of a woman. Knowledge of this is the aim of the *jñāna-prajñā*. The last initiation is not usually given a descriptive title, but is called simply 'the fourth'.

These Tantric initiations are correlated with body, speech, and mind, the basic division of the human being in Buddhism. The aim of the Vajrayāna, as of all forms of Buddhism, is Enlightenment; but the Vajrayāna speaks of Enlightenment in a particular way, in terms of the acquisition of the three *kāyas*. *Kāya* literally means 'body', but not body as opposed to mind; 'personality' would be a better rendering. According to general Buddhist teaching, the three *kāyas* represent different facets of the Enlightened mind, different aspects of Buddhahood as it appears on three levels. First there is the *nirmāṇakāya* or 'manifested personality', in other words Buddhahood as it appears on the human historical plane in the form of the specific historical teacher, Gautama the Buddha (or Padmasambhava in the case of the Nyingmapas). Then the *sambhogakāya*, which literally means 'the body of reciprocal enjoyment', or 'the glorious personality', represents Buddhahood appearing on higher celestial or archetypal planes, above and beyond the historical context. Thirdly, there is the *dharmakāya*, 'the absolute personality', or 'the body of truth'. This is Buddhahood in its ultimate essence, above the historical plane, and even above the archetypal plane.

So, the doctrine of the three *kāyas* is that the Buddha manifests or exists on these different levels of reality: the absolute level, the archetypal level, and the human historical level. The three *kāyas* also represent the body, speech, and mind of the Buddha. What in us is mind, in the Buddha is transformed into *dharmakāya*. What in us is speech, communication, in the Buddha becomes *sambhogakāya*. And what in us is physical body, in the Buddha becomes *nirmāṇakāya*. The object of the Vajrayāna is not just that we should gain Enlightenment in a general way. It is more concrete, more specific than that. The aim of the Vajrayāna is that we should become endowed with the three *kāyas*. Our body, speech, and mind should be transformed into the threefold personality of a Buddha.

The first three Tantric initiations and their associated practices are designed to bring this about. Our physical body is transmuted into the *nirmāṇakāya* of a Buddha with the help of the 'jar' *wong* and its associated meditations; our speech, our communication, is transformed into the *sambhogakāya* with the aid of the 'secret' *wong*, and our mind is transformed into the *dharmakāya*, the essence of Buddhahood, by means of the 'knowledge of *prajñā*' *wong*. The fourth *wong* represents the transmutation of body, speech, and mind, not just individually but collectively, into what is called the *svabhāvikakāya*, which means the 'self-existent body' or 'self-existent personality'. This is not really a fourth *kāya* but represents the collective transformation of body, speech, and mind into the three *kāyas* of a Buddha. Thus the fourth *wongkur* is itself not so much a separate *wong* as the totality of the other three.

The four Tantric initiations are also correlated with four yogas – not the *mūla yogas*, but quite different yogas sometimes known as the 'four tantras'. The first of these is *kriyāyoga*, the ritual tantra, which covers a whole class of practices, hundreds of different exercises. *Kriyāyoga* practice is usually described as consisting of one part meditation and three parts symbolic ritual. If a Tantric practice consists of, for example, a quarter of an hour's meditation and three-quarters of an hour's ritual, then it would be regarded as belonging to the *kriyāyoga*. The second yoga is the *ubhayayoga*, which means 'both sides' tantra, *ubhayayoga* practices being half symbolic meditation and half ritual. Thirdly, there is what is called simply *yoga tantra*, which consists of three parts meditation and one part symbolic ritual. Fourthly, there is the *anuttara yoga*, the unsurpassed yoga, which according to the traditional schema is devoted solely to meditation.

The correlation of the four initiations and the four yogas is not quite straightforward: there is not one initiation for each yoga. The first three yogas collectively comprise what is called the Outer or Exoteric Tantra, and the *anuttara yoga* comprises the Inner or Esoteric Tantra. If you want to practise anything belonging to the first three yogas, the Outer Tantra, you only need a simplified form of the first initiation, called the 'body' *wong* or 'little' *wong*, and then you can go ahead with the practice. But if you want to practise the meditations of the Inner or Esoteric Tantra, then you need all four initiations, which are collectively called the 'great' *wong* or the 'great Tantric initiation'.

Obviously there are limits in terms of space to what can be said about Tantric Buddhism in a few pages. But there are also limits in terms of appropriateness, or even propriety. In fact one of the conditions of initiation into the Inner Tantra is that you do not talk about its practices to anyone who has not received the same initiation. In any case, Tibetan Buddhists rarely talk or write about meditation – they're too busy practising it. It is only in the West that we have a lot of lectures and books on meditation. Of course there is no harm in having a sound knowledge of the theory, but sooner or later we have to start practising.

Though it is impossible to speak about the practices of the Inner Tantra, the Outer Tantra is more open and accessible. Its practices are followed by many lay people in Tibet as well as by the ordinary monks, those who are not teachers. There are many types of practice. When I myself first came into contact with Tibetan Buddhism, especially with Tantric meditation, I was bewildered by the profusion – even confusion – of material I found myself presented with. Having perhaps a rather methodical and tidy mind I wasn't quite happy with all these heaps of unorganized material that didn't seem to fit together in any neat fashion – until it became clear to me that it was never meant to be reduced to any sort of order at all. So probably the best thing I can do here is select one particular practice out of the heap, as it were, and concentrate on that.

One of the most popular practices of the Outer Tantra is the meditation on Green Tārā, Drölma in Tibetan. In the Hīnayāna and Mahāyāna, Buddhas and bodhisattvas are always male, but in the Vajrayāna we find just as many female ones, and Tārā is the most prominent of these. Her Sanskrit name means, literally, 'the one who ferries across', in the sense of the one who saves, and it is usually translated 'the Saviouress'. Each bodhisattva form represents one particular aspect of Enlightenment, and Tārā is the embodiment of compassion. More than that, we could say that she is even the embodiment of the embodiment of compassion, because she is in a sense the spiritual daughter of Avalokiteśvara, the great Bodhisattva of Compassion. He is one of the three main bodhisattvas of both the Mahāyāna and the Tantra, along with Mañjuśrī representing wisdom and Vajrapāṇi representing power or energy.

According to legend, once upon a time Avalokiteśvara looked out over the world from the terrace of his palace and saw the whole mass of humanity. He saw people enduring so many troubles, so much suffering. Some were engaged in protracted lawsuits, some were lying sick on their beds, while yet others were being attacked by robbers and highwaymen, or suffering bereavement, or dying painful deaths, even being devoured by wild animals. When he saw the great mass of human misery, the great bodhisattva Avalokiteśvara, out of compassion, could not help shedding tears. In fact he shed so many tears that a great lake formed. And in the midst of the lake appeared a huge white lotus, and when its petals opened, out came a beautiful green goddess – the bodhisattva Tārā, born, the legend says, out of the tears of Avalokiteśvara. So if Avalokiteśvara represents compassion, Tārā is as it were the essence, the quintessence, of compassion.

In Tibet she has many forms, but there are two principal ones, White Tārā and Green Tārā. They are both highly revered, but Green Tārā – also called the Khadiravaṇī Tārā[32] – is the more popular of the two. There are many ways of meditating on her, but the following is the standard evocation of Green Tārā. The general procedure is similar in other Tantric practices which evoke different Buddhas and bodhisattvas.

The meditation has ten stages. As with any Tantric meditation practice, you start off by Going for Refuge, as a brief recapitulation of the Hīnayāna. But the refuges are given a Tantric colouring. First you say, 'To the guru for refuge I go', because the Tantric view – as we saw in Chapter 4 – is that it is only through the guru that you can really come to know the other refuges. In this practice the guru refuge is Amitābha, the Buddha of Infinite Light, because he is the head of the spiritual 'family' to which Avalokiteśvara and Tārā belong. Tibetan paintings of Green Tārā show her with a tiny image of Amitābha in her hair.

You then repeat the refuge formula for the Buddha, Dharma, and Sangha, though in Tantric meditation these are given a Tantric flavour which varies according to the type of practice you are doing. In the Tārā practice, you consider Tārā herself as the Buddha; in other words, you take refuge in the compassion aspect of Enlightenment. Then the Dharma, in this practice, is Tārā's great compassion, as it is the compassion aspect of the Dharma with which you are particularly concerned. The Sangha in this context consists of the twenty-one manifestations or forms of Tārā. So you go for Refuge to Amitābha as the guru, to Tārā herself as the Buddha, to her compassion as the Dharma, and to her twenty-one forms as the Sangha. The same kind of pattern occurs in other practices. For example, if you were doing the Mañjuśrī practice you would go for Refuge to Vairocana as the guru, to Mañjuśrī as the Buddha, to his wisdom as the Dharma, and to his eight forms as the Sangha.

The second stage of the Green Tārā practice is the development of the four *brahma vihāras*, the four divine abodes or sublime states of mind. These are *maitrī*, that is, love in the sense of universal friendliness; *karuṇā*, compassion for all who suffer; *muditā*, sympathetic joy, in other words rejoicing in the happiness of others; and *upekśā*, peace and equanimity of mind. The *brahma vihāras* are also found in the Mahāyāna and Hīnayāna, but in the Hīnayāna they are seen only as *śamatha* practices, that is, as having simply the function of calming the mind. In the Mahāyāna they are also considered to be *vipaśyanā* practices, means of developing Insight, because when you develop these four sublime emotions and direct them towards all living beings, you realize at the same time that these beings are ultimately void or *śūnya*. This stage of the Tārā practice is seen as recapitulating the Mahāyāna in a Tantric context.

The next stage of the practice is the meditation on *śūnyatā* itself, also carried over from the Mahāyāna, where in fact it is seen as the main concern of meditation. This stage is extremely important. It is said that without some experience of voidness, some taste of *śūnyatā*, there is no real practice of the Vajrayāna. Yogi Chen, a friend and teacher of mine in Kalimpong, used to say that without the *śūnyatā* meditation, all the visualizations and rituals of the Vajrayāna are nothing but vulgar magic. Without the *śūnyatā* experience, your practice remains merely on the psychological level.

Fourthly, there is the visualization of the *bīja*, in other words of the seed syllable of Tārā. In the background, as it were, there is *śūnyatā*, the Absolute, the Unconditioned, visualized as a deep blue sky; then in the midst of this you visualize the seed syllable. Every Tantric deity has a seed syllable of his or her own which is regarded as constituting the heart or essence of the deity. Just as a whole tree is contained, potentially, in a seed, the Buddha or bodhisattva is contained in the *bīja*. Green Tārā's *bīja* is the syllable *tāṃ*. You visualize – in the midst of the void – this seed syllable, green in colour, in Tibetan or Sanskrit letters, standing upright on a horizontal moon disc on a white lotus, and radiating light in all directions.

Next we come to the central stage in the whole practice, the visualization of Green Tārā herself. She appears out of the seed syllable, green of course, with a beautiful smiling expression and wearing a crown ornamented with the five Buddhas, representing the five wisdoms. Her right hand rests on her right knee, palm outwards, representing generosity. Her other hand is held near her heart and holds a blue lotus with three blossoms which represent the Buddhas of the past, present, and future. One of her legs is folded in meditation posture, while the other hangs loose as though ready to step down. This symbolizes the fact that although immersed in meditation, in the experience of the Absolute, she is at the same time always ready to enter into the world to help people, out of compassion. Sometimes Green Tārā is said to embody three feminine archetypes: the virgin in the complete purity of her transcendental nature; the mother, in her love and compassion; and the queen, in her spiritual sovereignty and power.

There are different types or levels of visualization – in dreams or hallucinations one is visualizing – but the visualized image which one gets in meditation at this level should have a different quality. The visualized form of Tārā should not be solid and opaque, which would indicate a lower level of meditation. It should be visualized as delicate and diaphanous, like the colours of a rainbow. Or, as it is sometimes said, the colours should be seen like reflections in a mirror, quite evanescent and subtle.

Visualization plays an extremely important part in Tibetan Buddhist meditation. Generally speaking, its aim is to enable you to project from the depths of your mind higher aspects of yourself of which you are not as yet aware. The visualized image, in this case Tārā, acts as a focus for the corresponding qualities in you which are as yet undeveloped, but which are present in the unconscious. Tārā, representing compassion, becomes a focal point, at the level of the conscious or even supraconscious mind, for your own unrealized capacity for compassion. By means of the visualized image, these undeveloped feelings of compassion deep within you, which represent the higher part of your own nature, are enabled to cross the threshold of awareness and to be integrated into your conscious being at ever higher levels. To put it simply, through doing the Tārā visualization practice you become more compassionate yourself.

The sixth stage of the practice consists of the visualization and repetition of the Green Tārā mantra. In the heart of the visualized image of Tārā you see the seed syllable, *tāṃ*, and around it the ten letters of her mantra. You visualize these letters standing up vertically, emitting light and revolving in an anti-clockwise direction. (In the case of male deities the rotation is clockwise.) This is the most difficult part of the visualization, a stationary image being easier to see than one in motion. It is said that if you are mentally restless, you should visualize the letters of the mantra going round slowly, but that if you are feeling sluggish and sleepy they should be made to revolve briskly. As you visualize the letters going round, you repeat the mantra to yourself at least 108 times – the more the better. In between periods of meditation practice you can of course recite the mantra as often as you like.

In the next stage you dissolve the figure of Tārā, including the seed syllable and the mantra, back into the voidness, the 'blue sky', on which it has been superimposed. This is done gradually. You dissolve Tārā back into the lotus and 'moon mat' on which she sits, fade that into the mantra and then into the seed syllable, and finally allow the seed syllable to disappear into the voidness. This stage signifies the truth that all these forms, Buddhas or bodhisattvas, Tārā or Mañjuśrī or whoever, emerge from the void, from the depths of the 'One Mind', and do not exist apart from that. In other traditions it is often thought that the gods, goddesses, saints, sages, saviours, and so on appearing in meditation have a separate, objective existence of their own. But in Buddhism, in the Tantra, it is recognized that such forms and images are the products, ultimately, of one's own mind or consciousness, indeed of absolute mind itself. We impress this truth upon ourselves by dissolving the figure of Tārā back into the void from which she came.

Then the ninth stage consists of the double meditation of Tārā and the voidness. Here there is no build-up: the figure of Tārā appears instantaneously, like the silvery scales of a fish suddenly catching the light as it leaps from the water. Tārā springs up against the voidness, and you visualize the figure and experience the voidness at the same time. So far in the practice Tārā and the void have been concentrated on separately, but here you focus on their interpenetration, representing the identity of *rūpa* or form – represented here by Tārā – and *śūnyatā*. As the *Heart Sūtra* says, whatever is form, that is void, and whatever is void, that is form: there is no difference between them. In this stage you realize the truth of the *Heart Sūtra's* teaching. You realize, through actual experience, that the noumenal and the phenomenal, the Absolute and the relative, are not different. They are one. In this stage you also identify yourself and all other beings with Tārā, and you identify anything you hear with the mantra. If someone says something, you try to feel that this is Tārā herself speaking, this is the mantra of Tārā resounding. In this way, identifying yourself and all other beings with Tārā, you become yourself an embodiment of compassion.

The tenth and last stage of the practice is the dedication of merits, which is the conclusion to all Buddhist spiritual practices. Whatever merits you might have gained from this meditation practice, you resolve to share them with all living beings. There is nothing that you want to keep back for yourself.

This description gives at least some idea of the nature of the meditation on Green Tārā, but in order really to understand what it represents, what the experience involves, one has to practise it oneself. There is no other way to grasp what it is all about. The above description is only the meditation side of the practice – there are also ritual elements – but the whole thing is still quite simple by Tibetan standards. However, many ordinary practitioners, especially lay people, simplify it even further. They keep in their room, or on their shrine, an image or painted scroll of Tārā, to give them an idea of what they should try to visualize. Then every morning they lay out seven offering bowls and fill them with water, usually repeating the mantra, and they light a lamp and some incense, perhaps looking at the image or bowing to it as they do so. This usually suffices for the ritual part of the practice. Then they sit down cross-legged on a rug on a sort of plank bedstead, and start the practice.

They start by reciting what we might call hymns, praising Tārā and her great compassion. Usually in these hymns she is described almost limb by limb, ornament by ornament, so that one can build up a picture of her in one's mind. Then they recite verses expressing their Going for Refuge, their practice of the four *brahma vihāras* and their taking of the bodhisattva vow. And then just sitting there, perhaps looking at the picture and trying to see the image of Tārā in their minds, they go on repeating the Tārā mantra for half an hour or however long they can spare. They conclude by bowing down and dedicating their merits. This is how the ordinary person would do the practice. But if you are serious, especially if you have two or three hours to spare in the morning before you go to work, then you can go through the whole procedure.

These practices can certainly take some time to do. I remember, in connection not with the Tārā practice but with another one, that after the initiation I was given two written versions of the practice. My teacher said, 'Here's the short version, to be done every day, and here's a longer version for when you have two or three days to spare.' (Here he handed me twenty pages of instructions.) The Tārā practice is very commonly done among Tibetans, both monks and lay people. As they get older, as they have fewer and fewer responsibilities in the world, they devote more and more time to it, until eventually they may end up spending the greater part of the day in this way, not just with this particular practice but with a sequence of different practices. When I used to go and see my Tibetan friends in Kalimpong, very often I would arrive in the morning and the servant or disciple would say, 'Please wait a few minutes, he hasn't quite finished his meditation.' After a while I learned that they usually started at about six in the morning and would finish at around nine. Whether they were government officials, or busy abbots in charge of monasteries, or just ordinary people, they would often spend two to three hours on their meditation and devotional practice before starting the day's work.

You would often see people reciting their mantras during the day, especially during their evening walk. One of my most pleasant memories of Kalimpong is of going for an evening stroll in the direction of the bazaar, and seeing, on the way, elderly Tibetan men and women walking along the road with a prayer wheel in one hand and a rosary in the other, murmuring mantras as they went. Western writers on Tibet have talked of rituals being performed mechanically, but there was nothing mechanical about this sort of practice. You could tell by the way people were concentrating that they were completely absorbed in what they were doing. In this way, even the comparatively advanced practices of Tantric Buddhist meditation could become an integral part of the daily life of the average Tibetan.

8
THE FUTURE OF TIBETAN BUDDHISM

In the preceding chapters we have surveyed a rich and dramatic field, and covered a great deal of ground. We have looked at both the distant past and more recent times. Surely anyone would be inspired by the great traditions and spiritual disciplines of Tibetan Buddhism, and the organization of the whole country around its religion. Other countries have tended to gear their national life to commerce or politics, to conquest or the arts, but in Tibet, the whole of life – political, economic, social, and artistic – has been focused on religion, on the Dharma. So for Buddhists, particularly, there is much to wonder at, admire, and learn from in the past of Tibetan Buddhism. But what is its future?

Having asked this question, we might as well face the unpalatable facts of the matter at once. As far as one can see, Tibetan Buddhism has no future. This great tradition of Buddhism, in its fullness, as it has existed in Tibet for hundreds of years, has had its day. In Tibet itself there are many ancient prophecies about the future of Tibetan Buddhism, and one which is often quoted by Tibetans is to the effect that the Fourteenth Dalai Lama will be the last of his distinguished line. Tibetans who were well versed in the history and traditions of their country were, therefore, not altogether surprised when in 1959 the Dalai Lama had to flee from Tibet and seek shelter as a refugee in India. Unfortunate and tragic though it was, they knew that it had been prophesied that the Fourteenth Dalai Lama would be the last. And it is not as if everything else in Tibet can remain the same except that there will no longer be a Dalai Lama. This is impossible. When the queen bee has gone, the life of the hive cannot continue. The Dalai Lama is central to the system. He summarizes or embodies in his person the whole of Tibetan Buddhism, and if he goes – and the prophecy does seem likely to be fulfilled – then the whole way of life which he represents will come to an end.

Tibet has been under Chinese domination since 1950, a year I remember very vividly. I had arrived in Kalimpong in March, and all summer there were rumours of war from the borderlands between Tibet and China. We heard that the Chinese armies were on the march, that they were building roads and bringing up reinforcements. First they entered Kham in eastern Tibet; we heard that monasteries had fallen, that monks had been massacred. And then week by week, month by month, we watched almost breathless as they advanced ever nearer and nearer to the sacred city of Lhasa. When the Chinese communists eventually reached Lhasa, many people felt that the end of an epoch had come.

The Chinese have been in Tibet ever since – time enough for a couple of generations to have grown up there – and many changes have taken place. In material terms there have been some improvements: roads have been laid down, hospitals built, schools opened. There have also been great psychological changes in the outlook of the Tibetan people, especially the young. This is due partly, no doubt, to Maoist indoctrination, but also to the inevitable march of time. The industrial revolution – to which Asia has largely succumbed – has at last caught up with Tibet. In some outlying areas of the country, within living memory they didn't even have the wheel. People can live perfectly well without wheels, but technologically it meant that not very long ago parts of Tibet were still in the Stone Age. Now they have the wheel in some of its most complex forms – they have cars and aircraft. Tibet, we may say, is one of the last major traditional civilizations to have yielded to the onrush of industrialization.

This has resulted in a tremendous culture shock, whose force it is difficult for us to appreciate. Suppose you were living, say at the time of the Norman Conquest, in your village, with your priest, with your farm work, and so on. And suppose suddenly, by some miracle, you were snatched up from the middle of the eleventh century and set down in the middle of the twentieth. You can imagine the shock you would experience on seeing everything so changed, so industrialized and mechanized. In a way this is what has happened to many Tibetans. They've been lifted up from a very simple, albeit spiritually profound, civilization, and landed right in the middle of the twentieth century, exposed to all the technological and materialistic winds that blow. In many ways it is a very great pity that the traditional culture of Tibet has been disrupted and broken up in this way – but we can be pretty sure that it would have happened anyway, even if the Chinese had not invaded. The process might have been less dramatic, but it would inevitably have occurred.

In Kalimpong I often met young refugees fresh from Tibet. You could always spot the new arrivals because they would look around and take notice of things that others took for granted. The first time I took a party of my Tibetan students to Darjeeling, I remember how fascinated they were by the station and the railway engine. They were all men of about forty, but they were newly arrived, and hadn't seen a locomotive before. To them it was like an iron dragon, a great monster standing by the platform. In fact it was a tiny engine – the railway which goes up to the hills is called the 'Himalayan toy railway' – but they were very impressed by it. As they excitedly peered at it and underneath it, tapping the wheels and gesticulating to each other, suddenly it let out a loud hoot, and they sprang back in alarm as if they thought it might bite them.[33]

When they first arrived in Kalimpong, most of the refugees – some of them aged only eighteen or twenty – looked typically Tibetan. They wore their hair long, as Tibetan men traditionally do, tied into a braid around their heads. Often they'd wear an earring, usually of turquoise, and they'd be wearing a *chuba* (a kind of tunic) and tall boots. And of course they'd each have a *mālā* or rosary in their hand. Now Kalimpong is just a quiet little town of 15,000 inhabitants, and rather backward by western standards. Not everybody has electricity or running water. You wouldn't think there was much there to corrupt the innocent young Tibetan. But if you just waited six months and then took another look at those same Tibetans you'd find they had completely changed. They'd have cut off their long hair – that usually went first – and they'd be wearing sharkskin suits. They'd have given up their rosary, and you'd see them carrying around a transistor radio. You'd find them listening to pop music and wanting to learn to disco-dance. These were young men who six months before had been living in the Middle Ages. The women, incidentally, even the young women, were much more conservative. They might give up their *mālās* and prayer wheels, but you didn't often see them cutting their hair or changing their dress.

We can't blame the Chinese communists for all the changes in Tibet itself and among the Tibetans in exile. This is the march of time. It may not be progress – I'm sure that in many ways it is not progress – but such changes are inevitable. Even if the Chinese had not come, Tibet would eventually have undergone this sort of process. So even if Tibet does succeed, as one hopes it will, in regaining independence, and the Dalai Lama returns and takes up residence again in the Potala, it will nevertheless be impossible to put the clock back. Tibet will never be again what it was for so many hundreds of years. It is in this sense that we can say that Tibetan Buddhism has no future.

This is a very great loss, no doubt, but perhaps we shouldn't be too shocked. All Buddhists know that the law of impermanence – *anitya* – governs and controls all human affairs, and the institutional forms of Buddhism itself are no exception. Buddhism began in India, where the Buddha lived and taught, and Indian Buddhism endured for 1,500 years; but in the end it disappeared. Nowadays, apart from modern revivals, we find little trace of Buddhism in India. So we should not be surprised if Buddhism were to disappear from Tibet after a similar period.

This does not mean that no vestige of Tibetan Buddhism will remain. As the way of life of a whole nation it has already come to an end, and I do not believe there can be any question of its revival. But Tibetan Buddhism will survive among the Tibetan refugees, in India and elsewhere, and it will survive as an integral part of Buddhism in the West.

Most Tibetan refugees – about 100,000 altogether – are found in India, mainly in the hill areas. Tibetans, coming from a very high country, understandably haven't been very happy in the hot plains of India. As far as possible they have clung to the hills, settling in places like Darjeeling, Kalimpong, and Sikkim, as well as in various parts of the Punjab and the Himachal Pradesh. There are also some Tibetans in Europe, especially in Switzerland, which houses one of the largest Tibetan refugee communities outside India. There are also Tibetan communities in the USA and Canada.

For refugees everywhere, the first question is that of physical survival. For many of the Tibetan refugees it has been a difficult business just to scrape a living. But as conditions improve they can begin to take steps to preserve their culture and their form of Buddhism. Tibetan temples and monasteries have been built in several places – for example, the two Tantric colleges have been reopened in Dalhousie – and temples and monasteries have been built elsewhere in the foothills of the Himalayas. Handicraft centres have been opened by the refugees, producing paintings, carpets, metalwork, woodwork, and so on, along traditional lines – albeit with some corruption in the matter of colour and design. So there is no doubt that Tibetan Buddhism, in some form, will survive in exile.

In time its position in India will probably be rather like that of Zoroastrianism among the Parsis of Bombay. The Parsis are a flourishing Indian community whose ancestors fled from Persia (now Iran) about 1,000 years ago, at the time of the Muslim invasion. It was a question of being converted to Islam or perishing, and a number of Zoroastrians, followers of the ancient teaching of the Persian prophet Zoroaster, decided to flee. They came by sea to the area which is now Mumbai, and the Indians received them kindly, as the Indians usually do receive refugees. They were given land, settled down, and engaged in trade, and now are the richest communities in the whole of India. There are around 70,000 Parsis, and as a community they are enterprising, highly educated, and very charitable – they have endowed many schools and hospitals in Bombay. Above all, they preserve their ancient Zoroastrian faith which has virtually disappeared from its homeland.[34]

Something like this is likely to happen with regard to Tibetan Buddhism in India. No doubt it will be preserved among the Tibetans in exile, especially as the refugee community includes many monks of all grades. But in Tibet itself, if the Chinese communists remain in power for a few more generations, it is very likely that Tibetan Buddhism will entirely disappear. We may not like to think that a religion can be wiped out, but it can. Manichaeism, the teaching of the prophet Mani – a sort of universalist, all-embracing religion – was at one time practised right across Europe and Asia, from France to China. But now it just doesn't exist. It was a very inoffensive faith – it believed in complete non-violence, in love and compassion – but it was stamped out by Persian kings, by the Roman Catholic Church, and by Chinese emperors. So we shouldn't think that Tibetan Buddhism is so great, so glorious, that it can't be wiped out in Tibet.

In fact, the decline of Tibetan Buddhism would seem to be part of a general trend in the East. All over Asia, it would appear, Buddhism is capitulating. China is lost to Buddhism, to all intents and purposes. Communism has virtually destroyed Buddhism in Mongolia and several countries of South-east Asia. Thai Buddhism is vulnerable to the march of Westernization. Japan is threatened not from without but from within, by over-industrialization; Buddhism does still exist there, but not as it did in the past. And in other parts of the East, Islam swept Buddhism away several hundred years ago. Just because the East was Buddhist for 2,000 years clearly does not mean it always will be. As far as we can see, in all the Buddhist countries of the East, Buddhism is in retreat, if not actually vanquished. It might seem a fantastic thought, but it may be that one day there will be very little Buddhism in the East and it will be stronger in the West. Bigger changes than this have taken place in world history.

But this is not the only reason why it is important for us in the West to study, to practise, and if possible to preserve Tibetan Buddhism. It is equally important that it should survive to become an integral part of western Buddhism – indeed, of world Buddhism. Many different forms of Buddhism have been introduced into the West and are gradually spreading across the western world, and it is already evident that western Buddhism will not follow any one eastern tradition exclusively. Sometimes Buddhists from the East are hopeful that their particular brand of Buddhism will take root in the West, and that all western Buddhists will be strict Theravādins, or staunch followers of Sōtō Zen. But as far as we can see, this is not going to happen. It is certainly not happening at present. Western Buddhism is learning, and will continue to learn, from all the different oriental traditions of Buddhism as they become known. But people in the West will try to extract the essence of the teaching, the Buddha's real message, from all these different and differing traditions, and this ultimate and vital element in the teaching will be adapted to meet the psychological and spiritual needs of western people.

In the West, people who are interested in religion and philosophy are weary of orthodoxies, weary of too much importance being placed on things which are not necessary, even quite unrelated to the essence of the teaching. Westerners who turn to any spiritual teaching emanating from the East are too much concerned with ultimate issues, with real human problems, to waste their time on the inessentials and trappings that have been handed down by the various eastern Buddhist traditions.

Much of what passes for Buddhism in the East has no connection with the teaching whatever. In Myanmar (Burma), for instance, there has been a bitter dispute as to whether when monks go out from the monastery, they should have the left shoulder covered and the right uncovered, or whether they should cover both shoulders. This dispute dominated the Burmese monastic community for a whole century and it is still not settled.[35] Eastern Buddhists are often excessively preoccupied with such trivial matters; but such preoccupations are not going to go down very well in the West.

What we need is to encounter and get to grips with the essence of the Buddha's teaching, which is basically concerned with nothing other than the way to Enlightenment, mainly through ever-increasing awareness. This is what the Buddha was really talking about, and it is reflected and echoed in all the various traditions in different ways. It is to this essential theme that we need to pay attention, trying to adapt it to our own lives and to the lives of those around us. Which is not to say that in adapting the teaching there can be any question of compromising it or watering it down. On the contrary, we are concerned with the effective communication of the fundamental principles of the Dharma.

Tibetan Buddhism is just one of the forms of Buddhism with which we are currently becoming acquainted in the West. The main question we need to ask ourselves is: what can we learn from it? As we have seen, we can learn about Buddhism in general from its Tibetan form, by coming to understand how Buddhist teaching is reflected in Tibetan Buddhism. In this way one tradition can be a key to understanding the whole teaching. But we can also learn things which we may not learn from any other form of Buddhism, because Tibetan Buddhism is in many respects unique.

First of all, it represents Indian Buddhism at the height of its development. As we saw in Chapter 2, after 1,500 years Indian Buddhism was very rich and many-sided, including all three *yānas*, and it was this form of Buddhism which went from India to Tibet and was preserved there. So Tibetan Buddhism is the nearest we can get to Indian Buddhism as it was practised. It is all very well to read about ancient traditions in books, but it is much better to have some sort of contact, however indirect, with living traditions. Tibetan Buddhism is still a living tradition, albeit on a reduced scale, and it is our nearest contact with Indian Buddhism at its peak.

Dr Edward Conze had a rather interesting theory in this connection. He maintained that the nearer one is to the geographical centre of a religion, the nearer one is to its spirit. Tibet, Conze says, is closer geographically to the original centre of Buddhism than any other Buddhist country; and Tibetan Buddhism is therefore nearest to the spirit of Indian Buddhism. Whatever the merits of Conze's theory, it is certainly true that the spirit of Tibetan Buddhism seems remarkably close to that of Indian Buddhism during the last stages of its development in north-eastern India.

We can also learn from Tibetan Buddhism about all three *yānas*, not as unrelated paths, as it were side by side, but as aspects of a single path. The idea that the Hīnayāna, Mahāyāna, and Vajrayāna are not just different forms of Buddhism but successive stages on the path to Enlightenment is a major feature of Tibetan Buddhism. It is first mentioned in the *Hevajra Tantra*, and it is worked out in greater detail by Atīśa in his *Bodhipatha Pradīpa* or 'Lamp of the Way to Enlightenment'. This doctrine is also the basis of Tsongkhapa's *Lamrim Chenmo* or 'Great Stages of the Path'.[36] All Tibetan Buddhist schools teach that one progresses to Enlightenment through a course of training in which one recapitulates in one's own practice the historical sequence of the three *yānas*. This *triyāna* synthesis is not found elsewhere in the Buddhist world. In South-east Asia we find only the Theravāda, a form of the Hīnayāna. In China or Japan we find both Hīnayāna and Mahāyāna (and here and there the Outer Tantra, though the Inner Tantra is found only in Tibet), but they are usually constituted into mutually exclusive, even rival, schools. Japanese Buddhism is more sectarian than any other Buddhist tradition. It is only in Tibet that we find all three *yānas* existing not as separate sects, but as stages of the one path leading to Enlightenment.

Tibetan Buddhism is also perhaps the most intellectual form of Buddhism that we know today. Although Tibetans in some areas did not even have the wheel until recently, this does not mean that they were primitive or uncultured, and it certainly does not mean that they were stupid. Intelligence and understanding, in the real sense, are not necessarily correlated with technological or material sophistication. Tibet has been the only part of the Buddhist world which has kept alive the highly intellectual tradition of Indian Buddhist logic.

Moreover, the exegesis of the Prajñāpāramitā, the Perfection of Wisdom tradition, was continued and even elaborated in Tibet. The

Perfection of Wisdom *sūtras* are among the grandest and most sublime in the whole field of Buddhist canonical literature. They were produced in India and went to all the other Buddhist countries of the Far East, especially China and Japan. But it was only in Tibet that they continued to be studied, and that there was a tradition of teaching and explanation of the Prajñāpāramitā.[37]

In this connection I remember hearing Edward Conze relate how when he was in the USA he met a lama of the Sakya school, which is renowned for its learning. Dr Conze had devoted some thirty years of his life to studying and translating the Perfection of Wisdom *sūtras*, and he had been doing this more or less on his own. This was no mean task – it required tremendous understanding, much knowledge and scholarship. But there were just a few knotty points that even Conze could not clear up by himself.

So one day he went to see this lama and put some of these points to him. Whereupon the lama started explaining and expounding, and after he had been going on for a couple of hours, Conze was overwhelmed. 'I felt', he told me, 'that I really knew nothing about the Perfection of Wisdom. I became aware that there were vast stores of knowledge on the subject, the existence of which I hadn't even suspected.' And Dr Conze, it should be noted, was not given to handing out compliments. Quite the contrary, in fact. But this was his response to the Sakya lama, and it testifies to the tremendous intellectual tradition of the exegesis of the Prajñāpāramitā in Tibet.

At the same time, Tibetan Buddhism is highly devotional. All Tibetan Buddhists, including the learned *geshes* who are immersed in logic and the Perfection of Wisdom, have strong feelings of devotion for the Three Jewels. They have developed the intellect, perhaps as far as is humanly possible – but not one-sidedly. Their devotional side is also evident in all sorts of ways. One notices it in the way Tibetans handle images of Buddhas or bodhisattvas. They do so very reverently, often putting them to their heads as a gesture of respect. Similarly with the sacred texts; it is unthinkable to Tibetans to fling a book on the floor. They consider that to be disgraceful, especially where the sacred scriptures are concerned – and most of their books are sacred scriptures. In fact in Tibetan Buddhism, whether among ordinary Buddhists or learned monks and abbots, the intellectual and emotional aspects of the religious life are not really divided at all. Their intense intellectuality is combined with profound devotion and faith. This is something else that we can learn from Tibetan Buddhism.

We find a similar balance in Tibetan Buddhism between study and meditation. Some of the most learned men in the Buddhist world are or were to be found among the *geshes* and lamas of Tibet, whose knowledge is often encyclopaedic. I remember once going to see Jamyang Khyentse Rimpoche, from whom I received certain initiations. He was very interested in various aspects of Indian literature, and in the course of conversation he suddenly asked me, through an interpreter, 'Do you know anything about dancing?' I said, 'Well, no, not really,' wondering what he was getting at. He went on to say: 'I've read fourteen books on Indian classical dance and there are a few points I want to clear up.' He had come from a remote corner of eastern Tibet, and here he was studying texts on Indian dance in Tibetan translation – they were in the Tengyur – and wanting to clear up some queries. I subsequently learned that these texts were the basis of the famous 'lama dances', which he was very interested in, and I believe later he did procure some treatises on the subject. He was exceptional, even among Tibetan lamas, but they all typically have such many-sided interests.

At the same time, these monks and lamas included some of the greatest yogis and meditators in the Buddhist world. Perhaps the most remarkable example is Milarepa, Tibet's greatest yogi and also her greatest poet, but there are many instances in Tibetan Buddhism of this type of person – great scholars, with wonderful intellectual knowledge, who are at the same time profound meditators, understanding not only the theory but also the practice of the spiritual life. Jamyang Khyentse was himself of this type. He was by no means a 'dry-as-dust' bookworm. When he was not studying he was meditating, and he was famous for both.[38] It's rather as if someone like Bertrand Russell was also a sort of St John of the Cross. To our western way of thinking, this kind of combination is extraordinary, it breaks all the rules. We don't find it even in the Christian tradition in the Middle Ages. St Thomas Aquinas was a great scholar and theologian; it was only towards the end of his life that he turned to mysticism, and then, rather significantly, he gave up theology. St Francis, on the other hand, was a great spiritual soul, but he probably knew nothing about theology. But in Tibetan Buddhism we often find, combined in one person, the genius of the scholar and the simplicity and spiritual experience of the mystic.

This balanced approach is something else that we can learn from Tibetan Buddhism, not only in respect of intellect and faith, or study and meditation, but also in less important areas. In Tibetan Buddhism we find a combination of organization and freedom, two things which in the West we usually consider antithetical. Tibet had the biggest monasteries in the world, yet at the same time it had the loneliest, most isolated hermitages. There were monasteries with thousands of monks, but you could also go hundreds of miles out into the wilderness and find a cave, a shack, or a little temple with just one solitary hermit living in it.

There was another synthesis: of highly organized monasticism on the one hand and serious spiritual practice by lay people on the other. In a way, Tibetan Buddhism was the most monasticized in the world. There were monks everywhere. Just imagine walking down Oxford Street in London and finding that every other person you met was a monk. This is what it was like in Lhasa in the old days. Wherever you went there were monks. You might even think that they were rather monk-ridden. But although monks constituted a higher percentage of the population in Tibet than in any other country in the world, at the same time there was full participation by the laity in the spiritual life. No one thought that you had to be a monk in order to practise the Dharma. In fact, among the Nyingmapas the laity, including the lay lamas, practically ran the show. In Theravādin countries they tend to think that you can't be a real Buddhist unless you become a monk; but in Tibet, though they had so many monks, they never thought like this.

To generalize even more, one may say that while Tibetan Buddhists have their head in the clouds, at the same time their feet are firmly on the ground. They try to follow the most sublime and rarefied of all spiritual ideals – that of the bodhisattva, one who does not care for his or her own individual salvation but who is devoted to the spiritual welfare of all beings. This is their ideal, which everyone appreciates and to some extent tries to follow. At the same time the Tibetans are intensely practical in all affairs of life, whether it is to do with food, or clothing, or building, or making money in trade and business. We might go so far as to say that there's nothing mystical, nothing occult about the Tibetans at all, not in the woolly sense of those terms. Westerners have often tended to think of the Tibetans as wonderful mystical figures, living beyond the Himalayas in an aura of mystery, surrounded by all sorts of strange happenings. The idea that Tibetans ever thought of eating or drinking or making money was at one time almost blasphemy among some occult circles in the West, who would speak of 'the masters beyond the Himalayas' as if they were always immersed in meditation and never thought of anything else. But the Tibetans are not like this at all. They are mystical in the true sense. They have their heads in the clouds spiritually, but their feet are firmly planted on the earth. This is something we might emulate.

We can learn many other things from Tibetan Buddhism. For example, we can learn depth and sincerity. Tibetan Buddhists are remarkably sincere, in the full sense of that much-misused word. They really do believe in their religion. We can also strive to equal their thoroughness. It is very difficult to get Tibetans to commit themselves. If you ask them to do something, or to help in some way, they agree very slowly and reluctantly. They go through every step of it with you, making sure they understand exactly what you are asking them to do. Only then will they commit themselves and say 'Yes'; but when they have done so, you know you can depend on them. They are very thorough and reliable. We can aspire to their strenuousness too. I have often heard Tibetans say that there is no religious life without difficulty. They tend to think that if any religious practice is easy it can't be truly religious. They believe that there are no easy ways round, no short cuts. They are prepared to endure hardship and suffering for the sake of their spiritual life. We saw in Chapter 1 how King Yeshe-Ö of western Tibet sacrificed his life so that the Buddha's teaching might be revived in western Tibet.

We can therefore conclude that Tibetan Buddhism is a highly developed, fully articulated, balanced, and harmonious system of Buddhism. There is nothing one-sided in it. Moreover, we can say that it is the richest form of Buddhism, in the sense that, within its harmony and synthesis, it includes the greatest number of diverse elements. In the West we have perhaps only one form of religion which can compare with Tibetan Buddhism in respect of richness – and I'm only thinking of richness when I make the comparison – and that is Roman Catholicism. But there are of course many very weighty differences between them, and one respect in which they differ very much is that Tibetan Buddhism, unlike Roman Catholicism, is characterized by tolerance. Tolerance is characteristic of all forms of Buddhism, but one might think that the temptation to intolerance would be greater in Tibetan Buddhism inasmuch as its internal differences are greater. But it has not yielded to that temptation. The scholar does not look down upon the yogi, nor the yogi upon the scholar. There is no rivalry between the monks and the laity, but full cooperation. There are four schools, each proud of its own traditions and adhering to them faithfully, but they all display deep mutual courtesy. Their differences rarely degenerate into criticism, much less into hostility. In the course of all my contact with lamas of all schools I never heard from, say, a Nyingma lama a real criticism of the Gelug tradition, or vice versa. Of course they are human, and sometimes they have little jokes at each other's expense. I remember a Gelug joke about the Nyingma *wong* – the Tantric initiation – to the effect that the Nyingmapas had very powerful, esoteric *wongs*, such as they, the Gelugpas, didn't have: they even had a *wong* so powerful that you could give it to others without having practised it yourself. To appreciate the humour of this one has to understand the Tibetan attitude towards *wongs*; the point is that the joking is done in the friendliest spirit.

The tolerance of the Tibetans extends to non-Buddhists, and sometimes Tibetans are very shocked when they come to India and encounter Christian missionaries for the first time. They can hardly believe their ears. If they hear a Christian criticizing Buddhism, they see it as someone criticizing religion in any form, which *they* would never do. They are not averse to the free expression of religious differences, but in Tibetan Buddhism such differences are always expressed courteously. I remember a young lama coming to see me shortly after the influx of refugees into Kalimpong in 1959 and telling me he had just discovered that communism and Christianity were the same thing. When I asked him what had led him to that conclusion, he explained that he had just heard some Christian missionaries preaching in the bazaar (as they did every week) and vigorously denouncing Buddhism and Hinduism. In Lhasa the young lama had heard Chinese communists denouncing Buddhism in exactly the same terms. So obviously communism and Christianity were the same thing.

Western Buddhists can learn a great deal from this. As a living religion, Buddhism in the West is very recent. At first we just had some Theravāda, then a little Mahāyāna was added, including Zen, and more recently we've come to know about Tibetan Buddhism, including the Tantra. Western Buddhism will not and should not be confined to any one of these traditions – it will be a synthesis of them all. But we do not want it to be just a jumble. Perhaps we can learn from Tibetan

Buddhism how to achieve a harmonious synthesis of all the different elements in the total Buddhist tradition. Obviously this will not be achieved without mutual respect and tolerance, and this too we can learn from the Tibetans. We can't hope that all Buddhists in the West will see Buddhism in exactly the same way. We have to accept this, and work together nevertheless, reconciling our differences in the light of the one ideal, the one objective, which we all accept, which is Enlightenment or Buddhahood.

Nobody can say with any certainty what the future holds for Tibet. But we in the West have the opportunity to follow, however hesitatingly, in the footsteps of the Tibetans, who achieved in the past such a magnificent and rich synthesis of the total Buddhist tradition. If we can do this, then western Buddhism, though it may be confined to comparatively few people, may become as rich and many-splendoured as was the Buddhism of Tibet.

Creative Symbols of Tantric Buddhism

WITH ILLUSTRATIONS BY DHARMACHARI ALOKA

INTRODUCTION

In the course of some 1,500 years Indian Buddhism passed through three great phases, each with its own distinctive emphasis. The first phase was named the Hīnayāna, the 'lesser way', by followers of later Buddhist schools, but we can think of it simply as Early Buddhism. In this first flowering of the Buddhist tradition, the emphasis was placed on ethical observance and psychological analysis. With the development of what became known – at least to its own adherents – as the Mahāyāna, the 'great way', the focus shifted to devotional practice and what could be called metaphysics, although it was of a rather different kind from the metaphysics of the western tradition. But the third phase, the Vajrayāna, the diamond way – also called the Tantric path – placed special emphasis on the use of symbols, ritual, and meditation.[39]

Each phase emerged in response to, or even reaction against, existing tradition, but did not entirely replace it; the essential features of the preceding traditions were preserved in each new synthesis of the teaching. Even when a change of cultural setting was involved, when the Vajrayāna or Tantra was introduced into Tibet, the Tibetans elaborated upon the Indian Tantric tradition rather than changing it in any substantial way. The only real innovation was the incorporation of indigenous Tibetan deities into mandalas, but those figures never occupied a prominent position. Even the songs of Milarepa, which seem so distinctively Tibetan, have antecedents in Indian literature.

The Tantra went on developing in the Indian Buddhist community until the final disappearance of Buddhism from India. But the Indian tradition was always just one step ahead of developments in Tibet. For several hundred years Tibetan monks and scholars were coming down into India and eagerly enquiring after the latest Tantric teaching, so that they could study it, practise it, and take it back to Tibet. The Tibetans did not rely entirely on Indian forms of practice; they assimilated the spirit of the teachings and practised them in their own way. But before the introduction of Buddhism the Tibetans had very little culture of their own, so their culture has always been mainly Buddhist, and that included the adoption of Indian cultural forms. The situation was more or less the same in Sri Lanka, and even in Japan. The great exception was China; the Chinese did not always take kindly to the Indian culture that came along with Buddhism because they already had a highly developed culture of their own.

Our own position, as we adopt Buddhism in the West, is most akin to that of the Chinese; we too have a highly developed culture already, and that will have its effect on the way we approach Buddhism. We may be as eager as were the Tibetans all those centuries ago to acquire the latest teachings. But we may find that we experience – in a way the Tibetans never did – a clash between Buddhist tradition and the culture in which we have been born and which has exerted its influence on us throughout our lives. This is perhaps especially true when we try to come to an understanding of Tantric Buddhism, with all its symbols, rituals, and apparently arcane practices. The increasingly rationalistic and secular outlook of western society has given many people a thirst for more myth and symbol. All the same, we will need to make a special kind of effort if we are to grasp the true nature of those myths and symbols, so that they can become part of our lives in a creative and natural way.

This has been my own experience, anyway. When I first encountered the Tantra I was living in Kalimpong, a small town in the foothills of the eastern Himalayas. Thus I was surrounded by the great kingdoms of Tantric Buddhism – Sikkim, Bhutan, Nepal, Tibet – and Kalimpong itself was full of Tantric practitioners, mostly Tibetan refugees who had fled the Chinese invasion. But although I was surrounded by the Tantra, it took me some time to understand what that meant. At that time, in the 1940s and 50s, I had been a committed Buddhist for a number of years, but nothing had prepared me for the Tantra, and there were no books on it in English to be found anywhere, or at least no reliable ones. But in Kalimpong I began to meet people who were actually engaged in the practice of the Tantric path. I also came in contact, a little later on, with Tantric art and ritual, and I eventually met a number of great Tantric gurus, and came to experience Tantric initiation and practice for myself.

I well remember my early impressions of the Tantra. As I tried to penetrate a little into it, to see what it was about and how it connected with other forms of Buddhism and with modern thought – psychology, comparative symbolism, and so on – I felt more and more that it was a jungle – a jungle in which one could very easily get lost. There seemed to be so many different traditions within it. There were so many meditation methods and forms of ritual observance, so many kinds of offerings, even so many kinds of ceremonial robe – and, indeed, ceremonial hat.

I used to tell my Tibetan friends that I found the Tantra far too vast and complicated to study as a whole, and that I was therefore going to confine myself to the study of one little corner of it. My chosen field of study, I said, would be the hats, some of which were very weird and wonderful indeed. I would make a collection of at least a hundred kinds of Tantric hat, and then write a book about them. Of course, I never did. But even when I began to study the Tantra in earnest, there were so many images in the temples, so many scroll paintings, so many figures of Buddhas and bodhisattvas and gurus, and *ḍākas* and *ḍākinīs* and *dharmapālas*, that for a long time I continued to feel that the Tantra was truly a vast jungle.

This is likely to be the experience of any westerner beginning to investigate the Tantra, even in the very simple form of the limited number of symbols we will encounter in this book. The impression one gets of richness and variety, growth, fertility, and abundance is quite bewildering to begin with. But a feeling of being lost among the creative symbols of Tantric Buddhism is no cause for alarm. Indeed, to become *intellectually* lost in the context of the Tantra is quite a positive thing. One may find oneself moved or stirred by the symbols without being able to say exactly how or why. With more experience, one comes to discover that the Tantra is not really the jungle it appears to be. It is more like a garden or, rather, a complex of gardens. Despite the richness of the Tantra, despite its incredible profusion, its superabundance of material, and its exuberance, there is a pattern running through it, or a number of interlocking patterns. These patterns are not intellectual, but spiritual. They are not imposed on the Tantra from the outside, but unfold from within it, expressing its innermost nature and essential purpose.

What is that purpose? Tantric Buddhism is concerned not with theories or speculations, not with formal religiosity or external piety, but with the direct experience, in the depths of one's being, of what one truly and essentially is. It seeks to reveal to us our essential nature – not just psychologically but existentially, metaphysically, even transcendentally. So far as the Tantra is concerned, this experience cannot be mediated by concepts. In fact, concepts give no idea of it at all, do not lead to it or point to it in any way. It is beyond words, beyond thought, beyond the conscious mind and personality. But this direct experience can be evoked, conjured up, or at least glimpsed, with the help of symbols. The whole Tantric path to Enlightenment is strewn with symbolic images, mantras, and rituals. You stumble over them at every step; indeed, the Tantric path largely consists of them. And they are all intended to reflect, or lead to, or give a glimpse of, this direct experience.

What is a symbol? The very nature of symbols makes it impossible to define them; it is best to let them speak for themselves, and this is the approach we will be taking to the symbols of the Tantra. But we can at least make one generalization: a symbol is not a sign. It does not stand for something that could be known in some other way. The whole point is that you can only get at what the symbol represents, or develop any feeling for it, through the symbol itself. You don't know what it's a symbol of, you don't know what it stands for, because your only means of access to it is through the symbol itself. You can give a meaning to a symbol if you like – you can use your understanding or experience of it as a starting point for a series of ideas or concepts – but that is not to say that you have got in touch with what the symbol stands for. Symbols are not concepts, so their meaning cannot be exhausted conceptually. There is usually something quite concrete about them – they have form and colour – and they do communicate something. But it is not easy to put what they communicate into words. They are like dreams, which leave a vivid impression, a strong feeling, but cannot be expressed in conceptual terms.

To take one of the Buddhist tradition's favourite symbols, consider the lotus – or if it is more familiar to you, the lily, or the rose. Let your mind dwell on it, and then ask yourself what you are experiencing. What is this flower? What does it mean? Clearly it is not just a botanical specimen. It conveys something; it gives you a certain feeling that goes beyond its botanical characteristics. That is what makes it a symbol. But how does that work? Is it that we invest the innocent flower with qualities it does not possess, or does it really have some quality of its own, apart from our projection on to it?

When you see the lotus as a symbol, you are seeing it as being illuminated by some other, higher dimension of reality. This reality is described in some Buddhist texts by the term *śūnyatā*, emptiness, which is a synonym for the unfathomable, indefinable mystery of the true nature of things. However, we cannot come at that mystery except through what is around us every day. As the Perfection of Wisdom *sūtras* put it, we cannot experience *śūnyatā* except through *rūpa*, *rūpa* ('form') referring to the objects we can perceive through our senses.[40] A symbol is an object seen or felt or experienced as possessing a heightened significance that cannot be reduced to words or concepts. There is something there other than that form, that colour, or that sound, which is both communicated through that form and inseparable from it.

So it isn't quite accurate to say that a symbol stands for something. It is more that the symbol *is* that thing as it appears under a certain set of conditions, in a certain mode. The operative word here is 'appears'. What determines how something appears is the quality of perception of the person who sees it. For example, the figure of the Buddha is well known to be a symbol of Enlightenment. But how do we know that? We are unlikely to be able to recognize it from our personal knowledge of the Enlightened state. We may have some conception of what Enlightenment is, and we may also, if we are receptive, get some inkling of Enlightenment through the Buddha's symbolism of it. But that inkling will not necessarily coincide with our conception of Enlightenment.

And to get even an inkling, we have to be receptive to the symbol. It isn't that it definitely means this, that, or the other, and will deliver its meaning to us automatically. The symbolism is in the eye of the beholder. That is one of the differences between a symbol and a concept. In certain states of mind – the kind of states of mind developed in meditation – all experience is symbolic, and everything is seen as possessing a heightened significance. To continue to use the language of the Perfection of Wisdom, inasmuch as all forms are empty (all *rūpas* are *śūnyatā*), whenever we are in contact with *rūpa* we are in contact with *śūnyatā*. Everything we see – a tree, the sky, the clouds – is therefore symbolic: 'huge cloudy symbols of a high romance', as Keats says.[41]

Ultimately, nothing is any more significant than anything else. Things can't be divided into symbols and non-symbols. They simply become symbolic under certain conditions; a symbol is a particular thing seen under particular circumstances or in a particular way. In principle, anything can be a symbol. One might say that everything is symbolic, but some things are more symbolic than others. It is partly that we experience some things as being more significant than others for subjective reasons. Most people can see the significance of a beautiful sunset more readily than that of a heap of ashes. One cannot say that a lotus is more real than a dandelion, or that in itself it possesses more significance, but for subjective or cultural reasons it may make a more appropriate symbol. There may also be some objective reason; the way the lotus grows unsullied out of the muddy water, for example, makes it an especially appropriate symbol for purity. But one must be careful that the association is not just intellectual. You have to *feel* the purity of the lotus. If you have not personally seen one, and if you have difficulty imagining it, you could have the same sort of experience with any other beautiful flower that you happened to see with the dew shining on it in the early morning.

It is not as though you could make a list and check each symbol off against its significance. A symbol is not an inadequate copy of something that exists quite separately on some higher plane. It is not that the lotus symbolizes something that is quite other than a lotus and could just as well have been symbolized by something else. What we speak of as being symbolized by the lotus is in fact a deeper dimension of the lotus, so that when you see the lotus as a symbol, you are seeing it in a deeper and truer way.

This is what the spiritual life is about: trying to find more significance in our daily lives. When you can do that, there is never a dull moment. This is the experience of mystics and meditators who speak of seeing literally everything as being lit up from within, glowing with light. Light, significance, meaning, inner depth, symbolism – it all amounts to the same thing. In a certain state of mind, everything you see has significance. Not that the significance is reducible to a conceptual meaning – it just is significant.

We each need to explore what it is that makes something symbolic for us personally. We might all agree that a lotus – or indeed a dandelion – is symbolic in some way, but what is your actual experience of it? Setting aside whatever it is conventionally said to mean, what does it symbolize for you as an individual? You have to contact your own feeling about a symbol, otherwise it becomes just a counter that you manipulate: 'Oh yes, that symbolizes such-and-such.' There is certainly scope for dwelling on the meaning of symbols. Quite often, as we shall see, one finds oneself exploring the meaning of one symbol through others. For example, the significance of a particular Buddha figure may become clearer when we consider what he is holding in his hands. One should beware, however, of explaining symbols in a purely conceptual way.

In any case, the effect of symbolism is not *entirely* subjective. Whereas a sign simply points towards a reality, a symbol to a degree participates in it. And, as I said, some symbols are more symbolic than others. Some, as Jung discovered, are universal, archetypal, to be found in all cultures in various forms. There is what might be called a hierarchy of symbolism, and for Buddhists, the images of Buddhas and bodhisattvas are certainly to be found at the top of that hierarchy.[42] But in what sense are these figures truly symbols for us? We may have their pictures on our walls. We may even visualize them in meditation. But they are not necessarily symbols for us in the sense of being fully, powerfully, and emotionally stimulating. A symbol isn't just something you put up on a wall. It's only a symbol to the extent that you respond to it, that you feel for it.

Developing a feeling for a symbol may therefore mean establishing links from whatever we do have a feeling for, however mundane it may be, to more refined things which, by degrees, link us with the archetypal symbol itself and make it more real to us. The Buddha image is the symbol of spiritual growth *par excellence*, the most elevated symbol available to us, but we may still find it easiest to approach it through a whole series of other symbols. For example, a certain Buddha figure may be associated with the symbol of the elephant. While the Buddha may be beyond the reach of your vision, you may for some reason feel an attraction to elephants, and make your connection that way. We catch on where we can. This is where the profusion of symbols of the Tantra comes into its own; there is something to appeal to everybody.

At the beginning, we may have to accept that the Buddha image is not a symbol for us, but only a picture. It may still represent an inspiring ideal for us, but, to begin with, it is just that – an ideal – something conceived of mentally. If the Buddha image were really a symbol for us, it would move us powerfully, and rouse and harness all our energies. If we just admire it as a striking picture or conceive of it as an abstract intellectual ideal, it is clearly not a symbol for us yet. Not that it should not be, or cannot be, but that as a matter of fact it is not. It can become a symbol, it may become one, you may want it to become one, but all this does not necessarily make it one here and now.

Can words lead us to a deeper experience of symbols? We had better get that straight before embarking on this study, which – although it will include many word-pictures – will also involve, it must be admitted, at least some conceptual explanation. Concepts themselves are ultimately derived from sense experience, of course, and thus refer to the direct experience of things. Language is essentially metaphorical and, like symbols, metaphors point to something which cannot be referred to in any other way. When we use words, we are not usually aware of their metaphorical origins and symbolic associations. When we talk about 'understanding', for example, we don't usually think of 'standing under', which is what the word literally means. We don't think of it as a spatial metaphor, although that is what it is.

Even if we do realize the metaphorical nature of language, what are we to make of it? Take the word Enlightenment. Forgetting about the Sanskrit original for the moment and just considering the English word, it obviously contains the word 'light'. Although the word literally refers to the world of the senses, in this context 'light' obviously represents some kind of understanding that goes beyond the senses. But if we want to investigate the accuracy of the expression 'Enlightenment', what can we say? If it isn't literally light that is experienced when one becomes Enlightened, what is it? We can't say, except by means of some other basically metaphorical expression.

Sometimes words – poetry especially – do manage somehow to transcend words, or at least point to a reality beyond them. But we must not let our facility with words deceive us. Even if we concede that no verbal description can be exhaustive, we may still have the idea that we have at least described something. But the truth is that we haven't described anything at all – or if we have, we can't verify that by comparison with some alternative method of explanation.

In essence, then, our relationship with language is similar to our relationship with symbols. Just as we may use symbols in a conventional way, so we also tend to put words together in patterns which are conventionally accepted as meaningful, but which may not mean much to us. The aim of the following chapters is to introduce the creative symbols of Tantric Buddhism in such a way as to help the reader find real meaning in these symbols. The more receptive you can be to the resonances of the words, and the more you try to see in your mind's eye the pictures they conjure up, the more alive the symbols will become.

But it is not just effort on our part that will bring Tantric symbolism alive for us, and make these symbols meaningful to our lives – not intellectual or willed effort anyway. The symbols themselves will affect us, will work on us and transform us, if we are receptive to them. They stand for something of which we are not yet conscious, but of which we can become conscious, which we can come to know in a spiritual sense. Symbols are not dead, inert counters. They are full of energy, and give birth to life, spiritual life, in us. They are by their very nature creative. The creative symbols of Tantric Buddhism are not just of historical interest. They are not just creative in the abstract, or in the past, or in Tibet and India. They are creative for us. They can act on us, energize us, spark off developments in our own spiritual life, here and now, right now.

1

THE TIBETAN WHEEL OF LIFE

The Tibetan wheel of life is a well-known and colourful symbol, but that is not why I have chosen it to begin this exploration of Tantric symbolism. It is best to deal with it first for two specific reasons. Firstly, the wheel of life is only partly Tantric. It is described in early Buddhist scriptures and in Mahāyāna *sūtras*, and those traditions were preserved in the Tantric context,[43] while at the same time the symbol was imbued with a distinctively Tantric spirit. Secondly, the wheel is only partly symbolic. While some parts of its complex structure are true symbols, others are only illustrative, representing in pictorial form teachings that can be expressed in other terms. Here we shall be dwelling more on the symbolic than on the illustrative elements of the wheel.

Starting with a simple description, what do we see when we look at the wheel? Basically, we see a lot of little pictures. The wheel consists of four concentric circles – that is, four circles of different sizes, one inside the other. Within the innermost circle, at the hub of the wheel, are to be seen three animals: a cock, a snake, and a pig. They appear head-to-tail in a sort of triangular relationship, each animal biting the tail of the one in front.

The circle surrounding the hub is divided into two halves, one light, the other dark. In the light segment are human beings moving upwards as though on a sort of celestial escalator. They have peaceful, joyful expressions, and they are decently clad. In the dark segment there are what seem to be human beings too – but are they really human? They are plunging headlong as though into a pit, naked and chained together, with expressions of fear and horror on their faces.

Moving outwards, the next circle is divided into six equal segments. In the first segment, right at the top of the circle, we see the world of the gods. Heaven opens before our eyes: a world of pleasures and delights where the gods live in beautiful palaces among trees and gardens, a world where every wish is instantly gratified. As soon as the desire for something floats – however vaguely – into your mind, that thing instantly appears in front of you, or in your hands, or your mouth, or on your body. This is how the gods live.

In the second segment, moving clockwise, is the world of the *asuras*, the anti-gods, the Titans. These are fierce, war-like beings – usually depicted as well-muscled, not to say heavily built – and they are engaged in perpetual warfare with the gods, fighting especially for the possession of the *kalpataru*, the magic tree that grants all wishes and fulfils all desires.

The third segment depicts the world of the *pretas*, the hungry ghosts. These beings are naked and horribly deformed: they have enormously swollen bellies, very thin necks, and mouths no bigger than the eye of a needle. Suffering all the time from ravenous hunger, they grasp at food and drink, trying desperately to cram it into their needle-eye mouths, but as they do so, the food and drink turns into excrement and liquid fire.

In the fourth segment, right at the bottom of the wheel, is the world of tormented beings: hell. At the centre of this world is a fearsome figure sitting enthroned. This is Yamarāja, the King of Death, dark blue in colour, clad in a tiger skin and surrounded by flames. In his hand he holds a mirror – the mirror of karma – and as beings are dragged before him, beings who have just died, he looks into the mirror and sees everything they have done, everything they have said, everything they have thought. If they have done more evil than good in the course of their preceding life, he orders that they should be taken away and punished. It should be said that this world is more of a purgatory than a hell, because it isn't a permanent state – but even so, in it we see guilty people suffering torments so terrible that it is painful to think about them, let alone describe them. The air is full of the sound of wailing and roaring and lamentation.

In the fifth segment is the world of animals, both wild and domesticated. They are shown in pairs, male and female, and they seem to be living a peaceful, idyllic existence – almost like the lion and the lamb in the biblical story. It isn't a very Darwinian picture, at least as depicted in Tibetan Buddhist art. There's no nature red in tooth and claw – the animals all seem very placid. Perhaps it is intended to show the animal's life from the animal's point of view, because, after all, animals don't worry about what's going to happen tomorrow.

The sixth and last segment is the world of human beings, and there men and women buy and sell, read, talk, work in the fields, meditate under the trees, and are finally carried as corpses to the cremation ground.

There is one important feature in each realm that hasn't yet been mentioned. In each of the six worlds there appears a Buddha figure of a particular colour, offering to the beings in that world something they need. In the world of the gods there appears a pure white Buddha holding a stringed musical instrument – usually in the paintings it's an Indian vina, which is rather like a medieval lute. This Buddha plays to the gods a sweet, penetrating melody: the melody of impermanence. Nothing lasts, the tune is saying; everything changes. In the world of the *asuras*, there appears a Buddha of a beautiful emerald green colour, holding in his right hand a flaming sword. It is on fire because it is the sword of transcendental wisdom, and he brandishes it at the *asuras* as they're fighting. In the world of the *pretas*, the hungry ghosts, there appears a ruby red Buddha who showers upon the *pretas* food and drink that they are able actually to consume. In the world of tormented beings there appears a Buddha the colour of smoke, bluish-grey, and he regales the beings in hell with *amṛta*, the food or drink of the gods known in the western tradition as nectar or ambrosia. In the world of the animals there appears a dark blue Buddha who is showing something to the animals: a book. And in the human world there appears a golden yellow Buddha, bearing the twin insignia of the spiritual life in ancient India: the begging-bowl and the staff with three rings. These six Buddhas represent the introduction into the symbolism of the wheel of life of a Mahāyānistic element, the element of great compassion, which, conjoined with wisdom, sees and responds appropriately to the needs of all beings.

The outermost circle of the wheel is divided into twelve segments, in each of which is a tiny picture. Clockwise from the top, these are: (1) a blind man with a stick, (2) a potter with a wheel and pots, (3) a monkey climbing a flowering tree, (4) a boat with four passengers, one of whom is steering, (5) an empty house with five windows and a door,

(6) a man and woman embracing, (7) a man with an arrow stuck in his eye, (8) a woman offering a drink to a seated man, (9) a man gathering fruit from a tree, (10) a pregnant woman, (11) a woman in childbirth, and (12) a man carrying a corpse to the cemetery.

The whole wheel is gripped by a monstrous, demoniacal figure: his face peers over the top of the wheel, his clawed hands and feet grip the sides, and his scaly reptilian tail coils below. He is impermanence personified, and he wears a crown made of five human skulls, a Tantric touch that hints at radical transformation. (We shall be looking at this key aspect of the Tantra when we come to consider the symbolism of the cremation ground and the celestial maidens.)

Above the wheel and to the right is the figure of Śākyamuni Buddha, floating on clouds and stretching out his arm to point out the path to Enlightenment. On the left is the full moon, in which can be discerned the figure of a hare.

This is the Tibetan wheel of life as it is – or used to be – depicted on the walls of temples and monasteries, and on painted scrolls, all over Tibet and the adjacent Himalayan region. But what does it all mean? As to that, much of it – the symbols, at least – cannot, as we have said, be explained at all. The main thing for us to do is just look at the wheel: not only at it, but into it – because in fact the wheel of life is not a picture at all. It is a mirror, in which we see – what else? – ourselves. Perhaps we could say that the wheel of life is made up not of four concentric circles, but of four mirrors. Or we could say that we look into the mirror four times, each time seeing more and more of ourselves, experiencing more of ourselves, realizing more of ourselves. The wheel of life is a sort of magic mirror or crystal ball into which we can gaze.

So let us look now into that mirror – not just four times but as many times as may be necessary – and let us have the courage to see ourselves in it. Some courage, indeed, will be needed. The very first time we look into the mirror, we see the three animals: the cock, the snake, and the pig. Usually it is said that they represent greed, hatred, and ignorance and that these three poisons are present in our own hearts. But this explanation is letting us off far too lightly; it is a kind of defensive rationalization. It is much more of a shock to look into the mirror and see not the human face we expected, but the face of an animal – a bird, a reptile, a pig. That's us, and uncomfortable as it may be, indeed should be, we should take a long look. This reflection is giving us a direct experience of our own animal nature. We see that we are not quite so human, so civilized, as we had thought. We're just an animal, a beast. And this realization is the beginning of spiritual life. We see ourselves as we are on the most basic level, we accept ourselves, and we go on from there.

Going on from there means taking another look in the mirror: once we have recovered from the shock of seeing that animal face, we take a second look. This time we see two paths, one going up, the other going down, one light, the other dark. So we are faced with two alternatives: up or down. It's as simple as that. We can either evolve or regress; the choice is before us. And this choice is before us every minute of the day, in every situation in which we find ourselves. Shall we go up or shall we go down? Shall we follow the light path or the dark path? It's up to us to decide.

If we do decide, after thinking it over, to follow the light path, the next question is, how? What must we do to grow spiritually? What is the next step? This clearly depends on where we are now. And to find that out, we need to look into the mirror a third time. This time we see one of the six worlds: the world of the gods, the world of the *asuras*, the world of the hungry ghosts, the world of tormented beings, the world of animals, or the world of human beings. In other words, we see where we are at any given moment or over any given period of time. Sometimes when we look into the mirror we see a happy, peaceful, cheerful face: the face of a god. Sometimes we see the angry, aggressive face of an *asura*. Sometimes we see a famished, hollow-eyed face, with a pinched mouth and a dissatisfied expression: the face of a hungry ghost. Sometimes we see the miserable, tormented face of someone in hell. Sometimes we see a face with a long snout and whiskers or big sharp teeth: the face of an animal. And sometimes we see just an ordinary human face. But whatever we see, we see ourselves.

The six segments into which this circle of the wheel of life is divided can be considered literally as realms of existence into which living beings are reborn as a result of their karma and in which they live until that karma has been exhausted. But this is only half the truth that the symbol represents. The segments can also be seen as representing states of mind that we can experience here and now, in the course of our everyday human existence. Sometimes our experience of these states of mind is so strong that for the time being we seem actually to be living in heaven or in hell or among the hungry ghosts. In other words, we experience them almost as states of being rather than just states of mind.

Viewed in this light, the world of the gods represents a happy state of mind, a state of relaxation, content, and repose. It's a state in which everything seems to flow smoothly, and there are no obstacles or problems. It is a state of aesthetic experience and artistic enjoyment as well as of meditation in the sense of deep concentration or *śamatha*, though not in the sense of insight into reality or *vipaśyanā* (Pāli: *vipassanā*).

The world of the *asuras*, by contrast, represents an aggressive, competitive state of mind. Here there is a lot of energy – perhaps too much – and it all turns outward. There is restlessness, suspicion, jealousy. Just as the *asuras* fight for possession of the wish-fulfilling tree, the *asura*-like state of mind is one that strives for an ever higher standard of living, more and more money, and so on. It is a state of assertive egotism, a state in which one wants to be better or more distinguished than other people, and even to control and exercise power over them.

The world of the hungry ghosts is the state of neurotic desire. Desire is neurotic when it seeks from its object more than that object can give, or even something quite different from what it can give. An obvious example is the neurotic desire for food. Sometimes people gobble down huge quantities of food, especially sweet things, but they don't really want food at all. It's a substitute for something else – for affection, very often, psychologists tell us. Neurotic desire in this sense is very often present in personal relationships, especially those of the more intimate kind – to such an extent in some cases that the two people involved are like hungry ghosts trying to devour each other.

The world of the tormented beings is the state of acute mental suffering, nervous frustration, mental breakdown, even insanity. This state is brought about in various ways: by the long-continued frustration of natural human impulses, by sudden bereavement, by unconscious mental conflicts, and by many other conditions and causes.

The world of the animals represents the state of purely sensual indulgence, the state in which one is interested only in food, sex, and material comforts, all the pleasures of life. When these needs are satisfied, one is quite gentle and tame, but when they are frustrated, one becomes snappy and even rather dangerous.

Finally, the world of human beings is the state of distinctively human consciousness, the state which is neither ecstatic nor agonized, neither fiercely competitive nor mindlessly sensual nor yet neurotically desirous. It's a state in which we are aware of our own self and aware of other people, a state in which we satisfy our objective human needs but at the same time see that they have their limitations, a state in which we devote ourselves to spiritual development. We call it the human realm, but in reality the truly human state is one that most 'human beings' only intermittently – or perhaps never – experience.

Our third look into the mirror has shown us where we are, whether we are – for the moment – a god or an *asura*, a hungry ghost or a tormented being, an animal or a human being. When we have seen where we are, we know the next step we have to take – and that draws us to the six Buddhas appearing in the midst of the six worlds. According to the Tibetan Buddhist teaching, these Buddhas are all manifestations of Avalokiteśvara, the bodhisattva who embodies the compassion aspect of the Enlightenment experience. Each of these six Buddhas holds, as we have observed, a particular object, something needed by the beings of the world in which he appears. As we shall see, the nature of the object the Buddha holds gives us a clue as to how to move on from that world, or that state of mind.

In the world of the gods the white Buddha holds a lute upon which he plays the melody of impermanence. This suggests that when we are in a state of aesthetic enjoyment, the next step is to remind ourselves that it won't last and also that aesthetic pleasure, however great, is not to be mistaken for the supreme bliss of Enlightenment. Although things may be going well now, we still have a long way to go. The Buddhist tradition stresses that prolonged happiness can be spiritually dangerous, if not disastrous. If we are happy and contented all the time, if things go easily and we have our own way, we meet no problems or obstacles, we tend to become self-satisfied, complacent, and even careless. We tend to forget that we are mortal, that life is short and time is precious. This applies even to the enjoyment of meditation, as well as to the appreciation of the fine arts. We need to make the transition from the heights of mundane experience to the experience of the Transcendental.

Notice that the white Buddha doesn't stand up among the gods and deliver a lecture on impermanence; he conveys his message by playing a melody on a lute. Nor is this just a symbolic notion, if we are to believe a story told about Aśvaghoṣa, to whom tradition ascribes the seminal text called *The Awakening of Faith in the Mahāyāna*. As well as being a great philosopher and spiritual teacher, Aśvaghoṣa was also a great musician, and he travelled throughout the India of his day playing his lute.[44] The Chinese traveller Xuanzang, who followed in his footsteps a few centuries later, in the seventh century CE, reports in his account of his sojourn in India that the effect of Aśvaghoṣa's music was still remembered all those years later. Apparently, when people heard it, they immediately got a sense of the impermanence of things. Somehow the melody conveyed the message that everything conditioned is unsatisfactory, all worldly things are unreal and insubstantial, Nirvāṇa is the only reality. Just listening to Aśvaghoṣa's music gave people that direct understanding. The music played by the white Buddha in the realm of the gods has the same effect. It wakes up those who are in this complacent and self-satisfied state, making them aware of higher truths and realities, not through philosophy, religion, or intellectual discussion, but through music.

In the world of the *asuras*, a green Buddha appears, brandishing a flaming sword, the sword of wisdom, transcendental wisdom – not just intellectual knowledge, but penetration into reality as a spiritual experience. This suggests that when we are in a state of competitiveness and aggressiveness, the next step is to develop intellectual insight into truth and reality. The battle, in other words, is relocated to the intellectual front. But why is wisdom symbolized by a sword? In an essay on 'Hate, Love, and Perfect Wisdom', the great Buddhist scholar Dr Edward Conze asserts that there is an affinity between hatred and wisdom.[45] If you experience a lot of anger and hatred, he says, you should be able to develop wisdom fairly easily.

This sounds odd at first, but a little thought shows the sense of it. The characteristic of hatred is to seek to destroy the hated object. If you hate something or someone, you want to finish them off, to smash them to smithereens, to make just one big nothing where they used to be. We may not always admit it to ourselves, but this is what we would like to do. And the characteristic of transcendental wisdom is also to destroy: to destroy conditioned existence itself, to reduce to dust everything that isn't reality, isn't truth, isn't Buddhahood. This is why transcendental wisdom is symbolized by the *vajra*, the thunderbolt, which is said to smash and destroy all obstacles.

Thus there is this affinity between hatred and wisdom, although the one is highly unethical and the other entirely ethical. It is noticeable that a hot temper and a highly developed intellect often go together, even when that intellect is applied to Buddhism, which should be the epitome of equanimity. Scholars specializing in Buddhist studies can be bad tempered and quarrelsome to a remarkable degree, especially among themselves – an example being Dr Conze himself, who was celebrated not only for his tremendous scholarship and intellectual penetration, but also for his peppery temper. It is as though the destructive force that expresses itself in hatred can be diverted into intellectual channels and used to fuel the discovery and realization of truth.

Dr Conze points out that the Perfection of Wisdom tradition is associated with the Buddha Akṣobhya, called the Imperturbable, one of the set of five archetypal Buddhas whom we shall encounter later.[46] Akṣobhya is said to be the patron Buddha of people of predominantly choleric temperament. In this way the Tantric tradition seems to recognize an affinity between hatred and wisdom. It seems that an *asura*-like person has a natural ability not only to fight with the gods, but also to conquer truth itself, at least intellectually, more effectively than other people who may be easier to get on with.

Having said this, one must be careful not to make a necessary connection out of a mere correspondence between two quite separate spheres, between an aspect of psychological conditioning and an aspect of reality. This suggestion of an affinity between hatred and wisdom originates with Buddhaghosa, the great commentator on the Pāli canon who lived in the sixth century CE. But what he actually said – as near as we can make it out – was that just as hatred seizes upon the negative aspects of things, in the same way wisdom seizes upon the faults of conditioned existence.[47] He draws an analogy between hatred and wisdom, but no more than that. In other words, someone with a critical, intellectually aggressive mind may have a greater potential to follow the path of wisdom, but without actually doing so they are no closer to true wisdom than anyone else. By the same token, someone who is warmly affectionate is not, without taking steps to realize their potential, any closer to developing true compassion than less demonstrative people.

In the world of the hungry ghosts there appears a red Buddha who showers the suffering denizens of that state of existence with food and drink that they can actually consume. Now what does this mean for us in practical terms? It means that when we are in a state of neurotic desire, the next step is to get back to an accurately objective perception of the situation, which also means getting back to the present moment. We must see what the desired object can give us and what it cannot. We also need to discover what we really desire, and where that desire is coming from. Once we have done so, we can either give our desire its proper satisfaction, if that is possible, or – if it is inappropriate or unskilful – do our best to let go of it.

The *amṛta* or nectar with which the smoke-coloured Buddha regales the beings in hell can be interpreted in at least two – rather contradictory – ways. Most obviously it signifies that when we are in a state of intense mental suffering, the next step is simply to gain a respite from it, some ease and relaxation. That is often the best we can do in the circumstances. But at another level of meaning, this nectar is both more challenging and more profound. *Amṛta* is usually translated as 'nectar' or 'ambrosia', but in many Buddhist texts it is a synonym for Enlightenment itself: the *amṛtapada*, the state of nectar, the deathless, eternal state.[48] So the smoke-coloured Buddha gives the beings in hell not just nectar but Nirvāṇa. The suggestion – which in a way seems quite outrageous – is that when we are in a state of intense suffering, the next step is to gain Enlightenment. But it does make sense. There's nothing else for us to do. All worldly hope has foundered. All we can do is head straight for Enlightenment. It's as though there were another strange affinity between a supremely negative state and a supremely positive one – this time between intense mental suffering and an aptitude for the highest spiritual attainment.

In the world of animals, the blue Buddha shows the animals a book. Surely this suggests that when we are in a state of barbarism and savagery, our next step is to become civilized, to acquaint ourselves with the arts and sciences, with the cultural life of mankind, because these things have a refining influence. It is difficult, if not impossible, to go from a barbaric state straight into a life of spiritual development. This is one of the reasons why Buddhism has always been a bearer of culture. As well as spiritual teachings, Buddhists took Indian higher culture all over Asia, because that refined, humanistic culture provided a foundation for the spiritual life. Hence the bodhisattva, the ideal Buddhist, is presented in Mahāyāna texts as a master of arts, sciences, and even handicrafts – quintessentially in the figure of Mañjughoṣa, the great Bodhisattva of Wisdom, who is said to preside over the arts and sciences.

Finally, the yellow Buddha who appears in the world of human beings carries the begging-bowl and three-ringed staff that are the insignia of the religious mendicant and therefore of the spiritual life in general. The point of this is clear: when we find ourselves in a truly human state, the next step is to devote ourselves wholeheartedly to the task of spiritual development. Once we have reached the truly human state, this should be our main interest in life.

The general message from the presence of the different Buddhas is that within each of these realms or states of existence there is the potential for development. There is always a next step. One of the fundamental teachings of Buddhism, especially Mahāyāna Buddhism, is that all sentient beings are capable of Buddhahood. Indeed, above and beyond the world of time and phenomenal particularity, all beings *are* Buddha, *are* Enlightened. And within time all beings are capable – eventually – of gaining Enlightenment.

But beings are not all equally capable of becoming Enlightened from their present state, whatever it is. In the Chinese Mahāyāna tradition it is said that some people are endowed with more 'Buddha seeds' than others. According to this tradition, there are three kinds of seed, three kinds of potentiality, in sentient beings. There are good seeds (red seeds, as they are sometimes called), bad seeds (black seeds), and Buddha seeds (yellow or golden seeds). Buddha seeds represent potentialities for spiritual growth. The distinction between good seeds and Buddha seeds is a reminder that being good does not necessarily make you a Buddha, although if you are a Buddha you can't help being good, presumably. All three kinds of seed are present in all beings, in all six realms, in varying – and sometimes rather surprising – proportions.

In the world of the gods, there are no bad seeds. The gods have no potentiality for evil – and you do get people like that, people who wouldn't hurt a fly. Almost all the seeds in the god realm are good seeds because the gods really are very good – happy, holy, contented, peaceful, and kind. But what is perhaps surprising is the fact that they possess very few Buddha seeds; the potentiality of the gods for Enlightenment is very limited.

The seeds in the world of the *asuras* are two thirds bad, one third good, with only a single Buddha seed. In the world of hungry ghosts there are no good seeds at all and a predominance of bad seeds, but quite a lot of Buddha seeds. It's almost exactly the same in the world

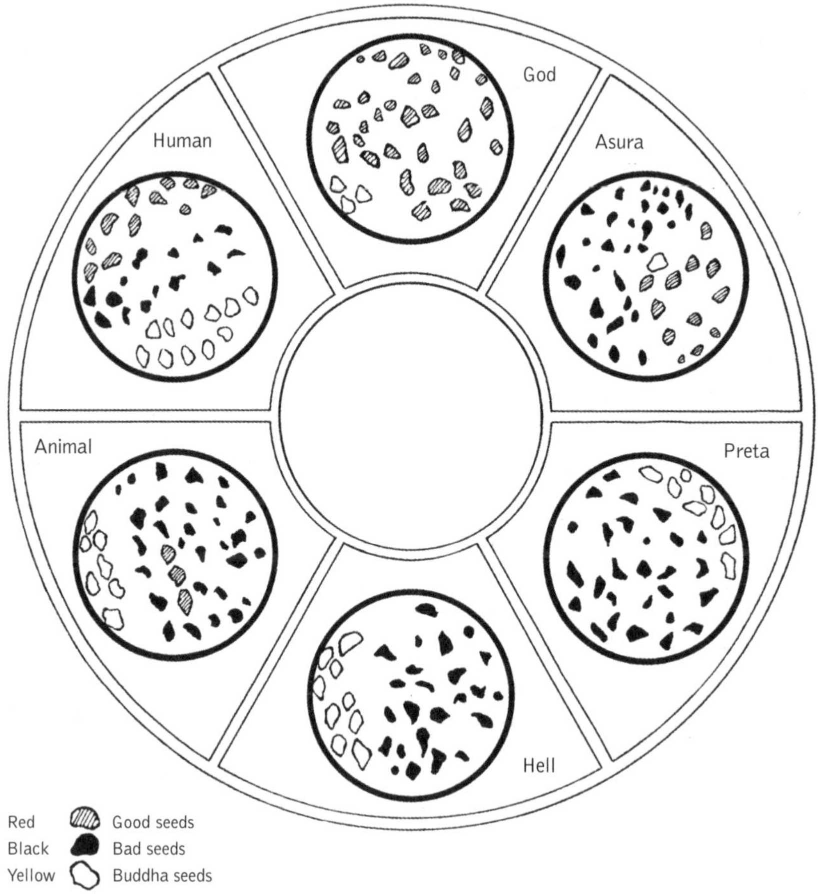

of tormented beings, except that there are even more Buddha seeds. In the world of the animals there are very few good seeds – so they don't have a very happy time of it after all, it would seem – a predominance of bad seeds, and a few Buddha seeds, about twice as many as the good seeds there. And in the world of human beings the three kinds of seed are present in roughly equal proportions.

Some of the conclusions that follow from all this are quite obvious. The *asuras* – warlike, competitive people – have the least potential for Buddhahood. By analogy, if you are in a highly competitive environment – big business, for example, or politics – you will have only the very smallest potential for Enlightenment, it would seem. This is not to say that all competition must be removed from the spiritual life. Competitiveness can be negative and destructive, but it can also be healthy and positive. It is possible to use the competitive spirit as a means of getting oneself to make more spiritual effort without having any antagonistic feeling towards the person with whom one is competing. For example, you might feel competitive with a friend about the relative consistency of your meditation practice. But if he or she manages to get up early to meditate more often than you do, you don't in the end mind being bested, because you have got the best out of yourself in the process, and that is what matters.

The competitiveness of the *asuras*, though, is completely antithetical to the spiritual life. It is not just using competitiveness in a playful way to get yourself to make more effort; it is aimed at victory, conquest, doing the other person down. This does sometimes occur even among those trying to live a spiritual life. It manifests most frequently in a reluctance to cooperate, but it can be expressed just through talking and joking. If we come to realize that we tend to be uncooperative, we need to make the effort to be more willing to go along with what other people want, and not to have very strong views about very small things. Bitter disputes so often arise over trivialities – because, of course, the issue isn't really whether to do this or that, but whether I have my way or you have your way. It is a good practice to be very slow to take a stand on anything other than a real matter of principle. Very often the situation isn't worth arguing about, but the *asura* element in one's nature whispers, 'Why should I do what he wants? Why should I always be following him?' It is a mistake to listen to that little voice. In most situations, the more wholehearted and warm the cooperation, the better it is for everyone.

It is sobering to observe that the gods have a smaller potential for Enlightenment than either the hungry ghosts or the tormented beings. It is very difficult, unfortunately, to gain Enlightenment from a state of unadulterated happiness and pleasure. It is much easier, though still extremely difficult, to make spiritual progress from a state of intense suffering. Suffering acts as a catalyst, it makes us more aware. People undergoing serious illness, going through physical changes and pain, or suffering intense distress, sometimes have spiritual experiences of a depth and intensity that do not occur so readily under more pleasant circumstances. We are more sensitive at such times, and thus more susceptible to spiritual influences. Self-inflicted suffering is, of course, another matter – the Buddha was clear that self-mortification takes one as far from the middle way, the path to Enlightenment, as self-indulgence, which is the other extreme.[49]

So has life in the god realm nothing to recommend it from a spiritual point of view? Is it just a waste of time? Not necessarily. It is analogous to sleep, which we know is not mere time wasting, but necessary to our good health and indeed our very existence. If you have led a healthy, positive life, a period in the god realm represents a rest from mundane existence, an opportunity to assimilate and digest experience. Then, as a residue of the skilful deeds that have caused you to be reborn among the gods, you may have a happy and positive human rebirth – like someone waking refreshed from a good sleep – and can make another positive spiritual effort. But while you are actually in the realm of the gods, as in dreams, it is difficult (though not impossible) to make any effort at all.

Contentment is, of course, perilously close to complacency, and this is the fatal flaw of life in the god realm. In *The Jewel Ornament of Liberation*, the Tibetan teacher Gampopa says:

> How is it that we have not already obtained Buddhahood? The fault lies in people like ourselves having come under the power of four obstacles by which the attainment of Buddhahood is prevented. They are: attachment to sensuous experiences during this life, to sensual pleasures in this world, to self-complacency, and to ignorance about the means of realizing Buddhahood.[50]

Hindered by the first of these obstacles, you take it for granted that your particular world will continue. Hindered by the second – taking pleasure as the highest value – you seize the pleasure of the moment and forget your long-term interests. And in the grip of the third – self-complacency – you are satisfied with yourself as you are, and what could be a greater obstacle than that? You say, 'Well, I'm all right, I'm quite happy, I'm doing well, I meditate every day,' – and you lose your sense of urgency with regard to spiritual development.

It is crucial to understand this obstacle *as* an obstacle. Once you feel established on the spiritual path, once you are meditating, going on retreat, and associating with people who share your values, you naturally and rightly feel very pleased about the state of affairs. But that is the time to say to yourself, 'I must beware of complacency. I must keep on growing.' You have to keep asking yourself if the situation you are in is helping you to keep growing spiritually.

At the same time you can't overcome complacency simply by making life difficult for yourself. It is also possible to be complacent about being someone who has to struggle and make a lot of effort in life. One is not necessarily growing just because one is struggling, especially if you feel quietly pleased with yourself because you are always the one who is making the effort. So while in general greed types are more prone to complacency than hate types, hate types are also susceptible to it in their own way.

If the teaching of the seeds is anything to go by, our best bet, if we want to make spiritual progress, would seem to be to seek rebirth in the human realm, where 'joy and pain are woven fine', as Blake says.[51] But this is not easy either. In the *Dhammapada*, the Buddha says, 'Difficult is the attainment of the human state.'[52] One can look at this statement in two ways, one traditional and the other more contemporary. The traditional view is that it is literally difficult to attain a human birth, and this view is illustrated by means of a simile. The chances of being born human are likened to the chances that a blind turtle who only emerges from the depths of the ocean once every hundred years will happen to put his head through a wooden yoke floating on the surface.[53]

This is probably not to be taken literally. No doubt the statistical probability that any living being will be born human is remote, given how many billions of insects, fish, and all sorts of other creatures there are – one could perhaps look at human birth as being rare in that way. But it is unlikely that those who have been human beings in previous existences will not be reborn human. In approaching this idea that it is difficult to attain the human state, it is more fruitful to ask what it really means to be a human being. This brings us to the more contemporary interpretation of the statement. What is the human state? Are you necessarily a human being because you bear a remote resemblance to the higher apes? What *is* a human being?

To speak of being *born* as a human being is clearly to refer to being human in the ordinary biological sense. But to speak of *attaining* the human state is to suggest that it is not enough to be human merely in the biological sense. You have to develop certain qualities to qualify as a human being. The process of becoming human consists in the full development of such qualities as self-awareness, emotional positivity, responsibility, fidelity, and cooperativeness. So it isn't easy to be human; the human state is, as the Buddha says, 'difficult of attainment'.

We have to ask ourselves the purpose of this teaching of the seeds. It is not saying that there are literally so many red, black, and yellow seeds in an animal, so many in a human being, and so on. It is not meant to be scientific. It is simply a reminder that as human beings we have great potential for spiritual development, and that we should therefore make the effort to develop whatever potential we have. Whether the six realms of existence are taken literally, or whether they are regarded as being contained within human life, the whole teaching is meant to be encouraging, meant to remind us that there is always some potential for Enlightenment. If you are a *human* human being, the potential is greater. But even if you are in a hellish or *preta*-like state of mind, even if you are neurotic or aggressive, your potential for spiritual development is not altogether obscured – you can still make progress. Inasmuch as you are a human being, Buddha seeds are there.

Having taken our third long look into the mirror, we have seen where we are, the mental state we are in, and the next step to be taken. Now we must look into the mirror again. This time we see the images depicted around the rim of the wheel of life: the blind man with his stick, the potter with his wheel and pots, the monkey climbing the flowering tree, and so on. These are the twelve *nidānas* or links that show how it all happens, how we pass from one state of existence to another, one state of mind to another.[54] This is the process of what I have termed the reactive mind.[55] And seeing it, really seeing it, we are free of it. We have seen through the reactive mind and we pass beyond it. And after a while, we look into the mirror again.

This time we see the monster in whose grip the wheel is tightly clutched. We come face to face with death, with the fact of universal, cosmic impermanence. We see that conditioned existence – that is to say, existence that comes into being in dependence on causes and conditions – is not only impermanent but also ultimately unreal. But we see at the same time, in the depths of the unreality of conditioned existence, gleaming like a pearl at the bottom of the sea, the real, the ultimately, absolutely real. It is not even really separate from the unreal, but constitutes another dimension of it.

When we look into the mirror once more, we see the Buddha – this time not up in the corner of the picture, but right in the centre of things.

We see, in short, Enlightenment itself. In Zen terms, we see our own original face. We experience directly what we truly and essentially are, in the depths of our being. And then we see the Bodhisattva. This is what the hare in the full moon represents: the Bodhisattva – that is, the Buddha in one of his previous lives. According to the traditional *Jātaka* stories, the Buddha-to-be was reborn as a hare, and sacrificed his body in the fire to provide a meal for a hungry guest. As so often in legends of this sort, the guest turned out to be a king in disguise – in this case Indra, the king of the gods. He restored the hare to life and drew his picture on the full moon as an everlasting testimony to his spirit of generosity and self-sacrifice.[56] This is why, according to Indian legend, you see the hare in the moon (not the man in the moon, as our legend is in the West), even today. Every time you look up at the hare in the moon, you are reminded of the Bodhisattva's generosity and self-sacrifice.

The Bodhisattva does not represent just one individual. Seeing the Bodhisattva means seeing the spirit of Enlightenment at work in the cosmos, and seeing ourselves as participating in that work. Having seen the Buddha, our own original face, outside time, we see that same Buddha principle at work within time, through time, in the activities of the Bodhisattva.

Looking in the mirror for the last time, we don't see anything at all. In fact, the mirror disappears. There's nothing to see and nobody to see it. And yet at the same time, mysteriously, everything is seen. Everything is heard. Everything is understood. Everything is realized. The symbolism of the Tibetan wheel of life has been transcended – and fulfilled.

2

THE TANTRIC STUPA

Gautama the Buddha, the founder of the spiritual tradition that we now know as Buddhism, lived in India some 2,500 years ago. Nevertheless, we know quite a lot about him – about the events of his life, and about the character of the man himself. We have voluminous records of his teachings. Also, there are available to us many descriptions of the people who were influenced by his example in the course of the forty-five years of his ministry: the men and women who formed the early Buddhist monastic community, and his lay followers – kings, noblemen, garland sellers, sweepers, scavengers, merchants, traders, priests.

From these records we can glean a good deal about how people reacted to the Buddha – both to his teachings and to the fact that, wandering the roads of India, there could be seen every day a man who was Enlightened. Some were very much impressed, even carried away by their joy that there was, walking about in the world in flesh and blood, an Enlightened human being. But there were others who didn't like the idea at all, who refused to see the Buddha as the Buddha. While some thought of him as the Enlightened One, others saw him simply as someone who had happened to leave his home with the Śākya clan to wander about as a religious mendicant. Some thought of him as just another spiritual teacher, others as a kindly sort of person, others as a great yogi, still others as a miracle-worker, while not a few criticized and reviled him as a notorious trouble-maker. We know from the scriptures that the Buddha created all these impressions in the minds of his contemporaries.[57]

We have, too, quite a lot of information about the cultural conditions that prevailed in north-eastern India at that time. It is clear that during the Buddha's lifetime there was a general shift from a republican to a monarchical form of polity. The social conditions, the stratification of society according to the caste system, and so on, are well documented. And we know about the economic condition of the country: what trades were carried on, by whom, and where. It seems that trading connections extended as far as Babylonia and perhaps even further than that. All these things we know.

But as regards the life of the Buddha we know most of all about two particular episodes. The first is of course his attainment of Enlightenment, when at the age of thirty-five the supreme reality of things at last dawned upon him in meditation. As for the second, this is the *parinirvāṇa*, his final passing away, the dissociation of that supreme Enlightenment experience from the physical body in connection with which – even through which – it was attained. Indeed, the *parinirvāṇa* has a complete and substantial text devoted to it, the 'scripture of the great decease', which exists in several versions (the Pāli version being entitled the *Mahāparinibbāna Sutta* and the Sanskrit the *Mahāparinirvāṇa Sūtra*). This great work contains a detailed, fairly connected description of the last few months of the Buddha's life.[58] It follows him almost step by step, telling us where he went, whom he met, what teachings he gave, and how he gave them. It is a solemn and moving account, culminating in this event, which was regarded as having profound significance.

At one point the text (in this case the Pāli *Mahāparinibbāna Sutta*) makes specific reference to this significance. The Buddha and his companion Ānanda are presented with robes made of cloth-of-gold, and the Buddha's complexion is observed to become so extremely bright as to outshine the brilliance of these new robes. The Buddha then explains that it is only twice in a Buddha's lifetime that his complexion becomes so bright: when he gains Enlightenment and when he is about to enter *parinirvāṇa*.[59] The symbolism of this story is clear: that the *parinirvāṇa* is paralleled in significance only by the Enlightenment itself.

Now why is this? It would seem that there was nothing particularly significant about it as far as the Buddha himself was concerned. For him it simply represented the 'dropping off' of the physical body; his experience remained the same. (This is obviously not a simple matter from a philosophical point of view, but we won't go into that here.)

For his disciples, though, it must have been a very different matter. When the Buddha gained Enlightenment there was nobody around, so the Enlightenment had no witnesses – or at least none are mentioned in the texts, except perhaps *devas*. But there were apparently many people present at the *parinirvāṇa*. Perhaps that fact alone gives it a special significance – not from the Buddha's point of view but as far as other people are concerned. Or perhaps the *parinirvāṇa* has come to be invested with so much significance because it is associated with death. It shows that even someone who is Enlightened has to die in the ordinary human way.

So let us follow the Buddha on that last journey. By the time he embarked upon it, he was an old man of eighty. He had lived a long and eventful life, and he knew that he was going to die soon, that Enlightenment did not exempt him from the general doom of humanity. Still, being the Buddha, he remained perfectly calm and objective. He apparently knew exactly when he was going to die, and he simply thought, 'What would it be most appropriate for me to do with the short time that is left to me?' He reflected, we are told, that it would not be fitting for him to attain *parinirvāṇa* without first having said goodbye to his friends and disciples and given them a few last words of exhortation and advice.

With Ānanda as his sole companion, the Buddha observed the 'rainy season retreat', that period during the rainy season when, making a virtue of necessity, one remains indoors, meditating or quietly talking with friends. Then the two friends set out on an extensive tour of north-eastern India, and as the *sutta* proceeds, the story unfolds towards a sublime and moving final episode. We see the Buddha and Ānanda arriving at a place called Kuśinagara – just a few miles from the present-day Nepalese border – where they make their way to a grove of *sāl* trees. *Sāl* trees are very beautiful, with tall, straight, smooth trunks, a few short branches, and lovely pale green leaves. This particular grove belonged to a republican tribe called the Mallas, who were well known to the Buddha, since many of his disciples and followers were from that tribe.

By now, the Buddha is very tired. He has been walking, perhaps every day, for many months, and exerting himself to the utmost, expending the last few ounces of his energy, visiting his friends and followers, talking with them, giving them his last words of advice. So, tired as he is, he asks Ānanda to prepare for him a couch between two *sāl* trees, and this

Ānanda does, taking off his own outer robe, which is quite thick, and making a rough couch from it on a stone platform beneath the trees. Here the Buddha lies down. Then, according to the *Mahāparinibbāna Sutta*, a miracle takes place. It isn't the time of year when *sāl* trees bloom, but suddenly they break out into blossom. And the blossoms – beautiful, pure white flowers, large and plentiful – start raining down on the Buddha's body. It is as though the *sāl* trees were offering these white flowers in worship, almost as though nature herself were worshipping the Buddha before his departure. Not only that: drifting down from the sky comes heavenly frankincense, and the ethereal music of gods and goddesses, so that the air is filled with beautiful sounds and fragrance, in worship of the Buddha. But the Buddha is apparently not in the least impressed by all these miracles – perhaps we can even surmise that after forty-five years he is rather tired of miracles. He just looks up and says to Ānanda that all this – the white flowers, the incense falling from the sky, the heavenly music – does not truly constitute worship of the Buddha. 'He who would worship me,' he says, 'Let him follow my teaching. That is the true worship.'

After a while Ānanda asks a question. It's a practical question – he's a practical man, and he can't help thinking ahead. He asks, 'Lord, when you are dead, when you have attained *parinirvāṇa*, what should be done with your body?' The Buddha says, 'Ānanda, don't worry about that. Get on with your own spiritual practice; that is far more important.' He goes on to say that there are faithful lay followers who will attend to the disposal of his physical remains. This illustrates the Buddha's objective, even severe, attitude. He would not tolerate sentimentality, he would not countenance for a moment the idea that anyone who was committed to the path of spiritual development should be distracted from what was really important.

But Ānanda, who is not yet fully Enlightened, finds it very difficult to accept this kind of objective attitude. In fact, he is very upset at the prospect of the Buddha's departing from the world – so upset that he cannot stay in the Buddha's presence at this point. He goes away into a nearby lodging and leans on the doorpost, weeping and saying to himself: 'I still have so much to learn and my teacher, who was so kind to me, is about to depart.'

Meanwhile, other disciples are arriving and gathering around the Buddha. The Buddha notices that Ānanda is uncharacteristically absent, and asks where he is. Hearing that Ānanda has gone away because he is so upset, the Buddha asks someone to fetch him, and one of the disciples goes and takes him by the arm and brings him back into the Buddha's presence. The Buddha consoles him, saying, 'Ānanda, don't feel regret that you are not yet fully Enlightened. You will be, very soon. Not long after my *parinirvāṇa*, you too will gain perfect Enlightenment.' Then, turning to the other disciples, the Buddha praises Ānanda for his many positive qualities, especially the tact with which he has always handled visitors.

By this time it is the middle of the night, and everybody knows that now it will only be a matter of hours before the Buddha departs. They are all sitting around, silent and solemn in the *sāl* grove of the Mallas, waiting for the *parinirvāṇa*. Then, in the midst of the silence and solemnity, an unexpected visitor arrives. The Buddha can't even die in peace, it seems. Ānanda remonstrates with the newcomer: 'The Buddha is about to pass away. You can't see him now; it's too late.' The Buddha overhears him, though, and he says, 'Ānanda, let him approach. He is a simple, straightforward man; as soon as I explain the truth to him, he will understand. Let him come near.' So the man – he was known as Subhadra the wanderer – becomes the last of the Buddha's personal disciples. He approaches, has a brief discussion with the Buddha, and as a result develops spiritual insight.

Now the Buddha's end is fast approaching. Rousing himself, he gives his final exhortation to his disciples. In particular he insists that they are not losing their teacher. He is leaving a teacher with them, he says – one that will be with them all the time. Their teacher will be the Dharma, the truth that he has taught. In other words, the Buddha is spiritually present in his teaching. If you are in contact with the Dharma, you are in contact with the Buddha himself. Finally, he reminds them that all things are impermanent. All things, all beings, even Buddhas, are transient. Everything, sooner or later, will flow away, like the water of a great river. He urges them to stay awake to this truth, not to fall asleep. And with that he passes into the state of deep meditation, and from that state he passes away.

However, so far as the *Mahāparinibbāna Sutta* is concerned, this is by no means the end of the story. The Buddha passes away, and his body is left lying beneath the twin *sāl* trees. Those of his disciples who are as yet unenlightened are very upset, weeping and lamenting, but those who are Enlightened just carry on sitting calmly round the corpse, their minds undisturbed even by the passing away of the Buddha. So they sit there, and the hours pass by, and the dawn comes. The Mallas, in whose *sāl* grove all this has taken place, hear the news that the Buddha has passed away, and in the course of the next few hours and days, they arrange for his body to be cremated with royal honours. After the body has been completely consumed by the fire, they search among the ashes and collect fragments of bone, which they seal in a golden jar. And they worship the relics in this golden jar with flowers and perfume and hymns of praise.

Then messengers arrive from every direction, from kings, nations, and tribes, all demanding a share of the Buddha's relics. But the Mallas are not ready to part with them, saying, 'The Buddha passed away in our territory, so the relics belong to us.' Various tribes demand their share of the relics, and a quarrel very nearly takes place. But there is at least one wise man around, and he talks with the representatives of these various kings and tribes, and makes them see how unseemly it is that they should be ready to resort to violence over such a sacred matter. In the end, they agree to the division of the relics, the golden jar is opened, the relics are reverently divided into eight equal portions, and everybody is happy. They all take their share of the relics to their own territory and enshrine them with great honour, heaping above them, in some chosen spot, an enormous mound of earth. These mounds were subsequently known as stupas.[60]

So this was the beginning of a tradition which was to become one of the most significant features of Buddhist life and culture throughout the Buddhist world. The stupa has a history throughout Asia coterminous with the history of Buddhism itself. Wherever Buddhism went, there went the stupa, and it became the most important and ubiquitous of all Buddhist visual forms. This may seem rather surprising. When one thinks of Buddhist art, the first thing that comes to mind is quite likely to be the Buddha image. But the stupa is the more ancient symbol, and even perhaps the more characteristic of Buddhism. The Buddha image did not come into existence in India until long after the *parinirvāṇa*. Indeed, among the early Buddhists there was a general feeling against representations of the Buddha. After all, in his essence the Buddha was the embodiment of ineffable reality. How could that possibly be represented? How could that experience be conveyed? Surely not by the image of a human body in some material medium. Moreover, the Buddha himself had said that people could not see him, could not truly understand him, even in his lifetime, because his nature was so deep and vast. The question of the nature of a Buddha after death – and this question was specifically addressed to the Buddha by various people at various times – was still more difficult to fathom. It was one of the 'inexpressibles', something about which it was impossible to say anything, whether in words or in any artistic medium.[61] For several hundred years after the Buddha's *parinirvāṇa*, therefore, no Buddha images were made.

But the stupa came into existence within days of the *parinirvāṇa*; in a sense it already existed even before the Buddha's time. In ancient India, as in many parts of the world throughout what may be described as the heroic age, it was the custom that when a great man died, a mound of earth would be heaped up over his remains. The ancient Greeks honoured their dead heroes in this way, and the ancient Britons heaped earth over the remains of the dead in the form of the long barrows and round barrows still to be seen in many parts of England. It was because such a custom prevailed in India to show honour to the memory of dead kings that the Buddha's followers erected stupas over the remains of the Buddha. They were moved to treat the Buddha after his death as though he had been a great king. In fact, this was what they felt he was: not an earthly king, but a king of the spiritual world, a king of truth, a *dharmarāja*. (This, indeed, became one of the Buddha's titles.)

According to an Indian tradition preserved in Tibetan sources, the question of building a monument over the remains of the Buddha after his death had been mooted even during the Buddha's lifetime. The story goes that the disciples had come to him and asked what kind of monument would be appropriate. Apparently the Buddha's response was rather Zen-like. He didn't say anything; he just showed them what he wanted. He was wearing the standard set of three robes: one round the waist, one over the shoulder, and an extra thick one which is used as a blanket at night and as a cloak when one is out and about. He took this thick outer robe and folded it into four and then into four again, to produce a rough cube of cloth. Then he took his begging-bowl, which was probably black and lacquered, and placed it upside down on top of the folded robe, saying, 'Make my stupa like that.'[62] And this is how the shape of the earliest form of stupa did in fact turn out: a cube surmounted by a hemisphere.

Over the centuries, the stupa became much more complicated. In fact, it became very complex indeed, architecturally, artistically, and in significance. Eventually, after several hundred years of development not only in India but also in Sri Lanka, Burma, Tibet, China, and Japan, it became a three-dimensional symbol of the Buddha's teaching itself, so that to tell the history of the stupa is practically to tell the history of Buddhism.

The stupa became more complex partly by way of the progressive incorporation of symbols. Fairly early in the history of the Indian stupa the hemisphere came to be surmounted by a box-like structure (sometimes surrounded by a railing), which may have represented the pre-Buddhistic Brahminical fire-altar. This in turn came to be surmounted by an honorific or ceremonial umbrella – in fact, by a number of umbrellas, one on top of the other, sometimes three, sometimes nine, and sometimes thirteen. These umbrellas may have represented the tree of life, the cosmic tree, beneath whose branches, according to some accounts, the Buddha sat on the night of his Enlightenment. And the thirteenfold umbrella which we find crowning the stupa very late in the history of its development represents the thirteen stages of spiritual progress through which the Bodhisattva passes on his way to supreme Enlightenment.

Thus far, there is nothing Tantric about the symbolism of the stupa – it has a long non-Tantric history. However, specifically Tantric elements were incorporated into the stupa during the Tantric phase of the development of Buddhism in India, and these are our primary concern here. We will focus on three of the symbolic features of the stupa, representing three main features of the Tantric path to Enlightenment: the five elements, the vase of initiation, and the flaming drop.

Of the five elements – earth, water, fire, air, and space – the first four between them make up the so-called material universe. In all Buddhist schools these so-called material elements are collectively known as *rūpa*, which is in turn the first of the five *skandhas*, the five aggregates or heaps into which the Buddha analysed the whole of conditioned or phenomenal existence. (The other *skandhas* are *vedanā* or feeling, *saṃjñā* or perception, *saṃskāra*s or volitions, and *vijñāna* or consciousness.)

Early translators of Buddhist texts into western languages, feeling their way through the unfamiliar thought-world in which they found themselves, translated *rūpa* whenever they encountered it, whether in Sanskrit or in Pāli, as 'matter' – meaning matter as opposed to mind. But this is very misleading. *Rūpa* literally means 'form' (though that translation can be misleading too) and it refers to what Dr Guenther has called the 'objective content of the perceptual situation'.[63] We talk in terms of 'having an experience', but it is more accurate to say that there is a situation in which perception takes place. Whenever we perceive something – when we see a flower, or hear a melody – we can distinguish two elements in that perceptual situation. First of all, there is what we ourselves contribute to it: the sensations mediated through our sense faculties, and whatever feelings – pleasant or unpleasant – arise as a result. But in that perceptual situation there is something that we do not contribute, something that the experience seems to be an experience *of*, something to which the perceptual situation seems to refer. This something, unknown and unidentified, is the objective content of that perceptual situation or that experience. It is this that Buddhism calls *rūpa*. So *rūpa* is definitely not matter as opposed to mind. Indeed, mind-matter dualism does not exist in Buddhism, least of all in the Tantra.

Rūpa is experienced in certain ways – that is, it is perceived as possessing certain qualities. It is perceived as (1) solid and resistant, (2) fluid and cohesive, (3) possessing a certain temperature, (4) light and moving. These four qualities are symbolized in Buddhist tradition by the elements earth, water, fire, and air. Here the elements really are symbols, not things. Earth doesn't mean a lump of rock, water doesn't mean the stuff that comes out of the tap. Rather, whatever is perceived as solid and resistant is symbolized by earth, whatever is perceived as fluid and cohesive is symbolized by water, whatever is perceived as possessing temperature is symbolized by fire, and whatever is perceived as possessing lightness and motility is symbolized by air.

These four qualities are known as *mahābhūtas*. The word means great or primary element, and these four are the basis of further, secondary elements of *rūpa*. But there are other interpretations of the term, referring to other very significant aspects of Buddhist thought. *Mahābhūta* sometimes refers to a great magical transformation or feat, such as the feat a magician performs when he makes you see one thing as something else. For example, a magician only apparently transforms clay into gold: the trick is that he makes you perceive as gold what is still in fact clay. Our experience of *rūpa* is similar: we come up against an experience of resistance and call it earth, but what the earth element is in itself we do not and cannot know.

Mahābhūta can also mean a great ghost, some terrible haunting spirit. Indian mythology tells of a terrible female sprite called a *yakṣiṇī* who appears one dark night as a beautiful maiden. You don't know it's a sprite who might gobble you up the next morning; you think it's the beautiful maiden it seems to be, unaware of the ghost reality underneath. This too points, in a rather sinister way, to the truth that we just don't know what *rūpa* is in itself. We don't experience it directly. We only experience it as these four great elements, these four primary qualities, through our five senses.

What about the fifth element: space? Space is that which contains the other four elements. It is what makes earth, water, fire, and air possible, what makes possible the existence of the whole material universe. In Indian thought, therefore, space is regarded as being more real or more ultimate than the four other elements. The word being translated as space here is the Sanskrit term *ākāśa*, which comes from the root *kāś*, meaning 'to shine'. There is a kind of light that is not the light of the sun, moon, and stars. It is the light that illuminates the *bardo*, the in-between world that one experiences after death, according to *The Tibetan Book of the Dead*. It is the light that pervades the astral world, the world inhabited by the astral body (which is the subtle counterpart of the physical body). *Ākāśa* represents space in that sense, illuminated by light in that sense. That space and that light are not two different things: space is light and light is space.

We all have some direct experience of *ākāśa*. When you see something in your mind's eye, it occupies space, but not Newtonian space – so what is the space that it occupies? Lama Govinda says that one's inner visionary experiences take place within an inner, imaginal space.[64] This is *ākāśa* – not the kind of space that Newton had to postulate in order to proceed further with his explanations of natural phenomena, but the space experienced at higher levels of consciousness. The distinction is not really between two kinds of space; it is between two orders of reality. Once we accommodate this idea of imaginal space, we come to see that the 'things' we habitually perceive as being 'out there' are perhaps not so much out there or so concretely existent as we like to think.

The conception of the five elements is very basic Buddhism, but it can seem a little abstract, and this is perhaps how it seemed to the practitioners of the Tantra. At any rate, they came up with a much more concrete way of expressing the symbolism of the elements, associating each of them with a particular colour and a particular geometrical form. Earth is associated with the colour yellow and with the cube. Water is associated with the colour white and with the sphere or hemisphere. Fire is associated with the colour red, naturally, and with the form of a cone. Air is associated with a pale green colour, and also with a hemisphere with its flat surface uppermost, a shape a bit like a shallow bowl. And space is associated with the golden or rainbow-coloured flaming drop.

Having come up with these associations, the Tantra incorporated the symbolism of the five elements into the structure of the stupa by placing the geometrical forms – the cube, the sphere, the cone, the inverted hemisphere, and the flaming drop – one on top of another. In fact, the Tantra did not merely incorporate the five elements into the structure of the stupa; it came to regard the stupa as essentially consisting of them, being built from them. The stupa came to be seen as an architectural symbol of the whole material universe, the whole of nature, the whole cosmos as existing in space.

But the symbolism of the five elements, and of the stupa itself, has an even deeper Tantric significance. The order in which these geometrical forms are arranged is not arbitrary. They are arranged in order of the increasing subtlety of the elements they represent, from the most gross at the bottom to the most subtle at the top. For the Tantric sages, this reflected not just the nature of the material universe but also the nature of the world of mind, which has its own levels, from the gross to the subtle. Thus, states of consciousness also came to be symbolized by the five elements, and the stupa came to be a symbol not only of the world without, but also of the world within: the world of mind, the world of successively higher levels of consciousness, successively higher stages in the transformation of psycho-spiritual energy.

In this world of psycho-spiritual energy, earth represents static energy – energy that is potential rather than actual, even energy that is blocked. To many of us, unfortunately, this state will be all too familiar. It is the way many people live much of the time. You feel that there is energy in you somewhere, but it has no way out, no channel through which it can express itself. It has been blocked, obstructed, shut down, and repressed for so long that it cannot come out. In a few people this goes on for years. The energy keeps congealing until it becomes a hard, solid, cold lump, and the person becomes more and more rigid. From time to time, there may be an explosion, and bits of rock may go flying in all directions. But usually this doesn't change much; no more energy is available than before. Few of us ever get into such a bad state as this; still, most of us only ever use a fraction of the energy we have – or rather, consist of. Every single human being is in fact made up of energy. But that energy is all too often potential rather than actual. This is the state of earth.

The state represented by water is one of slightly freed, slightly loosened up energy. Unlike earth, water moves, it flows – or at least it flows downwards; it can only flow upwards when under pressure, though it may flow backwards and forwards on the same level, like the waves of the sea. The mental state represented by water is much the same: one's energy is free to move, but it doesn't move far before coming back again, and it continues to ebb and flow. It moves between pairs of opposites – love and hate, attraction and repulsion, hope and fear, pleasure and pain. Energy is free, but only within definite limits. It is confined to a narrow circle of interest, a limited sphere of activity, like a goat tethered to a post. That is the state of water – energy just partly liberated.

Fire represents energy moving in an upward direction. Now something is really happening: energy is bubbling up, being liberated in ever greater quantities. As a result, the whole level of one's being and consciousness steadily rises, and one experiences overwhelming joy, ecstasy, bliss. When this happens – when the fire is blazing and energy is soaring upwards – mental conflicts are resolved and problems are transcended, to become just like dreams, or smoke dispersed by the wind. The state of fire is also a state of continuous creativity, the occasional, all too transient state of the artist and the mystic, as they reach out to that which is beyond.

It might seem impossible to go further than this. But we still have to consider the element air. Air represents energy too, energy that is moving not just upwards but in all directions. It expands as though from a central point, just as light and heat radiate from the sun. There is no limit. Energy flows in all directions at the same time, for ever. And even beyond this, there is the energy represented by the element space.

But this is in a state altogether beyond words, almost beyond thought. It has disappeared into another dimension.

These, then, are the five elements in this psycho-spiritual sense, the successive stages in the transformation of psycho-spiritual energy as symbolized by the Tantric stupa. We can get a sense of that liberative process by exploring the analogy of the physical experience of liberation in more detail. The state of earth, we could say, is like being bound hand and foot. You can't move, you can't stir. You can't even wiggle your little finger. Perhaps you are blindfolded as well. Perhaps you can't even blink your eyes. There is nothing you can do. Your energy is completely blocked.

Then someone comes along, cuts your bonds and takes the bandage from your eyes, and you find yourself in a little cell, about six feet across. Now you can move, you can walk up and down, six feet this way, six feet that way, all day if you like. In this state there is a little energy moving about within a circumscribed space, but that's all. This is the state of water, of energy oscillating between pairs of opposites. Sometimes we call it freedom.

But at the stage of fire, you succeed in making a hole in the roof and, like one of those famous Tibetan yogis, you go floating up through the hole, right up into the clouds. At the stage of air you discover that as well as going up, you can go sideways, in all directions, or even down and back up again if you like. Here our analogy breaks down, because in the state of air you go in all directions simultaneously. You would have to be a magician, or a yogi with the occult power to multiply yourself, so that there were millions of you going in millions of directions from this central point, all over the universe, into infinity for ever. Then, beyond that, there is space. There is no point in trying to extend the analogy further; words simply break down.

Having designated the stupa as the architectural embodiment not only of the world of so-called matter, but also of the world of mind and psycho-spiritual energy, the Tantra went further still. Eventually it came to identify the stupa with the human psycho-spiritual organism itself, establishing a kind of parallel between the elements and what are called the chakras (Sanskrit: *cakra*). Chakras (literally 'wheels') are centres of psycho-spiritual energy situated at various points along the spiritual equivalent of the median nerve or central channel, called the *avadhūtī* in Tantric terminology. They are often symbolized by lotus

flowers, each with a different number of petals. It is usually reckoned that there are seven chakras, but sometimes only five, four, or three are made use of. It depends on the type of spiritual practice you are doing and the purpose you have in mind for it; you don't have to work with all the chakras all the time, just as if you play the piano you don't have to use all the notes. The Buddhist Tantra usually operates with the set of five chakras. The bottommost chakra is situated on the *avadhūtī* at a point corresponding to the place on the physical body which is four fingers' breadth below the navel. The second chakra is at the level of the navel, the third at the heart, the fourth at the throat, and the fifth in or on the head. The lowest of these chakras is associated with the element earth, the second with water, the third with fire, the fourth with air, and the fifth with space.

Thus the stupa comes to represent the human body in the posture of meditation. We can see a hint of this in the Nepalese type of stupa. A pair of eyes is painted on each side of the *harmika*, the box-like structure that surmounts the hemispherical portion of the stupa. This gives the impression that there is a gigantic human figure seated inside the stupa with his psychic centres at points corresponding to the cube, the sphere, and so on. It's an awe-inspiring sight, especially when the stupa is hundreds of feet high, as some of them are, and the eyes look out across the landscape.

Another symbol the Tantra incorporated into the stupa is the vase of initiation. We have seen that the Tantra is concerned with direct experience of what one really and truly is, and that this experience is conceived in terms of the transformation of psycho-spiritual energy. For the Tantra, therefore, the spiritual life starts with, or is initiated by, the activation of one's energies. We don't typically think of the spiritual life in this way. We are more likely to think of it in terms of thinking something, or feeling something, or even doing something, or joining something, or committing ourselves to something. But the Tantra thinks of the beginning of spiritual life as the stirring up, the activation, of dormant psycho-spiritual energies. That's where the Tantric path really starts.

But how are we to activate our energies? How are we to stir ourselves up? If we feel like a lump of clay – as we sometimes do – how are we going to get ourselves going? The Tantra's answer to this is clear and unambiguous: through initiation. In Tibetan – and Tibet is where the

Tantric tradition flourished profusely in various forms well into the twentieth century – the word for initiation is *wongkur*, or *wong* for short. This is generally translated as 'consecration' or 'empowerment' but the word literally refers to the transmission, or even the giving, of power or energy. It corresponds roughly to the Sanskrit term *abhiṣeka*, which means 'a sprinkling with water'.

This transmission of power or energy takes place between the guru and the disciple, which is one of the reasons why the guru is so important in Tantric Buddhism, even as compared to the other forms of Buddhism, in all of which the guru has great importance. In Tantric Buddhism the guru isn't just a teacher; he may teach, or he may not. He is not an expounder of the scriptures; he may expound, or he may not. In Tantric Buddhism, the guru is essentially one who activates the energies of his disciples. In one way or another the guru stirs them up, and has such an impact on them that their energies cannot but be aroused.

We know from our everyday experience that different people have different effects on us. Sometimes we spend a few hours with someone – even our best friend, on a bad day – and afterwards we feel quite drained. We may even wish we hadn't seen them at all. This is the effect that people sometimes have on us – and the effect we sometimes have on other people too. But on other occasions, someone will have a tremendously stimulating effect on us. After spending time with them we feel brighter, more cheerful, more energetic, more vigorous, more alive; they stimulate our energies in a highly positive way. This is the kind of effect the Tantric guru has on us.

When I started studying the Tantra I heard quite a lot about *wong* and *wongkur*. Tibetan friends of mine were always going off into the mountains to get Tantric initiation. So I started asking them what initiation was. And everyone I asked – lamas and others – said more or less the same thing: it is like becoming a king. As I came to understand, they meant by this that the effect of Tantric initiation is to make one a spiritual king, invested with spiritual authority. But they would never explain it to me, or come up with a more conceptual or abstract reply – a good example of Tantric practitioners' use of symbolic rather than conceptual language.

I discovered, though, that the connection of the Tantric rite of initiation with kingship had a long tradition. The initiation ritual was apparently based on the ancient Indian ritual performed to consecrate a king, in the course of which priests would sprinkle the king with water from eight pots, thereby investing him with supreme power. (There could be a link here with the energies of the depths of the psyche with which water is universally associated.) It is this consecration – not lineage or conquest – that gives the king his sovereignty, so the ceremony itself has great power. But in a way the idea of lineage does apply to Tantric initiation. It is as though as an initiate you are the crown prince, the heir to the throne, the bodhisattva. Then, after the full initiation by the guru, you become virtually a Buddha – or at least you are supposed to think of yourself as a Buddha (in a purely non-egoistic way, of course). So this is what my friends meant when they said that to be initiated was like becoming a king.

But why have a ritual initiation at all? This was another question that puzzled me during the early years of my contact with the Tantra. While you may be given a particular meditation practice within the context of the *wongkur*, sometimes you are given a practice with just a guru's *chinlap* or blessing. So what difference does it make? The Tibetans seemed to feel that it did make a difference, though they weren't able to explain very clearly in what way. But one statement did give me a clue. I heard that a practice with a blessing from a spiritually developed guru was just as good as, if not better than, a full initiation from a less developed guru. This led me to the conclusion that the *wongkur*, the ritual empowerment, and the *chinlap*, the giving of the practice with a blessing, involved influences which did not differ in kind. The ritual empowerment gave a framework which provided both guru and disciple with a kind of support, and allowed the teacher transmitting the practice to do so more effectively than he could without that support. But a more spiritually developed guru could transmit as effectively without the ritual framework as a lesser guru could within it.

Let's suppose that someone wants to take initiation from a famous *rimpoche*, because of his reputation. They approach him and ask him for, say, the visualization of the bodhisattva Tārā, and accordingly he goes through the ritual. But it is quite possible that he has never done the Tārā practice himself; perhaps he hasn't even meditated on that deity before. He can look up the appropriate ritual in the book and perform it, but there will be almost no spiritual power involved. On the other hand, you might meet quite casually, walking along the road, some old monk who has practised for years and years, and who tells you about the practice and how to do it. You will get much more from that than from the *rimpoche* who went through all that elaborate ritual and purportedly gave you a transmission of power.

I came to the conclusion that even the Tibetans themselves can sometimes be misled by externals. Just because you get some incarnate lama roaming around giving initiations, it doesn't mean that you are necessarily getting very much. And it might be that in a corner of some refugee camp you might meet an old monk who has been getting on with his practice, and can transmit something to you and explain what to do without any fuss or bother. Of course, some effort on your own part is essential to the whole procedure. No one can literally hand on their spiritual experience, however experienced they are and however well they communicate. If that were possible, there would be nothing to stop the Enlightened Ones themselves from just going around giving people Enlightenment. Clearly some participation on one's own part would be required even if the Buddha himself was giving the teaching.

My own thinking on the value of initiation has been shaped by my realization of the centrality of Going for Refuge. I see Going for Refuge to the Three Jewels – the Buddha, Dharma, and Sangha – as the basic, definitive Buddhist act. The whole Buddhist tradition has grown or been elaborated out of the Going for Refuge. (We will be going into this in more detail in Chapter 4.) I therefore regard the initiation as being an *aspect* of Going for Refuge, representing the tremendous energy inherent in that act. It is not something you get as an extra goody, in addition to Going for Refuge. After all, there were no initiation ceremonies in the Buddha's day. None the less, the power of initiation must have been there, inherent in the act of Going for Refuge, which liberates a tremendous amount of energy. Going for Refuge was a spontaneous response to seeing the Buddha or hearing his teaching, but it is not that the Buddha literally wandered around handing out energy. Unfortunately that can sometimes be the way people talk about lamas and initiation. People say, 'I'm glad I got such-and-such an initiation from such-and-such a lama; he belongs to a very *powerful* lineage.' But the energy released by Going for Refuge is your own energy: it is as though you tap an inexhaustible source within yourself. Different people experience this in different ways, and some people do experience energy coming from the teacher to them. I have had a number of Tantric initiations myself, and I did have that experience once with one particular teacher – the energy seemed to come like a ray of light from him to me.[65] But what actually happens is that the impact of the guru's energy-full personality activates the energy in you. It is your own energy that you experience.

In the early Indian Tantric tradition, initiation, following the royal precedent, was performed with the help of water from a number of pots – one dedicated to the Buddhas, one to the bodhisattvas, and so on. Even now, in Tibetan Buddhist circles, some initiations are performed with a pot or vase which contains symbolically the nectar of immortality, the *bumpa* (Tibetan) or *amṛta kalaśa* (Sanskrit). During the ceremony the vase, which is of a certain stylized design, is placed on or against your head. The vase therefore came to stand for initiation in general.

And this symbol – to return to our main theme – eventually came to be incorporated into the Tantric symbolism of the stupa. In the case of the highly developed Tibetan version of the stupa (generally known as a *chorten*), the basic symbolism was modified in various ways. In particular, the sphere or hemisphere was often replaced by a vase of initiation, so that it was no longer just a symbol of the element water, even in a very refined sense. It came to be seen as a symbol of the plenitude of transcendental powers and energies, the life-giving stream of the *bodhicitta*, the will to Enlightenment, and the spiritual influence of all the Buddhas and bodhisattvas pouring down upon humanity.

This modification is of very great significance. It suggests that the progressive transformation of psycho-spiritual energy is the central business of the spiritual life. It reminds us of the need, in the course of our spiritual life and development, for initiation in the Tantric sense. It reminds us of the need for the good friend, the guru. And it reminds us that the spiritual life consists in both receiving and giving.

So the Tibetan version of the stupa has the usual cubic substructure, representing the element earth. But in the Tibetan *chorten* the cube is surmounted by four steps, on top of which stands the initiation-vase-shaped central portion. This central portion is crowned by a tall cone, often notched, representing fire, on top of which rests a small upturned hemisphere, representing air. On the flat surface of the hemisphere rests a white crescent moon, and in the inner curve of the moon is balanced a red sun disc from the top of which rises the flaming drop, representing the element space.

A clue to the meaning of this intriguing set of symbols is provided by the colours of the moon crescent and the sun disc. The moon crescent, being white, is the same colour as the pot-shaped central portion of the stupa representing the element water, and the sun disc, being red, is the same colour as the conical portion representing the element fire. This is no coincidence. Moon and water represent one and the same lunar energy, and likewise sun and fire both represent solar energy. These complementary forces or principles are sometimes referred to as masculine and feminine, although they have nothing to do with the conventional distinction between masculinity and femininity.

According to the Tantra, in the human psycho-spiritual organism these energies run within two nerves, which run either side of the *avadhūtī*, or subtle median nerve. The one on the left is known in the Buddhist Tantra as *lalanā* and is white, corresponding to the moon and to water; and the one on the right, known as *rasanā*, is red and corresponds to the sun and to fire. In Tantric practice energy is brought into the central channel through one or another of the chakras, and is thus liberated.

So the Tantric stupa represents the progressive unification of solar and lunar energies at higher and ever higher levels of being and consciousness: a unification of conscious and unconscious, reason and emotion, meditation and action, individualism and altruism. The flaming jewel represents the coming together of the white moon crescent and the red sun disc, the unification of the solar and lunar energies in their most refined forms – otherwise known in Buddhist tradition as wisdom and compassion. By wisdom is meant the direct experience of reality, face to face, without any obstruction or hindrance, illusion or delusion. And compassion is an overwhelming feeling of love for all living beings whatsoever, together with the desire to help them when they are in difficulties. The flaming drop, the unification of white moon crescent and red sun disc, wisdom and compassion, therefore symbolizes the *bodhicitta*, the will to Enlightenment, that which makes a bodhisattva a bodhisattva – symbolizes it not only in its inception but in its fulfilment. This fulfilment is, of course, perfect Enlightenment, the Enlightenment of a Buddha – the pinnacle of human experience, just as the flaming drop is the exquisite pinnacle of the Tantric stupa.

3
THE SACRED THUNDERBOLT

From the dawn of human consciousness, human beings must surely have been deeply impressed by the beauty of the world in which they found themselves. They must have marvelled at the astonishing sight of the sun, the moon, the stars, towering mountains, swiftly flowing rivers, swaying trees; the curious, splendid, dangerous, and fascinating forms of animals and birds; the vastness of the sky in tranquillity and storm, and the ocean in all its magnificence. Beauty was to be found in the depths of the ocean too, in the forms of astonishing sea creatures, and in the depths of the earth, in the strange structures of rocks and minerals. Prehistory is measured in terms of the successive technologies associated with the qualities of these substances: the stone age, the iron age, the bronze age. We can only imagine the amazement of the people who discovered the extraordinary nature and possibilities of these materials, making tools out of rocks, smelting glittering metals, and digging precious stones from the darkness of the earth. As history began, and the first civilizations developed, people started refining the metals and bringing out their beauty as much as their usefulness, especially in the case of gold. As for precious stones, these were valued for their beauty alone, and they were cut and polished and given names: diamond, ruby, emerald, and the rest. As they were named, appreciated, valued, it must have been like the revelation of a new world of light, colour, and radiance. Sometimes it must have seemed that these rare jewels were the most beautiful and wonderful things in existence. With the flourishing of culture, jewels were used to adorn the persons of kings and high priests, and to decorate religious images. In this way they acquired great significance, symbolizing whatever is rich and rare, beautiful, remote and mysterious, not of this world. Myths and legends spoke of the island of jewels, the philosophers' stone, the pearl of great price.

Among the traditions that came to see the jewel in symbolic terms was Buddhism; indeed, the symbolism of the jewel was present from Buddhism's inception as a historical phenomenon and has been at its heart ever since. In particular, this took the form of what tradition has called from the beginning the Three Jewels. The first of these Three Jewels is the Buddha, the Enlightened teacher, the embodiment in human form of the ideal of Enlightenment. Then, secondly, there is the Dharma, the truth, the path, the teaching, which guides one in the direction of Enlightenment. And thirdly, there is the Sangha, the community of those who have reached the higher stages of that path, and are near to Enlightenment. How, though, did these fundamentals of Buddhism come to be spoken of as the Three Jewels? Why not think of them simply as the three fundamental principles, or the three essentials? Or why not stick to the other traditional designation, the Three Refuges? It is as if the tradition wanted to convey not some abstract idea of these fundamental things, but a concrete image of something beautiful, colourful, sparkling, and infinitely precious.

Later on in Buddhist history, the Mahāyāna tradition gave us the symbol of the jewel in the lotus, representing the union of wisdom and compassion. Also from the Mahāyāna came the wish-fulfilling jewel, the *cintāmaṇi*. According to legend, if you hold this jewel in your hand and wish, it gives you at once everything you desire. And according to the Mahāyāna, what we really desire, did we but know it, is Enlightenment; so the wish-fulfilling jewel represents the *bodhicitta*, the will or aspiration to Enlightenment.

Out of the Mahāyāna there eventually developed the Vajrayāna, and in that tradition we find a Buddha especially associated with jewels: Ratnasambhava, the Jewel-Born One. He is one of the five archetypal Buddhas, each of whom presides over a different spiritual 'family'. Ratnasambhava is the Buddha of the jewel family, which includes a bodhisattva called Jambhala, who is popularly regarded as a god of wealth. Jambhala is represented as a stout, deep-yellow figure, and in his left hand he grasps a mongoose. The Indian mongoose is known principally as an animal that lives on snakes, but its iconographic role

here is to vomit jewels; it is shown with a whole stream of jewels pouring from its mouth as Jambhala gently squeezes it.

However, the most important contribution of the Tantra to the jewel symbolism of Buddhism is the *vajra*. It is a complex symbol, and the Sanskrit word itself has a double meaning. First, it means diamond, the hardest of all precious stones, which is traditionally said to cut through everything, but be cut through by nothing. It is absolutely pure and incorruptible. It doesn't rust or tarnish; it cannot be soiled or stained; it remains pure, untouched, undefiled, even under layers and layers of dust and dirt. Thus the symbol has all the qualities of jewels. But *vajra* also means thunderbolt – in particular, the thunderbolt wielded by Indra, the king of the gods of Indian mythology. Indra, or Sakra as he is sometimes called, is a very ancient Indian divinity. The *Rig Veda*, one of the main texts of orthodox Hinduism, which may go back to about 800–1000 BCE, contains a number of hymns to him, and he is quite an important figure in Vedic mythology generally.

From the hymns in which he is described and praised, we gather that Indra is a god of the storm, especially of the dark storm clouds that bring the seasonal rains upon which the existence of agricultural India depends. Sometimes in Indian poetry the storm clouds that come up when the rains are about to begin are referred to as Indra's cows. In art Indra is depicted as a robust and powerful figure riding on an enormous elephant and brandishing the thunderbolt or *vajra* in his right hand. The *vajra* is the most powerful thing in existence. Nothing can stand against it – no weapon, no armour, nothing at all. It is absolutely irresistible. And with this irresistible weapon, Indra annihilates his enemies – annihilates especially, according to the *Rig Veda*, the demons of drought and thirst.

In his commentary on *The Tibetan Book of the Dead*, Chögyam Trungpa sheds some light on this aspect of the symbolism of the *vajra*. He says:

> There was a certain sage who meditated on Mount Meru for centuries, and when he died his bones were transformed into *vajra*, and Indra, the king of the gods, discovered this and made his weapon out of it, a *vajra* with a hundred points. The *vajra* has three qualities: it can never be used frivolously, it always fulfils its function of destroying the enemy, and it always returns into your hand. It is indestructible, adamantine.[66]

Ancient Indian cosmography accorded Mount Meru the highest and most central place in the physical universe, and it may be significant that the sage was meditating in that particular place. His bones were transformed by his meditation, we can conjecture, and they were used to make Indra's special hundred-pointed *vajra*. But the qualities attributed to this *vajra* are the most interesting aspect of this description. To begin with, what does it mean that the *vajra* can never be used frivolously? The *vajra* is presented to us as a thing – a diamond or a thunderbolt – existing in the external world. But it is not really external; it represents a quality that you yourself have developed. If you are truly the possessor of the *vajra*, if you have that *vajra*-like quality, then using it frivolously is a contradiction in terms. If you were capable of using it frivolously, you wouldn't have it, and the fact that you *have* got it means that you are a person of a particular nature. It's like someone saying, 'Suppose you do gain Enlightenment, what is the guarantee that you won't use your Enlightenment for the wrong purposes?' To be Enlightened is to be of such a nature that you could not use it wrongly. Enlightenment is not a thing separate from the person realizing it. In the same way, the *vajra* cannot be used frivolously because the very acquisition of it means that one becomes *vajra*-like, and a *vajra*-like person is not frivolous.

The second attribute of the *vajra* put forward here is that it always fulfils its function of destroying the enemy, the enemy presumably being everything mundane, everything that stands in the way of Enlightenment.

And thirdly, the *vajra* is said always to return to your hand. Just as if you use one candle to light another, you don't lose the light of the first candle, so if you throw the *vajra*, you don't lose it. You may expend some energy, but you don't lose that energy – indeed, by expending it, you generate more.

The implication of these three attributes is that the *vajra* cannot be thought of as something objective or external, that it is a quality of one's inner nature. But what is meant by the *vajra*'s being 'indestructible, adamantine'? The Buddha Akṣobhya is said to represent the adamantine, indestructible aspect of the Enlightenment experience, but what does it mean to have these qualities? Certainly it is nothing to do with anything that is literally hard, tough, and solid. The *vajra*-like quality of Akṣobhya is tough without resistance, solid without inflexibility, powerful without coercion. Not that it *does* not coerce; it *cannot* coerce. It is not coercive power held in reserve; it is power that is non-coercive by its very nature. This is almost unimaginable to us. It is indestructible, but it is absolutely light and delicate at the same time. It is, in short, a good example of how difficult it is to talk about, or get any conception of, spiritual qualities.

The *vajra*, combining the qualities of the thunderbolt and the diamond, is infinitely powerful, capable of smashing through all obstacles; it is immutable, irresistible, indestructible. It is absolutely pure, and remains so in all circumstances. And it is full of light and brilliance.

Even though the *vajra* conveys the ideas of both thunderbolt and diamond, in Buddhist iconography it is always represented as a kind of stylized thunderbolt. It also appears in this form in Tantric ritual, in which it is the ritual implement that the lama, the guru or teacher, holds in his right hand. For this reason, and also because it represents spiritual power, spiritual sovereignty, even spiritual authority, it is sometimes referred to as the diamond sceptre.

Broadly speaking, the symbol of the *vajra* is specific to Tantric Buddhism; nevertheless, we find important prefigurations of the image much earlier in Buddhist history. Its first occurrence is in the *vajrāsana*, the diamond throne, references to which are to be found in the biography of the Buddha. The Buddha gained Enlightenment at the age of thirty-five, at a place now known as Bodh Gaya in the Indian state of Bihar. According to tradition, he awoke to the truth of things while he was sitting at the foot of a great peepul tree. The tree was thereafter known as the bodhi tree, the Enlightenment tree, and the spot on which the Buddha sat underneath it came to be known as the diamond throne, the *vajrāsana* – *dorje den* in Tibetan. Tradition has it that the *vajrāsana* was so called because all the previous Buddhas in previous world cycles had sat on that same spot and gained Enlightenment. To understand why they chose that particular spot – or at least *a* particular spot – and how this whole tradition arose, we need to consider briefly the rather arcane subject of Buddhist cosmology.

In Buddhism there is no such concept as a personal God, a supreme being, a creator God – which means that there can be no act of creation. The question therefore arises: how did the universe come into existence? The Buddhist teaching has always been that the universe evolved over a vast period of time, millions upon millions of years. According to the accounts of this process in Buddhist texts, there was at first, throughout the whole universe, a 'fire-mist', diffused in all directions. We are told that after millions of years had gone by, this fire-mist started cooling, condensing, solidifying. It began to cool at one particular point, and this became the central point, the axis, of the whole world-system. Just as this was the first point to emerge at the beginning of the cosmic process, it will be the last to disappear at the end. And the Buddha – a Buddha, any Buddha in this world system – gains Enlightenment seated on that spot, which became known as the diamond seat or diamond throne.[67]

This is how the *vajra* came to be associated with the symbolism of the central point (which is a whole separate subject), and thus to symbolize centrality, axiality, stability, imperturbability. It is not surprising therefore that the *vajra* is the special emblem of Akṣobhya, the dark blue Buddha of the eastern quarter, whose name means the Unshakeable, or Imperturbable.

Each of the five Buddhas is associated with one of the five mental poisons to be overcome. In the case of Akṣobhya this is hatred or aversion, which, as we have seen, can be said to have an affinity with wisdom. This brings us to the core significance of the *vajra* – its association with wisdom (Sanskrit *prajñā*), and more specifically with Prajñāpāramitā, the Perfection of Wisdom – the wisdom that directly intuits absolute reality. The Perfection of Wisdom is one of the most important themes of the Mahāyāna, and it is dealt with principally in the group of scriptures known as Prajñāpāramitā *sūtras*. There are more than thirty-five of these, some of enormous length and some very short indeed. One of the best known and most important of them is the *Vajracchedikā Prajñāpāramitā sūtra*, the discourse on the transcendental wisdom that pierces like the thunderbolt or cuts like the diamond.[68] What transcendental wisdom pierces or cuts is our illusions, our wrong ideas, our false notions, our projections. We can even go so far as to say that it is destructive. It destroys our intellectual assumptions, usually adopted so unthinkingly. It destroys the psychological conditionings in which we are enmeshed. It destroys the emotional hang-ups to which we are so attached. It destroys, in short, ourselves as we are at present.

It is not always understood that wisdom, the *experience* of reality, is destructive. It is tempting to think of it as a pleasant extra, something comfortably added on to what we already are. But it isn't like that at all. The experience of reality in what the Tantras call its 'nakedness' can be a shattering experience. One can even go so far as to say that *any* shattering experience has an element of reality in it. If an experience shatters, it is real – and if it doesn't shatter us, its authenticity may be questioned. This is not to say that this experience of breaking through or shattering needs to be traumatic – it can be very joyful.

Whether one can expect to have this kind of experience oneself all depends on the way one goes about one's spiritual practice. If you meditate for half an hour or an hour a day over a period of years, you will get results, but they will be slow in coming. However, if you meditate for ten or twenty hours a day, and keep that up, you can expect something much more dramatic to happen. Breaking through depends not so much on the kind of meditation you do as on the intensity with which you do it. And, of course, most people tend to take things quite easily. There is certainly room for a great deal more intensity in the spiritual practice of most western Buddhists. This includes, of course, concentrated attention upon the views that direct that intense practice, and a robust faith with which to meet the strong reactions and inner resistance that such intensity tends to provoke.

A lot of people experience psychological breakthroughs with the help of various kinds of therapy. However, breakthroughs achieved through psychotherapy must be distinguished from the kind of breaking through associated with the *vajra* – the breaking through of illusion, the breaking through into reality. In the hands of a skilled psychotherapist who has a definitely transcendental dimension to his or her work – and that is quite rare – you may come to recognize something about yourself which will give you the opportunity for a breakthrough in a vajric sense, but it is important to recognize two quite different orders or levels of breakthrough in such a context.

Meditation is not, of course, the only method of intensive spiritual practice. Work, for example, can also provide a spiritually intensive situation. The crucial thing, if you are to break through in the vajric sense, is that your intensive situation must pertain to insight. Simply working hard, day after day, month after month, does not by itself lead to breaking through. Intensity is not just about slogging away; it involves wholeheartedness and enthusiasm, even passion. For insight to arise in an intensive situation, you must reflect all the time upon what you are doing, looking very closely and deeply at the successes, problems, and even catastrophes that arise.

Suppose you are in business, and chasing a particularly big order. All your energies are bound up with that order, and you are doing everything possible to get it. You leave no stone unturned, and for weeks you think of nothing else. Then, just as you seem to be on the brink of success, suddenly the deal is off. At that point, you have to watch your mind very closely. Can you say to yourself, 'No, I am not going to be disappointed or upset: this is what life is like, this is what happens; I am going to maintain equanimity'? If, in Kipling's language, you can be determined to treat those two impostors, triumph and disaster, just the same,[69] then you may well make a breakthrough. But the breakthrough will only come if you are able to bring a depth of understanding to that disappointment.

It is possible to develop insight in all sorts of situations, but clearly if you have been after a million dollar deal and it suddenly falls through, that is going to present you with a bigger opportunity than some smaller matter. If you are living with great intensity you are more likely to encounter – or to create – situations in which it is possible for there to be a pronounced breakthrough than if you are just plodding along. Inevitably, though, the routine of life is sometimes interrupted by a potentially vajric situation. You may be going along steadily and methodically when one day you find out that you have cancer, and you have to face that – and thus, potentially, the full force of the shattering experience which is the nature of the *vajra*.

This destructive aspect of the Enlightenment experience is embodied in the awe-inspiring figure of Vajrapāṇi ('thunderbolt in hand'). Vajrapāṇi belongs both to the Mahāyāna and to Tantric Buddhism. He has many forms, some peaceful, some wrathful (though in Tibet the wrathful forms of this figure were far more popular than the peaceful ones). The wrathful Vajrapāṇi is depicted in painting and sculpture as stout and strong, with a powerful body, dark blue in colour, a protuberant belly, and thick, short limbs. He wears a crown of human skulls, and he is usually naked except for ornaments of human bone, though sometimes he is draped in the pelt of a freshly-skinned tiger. He has three eyes – two in the usual places and one in the centre of his forehead – and they are all red-rimmed and glaring ferociously. His whole expression is one of terrific anger, and he is surrounded by a halo of flames. He is depicted trampling on two human figures, usually said to represent ignorance and craving – trampling triumphantly on them because he has destroyed them. His right arm is raised, and in his right hand he grasps, as though ready to hurl it, the *vajra*, the diamond thunderbolt.

Vajrapāṇi's ferocious trampling on ignorance and craving suggests that such mental states are to be completely destroyed. However, he represents not just destruction and eradication, but transformation. Defilements – in this case anger – can be transmuted into wisdoms. This idea of transforming energy is no doubt an innovation on the part of the Tantra in terms of its presentation of the path, but the spiritual mechanism itself is not new. If you change a state of hatred into one of loving-kindness, for example, this means that the energy that formerly found a negative expression is now expressed in ways that are entirely positive.

In the Mahāyāna, on which the Vajrayāna is based to a great extent, there are many meditations on *śūnyatā*, teachings concerning which are to be found in texts such as the *Hṛdaya* or *'Heart' Sūtra*. The *Heart Sūtra* teaching that *rūpa* is *śūnyatā* and *śūnyatā* is *rūpa* – form is emptiness and emptiness is form – may sound like abstruse philosophy, but it is what makes transformation possible. If *rūpa* can be *śūnyatā*, then the *kleśas* – the poisons, the defilements – can be *bodhi*, Enlightenment. In the Vajrayāna you face the *kleśas* directly when you visualize the wrathful form of a bodhisattva. Anger is brought out into the open, and being integrated into the figure of the bodhisattva it ceases to be anger in the mundane sense, however fiery its nature.

Whatever the Tibetans may sometimes say, you have to do a lot of preliminary work before you can make skilful use of this perspective. In this, as in so many things, it is all too easy to have the words but not the experience. You can try to summon the vajric vision by saying, 'These faults and weaknesses of mine, these *kleśas*, are really *bodhi*, so there is no need to control them.' But you have to learn to control the *kleśas* in order to have the clarity of mind and heart that will enable you to see their fundamental emptiness. Thus the Pāli scriptures speak of the *kleśas* as hindrances to meditation; they talk about 'cultivating the opposite' rather than urging us to reflect that both the hindrance and its opposite are essentially *śūnyatā*.[70] However, in the vision of a wrathful form like Vajrapāṇi, anger has been sublimated to become pure energy devoted to the attainment of Enlightenment. When you visualize the form, you feel a kind of sympathy with that anger. As it draws the same quality of energy out of you in a highly sublimated form, you can enjoy it with a clear conscience. To the extent that you visualize the figure, it is in a way part of you, an aspect of your own psyche, your raw anger refined and integrated. It's similar when we talk about our anger: to the extent that we are able to admit it and bring it into the open, to that extent it ceases to exert its poisonous influence on us, and on what we do, say, and think.

The *vajra* as depicted in Vajrapāṇi's hand – or as made from metal for use in Tantric ritual – is quite an intricate object, reflecting the complexity of its symbolism. In the middle is a sphere – the handle of the sceptre, one could say, as this is where it is usually grasped. Out of this sphere, on either side, there grow two lotuses, sometimes with four petals, sometimes eight. From the centres and from each petal of these lotuses there spring 'ribs' or 'spokes', usually four in number. The central spoke runs through the whole *vajra* like an axis, and the other four on each side fan out in the cardinal directions, then curve inwards and converge onto the central spoke. The outward-turning section is meant to represent the head of a strange beast, from whose open mouth the inward-turning section emerges. In some *vajras* this can be seen very clearly, but usually the head of the beast has become so stylized as to be virtually unrecognizable, so that it looks rather like curling leaves. The typical *vajra* thus consists of four formal elements: a central sphere, two four-petalled lotuses, two sets of five spokes, and the head of the strange beast, repeated eight times.

The sphere – which is of course a universal symbol – represents completeness, totality, perfection, and therefore reality. In Mahāyāna Buddhism the word most widely used to denote reality is *śūnyatā*. As we have seen, *śūnyatā* literally means emptiness. This is emptiness not in the sense of vacuity or nothingness (the old translation 'the void' is very misleading), but in the sense that there is nothing to be identified as this or that by the rational mind, nothing that can be described as being or non-being, existence or non-existence. Reality is beyond thought, beyond speech, ineffable.

Even before the rise of Tantric Buddhism the *vajra* had become for the Mahāyāna a symbol of transcendental wisdom, the wisdom that intuits reality. Later on, the *vajra* became a symbol of *śūnyatā*, or reality, itself. It also became symbolic of anything connected with reality, or of that aspect of anything that is conterminous with reality. The Tantric path to Enlightenment itself came to be spoken of as the Vajrayāna, the path or the way of the *vajra*, the path of experiencing oneself as one really and truly is. The Vajrayāna is the path on which nothing matters except direct experience, on which one is prepared to abandon external traditions and conventions of every kind, even those of Buddhism, even those of the Tantra itself. It is the path on which you no longer care what people think of you. According to some Tantric sayings, it is the path on which you may at times appear to other people as being completely mad, or like an animal, or even like a ghost.

In the same way, the Tantric teacher came to be spoken of as the *vajraguru* or the *vajrācārya* – the real guru, the true, authentic guru, the guru who is concerned only with direct experience. He is the guru who means business, the no-nonsense guru. If you are the disciple of a *vajraguru*, he doesn't mind what he does to you. You can go mad or jump over a cliff; he wouldn't mind at all, provided that he pushes you in the direction of direct experience, gets you away from words, away from theories, away from books, away from your own ideas, away from yourself. This is famously how the great Tibetan guru Marpa dealt with his even more famous disciple, Milarepa. He got him doing all sorts of difficult and even dangerous things, he frustrated and tormented him, and in the end all this purified him of all his sins so that he gained Enlightenment.

Of course, as we are all too aware these days, the idea that a guru can behave in this way is open to misunderstanding and even abuse. In one of his songs, Milarepa himself says:

Before all appearances have become
Aids in one's meditation practice,
'Tantric Acts' will be
Worldly desires disguised.
You should thus strive for purity and non-clinging![71]

These 'Tantric acts' are unconventional modes of behaviour engaged in as being in accordance with one's higher realization, actions directed towards helping other people. They may on occasion be very bizarre indeed. But if you haven't reached the level at which 'all appearances have become aids in your meditation practice', your unconventional behaviour will just be worldly desires disguised, as the text says. If a lama takes a 'spiritual consort', this may be a 'Tantric act', but he may just be giving a lofty spiritual interpretation to an expression of ordinary desire; and the same sort of abuse can happen with respect to money.

Milarepa doesn't deny that there are such things as Tantric acts, and some of the gurus in his lineage – Marpa, Naropa, and Tilopa, for example – did some very strange things. But they had reached a very high level of spiritual realization, so that for them all appearances really were aids. There was nothing they had to avoid. They experienced no real distinction between *saṃsāra* and *nirvāṇa*. They could, in a way, do anything; they could appear to break any convention, any moral rule. Their Tantric acts really were Tantric – but only because of their high level of spiritual attainment.

The 'Tantric acts' I have personally observed gurus to perform have been of a comparatively minor nature. For instance, a Nyingma lama who used to come to stay with me in my vihara in Kalimpong would act in accordance with whatever came up in his morning meditation – once, I remember, it was the necessity of putting a banner of victory on the roof of the vihara.[72] This was a little unconventional, but to the best of my knowledge he never went to the extent of breaking the accepted moral rules. Another lama, whom I knew less well, was in the habit of drinking a lot of whisky. He was guru to the Maharajakumara of Sikkim, who used to say, 'I don't care if he's always drunk – as far as I'm concerned, he's the wisest lama I know.'[73] And I can think of a third lama who, despite his reputation for drinking and womanizing, was able to convey to a western woman with no previous knowledge of Buddhism a clear understanding of what amounted to Gaṇḍavyūha philosophy. Somehow, despite his disreputable behaviour, he could communicate in such a way that she really understood the teaching.[74]

So if you find in the case of a guru who drinks a lot of whisky and doesn't seem ever to study the Dharma that his disciples undeniably do make spiritual progress, you might conclude that, appearances to the contrary, there is something in his methods. You cannot completely rule out the possibility that he really is a guru. You have to have an open mind. But that open mind need not exclude a big dose of healthy scepticism. You're not obliged to believe everything that everybody says.

A guru might hold a deep conviction that in view of the powerful forces of conventionality ruling many people's lives, it is justifiable to go to any extremes to break them. He might well think, 'I don't care if people misunderstand me. I'm just not going to be a respectable religious teacher, and I'm going to discourage people who can't see what I'm really like.' On the other hand, a guru who is completely conventional may be just as much a guru as one who is completely unconventional. Gurus, as such, can't be pinned down like that. However they behave, you can't draw from their behaviour the conclusion that they must have insight and wisdom. You can only come to understand that from your own deep personal contact with them. The word guru means by its very definition someone with whom we have a direct personal relationship; a *vajraguru* cannot, therefore, be judged from a distance. We will be further considering the nature of the guru in the next chapter.

The epithet '*vajra*' came to be attached to various other things as well. Enlightenment itself, *bodhi*, came to be spoken of as *vajrabodhi*, and the heart or mind set on Enlightenment came to be called the *vajracitta*. Moving from the individual to the collective level, one finds the community of initiates spoken of as the *vajrakula*. *Kula* literally means family – family in the ordinary sense and, more especially, a spiritual family. A *kula* is a community of people following the same spiritual tradition, usually under the guidance of the same spiritual teacher. But the *vajrakula* is a spiritual community in a special sense: a community of people dedicated to the direct experience of reality. They are not together for social reasons, or to argue over texts, or to mull over their personal problems; they are dedicated to the direct experience of reality, and they are infused with a shared spiritual power. In the *vajrakula*, communication is completely authentic. It is said that in it everybody is naked, because there is nothing to conceal, everything is completely open. (We will return to the idea that nakedness is spiritually significant when we come to consider the symbolism of the cremation ground and the celestial maidens.)

We also have the term *vajragītā*. *Gītā* is 'song', and the *vajragītā* is the song – sometimes a whole series of songs – sung by the Tantric master, songs expressive of the direct experience of reality, songs that burst from his lips out of the fullness of his spiritual experience. Many of these Tantric masters, especially those in India during the Middle Ages, were very unconventional indeed. They didn't look like gurus, they didn't behave like gurus, and they didn't speak like gurus. Very often people didn't know they *were* gurus – they just roamed about like wandering minstrels or troubadours. They didn't teach in any formal way, they simply went about singing. Sometimes they would sing without anybody asking them to, whether people liked it or not. That was their way of communicating the Dharma.

An interesting parallel is to be found in the section of the Pāli scriptures called the *Udāna* (literally the outward-going breath). The *Udāna* consists of verses 'breathed out' by the Buddha at times of great spiritual exaltation. Something would happen to him, or rather develop within him, some tremendous experience, and a transcendental pressure would build up inside him so that he just had to speak out. Sometimes he would address whoever was present – men, women, even gods – but sometimes he would just speak to himself, to the air, to the cosmos at large.[75]

The songs of the *vajrācāryas*, these wandering minstrel-type figures in medieval India, were of much the same kind. These wanderers were engaged in yoga, meditation, and all sorts of more unconventional practices. Sometimes they stayed in hermitages, sometimes in the jungle, sometimes in cremation grounds, and sometimes they just lived at home with their families. Sometimes they plied trades, sometimes they lived on alms. But all the time there was a current of spiritual practice and experience running through them, and on some occasions it came surging up. They couldn't contain it – it had to find expression in song. There are several collections of these diamond songs, these *vajragītā*, in Tantric literature, the most celebrated being Sarahapāda's *Dohākośa* or Collection of Songs, and the songs of Milarepa, which continue the same tradition.[76]

The epithet *vajra* is also applied to various objects used in Tantric ritual. In all Buddhist ceremonies flowers are offered, but the flower offered in Tantric ritual is known as the *vajrapuṣpa*, the diamond flower. When you place that flower at the feet of the Buddha, you experience the ultimate reality of the flower, what it really is, what it really means. You offer the *vajrapuṣpa* – not just the phenomenal flower, but the transcendental flower, the flower in its transcendental essence. You experience what the flower is in the depth of its flower-being, and that is what you offer.

The *vajra*-bell or *vajraghaṇṭā* and all the other implements used in Tantric ritual have the same significance. In Tantric ritual everything you touch, everything you offer, everything you do, is imbued with this sense of ultimate reality. You don't just ring a bell, you ring the *vajra*-bell; you don't just light incense, it's *vajra*-incense; you're not just sitting in an enclosure, it's a *vajra*-enclosure; you're not just pouring water from pots, it's *vajra*-water from *vajra*-pots. Everything is *vajra*, everything is imbued with reality. In Tantric ritual you experience everything in its ultimate depth, its ultimate essence.

This is a paradigm of what one's life in the world should be like. The ritual concentrates everything within a certain area, it creates an ideal world, and that's all right for the time being – just as when you go on retreat, conditions are ideal for the time being. But eventually you have to come back into the world, and whatever you have experienced in the ritual area, whatever you have experienced on retreat, you have now to experience in the midst of your life in the world. This is what this *vajra* epithet means: that one must experience everything, all the time, under its *vajra* aspect, that one must live saturated by the experience of reality.

There is one thing used in the ritual that doesn't have the *vajra* epithet: the *vajra* itself. It doesn't have to be described as real because it *is* reality – as symbolized especially by the central sphere of the *vajra*. This is not just a sphere; it's also an egg or a seed, and it therefore represents not just reality, but reality as the ultimate source of the whole of existence.

The meaning of the two lotuses that grow out of the sphere should now be clear. The lotus generally symbolizes birth, growth, unfoldment, development; and the two lotuses growing out of opposite sides of the central sphere represent the emergence from non-differentiated reality of the basic duality of existence, the primordial splitting of reality into

two poles, two halves, two worlds. Once the process of growth and unfoldment has started, it continues until it reaches the very limit, until two whole worlds, two whole cosmoses, have come into existence. Paradoxically, this emergence of the lotuses, this splitting of reality, is not something that takes place in time or at a particular point of time – say, at the beginning of things. It takes place *all* the time. And the two worlds that emerge from this split are represented by the third element of the *vajra* – the two sets of five spokes.

One set of spokes stands for the five Buddhas, whom we shall meet in all their glory later on; they represent the archetypal, ideal world, the world of meditation, the world of Enlightenment. This set of five spokes also stands for the five wisdoms associated with these Buddhas: what the Buddha represents in image form, the wisdom represents in concept form. First of all, there is the wisdom of the *dharmadhātu*. This is absolute wisdom, and it is associated with Vairocana, the white central Buddha. In this context *dharma* means reality, and *dhātu* means a field, sphere, world, or cosmos, so the wisdom of the *dharmadhātu* is the vision or the experience of the whole of existence, conditioned and unconditioned, as pervaded by one absolute transcendental reality. It means seeing the whole universe as the playground of reality.

The 'mirror-like wisdom', or objective wisdom, associated with Akṣobhya, the dark blue Buddha of the east, is the wisdom that simply reflects: it sees everything just as a mirror reflects all forms. And just as a mirror reflects things exactly as they are, so this wisdom sees things as they are, with no distortion. In a mirror reflections come and go – the mirror doesn't hang on to them, they don't stick – and this is another characteristic of the mirror-like wisdom: it sees everything perfectly, clearly, objectively, and it is attached to nothing.

The 'wisdom of equality', or wisdom of sameness, is associated with Ratnasambhava, the golden yellow Buddha of the south. It is the wisdom that sees one reality everywhere, in everything. It sees everything as *śūnyatā*, as emptiness, just as all the waves of the ocean are equally water. The wisdom of equality or sameness is accompanied by love and compassion, which is felt equally for all beings.

The 'distinguishing wisdom', conversely, is the wisdom that sees the uniqueness of things. It is associated with Amitābha, the red Buddha of the west, and it represents the fact that, yes, the eye of Enlightenment sees things in their oneness, but it also sees them in their diversity. One sees everything as imbued with the same ultimate reality, but at the same time one sees everything in its minute particularity, individuality, uniqueness. There is no contradiction between the two. One sees both at the same time: everything is the same, and everything is utterly different. One has this double vision of reality. And from this distinguishing wisdom also, great compassion flows.

The fifth wisdom is the all-performing or all-accomplishing wisdom, the wisdom of activity, the wisdom that gets things done. This is associated with Amoghasiddhi, the green Buddha of the north. It is not activity in the sense of planning and organizing; it is spontaneous activity, like play or dance, activity that comes freely bubbling up.

The *vajra*'s second set of spokes represents three things, or rather three sets of five things. In the first place, the spokes stand for the five elements: earth, water, fire, air, and space. They also represent the five aggregates of conditioned existence: form, feelings, perceptions, impulses, and consciousness. Thirdly, they represent the five mental poisons. We have already encountered the five elements and (briefly) the five aggregates, but we haven't yet met the five mental poisons.[77] The first poison is infatuation: dullness, stupidity, unawareness, unmindfulness, mental confusion, bewilderment. This is a basic spiritual ignorance and darkness; it is sluggish and at the same time chaotic. Second on the list is aversion, which includes dislike, hatred, enmity, and ill will, the desire to harm another, the craving for revenge, and any negative, hostile attitude towards other living beings. The third poison is conceit. This consists in comparing oneself with others, thinking of others as superior, inferior, or even equal to oneself. According to this teaching, self-conscious humility is a form of conceit, and so is egalitarianism – which might be food for thought for some political thinkers.[78] Fourthly, there is passion, which includes insatiable craving for pleasure, enjoyment, amusement, luxury, uncontrollable sexual desire, and attachment to material things. And the fifth poison is envy: grudging others their good fortune, feeling displeasure and unease at their happiness. It is an attitude of carping, a refusal to give recognition, a refusal even to appreciate.

We can begin to see from all this what the two sets of five spokes stand for. They stand essentially for the world of Enlightenment and the world of non-Enlightenment. But the symbol of the *vajra* makes it clear that both worlds are in truth aspects of one and the same ultimate reality. Both poles have emerged from that reality, and the two worlds, therefore, despite their divergence, also correspond to each other, not only in general but in particular. The five Buddhas correspond to the five elements, the five wisdoms correspond to the five mental poisons, and there are one-to-one correspondences as well. Vairocana the Illuminator and his absolute wisdom correspond to consciousness among the aggregates, to space among the elements, and to ignorance among the mental poisons. Akṣobhya and his mirror-like wisdom correspond to water among the elements, to form among the aggregates, and to aversion among the mental poisons – and so on.

The suggestion is that the two worlds – the world of Enlightenment and the world of non-Enlightenment – though separate, are connected. There is a principle of unity running through them, just as there is a central axis running through the two halves of the *vajra*. This unity exists on a very deep level, the level of absolute reality itself, but according to the Tantra it can be made to operate on other levels as well. The forces of Enlightenment and non-Enlightenment can be united, integrated; the five mental poisons can be transmuted into the five wisdoms; the two worlds can be made to interpenetrate, to fuse. The achievement of this union, technically known as *yuganaddha* or two-in-oneness, is the work of the Tantra. At the highest level it is the two-in-oneness of wisdom and compassion (or skilful means), of *nirvāṇa* and *saṃsāra*.

Yuganaddha, the interpenetration of the two worlds, brings us to the fourth formal element in the symbol of the *vajra*: the head of the strange beast, known as the *makara*. This beast, which is somewhat like a crocodile, has its origin in Indian mythology, and it is often used as a decorative motif in art and architecture. The mystery of what on earth a crocodile-like beast is doing on the *vajra* is cleared up when it is remembered that crocodiles are amphibious, at home both in water and on land. The *makara*, bringing together water and earth, is thus a symbol of the union of opposites. Incidentally, the *makara* corresponds to the zodiac sign of Capricorn, which is sometimes represented by a fish-tailed goat, another beast that is a combination of opposites, the fish going down to the depths while the goat climbs up to the heights.

A connection can also be made with a story from Buddhist mythology. The story goes that originally various pairs of animals were inveterate enemies. For example, there was a settled antagonism

between the *garuḍa* and the *nāga*. The *garuḍa* is a mythical kind of great eagle which feeds on *nāgas*, which are snakes of a sort – dragon snakes – and there is a constant battle between the two. In a common motif, the fierce *garuḍa*, with its enormous parrot beak, is depicted gripping an unfortunate *nāga* in its claws. The otter and the fish are enemies too, obviously, and so are the tiger and the deer, and many other pairs of animals that have been linked together by ferocity and fear from the very beginning of things.

But one day, we are told, something wonderful happened, something that influenced the whole world: Gautama the Buddha became Enlightened. The effect was immediately felt everywhere. The feeling of love and kindliness and compassion flowing from the bodhi tree where the Buddha sat was so strong that it affected even those animals which were inveterate enemies. The *garuḍa* and the *nāga* became friends, and so did the fish and the otter, the tiger and the deer. So friendly did they become, in fact, that they mated and produced strange offspring: an eagle-snake, an otter-fish, a deer-tiger. In Indian and Tibetan art and mythology, these hybrid beasts came to be regarded as symbols of the union of opposites in a spiritual sense.

The union of opposites is also sometimes represented in the form of an androgynous human being, a figure that is half male and half female. In Hinduism this is depicted somewhat crudely: you get a human figure divided right down the middle, one side unmistakably male, and the other unmistakably female. But in Buddhism it is usually done more subtly. Representations of 'male' bodhisattvas have female characteristics, and can even be mistaken for female forms. But they aren't really male *or* female. The bodhisattva combines the two, the so-called masculine and the so-called feminine. We will go into this a little more in our final chapter.

An even more subtle representation of the union of opposites is to be found in that most mysterious symbol, the double or crossed *vajra* – the *viśvavajra*, as it is called. Although the *vajras* are not particularized as opposing principles, by crossing each other they create two opposing directions, one horizontal and the other vertical, again representing, one could say, the union of feminine and masculine. The crossed *vajra* is, as we have seen, the special emblem of the Buddha Amoghasiddhi, and the colour of this archetypal figure – as Lama Govinda has pointed out – is as mysterious as his emblem. He is deep green, a colour that is a mixture of the two primary colours, blue and yellow. There is a subtlety about it that the primary colours don't have – like twilight, Lama Govinda suggests, when the gold of the day and the blue of the night merge.[79] Likewise, the action of Amoghasiddhi is subtle, even esoteric – the almost indefinable type of action, refined and delicate, which is the activity of the Enlightened mind.

This, one could say, is the nature of the double *vajra* as well. Given that the *vajra* itself represents illimitable power, it is baffling to consider the potency of the double *vajra*, two *vajras* crossed. Although this power is echoed in the very meaning of Amoghasiddhi's name, Unobstructed Success, it is a subtle and entirely benign power, a non-polarized action with nothing crude or forceful about it.

Thus the symbolism of the *vajra* represents absolute reality, the basic polarity of existence, and the two worlds that emerge from that polarity: the world of spirit and the world of nature, one might say. It also represents the union of opposites. Above all it represents power, spiritual power: the power that is inherent in reality itself, that smashes through all the obstacles to Enlightenment, and that is generated by the experience of the union of opposites.

The *vajra* is a ritual implement. It is something to be used, something to be held in the hand. As you hold it, as you use it in Tantric ritual, if you do it properly, if you feel it fully, you have an experience. You experience the power of reality; and you experience what you truly and authentically are. Ultimately you become Vajradhara, the bearer of the *vajra*, the bearer of the power of reality, even the bearer of reality itself. Or, to put it another way, holding the *vajra*, you become what you truly always were.

Vajradhara is the Ādibuddha, or primordial Buddha, especially of the Kagyu schools of Tibetan Buddhism. Usually depicted as white or pale blue in colour, he wears a crown and his arms are crossed on his breast. In one hand he holds the *vajra*, in the other the bell. But there is another figure associated with the *vajra*, a figure even better known than Vajradhara: Vajrasattva. *Sattva* means an individual being, and in this context it is sometimes understood as consciousness, so Vajrasattva is the being whose consciousness is thoroughly saturated with the experience and power of reality. Vajrasattva is one who is the living embodiment of reality, who unites wisdom and compassion.

Vajrasattva was originally regarded as a bodhisattva, and he is always represented in bodhisattva form, even though he is in essence a Buddha. He is depicted as a man in what the Indians regarded as the most attractive period of life, that is to say, a young man of sixteen. The colour of his body is dazzling white, like bright sunshine on fresh snow, he has long black hair, and the expression on his youthful face is beautiful and compassionate. He is clad only in bracelets and rings, and in his hand he bears a *vajra*, which he holds to his heart.

In a common visualization meditation of Vajrasattva, you see him vividly and clearly, brilliantly white, in the middle of the sky before you, above your head. In his heart is to be seen a deep-blue syllable *hūṃ*, around which there revolve, in a clockwise direction, the blue or white letters of the hundred-syllable mantra, the mantra of Vajrasattva. The letters emit rays of light. From the syllable *hūṃ* and from the letters of the mantra there fall drops of nectar which converge into a stream. And the stream – cool, refreshing, cleansing – falls on the crown of your head and flows down through your body: through all the psychic centres, through the whole psycho-spiritual system. As it flows, it washes away all impurities and defilements, and as they are washed away, you feel cleansed, pure, bright, resplendent, crystalline. You begin to recover what is called your original purity, your original nature. You see, you realize, not just that you have become pure, but that in the depths of your being you were never defiled. In the depths

of your being you were pure from the beginning, absolutely pure, not touched, not stained, by anything at all. And as you realize that, you become gradually suffused with the sense of reality, and even with the power of reality. You become Vajrasattva. You become invested with the *vajra*, the sacred thunderbolt, the diamond sceptre of the lamas.

4
THE COSMIC REFUGE TREE AND THE ARCHETYPAL GURU

There is little in life of which we can be certain, but one thing of which we can be quite sure is that it involves a great deal of misunderstanding. One might go so far as to say that the world is one great big misunderstanding, or even mistake. We misunderstand ourselves, the world we live in, and, of course, each other; we don't really even understand people we think we know quite well.

One of the many targets of this universal tendency to misunderstand – and to criticize where that misunderstanding is greatest – is what is sometimes called the spiritual life. One of the commonest criticisms of the spiritual life is that it is escapism, and that those who try to practise some such thing as Buddhism are escapists. What people mean by this probably comes quite close to the dictionary definition of escapism: 'the tendency to seek distraction and relief from reality'. As we shall see, nothing could be less like a description of Buddhism.

But escape – 'to get away, as by flight or other conscious efforts; to break away, get free, or get clear, from or out of detention, danger, discomfort or the like, as to escape from prison' – *is* quite a good description of the spiritual life, at least as looked at from a certain point of view. It may not be the whole truth about spiritual life, but it is a substantial part of it. When one sets out to live a spiritual life, one is – or one should be – making a conscious effort to break away, to get free, to get clear of all sorts of entanglements, involvements, and complicated murkiness. Or, to put it another way, one is trying to make the transition from lower to higher states of being and consciousness, trying to develop, trying to evolve. This is what the spiritual life is substantially about.

So why might we try to do this? What makes us want to escape, to develop, to rise from a lower to a higher state of being and consciousness? We are impelled, even *com*pelled, to do it because we experience our present state as restrictive, cramped, limiting, confined, unsatisfactory, even dangerous. In our present state and circumstances, we feel only too often as though we are imprisoned, even caged, on a treadmill. Naturally we have the urge to get out, to *break* out if necessary, to get free and clear.

The Pāli canon contains a passage attributed to the Buddha in which he tries to explain to some of his disciples what it feels like to be Enlightened. Obviously they are very curious to know how it feels when you've got there. What does it feel like to be liberated? What does it feel like to be a Buddha? In his attempt to put across the inner content of the experience rather than offer a conceptual explanation, the Buddha chose to use three similes.[80] He said suppose that on a hot and dusty day you've been carrying an enormous burden for many miles; and suppose that after you've been staggering along with it for mile after mile, hour after hour, you are at last able to lift that load off your shoulders and put it down, free from that tremendous, oppressive weight. Becoming Enlightened, he said, is like that. You feel as though you have set down all your burdens. There's no weight for you to carry, nothing oppressing you. You are light and buoyant; you can float free.

Then again, he said, suppose you've been engaged in some trade, and suppose as the result of your business enterprise – or lack of enterprise – you've got heavily into debt. You owe a lot of money to a lot of people and you have no idea how you are going to pay them back. Your creditors are knocking on your door, following you about, wanting their money. Before you is the prospect of going to prison. Then one day, by some miracle, you suddenly acquire a large sum of money and can discharge all your debts. At last you can look everybody in the face again, free from that terrible anxiety. Becoming Enlightened, the Buddha said, is a bit like that.

Then a third image: becoming Enlightened, the Buddha said, is like being released from prison. Imagine how it might feel to have been shut up in prison for years on end. Then, one day, the door is flung open. Suddenly you are free to walk out into the sunlight and go wherever you please. Being Enlightened is just like that – you've escaped from the prison of the world itself.

Through these three similes, the Buddha tried to express something of how it feels to become Enlightened. You feel light, buoyant, carefree. You may even strike unenlightened people as being rather irresponsible, as not taking life seriously enough. You feel completely unconcerned about the past, because there is nothing left over that you have to deal with, and you are not concerned about the future either. Above all, you feel free, absolutely free, because you have at last escaped in the fullest possible sense.

It is therefore quite appropriate to describe the spiritual life as being, at least from one point of view, about escape. As for escapism, that is something else entirely. If an escapee is one who breaks out of prison, an escapist is one who tries to forget that he is in prison at all, who pretends to himself that the prison is not a prison, and that he is really free. Broadly speaking, this kind of escapism takes two forms: the non-religious and the religious. Of these two, non-religious escapism is probably the more common these days. It consists in trying to forget that one is in prison by becoming absorbed in whatever activities can be carried on within the prison walls. Religious escapism, on the other hand, consists in trying to forget that one is in prison by becoming absorbed in books on how to escape from prison.

Of course, one cannot escape unless there is a means of escape – a ladder or a rope, or a getaway car – and somewhere to escape to. And this is in fact the subject of an important passage in the *Udāna*, the book of the 'breathed out utterances', in which the Buddha calls his disciples together and speaks to them in a particularly solemn and impressive manner. He says

> There exists, monks, that which is unborn, that which is unbecome, that which is uncreated, that which is unconditioned. For if there were not, monks, that which is unborn, that which is unbecome, that which is uncreated, that which is unconditioned, there would not be made known here the escape from that which is born, from that which is become, from that which is created, from that which is conditioned. Yet since there exists, monks, that which is unborn, that which is unbecome, that which is uncreated, that which is unconditioned, there is therefore made known the escape from that which is born, from that which is become, from that which is created, from that which is conditioned.[81]

Closely related to the idea of escape in Buddhism generally, and much more familiar, is the idea of 'refuge', which the dictionary defines as 'that which, or one who, shelters, protects from danger, distress, calamity etc, a place inaccessible to the enemy'. In Buddhism, refuge – a means of escape and a place to escape to – is provided by the Three Jewels, or Three Refuges: the Buddha, the Enlightened teacher, the Dharma, the teaching, and the Sangha, the more highly developed members of the spiritual community. Between them the Three Refuges represent not only the means of escape from lower to higher levels of consciousness; they also represent what we escape to, those higher levels themselves. The act of Going for Refuge to the Buddha, the Dharma, and the Sangha is the central act of the whole Buddhist life; it is Going for Refuge that makes one a Buddhist. For the Buddhist tradition, therefore, Going for Refuge is identical with the following of the spiritual path itself.

All of this finds expression in the very earliest Buddhist texts, most famously in the *Dhammapada*, in which the Buddha is recorded as making a clear distinction between what could be called false refuges and true refuges, the main point being that no mundane thing can give refuge in an absolute sense. He says:

> Many people, out of fear, flee for refuge to sacred hills, woods, groves, trees, and shrines. In reality this is not a safe refuge. In reality this is not the best refuge. Fleeing to such a refuge one is not released from all suffering. He who goes for refuge to the Enlightened One, to the Truth, and to the Spiritual Community, and who sees with perfect wisdom the Four Ariyan Truths – namely, suffering, the origin of suffering, the passing beyond suffering and the Ariyan Eightfold Way leading to the pacification of suffering – for him this is a safe refuge, for him this is the best refuge. Having gone to such a refuge, one is released from all suffering.[82]

Just to clear up possible misunderstanding, it should be observed that the idea of Going for Refuge in the sense of escaping from all that is unsatisfactory does not do full justice to the ideals and practice of the spiritual life. The spiritual life also involves committing oneself to all that is truly satisfactory, and the point of escaping is to leave yourself free to make that commitment. There is nothing wrong in escaping if there is something to escape from, but to escape is not the be-all and end-all of the spiritual life any more than it is of worldly life. The fact that the word *śaraṇa*, refuge, is so firmly embedded in Buddhist tradition makes it extremely important to bring out its positive implications, otherwise we get a one-sidedly negative picture of the spiritual life, like talking about escape from the bud without mentioning the flower.

Going for Refuge in this full sense is common ground to all the three successive phases of the development of Buddhism in India, the phase of Early Buddhism (the 'Hīnayāna'), the Mahāyāna, and the Vajrayāna. Followers of all these three *yānas* venerate the Three Jewels and go to them for refuge. However, there are differences in their attitudes to them. So very different, indeed, is the Tantric Vajrayāna's way of looking at the Three Refuges that in addition to the Three Refuges of the general Buddhist tradition, it eventually established three special, esoteric, Tantric refuges.

The early Buddhist conception of the Three Refuges is comparatively simple and straightforward. The Buddha is seen simply as an Enlightened human being, a person who lived at a certain time in history. As a result of his spiritual struggles and endeavours he came upon or rediscovered the path to Enlightenment, and thereafter he showed that path to others, guiding his disciples to the same spiritual experience that he himself had attained. The Buddha is dead and gone. His memory can still guide and inspire, but that is all that remains of him – just his memory. Similarly, the Dharma is the actual teaching of the Buddha, the words the human historical Buddha actually spoke. According to the early Buddhists, the Dharma was passed on by word of mouth for hundreds of years and then written down in the form of what we now know as the Pāli canon. Followers of the early tradition strongly believe that if one follows this teaching – the letter and the spirit of it – one will gain Enlightenment, just as the Buddha did. As regards the Sangha, the third refuge, this is seen as being twofold. On the one hand there is the Āryasaṅgha, the 'noble sangha', which consists of the Enlightened and partly Enlightened disciples of the Buddha, past and present; and then there is the *bhikṣu* sangha, the community of monks.

The Mahāyāna, the second great phase, didn't so much change the earlier conception of the Refuges as universalize it. Mahāyānists tried to see the Three Refuges in a universal perspective, to understand what they were in principle, what they really meant, what they really involved, and they tried to express that in the most universal manner possible. They did not see the Buddha as just a historical figure, someone who lived in India at a certain time. For the Mahāyāna the Buddha became a spiritual principle, even a transcendental principle, the principle of Enlightenment. And by 'principle' I don't mean anything abstract or conceptual. For the Mahāyāna the Buddha became the living image of Enlightenment, abstracted or prescinded from history, having, in a sense, nothing to do with history, existing outside space and time, the living embodiment of the ideal of Enlightenment itself, quite apart from the 'where' and the 'when' and the 'by whom' of any particular attainment of Enlightenment by any particular historical individual.

Mahāyāna practitioners therefore see the Buddha as endowed with all imaginable perfections, virtues, and qualities. They see him living not on the stage of history, but in another world, a spiritual, even transcendental world. It is an ideal world, the expression in terms of a cosmos of what the Buddha himself is. Lavish descriptions in the Mahāyāna scriptures extol this ideal, pure Buddha-world in terms of radiant light and brilliant colour, beautiful music, jewelled trees, and expanses of lapis lazuli traversed by golden cords.[83]

In the same way, for the Mahāyāna, the Dharma is not just the teaching of the historical Buddha, not just words uttered in some obscure north-eastern Indian dialect by Śākyamuni and written down as scriptures. It is the great stream of spiritual influence that pours all the time from the eternal archetypal Buddha, the Buddha principle or ideal. It is an influence that is not just restricted to north-eastern India 2,500 years ago, but can be felt here and now, at any time, in any place, if one is receptive, and it can find form in words and be written down at any time, to create new scriptures.

And while the Mahāyāna conception of the Sangha also consists of two sections, they are entirely different from those of Early Buddhism. First, there are what are called bodhisattvas: beings of advanced spirituality who dwell on higher levels of consciousness and hear, at least sometimes, the words of the eternal Buddha, because they are attuned to the Dharma as an outpouring of the Buddha-nature sounding eternally on higher planes of existence. Then, lower down, on this earth, there are those who look up to the Buddhas and bodhisattvas, contemplate them, are devoted to them, aspire to be like them, wish to be drawn up to the bodhisattva level. All those who have that aspiration to become

Buddhas – to incorporate or manifest the Buddha principle – are part and parcel of the Sangha in the Mahāyāna sense, whether they are monks or lay people, male or female, spiritually advanced or not.

With the emergence of the Tantra came yet another way of seeing the Three Refuges. This did not involve a rejection of previous ways of seeing them: just as the Mahāyāna accepted the outlook of Early Buddhism and stepped beyond it, the Tantra accepted both earlier interpretations of the Three Refuges. But as we are well aware by now, the Tantra was concerned above all with direct experience. The Tāntrikas said, especially with regard to the Mahāyāna interpretation of the Three Refuges: That's all very well, but what does it amount to in terms of experience? Your conception of this archetypal Buddha living in this world of divine splendour is beautiful, impressive, and no doubt true. But we haven't seen that Buddha – indeed, we have to admit that we haven't seen any Buddha at all, whether archetypal or historical. We haven't even caught so much as a glimpse of a corner of that Buddha's robe, and perhaps we have no hope of ever catching a glimpse of it. As for the Dharma, we can't possibly study all the hundreds and thousands of scriptures, and we haven't been able to rise to the level at which we are able to listen to the eternal Buddha and come into contact with this great stream of spiritual influence. And we've never seen a bodhisattva in our lives – or at least we wouldn't recognize one even if we did see one. With no actual experience of the Three Refuges, what have we got? Are the Three Refuges totally non-existent for us? Is there nothing in our experience corresponding to them? Are there no points at which we can make contact with them?

Of course, the Tāntrikas concluded that they could indeed find such points of contact. They realized that they were able to encounter the Three Jewels through their own direct experience in the form of what are called the three Tantric or esoteric refuges: the guru, the *yidam*, and the *ḍākinī*. Guru here means one's own personal teacher, that is, someone with whom one is in regular personal contact, and from whom one receives inspiration, guidance, teaching, and especially Tantric initiation. As we saw in Chapter 2, Tantric initiation consists essentially in the transmission of power, the activation of one's own dormant energies as a result of the impact of the greater energies of the guru. As far as the Tantra is concerned, therefore, the guru is the Buddha. You may never have met, or even seen, the Buddha, whether historical or archetypal.

'Buddha' may be no more than a concept for you; you may have no insight into what it means. But you do have contact with the guru. According to the Tantra, therefore, the guru represents the Buddha principle within the field of the disciple's actual experience. To the extent that you are in contact with the guru, you are also in contact with the Buddha – indeed with all Buddhas, with the Buddha principle itself – and you receive through the guru the spiritual influence of all the Buddhas. This is the Tantric conception of the first of the three esoteric refuges.

There is an argument for avoiding the use of the word guru altogether these days, on account of the connotations of exploitation and authoritarianism it has acquired in the West. But the word is one thing, the principle another. To say that the Tantric guru stands in the position of the Buddha as far as you are concerned is not to say that the guru is Enlightened like the Buddha – though if he is, of course, so much the better. The point is that you are not in direct contact with the Buddha – the Buddha doesn't know you, as far as you know, and you don't know the Buddha – whereas your own guru at least has some personal knowledge of you and can thus act for you as an interpreter or translator of the vast mass of Buddhist literature and teachings, selecting those that will be helpful to you and putting the rest aside.

Thus in principle the guru is an interpreter, explicating the existing Buddhist tradition in such a way as to make it more accessible for those with whom he is in direct contact. It seems more appropriate today to think of a spiritual teacher in that way than to think in terms of a guru in a red robe and a lotus cap, ringing bells and waving *vajras*. It is the principle that is important – and the principle is translation. The Tantric guru is the person who makes the Dharma intelligible to *you* and practicable for *you*. To think of the guru as essentially someone who gives out esoteric initiations is to miss the point. It might be that for a particular person the essence of the Dharma is to be found in a particular Tantric practice, but the guru should not be identified exclusively with the imparting of such initiations and practices.

It is a question of the effectiveness of the teaching, and this cannot even be said to correlate very precisely with the extent of the guru's spiritual attainment. There is a well-known story that pleasantly illustrates the point. It is about a pious old woman whose son went on pilgrimage to the Buddhist holy places. She asked him to bring back a relic, a tooth of the Buddha, but he forgot her request until he was nearly home again. Then, so as not to disappoint her, he pulled out one of the teeth of a dead dog that happened to be lying nearby, wrapped it in silk, and took it home for his mother. Delighted, she put it on her shrine, and meditated in front of it. Before long there were rays of light coming from the tooth, and the old woman herself was Enlightened.[84]

In the same way, a lot will depend on one's own attitude to the guru. When you adopt the attitude that the guru is the Buddha for you, you are not desperately trying to convince yourself that the guru is Enlightened as the Buddha was. What you are really saying is that within your particular world the guru is the most Enlightened person you know. Of course, you must have some basis for saying that; there must be an appreciable difference between him and other people.

In a sense, though, anyone who teaches Buddhism functions as a Tantric guru. As a teacher you don't just repeat everything you have read on the subject. You consider the needs of the person or people in front of you, and you pass on to them as much as you feel they can understand and use. If you are explaining something to somebody, you can tell if they have understood what you have said – you can see by the expression that lights up their face that the penny has dropped, and that understanding has been transmitted. If there is a 'Tantric' aspect to this, it is perhaps simply in the fact that the teaching should be accompanied by a charge of energy, so that it is not just a theoretical explanation to impart intellectual understanding but has the life and energy of actual experience being transmitted.

The principle behind the idea of the Tantric guru is also what makes possible any kind of spiritual revival. A lineage of teaching doesn't inevitably peter out once it has been going for several hundred years. What has been lost can be regained; what has died out can be revived, if the necessary effort is made. To take a simple example, someone may give a very poor talk about Buddhism, reproducing Buddhist teachings in a lamentably mechanical fashion, but a person in the audience may nonetheless be uplifted and inspired, even transformed, because the words of the doctrine are able to communicate something, quite independent of the communicator's own understanding. Even in the absence of any real depth of understanding on the teacher's part, the disciple, if he or she is receptive, may manage to pick up something of great value to his or her own spiritual life.

In Indo-Tibetan Buddhism a pattern has developed whereby a certain teaching, which was originally taught as being capable of taking the practitioner all the way to Enlightenment, degenerates – or at least it appears to degenerate, because it is no longer practised effectively. Then a new teacher introduces a new practice which is, for a time, completely effective. He does not repudiate the old practice, but simply says that it was lower or more basic than the new one. This process of degeneration and revival recurs until there is a whole stack of practices or teachings, only the top one being considered to give rise to Enlightenment.

This process eventually resulted in the *triyāna* system of Indo-Tibetan Buddhism, which encompasses the doctrines of all three phases or *yānas* of Buddhist tradition, with all their practices and attainments. You are meant to go through the whole stack of teachings, but in practice people whizz through most of them very quickly and only practise the top one seriously. The stack has got so high by now that it would really make sense to drop all the later developments and go back to the original teaching of the historical Buddha himself (as far as we can tell what it was) – hence my own concern to stress the importance of Going for Refuge.

Tibetan Buddhists formerly believed that all the *yānas* were the personal teaching of the Buddha but that some were meant for a more highly qualified group of disciples, and kept hidden for that reason. With the historical perspective available to us, however, we can go back to the Going for Refuge and build on that. We are confronted by so many forms of Buddhism – Tibetan, Chinese, Japanese, Theravāda – all with their own ways of looking at things and their own stacks of teachings, but that is all the more reason to get back to basic principles – the simpler and more accessible the better. It would be disconcerting – as perhaps it is for, say, Tibetan or Japanese Buddhists – to read the Pāli canon and recognize little that related to one's own practice of the Dharma. We need not ignore the later developments, but we can base them more firmly on the earlier practices, appreciating them as growing out of those early forms and rounding them out, illustrating them. Otherwise, you end up trying to practise teachings which are so far beyond you as to be barely intelligible.

The second esoteric refuge is the *yidam*. This is a Tibetan word which literally means 'oath-bound'. It is sometimes translated as 'guarantor', that is, one who guarantees that the disciple will eventually gain

Enlightenment, and it is equivalent to, though not an actual translation of, the Sanskrit term *iṣṭa devatā*, which means 'chosen or selected divinity'. The *yidam* is thus that special aspect of the Dharma, that special aspect of reality, through which the disciple approaches the Enlightenment experience. The *yidam* is not an abstract concept or an idea but a figure – a figure of a Buddha or bodhisattva, embodying a particular aspect or attribute of Enlightenment. Your *yidam* could be Amitābha, the red Buddha of infinite light and eternal life; or Mañjughoṣa, the golden Bodhisattva of Wisdom with the flaming sword; or Tārā, the saviouress, usually white or green in colour, carrying lotus flowers; or Vajrasattva, the embodiment of the innate purity of one's own mind. Whichever figure it is, as a disciple of the Tantra, the whole of the Dharma is contained, embodied, in your *yidam*, and you direct all your attention to that. You don't bother too much about scriptures, studies, teachings, doctrines. The centre of your attention, spiritually speaking, is occupied by the figure of the *yidam*, and you devote yourself to becoming familiar with that figure.

You first make the acquaintance of the *yidam* in the course of Tantric initiation. In effect, in giving you the initiation of, say, Tārā, the guru is introducing you to her, saying to her, 'Tārā, this is So-and-so,' and to you, 'This is Tārā. Now I've introduced you to her, you know each other and there is a connection between you.' Once you have made the acquaintance of a *yidam* in this way, your practice is to keep the *yidam* at the centre of your attention. One way of doing this is to visualize the figure in meditation. With your inner eye you see the *yidam* before you, and you contemplate and become absorbed in that figure, and chant the *yidam*'s mantra. Becoming absorbed in the *yidam*, you thereby absorb the spiritual qualities and principles and experiences which the *yidam* represents, which the *yidam is*. Eventually, you are absorbed into the *yidam*, or the *yidam* is absorbed into you, so that the two of you become one. If you have been focusing on Mañjughoṣa, for example, you absorb the wisdom that Mañjughoṣa represents, while if your *yidam* is Tārā you develop the purity, the tenderness, the compassion, which is Tārā, and if you have Vajrapāṇi as your *yidam*, you acquire the energy, strength, courage, even spiritual ferocity he stands for. For you, your *yidam* is the whole Dharma, the whole teaching, distilled into a single figure with which you become spiritually intimate, and into whom, or into which, you are incorporated.

Your *yidam* is your *iṣṭa devatā*, the chosen divinity. But who or what does the choosing? The important point here is that you do not choose a *yidam* with your conscious mind. Your *yidam* is chosen by your nature, your needs, your spiritual requirements, or even weaknesses to be corrected. So you can't be trusted – that is, your conscious mind can't be trusted – to make the choice. Usually, therefore, your guru does it for you, saying, 'This is what you need. This is the divinity chosen not by what you think or what you want, but what you are.' The guru, of course, knows what you are better than you know it yourself. If your guru doesn't choose your *yidam* for you, the Tibetan tradition says that it is better to leave it to chance than to make the choice yourself. Chance is more likely to be right.

In the end it doesn't really matter which Buddha or bodhisattva is chosen, or whether or not you make the choice yourself. In the course of ordaining people and passing on these practices in that context, I have found that it is comparatively rare for there to be a strong affinity between a particular person and a particular visualized form. People do have their preferences, and sometimes the preference is for quite a superficial reason – but that doesn't actually matter, because as you do the meditation, your relationship with the figure will deepen. The important thing is that the choice is made, that you make a start and get on with the practice – with the guidance of the person who has given it to you.

The third Tantric refuge, the *ḍākinī*, literally means 'sky-being', or 'space-being', and we will be considering *ḍākinīs* in this sense in the next chapter. But in the context of the esoteric refuges, the *ḍākinī* signifies something like spiritual companion – a spiritual companion in a rather special sense. A *ḍākinī* is someone whose company you find spiritually stimulating and energizing, and who therefore helps to release, to spark off, your energies, to free them for the living of the spiritual life. Such a spiritual companion, according to the Tantra, can be either male or female – *ḍākinī* is the feminine form of the noun, and *ḍāka* the masculine form. Just as the guru represents the Buddha principle within the context of your actual experience, and the *yidam* represents the Dharma principle, the *ḍāka* or *ḍākinī* is the embodiment of the Sangha principle.

Like the *yidam*, the *ḍāka* or *ḍākinī* needs to be selected by the guru, and – according to strict Tantric tradition – initiated by him as well. In the Indian Tantric tradition it did apparently sometimes happen that the guru would literally present the initiate with a *ḍāka* or *ḍākinī*, and it happened occasionally in Tibet too. The *ḍāka* or *ḍākinī* (usually the practitioner was male, so usually it was a *ḍākinī*) had to be properly identified and initiated by the guru; she wasn't just someone you happened to meet at a party. As a disciple you may obviously make mistakes; you may think you are being spiritually energized when you are only being amused and distracted. And, of course, if the spiritual companion happens to be of the opposite sex, you may think you have found a *ḍāka* or *ḍākinī* when you have only fallen in love – quite a different matter.

As Buddhists today it is probably safest for us to disregard the Indian or Tibetan form of the tradition and just think in terms of spiritually stimulating company. It is the quality of stimulation that is important – *spiritual* stimulation, which goes much deeper than mere liveliness – and this is the quality to look for in your communication with your spiritual friends. No doubt in a broad sense the whole sangha has this kind of effect, but within it there may be just a few people whose company you find so stimulating that they can be the third esoteric refuge for you. In such friendship you may, for instance, find it very easy to talk about your meditation, or about the Dharma generally. You may find that communication brings up all sorts of things, and that you can talk very freely – not just unburdening yourself, but finding genuine inspiration. The more you communicate with such a friend (which doesn't mean just talking a lot), the more intensely you experience the spiritual life itself.

Having said that, it is not generally appropriate actually to label particular people as *ḍākas* or *ḍākinīs*; it is better to bear in mind that this is something that our spiritual friends are able to be, at least occasionally. Just as the Dharma is not always the Dharma – when, for example, you pick up a beautiful Dharma book and find as you start reading it that it doesn't mean much to you at that particular moment – in the same way, a spiritual friend will not always spark you off. Sometimes they do act as a *ḍāka* or *ḍākinī* for you, sometimes they don't. Rather than thinking of *this* person as being a *ḍāka* or *ḍākinī*, and *that* person as not being one, it is perhaps more useful to look out for the *ḍāka* or *ḍākinī* as a possibility that might arise in quite unlikely contexts of communication. In Tantric legend, ugly old women were sometimes *ḍākinīs* in disguise and, if approached in the right way, became beautiful young women. We can all too easily mislead ourselves as to who or what is a *ḍāka* or *ḍākinī*; he or she is not necessarily going to resemble a film star or a pop idol.

This third esoteric refuge balances the 'vertical' relationship that you have with your guru with a more 'horizontal' kind of relationship among what we would call a peer group, known in the Vajrayāna as the *vajrakula*. The *vajrakula* consists of all those who have taken initiation from the same guru, and who thus become *vajra* brothers and *vajra* sisters. It should be said that while this tradition has continued to be maintained in some forms of Tibetan Buddhism, in certain cases it seems that all the emphasis is on the relationship with the guru to the neglect of the esoteric Sangha refuge, with the result that practitioners do not relate to each other very much. It is difficult to be inspired when you are feeling rather lonely and isolated.

These three Tantric refuges are not in addition to the original Three Refuges; you don't go for Refuge to the Buddha, the Dharma, and the Sangha, and then also to the guru, the *yidam*, and the *ḍākinī*. The guru, the *yidam*, and the *ḍākinī* represent the Buddha, the Dharma, and the Sangha in terms of our own, actual experience, here and now, as we try to follow the path. So if a Tantric tradition neglects the esoteric Sangha refuge, it does not have another Sangha refuge to fall back on.

All of this discussion of the Three Refuges is by way of providing the context in which the cosmic Refuge Tree and the archetypal guru are to be understood. The visualization we will look at here is taken from the Nyingma tradition. The first thing to say about the Refuge Tree, as it is called in the Tantric tradition, is that in the form in which it is traditionally visualized, it is not a tree at all, but more like a lotus plant. As in any visualization practice, you see, first of all, with your inner eye, just a great expanse of blue, vivid and shining. The blue sky is traditionally said to symbolize *śūnyatā*, emptiness; it can also be said to represent the complete absorption of all wandering thoughts into a higher dimension of consciousness, undifferentiated and pure. In the midst of this blue sky, you see a rainbow-coloured cloud, flashing and glowing in all the colours of the rainbow. From the cloud there rises up a vast stem or trunk several hundred feet high, and from this central stem there emerge four great branches, one at each of the cardinal points. The central stem and the four branches terminate in five enormous lotus flowers, so that the whole thing looks rather like a gigantic candelabrum.

As you bring the image more and more intently to mind, you see that on the lotus flowers there are many figures. The different traditions describe these figures in slightly different ways, the description that follows being taken from the Nyingma tradition. According to this, on the 'southern' lotus, the one immediately in front of you, there appear three figures in a row. These are the Buddhas of past, present, and future, representing the succession of human historical Buddhas. On the left as you look is Dīpaṅkara, the light-maker or light-bringer, the Buddha of the remote past. In the centre is Śākyamuni, our own Buddha, the Buddha of the present age. And on the right is Maitreya, the friendly one, the Buddha of the future, the Buddha yet to be. They are all sitting there, side by side, clad in saffron robes and carrying begging-bowls.

The western lotus, the lotus to your left, is occupied by eight to twelve figures. These are the great bodhisattvas of the Mahāyāna sangha: Avalokiteśvara, the Bodhisattva of Compassion, Mañjuśrī, the Bodhisattva of Wisdom, Kṣitigarbha, and the rest. They are all depicted as youthful, slender, graceful, and beautiful, with smiling expressions and long, black flowing tresses, and they are clad in silks and jewels and magnificent jewelled headdresses.

The northern lotus, the one at the back behind the central lotus, has no figures at all, but a huge pile of books: massive Tibetan xylograph volumes – you are meant to visualize 108 of them – representing the Buddhist scriptures.

On the eastern lotus, to your right, you see another group of figures, very different in appearance from the bodhisattvas. They are old men, wrinkled and bald, clad in saffron robes and carrying monastic staffs. Among them we see Śāriputra, the Buddha's chief disciple, Maudgalyāyana, Kāśyapa, Ānanda, and the other great *arhant* (i.e. Enlightened) disciples of the historical Buddha: in short, the great figures of the early Buddhist sangha.

The central lotus is much bigger and more splendid than the other four, and on its calyx, which is said to be like a mountain of gold, you see the figure of Padmasambhava, the great Tantric guru of India and Tibet, the founder of the Nyingma tradition. He is seated cross-legged, clad in rich and colourful garments, and he wears on his head his famous lotus cap, which terminates in a *vajra* and a vulture's feather. His expression is benign, compassionate, and smiling, though not without a touch of ferocity. In his left hand, which rests in his lap, he holds a skull-cup

filled with nectar, and in his right hand he holds a golden *vajra*. In the crook of his left arm is a long staff with streamers, surmounted by three severed human heads and a trident.

From the calyx of this central lotus open out layer upon layer of petals, forming a series of tiers or rows which hold a multitude of disparate seated figures. Immediately below Padmasambhava you visualize various gurus – mainly from the Nyingma lineage, but also gurus of other lineages, and your own personal teachers as well. You see them all seated cross-legged there side by side on the tiers of petals. Some are wearing monastic dress of various kinds, others are wearing hardly anything. Some are wearing the tall red pandit cap, others are wearing square caps, while many are bare-headed. Some have shaven heads, some have long flowing hair. Some are holding books, others grasp the *vajra* and the bell, while many sit empty-handed. Some seem to be preaching, others are meditating or making ritual gestures. If you look closely, you see that some of these gurus look very holy and pious, with calm contemplative expressions, while others have quite a disreputable appearance. You see, in short, Tantric gurus of every conceivable kind. In a large representation of the Refuge Tree there may even be hundreds of them.

Lower down, on the next set of petals, come the four orders of Tantric divinities – that is, Buddhas and bodhisattvas belonging to the main subdivisions of the Tantra. All of these – and there are several hundred of them – can be used or chosen as *yidams*. Some have peaceful smiling faces, while others are wrathful, with ferocious, terrifying expressions. Some have two arms, while others have four, eight, sixteen, or thirty-two. They can be bright red in colour, or green, blue, yellow, white, or black. Most of them have human heads, whether one or more, but a few have the heads of animals. Each in his or her own way embodies a different aspect of the Dharma, a different approach to the Enlightenment experience.

Below the *yidams*, on yet more layers of petals unfolding from that central calyx, you see the 'spiritual companions', the *ḍākas* and *ḍākinīs*, depicted according to the conventions of Tantric art as young, beautiful, and naked or nearly naked. On the tiers of petals below these, you see guardian deities or protectors of the Dharma, usually very fierce in form. These represent the powerful spiritual influences that shield the Tantric disciple from psychic danger and disaster. Usually when you receive a powerful Tantric initiation, you are also given the initiation of a guardian to ward off any undesirable influences that may get in the way of your practice – or even be activated by it. The protectors are of different colours, but they are all powerfully built, ferocious in appearance, and armed with weapons of many kinds, and some of them are represented as trampling underfoot the enemies of the Dharma.

The Refuge Tree may already seem rather overpopulated. But there are still more figures to be seen, above the head of Padmasambhava. These are the gurus of the telepathic lineage, in which initiation and teaching is imparted mind to mind, heart to heart. In this lineage one encounters the 'archetypal' Buddhas: Amitābha, the red Buddha, the Buddha of infinite light and eternal life; above him the shining white figure of Vajrasattva; and beyond even Vajrasattva, the dark brown figure of the Ādibuddha, the primordial Buddha, Samantabhadra, the 'All-Good', cross-legged, naked, and embracing his female counterpart.

This, in brief, is the cosmic Refuge Tree according to the Nyingma tradition. As you look at it, what should become clearly apparent is that it is formed by the intersection of the horizontal and vertical dimensions – or, one might say, the exoteric and esoteric dimensions, the horizontal, exoteric dimension comprising the Buddha, the Dharma, and the Sangha, while the vertical, esoteric dimension comes in the form of the gurus, the *yidams*, and the *ḍākas*, *ḍākinīs*, and guardians. The cosmic Refuge Tree thus represents in vivid, detailed symbolic form the whole conception of refuge, in its historical background, its universal perspective, and its immediate practical application. It is one of the richest and most complex symbols in the whole field of Tantric Buddhism, a symbol that would repay a lifetime's study.

Rich and full and glowing as the Refuge Tree is in itself, there are still a few details to be filled in to complete the visualization. Up in the sky, all round the tree, there are clouds on which float gods and goddesses, making offerings to the Refuge Tree, offering flowers, lights, incense, parasols, and so on. And right in the foreground, where you might easily miss it, is a single, tiny human figure, confronting all those Buddhas, bodhisattvas, gurus, books, and so on. This figure has his back to the spectator – in some paintings you just see the head and shoulders. But if you look closely you can see that the hands of this figure are clasped above his head, and even that there is a string of *mālā* beads on his wrist, signifying that he is in the act of prostrating himself in the direction of the Refuge Tree. Who is this? It is you – you in the act of Going for Refuge.

It is with this very significant figure that we come at last from the description of the Refuge Tree to the way in which it is used in spiritual practice. The tree is visualized, recreated in a sense, with one's own inner vision in the course of a very important Tantric practice known as the Going for Refuge and Prostration practice. This is one of the *mūla yogas* or foundation yogas of the Vajrayāna – practices or exercises that one must go through before one can embark on the practice of Tantric meditation proper. At least, this is the way the Going for Refuge and Prostration practice is often presented in the Tibetan tradition – as something you do as a preliminary practice and leave behind. However, as a Going for Refuge practice, it is the fundamental act of the Buddhist, not just something to get over with before you move on to something else. Many Buddhists therefore find themselves sustaining the practice, or returning to it, throughout their lives.

All the Tibetan schools have their own version of the tree, and there is no reason why other versions cannot be devised. Indeed, one has been specially created for use in the context of the Triratna Buddhist Order. This one is much simpler than many of the traditional trees, in that it involves far fewer figures. It has Śākyamuni Buddha, together with the Buddhas of the past and future, on the central lotus, and the teachers it depicts are the great teachers of many traditions – Indian, Tibetan, Chinese, and Japanese. Another feature of this tree is that it includes a female *arhant* – the Buddha's gifted disciple Dhammadinnā – and a female bodhisattva, Tārā. But whether the Refuge Tree visualized is a traditional Tibetan version or a new one, this practice is entirely suitable for use by western Buddhists. It helps to make the whole act or practice of Going for Refuge much more concrete, impressing it powerfully on one's mind (and indeed on one's body, as we shall see).

Depictions of the Refuge Tree are rare simply because artists don't like to do them – they are very fiddly, with all those hundreds of tiny figures, and quite a strain on the eyes. They are expensive too, because Tibetan artists usually charge according to the number of figures and the amount of gold used. However, you do come across them from time to time, and some of them are among the masterpieces of Tibetan religious art. Every figure, even though it may be no bigger than a quarter of an inch in height, is painted meticulously in the finest detail, as though

with a single hair of the brush, and the overall effect of this richness of detail can be awe-inspiring.

For all that, a painted scroll of the Refuge Tree is not just for decorating the shrine or the temple. It is not even just for general devotional purposes. It is intended as a guide to actual visualization. First of all you visualize the Refuge Tree, building it up bit by bit. As we have seen, you start by seeing the expanse of blue and, in the midst of it, the rainbow-coloured cloud, out of which springs the lotus plant upon which the figures assemble. In this way you build up the whole Refuge Tree, figure by figure, until it is complete. In the end you are supposed to see it clearly before you, as you sit there in meditation. If you can't visualize it very well, if all you get is an occasional glimpse of a single figure or a lotus petal, you should at least *feel* that it's all there. In particular, you should feel, or if possible see, the central figure of Padmasambhava. It is important to be particularly aware of him because, for the Nyingma tradition, he is the embodiment of all the refuges, exoteric and esoteric.

Once you have got the Refuge Tree in view, or the feeling of its being there, with Padmasambhava at the heart of it, you are meant to cultivate the sense or feeling that Padmasambhava embodies all the refuges in his own person, that he *is* the Buddha, Dharma, and Sangha, the guru, *yidam*, and *ḍākinī*, that they are all concentrated in this one awe-inspiring figure. You then cultivate a heartfelt determination that until you attain Enlightenment you will go for Refuge to Padmasambhava as the embodiment of all the Refuges, with your whole being, your body, speech, and mind, with all your energies flowing in that direction.

At this point in the practice, you repeat aloud some verses expressive of your Going for Refuge to Padmasambhava, and after each recitation, you prostrate yourself. You join your hands, which are supposed to represent a lotus bud, and then with your joined thumbs you touch first the centre of your forehead, then your throat, and finally your heart. Then you drop onto your knees and shoot your hands forward until you find yourself flat on the floor, having thrown yourself before the Refuge Tree. You raise your joined palms above your head in salutation, recite the verse or verses, and prostrate yourself in this way 100,000 times; not all at once – you are allowed to spread the total number over a certain length of time – but you should do at least a hundred recitations and prostrations daily until the total is complete. It goes without saying that the Going for Refuge and Prostration practice is a rather strenuous exercise. Tibetans believe that it is a cure for tuberculosis.

Besides, as you go down flat in front of the Refuge Tree, keeping the visualization in mind, you are exercising not only your body but also your imagination. You have to imagine, to feel, that all living beings, especially all human beings, are prostrating themselves with you. At your right shoulder you imagine your father, at your left shoulder your mother, and behind your father all the men in the world, behind your mother all the women in the world. In some forms of the tradition you imagine your parents literally *on* your shoulders, as though you are carrying them. Behind you are all your friends and acquaintances, and in front of you all your enemies. As you prostrate yourself and recite the verses, they all recite and prostrate themselves with you.

The idea of this is that all living beings are doing the practice with you. You are taking the lead, but everybody is doing it, the whole cosmos is involved. This is one of the reasons why we speak of the cosmic Refuge Tree – not only because it embodies all the Buddhas, bodhisattvas, gurus, *ḍākinīs*, and so on, of the three periods of time (past, present, and future), but also because the whole of sentient existence is involved in the practice through your imaginative identification. You feel that you are not doing it on your own, it's not just for you; in the compassionate spirit of the Mahāyāna, you are doing it for the benefit of all beings, and indeed all beings are doing the practice with you. Of course, this can be interpreted psychologically. In some cases, psychologically speaking, you've definitely got your father sitting on one shoulder and your mother sitting on the other, and you can't do anything about it, you can't get rid of the psychological conditioning that comes from them. In some sense they will always be with you. But never mind – let them prostrate themselves with you. Let the whole world, let all sentient beings, be involved.

If this vision seems difficult to engage with, it may be helpful to introduce a specifically western idea that I have certainly found quite useful when thinking about the larger Buddhist view of things – that of evolution. Just as one can see the development of biological life in terms of the evolution of species, by analogy one can think of the spiritual life as an evolutionary process, whereby one develops ever higher and more refined states of consciousness. This process, which I term the higher evolution, of course depends on the lower evolution, in that it is from the lower evolution that consciousness emerges in the first place. Lower and higher evolution differ from each other, however, in that the lower evolution is collective and unconscious whereas the higher evolution is individual and a matter of conscious effort.[85]

One could see this whole process as being represented by the cosmic Refuge Tree. The figures on the tree of course represent the evolutionary process at the very highest level. You could imagine that around and behind you as you prostrate yourself are all the other forms of life: human beings and animals, plants and trees. As you prostrate yourself, you could imagine not only that all human beings are prostrating themselves with you, but that all life is participating in this great process, the cosmic Going for Refuge. We can trace our existence not just through our human ancestors but right back to primitive man, and to apes before that, and all the other forms of life through which we have evolved over so many millions of years.

However you imagine it, you do the recitation followed by the prostration – a hundred times, or two hundred, or even a thousand times if you want to make it a longer session. Then you stop, sit down again in meditation posture, and continue seeing – or at least feeling the presence of – the Refuge Tree. At the conclusion of the session you see – or again you feel a sense of – white light shining forth from all the refuges in front of you, streaming from the central figure of Padmasambhava, from the Buddhas and bodhisattvas, from the books, from the *arhants*, from the gurus, the *ḍākinīs*, the guardians, the *yidams*, the archetypal Buddhas. This pure white light falls on to you, and onto your father and all men, and your mother and all women, and in its dazzling beams all defilements and faults are dissolved, so that the whole assembly of beings is completely purified. The light is then drawn back into the body of the Refuges, and then all the figures on the four lotuses are absorbed into the central figure of Padmasambhava, so that only he is left, suspended in the midst of that blue expanse. He stays there for a few minutes more, and then you see him too dissolve into emptiness, so that only the blue expanse of the empty sky remains.

This, at least, is a form of the practice as carried out in the Nyingma tradition. In the other Tibetan traditions – the Kagyu, the Gelug, and so on – the Refuge Tree is more or less the same, with just a few variations from tradition to tradition and from school to school. But there is one variation which is quite important – not a variation in

principle, but in the particular embodiment of the principle. In the Nyingma tradition, the calyx of the central lotus is occupied by the figure of Padmasambhava because he is regarded as the founder of the Nyingma tradition. But in the Kagyu tradition that central position is sometimes occupied by Milarepa. He is depicted as either white or green in colour – green because, according to his biography, he lived for years on nothing but nettles, which turned his whole body green. He is represented as naked except for a small piece of cotton cloth, his only covering in the bitter cold of the Tibetan winter, in the Himalayan ranges, well above the snow line. His hand is held to his ear, and his mouth is half open, to indicate that he is singing – singing, of course, one of his famous songs.

In the Gelug tradition the central figure, and founder of the tradition, is Tsongkhapa, whose strict commitment to formal monasticism makes a powerful contrast with Milarepa. Clad in monastic robes of red and yellow, he wears a tall pointed yellow pandit cap, being the special cap worn at the time of giving initiation. His hands are in the *mudrā* of exposition or teaching – he was a great teacher and commentator on the scriptures – and he holds the stems of two lotuses that blossom at his shoulders, one bearing a flaming sword, while on the other rests a book of the Perfection of Wisdom. These are the insignia of the Bodhisattva of Wisdom, Mañjuśrī or Mañjughoṣa, and Tsongkhapa is depicted with them because he is believed by his followers to be a manifestation of this bodhisattva.

Gelug representations of the Refuge Tree are rather different in character, at least artistically speaking, from Nyingma ones. All the same features are there, but their arrangement is much more schematic and geometrical, suggesting even a certain rigidity of approach. If you see a Gelug representation of the cosmic Refuge Tree from a distance, it's as though Tsongkhapa is seated in the midst of the four arms of a cross. On closer inspection you see that the cross is made up of scores of tiny figures which sometimes seem to be sitting in little cubicles or compartments.

Just as the Mahāyāna Buddha embodies the Buddha principle in its perfection, so the figures of Padmasambhava, Milarepa, and Tsongkhapa embody for their respective traditions the guru principle in its perfection, the ideal universal or archetypal guru. Each is the embodiment of all the Refuges, as well as being the founder of the particular school to which one's own guru belongs.

Lineage is a very important aspect of the whole Tantric Buddhist tradition, as well as of Chan or Zen, though there is always the danger of its becoming formalized. We have already seen that the Tantric guru is one who gives initiation, and that this is more like a transmission of power or activation of dormant energy than the giving of a teaching or the explanation of a doctrine. But although the experience may be primarily like the giving of energy, it is also – so it is said – like the planting of a seed. At the time of initiation, the guru plants a seed in the soil of the disciple's heart. The seed comes from outside, from the guru, but as a disciple you yourself have to tend it, cultivate it, water it, give it light and warmth. If you do this, the seed will sprout and grow into a plant, the plant will produce buds, and in time, given the right conditions, the plant will blossom into a magnificent lotus – indeed, into the thousand-petalled lotus of Enlightenment itself.[86] With energies fully activated, and endowed with the plenitude of spiritual power, the disciple will become Vajradhara, the bearer of the *vajra*, or Vajrasattva, the *vajra*-being, the adamantine being: the disciple himself or herself will become a guru.

Having become a guru, the former disciple is able to transmit power to his or her own disciples. In this way, a chain reaction is set up, beginning with the original guru – Padmasambhava, in the case of the Nyingmapas. However, although this spiritual chain reaction, from generation to generation, is called a lineage, or a line of transmission, it is important not to imagine that there is any thing which is transmitted. It isn't that the guru gives you something which you hand on to somebody else, who hands it on to yet another person. Much less is it a question of giving a robe or a certificate. So what is transmitted? It is what can only be described as a current of spiritual energy, spiritual electricity even. It is a direct experience that is sparked off.

The transmission from generation to generation is not a one-to-one linear process. Any guru may have had many teachers and received many transmissions. All the energies of all these transmissions converge in him just as many rivulets form a great river, and the guru transmits all these energies. The guru does not lose energy by this transmission. If anything, in transmitting spiritual power, the guru gains more energy: sometimes it is said in the Tantric tradition that the giving of initiation to a worthy disciple is very helpful and beneficial to the guru. However, this is rather an esoteric aspect of the subject; the important thing to recognize is that lineage is not just an idea, not just of historical interest. It isn't just that it is nice to be able to trace your spiritual descent back to Padmasambhava. Lineage is a truth, a fact that can be experienced as a living spiritual reality.

To help one experience this living reality is the purpose of a meditation practice called the *guru yoga*. The practice has many forms, some of them rather complex; here I will describe one of the simpler forms. To begin with, you imagine yourself transformed into a mass of light. You feel, you imagine, that you are nothing but light, that your body – your bones, flesh, blood, marrow, skin, heart – and your mind, your thoughts, are transmuted into pure, brilliant, blazing light. This light gradually assumes a certain form, the beautiful female form of a figure known as Vajrayoginī. (Whether the disciple is male or female doesn't matter.) You feel yourself to have become – you feel yourself now to *be* – this beautiful female form, brilliant red in colour, naked except for ornaments of human bone, and surrounded by a halo of rainbow-coloured light shining in all directions. The assumption of the female form here is significant, in that it suggests receptivity to the guru's influence: especially at the time of initiation, the disciple – of whichever sex – is female in relation to the guru. She is red because, in the Tantric tradition as in western culture, red is the colour of love, passion, and fascination. As for the nakedness of the figure, this represents sincerity, openness and freedom from all disguises. And the ornaments of human bone represent renunciation, freedom from attachment, fearlessness in the face of death.

Seeing yourself in the form of Vajrayoginī, you visualize above your head your own personal guru, and above him you see, or imagine, the figure of the great guru Padmasambhava. Above him in turn you see Avalokiteśvara, the Bodhisattva of Compassion – not in his more usual two-armed or four-armed form, but with eleven heads and a thousand arms, looking or extending in all directions – an important form of the bodhisattva which represents the omnipresence of compassion. Above even Avalokiteśvara you see the figure of Amitābha, the red Buddha, the Buddha of Infinite Light and Eternal Life. All around you there appear the gurus of India and Tibet, but your attention is mainly fixed on the line of gurus above Vajrayoginī's head – that is, above your own head. Seeing, feeling, this lineage extending upwards into space, you pray to all these figures. You pray for their blessing, and that you may gain Enlightenment for the sake of all living beings. (In the course of doing this practice over time, you recite this prayer 100,000 times.)

At this point all the gurus dissolve into light. Then Amitābha also dissolves into light and becomes absorbed in the figure of Avalokiteśvara, which dissolves into light and is absorbed in the figure of Padmasambhava, which is dissolved into light and is absorbed in the figure of your own guru. Next, you see brilliant light radiating from the form of your own guru in all directions. You experience the compassion of the guru and feel his blessing, his *adhiṣṭhāna*, as it is called, descending upon you. You feel this, you experience this.

But this is only the preparation. In the Tantra you want more than a blessing; you want initiation. So next you visualize a white *oṃ* on the guru's forehead, from which issues a ray of pure white light, which falls onto your forehead and bestows upon you the vase initiation. You feel that all the sins of your body, all your sins of action, have been wiped out. You are enabled now to practise the *mahāyoga*; the seed of the *nirmāṇakāya* Buddha has been sown. Then you visualize at the guru's throat a red syllable *āḥ*, and from it comes a ray of burning red light, which falls on your own throat centre, conferring the secret initiation, wiping out your sins of speech, enabling you to practise the Anuyoga, and sowing the seed of the *sambhogakāya*. Then at the guru's heart you visualize a deep-blue *hūṃ*, and from it there issues a ray of smoky blue light. This falls on your heart centre, conferring the wisdom initiation, wiping out sins of mind, enabling you to practise the *atiyoga*, the supreme yoga, and sowing the seed of the *dharmakāya*. Finally, from all the guru's centres there issue rays of light which make up a rainbow. This rainbow of light falls on all your centres, conferring the knowledge initiation, wiping away sins of body, speech, and mind together, and sowing the seed of the capacity for sharing in the *svabhāvikakāya*, the self-existent body, the unity of the previous three *kāyas*. At the same time you spontaneously gain the power of experiencing absolute *samādhi*.

Then you see, you feel, the guru descending through the crown of your head, down the central channel, into your heart, and taking his seat there. As the guru descends into your heart, you feel, coming down through your body – or rather through your whole psychophysical organism – a flood of what is called knowledge nectar. You feel as though you have absorbed transcendental wisdom, as though you are becoming filled with nectar, until it fills your whole body, your whole being. As that happens, the guru in your heart is transformed into the light of great bliss, overwhelming ecstasy, and you feel your body, speech, and mind becoming one with the body, speech, and mind of the guru.

In that state you remain as long as you possibly can, and then you conclude with a prayer – with which we shall also conclude this study, or rather this visualization, of the cosmic Refuge Tree and the archetypal guru. With the help of one of my own gurus, I translated this prayer many years ago at a time when I was engaged in some of these practices.[87] It runs as follows:

O my own immediate holy guru, O great jewel abiding within the lotus of my heart, may you never separate from me, but remain inseparable.

Grant me accomplishment of body, speech, and mind.

Throughout all births may I have an excellent guru, and from him never separated, may I practise the holy Dharma and, fully accomplishing the good qualities of the path and the stages, may I speedily attain the Vajradhara state.

From this evil mind of mine quickly liberated, may I speedily become the Guru-Buddha, and may I lead all beings, without exception, to the Guru-Buddha's abode.

O, holy guru, as are your body, length of life, and abode, so also may I be.

5
THE CREMATION GROUND AND THE CELESTIAL MAIDENS

In the West we don't usually regard funerals as being pleasant occasions. Among certain communities they can be quite festive, but in general they are rather dismal affairs. However, in the area of the Himalayas where I used to live, people do not find funerals at all unpleasant. Indeed, during all my years in India, some of my most enjoyable experiences were in connection with them. Of course, when you hear that somebody has died you feel sadness, perhaps shock, even grief, especially if the person was a close friend or relative. But that personal response is quite apart from the public occasion of the funeral, which does not have to be at all mournful or depressing. Indeed, the popular consensus in places like India and Tibet is that cheerfulness is salutary for everyone concerned. By the time the funeral takes place, two or three days or even a week after the death, even those who have lost someone near and dear to them have usually got over the worst of their grief. Drying their tears and recovering from the initial shock, they begin to accept the fact that their loved one is dead. By the time of the funeral, the atmosphere is often one of solemnity tinged with a strange kind of exhilaration, even joy. The deceased person usually lies in state in their own home for a couple of days, and all their friends, relations, well-wishers, acquaintances, and colleagues come to pay their last respects with a garland of flowers or a ceremonial white scarf. But at last all that is over, and the funeral procession is ready to leave the house. Four, or perhaps eight, men raise the body onto their shoulders on a bier and carry it forth, feet foremost, from the house. The face is usually left uncovered; we might consider it indecent for a dead body to be carried through the streets like that, but in India it is accepted as perfectly right and natural.

Accompanied from the house usually only by the menfolk, the dead body is slowly borne through the town or village. As the funeral procession moves through the streets, the word spreads, and people come out from the shops and houses to see who is being carried to the cremation ground. The ground itself is usually situated on the outskirts of the village, or even some distance away, often at a beautiful spot on the bank of a river. It is, of course, a quiet place. It is remote, and in any case people don't usually go there, so it has a solitary feel. Even during the day, even when the sun is shining, especially if you go there on your own, the cremation ground has a strange atmosphere – a quivering, a vibration in the air that you can almost see. It is alive in a way that other places do not seem to be. As you look around, you see here and there little heaps of charred wood, left over from funeral pyres. If you look more closely, you may even see part of a skull, or a thigh bone, or a finger bone. And if you happen to visit late in the day, when the shades of night are falling, you may see the shadowy, slinking figure of a jackal, who may look at you with glowing green eyes and then disappear with a short bark.

To this place the body is brought to be committed to the flames. First of all the pyre has to be built, and this is usually done by the people of the funeral party themselves, using logs they have brought along, or purchasing them on the spot from a vendor. They dig a trench and put great stones on either side, then they lay the logs across the trench, and place more logs in the opposite direction, leaving plenty of room in between for the air to circulate. Upon these criss-crossed logs they place the corpse itself, having removed most of the clothing. On top of it are placed some lighter pieces of wood, and finally the whole pyre is sprinkled with ghee (clarified butter), if the money can be found for it, or with oil, or – nowadays – with tins of kerosene.

If there is a priest present – a brahmin, a lama, or some such officiant – mantras are chanted and prayers are recited. Then the next of kin, usually a son or a brother, takes a torch and lights the funeral pyre. Within minutes, especially if there is a good wind, the pyre is burning merrily, sending up showers of sparks into the heavens. When the cremation is well under way – when the pyre is blazing and the body is a molten mass, bright and glowing – everybody starts to relax. They start talking – talking, of course, about the deceased, about his loveable characteristics and his little foibles; then they start swapping stories about him – something he said or did, a scrape he once got into, some little adventure that someone had with him years ago. Talking about him in this way, they generate a friendly, cheerful atmosphere, with plenty of goodwill towards the dear departed.

Then cups of tea start circulating – a vendor appears, as if by magic, proffering a teapot and little cups – and everybody starts drinking tea and eating biscuits. In some circles, they circulate something rather stronger than tea. Before you know what has happened, everybody is having a thoroughly good time, without the slightest feeling of anything being out of place, or any sense of guilt or impropriety. After all, to die and be cremated is just as natural and inevitable as to be born. Life and death, so people feel at such times, are both to be accepted, and ultimately to be reconciled. They are two sides of the same coin. Not that such people will be likely to think such thoughts at the time, if they ever do – they may not be very philosophical or metaphysically inclined – but this is what they feel, inarticulately, when they are enjoying themselves after a cremation. It's all part of life. You've got to accept it cheerfully, or at least tranquilly. There's no time or place for grief, or at least not much time and not many places.

The talk goes on for an hour or two, and eventually the fire starts dying down, and the cremation is nearly over. Once people have satisfied themselves that the corpse is going to be completely consumed, they leave it smouldering and go home. Even for those who have just witnessed the cremation of someone near and dear to them, it has been on the whole a not unpleasant experience, even a rewarding and uplifting one.

Thus the cremation ground has deep and positive significance for Indian culture. But what further significance might it have as a symbol? What does the cremation ground symbolize in the Tantra? And what might the celestial maidens of the chapter title – by which I mean *ḍākinīs* – be doing there? To understand this, we have to go back to the sources of the Tantric tradition, the Nyingma tradition in particular, back to the legendary life – the symbolic biography – of Padmasambhava, the Tantric guru of India and Tibet.

This great teacher of the eighth century CE had a chequered career, to say the least. He began life as the adopted son of a king, was brought up as a prince, got married but left his wife, became a monk, studied all forms of Buddhism, practised meditation extensively, especially Tantric meditation of various kinds, travelled widely, even outside India, and eventually became Enlightened. He was known throughout India and Tibet and beyond as the greatest master of the Tantra of his day, and he is credited with driving out the demons opposed to the Dharma and establishing Buddhism in Tibet. A brief résumé cannot do justice to the wealth of incident narrated in his biography. But the episode we are concerned with here is the period of his career, while he was still treading the Tantric path in quest of Enlightenment, when he spent a great deal of his time in cremation grounds in different parts of India. According to the rumours that circulated at that time, he lived there with the *ḍākinīs*, singing, dancing, and drinking wine.

Whether these stories are to be taken as historical fact or as legend is difficult to tell. In the biographies of Padmasambhava that have come down to us, historical fact and symbolic statement seem to shade into each other.[88] Sometimes it is quite clear whether something is fact, or whether it is meant symbolically, but sometimes it could be either, or both. And perhaps the stories of Padmasambhava in the cremation ground are of this latter kind, to be taken as historical fact, but also as possessing symbolic meaning. What is not in doubt is that the picture of Padmasambhava in the cremation ground, surrounded by the celestial maidens, captured the imagination of later generations of Tantric devotees. With the passing of time it became richer and richer in spiritual content, and the symbolism of the cremation ground and the celestial maidens assumed greater and greater significance.

The associations of the cremation ground are fairly obvious. The one that springs most readily to mind is, of course, death. Even thinking of the cremation ground stimulates thoughts of death, and when you visit one and look around, you can't help thinking of all the people who have been cremated there in the course of many years – even hundreds of years, if it's an old site. If you are very quiet, especially if you are on your own, you can sometimes almost feel them there, as if they have left some trace in the psychic atmosphere, as if you can actually feel the presence of those numberless dead people pressing round. In such a place, you can't help reflecting in a sober and serious way that everyone will die one day – including yourself. You can't help realizing that one day your own body will be carried to the cremation ground and burned there, and that you will have to leave behind possessions, relations, and friends for ever. Little by little your own physical body will be consumed, will disintegrate and sink into ashes.

Reflections of this sort were systematically cultivated in Early Buddhism. The serious disciple was advised to go, on his own, to the charnel ground, where people's bodies were left to rot, or to become carrion for wild beasts (rather than being burned, for in the Buddha's day cremation was not widespread). The disciple would see lying all around him not the remains of cremated bodies but bodies in various stages of decomposition. He was urged not to shrink or shudder, not to turn away, but to look at them, even study them, and apply the lesson to himself, to tell himself that his own body was equally liable to decay.

As this practice became more systematized, meditation teachers started distinguishing ten stages in the decomposition of a corpse. The disciple was asked to look at and reflect on each stage in turn, and tell himself, convince himself, that one day his own body would pass through that very same process. The practice was known as the meditation on the ten stages of impurity of a corpse. (The word for impurity in Pāli is *asubha*, which also means loathsome, disgusting, and unbeautiful.) The practice of this corpse meditation led, it was said, to detachment, especially detachment from the body, and provided an antidote to the craving for sense experience.[89]

It is worth enumerating the ten kinds of corpse the practice involves, just to give an idea of what the early Buddhists were up against, how seriously they took their spiritual life, and how radical, even drastic, they were in their practice. The first kind of corpse you would look out for would be a swollen and bloated one – because a few days after death, the gases produced inside a corpse make it start to swell. Secondly, you would seek out a discoloured corpse, one that has become a blueish green colour. The third stage is when the corpse begins to fester and liquescent matter starts to flow from its apertures, the unpleasantness of which I can confirm personally, having gone as far as observing this stage myself. Then fourthly, you look for a fissured corpse, one that is split, perhaps even split in two; and fifthly, a mangled corpse, a corpse torn by dogs and jackals. Sixthly, you might come across a dismembered corpse, the limbs of which are scattered in all directions; and seventhly, a corpse cut up into small pieces, presumably for disposal. Eighthly, you are directed to seek out a blood-smeared corpse, or one streaming with blood; and ninthly, a corpse infested with thousands of tiny worms. Then, the last stage of all is, of course, the skeleton – just a few bones, all that is left at the end of Death's feast.

This meditation on the ten stages of the decomposition of a corpse is still kept up in some parts of the Buddhist world, especially by monks. It isn't always possible these days, even in India, to find corpses in all the stages of decomposition, but it is generally considered sufficient simply to go to the burning ground or charnel ground and look for a while at the skulls and bones lying there, or at the charred wood of the funeral pyres. If one is sensitive and aware, this will produce the required effect. Sometimes, to aid one in this practice, paintings are made of the ten stages of decomposition – and I remember all too vividly how I discovered this custom. I had been invited to a small vihara, situated on the outskirts of Kalimpong and inhabited by just one old Nepalese monk. The invitation was for lunch, and as I sat eating, I looked round and saw on the walls a series of almost life-sized depictions of the ten kinds of corpse, depicted in the most gruesome and realistic detail.

If you practise this kind of meditation, in the end you start seeing everybody you meet as a walking skeleton. You don't see flesh and blood, you don't see *people*, just skeletons. Eventually you may be rewarded in your meditation with a *nimitta* or sign, of a particular character appropriate to this practice. This appearance of the *nimitta* is an element of many meditation practices. The procedure is that first you concentrate on the external object of meditation – it could be a coloured disc called a *kasiṇa*, to take one example from many, but in this case it is of course the corpse. Next, you close your eyes and try to see or experience the object of your meditation with your inner eye. After a while, there emerges from this 'mental replica' a shining 'counterpart', and you become absorbed in that, an absorption that becomes the nucleus for the states of meditative concentration called *dhyāna*. The sign is not necessarily brilliant – sometimes one is meant to see a smoky sign. And sometimes the sign is not visual at all, but auditory, or even a physical sensation, or a smell. The mind seems to produce these subtle sense experiences as part of the process of becoming more deeply concentrated. In the case of the corpse meditation, you just see bone – white, shining, pure – and that becomes the object of your concentration in the next stage of the practice.

It goes without saying that this type of meditation practice is not suited to everybody. The so-called corpse meditations are traditionally recommended for people of the greed type, the passionate type of person, because if you have always concentrated on the bright, agreeable, pleasant side of human life, you must remind yourself that there is another side. You may be very much attached to someone physically, for example, but if you are going to be truly aware of what you are attached to, you must ask yourself what is going to happen to it in ten, fifteen, thirty, a hundred years' time. The point of cultivating a deeper awareness of the more challenging aspects of human experience is not to take the sparkle out of life, but to help detach yourself from an over-preoccupation with the kind of beauty that is bound up with craving, and thus make yourself free to experience a more refined beauty.

But if you are of the hate type, it might not be good for you to practise these meditations because you already see life as essentially disagreeable, or even disgusting. You will need rather to remind yourself that life, and especially the aspect of life that concerns other people, has a bright side, an agreeable aspect. In such a case, the *mettā bhāvanā*, the development of loving-kindness, will be a more suitable meditation practice.

Even if you are of the greed type, going out in search of corpses to meditate on is not necessarily the best approach. If you are so greedy by temperament that you are completely obsessed with material things and with other people on the purely physical level, then a visit to the cemetery, or a burning ground if you could find one, might be salutary (though with such a temperament you would be unlikely to go out of choice). But if you aren't of that extreme type, you can reflect upon death or even just upon impermanence. It will not have the kind of dramatic effect that trying to force oneself into an awareness of death may have. However, simply taking note of certain objective facts about existence is crucial to the process of growing up, of maturing in a truly human way. If you apply what you understand and experience to yourself, you will gradually deepen that awareness of impermanence to allow real insight to emerge.

Merely taking in one's natural surroundings can help with this exercise. It is easier in the countryside than in the city, but even in the city you can see impermanence as an immediate reality. When I lived in the East End of London there was a tree outside my window which I used to enjoy looking at, noticing its annual flourishing and withering: in the spring covered in blossom, in the summer in full leaf, and in the winter with no leaves at all. Even where there is no turning of the seasons to observe, one can still catch striking glimpses of the same reality. When I visited New Zealand, for example, although the native bush was virtually all evergreen, in the midst of the green I noticed skeletons of trees, bleached white by the sun. That was quite odd, a real memento mori, a skeleton at the feast. It was as if you were to go down to a beach full of healthy, bronzed people sunbathing and see at intervals human skeletons, bleached white, reclining among the sunbathers.

The Romans allegedly had skeletons at their feasts, dressed up with garlands of roses, to remind them that the feasting was going to end one day, for everybody. To us this would no doubt seem an unnecessarily morbid addition to our guest list. We don't even keep flowers in our rooms once the petals have begun to fall. But if you live in the countryside, you cannot pick and choose from its seasons, and that does give you a sense of the evanescence of things, if you are observant. You can also nourish this sense with the arts: reflections on transitoriness are of course the constant theme of both English nature poetry, and Chinese and Japanese Zen Buddhist poetry.

In all these different ways one may deepen one's awareness of one's own existence, becoming more alert to the shortness of one's life, and learning to see things more constantly from this truer perspective. Nor is such a perspective at all negative – rather the opposite. As you start recognizing the impermanence of things, you realize that change is not just about decay and deterioration – things can also change for the better. Indeed, you can *make* them change for the better, so that change becomes not just change but transformation. This is symbolized by the Hindu figure of the dancing Shiva: although Shiva is apparently a violent, destructive figure, the symbolism is essentially positive because it represents the potential for transformation. Likewise, in Buddhist tradition, the bodhisattva Avalokiteśvara who appears in all the six realms of existence of the wheel of life reminds us that the possibility of transformation exists in every one of those realms.

Facing up to impermanence before old age forces us to do so helps us to make the most of life. Whereas many people start to take full advantage of life only when they get older and a bit wiser, if you are fortunate enough still to have youth on your side, you can reflect, while you are still young, 'Here I am, alive, and with luck I will live for a few more years. In that time, I can really do something with my life, make it something worthwhile, so that at the end of it I can look back and think, "Well, I have had a wonderful opportunity, and thank heaven I have been able to take advantage of it."'

The corpse meditation is therefore only the most hair-raising way of contemplating impermanence. There are many other practices concerned with the same basic theme and purpose that are better suited to most people's spiritual needs. It is said that one should do the corpse meditation in the full manner only if one has strong nerves – and indeed one should approach any version of the practice with caution and seriousness and a firm foundation of mindfulness and *mettā* – especially *mettā* towards oneself.

If the first association of the cremation ground is death and impermanence, following hard upon its heels comes the most immediate emotional association: fear and terror. As I mentioned, cremation grounds are lonely places, situated on the outskirts of the town or some distance away, on the edge of the forest or by the side of the river. All sorts of superstitions about the cremation ground circulate among the local people – stories of people who saw ghosts there, or said they saw them, or heard voices, or felt strange uncanny sensations. And as with some isolated country churchyards in England, no one likes to go there on their own, especially at night, or even to pass very near, except when it is broad daylight and they are in the company of a crowd of other people on the occasion of a funeral.

However, according to the Tantric tradition, if what you wanted was not to give in to your fear but to overcome it and become completely fearless, you would make a point of going to the cremation ground precisely because that is what everybody is afraid of. You would go there at night, preferably when there was no moon and it was completely dark, and you would go alone. In India to this day, yogis do just this. They not only go to the cremation ground; sometimes they live there, for days, weeks, or months on end. In order to overcome fear they force themselves into the very situation in which fear is most likely to arise. They deliberately induce the fear, and allow themselves to experience it fully – even making it familiar, like a constant companion. And because they face it, they can deal with it, and overcome it.

Fearlessness is not a Buddhist virtue we hear much about, but it figures prominently in the scriptures, and the Buddha himself is often depicted making what is called the *abhaya mudrā*, the gesture of fearlessness. This gesture – hand held up at the level of the heart, palm facing outwards – says, 'Fear not; don't be afraid.' Bodhisattvas too are regarded as embodiments of fearlessness. The Mahāyāna tradition insists that they should have confidence, courage, enterprise, and a spirit of adventure, that they should be firm of heart. In fact, in all forms of Buddhism, great importance is attached to the heroic virtues: courage, self-confidence, self-reliance, energy, initiative. This is not always realized – not in the West, anyway. We tend to think of the spiritual life primarily in terms of the more passive, so-called feminine virtues: love, compassion, patience, sympathy, tolerance, gentleness. But according to Buddhist tradition, the heroic virtues are no less important – even, in some ways, more important. And the cremation ground came to be regarded as the training ground for fearlessness, a centre for the development of a heroic spiritual attitude.

The extent to which people fear death seems to be determined by a combination of imagination and cultural conditioning. In Holbein's engravings of the Dance of Death, for example, one can see the way death was commonly envisaged in late medieval Christianity – as a skeleton, dancing with all sorts of people, with a young woman, a rich merchant, a monk, the pope.[90] The message was clear: everybody would die, and death was a horrible thing. Dying meant being embraced, clutched, by this horrible, grisly, leering, repulsive figure. Death was like going to bed with a skeleton. This was how it was seen in the popular imagination. But this was a time when, according to official theology, if you had been a good Christian you went straight to heaven. Why should death have been so terrible? Why should people be so afraid of it? In fact, this fearful vision was apparently conjured up by the Church to concentrate people's minds on the uncertain end in store for their souls by reminding them of the certain fate of their physical bodies.

By contrast, in classical Greek imagery death was represented as a beautiful winged youth, suggesting that the Greeks accepted death much more easily and naturally. For them it was a falling asleep. They didn't expect great things afterwards; there was a vague conception of heaven called Elysium for a few, and a dim and ghostly post-mortem existence for the majority. They certainly preferred life to death, but they didn't have the macabre vision of death that Christians had developed by the late medieval period.

Not only do you face fear in the cremation ground. There is also loneliness. You are there at night, with death, with fear, on your own, isolated, and your loneliness seems to foreshadow the loneliness of the grave. And then you come face to face with the possibility of insanity too. Sometimes you may feel as though your reason is breaking down, that you can't stand it any more, you're cracking up. You have to come to terms with that possibility. In the cremation ground you can take nothing for granted – not even your reason – for in the cremation ground you finally come face to face with yourself, with your weaknesses and your strengths, with who and what you are – and this is never a comfortable thing for the mind.

Moreover, the cremation ground is a place you choose to enter. You don't wait for death to come to you, for the corpse to pass by in the street outside. You go looking for death, you go seeking out fear. You court them, invite them: 'Come on, do your worst, I'm ready.' So the cremation ground represents a crucial situation, a situation of crisis into which you deliberately plunge yourself, and in which you are compelled to change, in which you must develop or die. In short, it is the place where you deliberately seek out whatever other people avoid – indeed, whatever you yourself want to avoid. The cremation ground is therefore a symbol of transformation – the transformation of your whole being from the depths to the heights, the transformation of every aspect of your consciousness.

Of course, there is no need to go off to India and start seeking out cremation grounds to provoke crucial situations. It is quite important to recognize the principle here and not be misled, even while one may be inspired, by the Tantra's colourful realizations of the principle. Yes, you can quite literally experience the cremation ground, if not the celestial maidens. But you can experience your own cremation grounds in the course of your ordinary life – when an important deal falls through at the last minute, or when you suddenly have to go into hospital, or when someone dies.

The Tantric cremation ground is essentially an inner experience. Being alone, for example, is not in itself a crucial situation. Fear may arise when you are alone, but this may be because you do not have company to distract you from the fear that is always there. In other circumstances it may be the very presence of someone else that gives rise to the crucial situation, as in the case of hatred or jealousy. Jealousy, especially sexual jealousy, is one of the most powerful emotions, and it comes up, or threatens to come up, particularly within the context of sexual relationships. The emotion can be so powerful that you feel like murdering the person you supposedly love, not to mention the person who seems to be taking them from you. But when the feeling of jealousy arises, you should say to yourself: 'Aha! This is the crucial situation. I am approaching the cremation ground, the place where my ego could die.' Jealousy, based as it is on projection and possessiveness, is a powerful assertion of the ego. It is a very unpleasant emotion – in some ways more unpleasant than fear, because it threatens another person, or even more than one. It can provoke murder just as much as intense fear can. But even jealousy can be transformed if you see it for what it is. We will come back to this later.

Another example of a common crucial situation is that presented by a lack of self-confidence. Here again, it is not so much the lack of confidence itself, nor the objective situation calling for confidence – like, for example, speaking in public – that is the crucial situation. The crucial situation is when you are forced to confront your lack of self-confidence. You may have always avoided giving a public talk, but then for some reason – to respond to a need, or to challenge yourself – you agree to give one, against what may seem to be your better judgement. When the day comes you are quite likely to think, 'Oh no, I just can't go through with this.' You can then either conveniently 'fall ill', or face up to the fact that your self-image was an illusion. *That* is the crucial situation. If you can confront your fear of failure and take the risk of going on to give the talk, that is a further cremation ground.

The cremation ground as a symbol of transformation is elaborated in what are known as the eight great cremation grounds. All over India there are cremation grounds – every village has one, and every town has two or three – so there are tens of thousands of cremation grounds up and down the length and breadth of the country. Where there are human beings, there is death, and where there is death, there is a cremation ground. But in Indian tradition, out of all these cremation grounds there were eight that were especially renowned as places where yogis and *ḍākinīs* regularly gathered, and where initiations were given at night in darkness and secrecy.

These eight great cremation grounds often appear in the mandalas of the Tibetan Buddhist tradition. If you look at almost any mandala, you will see that it is surrounded by a halo of flames. Within the flames is a circle – or, if you look at it three-dimensionally, a wall – of *vajras*. Within the *vajras* is a circle of lotus flowers, and – sometimes within the lotuses and sometimes outside the flames – are the eight great cremation grounds: one at each of the four cardinal points, and one at each of the four intermediate points. They are depicted very vividly, usually with lots of skulls, bones, corpses, and burning funeral pyres. Against this macabre background you see the yogis and *ḍākinīs* meditating, dancing, embracing, and drinking.

The fact that there are cremation grounds in all the eight directions of space is significant. It suggests that there are cremation grounds everywhere, that the whole earth is in fact one vast cremation ground, that the universe in its entirety, all of conditioned existence, is a cremation ground. It's a place where we are confronted by death and fear, where we have to evolve or perish. The symbolism is telling us that life itself – death in life, life in death – is the crucial situation, a situation into which we thrust ourselves when we take birth as a human being.

Beyond this, the eight great cremation grounds also have a more precise meaning. They represent the transformation not just of consciousness or *vijñāna* in general, but specifically of the eight consciousnesses that are enumerated as the basis of their teaching by the Yogācāra school of Mahāyāna Buddhism. The first five of these eight consciousnesses are simply the five senses: consciousness, or discriminating awareness (to translate *vijñāna* more directly), through the eye, of form and colour; through the ear, of sound; through the nose, of smell; through the tongue, of taste; and through touch, of heat, cold, hardness, and softness. Sixthly, there is mind-consciousness – discriminative awareness, through the mind, of ideas. In Buddhism the mind is usually regarded as a sixth sense along with the other five; it isn't given a special position. Seventhly, there is the 'defiled mind consciousness' – that is, the mind consciousness defiled by a dualistic outlook. The defiled mind consciousness interprets experience in terms of a subject and an object, an external world out there and an ego-self in here; the defilement consists in this erroneous interpretation. And eighthly, there is the 'store consciousness', which has two aspects – relative and absolute. The relative aspect of the store consciousness

consists of the impressions left by all our past experiences, not only in this life but in previous lives. It is called store consciousness because it represents the level of mind at which all these impressions are stored up – something like Jung's collective unconscious. The store consciousness in its absolute aspect is reality itself, pure awareness – no subject or object, but One Mind.[91]

The Yogācāra school, like the Tantra, is concerned primarily with direct spiritual experience, and especially with the experience that it calls the 'turning about', the *parāvṛtti*. This turning about or turning around is an overwhelming experience that takes place in the very depths of one's being, at the level of the store consciousness. As a result, one's whole being – the whole system of consciousness – is changed, turned around, turned upside down, transformed.

What the eight consciousnesses are transformed into is of course very difficult to put into words. The short answer is: they are transformed into wisdom – more specifically, into the five wisdoms or knowledges (the Sanskrit word is *jñāna*) associated with the five Buddhas. The five sense consciousnesses are collectively transformed into the all-performing wisdom of Amoghasiddhi, the green Buddha. Mind consciousness is transformed into distinguishing wisdom, the wisdom of Amitābha, the red Buddha. Defiled mind consciousness is transformed into the wisdom of equality, the wisdom of Ratnasambhava, the yellow Buddha. Relative store consciousness is transformed into the mirror-like wisdom of Akṣobhya, the dark blue Buddha. As for the absolute store consciousness, this, of course, is not transformed at all – it doesn't need to be. It corresponds to absolute wisdom, the wisdom of Vairocana, the central Buddha, the white Buddha. This transformation is an important symbolic association of the eight great cremation grounds.

Thus there are many aspects to the symbolism of the cremation ground, and they are all connected. The cremation ground stands for death, for fear, and for fearlessness – in fact, for all the heroic emotions. It is your spiritual centre, the place where heroic emotions are cultivated. It is the deliberately sought out crucial situation. It is the world itself, as the theatre of death and destruction, the arena for spiritual development. And it symbolizes the process of radical transformation that we call the spiritual life – a transformation which, as the Tantra insists again and again, comes about only as a result of direct experience.

Against the background of the cremation ground, there rises a mysterious figure: the *ḍākinī*, the celestial maiden. The words *ḍāka* and *ḍākinī* are derived from a Sanskrit root meaning direction, space, sky, and when Tantric texts were translated into Tibetan, *ḍākinī* was rendered as *khadroma*, which is usually translated 'sky-walker' or 'traveller in space'. As we have already seen, empty space represents absence of obstruction and therefore freedom of movement. If space is absolutely empty, you can move freely in it, in any direction. So the *ḍākinī* or *ḍāka* symbolizes complete freedom of movement. This is not, of course, literal movement within space. Space or sky also represents mind in its absolute aspect; so the *ḍākinīs* represent the free-moving energies of the mind itself – they are the thrills or tremors of emotional energy that pass quivering through the mind, bubbling up from its very depths.

In developed Tantric Buddhism, especially in its Tibetan form, there are said to be three kinds of *ḍākinī*, representing three levels on which the *ḍākinī* principle, as we may call it, is experienced. First, there is the *ḍākinī* as female Buddha form. In Early Buddhism, the Enlightenment principle, Buddhahood, was usually represented in the form of a perfect human body sitting cross-legged as though in meditation – and the body was usually male. But there is no reason why it should be male rather than female, and in the case of the *ḍākinī* as female Buddha, it happens to be female. We will go further into this in our final chapter, in the context of considering the symbolism of the five Buddhas, male and female. Secondly, the *ḍākinī* is the embodiment of one's own upsurging energies. This is the kind of *ḍākinī* with which we are mainly concerned here. And thirdly, the *ḍākinī* can be seen as a spiritual companion, and as representing, as we saw in the previous chapter, the esoteric Tantric form of the third refuge – the refuge in the Sangha.

The *ḍākinī* in this sense, as encountered in, for example, *The Life and Liberation of Padmasambhava*, is a highly advanced female spiritual practitioner in association with whom a male practitioner practises the Dharma and whose company is spiritually inspiring. She has a highly developed moral awareness, though not in a conventional sense. *Ḍākinīs* are usually described as being youthful and extremely beautiful, as well as having intense faith and devotion, and being pure-minded and given to meditation. As such, they are not at all common.

In considering the second of these versions of the *ḍākinī*, which is our theme here, we must remind ourselves that the Tantra is concerned above all with the direct experience of what one really and truly is in the depth of one's being, and with the direct experience of what we can only call reality, if we have to find a word for it at all. To achieve this experience of oneself, and of reality, requires a tremendous, almost explosive, charge of energy, and it remains beyond us so long as our energies are unavailable to us, scattered, dissipated, submerged, allowed to leak and drain away. If we are to experience ourselves fully, all these energies will have to be gathered together, conjured up from the depths, merged into a single stream. And these energies are symbolized by the *ḍākinīs*.

Padmasambhava is described in *The Life and Liberation of Padmasambhava* as teaching the *ḍākinīs*, and at the level of meaning we are concerned with here, it is clearly his own high-level energies he is educating.[92] In our own case, we could say that the *ḍākinīs* represent the more passionate side of our nature, all our more powerful emotions, including negative emotions, which are potentially helpful inasmuch as all of them express a charge of energy which can be turned in a different direction and made helpful to the spiritual life. Teaching the *ḍākinīs* means bringing those energies under control one way or another, sometimes gently, sometimes roughly – not just holding down, but guiding, directing, integrating – and there are many ways of doing that. It is also a question of freeing one's energies. If you are going to teach the *ḍākinīs*, you have to find them first. If we don't have the sense of being surrounded by our energies – and most of us don't, except perhaps in dreams – maybe they are all hiding in the cellar, and need to be cajoled out.

Another way of describing *ḍākinīs* might be in terms of moods. Everyone has moods, of course, some positive, and some negative. Jung's view was that in the case of a man, a mood is his anima troubling him. If you find yourself in an argumentative mood, or a dull mood, or a depressed mood, or a cheerful mood – and of course moods change, sometimes quite fast – according to Jung it is the work of your anima. From this conception it is a small step to viewing these moods as *ḍākinīs* that need to be brought under control. In the case of a woman, again according to Jung, she is more likely sometimes to be possessed by ideas – she just gets ideas in her head which she hasn't thought about, but which she has picked up somehow and which take possession of her. For Jung this is the expression of her unintegrated animus.[93]

The first thing to do if you are going to deal with a mood is to recognize it *as* a mood, recognize that there is a *ḍākinī* lurking in the shadows who needs to be brought out and trained. If you start feeling jealous, to return to that example, you could say to yourself, 'Aha! Here's the green *ḍākinī* appearing. She needs to be tamed, to be made more genuinely *ḍākinī*-like, more like a bodhisattva.' However, it is one thing to know you need to bring her under control; actually to do so requires a deeper realization. You have to ask yourself, 'Why am I jealous? What does it mean to be jealous?' Suppose you are jealous because your lover is going out with somebody else and neglecting you. You have to say to yourself, 'Look, this is just possessiveness. Does she (or he) belong to me? Is she my slave or my exclusive property? If someone else goes out with her and enjoys her company, do I lose anything? She may come back cheerful and happy, all the more ready to enjoy my company. Am

I going to meet her with a gloomy face and reproach her for having spent time with someone else?'

Of course, you won't succeed first time, but you should continue to talk to your jealousy *ḍākinī* in this way. You could say to yourself, 'Suppose I didn't know she had been seeing somebody else. I wouldn't be worried then, I wouldn't be conscious of having lost anything – especially if she was just as friendly to me as before. Why should it make any difference when I know about it? It seems so absurd to be jealous.' Even if you do actually lose your lover, that is all the more reason to look for the *ḍākinī* in the situation. Consoling yourself with mundane reflections like 'there's plenty more fish in the sea than ever came out of it' might perhaps be unhelpful from a spiritual point of view. But you can reflect, 'She is also a human being. Surely I wish that she should be well and happy. If she is happier with somebody else than she is with me, that's fine. I can just let her go with my best wishes.'

If reasoning with yourself in this way is difficult, you again need to grasp the opportunity that only painful experiences like this can provide to see your own possessiveness, see that you have invested part of yourself in that other person. That is why the situation is so painful. It is not as though your lover is just taking herself away; she is taking you with her, and that is your fault, because you have invested part of yourself in her. Of course, ideally, you would see that investment, that projection, and withdraw it before suffering the consequences. But perhaps if she had never had that affair with somebody else, you would never have had that insight, so you should be grateful to her. (Of course, the more usual response is much less positive than that, to say the least.)

This should not be merely an intellectual exercise. You have to find some link between your understanding and those powerful, potentially destructive, emotional forces. To start with, you have to let yourself just feel the emotion. It's no good saying to yourself, 'I'm not jealous. I'm a civilized human being.' It's a question of coaxing that green *ḍākinī* – or whichever of the other *ḍākinīs* that are liable to crop up in one's psyche from time to time – into line by setting up a dialogue with her. The symbolism of the *ḍākinī* thus offers a way of integrating one's unconscious contents by personalizing them and conducting a dialogue with that personalized form. I had this kind of experience myself once. I used to have dreams in which a very angry woman was telephoning me. I eventually worked out that this was because I wasn't spending enough time on purely creative work. If I engaged in writing, especially poetry, I didn't get those angry calls, but if my life had become too intellectual, I started getting them again, and it became clear that this was a muse-type figure that was trying to re-establish contact.

To get a real feeling for the *ḍākinī*, we can do no better than encounter one. I propose, therefore, simply to give a description of a particular *ḍākinī* figure, one who occupies an important place in the Tantra as practised in Tibet. We have already encountered her in the context of the *guru yoga*. She is known as Vajrayoginī, and in Tibetan Narokhachö, and also described as Sarvabuddhaḍākinī. *Sarva* means 'all', and *Buddha* of course means 'Enlightened one', so Sarvabuddhaḍākinī is the *ḍākinī* of all the Buddhas, the embodiment of all the energies that have carried all the Buddhas, past, present, and future, to Enlightenment. She is thus a very powerful figure indeed, as her appearance dramatically demonstrates. She is also, in a way, a Buddha figure in her own right.

She is not depicted sitting down meditating. She stands with her legs wide apart, her right leg straight and her left knee bent. She is moving towards the right, with her breasts, which are very full, thrust out, and her head tilted back. Her right arm hangs a little away from her side, while her left arm is raised above her head and bent back, the hand almost touching the head. The whole figure is brilliant red in colour, and completely naked. She wears only a few ornaments – which are of human bone – and an enormous garland of human skulls that hangs down below her knees. She has long dishevelled hair which falls straight down her back to her waist. In her right hand she holds a chopper with a *vajra* handle, while with her left hand she lifts a skull-cup filled with blood to her mouth and drinks it with evident enjoyment. She has what is called a wrathful smile, and three eyes, the extra one being in the middle of her forehead. She wears a crown of five human skulls, and on her left shoulder, lying horizontal and passing behind her upturned head, is a long staff, from the top of which there hangs down a type of small drum, called a *ḍamaru*, and a bell, with streamers. The head of the staff is formed by the vase of initiation, which is surmounted by crossed *vajras*, and, above them, three human heads, one on top of the other: a freshly severed head, a head that was severed some time ago and has begun to dry out and go yellow, and – at the top – a skull, on top of which a *vajra* stands upright. She tramples underfoot two figures, one red, the other black. Each has four arms. Usually the red figure holds a

skull-cup filled with blood and a staff like the *ḍākinī*'s, while the black figure holds a small drum and a curved sword. Each has one pair of hands raised in supplication. And surrounding the naked red figure of the *ḍākinī* is a halo of flames.

I am not going to say what the *ḍākinī* 'means' – the figure makes its own impact. I will just elaborate a little on some aspects of the symbolism, and suggest a few associations. First of all, the *ḍākinī* is red in colour. In Tantric Buddhism, red is the colour of love, passion, and emotional arousal – which, in the case of any *ḍākinī*, is total. Blood suffuses not only her face; her whole body blushes crimson. So the *ḍākinī* represents the state of total emotional involvement in the spiritual life. This is also why her hair is dishevelled. She doesn't care about decorum, about keeping tidy, about what people may think or say. She just abandons herself. Sometimes it is said that the *ḍākinī* throws herself into the spiritual life just as a passionate woman flings herself into the arms of her lover. She represents that spiritual ideal of self-abandonment to the Three Jewels.

Usually people find it very difficult to give themselves in this way, not just to the spiritual life, but to anything. They find it difficult to plunge in, commit themselves, get totally involved, put all their emotions into what they are doing. As a result they don't achieve much in any direction, certainly not in a spiritual one. In many cases people can't give themselves in this way because they are emotionally blocked. They have to learn to loosen up, get their emotions flowing more freely – flowing, ultimately, in the direction of Enlightenment. This is what the red colour of the *ḍākinī* suggests – that in the spiritual life one should not be afraid to feel.

And the *ḍākinī* is naked. She is concerned only with direct experience, reality, truth. She has nothing to hide. She is completely open, completely honest. Nakedness is a prominent feature of Tantric symbolism, to underline the importance in the Tantra of being direct, unveiled, radical. In Tantric art, yogis, *ḍākas*, and *ḍākinīs*, even Buddhas, are often depicted naked, which is entirely scandalous from the point of view of Theravāda Buddhism, or even Zen. The nakedness is, of course, spiritual nakedness, nakedness of one's emotions, of one's being. However, it is not in the spirit of the Tantra to hide behind the idea of symbolism, and sometimes even literal nakedness is not without its significance, and even value.

This reminds me of a famous story about the beat poet Allen Ginsberg. I thought at first that it was just the sort of story that is made up about famous people, so when I met him once I asked him whether it was true. He said it was, and proceeded to give me his own version. He had been reading some of his poems at a big public meeting in California, and after the reading he was talking and answering questions. As he was speaking, every now and then he used the expression 'the naked truth' or 'the naked reality'; he said it quite a number of times. In the end, inevitably, some intellectual asked him: 'Mr Ginsberg, what do you mean by the naked truth? What do you mean by naked reality?' Ginsberg looked at him, and just didn't know what to say. So, standing up there on the platform, he simply stripped off all his clothes and said: 'That's what I mean by the naked truth.'[94] This is using nakedness as shock therapy, jolting the questioner's mind from the abstract to the concrete – bringing him back to reality.

Not only is the *ḍākinī* naked; she is wearing a garland of human skulls. Each skull represents a dead body – no skull without a body – and each body, which was once alive, represents a life. One way of interpreting the garland of skulls is therefore to say that it represents the whole cycle of one's previous lives – and the *ḍākinī* is breaking through this cycle. There is a powerful, almost volcanic upsurge of energy, bursting through all previous psychological conditionings, through the vicious circle of self-created and self-induced problems, in which almost all of us live, and leaving them hanging there, like the garland of skulls, dead.

The *ḍākinī* also wears delicately carved ornaments of human bone. Bones, of course, figure rather a lot in the Tantra. Tantric practitioners make great use of objects made of human bone: trumpets made of thigh bones, rosaries made of little discs of human bone, drums covered with human skin, and skull-cups. The reason for all this is obvious enough: bones suggest death – which is why most people are unhappy about handling them, especially human bones. The Tantra wants us to confront our distaste, to familiarize ourselves with death and overcome our fear of it. So it encourages us to familiarize ourselves with bones – to handle them, use objects made of them, especially in Tantric ritual, wear ornaments of bone, and drink from skull-cups.

The *ḍākinīs* are not all as attractive and fascinating as Sarvabuddhaḍākinī, by any means. There are *ḍākinīs* with the faces of lions.

You get descriptions of headless *ḍākinīs* carrying their bleeding heads under their arms, and *ḍākinīs* cutting open their own bellies. What are we to make of these strange figures? We will go into the apparently bloodthirsty aspects of *ḍākinīs* a little in the next chapter. As for the animal-headed ones, these are no doubt figures from indigenous mythology, representing primitive animal energies. They came to be associated with the higher Tantra because the higher the realization, the deeper the energy that has to be transformed. The one shown here is Siṁhamukta, the *ḍākinī* form of Padmasambhava.

These *ḍākinīs* remind me of the animal-headed deities of ancient Egypt, whose impressive images are still to be seen in the British Museum. What is notable about such figures is that they seem to have definite personalities. The Egyptian lion-headed goddess Sekhmet sits on a throne and looks noble and majestic, with no suggestion of animality in the ordinary sense. It's the same with the Sphinx, who is the other way round – human head and lion's body; you get the sense that you could really believe in these figures. In ancient days human beings did not always regard animals as inferior. In evolutionary terms they are, but in those days people knew nothing about evolution, of course. They didn't know that they themselves had developed from animals. Animals were just different from humans – more powerful, or more beautiful, or swifter. There was no reason to regard humans as being superior. Ancient men and women could therefore see divinity in an animal form just as easily as the ancient Greeks saw it in the human form, and they could combine the human and the animal without the sense of incongruity that we might experience. Often the animal represented something other, something numinous. This sort of symbolic hybrid might be something of a culture shock for us initially, although there is a little of it in Christian symbolism, which sometimes represents the Evangelists in semi-animal, semi-human form, for example. But it is possible, with a little effort of the imagination, to get used to seeing such figures as the ancient Egyptians saw them.

The wrathful type of *ḍākinī* figure seems to have a special appeal for some Buddhist women in the West. Perhaps this is a response to feeling that their energies are repressed. A lot of women quite rightly also object to the traditional classification of women as either Eve or the Virgin Mary. The *ḍākinī* figure could represent an attempt to find something very different from either. But also, women do often feel

that they suffer from a lack of positive spiritual role models, and it is here – as an idealized role model or Buddha, rather than as an idealized embodiment of one's own energies – that the appeal of the *ḍākinī* seems to lie. It is certainly understandable that it might be difficult for some women to identify with a masculine Buddha figure, and that the figure of a *ḍākinī*, or of the bodhisattva Tārā, might be more appealing to them.

The extra appeal of the *ḍākinī* to women is of course that she seems to embody qualities not commonly associated in a positive sense with women. It is very doubtful, though, whether ecstatic, wrathful wild abandon in the literal sense can be described as a spiritual quality. Nor are we really any closer to the spiritual qualities that it does symbolize than we are to the apparently much more remote and unearthly qualities of the peaceful deities. But if we *feel* that we are, this can be helpful in itself. If the wrathful deities help to put us in touch with primal energies, that is probably a good start, so long as we understand that it is only a start, and that our real task is to put all that energy into the spiritual life, that is, to direct it skilfully. The danger is that we will summon up a lot of wild energy and then not be able to direct it.

As well as having their separate symbolism, the cremation ground and the celestial maidens carry a further symbolic meaning in conjunction with each other. The two symbols are at first glance very different – one is rather terrifying, the other rather attractive, not to say fascinating – but they are closely associated. The connection between them can be summarized by a single iconographic detail: the skull-cup that the *ḍākinī* holds, and the blood she drinks from it with such relish. This epitomizes the whole symbolism of the cremation ground and the celestial maidens: the cup carries with it all the associations of the cremation ground, while the blood encapsulates all the associations of the *ḍākinī*. The skull-cup represents death, reality, the void – that is, the spiritual death of the ego – while the blood represents the great bliss that arises in the heart of the Tantric practitioner when he or she plunges into the void, meets spiritual death, and experiences reality.

The *ḍākinīs* frequent the cremation ground: that is where they sing and dance with Padmasambhava, or with any yogi who cares to go there. But why the cremation ground? Why couldn't they go to some beautiful garden and dance and sing there? As we saw, the cremation ground is the crucial situation deliberately sought out, and the *ḍākinīs* are the energies that arise once you are within the crucial situation. They can arise, in fact, nowhere else. This symbolism bears an important implication: it suggests, in simple terms, that we are capable of far more than we usually think. Rather than finding the energy and then using it to do the job, we can take up the job knowing that the energy will come. We can plunge into the crucial situation, knowing that the emotional response, the upsurge of energy from deep within us, will be there when it is needed. We can take our seat in the cremation ground knowing that the *ḍākinīs* will gather round. It requires tremendous courage and confidence, but it is what Padmasambhava had to do, and did, what every Tantric yogi has to do, whether literally or symbolically. The follower of the Tantric path to Enlightenment lives in the cremation ground with the *ḍākinīs*, with everything that such a situation implies. From the Tantric point of view, this is the essence of the spiritual life.

Hence the popularity in Tantric art of the scene of Padmasambhava living in the cremation ground with the *ḍākinīs*. When he is depicted in this context, it is not in his most familiar guise, wearing his robes, his lotus cap, and so on. He is depicted in what is called his *heruka* form – as a naked yogi, seated on a carpet of human skin or a pile of human bones. On all sides there are dead bodies and blazing funeral pyres. In one hand he rattles a small drum, the symbol of fearlessness, and with the other he drinks wine from a skull-cup, symbol of the great bliss. All around him are the *ḍākinīs*, some dancing, some singing, some flying through the air, some encircled by rainbows, some embracing him. The atmosphere of the place is awe-inspiring and sublime, and the mood of the naked yogi is fearless and heroic. He represents human consciousness itself – human consciousness deliberately seeking out the crucial situation, human consciousness face to face with death, with fear, with reality. He is human consciousness surrounded by its newly awakened energies, aware of its own strength, determined to follow the Tantric path, determined to gain Enlightenment.

6
OFFERINGS AND SELF-SACRIFICE

The setting is India, 2,500 years ago: cloudless blue skies, vast tracts of jungle, and little paths threading their way through the trees. Into this scene enters the Buddha, walking along the jungle paths from village to village, sometimes even venturing into the towns, and lodging on their outskirts. As he goes from place to place – on foot, of course – from time to time the Buddha meets some fellow traveller. Perhaps his path crosses theirs in the depths of the forest, or perhaps he is discovered sitting at the foot of a great banyan tree with vast overspreading branches, or at the door of a palm-leaf hut, or the mouth of a cave. As he sits there in the cool of the evening, we see someone coming to see him – or perhaps someone just happening to pass by whose attention is arrested by the sight of the Buddha sitting there calmly, peacefully, radiantly.

However it happens, there is a meeting. As the ancient Indian custom was, especially among wanderers, and as in fact it still is, friendly greetings are exchanged and polite enquiries about health and well-being are made. Then, formalities having been observed and identities established, some kind of discussion ensues. Eventually, when he finds the other person attuned and ready, the Buddha starts talking about the Dharma. What he talks about isn't just a ready-made idea, or concept, or philosophy, or view, or doctrine. It isn't even a teaching, strictly speaking. It is nothing other than his own direct experience of Enlightenment and the way leading to that experience.

In order to create a medium of communication, he might speak about the Four Noble Truths, or the Noble Eightfold Path; according to the scriptures, he spoke on these topics very frequently. Alternatively, he might speak about mindfulness, or meditation, or the experience of higher states of consciousness, or even the supernormal faculties that pertain to them. If his listener is particularly receptive, the Buddha might even start speaking about Enlightenment itself.

Depending on the occasion, and the temperament and background of the person to whom he is speaking, the Buddha might speak no more than a very few words. On the other hand he might deliver a discourse lasting for several hours. Occasionally, according to the records, when he was particularly moved, or the topic under discussion was of a particularly solemn nature, or the listener seemed to be extraordinarily receptive, the Buddha would break into verse. Whatever he said, and however he said it, he would be communicating, directly or indirectly, his own experience of reality. He would be communicating what it was that made him what he was, a Buddha. In a sense he would be giving himself. One of the most significant things that can be said about the Buddha's teaching is that it is a communication from one individual to another, from an Enlightened individual to a not yet Enlightened individual, who is nevertheless *potentially* Enlightened. What we call the Buddhist scriptures are just so many records of that communication.

What would be the effect of all this on the listener? He or she might be anyone: a nobleman or a priest, a wealthy merchant or a humble tiller of the soil, someone deeply versed in metaphysical subtleties and abstruse discussions, or someone with no capacity at all for that sort of thing, someone who had spent many years in self-mortification, a pious hermit, a playboy, or a robber. Whoever it was, the Buddha's communication almost always had a powerful effect. The listener would be deeply impressed, often moved, on some occasions completely overwhelmed. Sometimes those who encountered the Buddha are reported as saying that they felt as though a light had been brought into a dark place, or as though something that had been knocked over had been set upright, or as though they had been wandering astray and the path had been pointed out to them.[95] When the Buddha finished speaking, some people would be moved to utter exclamations of wonder and delight, others would burst into tears. People who had something on their minds – some crime or misdemeanour committed in the past – would spontaneously confess it. Some would experience a profound spiritual convulsion, they would feel themselves stirred to their very depths, as though an earthquake had taken place at the very centre of their being. A few might even develop transcendental insight on the spot, having briefly glimpsed reality itself.

As a result of what they had heard from the lips of the Buddha, most people felt that they wanted to commit themselves to the Three Jewels. To use the traditional expression, they would feel that they wanted to go for Refuge. But in the case of some of them, even going for Refuge did not fully express what they felt. The listener, the disciple – in Pāli the word is the same, *sāvaka* – felt something else that needed to be expressed: an intense gratitude, love, and respect towards the Buddha for opening his or her eyes to a whole new world of spiritual experience – opening, that is to say, the spiritual eye, the third eye. Out of this sense that the Buddha had given so much of himself, as much of his own Enlightened being as his interlocutor was able to receive, a common response would be to want to give something to the Buddha, or do something for him.

But what can you give a Buddha? What had the listener to offer? Obviously, nothing spiritual. It would have to be something material: a piece of cloth, or an article of clothing, or – from someone with a bit more imagination – a garland of flowers, or even a single flower. Those who could afford it even offered gardens and parks for use as retreats by the Buddha and his wandering disciples. One wealthy woman, after hearing a particularly edifying discourse, offered what the early translators unhelpfully call her 'parure', which would appear to be something extremely valuable made of jewels. We are not told what the Buddha did with it.[96] But often it happened that at the moment when he or she wanted to give something to the Buddha, the listener had nothing to hand. In that case, he or she would usually invite the Buddha home for a meal the following day. In that very simple, human way, joy and gratitude would be expressed.

Forty-five years separated the Buddha's Enlightenment from what tradition calls the *parinirvāṇa*, the final passing away, the dissociation of the Enlightened consciousness from the physical body. After his *parinirvāṇa*, people continued to feel intense gratitude towards the Buddha. If anything, as the teaching spread, and people found it more and more effective in practice, the gratitude and the desire to express it were greater than ever, even though the Buddha was no longer present in the flesh to receive their offerings. In the century or so after the *parinirvāṇa*, the practice therefore developed of making offerings to the relics of the Buddha, to the ashes and fragments of bone that had been enshrined in stupas, or to the stupas that had been built in memory of the Buddha.

This practice is often referred to as 'stupa worship'. The expression is a little imprecise, because if anyone or anything is being worshipped through making offerings to a stupa, it is the Buddha, and that worship – if we can use that term at all – is one's expression of gratitude for the teaching. At all events, for several hundred years after the *parinirvāṇa*, 'stupa worship' was a prominent feature of Buddhism, and occupied an important place in the religious life of the many people, alongside study and meditation. We know from literary records and archaeological evidence that the stupas during this period were not only worshipped, but also elaborately decorated: festooned with garlands of flowers, and hung with flags, banners, and bells.[97] Eventually they became the focal points of great religious festivals. People would spend years building a magnificent stupa, months decorating it, and then weeks on end celebrating festivals, circumambulating the stupa the whole day, whilst chanting, making offerings of various kinds, and lighting lamps.

Then, after a few hundred years, a crucial change took place. The Buddha image appeared. There is no general agreement among historians as to where the first representation of the Buddha in stone was made, whether in Gāndhāra, Mathura, or even Sri Lanka, because the practice quickly became popular throughout the Buddhist East, and has remained so right up to the present day, to the extent that we can hardly think of Buddhism without bringing the Buddha image to mind. For some people, indeed, the Buddha image *is* Buddhism.

The introduction of the Buddha image had far-reaching consequences for the whole of Buddhism, as stupa worship declined in popularity, and devotion was to some extent transferred to the Buddha image. The stupa was by no means neglected – in fact, it has continued to be venerated until modern times – but the Buddha image became the principal object of devotion. The offerings formerly made just to the stupas came to be made to the images as well, becoming more and more elaborate, and assuming deeper and deeper significance as they did so.

In this chapter, we will briefly be considering the symbolism of offerings and self-sacrifice in Early Buddhism, and in the Mahāyāna, before taking a more detailed view of the subject with respect to the Tantra. In its early days the Buddhist monastic sangha consisted of eighteen different schools, only one of which survives as an independent entity. This is the school known as the Theravāda or the Tradition of the Elders (elders here meaning the senior monks), the form of Buddhism that now prevails in Sri Lanka, Burma (now Myanmar), and Thailand. In the many beautiful temples to be found in these countries are enshrined an enormous number of Buddha images, to which offerings are made every day.

Usually in Theravādin countries three things are offered: flowers, sticks of incense, and lamps or candles. The offerings are made individually; there is no such thing as congregational worship. You go along in your own way, at your own convenience, with your little tray of offerings, and you offer them at the feet of the Buddha. There may be a number of people making their offerings at the same time, or you may be entirely on your own. As you offer each item, you recite appropriate verses in Pāli to remind you of the significance of what you are offering. For instance, when you offer a lighted lamp or candle, you may recite a verse that says, 'I offer this light to the Buddha who is the light of the three worlds,' to remind you that the Buddha illuminates the whole of mundane existence with the light of his wisdom. But the light also suggests something else: that just as one lamp can be lit from another, we can light the lamp of wisdom in our hearts from the already kindled light that is the Buddha's wisdom. In some ceremonies in Theravādin countries, thirty-seven candles are placed on the offering-table, symbolizing the thirty-seven *bodhipakkhiyadhammas*, the practices leading to Enlightenment.[98] In the course of the ceremony, each candle is lit from a larger central candle, symbolizing the Buddha.

Secondly, flowers are offered. Here there are quite a number of verses to choose from, or you can even recite them all. One of the verses reminds us that although when they are offered, flowers are fresh and beautiful, perhaps with the dew still glistening upon them, later on, even by that very evening, they will be withered and dry. It goes on to say that all mundane things are like that, today bright, beautiful, and attractive, but tomorrow already beginning to fade. The offering of flowers thus becomes a reminder of the truth of universal impermanence: nothing lasts, nothing stays; everything fades, everything flows. The action may also remind us of the deeper implication of that truth – that attachment to anything that is impermanent can only bring grief, that it is useless to try to hang on to anything. Experience it, enjoy it, but let it go, don't cling to it, don't make the impossible wish for something that is essentially impermanent to be made permanent. At the same time, as you make your offering, you try to sense beneath the flow of transient things the deeper reality, like the still depths of the ocean beneath the waves.

Thirdly, you offer lighted incense sticks. Here too there is a variety of verses to choose from. One of them observes that the sweet fragrance of the lighted incense stick spreads in all directions, and that a little of it spreads a very long way. Scent is a remarkable thing – it is extraordinary that microscopic particles can exert their influence over such a wide area – and the practice of the Dharma has a correspondingly subtle but powerful effect. Even a little Buddhist practice has an effect that carries beyond the individual psyche of the practitioner into their environment. The effect may not be tangible, but when your state of consciousness starts changing, it is as though the vibrations spread out into the surrounding atmosphere in ever-widening circles, having a positive influence on other living beings, whether they know it or not.

These three offerings of the Theravāda have an additional set of associations: the offering of lights with the Buddha, flowers with the Dharma, and incense with the Sangha. In very simple terms, this is the symbolism of offerings of traditional Early Buddhism, especially in its contemporary Theravādin form.

Broadly speaking, in the Mahāyāna, offerings are divided into two groups: internal offerings and external ones. The internal offerings represent the offering of the five physical senses. The sense of sight is represented by a mirror, usually circular in shape and made of metal; hearing, by a small pair of cymbals, or a bell; smell, by an incense stick; taste, by a sacrificial cake made of dough; and touch, by a roll of silk. To these five objects is sometimes added a sixth: a page of printed text from the scriptures to represent the sixth sense, the mind.

The significance of these offerings is quite clear. They constitute a reminder that one must be dedicated to the ideal of Enlightenment on every level of one's being. Not just the mind, not just the emotions – the physical senses too must be involved in the spiritual life, so that you are not leaving any part of yourself undedicated, unoffered. In this context the senses stand for your active existence. According to the Yogācāra system, the offering of the senses can also be connected with the transformation of the sense-consciousnesses into the all-performing wisdom of Amoghasiddhi, because through them you have contact with the material world. When you dedicate them, you are in effect dedicating your whole life and activity to Enlightenment.[99]

The external offerings of the Mahāyāna are the seven things offered to an honoured guest. According to ancient Indian tradition these are water for drinking, water for washing the feet, flowers, incense, lamps, scented water, and food. Sometimes music is added to these to make eight items. If you imagine the scene – a house in ancient or even modern India, and a visitor or traveller suddenly turning up – how would you receive your guest? How would you entertain him? It is possible that the traveller has come a long way in the heat of the sun, in which case he will be thirsty, so the first thing you do is offer him a drink of water. If he has come on foot, perhaps even barefoot, his feet will be dusty, so you offer him water for washing his feet – a custom that is still very much kept up. Then, when he has refreshed himself and taken his seat inside the house, you welcome him by placing a garland of flowers round his neck. After a few minutes you might light a few sticks of incense, to create a pleasant atmosphere and keep the mosquitoes away.

In India people are very hospitable, and guests usually stay not just for an hour or two, but for a whole day, a week, or even longer. So your guest is sure to be there when evening falls. Naturally you light lamps, and you may sprinkle your guest with perfumed water – rosewater, say – which in a hot climate is cooling and refreshing at the end of the day. When the guest has had a chance to relax and recover from the journey, you serve food. Traditional Indian etiquette does not allow you as host to sit and eat with your guest, as you should be far too busy looking after him. He sits down by himself, and the whole household helps to serve him. To be on the receiving end of this, as a guest, can be slightly unnerving if you are not used to it. There you are, sitting at the centre of all this bustling attention, all this coming and going with little dishes and delicacies, and you are slowly stuffed – there is no other word for it. When you have been fed to absolute repletion, and have perhaps been given betel to chew,[100] if you are visiting a cultured family, especially one with teenage daughters, one of the girls will fetch her vina or her sitar, and you will be entertained with music.

This whole procedure still takes place in India in many families and, exotic and oriental as it may seem, there are obvious parallels with contemporary western social customs. Here too, if someone comes to visit, you make them welcome with a cup of tea and show them where they can wash their hands. At nightfall, though you might just switch on the light, you might perhaps light a candle. You will offer your guest food, and after the meal you might put on some music. Different as they are from the Indian traditions, we have our own ways of treating an honoured guest.

The traditional Indian manner of welcoming a guest is reflected in the offerings made throughout the Mahāyāna Buddhist world. On special occasions Tibetan Buddhists present the seven external offerings literally, arranged in a row on the shrine. First, there are two bowls of water, one for drinking, one for washing the feet. Next is a bowl of rice with a flower stuck in it. Not many flowers grow in Tibet, so the Tibetans generally use a large, flat, papery kind of seed they call a 'white flower', which comes from the 'flame of the forest' tree. Next comes a bowl of rice with lighted incense sticks in it. Then there is a lighted butter lamp, and a bowl of perfumed water. Finally there will be a sacrificial cake on a plate, or sometimes a bowl of rice with a small fruit on top. If the eighth item, music, is included, a pair of small cymbals will be placed at the end of the row.

For everyday purposes seven bowls filled with water are placed on the offering-table to symbolize the seven offerings. But the significance is the same: that the Buddha is being welcomed as an honoured guest, just as we might have invited him into our home 2,500 years ago. Once he takes his seat in our home, we give him our very best, out of gratitude for the teaching. In the East people seem often to feel this quite literally when they are making offerings. Whether they are offering the simple lighted candle, flower, and incense-stick of the Theravāda or making the more elaborate offerings of the Mahāyāna, I have been told that they feel definitely as though the Buddha is actually present and that they are receiving him as a guest. I have noticed people being very deeply moved on such occasions. If we are honest, we may have to admit that it isn't easy, or even natural, for us to enter into this sort of feeling ourselves. We cannot force ourselves into it. What we can do is try to appreciate how people in the East feel, and understand the general principle involved, which is the expression of gratitude to the Buddha for the teaching. We can then try to find some way of expressing our own feelings of gratitude, in accordance with our own temperament and cultural tradition.

There is, however, a further, deeper meaning to this practice of treating the Buddha as an honoured guest. The Sanskrit word for guest is *atithi*. *Tithi* means a time of day, or a period of the day, and *a-* is simply a negative prefix, so *atithi* is someone who does not come at an appointed time – they just turn up. This is what usually happens in India. You don't make appointments or arrangements. It doesn't matter that the person you are planning to visit may not know that you are coming, may not even have heard of you. You just turn up, out of the blue. That is what makes you a guest, *atithi*. And the Buddha is just like that. He just appeared. The world wasn't expecting him, nobody knew he was coming – he just turned up.

The ancient Indian custom when an unexpected guest arrives is to drop everything. You don't go to work that day. That would be ridiculous – you have to entertain your guest. If you were about to set off for the fields, you ask somebody else to look after your crops. If you were about to teach your children, you give them a holiday. If you were about to go out for a little exercise or to visit friends, you forget it. You drop everything and devote yourself entirely to your guest. That is the old Indian custom, and sometimes even now people will say, 'Please treat everything in the house as your own. I'm just here to serve you.' There is never any question of inconvenience. No one would dream of saying, 'Fancy turning up like that, without giving me any notice!' No one minds; in fact, they are overjoyed. When an unexpected guest has arrived, I have even heard the head of a household say – this was in South India, where the people are particularly religious and traditionally minded – 'I feel just as though God himself had come to my house.' This shows how seriously Indians take the duty of hospitality.

Clearly, our own lives in the West today are very different. Our time is usually carefully allocated; if someone were to turn up unexpectedly, it would disrupt our entire schedule, and we might feel quite put out. Life is not so leisurely or spacious as it was a few centuries ago – or

as it still is in some parts of the world. However, this is all the more reason, of course, for us to make the necessary changes to our attitude and way of life, so that we are never too busy to be hospitable.

The Buddha as guest represents the transcendental as something unexpected and unprecedented, suddenly erupting into our humdrum lives, breaking in from some other dimension and catching us completely off our guard. And the seven offerings of the Mahāyāna represent our response. When the Transcendental appears and takes us by surprise, we drop everything and attend only to the Transcendental, to the Buddha. That undivided attention is expressed by giving the best we have, not holding back but giving everything we have, giving out of unbounded gratitude, unbounded love and joy.

The spirit of our response to the Buddha is symbolized by eight beautiful figures, the eight 'offering goddesses' – one for each of the eight offerings (including music) of the Mahāyāna – which can be made the subject of visualization in the course of meditation practice. One sees, one feels, emerging from one's heart, eight rainbows, which pass through the crown of one's head and fan out. At the end of each rainbow is a goddess, an exquisite sixteen-year-old female figure, bearing the appropriate offering. These eight goddesses make their offerings – water for drinking, water for washing the feet, incense, and so on – to the Buddhas and bodhisattvas, who are visualized as seated on lotus thrones in the midst of the sky. The offering goddesses, in the brightness of their beauty, represent the essence of worship, the powerful upsurging of devotional feelings, pure and strong.

With the Tantra, the symbolism of offerings and self-sacrifice takes off in some surprising and strange directions. Just as the Mahāyāna offerings include those of the Theravāda – the same lights, incense, and flowers reappear in a slightly different way – in much the same way, the Tantric offerings include the offerings of the Mahāyāna. But there is an important development. Offerings are made in the Theravāda and the Mahāyāna to the Buddha, the Enlightened One, and in both the Mahāyāna and the Tantra to all the Buddhas and bodhisattvas, to the principle of Enlightenment in all its innumerable forms and guises. But in the Tantra, Buddhas and bodhisattvas are of two kinds, or rather manifest under two aspects: peaceful and wrathful.

When we think of Buddhas and bodhisattvas, we perhaps naturally think of them as calm, peaceful, compassionate, and beautiful. But in the Tantra many Buddhas and bodhisattvas have wrathful, fierce, even terrible aspects, representing – as we saw when we encountered Vajrapāṇi – Enlightenment's function as the destroyer of ignorance. The invocation of and meditation upon 'wrathful deities', as they are sometimes called, is central to Tantric Buddhism, especially the highest Tantra, the *anuttara yoga* Tantra. One is directed to study painted *thangkas* depicting these wrathful forms, to meditate upon them, to occupy one's mind with them, to become familiar with their forms, for quite a precise reason: because such practices help develop one's heroic virtues.

In the Tantra, the Buddhas and bodhisattvas in their peaceful manifestations are worshipped with the usual Mahāyāna offerings: the five objects representing the five senses and the seven items offered to the honoured guest. But when it comes to the worship of the wrathful deities, there are specifically Tantric offerings, both internal and external. The internal offerings of the Tantra are often represented by what is usually referred to as 'the flower of the senses'. As offered in ritual worship, this is made of dough, fashioned and coloured to resemble a skull-cup which contains some strange and unpleasant objects: a human heart, a tongue torn out by the roots, a nose and a pair of ears that have been cut off, and a pair of eyes that have been gouged out. These five items made of dough – representing the five senses, the heart standing for the sense of touch – are artistically arranged in the skull-cup to form a sort of bouquet; hence, the flower of the senses. This, the first of the specifically Tantric offerings, in fact carries the same meaning as the internal offerings of the Mahāyāna, only much more dramatically

expressed. The senses themselves – heart, tongue, nose, eyes, ears – are to be dedicated to Enlightenment.

As for the external offerings of the Tantra, one might list six of these. First of all, there is what is known as a cemetery flower, a flower that supposedly grows only in cemeteries, that blooms out of the bodies of the dead. Secondly, you offer incense made of singed human flesh. Anyone who has attended a cremation – not the hygienic kind we have in the West, but one where you see and smell the corpse burning, as you do in India – will know that the smell of singed flesh is very distinctive and never to be forgotten. The other offerings are a lamp made of human fat, scent of bile, beverage of blood, and food of human flesh. These offerings obviously represent an extension of the cremation ground symbolism with which we were concerned in the previous chapter.

In addition to the internal and external offerings, there are various 'secret offerings'. One set of five comprises human flesh, heart, blood, brain, and entrails. The general significance of these offerings is again the same as that of the other Tantric offerings, and even more emphatic. The message is that it's not enough to have pious, devotional feelings. It's not even enough to dedicate your very senses; even that doesn't go far enough. Making these secret offerings of flesh, heart, blood, brain, and entrails, you are acknowledging that you've got to dedicate yourself, give yourself at a raw, visceral level, give yourself blood and guts and all. At the other end of the scale from these is the single offering of *amṛta*, the nectar of immortality, which symbolizes Enlightenment or Buddhahood itself and is represented by a skull-cup filled to the brim with beer or spirits. This is offered only to the wrathful deities, who are often depicted drinking it.

All these offerings have an important place in Tantric practice, but more important still is the offering of the mandala. This practice is one of the foundation yogas of the Tantra.[101] In this context the term mandala has a slightly unusual meaning, referring to the universe, the cosmos, as represented in traditional Buddhist cosmology. Thus the offering of the mandala means the offering of the whole universe. When you offer the mandala, you offer the whole of material existence to the Buddhas and bodhisattvas.

The suggestion behind this particular form of external offering is that your gratitude to the Buddha, to the Three Jewels, is intense to the point of being overwhelming. You feel so grateful for what you have received that in response you would like to give everything you have and experience, everything you could possibly own or enjoy or imagine. If you owned the whole world, you would want to give even that. You could think of nothing better to do with it than offer it to the Buddha. Although you can't do this literally, you can offer it symbolically. In this, as in the spiritual life as a whole, it is the heartfelt intention and the attitude that count.

The mandala represents not just the physical universe, but a system of intersecting planes or dimensions of being and consciousness, only one of which is identical with our own physical universe. It is usually said to consist of thirty-seven parts, but this is simply to give an idea of its most prominent aspects, and is not meant to be a comprehensive survey. Perhaps the number thirty-seven was chosen to correspond with the thirty-seven practices leading to Enlightenment, the *bodhipakkhiyadhammas* – but sometimes only twenty-five parts are enumerated, and one list from Tibetan sources puts the number at thirty-nine.

The mandala has a foundation, called the 'diamond ground', which represents the ultimate reality that is the basis of the whole of phenomenal existence. Then there is a wall of iron, which marks the outermost limit, or (thinking three-dimensionally) the outermost shell of this universe. Within the wall there are seven concentric circles of golden mountains, alternating with seven concentric circles of ocean. In this context are found, according to the list of thirty-seven, the constituent parts of the mandala. The first part is Mount Meru, the king of mountains, the axis of this whole system, which rises up from the innermost circle of ocean. Meru is popularly identified with a certain peak in the western Himalayas, but in reality it is not to be identified with any earthly mountain at all. Below Mount Meru are the lower worlds of suffering, the purgatories and hells, and above it are the worlds of the gods. Upon Mount Meru itself are four realms, the topmost of which is inhabited by the *asuras* or Titans, who are perpetually attacking the gods. (It is beginning to be clear that this world-picture shares many features with that other symbol of conditioned existence, the Tibetan wheel of life.)

Parts 2–5 are the four islands or continents situated in the outermost circle of ocean, immediately inside the iron wall. The eastern continent is white in colour and shaped like a crescent moon; its inhabitants have crescent-shaped faces, and are tranquil and virtuous. The southern continent is blue, and shaped, we are told, like the shoulder blade of a sheep – and the faces of its inhabitants are apparently this same shape. This continent – in which riches abound and both good and evil exist – is said to correspond roughly to our own world. The western continent is round like the sun and red in colour, with red-faced denizens who are powerful in constitution and greatly addicted to the flesh of cattle. The northern continent is square and green; its inhabitants have square faces like the faces of horses, and they get all they need from the trees that grow on their continent.

Parts 6–13 are the eight subsidiary continents. There are two of these to each of the main continents, and they are of the same shape as their parent continent. The fourteenth part of the mandala is the mountain of jewels, and the fifteenth is the wish-fulfilling tree, possession of which the Titans are constantly trying to wrest from the gods. The sixteenth part is the wish-fulfilling cow, the cow of plenty; the seventeenth is the crops that grow without the necessity of cultivation. Parts 18–24 are the seven jewels of the universal monarch, the word jewel here meaning 'the best of its kind'. This is a well-known list: the wish-fulfilling jewel, the precious wheel, the precious queen, the precious minister, the precious elephant, the precious horse, and the precious general. The twenty-fifth part is the wish-fulfilling jar, a kind of Aladdin's lamp, sometimes considered to be identical with the vase of initiation. Parts 26–33 are the eight offering goddesses, who live in their own heaven worlds, adjacent to the paradise of Indra. Parts 34 and 35 are the sun and the moon – not just in the literal sense, but more as they appear at the top of the Tantric stupa – as symbols of the complementary influences in the universe. The thirty-sixth part is the ceremonial umbrella, the umbrella of victory and sovereignty, which crowns the whole mandala, and the thirty-seventh part is a banner of victory, which flies from the top of the umbrella. Between them, these thirty-seven parts of the mandala represent the whole multidimensional universe.

According to the Nyingma tradition, the mandala is offered thus: First you visualize the cosmic Refuge Tree, as described in Chapter 4. You see in your mind's eye the glorious figure of the great Tantric guru Padmasambhava surrounded by the exoteric and esoteric refuges. Above him you see the gurus of the spiritual lineage up to the Buddha Amitābha and the Ādibuddha Samantabhadra, below him are gurus, *yidams*, *ḍākinīs*, *dharmapālas*, and so on, in front of him the Buddhas of the three periods of time (past, present, and future), behind him the sacred books, and on either side the two wings of the sangha. You visualize all this in the sky before you, and as you do so, you recite a special esoteric version of the sevenfold puja, of which the following is a rendering into English that I made many years ago with the help of one of my Tibetan teachers, Dhardo Rimpoche:

> To that Trikāya which is the true nature of all Dharmas, non-dual, limitless, profound and vast, I make obeisance.
> I worship the unmade, the unlimited, and the eternal.
> I make confession of the sin of not knowing that my own mind is the Buddha,
> Rejoicing in the natural state, the self-aware.
> I request the Buddha to revolve the ungraspable, omnipresent and all-accomplished Dharmacakra.

I pray that the mundane and the transcendental may be
established in oneness.
Whatever obeisance and worship I have performed, I transmute
into the voidness.
May all beings attain both voidness and great bliss.

This should be repeated many times, and as you recite it, you should feel that all living beings are repeating it with you. After that, you actually offer up the mandala. First you visualize it in your heart – the diamond ground, the iron wall, the golden mountains, the circles of ocean, Mount Meru, and so on, adorned with all the other items – and then you offer it in worship to the Buddhas, bodhisattvas, gurus, and *ḍākinīs* of the cosmic Refuge Tree.

To visualize all this in detail is very difficult, even with a lot of practice. But there is another way of doing the practice which is commonly resorted to in Tantric circles. This is literally to construct a simplified three-dimensional model of the universe. You take a round metal base, like a deep tray turned upside down, to represent the diamond ground of existence, and you usually begin by symbolically cleaning it a few times. Then you recite a mantra, '*oṃ vajra bhūmi āḥ hūṃ*' (*vajra bhūmi* meaning 'diamond ground'). As you do this, you try to realize, to feel, that this is the underlying reality of the whole phenomenal world. On this base you place a large metal circle or ring about one inch high, to represent the wall of iron enclosing the universe. You fill this ring with rice, and place on the rice a second ring, smaller than the first, to represent Mount Meru. After filling the second ring with rice, you place upon it a third ring, smaller still, to represent the higher heavenly realm. Around this stepped pyramid structure you then deposit a few grains of rice to represent each of the other parts of the mandala. Finally, you crown the whole edifice with a jewel mounted on a silver *dharmacakra*. Having constructed the mandala, you are now ready to offer it up. The act of offering consists simply in lifting up the mandala you have created in the direction of the shrine and the figure of the Buddha or guru upon it, or actually placing it on the offering table. The whole procedure, from beginning to end, is to be repeated 100,000 times. It is important to remember that, although it involves physical actions, this practice is really an act of the imagination, and of the emotions. Furthermore, all these apparently solid phenomena, represented by rice

and metal, are not as solid as they seem; the very 'ground' on which they are based is insubstantial, being represented in some descriptions of Buddhist cosmology by nothing more than two winds blowing across each other.

If you don't have time for this, there is a still more simplified form of offering the mandala. To do this, you just fill the palms of your hands with rice and make a certain ritual gesture or *mudrā*, to symbolize the mandala. To make this *mudrā* you place the backs of your two ring-fingers together, so that they are sticking up into the air, to represent Mount Meru. Then you cross your middle fingers and grasp their tips with your forefingers, and cross your little fingers and grasp their tips with your thumbs. You have thus made four corners, to symbolize the four continents. Holding your hands together in this way, you recite this verse:

The ground is purified with scented water and strewn with flowers.
It is adorned with the king of mountains, the four continents, the sun and the moon.
Thinking of it as the Buddha realm, I offer it to the Buddha.
By virtue thereof may all human beings attain to the realm of bliss.

Having offered the universe, you might think there was nothing left to give, and this is true as far as external offerings are concerned. But it does leave one thing not yet offered, and that is your own self, especially your body. Offering the whole world isn't enough. You must offer the offerer. You must give yourself to the Buddhas and bodhisattvas, and to other living beings. Even if you give the whole universe 100,000 times, you are really only giving fully when you give yourself. It all comes down to that old and – for some – rather problematic idea of self-sacrifice. Those of us born and brought up in western cultures may have to approach this with some care. In the early days of the Christian church, after you were baptized (baptism took place in adulthood then), you were supposed never to sin again – and some churches believed that if you did, there was no possibility of redemption. But eventually a belief grew up that there was one way of redeeming yourself, which was to become a martyr for your faith – to wash away your sin in a baptism of blood. In time this came to mean that out of a sense of guilt some Christians began actively to invite martyrdom, and even to insist on it when the authorities concerned gave them every opportunity of avoiding a painful death.

In the course of time, Christianity became the established religion of the Roman Empire, which drastically reduced opportunities for martyrdom, and left sinners without the means of saving themselves from damnation. According to some authorities this is one of the reasons why Christian monastic and eremitic traditions sprang up: the austerity and self-mortification they involved was meant to be a substitute form of martyrdom. If nobody was prepared to martyr you, you had to take steps to inflict pain and suffering on yourself – so you became a hermit and wore chains or lived on top of a pillar, or else you did it in more discreet style, with a hair shirt under your monk's habit. In the West an idea prevails even today that the monastic life is, or should be, a life of penance and asceticism.

It is unlikely that many of the martyrs and self-flagellating monks would have been genuinely trying to transcend themselves. There were certainly some individuals who, even under those circumstances, did manage to feel and give expression to genuine concern for other people. In others, though, there seems to have been an overriding preoccupation with saving their own soul, motivated by fear of punishment or hope of reward. As we look at the Tibetan Tantric practice of self-sacrifice known as *chöd*, it may be useful to bear in mind the ways in which it differs from the Christian tradition of martyrdom, even though both focus specifically on the sacrifice of the physical body.

Chöd is a Tibetan word which means 'cutting', and it corresponds to the Sanskrit *chedana*. This same word is part of the title of the *Vajracchedikā Sūtra*, known in the West as the *Diamond Sūtra*, the teaching of the transcendental wisdom that cuts like the diamond. However, whereas the *Diamond Sūtra* is meant to cut off ignorance at the root, the *chöd* practice is concerned simply with the cutting off of ego or, to be more precise, with the cutting off of attachment to the ego or self, especially attachment to the physical body, with which we so firmly identify ourselves much of the time.

Before we look at what happens in the *chöd* practice, we should pause to consider briefly what is meant by ego. In one of his songs, the Tibetan yogi Milarepa refers to what the translator calls 'the demon of egotism',[102] but we have to be rather careful with this language. There is much talk of the ego in spiritual circles: people say things like, 'Oh well, I mustn't let my ego get in the way,' or, 'I suppose my ego just caught me napping,' as though the ego were a mischievous entity, like a disruptive sprite. Such expressions reflect and reinforce a subtle confusion of the point at issue, suggesting as they do that the ego is not you, when that is exactly what it is. It *is* you. It is you adopting a particular attitude, being rigid, or unreceptive, or stubborn. Egoism is not an entity, but an attitude. One may say for example that generosity counteracts egoism, but not that it gets rid of your ego (or the demon of egoism). The obvious problem of using language that seems to postulate a separate ego identity is that it can allow you to abdicate responsibility for your own selfishness: 'It isn't me, it's my ego.' The ego is like the 'it' in the phrase 'it's raining'; the psychological or spiritual reality is simply that one behaves egoistically. It is this egoistic attitude that the *chöd* practice is designed to cut off.

The *chöd* practice was originated by Phadampa Sangye and Machig Labdrön.[103] To do the practice, the Tantric yogi leaves the town, leaves his friends and companions, and goes far away, to a wild and solitary place, preferably to one that is haunted, such as a cremation ground. He takes with him various articles that he will need in the ritual part of the practice, including the skin of a beast of prey, complete with claws, a tent, a staff surmounted by a trident, a trumpet made of a human thigh bone, and a large double-sided drum.

This yogi settles himself in that solitary spot, perhaps with corpses and bones round about, seeing the occasional glimpse of glowing eyes in the dark from the quick stare of the resident jackals, or even having a sense of supernatural beings around as well. In this eerie setting, he starts upon various preliminaries to the *chöd* practice, and offers up a prayer to the great Tantric guru Padmasambhava. He then turns his attention to his physical body, beginning to identify it with the corpses lying around him in various stages of decomposition. Next, he tries to experience his mind, his true mind, as being separate from his body, visualizing it as the 'knowledge *ḍākinī*' or 'awareness *ḍākinī*'. Like the *ḍākinī* we met in the last chapter, she is completely naked, except for a few ornaments of bone, though this *ḍākinī* is usually black in colour. She has a wrathful expression, and three eyes, the third eye being the eye of wisdom. She holds a kind of chopper in one hand and a skull-cup in the other. Identifying yourself with this knowledge-*ḍākinī*, you see your physical body lying there dead, a fat, luscious-looking corpse, while your true mind stands beside it, independent from it, imagined as the knowledge or awareness *ḍākinī*.

This terrible *ḍākinī* proceeds to wield her chopper. Suddenly, she chops off the head from your own dead body. Your severed head rapidly becomes a skull, which the *ḍākinī* turns upside down and places on top of three smaller skulls, thus creating a sort of three-legged cauldron.

She then cuts your corpse into bits, and throws them into the skull cauldron as an offering to the deities. This done, certain mantras are pronounced – that is, you, the yogi, pronounce them – and as you do so, the pieces of flesh and bone in the skull cauldron are transformed into *amṛta*, the nectar of immortality.

Next, you invite the Three Jewels, and the guardian deities together with spirits of various kinds, to come and partake of the feast of nectar. You tell them that you are sacrificing your physical body because it is the root of duality, making you distinguish between subject and object. Your mood is happy and triumphant, even heroic, as you call upon a disparate array of spiritual beings, high and low, to come and enjoy the nectar in whatever form they please, peaceful or wrathful. As a Tantric yogi you must actually experience all this. It isn't just an idea, or a fantasy to read about in a well-lit room. It is something you actually go through, on your own in some solitary spot, by conjuring up all this terrifying imagery. Its meaning is to be found only in the doing of it.

Chöd practitioners are usually wandering yogis; whenever they find a suitable spot, especially a cremation ground, they stay there for a few days to perform the *chöd* practice. Over time, if you do this practice consistently, you come to feel as though your body is a corpse already, and your attachment to it starts to wane. You see more and more clearly that only the mind, in the sense of a pure and radiant reality, exists – whether or not it is realized in its red *ḍākinī* form.

Not many of us are prepared to go as far as this. Not many of us, indeed, want to sacrifice ourselves in any sense at all – and we may not be inclined to offer anything else either, let alone a mandala representing the whole universe. Indeed, the whole subject of devotion, gratitude, making offerings, and self-sacrifice can be quite difficult for western people. The long Buddhist tradition of what Nāgārjuna calls honouring the honourable[104] sits uncomfortably with our egalitarian principles; a common instinct these days seems to be to want to pull down, denigrate, and deflate.

Consequently, we may be liable to misunderstand the statements sometimes made by Buddhist teachers apparently disparaging the making of offerings. In fact such statements are made to warn against the making of offerings as the be-all and end-all of Buddhist life and practice, because for some Buddhists at some times and in some places it has come close to being viewed as such. Good though it is to make offerings, there are other forms of Dharma practice that are even more beneficial. The great Tibetan teacher Gampopa (who was Milarepa's foremost disciple) makes the point with traditional Tibetan hyperbole in his *Jewel Ornament of Liberation*:

> Whatever immeasurable offerings there may be and however varied,
> Filling millions and millions of universes –
> Offering them to the most sublime being (the Buddha)
> Does not equal the merits of Benevolence.
>
> The merits accruing from having practised Benevolence only for a little while also cannot be measured. As is written in the *Ratnāvalī*:
>
> Even if one were to give out food
> Cooked in three hundred pots, daily thrice a day,
> This would not equal the merits
> Of one moment of Benevolence.[105]

Gampopa is in no way dismissing the making of offerings and the practice of generosity, *dāna*, which are extolled in all Buddhist traditions. For the bodhisattva – and it is the practice of the bodhisattva, or would-be bodhisattva, that is being described here – the practice of developing *maitrī* and *karuṇā* (benevolence and compassion) represents a commitment to the happiness of all sentient beings, in the sense of helping them to gain Enlightenment. As such, its benefits, both for you as the novice bodhisattva and for other people, are infinite. In a sense Gampopa is explaining where the real importance of devotion and generosity lies – as the natural expressions of benevolence and compassion.

It is possible – and highly beneficial – to extend this feeling of benevolence not just to our fellow human beings, but to the universe as a whole. In the *Ratana Sutta* the Buddha is reported as saying:

> Hence, all ye spirits, hear attentively.
> Look lovingly upon the race of men,
> And, since they bring thee offerings day and night,
> Keep watch and ward about them heedfully.[106]

This verse clearly reflects an animistic attitude to nature. It is perhaps not easy for us, with our Christian conditioning, to imagine having such a strong feeling for nature and for the things of nature. The people of India are much closer to their pagan roots: if you give them half a chance to worship anything, village people especially will happily take it. This at least was the view of my teacher Bhikkhu Jagdish Kashyap, who told me once of a curious example of it that he observed as a boy in a village in a remote part of the Indian state of Bihar. A new road was being built and marked out with milestones, and one morning he saw a woman making her way from the village to the nearest milestone, carrying a tray upon which she had placed some vermilion, some flowers, and a few sticks of incense. On reaching the milestone she anointed it with the vermilion, scattered the flowers, and stuck the sticks of incense in the ground in front of it. She then bowed to the milestone with folded hands. She thought it was a new kind of god.

The attitude behind such undiscriminating devotion is essentially animistic, and for all its primitiveness and simplicity, it is a healthy basis for spiritual life. You feel that everything is alive; you feel a rapport with the forces of nature, and you want to propitiate them, be on friendly terms with them. Mechanistic materialism suggests that everything is just dead matter, but it is surely much better to think that all things – trees, stones, streams, clouds – are alive, even if you personify them in a rather childish way.

Some western scholars are disturbed to find that in some traditional Buddhist cultures, the pure philosophical and ethical teachings of Buddhism have been corrupted, as they see it, by being mixed up with a lot of animism and spirit worship. I myself do not share their unease. At a certain level we *are* a part of nature, we are surrounded by all sorts of natural forces and energies that are also present within us, and we cannot help feeling and experiencing them, even in the form of spirits and gods of the earth and sky. And if you do experience them in that way, you naturally want to keep up a positive relationship with them: you give them offerings and in return they protect you.

In this verse from the *Ratana Sutta* the compiler of the *sutta* is taking up this archaic, pagan, animistic way of looking at things and giving it wider significance. He is saying, 'Be on friendly terms with the universe. If you feel friendly towards the universe, the universe will feel friendly towards you.' It's as though the universe (in the form of the gods) is prepared to strike a bargain with us. We agree to worship the gods and provide them with oblations, and in return they agree to protect us. Today it is considered more realistic to regard the universe as implacably hostile and threatening, but really this view is just more paranoid, the natural result of living in a universe conceived of as impersonal.

It is difficult to feel good will and love towards something you think of as impersonal. Before you can feel positive emotion towards it, you have to invest it with personal qualities, and you can see this in the way some people love their car or motorbike almost as though it were human. Making a living connection with something whose workings are ultimately perhaps a bit of a mystery involves personalizing it, calling it 'he' or 'she'. You may end up saying things like 'She's not going very well today. I don't think she's very happy. Maybe she doesn't like the change in the weather.' Similarly, to the extent that you feel positive towards life as a whole, you will start personalizing things, so that they are not just things but 'spirits' – spirits at least in a poetic sense. If you want to enter into relationship with the universe, if you want to love it, you have to see it as personal.

Throughout the Buddhist tradition one finds this same sense of the importance of propitiating local spirits. For example, in one of his songs Milarepa sings:

> Ye local demons, ghosts, and gods,
> All friends of Milarepa,
> Drink the nectar of kindness and compassion,
> Then return to your abodes.[107]

These gods and goddesses and spirits can also be seen as representing aspects of oneself. The basic energies that find their expression in nature through the primitive folklore of our indigenous culture also exist in us, and we cannot afford to ignore them or cut ourselves off from them. Instead, we can take notice of them, absorb, assimilate, and direct them, as Padmasambhava is said to have harnessed the demons of Tibet. And just as we must harness our inner drives, so we must harness the same forces as they express themselves through the indigenous culture. For example, rather than building an exact replica of a Tibetan or Japanese Buddhist temple in England, which might seem somewhat alien, one could build it in an English style. You would still want to centre it upon a Buddha image, but you could introduce motifs or symbols with indigenous significance. Instead of *bodhi* leaves, for example, you could decorate the shrine with carvings of oak leaves, which have deep associations for the English. Druids worshipped the oak tree, and the mistletoe that grows upon it, and in more modern times the oak has developed associations of strength and stability – 'hearts of oak' – based on the extraordinary success of the English ships that were built from it. All the energy bound up with these old associations would contribute to whatever was done in the temple.

In India, when Buddha images were first made, the principal gods of the indigenous tradition, Indra and Brahmā, were not banished completely. You find for example, in images of the Buddha descending from the *devaloka*, that he comes escorted by these two deities. They are smaller than the Buddha – very much attendants – but they have not been excluded, they have been given their place. The ethnic, one might say, has been integrated with the universal, the lower ideal with the higher. The universe we know and love in the form of our native land and folklore puts heart into our highest ideals, making them personal, something we can love.

As Buddhists, more than anything else, we should love the Dharma. When we make our offerings, when we sacrifice ourselves, it should not be out of a dull sense of duty, but out of love, even passionate love. In the *Parābhava Sutta* of the *Sutta-Nipāta* the Buddha says *dhammakāmo bhavaṃ hoti*, which means something like, 'One who loves the Dharma passionately, progresses.'[108] This is very important. If you think of yourself as a Buddhist, you have to ask yourself whether you really do love the Dharma. The word here is *kāma*, which is the Pāli term for the love of a passionate lover. And the signs of love for the Dharma are just like the signs of passionate love for a man or woman. Just as when you love someone, you want to spend time with them, do things for them, give them presents, if you love the Dharma, the Buddha's teaching, you will want to spend time with it, and give to it. This is what is really meant by practising the Dharma – you will want to read about it, study it, practise it, hear about it, associate with people who are interested in it.

If you see the Dharma as something rather dull which is supposed to do you good, you won't get very far. Being convinced intellectually that Buddhism is good for you may prepare the ground, but to make much progress you have to have a real love for it. Just as nobody needs any encouragement to talk about the object of their affections to anyone who will listen, you will find yourself wanting to talk about the Dharma on all possible occasions. And just as you like to give presents to the person you love, even squander all your money on them, if you love the Dharma you will want to squander all you have on it. Not that it is really squandering – in fact it is the best possible investment – but you don't think of it as an investment; you just want to give. That is the real secret of Buddhist offerings and self-sacrifice.

7
COLOURS AND MANTRIC SOUND

Anyone who gives talks or writes books on Buddhism soon discovers that certain words have a special drawing power. 'Secret' is one such word, as I once learned from a friend whose work as a publisher's reader on oriental subjects involved advising authors about book titles. What he said to me was that if he thought that a book wasn't likely to sell very well, he usually advised the author to include the word 'secret' in the title. Apparently, people rather like the idea of penetrating into secrets, finding out things they are not supposed to know. Another word that rather seems to arouse people's curiosity is 'sex' – maybe they think they're missing something – and of course the word 'Tantra' or 'Tantric' is also of perennial interest, apparently more so even than 'Zen'.

Most tantalizing of all, perhaps, is the word 'magic'. This seems to have a very wide appeal, especially when juxtaposed with one or more of the other words I have mentioned. (Let us hope that no one will ever put them all together, to enthral us with a title like 'The Secret Zen Yoga of Tantric Sex Magic'.) However – even at the risk of appearing sensationalist – one cannot help referring to magic at least once when dealing with the theme of the Tantric path to Enlightenment. The reason for this is that a lot of the symbolism of the Indo-Tibetan Tantric tradition has its origins in Indian magical practices, which can still be encountered all over the subcontinent.

It must be admitted that this popular magic is not of a very elevated type. It has little philosophical underpinning, and it is not spiritual in intent, not as understood by most people, anyway. For the most part it is concerned with the attainment of purely worldly objectives with the help of supernatural – or at least supernormal – means and methods. Suppose, for instance, that you live in a village and you have a feud going on with one of your neighbours: you want them out of the way, perhaps even dead. Under normal circumstances it is not (fortunately) at all easy to bring this about. The tranquillity of Indian village life hides all sorts of intrigues, but you can't very easily dispose of someone by ordinary means, not unless you have considerable influence. Instead, you will turn to magic. You will have what is known as the rite of destruction performed by an expert in the magic arts, or you may even perform it yourself. Either way, you will hope thereby to bring about the death of your enemy.

When I lived in Kalimpong there was quite a lot of magic of this sort going on. On the night of the new moon I would very often hear from my vihara the sound of little drums beating some few hundred yards away: tuck tuck tuck, tuck tuck tuck, tuck tuck tuck, sometimes all night, with a horrible wailing and shrieking, as the magician or sorcerer (the *jakri*, as they called him) uttered his incantations, dancing and beating his drum. The aim would not usually be to cause somebody's death, but certainly he would be performing his ritual for some nefarious purpose. Quite often a death in that area would be attributed to some kind of witchcraft, or black magic, as we would call it. In India, and especially along the Himalayan border, practices of this sort are not unknown even today.

As well as the need to eliminate, or at least harm, your enemies, magic serves other dubious, if less criminal, motives. Suppose, for instance, you have the misfortune to fall in love, and you find that the object of your affections doesn't show any interest in your advances. What do you do? The time-honoured remedy is to resort to love magic – which, unsurprisingly, is even more popular than death magic. You perform – or you have performed for you – the rite of fascination, and as a result, the person in whom you are interested is supposed to be inexorably drawn to you despite themselves – perhaps even against their better judgement – as though by some irresistible force. People in India who see you as some kind of holy man – young women especially – are quite likely to ask you if you have any magic powers in this line.

There is, of course, something else that has the same enduring interest as love for most people: money. Suppose you live in a village in India, in a miserable hut, with little more than a few pots and pans, a few pieces of cloth and an old bedstead, and no prospect of making money by ordinary means, but a strong hankering after wealth. There is no need to despair; you always have the option of performing the 'rite of prospering' – or, more reliably, having it performed for you. The only snag in this kind of get-rich-quick plan is that such rites are usually rather expensive.

Many other magic rites, for all sorts of worldly purposes, have been handed down in Indian villages from ancient times down to the present day: rites for gaining offspring, rites for paralysing people, rites for pacifying enemies and evil spirits, rites for winning law suits, rites for warding off misfortune, rites for curing disease, and so on. As it developed, the Indian Buddhist Tantra adopted and adapted quite a number of these rites, taking over their symbolism and refining it, imbuing it with new meaning. For instance, it came to associate rites of various kinds with the different Buddha families. All the Buddhas and bodhisattvas are organized, according to their spiritual affinities, into these groups – the *vajra* family, the jewel family, the lotus family, and so on – and each magic rite came to be associated with one or another of them.

Furthermore, each of the important rites came to be regarded as symbolizing a certain activity of the Enlightened mind. In the Tantra, Enlightenment is conceived – and experienced – not as a passive or inert state into which you become absorbed, but as something active, dynamic, almost vibrating, and expressing itself in terms of action. In the Indian Buddhist Tantra even the old magical rite of destruction symbolizes one of the Enlightened mind's principal functions – the destruction of the real enemy: ignorance. The rite of fascination, on the other hand, symbolizes the activity of charming the hearts of living beings. According to this way of looking at things, the Enlightened mind exercises on all living beings an unrivalled – if subtle – fascination. Enlightenment is not only truth, reality, the supreme good, not only profound compassion; it is also what everybody truly desires, whether they know it or not. When you are attracted by something beautiful, whether in nature or in art, what you are really being attracted by is the transcendent beauty of which all these particular beauties are reflections. Enlightenment is experienced and described as pure beauty, a beauty that may be experienced through all things, and to which all living beings are drawn.

Out of the ancient Greek trinity of ideals – the good, the true, and the beautiful – we are perhaps inclined to think of beauty as being a little less important than the other two. The Puritan tradition in the West tends to look askance at an ideal that is expressed in terms of beauty and fascination, and the Buddhist Theravāda also tends to be somewhat suspicious of beauty. Theravādins tell very approvingly the story of a monk who occupied a cell for forty years and, when a visitor commented on the frescoes on the walls, said, 'What frescoes?' Similarly, St Bernard famously made a point of ignoring the Alps when on his way to Rome. But for the Greeks the beautiful was unquestionably linked with the ethical, and beauty also developed a definitely transcendental dimension in Sufism, in Neoplatonism, and in some forms of Hinduism. Indeed, despite Theravādin strictures, traces of this ideal are to be found in the Pāli canon itself. In Pāli, *subha* (Sanskrit *śubha*) means 'pure' as well as 'beautiful', and 'the release called the beautiful' is the third of what are called the eight *vimokṣas*, (Pāli *vimokkhas*) the eight liberations.[109]

The link between beauty and the positivity that is the hallmark of spiritual life is not hard to see. If you take beauty as your goal, you begin to see beauty everywhere, to see everything as beautiful, and thus to take delight in everyone and everything, and to act positively towards them. If you develop *mettā*, loving-kindness, you will naturally see beauty in people, even in those who would conventionally be regarded as ugly. The obvious danger of being susceptible to beauty is that it is usually appreciated very definitely on the *kāmaloka* level, the level of merely worldly pleasure, or as a more refined aesthetic experience, on the level of the *rūpaloka*, the level of subtle, archetypal form. But is beauty limited to that which has form? Could you not say that infinite space has its own beauty – or infinite consciousness, for that matter? Plato speaks in the *Symposium* of a progression from beautiful forms to beautiful characters,[110] while the link between beauty and truth is acknowledged by scientists in search of 'elegant' proofs. Likewise, in the visualization of a Buddha or bodhisattva, the colour and beauty of their forms is not just a sweetener, to make them attractive; it is expressive of the wisdom, compassion, and energy that they embody. Their beauty represents the real beauty of those qualities – and our aesthetic response should not stop at the level of light and colour.

To the rites of destruction and fascination, the Tantra added a further two rites garnered from the old magical traditions, which they saw as also corresponding to functions of the Enlightened mind. There was the rite of prospering, which symbolized the Enlightened mind's capacity to encourage unenlightened minds to grow in the direction of Enlightenment, together with the rite of pacification, which is connected with the soothing calm imparted by the Enlightened mind – as, for example, when the historical Buddha tamed an elephant that had been made to charge at him.[111]

The Tāntrikas came to associate these rites with particular colours. Colour possesses not only aesthetic but also symbolic value, and the colours associated with each rite expressed the mood of the rite and the type of transcendental activity it had come to represent. The rite of destruction was said to be black, the rite of fascination red, the rite of prospering yellow, and the rite of pacification white. When considering the symbolism of colours, we must be careful to remember the nature of symbolism in general. We are not trying to attach a fixed meaning to each and every colour. The idea is more to conjure up, to feel, whatever emotional and spiritual associations the colours may possess. We will find that the Tantric symbolism of colours does not always correspond to the symbolism of colours in the West, or even in other parts of the East.

So, to begin with, what are the associations of the colour red? It is the colour of blood and hence the colour of life – physical life and, by implication, life in general. No blood, no life. And just as blood is hot, red is the colour of warmth, both physical and emotional. Red, indeed, is the colour of all the positive emotions – and in particular, according to the Tantric tradition, the colour of love.

The word 'love' can of course mean many different things. We can get a better idea of the emotion the Tantra associated with the colour red by considering the Sanskrit word used by the Tantra in this context: *mahā-rāga*. *Rāga* in the ordinary literary or psychological context is a word for strong, even violent, passion, and *mahā-rāga* thus means 'great passion'. But *mahā* has a special meaning in Buddhism, especially in the context of the Mahāyāna and the Vajrayāna. It usually stands for or suggests *śūnyatā* – which is another term that is difficult to translate into English. *Śūnyatā* means emptiness. It also means fullness. It means the relative, and also the absolute. Probably the best way to translate it in this context is 'reality' or 'truth', 'the ultimate' or 'the transcendental'.

This term *mahā*, used as a prefix, therefore suggests that whatever is referred to by the word to which it is prefixed partakes of the nature of *śūnyatā*; that is, it has been purified by passing through the flames of the *śūnyatā* experience. If a word is prefixed by *mahā*, it is not to be understood in its ordinary sense, but as representing something that has been merged with reality, or plunged into reality, or purified by the experience of reality. Hence the word Mahāyāna – to take an obvious example – doesn't just mean the great *yāna* (way) as opposed to the small *yāna*. It means the *yāna* that consists in the experience of ultimate reality, or that is at least heading in the direction of ultimate reality. Likewise, the expression *mahāsattva*, as in *bodhisattva-mahāsattva* (a term found in the *Diamond Sūtra*, for instance) doesn't just mean a great being. It means a being whose whole nature has been transformed through immersion in the experience of *śūnyatā*. A *mahāsattva* is a transcendentalized being – a *śūnyatā*-ized being, one might say.

So *mahā-rāga*, in the context of the Tantra, doesn't mean great passion in the sense of an excessive passion. It means a wholly spiritualized emotion. The strength of the emotion – the emotionality – is undiminished, but it has been purified, plunged into the depths of *śūnyatā* and thoroughly transformed. *Mahā-rāga* is a spiritualized, even transcendental, passion. We can describe it – if we have to describe it at all – as an uninterrupted stream of powerful, positive feeling that flows spontaneously from the very heart of Enlightenment in the direction of all living beings. All this is symbolized in the Tantra by the colour red.

The colour yellow brings with it a very different set of associations. It is the colour of sunshine, the colour of the ripened grain, of harvest – deep, rich, and golden. It is therefore the colour of growth, maturity, even perfection. In agricultural communities, a good harvest means prosperity, so yellow is also the colour of riches, abundance, profusion, plenty – not just in a limited material sense, but also spiritual riches. Yellow therefore suggests an abundance of good qualities, and especially an abundance of merits. By extension, yellow also comes to signify whatever is rare, precious, and valuable. And because what is precious gives delight, yellow also comes to have associations of delight, exuberance, and beauty of every kind, physical and spiritual. At the highest level yellow comes to represent the inexhaustible wealth and incessant creativity of the Enlightened mind, a creativity that overflows in a shower of plenty on all living beings.

Green conveys very different emotions again, though still entirely positive. It is the colour of grass, the tender shoots of young rice plants, and the leaves of the great forests. It is the colour of nature – not nature red in tooth and claw, but nature in its most restful and tranquil aspect. Green is thus the colour of freedom from danger, distress, fear, and anxiety, and therefore also of refuge, shelter, protection – indeed, the colour of Going for Refuge. It is the colour of harmony, balance, and healing – and also, paradoxically, the colour of action, especially action taken to restore an equilibrium that has been lost. As such, it is the colour of justice and even of karma. It might seem strange to distinguish an abstract term by its colour, but that is where colour considered in symbolic terms leads us – in this case, to say that karma is, as it were, green. Green therefore represents the harmonizing, reconciling, balancing aspect of the Enlightened mind – the aspect that rounds off the corners, brings things together, and smoothes irregularities. It also represents the restorative, healing aspect of Enlightenment.

Blue is most obviously the colour of the sky – and the word sky instantly suggests vastness, limitlessness, even infinity, so blue has these connotations too. A clear blue midday sky, free of clouds – the kind of sky you get in the tropics – suggests freedom from all obscurations. This is no theoretical symbolism: you can really feel that sense of freedom when you see such a sky, as one often does in India or Tibet, like a vast dome of pure deep brilliant blue, with not a fleck of cloud obscuring it anywhere. Through its association with the cloudless sky, blue comes to symbolize truth – truth in its nakedness, unclouded, unveiled, truth that is like the blue sky, shining and infinite. Even when there are clouds in the sky, they come and go, while the sky behind them remains unchanged. So blue is not simply the colour of reality, of truth, but more specifically the colour of reality in its eternal, unconditioned aspect – that which does not change, that which remains when all transitory things have passed away. Thus it represents not just an *aspect* of the Enlightened mind, but the Enlightened mind itself.

White is the colour of snow, of the snow peaks of the Himalayas – peaks that have remained untrodden from age to age, and remain untouched, unsullied. White is therefore the colour of peace, purity, freedom from disturbance. It is also the colour of centrality. More actively, it represents the removal of all obstacles and difficulties, and thus the calming, pacifying aspect of the Enlightened mind as the allayer of all ill and the remover of all sorrow. The sixteenth-century English poet Edmund Spenser captures well this kind of feeling in two famous lines from his epic poem, *The Faerie Queene*:

> Sleep after toil, port after stormy seas,
> Ease after war, death after life, does greatly please.[112]

White represents this peace that greatly pleases, the peace that passes all understanding, as St Paul put it (referring to the peace of God).[113]

Finally, black is the colour of night, midnight, the colour of the charred wood of the cremation ground. In the context of the Tantra it stands for death and destruction – not just physical death but spiritual death, the destruction of the ego, of ignorance, of all that stands in the way of Enlightenment.

These, then, are a few of the associations of the principal colours in the Tantric tradition. There are many other colours that occur in Tantric art and meditation – grey, brown, orange, light blue, pink, pale green – and these too have symbolic associations, although they are rather less clear-cut than those of the principal colours. Indeed, all colours have associations of some kind, because no colour exists in the abstract, least of all in the Tantra. Colour is always found in association with an object – it is always the colour *of* something – and that something has its own significance. We have already come across this in relation to many of the symbols we have encountered. For example, a different colour is assigned to each of the five elements symbolized by the stupa: yellow for earth, white for water, red for fire, pale green for air, and gold or rainbow-colour for space. In the last chapter we saw that each of the four continents of traditional Buddhist cosmology has a colour. Moreover, the six worlds of the Tibetan wheel of life into which beings can be reborn as a result of their karma, and which also represent mental states that can be experienced here and now in this life, are associated with light of a particular colour: the world of the gods with a dull white light, the world of the Titans with a dull red light, the world of the hungry ghosts with a dull yellow light, the world of tormented beings with a smoke-coloured light, the animal world with a dull green light, and the human world with a dull blue light.

In the Tantric tradition every symbol is carefully assigned a colour. It is as though the Tantra is trying to remind us of something we are inclined to forget: that everything in the universe has colour, or is experienced as possessing colour – and not just possessing it, but alive and glowing and radiant with it – and that colour has an emotional effect on us. This is only just beginning to be understood in the West, but it has been known to the Tantra for centuries. Suppose, for example, that instead of being blue, the sky was a bright emerald green, and that instead of being green in spring and golden in autumn, the leaves on the trees were bright red throughout the year, to match the bright red grass. Surely it would feel entirely different to go out into the countryside under an emerald green sky, with red trees and red grass around us.

Many philosophies see existence in black and white rather than in glorious Technicolor. Theravāda Buddhism, for example, is content to make certain black and white distinctions: skilful and unskilful, for example. But there are all sorts of beautiful colours to be seen in the spiritual life, and this comes out in Mahāyāna *sūtras* and Vajrayāna art, which are full of light and colour. Visionary art is always made of pure, bright, transparent, luminous colours, most obviously in the stained-glass windows of the great French cathedrals. By contrast, when you look at some eighteenth-century European paintings, you can tell from the sobriety of their colouring that they were painted in a rationalistic age. Colour came back into western art with the advent of a new age of faith, in the works of William Blake, Turner, and the Pre-Raphaelites. It has been said that the pure, bright colours of Persian miniature paintings correspond to visionary experience on the part of the painter. Gold leaf plays an important part in these paintings, as it does in medieval Christian art; it is as if the gold represents the transcendental itself breaking through into the archetypal world of the paintings. In Japanese paintings, similarly, you will sometimes see the figure of the Buddha Amitābha appearing from behind mountains like a rising sun, with rays emerging from his body against a pure gold background, like the vision of Enlightenment dawning on the purified human consciousness.

Thus, if we have to choose between thinking of reality as colourless and thinking of it as colourful, it is far better to think of it as colourful – better, at least, for most people. It is better for the same reason that an image will give us a better idea of what Buddhahood or Reality is like than will an abstract conceptual definition. Mathematicians may be moved by the concept of infinity, but it leaves most of us cold. We don't want the transcendental merely to convince us; we want it to inspire us, coax us, even seduce us. So, the more vivid, poetic, and colourful, the better. Nor is it enough to *think* of reality in that way; we must *see* it in that way – because it *is* like that: it is fascinating and alluring as much as it is a matter of abstract concepts.

From the way the Tantra assigns colours to the forms of Buddhas and bodhisattvas, it is evident that this is how Tantric practitioners saw things. In Tantric Buddhist art these figures are never envisaged naturalistically. The depictions are not meant to tell you what a Buddha or bodhisattva or *ḍākinī* or *dharmapāla* looks like on the material, historical plane; this art is symbolic, not representational. Strange as it may seem to have a Buddha or bodhisattva whose face and body are emerald green, or ruby red, or sapphire blue, this is how the Tantra sees them – in full, brilliant colour. Every Buddha or bodhisattva has a colour – indeed, *is* a luminous, transparent, jewel-like colour.

Not only this: some of these figures have varying forms, of a multitude of colours. For instance, Tārā, one of the most popular bodhisattvas, appears in many forms, including a well-known set of twenty-one, and according to some traditions Avalokiteśvara, the Bodhisattva of Compassion, manifests through 108 forms. In each case the specific colour is as significant as – if not rather more significant than – every other detail of the symbolism.

Faced with all these forms and colours, it is reasonable to ask why there are so many. To understand this, we have to remember the Tantra's emphasis on direct experience. The experience of oneself in the ultimate depths of one's being is to be achieved, according to the Tantra and all other Buddhist traditions, with the help of meditation. There are very many methods of meditation, and the Tantra has certain methods of its own (in some cases developed from Mahāyāna techniques). One of the best known of these is visualization. It is considered that we can only conceive of the Enlightened mind, ineffable and absolute as it is, in terms of a variety of aspects. It may be approached under the aspect of love, of compassion, of beauty, of primordial purity, of complete peace, of wisdom, or of spiritual power and sovereignty; and each of these aspects of the Buddha mind can be – in a sense, *is* – personified in the form of a particular Buddha or bodhisattva. Love, for instance, is personified as Kurukullā, compassion as Avalokiteśvara, wisdom as Mañjuśrī, and purity as Vajrasattva.

This superabundance of divine forms appears on the horizon of Tantric Buddhism, and you select for yourself – or your guru selects

for you – a form that corresponds to some quality you especially need to develop, or towards which you are especially drawn – love, wisdom, energy, or whatever it may be. After all, bodhisattvas are within us potentially, just as the Enlightenment experience is within us potentially. When we repeat the mantras of bodhisattvas, we are therefore in a way calling up our own inner forces, trying to get in touch with them. When we repeat the mantra of Mañjughoṣa we are invoking our own innate undeveloped wisdom, and when we repeat the mantra of Avalokiteśvara we are trying to make contact with our own innate compassion.

The selection made, you learn to visualize that figure in meditation. You practise until you can see it in your mind's eye: the shape, insignia, dress, and – perhaps more than any other aspect – the colour. Sometimes when you start visualizing you just see an undifferentiated patch of colour before it gradually assumes, with practice, the definite form of the Buddha or bodhisattva. But to see the colour, and even to feel it, is very important in this type of practice, because it is the colour that gives you the inner feeling of that particular Buddha or bodhisattva, so subtle a feeling that it cannot be put into words. In the course of time, however, if you are meditating on, say, a red Buddha, or a green bodhisattva, or a white *ḍākinī*, you will experience something rather strange. For example, if you have been doing the visualization practice of Green Tārā, you eventually experience what might be described as the spiritual equivalent of greenness. Or, to put it the other way round, the colour green is the equivalent in terms of colour of the spiritual experience known in its personified form as Tārā – the very quintessence of tenderness and compassion. When you start to experience greenness as more than a colour, as a symbol, to that extent you experience Tārā. As a symbol, the colour becomes a vehicle for the experience of the spiritual state that it symbolizes. If this idea seems mysterious, it should be reiterated that such symbolism can be understood only from one's own practice and experience.

The symbolism associated with these figures is not only that of form and colour. There is also the symbolism of sound, specifically mantric sound. Mantra used to be translated as 'magic words', which is as unhelpful as the old translation of mandala as 'magic circle', and sometimes even now mantra is, again rather less than usefully, rendered as 'spell'. The traditional etymology of mantra is 'that which protects the mind', and it is undoubtedly true that reciting a mantra has this effect, but so does every other spiritual practice, so this doesn't get us very far either. The most important thing to understand about a mantra is that it is a sound symbol, just as the figure of a Buddha or bodhisattva is a form and colour symbol. It is a sound symbol, that is to say, of a particular aspect of the Enlightened mind. Just as the figure of Avalokiteśvara is what compassion would look like if we could see it, the mantra associated with Avalokiteśvara is what compassion would sound like if we could hear it.

Some people explain the efficacy of mantras in terms of physical vibrations: after making certain measurements, technicians have pronounced that if you recite such-and-such a mantra you produce such-and-such a density of sonic vibrations, and that the mantra that produces the highest density is the most spiritually efficacious. Such crude and materialistic calculations have rightly been ridiculed by Lama Govinda, who pointed out that if the efficacy of mantras were a matter of physically measurable sonic vibrations, all you would need to do in order to derive benefit from them would be to get a recording of mantras being chanted and play it over and over again.[114]

But although mantric sound can be external, in the sense of being produced by the voice, its significance does not lie in the actual physical sound. A mantra is essentially an inner sound, an inner vibration, even an inner feeling. Not that the external sound has no significance at all – there is certainly a place for reciting mantras aloud – but the recitation is only a means to the subtle internal experience of the mantra. The relation between the two is rather like that between a painting of a Buddha or bodhisattva and the same figure as visualized in meditation. In both cases the gross leads to the experience of the subtle, or acts as a catalyst for it.

The recitation of mantras occupies an extremely important place in the Tantra, so much so that an early term for Tantric practice, predating 'Vajrayāna', was 'Mantranaya', the path of mantras (generally referred to nowadays as Mantrayāna). Mantranaya was paired with Pāramitānaya, the path of perfections, and together the two paths were considered to constitute the Mahāyāna. Spiritual progress was said to be more rapid on the Mantranaya than on the Pāramitānaya – but it is not obvious why this should be so, given that the practice of the perfections is itself said to represent a complete scheme of ethical and spiritual development. One reason for this is that the practice of the

perfections, at least in its early stages, is aimed at the conscious mind, while the Mantranaya, by contrast, is directed more to the unconscious depths. It is aimed at contacting the spiritual forces latent within us, the forces that are ultimately the various aspects of the Enlightened mind and are personified, or crystallized, in the form of Buddhas and bodhisattvas. These forces can be contacted, according to the Tantra, through the joint practice of visualization and invocation: visualization of form and colour, and invocation with mantric sound.

It is possible to get very technical about mantras, and to classify them in a variety of ways, but I propose to attempt a definition by means of a short, simple description. First of all, a mantra is a string of syllables from the Sanskrit alphabet, sometimes, but not always, including Sanskrit words.

Secondly, mantras are not susceptible to conceptual analysis, and it is therefore traditional not to translate them, even though it is in some cases possible to give them a literal rendering. In a sense, they are meaningless; that's the point of them, in a way. Take, for instance, the Tārā mantra. It consists of just a series of modulations of the vocative form of the name Tārā. There is no analysable meaning; you are just juggling with the sound of the name. Some mantras do contain meaningful words; for instance, in the famous mantra '*oṃ maṇi padme hūṃ*,' *maṇi* means 'jewel' and *padme* means 'lotus', so that while you can't translate the initial *oṃ* or the concluding *hūṃ*, *maṇi padme* has often been translated as 'the jewel in the lotus' (though as Donald Lopez makes clear in *Prisoners of Shangri-la*, the translation should really be 'Jewel-Lotus (One)').[115] In any case, the meaning of the words doesn't give the real – much less the total – meaning of the mantra. Either 'the jewel in the lotus' or 'Jewel-Lotus One' is perfectly plausible philosophically, with all sorts of ramifications in Buddhist thought and practice, but to say that the mantra *means* that doesn't give the real – much less the total – meaning of the mantra; it gives just a facet of it, and not even the most important one. Mantras cannot be logically analysed; they don't have a meaning in the ordinary conceptual sense. Even when they do contain words with an assignable meaning, these only suggest the spirit of the mantra and the general direction in which its meaning may be found.

Thirdly, and most importantly, a mantra is the sound symbol of a particular Buddha or bodhisattva. When that divinity becomes or manifests as a sound, which according to the Tantra he or she can and does, that sound is the mantra. Just as the visualized image is the equivalent of the Buddha or bodhisattva in terms of form and colour, so the mantra is the equivalent in terms of sound. The mantra is therefore, in a sense, the name of the divinity. It may or may not include the name usually used to refer to the divinity – that doesn't matter. When we call people by name they come, and when we invoke a Buddha or bodhisattva with a mantra, the divinity appears, or manifests, or becomes – in a sense – present.

Fourthly, the mantra is given by the guru at the time of initiation, otherwise it is not really a mantra. In fact, traditional initiation can consist wholly in the giving of a mantra. Usually one repeats the mantra three times after the guru, by which means energy is transmitted. Of course, it is possible to learn a mantra through hearing it chanted in a puja, and start reciting it yourself. You will get some benefit from this, but what you are reciting is not really a mantra. Mantra includes as part of its meaning that you are empowered to use it by the guru. The usual method is to receive it from a living human teacher, though it is possible to be given a mantra in a dream or in meditation by a guru figure or even by a Buddha or bodhisattva. If you get the mantra in any other way, it may be a good religious practice, but it isn't Tantric recitation.

Fifthly and lastly, a mantra has to be repeated. Having received it from the guru, you must repeat it with the energy with which it was transmitted to you; otherwise, the energy is eventually lost. Sometimes it is said that if you neglect to repeat the mantra for three years, its original energy is entirely lost, and reinitiation is required. But if you repeat the mantra regularly the energy increases and eventually repetition becomes spontaneous, continuing without conscious effort.

The reason visionary colours and mantric sound figure so prominently in Tantric meditation and ritual isn't difficult to determine. As we saw in the previous chapter, all the physical senses are to be dedicated to Enlightenment, and of these, sight and hearing are more subtle and refined, at least in human beings, than the other three. The senses have both gross and subtle forms, and the subtle counterparts of sight and hearing are more highly developed than those of smell, taste, and touch. It is with subtle sight that we see in meditation the forms of Buddhas and bodhisattvas, and with subtle hearing that we hear their mantras. It is possible to experience the subtle counterparts of the other senses too – when you are meditating you may, for instance, smell a perfume that isn't physically there or feel a breeze that is not blowing – but these experiences are exceptional, and even when they do occur, they are usually faint and intermittent.

In visualizing form and colour and reciting the appropriate mantra, we are approaching an aspect of the Enlightened mind through the medium of two different senses, and thus converging on the experience from two directions. This makes it much more likely that we will actually experience that aspect. It is like holding something between two fingers instead of just touching it with one. This is why in the Tantra visualization and mantra recitation are so important in conjunction with each other, and why Tantric ritual, in which sound and colour are invariably brought together, is such an important part of the whole Tantric tradition.

Tantric ritual seems to work in somewhat similar ways to the equivalent practices of other traditions. Later Neoplatonist 'theurgy', for example, is based on a system of correspondences: you manipulate things lower down the scale in such a way as to provide an effective basis for the manifestation of the corresponding reality higher up; and perhaps this is how all ritual works.

Thus, if you wanted to invoke the figure of Green Tārā, the bodhisattva in female form who embodies the quintessence of tenderness and compassion, you could start by including in your ritual whatever seemed to correspond to the qualities of Tārā in terms of the ordinary objects, colours, and sounds to which we have access in the world of the senses. The colour green would presumably play a prominent part in the decor, with green vases, green carpets, green hangings and robes – perhaps the walls could even be painted green for the occasion – while any music you played would be gentle, pleasing, and charming, as Tārā herself is said to be. All this would focus attention and energy on your recitation of the litanies of Tārā, and on the image of her on the shrine, to create a context within which you could invoke Tārā and experience her, or what she represents, more intensely. (Of course, the theurgic type of approach will not be appropriate and helpful for everybody.)

Incidentally, Tārā is a suitable deity to start with, if one is considering experimenting with rituals of this kind. She is traditionally regarded as a 'safe' deity; the Tibetans say that even if you perform her puja wrongly or mispronounce her mantra, she won't mind; there will never be any repercussions; Tārā will overlook all mistakes. Nor is it at all wrong to think in terms of experiment in this kind of context, providing that you really do regard it as an experiment – that is, you take notice of the spiritual effect of what you do.

The founder of Neoplatonism, Plotinus, seems to have had no interest in ritual, instead favouring meditation and reflection, and even the development of insight, as a Buddhist might say. But later teachers such as Iamblichus either found that meditation and reflection was too difficult, or felt that it was not suited to everybody, and they brought in theurgy in various ways, so that it became more or less a substitute for meditation. Some of them were influenced by Egyptian magic and symbolism – in much the same way that we are influenced by Buddhist symbolism – and took various Egyptian rites for their models.

Almost all writers on Neoplatonism fail to recognize the spiritual function of theurgy at all, and treat it as a sign of degeneration and an irruption of superstition, in the same way that writers on Buddhism used to condemn the Tantra. But in the case of the Tantra it is not that you throw away Mahāyāna philosophy in favour of Tantric ritual; the ritual is one of the means of implementing the realization of the philosophy.

So far we have examined only the theory; it is all very different in practice, and no description in words can be a substitute for that. But we can perhaps get some idea of the experience by means of a closer look at how the Tantra uses colours and mantric sound in the context of *sādhana*. *Sādhana* practice, the visualization of a Buddha or bodhisattva, with accompanying mantra recitation, involves a similar convergence of colour and sound, but in a much more subtle way than can be achieved in the collective, external setting of ritual. Here, then, is a résumé of a Mañjughoṣa *sādhana*, the visualization of Mañjughoṣa, the sweet-voiced one, the Bodhisattva of Wisdom.

The practice begins, as all such exercises do, when you see before you with your inner spiritual vision a vast blue sky – blue sky in all directions. You see it, concentrate on it, become absorbed in it. Then, in the midst of the blue sky, you see rainbow-tinted clouds massing, and drifting together. Framed by the clouds, you see a pale-blue lotus throne with beautiful unfolding petals, on which is spread what is known as a moon mat. It looks like an oval because you are seeing it from the side, but it is round, white and very brilliant, just like the moon. On this moon mat is seated cross-legged the figure of Mañjughoṣa. He appears in the form of a beautiful sixteen-year-old youth – sixteen being the ideal age as far as beauty is concerned, according to the Indian tradition. He is a deep rich yellow colour, not opaque like paint on a wall, but luminous, transparent, diaphanous, like a reflection in a mirror, or a section of rainbow – delicate, tender, subtle.

The figure is clad in the silks and jewels of a bodhisattva, and the long black tresses of his hair spread across his shoulders, while on his head he wears a garland of five pale blue lotus blossoms. His face wears a smiling and compassionate expression. This figure of Mañjughoṣa, the sweet-voiced one, sitting there on that moon mat, on that pale blue lotus throne, beautiful yellow in colour, is the embodiment of transcendental

wisdom, the lord of speech, the patron of the arts and sciences. His right arm is uplifted, and in his right hand he flourishes above his head the flaming sword of knowledge with which he cuts the bonds of karma and ignorance. In his left hand he holds the book of the Perfection of Wisdom, pressing it to his heart. The whole figure is surrounded by a shining aura of blue and green and golden light.

At the heart of the bodhisattva you see a letter, a seed syllable, *dhīḥ*, which represents the essence of wisdom. It is fiery orange-golden in colour, and from it comes a ray of amber light, which falls on the top of your head and from there passes down into your heart. Along that ray, from the heart of Mañjughoṣa into your heart, the syllables of the mantra descend: *oṃ a ra pa ca na dhīḥ, oṃ a ra pa ca na dhīḥ*. Having received the mantra into your heart, you go on reciting it, and as you do so, you feel that you are absorbing wisdom, that wisdom is flowing from Mañjughoṣa into your own heart, your own being. You feel that your ignorance is being dispelled, that you are being transformed, transmuted, into the image of Mañjughoṣa. As you feel the presence of Mañjughoṣa, you become more and more like that presence: you assimilate it, or it assimilates you. It's as though you and Mañjughoṣa are coming closer and closer together, even merging, or at least touching, as though you are in the process of becoming wisdom itself. When that happens, or when that begins to happen, you are realizing the wisdom aspect of the Enlightened mind, and through it, entering into the Enlightened mind itself. And at that point you are really beginning to understand, to some extent at least, the Tantric symbolism of colours and mantric sound.

8

THE FIVE BUDDHAS, 'MALE' AND 'FEMALE'

At the very beginning of this exploration of the creative symbols of Tantric Buddhism, we saw that the Tantra is characterized by a variety of interlocking patterns that unfold from within it, expressing its essential nature. The subject of this chapter is one of the most important of these, and unless we are familiar with it – not just intellectually, but emotionally and spiritually – we have little hope of finding our way around in the apparent jungle of the Tantra. To understand the symbolism of the five Buddhas, however, we need to go back to the fundamentals of Buddhism. In fact, we need to go right back to the Buddha, to the individual who gained supreme perfect knowledge and made his knowledge known. It is to one who has broken through to this achievement that the term 'Buddha' refers. A Buddha is still a human being, but he is the highest kind of human being possible, having transcended in his spiritual development the rest of humanity.

In western thought we have the concept of humanity, the concept of God, and the concept of reality, but we don't have any concept equivalent to 'Buddha', and we therefore have to shift our mode of thinking to accustom ourselves to it. The idea that a human being can become an embodiment of reality by his or her own efforts presupposes a conception of the possibilities of human development such as has not been envisaged in the West until very recently. Christians, and ex-Christians, tend to think of the Buddha as a sort of oriental Jesus; this is how his status was explained by the Theosophists at the end of the nineteenth century, for example. Others took up the Hindu idea of the Buddha as an incarnation of God, an avatar. Alternatively, there is the mistake of thinking of the Buddha as being no more than a very good and wise man, perhaps a bit like Socrates.

This difficulty in categorizing the Buddha in fact dates back to the Buddha's own time. The Pāli canon recounts his meeting with a Brahmin called Doṇa who tries to understand what kind of being the Buddha might be. 'Are you a god?' 'No.' 'Are you a *gandharva*?' 'No.' 'Are you a *yakṣa*?' 'No.' 'Are you a man?' 'No.' Eventually the Buddha says, 'Those karmic tendencies on account of which I might have been placed in one of those categories have been exhausted. Therefore I am a Buddha.'[116] One is born as a god or a human being or an animal or some other kind of being on account of one's skilful and unskilful actions in previous lives. But if you have transcended all karma, if all those individualizing tendencies have been brought to an end, how are you to be described? You may still be associated with the body which is the product of those tendencies, but it no longer represents you. In the notion of Buddha, humanity and the absolute coalesce. In a sense, humanity ceases to be humanity as we understand the term. At the same time, the absolute ceases to be the absolute in a merely abstract sense: it becomes realized, even embodied.

The Buddhist tradition has a technical term that encapsulates all this: one can say that a Buddha is a human being who has attained *samyak-sambodhi*. *Bodhi* means knowledge, understanding, awakening, and *samyak* means 'supreme' or 'perfect'; so *samyak-sambodhi* is supreme perfect knowledge, or understanding, or awakening. *Bodhi* can be said to have three main aspects: cognitive, volitional, and emotional.

From the cognitive point of view, it is a condition of insight, a state of wisdom or awareness. In the first place, this awareness consists in a clear understanding of yourself. It involves seeing yourself thoroughly and deeply, taking a long, close look at yourself, and seeing that you are conditioned on every level of your being, that you are not free, that you are just reacting mechanically on account of various psychological factors of conditioning of which you are largely unconscious. As your insight deepens, you also see the extent to which you are governed, dominated, directed even against your will or without your knowledge, by the negative emotions.

The cognitive aspect of *bodhi* also encompasses insight into others. You extend your vision to take in other people and see the ways in which they also are conditioned, just as you are. Then, ranging even further afield, you take into account all phenomena, the whole of nature, the whole of conditioned existence, the universe itself on all its levels, and you see that everything is conditioned, that the universe itself is transitory, ever-changing, frustrating, and unreal.

Beyond this the cognitive aspect of *bodhi* is a developing insight into the Unconditioned. Having seen how you yourself are conditioned, and how other beings, and the universe as a whole, are conditioned, you see right through the conditioned nature of things, penetrating into the depths of the conditioned and finding there the Unconditioned. In the depths of the transitory, you see the eternal; in the depths of the unreal, you see the real. Ultimately, you see the two as different facets of one and the same reality. This is insight, awareness, wisdom – the cognitive aspect of *bodhi*. And if these words sound merely baffling – well, they are just words, and words cannot convey the profound nature of this experience. For *bodhi* is not just a state of knowledge; it also has what can be called a volitional aspect. It is a state of untrammelled freedom, that is at once subjective and objective. Subjectively, it is a state of freedom from all moral and spiritual defilement, from all negative emotions, from the five mental poisons, from the whole process of the reactive mind, while objectively it consists in freedom from the consequences of defilement and the mental poisons – i.e. freedom from karma and rebirth, from the turning of the wheel of life and death. More positively, the volitional aspect of *bodhi* is a state of uninterrupted creativity and spontaneity.

Thirdly, *bodhi* has its emotional aspect. It is a state of positive emotion subjectively, an experience of supreme joy, bliss, happiness, and ecstasy, and objectively, a state of unbounded love and compassion for all living beings.

Bodhi is thus a state of full insight – into self and others, into conditioned and unconditioned. It is a state of absolute freedom, both liberation within and objective freedom. And it is a state of supreme bliss, infinite love, and unbounded compassion. A Buddha is a human being who has attained this state, who is the human embodiment of insight, freedom, happiness, and love.

At the beginning of the Buddhist tradition in the current historical era there was only one Buddha – *the* Buddha, as we usually say: Śākyamuni, the prince who gained Enlightenment 2,500 years ago. Even once the Buddha's followers began to break through into the nature of reality themselves, it was still clear – to them and to others – that there was a vast difference between them and the Buddha. Some of the Buddha's disciples apparently attained transcendental insight just in one lifetime, sometimes in the course of a few hours, or in a single instant. But the Buddha himself had clearly attained a much higher level of Enlightenment than anyone else, to the extent that it seemed impossible that he should have achieved it in one lifetime, and much more likely that it had been achieved over many, many lifetimes. People went on enlarging their conception of the Buddha's Enlightenment in this way, and making more and more elaborate the process by which he attained it, until it was reckoned that the whole process had taken three *asaṃkhyeya* (unreckonable) aeons.

From there it was a short step to the idea of the 'magical body'. Even in the Pāli scriptures the Buddha refers to a *manomayakāya*, a mind-made body, and subsequently it came to be felt that somewhere in the course of those unreckonable aeons, along with the development of all manner of supernormal powers, the Buddha must have developed a highly subtle and rarefied 'personality'.[117] (The term is not altogether satisfactory, in that *kāya* has none of the associations that – under the influence of Jung – the word persona, meaning literally 'mask', has come to have, but it is a somewhat better translation of *kāya* than 'body'). Mahāyānists felt that by the time the Buddha-to-be had reached the last life before the one in which he gained Enlightenment, he could not have been an ordinary human being at all. They acknowledged that he had started out as a human being, but that, they said, had been many, many lifetimes ago, when he was born as a man called Sumedha, who became an ascetic and met the previous Buddha, Dīpaṅkara, as a result of which meeting he formed the resolution to attain supreme Enlightenment. Then, after life upon life upon life of spiritual development, he finally came to reside in one of the god realms, the Tuṣita *devaloka*, as this supernormal, arguably transcendental, personality – and it was that personality that descended to earth and appeared to be an ordinary human being.

Although this doctrine is an essentially Mahāyāna development, the view may have had its antecedents in Buddhist history, with the Lokottaravādins. A distinguishing characteristic of Lokottaravādin thought was that all worldly phenomena are unreal, and that the only reality is to be found in supramundane or transcendental (*lokottara*) phenomena. In their view, the Buddha-to-be, having started out as a human being, reached such a high level of development that he was able to emanate a form into the world to perform the task of salvation. That emanation we know as the historical figure of Śākyamuni Buddha, who was born in Lumbinī – while the Buddha himself remained, in a manner of speaking, in some other world. If this doctrine suggests a resemblance to the docetic heresy of Christianity, the resemblance is only superficial.[118] The Lokottaravādin idea was not of God descending and appearing to be a man, but of someone who had originally been a man reaching such an elevated state of existence as to be able to emanate a personality in a yogic way on a lower human level.[119]

All this is based on the supposition of the vast difference between the Buddha's Enlightenment and that of his disciples – a supposition that is contradicted by certain passages in the Pāli texts that equate the Buddha's Enlightenment quite specifically with that of his disciples.[120] This obviates the need to infer all those previous lives in order to account for the difference between the Buddha's Enlightenment and that of his disciples, and you are left with an apparently ordinary human historical personality.

It is certainly hard for many Buddhists to accept that the life of the historical Buddha – 'our' Buddha – was no more than a kind of charade or play, which is how it is presented in Mahāyāna texts such as the *Lalitavistara*.[121] But this way of seeing the Buddha's life should not be taken too simplistically. It is a metaphysical interpretation of the historical facts which does not negate history and should not be confused with it. It is analogous to reflecting that the people you meet in the street are all magical illusions. That may be metaphysically true, but it doesn't mean that you experience them as ghostly or wraith-like; you can't see through them, and if you bump into them, they are pretty solid. The historicity and the metaphysical nature of the Buddha's life can be similarly reconciled. Even as a good Mahāyānist there is no reason to imagine that had you been around to meet the Buddha and shake hands with him, your hand would have passed straight through his.

As well as the difference between the Buddha and his Enlightened followers that some people observed, an important distinction was drawn by the Buddha himself between the Enlightened human individual and the abstract principle of Enlightenment, between Buddha and Buddhahood. This distinction found expression in certain technical terms, the Enlightened human historical personality being known as the *rūpakāya* (literally 'form body'), while the principle of Enlightenment, independent of the person realizing it, was known as the *dharmakāya*, the body of truth or body of reality. Note that this is a distinction, not a difference: both the form body and the Dharma body were bodies of the Buddha, in a sense. Although the distinction was made during the Buddha's lifetime, it was not insisted upon very strongly, because in the historical Buddha, *rūpakāya* and *dharmakāya* were united. After the *parinirvāṇa*, however, the distinction between form body and Dharma body became more pronounced. The form body, the Buddha in the flesh, was dead and gone, but the Dharma body was eternally present, as much so after the Buddha's death as during his lifetime.

When the early practitioners of the Mahāyāna turned their attention to this distinction, we can imagine them thinking of it 'vertically'. They thought of the form body as being below, in time, in the past, and the Dharma body as being above, out of time, transcending time, so that there was a vertical relationship between the Enlightened individual and the principle of Enlightenment, between Buddha and Buddhahood.

Later Mahāyānists continued to think in this way, but within that thinking a development took place. A third Buddha appeared – or rather a third *kāya*, a third body, appeared in between the other two. This third *kāya* was known eventually as the *sambhogakāya*. The term literally means 'body of mutual delight or mutual enjoyment', but in this context it is more helpful to translate it interpretively as the ideal Buddha or archetypal Buddha. This ideal Buddha is not an impersonal, abstract principle like the *dharmakāya*. At the same time, he is not a human historical individual. He is the ideal person, the archetypal person – below the level of the Absolute, but above and beyond history.

Thus, at this stage of the development of the tradition, we find three *kāyas* or bodies, all vertically aligned: Dharma body, ideal body, and created body. The last, the historical Buddha, now came to be called the *nirmāṇakāya*, the old term *rūpakāya* being applied to the ideal Buddha and the historical Buddha collectively. Thus arose the famous *trikāya* doctrine, which became very important as the basis for further development in both Mahāyāna and Vajrayāna Buddhism.

This development involved something rather dramatic. The human historical Buddha disappeared into the past – indeed, went almost out of sight, with the result that in Mahāyāna countries today the historical

Buddha, Śākyamuni, occupies a comparatively unimportant place. At the same time, Buddhahood as an abstract principle also receded into the background, perhaps because it was abstract to the point of being vague and difficult to grasp. All that was left, occupying centre stage, was the ideal, archetypal Buddha, and this became the Buddha of the Mahāyāna, as for example in the *Saddharma Puṇḍarīka* or *Lotus Sūtra*. In this text, Śākyamuni does appear, but he is obviously no longer the human historical personality. He has become the ideal Buddha, the archetypal Buddha.[122]

To us it might seem that myth is an integral part of Buddhism, but in fact it was quite a late development. By contrast, in the historical development of Christianity the myth came first – the myth of the saviour, the son of God who is slain by his enemies, then comes back to life and returns to his father in heaven, taking his worshippers with him. The strength – and the weakness – of Christianity is that it is based on a myth of this kind. As time went on, the myth was gradually turned into history; ethical and spiritual teachings were incorporated into it, but the myth came first. Then, the myth being firmly established as history, came the teaching. This is reflected in the Apostles' Creed, which is still recited today: the striking thing about it is that it is nothing but myth. The teaching, a certain amount of which evidently did take place, according to the Gospels, is just passed over, apparently regarded as being of no significance. A Christian is not someone who believes in the Sermon on the Mount – after all, such teachings are found in other religions too – but someone who believes in the Virgin Birth, the Crucifixion, the Resurrection, and the Ascension – in other words, someone who believes in myths.

In Buddhism it is the other way round: first teaching, then myth. The Buddha is clearly a historical figure who is concerned with teaching individuals how they may develop as human beings. It is only later on, especially in the Mahāyāna and then in the Vajrayāna, that myth appears. This is illustrated by the development of the mandala of the five Buddhas. First of all you simply have the Buddha Śākyamuni, in the different phases of his career: in meditation under the bodhi tree, then calling the earth to witness, then teaching, then reassuring his disciples, then offering the gift of the Dharma to his disciples and to the world. From this naturalistic basis developed specific Buddha icons, each Buddha making a gesture or *mudrā* to illustrate each situation. If

the Buddha was depicted with his hands folded in his lap, that would represent him meditating under the bodhi tree, and if the tips of his fingers were touching the earth, that would represent calling the earth to witness, while if he was displaying a *mudrā* as though turning a wheel, that would represent the turning of the wheel of the Dharma.

In this way there emerged a set of five episodes with five *mudrās*, and these gradually became almost like five different Buddhas. The whole idea of Buddhahood was gradually raised to a more ideal or archetypal level, giving a richer and more multifaceted – even multidimensional – expression to the content of the original, historically embodied Buddha ideal. Thus was formed the mandala of the five Buddhas. In the centre was *the* Buddha – the primary Buddha, you could say. To his right and left were the Buddhas of the east and west, representing respectively wisdom and compassion, or the intellectual and emotional aspects of Buddhahood. This was a development of the Mahāyāna. Then, with the Tantra, appeared the Buddhas of the north and south, representing further aspects of Enlightenment – compassionate action and beauty. So now there were five: one at the centre and one at each of the cardinal points.

The five Buddhas are sometimes referred to as the *Dhyāni* Buddhas, but this is not a truly Buddhist term, and never occurs in Buddhist texts. It was used by someone writing about Nepalese Buddhism in the nineteenth century, and then taken up and popularized by the Theosophists.[123] The five Buddhas are more correctly spoken of as the five *Jinas* – that is, the five Conquerors – or the five *Tathāgatas*. Each *Jina* or Buddha can be regarded as having an active aspect, personified in the form of his attendant bodhisattva, or even two attendant bodhisattvas, representing his compassion and his wisdom, or his wisdom and his activity, or his activity and his compassion. These were sometimes split up into further aspects, each of which was separately represented. In the Vajrayāna a major development was the introduction of female counterparts to all these aspects.

All these developments represent a gradual filling out of the original Buddha ideal. It is as though you had an uncut diamond: its surface would not catch and reflect the light, and consequently its true beauty would easily be missed. But worked upon by a master jeweller, its facets would sparkle with reflected light and iridescent colour, and its beauty would be revealed. That is how the mandala of the five Buddhas gradually took shape.

The five Buddhas represent an attempt to communicate something of the multifaceted nature of Enlightenment. If you define Buddhahood as 'the wisdom of reality', this description may be true, but it is hardly very beautiful or inspiring. What kind of wisdom is it, what kind of reality? To illuminate this, as we have already seen, the wisdom of the Buddha is described as having four principal aspects – the mirror-like wisdom, the wisdom of equality, the discriminating wisdom, and the all-performing wisdom – and this gives a fuller and richer idea of what Buddhahood is like, bringing out its nature more explicitly so that it can be seen more clearly.

Many of the Buddhas and bodhisattvas within the mandala became the objects of cults; they were visualized and meditated upon, and their mantras were recited, until in Vajrayāna Buddhism, and Tibetan

Buddhism especially, they became the foundation of a vast range of spiritual practices and experiences, as if refracting rainbow light from the thousands of facets of the mandala.

As for dividing each Buddha into masculine and feminine, into a Buddha and his consort, this helped to bring out the passionate engagement that is part and parcel of transcendental wisdom. If the wisdoms of the Buddhas seem a bit cold, the Buddhas themselves, with their consorts, counteract that feeling. The attendant bodhisattvas who also appear in the mandala have their own effect too, each bringing out a specific aspect of the activity of the Buddhas. The *dharmapālas*, the guardians of the Dharma, bring out further aspects still. And then, in a rich and complex mandala, there may be wrathful as well as peaceful Buddhas to bring out more and more aspects of Enlightenment.

Let us try to catch a glimpse of this splendour, and – returning to the mandala in its simplest form – try to see the five Buddhas in our mind's eye. I will not offer much explanation of the figures; they are creative symbols and as such quite capable of producing a direct impression without having to be translated into their conceptual equivalents – equivalents which are in any case only approximate.

There are various forms of the mandala, with the five Buddhas appearing in different configurations. In many early forms, the Buddha Vairocana appears at the centre of the mandala. He is seated cross-legged, and he wears monastic-type robes, but they are richly embroidered, because we are now on the archetypal plane. He has black curly hair, closely cropped, and long ear lobes. Sometimes he has a slight protuberance on the top of his head, and a white curl of hair between his eyebrows. He is brilliant white in colour, like pure white light.

As we saw in the last chapter, in the Tantra white is often the colour of centrality, and in the mandala we find that some bodhisattvas change colour and become white as they move towards the centre. For example, the original colour of Avalokiteśvara, the Bodhisattva of Compassion, seems to have been red, but in the course of time, in Tibet especially, Avalokiteśvara became more and more important – so much so that he became a kind of Buddha, and many people worshipped him and meditated upon him to the exclusion of all the other Buddhas and bodhisattvas. He occupied the centre of the mandala, so far as their spiritual life was concerned, and his colour thus became white. The same thing happened in the case of Tārā. Her colour is green, but as she became more and more important, her position as a bodhisattva of a particular Buddha family was forgotten and she moved into the centre of the picture to become white, to become *the* Buddha form. This is why there are two main forms of Tārās: White Tārā and Green Tārā. Green Tārā is Tārā keeping her proper place in the mandala, as it were, while White Tārā is that same Tārā moving to the centre of the mandala, and there assuming the colour white and becoming, for her particular devotees, all in all.

Vairocana, on the other hand, is defined by virtue of his position at the centre of the mandala. His name literally means the Illuminator: the one who sheds radiance, pours it forth on the universe. The name Vairocana was in Indian Vedic times an epithet of the sun, and in Japan, where the cult of Vairocana became very popular, he is known as the Sun Buddha, because he is a sun of the spiritual universe, the *dharmadhātu*. Vairocana has his own special emblem, the eight-spoked golden wheel, the wheel of the Dharma, of Truth, of the Teaching, and sometimes he is depicted holding this wheel in both hands against his chest. His *mudrā* – the gesture of his hands – is therefore the *dharmacakrapravartana mudrā*, the *mudrā* of turning the wheel of the Dharma.

Mudrās of various kinds occupy a very important place in Tantric practice. The kind we are concerned with here, to give a necessarily approximate definition, is a symbolic ritual gesture, representing the permeation of one's whole being by the truth. When one makes a *mudrā* in the course of a ritual one deliberately places one's fingers in a particular position. In origin, however, *mudrās* are spontaneous rather than deliberate. A spiritual experience flowers in the depths of your being, and you begin to be transformed by it, bit by bit, on all levels – spiritual, emotional, intellectual, even physical, until eventually the experience penetrates to your very fingertips, just as the sap spreads through the branches of a tree until it reaches the tiniest twig. Everything you do – the way you walk, the way you stand, the way you speak – is expressive of your inner spiritual realization. A *mudrā* is essentially Enlightenment expressed by the hands: hence Vairocana's *mudrā* – the *mudrā* of turning the wheel of the truth. It was originally associated with the historical Buddha's proclamation of the truth in the Deer Park at Sarnath, and in early depictions of the scene he is shown making this *mudrā*. But in the figure of Vairocana, the *mudrā* has come to be expressive of the very nature of this archetypal Buddha.

Like the other *Jinas*, Vairocana is associated with a particular animal, in his case the lion. This association is again to do with the proclamation of the truth. In the scriptures, the Buddha's utterance of the truth is sometimes referred to as his *siṃhanāda*, his lion's roar. Just as the lion roars at night without fear of any other beast, to proclaim his lordship over the whole jungle, the Buddha's fearless proclamation of the truth declares him the spiritual sovereign of the universe.[124]

As a *Jina*, Vairocana is the head of a particular family of bodhisattvas. He is in fact the head of the Tathāgata family, or Buddha family; which suggests that Vairocana is *the* Buddha, while the others represent only aspects of Buddhahood. One of the most important members of Vairocana's Tathāgata family is Mañjughoṣa, the Bodhisattva of Wisdom, with whose visualization we concluded the previous chapter.

But why isn't Śākyamuni the central Buddha? Why is a new archetypal form chosen? It is because the mandala operates on an ideal level, free from ordinary limitations. Being the human, historical Buddha, Śākyamuni exists within the limitations of time and space. He is limited to a particular spot on the Earth's surface, in a certain epoch of history. But the ideal Buddha, the *sambhogakāya*, is not limited in that way. He embodies the same ideal, but liberated from the historical limitations within which the Buddha Śākyamuni realized it. The fact that Śākyamuni lived in India 2,500 years ago has nothing to do with Buddhahood; the conditions under which it is attained are ultimately irrelevant. The *nirmāṇakāya* is Buddhahood realized under certain specific historical conditions. The *sambhogakāya* is Buddhahood as realized eternally under absolutely ideal conditions; that is why the *sambhogakāya* Buddha sits enthroned in a Pure Land. And the *dharmakāya* is Buddhahood free from all limitations whatsoever, even ideal limitations. The five Buddhas of the mandala are all *sambhogakāya* Buddhas, aspects of the one ideal, universal, eternal Buddha.

In practice any Buddha can occupy the centre of the mandala because any aspect can be considered central, just as you can turn a faceted jewel in such a way that any facet can become the central one from your point of view. If you are particularly devoted to Amitābha, you can make him the centre of your mandala and put Vairocana in the west. The fact that the centre of the mandala is usually occupied by Vairocana or Akṣobhya is just historical accident, reflecting the popularity of those two Buddhas with the practitioners of the past. Sometimes a bodhisattva like Avalokiteśvara is placed in the centre of the mandala, or even a *ḍākinī* like Vajrayoginī. Sometimes a peaceful Buddha is placed in the centre, sometimes a wrathful one; sometimes a single Buddha, sometimes the male-female form in sexual union. Which figure you place at the centre of the mandala depends on the Buddha or bodhisattva who is at the centre of your own practice. Usually one does find oneself drawn to one or two figures more than others, and the tradition recognizes that. If you find yourself especially attracted by Tārā, then you can do the Tārā *sādhana*, recite the Tārā mantra, and put Tārā in the centre of the mandala. You can even have a mandala of Tārās, with all the figures in the mandala in Tārā form – Tārās of different colours and with different *mudrās*.

But in the earliest forms of the mandala of the five Buddhas, it is Vairocana who appears at the centre, and the Buddha Akṣobhya who occupies the eastern quarter. Akṣobhya is dark blue in colour, the colour of the midnight sky in the tropics. His name means 'unshakeable', 'immoveable', 'imperturbable', and his emblem is the *vajra*, the sacred thunderbolt or diamond sceptre of the lamas with which we were concerned in Chapter 3.

Akṣobhya's *mudrā* is the *bhūmisparśa*, or earth-touching *mudrā*. This recalls an important incident in the life of the historical Buddha. We are told that before his Enlightenment the Buddha-to-be took his seat on the diamond throne, the central point or axis of the whole universe. But then, just as he was on the threshold of Enlightenment, something dramatic happened – the kind of thing that usually happens when someone is on the threshold of Enlightenment: the forces of evil appeared. Māra, the Evil One, challenged him: 'What right have you to sit on that spot, where the Buddhas of old sat when they gained Enlightenment? Who are *you*? Do you really think you are ready?' And the Buddha-to-be said, 'Yes, I have the right, I am ready. I have spent many lives as a bodhisattva, practising the perfections. I know that I am about to gain Enlightenment.'

But Māra was sceptical. He said, 'Well, you can talk about all these previous lives in which you have been a bodhisattva. But who has seen all these previous lives? Who is your witness?' So the Buddha-to-be said, 'The Earth is my witness. I have lived all these lives on the Earth, and the Earth has seen my practice of the perfections. The Earth will be my witness.' With the tips of his fingers he touched the Earth and, according to the legend, up rose the Earth Goddess, bearing a golden pitcher. She said, 'Yes, I have seen it all. From generation to generation, from age to age, I have seen all the hundreds and thousands of lives during which he practised the perfections. He is ready; he is worthy to sit on that spot.' Māra was discomfited and, of course, the Buddha proceeded to gain Enlightenment.[125]

Akṣobhya's animal is the elephant – appropriately, because the elephant is the biggest and strongest of all land animals, and according to tradition the wisest. Akṣobhya is the head of the *vajra* family, which includes the bodhisattva (or Buddha) Vajrasattva and many *yidams* in wrathful or semi-wrathful form, for instance Cakrasaṃvara, Hevajra, and Vajrabhairava. There are more wrathful deities in Akṣobhya's *vajra* family than in the family of any other Buddha, perhaps due to the powerful associations of the *vajra* as an instrument of destruction – destroying the poisons and hindrances and fetters.

Ratnasambhava occupies the southern quarter of the mandala, and he is golden yellow in colour. His name means the Jewel-Born One or Jewel-Producing One, while his emblem – naturally – is the jewel. His *mudrā* is the *varada mudrā*, the symbolic gesture of supreme giving – just an open hand, representing unlimited generosity, both material and spiritual, and especially the gift of the Three Jewels. Ratnasambhava's animal is the horse, which associates him with the departure from home of the historical Buddha-to-be, who left home on horseback at night, accompanied only by his faithful charioteer.[126] In Tantric Buddhism the horse is the embodiment of speed and energy, especially energy in the form of *prāṇa* or vital breath. In Tibetan Buddhist art one very often finds the figure of a galloping horse seeming to rise through the air, carrying the Three Jewels on his back.[127] The symbolism suggests that only through the concentration and direction of all one's energies can one gain Enlightenment. Ratnasambhava is the head of the jewel family, which includes the bodhisattva Ratnapāṇi, as well as Jambhala, the so-called god of riches, and of course the Earth Goddess.

Amitābha, whose name means Infinite Light, occupies the western quarter of the mandala. He is red in colour, and his emblem is the lotus flower, which signifies spiritual growth. Amitābha occupies a particularly important position in the Jōdo Shinshū school of Japanese Buddhism, in which he is the only Buddha worshipped, and in which his invocation is recommended as an expression of gratitude for what he has done for us, spiritually speaking. You don't repeat his name in order to gain Enlightenment, but to express your gratitude for the gift of Enlightenment that has (as it were) already been received. Some devotees of Amitābha aspire to be reborn after death in his Pure Land, known as Sukhāvatī, the realm of bliss, and said to be situated in the western quarter of the universe. People aspire to be born there after they die because conditions for gaining Enlightenment are said to be so favourable there. The climate is perfect, and food and drink appear of their own accord. And all the time you hear the Buddha Amitābha teaching, so that spiritual progress is assured.[128]

The *mudrā* of Amitābha is the *dhyāna mudrā*, one hand resting on the other, the *mudrā* of meditation. Amitābha is especially associated with meditation, and this connects with his usual position in the mandala. As we have seen, he is associated with the West and thus he has a connection with the setting sun. Just as at sunset the light gradually disappears, in meditation the mind withdraws from external objects to enter a kind of twilight, a higher state of consciousness that the lower mind can only regard as unconsciousness from its limited point of view.

Amitābha's animal – or rather bird – is the peacock, the most splendid of all birds. It is not quite clear why the peacock is associated with Amitābha, although various explanations have been offered. Sometimes, on account of the eyes in its tail, the peacock is associated with consciousness, but that doesn't seem relevant here. The association may be that the peacock lives, indeed thrives, on poisonous snakes, and thus as a symbol suggests immunity from poison, contamination, and defilement. Peacock feathers are often used in Tantric ritual – you see them sticking up like a bunch of flowers from the vessel that contains the consecrated water. Amitābha is the head of the lotus family, which includes a number of well-known figures, for example, Kurukullā, Padmanarteśvara, and Padmasambhava, and the most important of all, Avalokiteśvara.

Amoghasiddhi occupies the northern quarter of the mandala. He is green in colour, and his name means Infallible Success or Unobstructed Accomplishment. His emblem is the double *vajra*, two *vajras* crossed – a powerful and mysterious symbol which, as we saw when considering the *vajra*, is connected with a special aspect of the union of opposites. Amoghasiddhi's *mudrā* is the *abhaya mudrā*, the *mudrā* of fearlessness; his upraised hand says, 'Don't be afraid.' Fearlessness is emphasized in all forms of Buddhism, but most of all in the Tantra, particularly in the symbolism of the cremation ground. Amoghasiddhi's animal – or rather mythical beast – is the bird-man, a fabulous hybrid called a *shang-shang* bird, which is human (either male or female) from the waist upwards, but has the feet and wings of a bird. Amoghasiddhi is the head of the karma or action family, the best-known member of which is Green Tārā.

Usually you enter the mandala from the east and move around clockwise, the east being where the sun rises, where things begin. Akṣobhya, the Buddha of the east, is usually shown at the bottom of the mandala because it is organized from the point of view of the person entering it, and when you are imagining it yourself, that is one way of doing so; you can imagine entering at the eastern gate of the mandala, and moving round clockwise until you get to the centre. Alternatively, you can start by visualizing the centre and then see the other Buddhas appearing around that central point. Indeed, it is possible to look at these Buddhas from many points of view, and in many different ways – according to their *mudrās*, for example, or their colours. You can consider them in pairs: for example, when you compare the Buddhas of the north and south, you see that Amoghasiddhi's gesture of fearlessness and Ratnasambhava's gesture of giving both face outwards, but that the one seems to be a gesture of warding off, keeping at bay, protecting, while the other expresses the outward-going spirit of generosity. Or again, comparing the Buddhas of the west and east, you see that Amitābha's palms are facing up to the heavens while Akṣobhya's earth-touching hand stretches down to the earth. You can play around with the symbolism in all sorts of ways, and this – together with a factual acquaintance with all the attributes of the Buddhas, their names, their positions, their colours, their *mudrās* – can help you to get a stronger feeling for these five Buddhas and the five wisdoms they represent.

The basic pattern of the mandala was further developed within the Tantra. To begin with, all five Buddhas were envisaged in male form. But the Tantra now took a dramatic new step. It started envisaging the two principal aspects of Enlightenment in male and female form respectively, and then seeing these two figures, male Buddha and female Buddha, as being in sexual union.

We have to be careful not to misunderstand what such an image signifies. We are concerned here not with sex in the literal sense but with sexual symbolism, which is a very different thing. What the Tantra is

trying to express by means of this symbolic shorthand is the inseparable two-in-oneness of compassion and wisdom, *karuṇā* and *prajñā*, the very essence of Enlightenment. Tantric practitioners had no particular hang-ups about sex, and therefore saw no objection to the use of such symbols.

In Tibet, the male and female Buddha figures in sexual union are known as *yab-yum* – father-mother – and in Tibetan monasteries one finds (or used to find) many beautiful scroll paintings depicting them. For the Tibetans there is no erotic suggestion in these images. Indeed, they are considered as being especially sacred, inasmuch as the symbolism pertains to the highest level of spiritual experience, that on which love and wisdom are completely and finally integrated. If you see Tibetans going around their temples, when they come across a picture or image of this sort, they seem to feel and express more reverence and devotion than ever. For them these figures are symbolic representations of a profound spiritual truth. Perhaps surprisingly, the male figure represents the compassion aspect of Enlightenment, and the female figure the wisdom aspect. These two united figures are sometimes symbolized by the *vajra* and the lotus, or by the *vajra* and the bell.

Not only does the central archetypal Buddha divide into two figures, male and female; the other four Buddhas divide in the same way, so that there are not five Buddhas, but ten – five so-called male Buddhas and five so-called female Buddhas, the female Buddhas being regarded as the consorts of the male ones, and as being spiritually united with them. These five female Buddhas, together with their male counterparts, represent different aspects of the one Enlightenment experience, which is in its essence an experience of the inseparable two-in-oneness of wisdom and compassion.

The first of the female Buddhas is Ākāśadhātvīśvarī, the consort of Vairocana. Her name means Sovereign Lady of the Sphere of Infinite Space. If Vairocana is the sun of the spiritual cosmos, radiating the light of wisdom and the heat of love in all directions, Ākāśadhātvīśvarī embodies the infinite space through which the light rays of Vairocana fall. She can be said to represent unlimited spiritual receptivity; to use the language of *The Awakening of Faith in the Mahāyāna*, she represents the whole of phenomenal existence as thoroughly perfumed by the Absolute.[129] Like Vairocana, Ākāśadhātvīśvarī is white in colour, and she is represented in *ḍākinī* form, with loose flowing garments and long dishevelled hair.

Locanā is the consort of Akṣobhya, the deep-blue Buddha of the east. Her name means Clear-Visioned One, or, literally, 'the one with an eye', and she is the embodiment of clear awareness, representing pure, simple, direct awareness of things. Akṣobhya is especially connected with transcendental wisdom – he is practically the only Buddha to appear in the Perfection of Wisdom *sūtras* – and his association with Locanā suggests that there is no wisdom without awareness, and no awareness without wisdom. The two are inseparably connected, different aspects of the same spiritual experience. Locanā is light blue in colour.

Māmakī is the consort of Ratnasambhava, the yellow Buddha of the south. Her name means Mine Maker, and she is the one who makes everything 'mine', not in a selfish egoistic way, but regarding everything and everyone as her own, near and dear to her, precious to her. Māmakī enjoys everybody, delights in everybody, rejoices in everybody – even regards everybody as her own self. She sees no difference between herself and others: they are all 'mine', or even 'me'. Her colour is yellow.

Pāṇḍaravāsinī is the consort of Amitābha, the red Buddha of the west. Her name, which means White-Robed One, suggests one who is vested in purity, even insulated by purity. This recalls an image connected with the fourth *dhyāna*, the fourth state of higher consciousness. The Buddha said that one's experience in this *dhyāna* is like that of a man who, on a hot day, when he is tired and dusty, goes to bathe in a beautiful pond full of lotuses, and after bathing, wraps himself in a pure white sheet. This represents the concentration and gradual accumulation of one's energies, especially emotional energies, and the insulation of oneself from harmful outside influences.[130] Pāṇḍaravāsinī, the symbolism would suggest, is protected in the same way. She is light red in colour.

Tārā is the consort of Amoghasiddhi, the deep-green Buddha of the north. Her name means 'one who ferries across' – ferries across the river of birth and death, the river of *saṃsāra*. This recalls the Buddha's parable of the raft, in which he said that the Dharma is like a raft that helps you to get across that river.[131] The name Tārā is often translated as 'saviouress', but this can be misleading; it is better to say that Tārā represents the attitude of helping people to help themselves.

We come now to the final development in the symbolic pattern of the mandala of the five Buddhas. We have encountered the five Buddhas, male and female, under their peaceful aspect. But in the esoteric Tantra, the Buddhas and bodhisattvas appear under two aspects, peaceful and wrathful. The wrathful forms of the five Buddhas, male and female, are much less individualized than their peaceful forms. In their wrathful forms, the five male Buddhas are known as the five *herukas*, and they are named after their respective Buddha families: the Buddha-Heruka, the Vajra-Heruka, the Ratna-Heruka, the Padma-Heruka, and the Karma-Heruka. Each is represented as powerfully and massively built, each is naked, except for a tiger skin or an elephant hide, and each wears a garland of human skulls. Round their bodies and their arms snakes are twined. They usually possess at least six arms, sometimes many more, and each has three bulging inflamed eyes, and a wrathful expression. They are usually represented as trampling on their foes, the enemies of the Dharma, and as moving violently to the right. Each one is surrounded by a halo of flames. The Buddha-Heruka is maroon or wine-coloured, and the others are blue, yellow, red, and green respectively.

The consort of the Buddha-Heruka is known simply as Krodheśvarī, which may be translated as 'Lady of Wrath', and the consorts of the other *herukas* are also named after their respective Buddha families: the Vajra Lady of Wrath, the Jewel Lady of Wrath, the Lotus Lady of Wrath, and the Action Lady of Wrath. They are all depicted naked, or practically naked, and as being of the same colour as their consort, but lighter, and somewhat smaller in size. In each case they cling to the front of their consort, sometimes with their arms clasped round his neck.

Such is the symbolism of the mandala of the five Buddhas, male and female, peaceful and wrathful. It is one of the most beautiful and meaningful patterns in the whole range of the Tantra, a pattern that organizes some at least of the riches of the Tantra into a form that we can appreciate and assimilate. As we reflect on this complex and beautiful form, we see reflected the complexity but also the potential beauty of our own lives. Indeed, it is an interesting and fruitful exercise to consider one's own life in terms of a mandala. What is at the centre of your life? What gives it meaning? And what surrounds that central point? Is there anything that doesn't seem to fit into the mandala of your life?

In the centre of your life will ideally be whatever is most important to you, your ideal – for Buddhists, the Buddha in some form. You can see the process of spiritual change in terms of making the effort to place that ideal at the centre of everything. Naturally, other objects of your attention will tend to inch their way into the centre of the mandala, although as you yourself will admit, they are of lesser value and should therefore be peripheral. It takes constant effort to stay focused on what is really most important to you, to gather your interests around that central point and make a truly creative mandala out of your life.

Some people have relatively simple, uncomplicated natures, and will therefore have simple, even austere mandalas, with very few things in them – just the right things in the right places. But other people have hundreds of things to find room for, and it will take them a long time to find the right place in their mandala for all their different interests and possessions. If you are interested in music, and painting, and biology, and mathematics, and gardening, it is fair enough to want to fit it all into your mandala, but it will take time to do so. Provided you put the right things in the right places – especially making sure that you put the things of greatest importance in the middle – you can create an elaborate, complex mandala which is in some ways no less beautiful than a simpler one, and perhaps in some ways even more beautiful.

Of course, we have our own mandala – we have our life – all the time, but when we come to look at it, we may find that it is distorted in some way. Perhaps there is something rather insignificant in the middle – perhaps, indeed, that something is ourselves.... The task for each of us is to reorganize and rearrange everything in our mandalas around what is most important. You may have to leave certain things aside for the time being; perhaps you can't quite see where they are going to fit. There are some things you will have to throw out because they are unskilful and there can be no place for them. But it is important to be quite careful about what you throw out. In many cases it is just a matter of assigning everything its appropriate place.

The Theravādin approach, one might say, is to throw out from the mandala everything except the one central item, the Buddha; and sometimes it isn't even the Buddha, but the figure of the *arhant* in a rather limited way. But the Mahāyāna and Vajrayāna way is to put the Buddha firmly in the centre and then fill the rest of the mandala with all your other interests, arranged in a beautiful, harmonious way around the central figure. All the different bits are part of you. The reorganization of the mandala is your reorganization of yourself around your highest potential. In a sense you do have to put yourself at the centre of the mandala – but it's the real you, the person you have the potential to become if you make the right kind of spiritual effort.

It is going to take time. If you are too desperate to achieve a synthesis, you can end up throwing away the things you should be trying to synthesize. For example, you may try to get rid of anger – but no, anger has its place in the mandala, in the form of the wrathful deities that stand at the four corners. They have their place; your anger – or rather the energy of your anger, directed skilfully – has its place.

Perhaps this is a good note on which to end our exploration of the creative symbols of Tantric Buddhism. Even while we are in the midst of all the myriad forms of the mandala of the five Buddhas as it is traditionally visualized, we must never forget that all of them, whether male or female, peaceful or wrathful, represent different aspects of the Enlightenment experience. We must never forget that they all embody spiritual experiences – are the product indeed of spiritual experiences – and thus reflect, in their own unique way, our spiritual potential. If we make the effort, the mandala of our own life can gradually be transformed into the mandala of the five Buddhas. This symbol, exotic though it may seem at first sight, is thus specifically and personally relevant to us – and this is true of all the symbols of the Tantra. If we remember this, perhaps we shall be able to respond to them. And if we respond to them, they will be of immeasurable help and value to us at every step of our journey on the Tantric path to Enlightenment.

The Essence of Zen

PREFACE

After spending twenty years in the East, mainly in India, I returned to England in August 1964 at the invitation of the English Sangha Trust, and was for two years Incumbent of the Hampstead Buddhist Vihara, London. During this period I delivered at the Vihara upwards of a hundred lectures on various aspects of Buddhism, including five talks on 'The Essence of Zen'.

The present work is a transcription of these talks, which were given towards the end of 1965. Though the passage from the spoken to the written word has inevitably resulted in a certain amount of condensation, I have tried to resist the temptation to recast the substance of these talks in more 'literary' form. In this way, I hope I have not only remained closer to the heart of Chan but also avoided the obvious inconsistency of producing yet another 'book on Zen'. Despite the fact that you are now reading with your eyes rather than listening with your ears, in the following pages I am still just talking.... I wonder if you can hear me.

Freathy Bay, Cornwall. 26 April 1973

1

INTRODUCTION

Zen is one of the best known and most important forms of Buddhism, and for a long time I have been wondering whether to speak on the subject. I was aware that, in venturing to speak on Zen, I would be treading on very dangerous ground. Some people, indeed, might regard me as a trespasser on their own special preserve. However, after pondering the matter for some time I decided to take my courage in both hands and speak on Zen. There will, therefore, be a series of five talks on 'The Essence of Zen', of which the first talk in the series, the one I am giving today, will be of an introductory nature.

My reluctance to speak on Zen was certainly not due to any feeling of disrespect towards this form of Buddhism. I have in fact the greatest admiration for Zen. Along with the *mahāmudrā* and *atiyoga* teachings of Tibet it represents, in my opinion, the peak of Buddhist spirituality. My reluctance was due rather to an awareness of the extreme difficulty of doing justice to the subject. I was also aware of the numerous misunderstandings surrounding Zen, some at least of which would have to be dispelled before Zen itself could be approached. However, having given series of lectures on the Theravāda and Mahāyāna schools, as well as on Tibetan Buddhism – not to mention an odd lecture on Shin – I eventually decided that, for the sake of completeness at least, I ought to overcome my reluctance and speak on Zen too.

A few words about my personal connection with Zen might be of interest here. At the age of sixteen I happened to read the *Diamond*

Sūtra and the *Sūtra of Wei Lang* (as the *Platform Scripture* was then called) and immediately had the intuitive perception that here was the absolute truth which, far from being new to me, was what I had really known and accepted all the time.[132] Like many others, I also read the writings of Dr D. T. Suzuki and his imitators. Suzuki's own words on Zen, with their combination of erudition, intellectual brilliance, and spiritual profundity, impressed me deeply, and I have returned to them for inspiration throughout my Buddhist life. For more than twenty years, mainly in the East, I studied and practised forms of Buddhism other than Zen. In particular, I practised meditation according to Theravādin methods and according to the Tantric traditions of the Tibetan Buddhist schools. These studies and practices, and the spiritual experiences to which they led, deepened my understanding and appreciation of Zen. This will seem strange only to those who tend to regard the different forms of Buddhism as so many mutually exclusive entities each of which has to be approached independently and as it were *de novo*. Far from being mutually exclusive, all the schools of Buddhism, despite their immense diversity, have a great deal of ground in common, so that to experience the truth of any one of them is to some extent at least to grasp the inner meaning and significance of all the others. All are concerned, ultimately, with the attainment of Enlightenment. Having known the truth of Buddhism by practising, for example, a form of Tibetan Buddhism, it is therefore possible to understand and appreciate the Theravāda or the Jōdo Shinshū. Knowledge of the whole includes knowledge of the parts. In order to understand the spirit of Zen one does not always have to read books on 'Zen Buddhism', or stay at a monastery labelled 'Zen monastery', or even practise 'Zen meditation' – much less still learn Japanese or sit on cushions of a particular size and shape.

However, had that been all, had my connection with Zen been limited to my experience of the *Diamond Sūtra* and the *Sūtra of Wei Lang*, my reading of Suzuki's works, and my general understanding of Buddhism, it is very doubtful whether I should have ventured to speak on the subject. But fortunately there was one more link. Before returning to England in 1964 I was in contact with a very remarkable man. This was a lay Buddhist hermit living on the outskirts of Kalimpong in two small rooms which he has now not left for at least fifteen or sixteen years. From five in the morning until five in the afternoon he sat, and I am sure still sits, in meditation, with a short break for lunch. Visitors are allowed only in the evening, by appointment. For several years I saw him regularly, usually on Saturday evenings. Besides possessing a thorough knowledge of the canonical literature of Buddhism he was, I soon found, an advanced practitioner of the Vajrayāna, which he had studied in eastern Tibet, as well as of Zen or, as I ought to say – since he was Chinese – of Chan. He was moreover a prolific writer, publishing numerous books on Tantric Buddhism and Zen, though he allowed himself only half an hour a day for literary work. Despite the fact that he refused to act as a guru, and accepted no disciples, in the course of talks and discussions I was able to learn a great deal from him. In particular I was able to imbibe the spirit of Zen in greater measure. Had it not been for this contact I probably would not have felt able to speak to you about Zen at all.[133]

Now you may have noticed that so far as these talks are concerned I have arrived at the subject of Zen as it were schoolwise. That is to say, having given courses of lectures on the Theravāda, on the Mahāyāna, on Tibetan Buddhism, and so on, I finally decided to give, for the sake of completeness, a series of talks on Zen. This brings us to an extremely important point, a point directly affecting the nature of the Buddhist movement not only in this country but throughout the western world. Buddhism has a long history. It has flourished in the East for 2,500 years, and during this time, in India, China, Japan, Tibet, and elsewhere, numerous sects and schools have sprung up. Nobody knows exactly how many of them there are or were, for some are extinct. Probably there are several hundred still in existence. These schools present a picture, or pattern, of unity in diversity, and diversity in unity. All aim at the attainment of Enlightenment, or Buddhahood. At the same time they approach it in a number of ways and from many points of view. They are either predominantly rationalist or predominantly mystical, inclined to activism or quietism, situating their teaching in a historical or a mythological context, and so on. These schools, or at any rate some of the most important of them, are now in process of being introduced into the West. Partly on account of the reasons already adduced, and partly through being associated with different national cultures, they at first present, to the western student, a spectacle of unmitigated difference, not to say disharmony. But we should not allow ourselves to be misled by appearances. Despite their apparent differences, even mutual opposition, we should study and learn to appreciate them all, thus making ourselves acquainted, as far as possible, with the whole vast range of Buddhist thought and practice. Only in this way will it be possible for us to obtain a balanced picture of Buddhism. Otherwise, we might commit the mistake of identifying Buddhism with one or another of its expressions, maintaining that this, and this alone, was the true embodiment of the Buddha's teaching. Such a course would be unfortunate as it would mean, in effect, adopting an attitude of sectarian exclusiveness which, though unfortunately characteristic of most forms of Christianity until recent times, is quite foreign to the spirit of Buddhism.

In this place we do not identify ourselves exclusively with any particular school. Therefore, having dealt with so many other forms of Buddhism, it was inevitable that sooner or later we should get round to Zen. This synoptic kind of approach is, of course, a very difficult, even confusing, one to follow.[134] It demands ability to discriminate what is essential from what is inessential in Buddhism. It demands objectivity and power of judgement, as well as a considerable amount of hard study. Most of us shrink from the effort involved. After all, it is so easy, in comparison, to 'take up' the form of Buddhism to which we are most strongly attracted, to identify ourselves wholeheartedly with it, to derive emotional satisfaction, perhaps, from proclaiming this, and this alone, to be the true Dharma, and all the other forms travesties, misrepresentations, and corruptions! But the temptation must be resisted. We must remember that, as Buddhists, we take refuge in the Dharma, not in the teachings of this or that particular school. Our line of spiritual practice may, indeed must, be specialized, at least to some extent: we either recite the *nembutsu*, *or* practise mindfulness of breathing, *or* visualize a mandala of Buddhas, bodhisattvas, and other deities. But our general approach, our overall attitude, to Buddhism, should be as broad as possible. Indeed, it should be universal.

In this connection I remember my experience at the Buddhist Society's summer school in 1964, shortly after my return from India. There were lectures and classes on the Theravāda, Mahāyāna, Zen, and Tibetan Buddhism. Going from one meeting to another, as most of them did, some of the newcomers very quickly became disheartened and confused. Sometimes it seemed as though Buddhism was severely rational, strictly ascetic, and rather dry; sometimes as though it was warm, mystical, and ethically permissive. In one class they would be told to think; in another, to use their intuition. One speaker would sternly exhort them to rely on their own efforts for salvation; immediately afterwards, perhaps, another would invite them to rely solely on the compassion of Amitābha, the Buddha of Infinite Light, who in ages long gone by had already graciously accomplished their salvation! Some, indeed, were heard to remark that they had learned a lot about the Mahāyāna, the Theravāda, and various other schools, but where, they asked, was Buddhism? When were they going to hear about *that*? For most of them, however, light eventually dawned, and by the end of the week they had begun to realize that, despite their contradictions, all schools aimed at Enlightenment, all were concerned with one or another aspect of the same transcendental reality.

We have had the same type of experience in our speakers' class. On one occasion four people, two men and two women, were asked to speak for twenty minutes each simply on 'Buddhism'. Though the subject was the same, they produced four completely different talks. In fact, the talks could hardly have been more dissimilar. To begin with, the two men's approach to the subject was noticeably more intellectual; that of the women, more intuitive. While one speaker gave a systematic exposition of the Four Noble Truths and the Noble Eightfold Path, another devoted the whole of her talk to the subject of meditation. One of the four included a detailed account of the life of the Buddha. Another did not mention the Buddha at all. At the same time, despite their different approaches, all four talks were recognizably about the same thing – Buddhism. It was as though all, while inevitably falling wide of the central point of the incommunicable essence of Buddhism, in aiming at it drew, at different angles, lines which between them demarcated an area, or described a figure, within which Buddhism could be found and experienced. However comprehensive and objective we try to make them, our approaches to Buddhism are inevitably limited and conditioned – in short, one-sided. As my experience at the summer school, and in the speakers' class, illustrates, one way in which we can transcend this one-sidedness is by juxtaposing contradictory formulations of Buddhism in such a manner that we not only experience their contradictoriness but realize that they are equally valid expressions of a spiritual experience that forever eludes the logical categories of the discriminative mind. This is one of the benefits to be derived from a comprehensive study of different schools of Buddhism. We should not be afraid of contradictions. 'A foolish consistency,' said Emerson, 'is the hobgoblin of little minds.'[135]

On the psychological plane Buddhism attaches great importance to harmony and balance. Human nature has a number of different aspects, intellectual and emotional, active and contemplative, and so on, and justice must be done to them all. In the spiritual as in the secular life, all must be cultivated and developed, and a perfect equilibrium maintained. This is illustrated by the doctrine of the five spiritual faculties, one of the most ancient and important of the 'numerical lists' in which, from an early date, the Buddha's teaching was preserved. The five spiritual faculties are faith (*śraddhā*), wisdom (*prajñā*), vigour (*vīrya*), concentration (*samādhi*), and mindfulness (*smṛti*).[136] Faith, representing the emotional and devotional aspect of the spiritual life, must be balanced by wisdom, otherwise it runs riot in religious hysteria, persecution mania, fanaticism, and intolerance. On the other hand wisdom, which stands for the intellectual – better, cognitive or gnostic – aspect, must be balanced by faith, without which it speedily degenerates into hair-splitting scholasticism. Vigour, or the active, kinetic aspect of the spiritual life, must be balanced by concentration, representing the introspective, contemplative counter-tendency, without which vigour is either animal high spirits or neurotic restlessness, and concentration itself by vigour, divorced from which concentration is aimless reverie, morbid introspection, or neurotic withdrawal. Mindfulness, the remaining faculty, being by its very nature incapable of going to extremes – one can't have too much mindfulness – requires no counter-balancing faculty to hold it in check. Mindfulness it is, indeed, that keeps faith and wisdom, and vigour and concentration, in a state of equilibrium. 'Mindfulness is always useful,' the Buddha once declared.[137]

Besides being one of the schools of Buddhism, Zen is, more specifically, also one of the schools of the Mahāyāna – the second of the three great stages of historical development into which Indian Buddhism traditionally falls. In the Mahāyāna four major schools, or types of approach, can be distinguished, and these, as I have explained in detail in my book *A Survey of Buddhism*, correspond to the five spiritual faculties.[138] What Conze terms the Buddhism of faith and devotion, with its highly emotional worship of the Buddhas, both historical and 'legendary', and of bodhisattvas such as Avalokiteśvara, Mañjuśrī, and Tārā, represents a specialization, as it were, in the faculty of faith.[139] The Madhyamaka school, or 'School of the Mean', with its rigorously dialectical approach to reality, represents a specialization in the faculty of wisdom. Similarly the Tantra, which in its esoteric form integrates not only the mind but the physical energies of breath and semen, concentrates on the faculty of vigour. The fourth spiritual faculty, that of concentration, is represented on the theoretical side by the Yogācāra and on the practical side by the school which is known, in its Japanese form, as Zen. The faculty of mindfulness is represented by the spirit of tolerance which is diffused through all the schools and which holds them together as 'moments' in the Mahāyāna-concept.

This correspondence between the schools of the Mahāyāna and the five spiritual faculties gives us an important clue to the nature of Zen. Quite simply, it is that aspect of Mahāyāna Buddhism which emphasizes the importance of meditation, and specializes therein. This is indicated by the very name of the school. The Chinese term *chánnà* is a corruption of the Sanskrit *dhyāna*, the general Indian word for meditative practice and experience, while *zen-na*, *zen* for short, is the Japanese corruption of the Chinese corruption. Thus the Zen school is really the Dhyāna or Meditation school.

At the same time, Zen has its own distinctive features. This becomes obvious as we go a little deeper into the meaning of the word meditation. According to the remarkable man previously mentioned there are four kinds of Chan or Zen. So far as I know, this extremely important traditional classification, which sheds much light on the nature of Zen, has never appeared in English before, and it is unknown to western Buddhists. I therefore hope it will be of interest to you.

Firstly there is *Tathāgata Chan* – the classical methods of concentration such as counting the breaths and cultivating a spirit of universal love which were taught by Gautama the Buddha and are common to practically all forms of Buddhism, including Zen. In Zen monasteries the beginner is taught these methods and often practises nothing else for several years.

Secondly, *Patriarchal Chan*, i.e. the Chan of Huineng, the sixth Chinese patriarch of the Zen school. This refers to the *Platform Scripture*'s teaching of the identity, or at any rate the inseparability, of *samādhi* and *prajñā*. Huineng says,

> Learned Audience, in my system *samādhi* and *prajñā* are fundamental. But do not be under the wrong impression that these two are independent of each other, for they are inseparably united and are not two entities. *Samādhi* is the quintessence of *prajñā*, while *prajñā* is the activity of *samādhi*. At the very moment that we attain *prajñā*, *samādhi* is therewith; and vice versa.... A disciple should not think that there is a distinction between '*samādhi* begets *prajñā*' and '*prajñā* begets *samādhi*'.... *Samādhi* and *prajñā* ... are analogous to a lamp and its light. With the lamp, there is light. Without it, it would be dark. The lamp is the quintessence of the light and the light is the expression of the lamp. In name they are two things, but in substance they are one and the same. It is the same case with *samādhi* and *prajñā*.[140]

Prajñā of course means wisdom, in the sense of transcendental wisdom. But what does *samādhi* mean? Here there is a great deal of confusion to be cleared up. As one of the five spiritual faculties, *samādhi* means simply one-pointedness of mind, or concentration. This is the meaning of the term in what we may call general Buddhism, the type of Buddhism codified in, and nowadays represented by, the Theravāda, and it is in the same sense that *samādhi* is to be understood when it is enumerated as the second of the three great stages of progress into which the spiritual path is divided, the first stage being *śīla* or morality and the third *prajñā* or wisdom.[141] In the Mahāyāna *sūtras* which form the background of Huineng's teaching, however, *samādhi* has a quite different meaning. Confusion has been created in the minds of western students of Zen because they wrongly assume that the *samādhi* which Huineng was equating with *prajñā* was *samādhi* in the sense of mental concentration, thus making nonsense of the entire scheme of Buddhist spiritual self-development. In the Mahāyāna *sūtras samādhi* corresponds to the *cetovimutti*, or state of conscious spiritual emancipation of the Theravādin texts, rather than to *samādhi* in the sense of concentration.[142] Mahāyāna *samādhi* may well be said to be Enlightenment in its subjective aspect of personal realization. *Prajñā* or wisdom is the objective aspect of actual manifestation and function in the world, the two of course being inseparable.

This *prajñā* is not the ordinary *prajñā* of the general Buddhist teaching, consisting of insight into the unsatisfactory, impermanent, and unsouled nature of conditioned things, but *mahā-prajñā*, or great wisdom, realization of the Voidness – not emptiness but absolute unconditioned reality – of all the phenomena of existence. Collating the general Buddhist teaching with that of the Mahāyāna *sūtras* we may say that, according to Huineng, the entire system of Buddhist spiritual training may be expressed in the formula *śīla* (morality) → *samādhi* (concentration) → *prajñā* → *samādhi-prajñā* = Buddhahood.

While Tathāgata Chan is concerned with the practice of concentration, the second term in the series, Patriarchal Chan, is concerned with the realization of *samādhi-prajñā*, the fourth.

Thirdly, *Offspring Chan*. This is Chan as taught by the spiritual descendants of Huineng, especially by the great masters of the fourth, fifth, sixth, and seventh generations, who became the founders of the five Chan 'sects' of China. Whereas Tathāgata Chan and Patriarchal Chan are Indian in form, Offspring Chan is characteristically Chinese. Instead of quoting the scriptures and discoursing at length on the philosophy and practice of Zen in the traditional manner, as even Huineng does, this kind of Chan tries to bring about the experience of Enlightenment in a more direct and concrete manner with the help of seemingly eccentric and bizarre words, sentences, and actions. These are the celebrated *kung-an* (Japanese *kōan*: literally 'public documents') or 'concurrent causes' of Enlightenment, such as a sudden shout, a roar of laughter, a gesture, or a blow with a staff.

Fourthly, *Mouth Chan*. This is the Chan of people who merely talk about Zen, or write books and articles about it, and never do any practice. When my friend in Kalimpong told me about this kind of Chan I remarked that it was very common in the West, where it was the dominant school, with many distinguished masters, and almost a patriarchal succession of its own. He replied, rather sadly, that it was common enough in China too, even in the old days. On another occasion, when I showed him an article on Zen in a western Buddhist magazine, he burst into roars of laughter after reading a few sentences. But soon the laughter changed to tears, and he wept bitterly, out of compassion for sincere seekers after truth who were being deceived and misled by the exponents of Mouth Chan.

In the course of the next four weeks I shall try to do justice to what Zen has in common with other schools of Buddhism as well as to its own distinctive features. The subject will be dealt with by way of a consideration of a popular traditional verse widely regarded as embodying the essence of Zen. By this means, it is hoped, misunderstanding will be avoided. Before telling you what this verse is, let me briefly touch upon what are, so it seems to me, the three causes for much of the current western misunderstanding of Zen.

The first cause is our purely intellectual approach. Most western students derive their knowledge of Zen from books, usually those of Suzuki. In the beginning this is, of course, unavoidable. Fortunately, at present a number of books on Zen are available which are probably as reliable as books on Zen can be. Such, for example, are the three volumes of Charles Luk's *Ch'an and Zen Teaching* and Trevor Leggett's *First Zen Reader* and *The Tiger's Cave*.[143] Thoughtfully – one might even say contemplatively – read, works of this nature, besides conveying something of the spirit of Zen, make the sensitive reader aware of the limitations of the intellectual approach. As though with one voice they urge him to practise Zen. Unfortunately, only too many people seem to have a perfect intellectual understanding of the fact that Zen cannot be intellectually understood. So thoroughly do they understand the need for practice that the idea of actually practising Zen themselves never occurs to them. Instead, on the basis of their reading and their intellectual knowledge of Zen, they set to work and produce yet another book on the subject. In these books they usually argue at great length, as if to convince the unconverted, that books cannot tell you anything about Zen, that the intellect is a hindrance, and that one should cultivate one's intuition. After several hundred pages of discussion, Zen is usually defined, very much to their own satisfaction, as 'the indefinable'. If questioned about meditation, Zen intellectuals of this type are liable to snap back, 'I do my meditation while I'm waiting for the traffic lights to change.'

Secondly, we try to understand Zen apart from Buddhism. This is like trying to understand the acorn apart from the oak, and is absolutely futile. Zen is an integral part of the total Buddhist tradition. As we have already seen, it is that aspect of the Mahāyāna which specializes in the practice of meditation. The terminology and techniques of Zen, as well as its doctrines, its scriptures, its spiritual ideal, and its monastic organization and ordination lineage, have all been taken over from Buddhism, and even after being given the special development, the characteristic emphasis, that makes them Zen, cannot be understood independently. If we are in personal contact with an enlightened Zen master and are prepared to follow his instructions implicitly, we need not bother about Buddhism. We need not bother even about Zen. But so long as we do not have this advantage we have no alternative but to study Zen as part of Buddhism. Any other course would be as futile as trying to understand the origins and nature of Methodism without reference either to the Church of England or to Christianity.

The last of the three main causes for our misunderstanding of Zen is that we mistake the finger for the moon. According to the Buddhist saying, when one asks, 'Where is the moon?' and somebody points it out with his finger saying, 'There it is!' one does not stand with eyes riveted on the finger. One looks from the finger to the moon. In the same way all the teachings and methods of Zen are so many pointers to the experience of Enlightenment. The disciple does not take them for ends in themselves. He utilizes them as helps to the attainment of liberation. Some western students of Zen, however, fascinated by the apparently bizarre sayings and doings of the later Zen masters, think that *this is Zen*. For instance, they read that when disciple so-and-so questioned Master such-and-such about Zen, the latter, instead of answering, gave him thirty blows with his staff.[144] Giving thirty blows, they think, is Zen. Whenever anybody mentions Zen, therefore, they explain triumphantly, 'Aha, thirty blows for you!' and think that they have thereby demonstrated their superior understanding of Zen. Others think that the tea ceremony is Zen, or judo, or kendo, or karate. They fail to realize that these are not Zen itself but only expressions of Zen within a certain Far Eastern cultural context. Some even think that Zen is Japanese. If one wanted to be paradoxical, not to say provocative, one could go so far as to say that Zen had nothing whatever to do with Japan.

In the coming weeks we shall try to avoid misunderstandings of Zen such as those I have described. Now for our verse. It is said to have originated during the Tang dynasty in China, but nobody knows who composed it. The verse reads:

A special transmission outside the scriptures;
No dependence upon words and letters;
Direct pointing to the mind;
Seeing into one's own nature and realizing Buddhahood.

Each of the four lines of the verse represents a fundamental principle of the Zen school. Each week, therefore, we shall take up one line for study. In this way, I hope, we shall acquire some insight into the essence of Zen, thus approaching nearer to Enlightenment and broadening and enriching our understanding of the whole Buddhist tradition.

2

A SPECIAL TRANSMISSION OUTSIDE THE SCRIPTURES

At first sight the idea of a special transmission outside the scriptures seems quite simple and easy to understand. Had we encountered it in a book we probably would not have given it a second thought, assuming as a matter of course that we understood what was meant. But is this line, the first line of our verse, really so simple as it appears? '*A special transmission outside the scriptures.*'... If we give ourselves time to think, a number of questions suggest themselves.

What are the scriptures? What is meant by a 'transmission', or a 'special transmission'? What is meant by 'outside'? Let us examine each of these in turn.

First of all the *scriptures*. All the religions of the world possess sacred books. Christians, for example, have the Bible, Muslims the Koran, and Hindus the Vedas. Similarly Buddhists have what is known as the Tripiṭaka. *Tri* means 'three', while *piṭaka* means 'basket' or, by extension of meaning, 'collection'. The Tripiṭaka is therefore the 'three basketfuls' or 'three collections' of Buddhist sacred texts. According to some authorities, in the early days of Buddhism the bundles of palm-leaf manuscript on which the texts were inscribed were divided, according to subject matter, into three groups that were kept, for convenience of reference, in three wicker containers. Some, however, suggest that the term refers to the way in which earth and other excavated material was passed from hand to hand in baskets down a line of workmen. In the same way the monks handed down the sacred traditions, first in oral and then in literary form, from generation to generation.

The 'three basketfuls' or 'three collections' are, firstly, the Vinaya Piṭaka or 'Collection of Monastic Discipline'. In its present form this consists mainly of the rules governing the monastic order, including the circumstances in which these are promulgated, interspersed with a great deal of biographical, historical, and doctrinal matter. The original nucleus of this *piṭaka* seems to have been a short life of the Buddha.[145] Secondly, there's the Sūtra Piṭaka or 'Collection of Discourses, Dialogues, and Sayings of the Buddha' on various moral and spiritual topics. This is the most important collection. Thirdly, there's the Abhidharma Piṭaka or 'Collection of Higher Doctrine'. This is a systematic arrangement and scholastic analysis of material found in the Sūtra Piṭaka.

Traditionally the entire contents of the *Tripiṭaka* are regarded as *Buddhavacana* or the 'word of the Buddha'. The Buddha himself, of course, wrote nothing. Like Socrates and Christ, he taught orally. Those who remembered what he had said told his sayings to their disciples; they told theirs and in this way the teaching was transmitted to posterity. Only after five hundred years, approximately, of oral transmission was the teaching committed to writing. Much, no doubt, had been added. Much, perhaps, had been lost. At present there are extant in the Buddhist world three major editions of the *Tripiṭaka*: firstly, the Chinese *San Zang* or 'Three Treasuries' (i.e. *Tri-piṭaka*) in 55 volumes; secondly, the Tibetan *Kangyur* ('*Buddha-vacana*') in 100 or 108 volumes. Both these editions consist mainly of translations from the Sanskrit, many of the original texts having since been lost. The third edition is the Pāli *Tipiṭaka* in 45 volumes (Royal Thai edition). This is the only version of the canon to have survived complete in the language in which it was originally compiled.

The three editions of the *Tripiṭaka* possess a great deal of material in common. The biggest difference is that while the Chinese and Tibetan editions include the Mahāyāna *sūtras* the Pāli edition omits them.

Even when allowance is made for overlapping, the Buddhist scriptures are far more voluminous than those of any other religion. The Bible consists of 64 books; but the Chinese *San Zang*, for example, contains 1,662 independent works, several of them almost as long as the entire Bible. Though much of this vast literature has been translated into English and other European languages, an even greater part of it remains untranslated. Thanks to the labours of the Pali Text Society, the Pāli *Tipiṭaka* has been translated almost in its entirety. A number of the most important Mahāyāna *sūtras* are also available. Kern has translated the *Saddharma Puṇḍarīka*, Izumi the *Vimalakīrti-nirdeśa*, Suzuki the *Laṅkāvatāra*, Lamotte the *Saṃdhinirmocana* (in French), Luk the *Śūraṅgama*. Above all, in the greatest individual achievement in this field in modern times, Conze has translated the whole Prajñāparamitā or 'Perfection of Wisdom' group of *sūtras*, consisting of more than thirty independent works.[146]

A great deal of basic material is thus available for study. Unfortunately, the majority of English Buddhists and students of Buddhism fail to take advantage of the fact. Very few study regularly and systematically even a tithe of what has been translated. Consequently their knowledge of Buddhism remains vague and superficial. Some, indeed, appear to read anything rather than the scriptures. Classics of Christian mysticism, books about Pak Subuh, even the romances of Lobsang Rampa, are eagerly devoured, while essential texts like the *Diamond Sūtra* and the *Sutta-Nipāta* remain unread. This is not to say that there is anything wrong in reading the classics of Christian mysticism and deriving inspiration from them. But if one considers oneself a Buddhist and claims to be seriously following the path of the Buddha, it is strange that one should not make every effort to acquaint oneself with the basic literature of the subject. No doubt the Buddhist scriptures, even in the best translation, are often unattractive in form and obscure and difficult in content. But if we want to participate in the spiritual riches of Buddhism the effort to understand them must be made. After all, if we want to take up engineering, or medicine, or even pig-breeding, we have to put in a certain amount of intellectual hard work: we have to study. Buddhism demands no less. Ask yourselves, therefore, those of you who consider yourselves Buddhists, when it was that you last read a translation of one of the Buddhist sacred books. The answer might surprise you.

Some, of course, try to rationalize the situation and justify themselves. Western advocates of Zen, for instance, are fond of citing the example of Huineng, the Sixth Chinese Patriarch, whom Far Eastern Buddhist art sometimes depicts in the act of tearing up the *Diamond Sūtra*. They forget that if he did in fact do any such thing (there is no mention of the incident in the *Platform Scripture*) it was only after realizing the import of the *Sūtra* and that, in any case, he probably knew the entire text by heart. In Zen monasteries scriptures like the *Diamond Sūtra*, the *Heart Sūtra*, and the *Kwannon Sūtra* are not only studied but learned by heart and liturgically recited as an aid to the spiritual life. It is interesting to observe that those who neglect, and then depreciate, the primary sources, can be fanatical in their devotion to quite secondary ones. The word of the Buddha resounds unheeded, but Suzuki and a host of lesser lights are hearkened to with eager attention.

Whether our interest is in Buddhism in general or in one or another of its special forms, we cannot bypass the scriptures. In them are contained the original records of the transcendental experiences of the Buddha and his Enlightened disciples. Without a preliminary intellectual understanding of these records we have no means of knowing what it is that we, as Buddhists, including followers of Zen, are trying to attain and what is the method of its attainment. The only thing that can absolve us from study of the scriptures is regular personal contact with an Enlightened teacher, who is the living embodiment of the scriptures. Such a teacher is difficult to come by even in the East. In the absence of personal contact of this kind the scriptures are indispensable.

So much for what is meant by the scriptures. Now we come to the *transmission*, or *special transmission*. What is meant by this? According to the dictionary the literal meaning of the word transmit is 'to send across', also to pass on or hand down. Here we have the idea of Buddhism itself as *something transmitted*, something handed down. On the biological plane, life is transmitted from parents to children. On the spiritual plane, there is a transmission of Buddhism, or the Dharma. This transmission takes place between master and disciple. Hence the importance of this relationship. It is, in fact, the axis upon which the whole world of Buddhism turns. There are a number of different types of transmission of Buddhism, or rather, the transmission can take place on different levels. Four principal transmissions are enumerated:

1. *Transmission of Ordination.* Broadly speaking ordination is of three kinds: as a lay brother or lay sister (*upāsaka, upāsikā*), as a monk or nun (*bhikṣu, bhikṣuṇī*), and as a bodhisattva. These three categories of ordained persons make up the sangha or spiritual community in the socio-ecclesiastical sense of the term. Each ordination involves the adoption of a certain spiritual attitude and the observance of a certain rule. The lay brother or lay sister, who can be ordained by any monk,

nun, or bodhisattva, goes for Refuge to the Buddha, Dharma, and Sangha and undertakes to observe the ten precepts, that is to say, to abstain from harming living beings, from taking what is not given, from sexual misconduct, from false, harsh, frivolous, and backbiting speech, as well as from greed, hatred, and wrong views. A monk must be ordained by a chapter of not less than five other monks including an elder (*sthavira*) or monk of at least ten years' standing in the order. Nuns require a double ordination, once by a chapter of monks and once by a chapter of nuns. Both monks and nuns renounce the household life, devote all their energies to the realization of Nirvāṇa, and observe a basic rule of 150 clauses. The four most important clauses relate to abstention from sexual intercourse, from theft, from murder and incitement to suicide, and from making false claims to spiritual attainments. A bodhisattva is ordained ideally by a Buddha, but in practice by any senior bodhisattva. In special circumstances self-ordination is permitted. He (or she) develops the will to Enlightenment for the sake of all sentient beings and observes a rule consisting (according to the Indo-Tibetan tradition) of eighteen major and forty-six minor provisions, all strongly altruistic in emphasis. The three kinds of ordination are not mutually exclusive. A lay brother or lay sister, or monk or nun, may in addition be ordained as a bodhisattva. In the Mahāyāna Buddhist world bodhisattva ordination tends to supersede all other kinds of ordination.[147]

2. *Transmission of the Scriptures.* As we have seen, the Buddha himself wrote nothing. After centuries of oral transmission his words were committed to writing and preserved in the form of palm-leaf manuscripts. Eventually the manuscripts were printed in book form. These books, in the three editions described, constitute the Buddhist scriptures. Traditionally, one of the principal functions of the monks was to preserve incorrupt the pure and authentic word of the Buddha, first in oral and subsequently in literary form. They alone had time for the prodigious feat of memorization required to preserve the teachings orally. Once the 'scriptures' had been committed to writing, though, the importance of the monks as preservers and transmitters diminished. But they continued to be the custodians of the correct interpretation of the texts. This interpretation was often embodied in commentaries, which gave not the author's personal understanding of the texts so much as the traditional interpretation which he had received from his teachers along with the texts themselves. In some parts of the Buddhist world

one is still not considered to have mastered the scriptures unless one has studied them with a teacher. Reading the printed page by oneself is not sufficient. One has to learn, at the same time, the correct interpretation, which can be done only with the help of a teacher 'in the succession'. Tibetan Buddhism still retains the institution of *lung* or 'authorization'. Students are permitted to read or recite a sacred text only after it has been read aloud in their ear, with explanations, by their teacher. Some texts, of course, require more explanation than others, but in all cases the principle of a proper *transmission* of the scripture *and* its meaning is upheld.

3. *Transmission of the Doctrine.* By 'doctrine' is meant, in this context, the systematic presentation of the teaching, as contained in the scriptures, in terms of a logically coherent intellectual structure. The expression may be considered roughly equivalent to the terms 'Buddhist thought' and 'Buddhist philosophy'. Such presentations seem to have originated with the 'lists of lists' which were compiled after the Buddha's death, perhaps even during his lifetime. These were more or less complete enumerations of the various sets of related doctrinal topics – the five aggregates, the nine holy persons, the twelve links, and so on – in which, for mnemonic purposes, the teaching had been cast. As presentations of the teaching the 'lists of lists' were systematic only in the purely formal sense. More truly systematic are the *śāstras*, such as the Abhidharma treatises, the Five Books of Maitreya, and *The Awakening of Faith in the Mahāyāna*. In India there were four different, practically simultaneous, transmissions of the doctrine, in the form of the four 'philosophical' schools of the Vaibhāṣikas, the Sautrāntikas, the Vijñānavādins, and the Mādhyamikas. These were systematic presentations of the teaching in terms, respectively, of naive realism, critical realism, idealism, and absolutism. All four transmissions continued, with amplifications and extensions, in Tibet and the Far East. In China the transmission of the Doctrine was safeguarded by the great indigenous schools of the Huayan (the Avataṃsaka or 'Flower-Ornament') and Tiantai, characterized respectively by Takakusu as the totalistic and phenomenological (Mahayānistic) schools.

4. *Transmission of the Spirit of Buddhism.* This is the most important transmission of all. It is to this type of transmission that the verse refers when it speaks of a special transmission outside the scriptures. Though only the scriptures are actually mentioned, the

transmission is to be understood as taking place outside ordination and outside doctrine as well.

How did this transmission of the spirit of Buddhism begin? According to Zen tradition, the Buddha was once seated in the midst of a great concourse of his disciples. Hundreds of bodhisattvas and *arhants*, monks and nuns, lay brothers and lay sisters, were present, as well as various orders of celestial beings. All were silent, waiting for the Buddha to speak. This is, of course, the customary setting for a discourse by the Buddha, but on this occasion, instead of speaking, the Master simply held up amidst the silence of the assembly a golden flower. Only Mahākāśyapa, one of the oldest disciples, famed for his austerity, understood the meaning of the Buddha's action, and smiled. The Buddha then said, 'I am the owner of the eye of the wonderful Dharma, which is Nirvāṇa, the Mind, the mystery of reality and non-reality, and the gate of the transcendental truth. I now hand it over to Mahākāśyapa.' This was the transmission.

What happened? It is very difficult to explain. When the Buddha held up the golden flower (not when he spoke, which was only for the benefit of the other disciples, who had failed to understand the significance of his action) there took place a direct communication of truth from one mind to another, from a supremely Enlightened mind to one that was almost so, and needed only the most delicate of touches to bring it to perfection. The transmission from the Buddha was analogous to what happens, at an infinitely lower level of experience, between two people who understand each other very well. A sign or a look, the significance of which is a mystery to everyone else, suffices to convey a whole world of meaning. So it is on the highest spiritual plane.

Mahākāśyapa transmitted the spirit of the Dharma to Ānanda, who had been the Buddha's personal attendant during the last twenty years of his earthly life, he to his disciple Śānavāsa, and so on. From Mahākāśyapa in the fifth century BCE to Bodhidharma in the sixth century CE it continued to be transmitted down a long line of spiritual masters, some otherwise unknown to fame, others among the most distinguished names in Indian Buddhism. The list of these masters, who are traditionally regarded as the twenty-seven (including Bodhidharma, twenty-eight) Indian 'patriarchs' of the Zen school, is as follows:

(1) Mahākāśyapa, (2) Ānanda, (3) Śānavāsa, (4) Upagupta (spiritual teacher of the Emperor Aśoka), (5) Dhṛtaka, (6) Miccaka, (7) Vasumitra

(the earliest historian of Buddhism), (8) Buddhanandi, (9) Buddhamitra, (10) Pārśva (?President of the Fourth Council, the Council of Kaniṣka), (11) Punyayaśas, (12) Aśvaghoṣa (author of *The Life of the Buddha, The Awakening of Faith in the Mahāyāna*, etc.), (13) Kapimala, (14) Nāgārjuna (rediscoverer of the 'Perfection of Wisdom' *sūtras* and founder of the Madhyamaka school), (15) Kānadeva (=Āryadeva, co-founder of the Madhyamaka school), (16) Rāhulata, (17) Saṅghānandi, (18) Gayasata, (19) Kumārata, (20) Jayata, (21) Vasubandhu (author of *Abhidharmakośa*, etc., and founder of the Vijñānavāda school), (22) Monorhita, (23) Haklena, (24) Āryasiṃha, (25) Basiasita, (26) Puṇyamitra, (27) Prajñātāra, and (28) Bodhidharma.[148]

A study of this list reveals the close connection between Zen and what may be termed the central tradition of Indian Buddhism.

It was the celebrated Bodhidharma, the twenty-eighth Indian Patriarch – whom tradition depicts crossing the ocean on a reed – who 'took' Zen to China, thus becoming the First Chinese Patriarch of the school. What he took to China, of course, was not the Zen school as we know it today, complete with doctrines, scriptures, and temple organization, but the living spirit of Buddhism. This spirit he transmitted to his disciple Dazu Huike, he to his disciple, and so on down a succession of altogether six spiritual masters. These masters are known as the Six Chinese Patriarchs of the Zen school, as follows:

(1) Bodhidharma, (2) Dazu Huike, (3) Sengcan, (4) Dayi Daoxin, (5) Daman Hongren, (6) Huineng (Wei Lang).[149]

Such was the spiritual genius of Huineng, the sixth and last Chinese Patriarch, that he was able to transmit the spirit of Buddhism not to one disciple only, as the custom apparently had been hitherto, but to forty-three. Thereafter there were many different lines of transmission, no one of which could be regarded as the main one. Five lines were however of special importance, of which two continue down to the present day. These two lines are represented by the Sōtō and Rinzai schools of contemporary Japanese Buddhism.

Zen is essentially concerned with the fourth type of transmission, the transmission of the living spirit of Buddhism. This transmission is made possible through the high level of spiritual communication existing between master and disciple, usually within a context of meditation and study. Ordination and observance of the monastic discipline, scriptural studies, and doctrinal knowledge are all important, but only as means to an end, never as ends in themselves. The real thing, the only thing that ultimately matters, is the spiritual – better, transcendental – experience, the experience of Enlightenment. If this is not transmitted the transmission of all the rest is a waste of time. At best it is a cultural curiosity. Amending our previous definition, which was provisional, we may now say of Zen not merely that it is that aspect of the Mahāyāna which specializes in meditation, but that it represents a transmission of the living spirit of Buddhism with the help of the three main kinds of Chan described in the previous talk.

Thirdly and lastly, what is meant by *outside* the scriptures? The scriptures consist of words. Words convey ideas. In the case of the scriptures these ideas point in the direction of a spiritual experience. Zen, we have seen, is concerned primarily with this experience. It is not concerned with ordination, scriptures, or doctrine; or rather, it is concerned with them only as a means to the experience of Enlightenment, not as ends in themselves. But it certainly does not dispense with them altogether, on principle as it were. Instead, it follows a middle path. Distinguished from the scriptures but not divided from them, its own distinctive transmission makes use of the scriptures without becoming attached to them and without being enslaved by them. This is what is meant by 'outside'.

We have now answered the three questions which suggested themselves at the beginning of this talk, and have understood, I hope, the sense in which Zen is said to be 'a special transmission outside the scriptures'.

3
NO DEPENDENCE ON WORDS AND LETTERS

This week we are faced by a difficulty. '*No dependence on words and letters*,' declares the second line of our verse, continuing its definition of Zen. This means I shall have to talk about not depending upon words and letters, but in so doing I shall in fact be dependent on words and letters, or at least upon words and sounds. This is self-contradictory. Ideally I ought to expound the line by sitting in absolute silence for an hour. And an excellent exposition it would be! But if I did this you would probably all become restless and dissatisfied, and wouldn't put anything in the collection plate when you left, or at any rate not so much as usual. People value words; they do not value silence. So I suppose I shall have to do my best with words.

'No dependence on words and letters.' The line suggests that usually there is such a dependence. Let us examine the matter a little, first with regard to our dependence on words and letters in a general sense, and then with regard to our dependence on them where spiritual things are concerned.

Take the case of what we call our knowledge. We say we know this or know that. But what do we really mean? We mean, surely, that we have read it somewhere, or heard about it, or seen it on television. We have no *direct* knowledge. It is all based on hearsay, on second-hand, third-hand, and tenth-hand information, on conjecture and gossip. We consider, for instance, that we know what is going on in the world at large, what is happening in distant places – India, Rhodesia, Indonesia, etc. But whence is our 'knowledge' derived? From words and letters. From the radio and the newspapers, from snatches of conversation overheard on the Tube, from chance remarks at parties. How great is our dependence! The thought is quite a horrifying one. Supposing there were no radios, no newspapers, we would 'know' very little of what went on in the world. We would have fewer thoughts, fewer ideas. Being less cluttered up mentally, we would be better able to concentrate on things near at hand. We would be able to live more intensely. Perhaps we would be closer to Reality.

This was, of course, the condition of our ancestors in bygone days, even as it is still the condition of many people in the 'undeveloped' countries. Compared with us, our ancestors knew very little of what was going on in the great world that lay outside the gates of their own village or township. Vague rumours reached them from the distant capital, and usually that was all. Sometimes, of course, they saw armies marching past, and sometimes armies devastated with fire and sword, but despite beating drums and flying colours ordinary folk did not understand what the war was about or who was fighting whom. Occasionally men were conscripted. Otherwise, apart from natural calamities, the stream of life flowed on placid and undisturbed from year to year and from generation to generation. I am not trying to idealize the past. I am only trying to point out how much our knowledge depends upon words and letters and how little on direct personal experience, and that this dependence is, moreover, both proportionally and absolutely, greater now than ever before in history.

This is true in all fields. Take any subject that we think we 'know'. Take botany, or the history of art, or any other branch of human knowledge, from astronomy to zoology. By far the greater part of our knowledge of these subjects, if not the whole of it, is second-hand. Hardly any of it is original, the result of our own independent thought and discovery. Inheriting as it were a great stockpile of knowledge from the past, we go through life, for the most part, without adding to it so much as a single grain of our own. Originality would seem to be the prerogative of genius.

In everyday life all this, though perhaps regrettable, does not matter very much. We manage to get along somehow. From the Zen point of view, however, it is nevertheless important to realize what is actually happening. It might be interesting to perform an experiment. As you sit here, fold your hands and close your eyes, just as you do for meditation. Forget all you have ever learned from books, newspapers, magazines, radio, television, and advertisements. Forget even talks, lectures, and discussions. How much knowledge would you then have left? Very little indeed. If we were to perform the experiment regularly the experience would be a very salutary one. We should then realize how little we really know. To know that we do not know is the beginning of wisdom.[150]

From our general dependence on words and letters let us now turn to our dependence on them where spiritual things are concerned. We have, let us assume, a certain amount of religious knowledge. We know about Buddhism. We know about the Four Noble Truths and the Noble Eightfold Path; about karma and rebirth, Nirvāṇa and dependent origination; about *śūnyatā*, bodhisattvas, and the Pure Land. What a lot we know! We even know about Zen. Now where has all this knowledge come from? From books and lectures. Ultimately, of course, it comes from the scriptures, a survey of which I attempted to give last week. Now the scriptures consist of words and letters. On words and letters, therefore, is our knowledge of Buddhism dependent. Hence it is all second-hand, not based on direct, personal experience and perception.

Let us perform another experiment. Let us put aside all knowledge of Buddhism that depends on words and letters, all that we have not experienced and verified for ourselves. Probably we shall have to discard quite a lot. Do we really *know* what Nirvāṇa is? What about *śūnyatā*? Put them aside too if necessary. At the end of the experiment how much real knowledge is left? Perhaps none at all.

We should not think we have lost anything, however. In fact there is a great gain. As we saw last week, Zen is concerned with the experience of the living spirit of Buddhism, and with the transmission of that spirit. For Zen nothing else matters. Nothing must be allowed to stand in the way. This is what makes Zen so 'ruthless'. Zen has no hesitation about burning holy Buddha images or tearing up sacred books if these get in the way. But what is it that gets in the way more than anything else? What is it that most of all prevents us from having a real knowledge of Buddhism, based on our own experience? Can anybody tell me?... You are all silent. Surely the greatest obstacle is *to think that we know*. Until this obstacle has been removed, no progress is possible. Here, more than anywhere else, is the beginning of wisdom. It is also the beginning of Enlightenment, the beginning of progress: *to know that we do not know*.

Such knowledge involves distinguishing between what we know at second-hand, from the scriptures, and what we know from experience. This is what Zen means when it urges us not to confuse the two kinds of knowledge. If we do confuse them no spiritual progress is possible. Unfortunately we are guilty of this confusion all the time. It is, in fact, part of our general psychological conditioning. Having failed to distinguish thoughts from things, we then fail to distinguish words from thoughts. We think that if we can label a thing we have understood it. Take, for example, Nirvāṇa. This is essentially a spiritual principle, or transcendental reality, and can be thought of in various ways. For instance, it can be thought of in terms of the complete cessation of craving. Since we understand what is meant by the words 'cessation of craving' we think that we know what Nirvāṇa is! When, therefore, in some non-Buddhist work, we come across the idea of freedom from craving, we at once triumphantly exclaim, 'Ah yes, Nirvāṇa!' At once we slap on the label. We think we 'know' that the state of freedom from craving mentioned in the non-Buddhist work and the Buddhist Nirvāṇa are one and the same. All that we have in fact done is to equate thoughts and words. We are not dealing directly with things, with realities, at all. At best we are dealing with thoughts about things, or often with just words.

Conceptualizing and verbalizing activity of this sort is only too common in the West. People talk far too much. They always want to affix ready-made labels to their experiences. It is as though they were unable to enjoy the beauty of a flower until they had given it its correct botanical classification and a Latin name. We have to learn the value of silence, not only physical silence but the silence of thoughts, the silence of the mind. In this connection I remember an anecdote told me, many years ago, by an Indian friend of mine, an elder brother in the Order. Some years previously this friend had paid a visit to Germany, where he gave some lectures on Buddhism. One morning a German Buddhist lady came to see him. As he was in the middle of writing a letter, and wanted to catch the post, he asked her to wait in an adjoining room. He had only been writing for a few minutes, however, when the door suddenly burst open, and the German lady violently exclaimed, 'I shall go mad if I stay here much longer. *There's no one to talk to!*' As he came to the end of the story my friend threw up his hands in mock despair, as if to say, 'What hope is there of spreading Buddhism among such people?'

Some things there are which can be experienced and also thought about and described in words. Others, though capable of being experienced, transcend thought and speech. At best they can only be indicated, or suggested, or hinted at. Such are the realities, or aspects of reality, of which we speak in such terms as 'Enlightenment', 'Nirvāṇa', 'Buddhahood'. All these terms are used only provisionally. They give us a certain amount of practical guidance, some idea of the quarter in which to look, the direction towards which we have to orient our spiritual strivings, but their validity is only relative. They do not really define the Goal. In using them we say, therefore, in the absolute sense, nothing at all. Hence in the *Laṅkāvatāra Sūtra* the Buddha declares that from the night of his supreme Enlightenment to the night of his final passing away he did not utter a single word.[151] Between the two events lay forty-five years of untiring earthly ministry. During that period he had taught thousands, perhaps hundreds of thousands, of people. Hardly a day had gone by without discourses, dialogues, answers to questions. Yet in reality nothing had been said because nothing can be said about reality. All his words had been pointers to what is beyond words. As Aśvaghoṣa says, 'We use words to get free from words until we reach the pure wordless Essence.'[152]

Even better known and more striking is Vimalakīrti's 'thunderlike silence'. Vimalakīrti, the great householder bodhisattva of Vaiśālī, is sick, and the Buddha asks Śāriputra to go and enquire after his health. The great disciple declines, however, as he had once been admonished by Vimalakīrti and feels unworthy of the mission. All the other disciples, including the bodhisattvas, also protest their unworthiness, and for the same reason; all have been severely discomfited by Vimalakīrti at some time or another. Eventually Mañjuśrī, the great Bodhisattva of Wisdom, agrees to comply with the Buddha's request, and goes to see Vimalakīrti with a vast retinue. There is a great deal of discussion, and much subtle dialectic. Eventually the nature of the 'not-two doctrine' comes up for discussion. Various interpretations are given by those present. One says, 'Purity and impurity make two. If you see the real nature of impurity, then there is no state of purity, and you conform to the state of purity. This is entering the gate of the Not-Two Doctrine.' Another says, '*Saṃsāra* and *nirvāṇa* make two. See the (true) nature of *saṃsāra*, and then there is no *saṃsāra*, no bondage, no liberation, no burning, and no cessation.' Finally Mañjuśrī is asked for his opinion and replies, 'According to my idea, to have no word and no speech, no showing and no awareness about any of the *dharmas*, and to keep away from all questions and answers, is to enter the gate of the Not-Two Doctrine.' His interpretation is greatly applauded. Mañjuśrī then asks Vimalakīrti to speak. But 'Vimalakīrti kept silent, without a word.' This is the 'thunderlike silence' of Vimalakīrti.[153]

So long as we are dependent on words and letters, allowing ourselves to become enslaved by them instead of making use of them, we shall be unable to realize that which transcends words and letters. We shall, at the same time, confuse the two kinds of knowledge, thinking that we know something when we have merely heard it or read about it. For this reason Zen insists that there must be 'No dependence on words and letters'. Not that words are entirely useless. As I have said at the beginning of the talk, in communicating the truth of no dependence on words and letters one is inevitably dependent on words and letters. Thus we find ourselves back where we started from.

At this point an important question arises. If in Zen there is no dependence on words and letters, then on what *are* we to depend? This question will be dealt with next week, when we consider the third line of our verse.

4
DIRECT POINTING TO THE MIND

Today we are dealing with the third line of our verse, '*Direct pointing to the mind*,' and hoping to find there an answer to the question with which we concluded last week's talk – the question of what, according to Zen, we are to depend on, if there is to be no dependence on words and letters. Like the two previous lines of the verse, the line with which we are now concerned appears, at first sight, to consist of a quite simple and straightforward statement, something that everybody can understand. But this is not so. Before its meaning can become clear to us there is, in fact, a certain amount of obscurity to be resolved. This obscurity is not due to any vagueness on the part of the unknown composer of the verse, much less still on the part of Zen itself, but is simply the result of a characteristically Chinese attempt to pack the maximum amount of meaning into the minimum number of words. The meaning of the line can be clarified by a consideration of three questions, all of which are interconnected.

What is meant by 'mind'? Why does Zen insist on pointing to the mind rather than to anything else? What is the significance of *direct* pointing?

First of all, the meaning of the word 'mind'. In the original Chinese, this is *xin*. When I was in Kalimpong the hermit friend about whom I told you in the first talk once gave me a detailed explanation of the nine principal meanings of the word in Chinese literature, including Buddhist literature.[154] Fortunately, in the present context, we do not need to concern ourselves with all of these. Broadly speaking *xin* corresponds to the Indian (Pāli and Sanskrit) word *citta*, which it usually translates. *Citta* is mind in the widest and most general sense of the term, emotional and conative, as well as intellectual and rational. Some scholars, however, prefer to render *citta* or *xin* by 'heart', others by 'soul'. Suzuki, for instance, in some of his early works, such as his *Outlines of Mahāyāna Buddhism* and his translation of Aśvaghoṣa's *Awakening of Faith in the Mahāyāna* regularly translates *citta* as 'soul'.[155] Both renderings are apt to be misleading. In this context *citta* or *xin* is not heart as opposed to brain, in the sense of intellect, but rather the totality of mental life and activity which includes them both. It is more like the *psyche* in the Jungian sense of the term. Similarly *citta* or *xin* is not 'soul', because this term has, in English, connotations that are quite foreign to Buddhism. Today we are therefore sticking to 'mind' as the best working equivalent of both the Chinese and the Indian term. In any case, at this stage of our enquiry it is unnecessary for us to pay much attention to subtle differences of psychological terminology, and the general English term 'mind' will serve our purpose quite well.

Having warned us not to depend upon words and letters, that is to say on second-hand knowledge of reality, Zen tells us, as it were, to depend on the mind. This answers the question with which we were left at the end of last week. Zen declares, in effect, *depend on your own mind*. That is to say, depend on yourself, for psychologically speaking the mind is the self. Don't look without, don't allow your attention to be distracted by the multiplicity of external phenomena. Look within. This idea is of course not peculiar to Zen. It runs through the whole of Buddhism. In the *Dhammapada*, for instance, the Buddha declares that self-conquest is the greatest of all victories, that the self is its own refuge, its own master, and that purity and impurity depend upon one's own self.[156] Here attention is clearly directed to the subject of experience rather than to its objective content – to the feeling, knowing, willing mind rather than to the external universe. Similar in spirit are the maxim inscribed in the Temple of Apollo at Delphi, 'Know thyself,' and the *Dao De Jing*'s saying, 'He who knows others is wise; he who knows himself is enlightened.'[157] In pointing to the mind, and suggesting that we depend on that rather than on anything else, Zen gives the well-known idea its own special emphasis.

This emphasis is by no means superfluous. Indeed it is necessary at all times. People who have reached a certain level of maturity, or who enjoy a certain amount of leisure, tend to become bored and dissatisfied. They become bored and dissatisfied with their jobs, with their wives or husbands and families, with books and theatres, with radio and television, with work and with play, with the society to which they belong and the age into which they have been born, with laughter and with tears, with poetry, music, and art, with the face of nature and the form of man. Eventually they become bored and dissatisfied with themselves. In this state of boredom and dissatisfaction, of weariness and disgust, even, they start vaguely searching for something – they know not what. Giving it a name, they call it Truth, Reality. Others speak of it in terms of peace, happiness, ultimate satisfaction. Yet others make use of a specifically religious terminology. They speak in terms of God, salvation, Enlightenment, and so on. They even speak in terms of Zen. But however different the ways in which they speak of that for which they are searching, they all agree in searching for it *outside themselves*. Sometimes, of course, they find what they are looking for and establish a relation of dependence on it. They then think that they have succeeded in their quest, that boredom and dissatisfaction have been dispelled. But in reality they have failed. All that has happened is that they have fallen victim to a projection.

As a psychological phenomenon projection is quite familiar to us. In order to avoid having to recognize, and possibly come to terms with, something in ourselves, we unconsciously attribute it to other people. This repressed and projected factor is usually something that we experience as unpleasant or bad, something of which we are ashamed or afraid. We may be, for example, cold, hard, and selfish, completely lacking in warmth and affection. So we criticize other people for being like this. We complain, sometimes with bitterness, that our friends and relations are unkind and unsympathetic, that they trample upon our feelings, that they do not love us. We may even attribute feelings of coldness and hostility to the universe as a whole. All that we are really doing is projecting onto other people, or onto the outside world, our own personal defects. This sort of psychological projection goes on the whole time. Though extreme cases are rare, an element of projection enters into almost all our negative assessments of other people. If we are watchful we can often catch ourselves out. Just as another experiment, in the course of the coming week try to discover what it is you most dislike in others, what you most often criticize and condemn them for.

A little elementary self-analysis may reveal that those very qualities are hidden in the depths of your own mind and that in criticizing others in this way you are, in fact, unconsciously criticizing yourself.

Not only bad qualities but good ones too can be projected. These are not things of which we are ashamed or afraid, but capacities existing at a very deep level which we have so far been unable to develop. Sometimes we may be unaware of the possibility of developing them. We project, for example, the quality of love. Feeling the need for love, but being unable to develop it within ourselves, we try to find it outside and receive it from there. In other words we project. Good though a quality may be in itself, the projecting of it, however, is bad inasmuch as this projection stands in the way of full self-integration. In the case of love we cannot, in fact, truly receive it until we are able to give it, and we cannot give love until it has been developed.

It is possible to go even further than this. Projection is not only psychological but spiritual. All human beings are capable of developing their vague glimmerings of understanding and their intermittent impulses of kindness into the supreme wisdom and infinite compassion of perfect Buddhahood. All are capable of gaining Enlightenment. But we do not do this. Instead, we project our own potential Enlightenment as it were outside ourselves, on to another person, on to the figure of the Buddha for instance, and then proceed to establish a relationship with it, that is to say, to worship the Buddha, or at least to venerate him as the supremely wise and infinitely compassionate teacher. This does not mean that the Buddha was not Enlightened, or that the Buddha-ideal of our religious imagination is nothing but a projection, even a spiritual projection. It means that in the last resort we have to satisfy our need for Enlightenment by developing it within ourselves rather than by becoming parasitic on the Buddha's Enlightenment. Not that spiritual projection has no place at all in the religious life, or that faith and worship are all wrong. Spiritual projection represents a very important stage, and as such it has its legitimate place in the total scheme of spiritual development. But *ultimately* it is a hindrance.

Zen, which adopts the absolute standpoint, therefore points to the mind. It calls for a complete withdrawal of *all* projections, positive and negative, psychological and spiritual. It says, 'Depend on the mind, depend on yourself.' Within this context Enlightenment could be defined as the complete absence of projection.

So far we have considered Zen's pointing to the mind in a very general way. The time has come to be more specific. Zen points to the mind – but to which mind? Mind exists on many different levels, many different planes; it has various aspects, various functions. For instance there are the perceiving mind, the thinking and considering mind, and absolute mind. To which of these does Zen point? In a general way, of course, it points to them all, to mind as distinct from matter, as distinct from the external world. But specifically it points to absolute mind. It points to the Mind beyond the mind, to the Buddha-nature within, and tells us to rely upon that.

At this point our first question, 'What is meant by mind?' starts overlapping the second, 'Why does Zen insist on pointing to the mind rather than to anything else?' Mind is the point of contact with Reality. Absolute mind *is* Reality. In pointing to the mind, therefore, Zen points to Reality, points to Enlightenment, which is the experience of Reality, points to the Buddha-nature. This is why it points to the mind in preference to anything else.

We can now see more clearly the nature of the connection between Zen and meditation. We can understand why Zen is the *Meditation* school. Contrary to what is sometimes thought, meditation is not just a matter of concentration exercises successfully performed. Meditation may be defined as the persistent and methodical attempt to see reality within. Ordinarily our attention is directed outwards, towards the world. When we take up the practice of meditation, however, we learn to withdraw our attention from external objects, to disengage the senses from their respective stimuli, and to centre attention within. This attitude of withdrawal finds expression in the posture normally adopted for meditation, when we sit with legs folded beneath us and hands resting, one above the other, on top of the crossed ankles. The eyes are closed, representing the exclusion not only of visual stimuli, but of all sense impressions whatsoever. With practice it becomes possible to keep the mind centred within for longer and longer periods. This eventually results in a permanent shifting of the centre of attention from the external world to the mind itself, so that even when we are engaged in external activities a degree of inner recollection and awareness persists.

The next step we have to take is to make the mind progressively purer, clearer, and more luminous. That is to say, having turned from the external world to the mind, we now have to turn from the lower mind to the higher mind. In the general tradition which Zen shares with all other forms of Buddhism, this progress is represented by the four *rūpa dhyānas*, or states of meditative consciousness associated with the world of form, and the four *arūpa dhyānas*, or states of meditative consciousness associated with the formless world. These are usually regarded as together constituting one continuous series.

The first of the four states of meditative consciousness associated with the world of form consists of the five psychic factors of thought, both initial and sustained, rapture, bliss, and one-pointedness. In the second of these states thought is eliminated, and in the third, rapture. In the fourth, bliss is replaced by equanimity. One-pointedness is the only psychic factor that remains constant throughout. Indeed, it grows in intensity as the other factors are eliminated and it absorbs the energy invested in them.[158]

The four states of meditative consciousness associated with the formless world are known as the sphere of infinite space, the sphere of infinite consciousness, the sphere of no-thingness, and the sphere of neither perception nor non-perception.[159] These names tell us very little about the real nature of these states, which represent still higher and more refined experiences of one-pointedness and unification.

Even when the ascent has been made from the lower to the higher mind, and the eight states of meditative consciousness have all been experienced in their fullness, the limits of meditation have not been reached. The eight states are relative or mundane in character. They are not absolute, not transcendental. Reality has not yet been seen. Having turned from the lower to the higher mind we must finally turn, therefore, from relative mind to absolute mind. As relative mind and absolute mind are, from the standpoint of the relative mind, absolutely discontinuous, this transition can be brought about only by means of a kind of existential leap from the one to the other. There is no longer any question of a path with clearly marked steps and stages. The path that we have so far followed ends at the brink of an abyss, and from here we have no alternative but to take a leap in the dark. Taking the leap, we find ourselves in the midst of the Void. Darkness changes to light. Suddenly and mysteriously, relative mind is replaced by absolute mind. This absolute mind is not subject as opposed to object, nor can it be itself the object of thought. Rather, it is that pure, brilliant, and transparent awareness within which the distinction of subject and object does not exist. The goal of meditation has now been reached. Reality has been 'seen'. In pointing to the mind, Zen has pointed to Reality, to Enlightenment, to Buddhahood.

Having understood what is meant by mind, and why Zen insists on pointing to the mind rather than to anything else, we come now to our third and last question: What is the significance of *direct* pointing? This is not very difficult to see. Direct pointing means referring everything back to the mind itself – referring it, in the first place, to the thinking and perceiving mind rather than to the object of its thought and perception. It means throwing the disciple back again and again on his own personal problems and his own individual resources. It means refusing to go from Hampstead to Highgate via the whole universe.[160] The latter is, of course, just the sort of detour that people love to make. Despite protestations to the contrary, they do not really want to get to Highgate at all. They do not want to face up to the challenge of existence. They want to avoid it.

There are many ways in which this can be done. One of the most popular ways, especially in western Buddhist circles, is by asking questions. Now you may have been thinking that people ask questions in order to dispel their doubts and clear up mental confusion and arrive at the truth, and admittedly this does sometimes happen. But most of the time people ask questions in order *not* to receive an answer. A real live answer is the last thing they want. Even if they got it they would not know what to do with it. Probably they would feel like a small boy playing at hunting lions and tigers in the garden who was confronted by a real live lion or tiger escaped from the zoo. So they go on asking questions. What is the nature of Nirvāṇa? How can the law of karma operate when there is no permanent self? What is the evidence for rebirth? How shall we know that we have gained Enlightenment? Where does ignorance come from? Can one really desire not to desire? How is it possible to be fully aware, when awareness means being aware that you are aware, and so on *ad infinitum*? Has a dog Buddha-nature? Why did Bodhidharma come from the West?[161] To questions of this kind Zen gives no answer, at least it does not answer them on their own terms or from their own point of view. Generally, it prefers to put a counter-question, saying, in effect, 'Why do you ask the question?' Or, more challengingly, 'Who is it that asks?' In this way the exchange is at once placed on an entirely different basis. From being abstract and theoretical it becomes concrete and existential. The questioner is forced to realize, however dimly, that far from being motivated by a disinterested 'scientific' desire for the truth he is influenced by factors of which he is largely unconscious and that what he is really trying to do is to escape from the truth.

Most people, of course, resist this realization. Their own motives are the last thing they are prepared to scrutinize. But Zen does not let them get away with it so easily. By one means or another, with the help of slaps and shouts if words fail, it drags them back from philosophy and religion and psychology, even from Zen, and compels them to look where perhaps they never thought of looking before – at their own mind.

This is just what each one of you should do. Otherwise this talk will have been wasted. What I have said should be taken, however, as being itself a direct pointing to the mind. Take it as a talk *about* direct pointing to the mind, and you will miss the whole point.

5
SEEING INTO ONE'S OWN NATURE AND REALIZING BUDDHAHOOD

Today we come to the fourth and last line of the traditional verse with the help of which we have been trying, during the past few weeks, to gain some insight into the essence of Zen. The line reads, '*Seeing into one's own nature and realizing Buddhahood*.' The expression 'one's own nature' corresponds to the Sanskrit *svabhāva*, literally 'own-being' or 'self-nature', and in this context stands for the mind on which the previous line asked us to depend. One could, therefore, also render the line as 'Seeing into one's own *mind* and realizing Buddhahood.' The word 'and', however, does not appear in the original Chinese. Indeed, I believe the Chinese language dispenses altogether with conjunctions. What one has not divided one is under no necessity of joining together again. Here the omission, as we would regard it, of the word 'and' suggests that 'seeing' into one's own nature or into one's own mind and 'realizing' Buddhahood are not two distinct, even if parallel, activities, but simply different aspects of one and the same spiritual process.

In order to understand how this process takes place let us refer to the *Śūraṅgama Sūtra*, one of the most distinguished of the great Mahāyāna scriptures. The scene of the *sūtra* is laid at Śrāvastī, in north-western India, in the orchard which Anāthapiṇḍika, the rich merchant, had acquired from Prince Jeta as a retreat for the Buddha. Soon after the *sūtra* begins the Buddha and his disciples are all invited to a great feast by the king, it being the anniversary of his father's death. At the appropriate time all therefore depart for the palace. Only Ānanda, the Buddha's personal attendant, is missing. He has gone out on an errand, and returns only after the others have left. Finding the monastery deserted, and nothing to eat, he takes his almsbowl and goes begging from door to door in the streets of the city. Being a conscientious monk, he begs from all alike, without discriminating between rich and poor, or between high-caste and low-caste, and in this way eventually comes to the house of a low-caste woman called Mātaṅgī who has a beautiful daughter called Prakṛti. As soon as she sees the young and handsome monk Prakṛti falls violently in love with him, and begs her mother to cast a love-spell upon him. This Mātaṅgī does. Ānanda, though a conscientious monk, is not proof against the assaults of magic, and not only becomes fascinated by the maiden's charms but is lured into the house and into her room.

Meanwhile, the Buddha has returned to his orchard retreat, where he discourses to the king and other notabilities, who have accompanied him back from the palace. Knowing all the time what was happening to Ānanda, however, he calls the bodhisattva Mañjuśrī, the embodiment of wisdom, and bids him go and save Ānanda by repeating the Great Dhāraṇī at Mātaṅgī's house. As soon as Mañjuśrī does this Mātaṅgī's spell loses its power, Ānanda comes to his senses, and the crestfallen monk and repentant maiden accompany the great bodhisattva back to the feet of the Buddha.[162]

Now all this obviously has an allegorical meaning. To begin with, Mātaṅgī is a *low-caste* woman. She occupies a place, that is to say, at the very bottom of the Indian social system. Since there exists a clear correspondence between the higher and lower castes, on the one hand, and higher and lower states of consciousness, on the other, she may be said to represent the unrecognized or repressed side of one's nature. In Tantric Buddhism, indeed, the low-caste woman is the regular symbol for all the crude, unsublimated psychic energies which, according to this tradition, should not be repressed but brought out into the open and united with one's conscious spiritual attitude.[163] It is also significant that Mātaṅgī's daughter is called Prakṛti, for Prakṛti means 'Nature'. Ānanda is very learned and very conscientious but he is not Enlightened. He has not succeeded, that is to say, in integrating the different sides of his own being. Head is still at war with heart, conscious with unconscious. The casting of the spell represents not an assault from without, but rather an attack coming from forces deep within his own unconscious mind, forces with which he has not yet come to terms. Mañjuśrī, of course, represents transcendental wisdom. The conflict between head and heart, reason and emotion, conscious and unconscious mind, can be resolved only by the emergence of a higher faculty, wherein the light of reason and the warmth of emotion are not only fused but raised to the highest possible degree of intensity. Only when the bodhisattva recites the Great Dhāraṇī does Mātaṅgī's spell lose its power. But this does not mean that the natural forces which the spell represents are simply thrust back into the darkness of the unconscious. Mañjuśrī is no St Michael triumphantly holding down the powers of evil. Mañjuśrī brings Ānanda back to the feet of the Buddha. But he brings Prakṛti too. In other words, Nature is not to be repressed but recognized, not to be rejected but purified and assimilated.

On coming into the Buddha's presence Ānanda prostrates himself before him, confesses his shortcomings, and asks for help. The Buddha says that he will question Ānanda, and that the latter should *answer spontaneously*, without recourse to discriminative thinking. The qualification is important. Ānanda is a very learned man, he has 'heard much', but the Buddha does not want him to answer out of his acquired knowledge, which is after all second-hand, but out of himself, out of his personal perception and realization. He wants him to speak with his own voice, not a borrowed voice. This sort of spontaneity is, of course, very rare. Usually, when questioned on matters of fundamental concern, we reply after much thought and deliberation. That is to say, we reply from a comparatively superficial level of our being, from one made up of accretions from without rather than creations from within, from opinion and hearsay. Only in moments of crisis, or when deeply moved, do we in a sense really speak out. It is this sort of spontaneity, only coming from even deeper, coming from the existential depth of the disciple, that the Zen *mondō* or 'exchange' between master and disciple, or between one master and another, is designed to elicit. So long as the disciple speaks from anything less than his own true mind, or Buddha-nature, the master remains unsatisfied.

Step by step, relentlessly, the disciple is therefore forced into a corner, into an impasse. All his answers rejected, his mind baffled, his intellectual resources exhausted, in a state of near collapse, he can escape from the impasse only by waking up to the reality of his own true mind, and speaking out from that, saying – whatever comes. Perhaps, indeed, what comes will not be words at all, but a laugh or a smile, a polite bow or a sudden blow. But it must be spontaneous, and it must come from the deepest possible level of his being.

It is in this manner that the Buddha wants Ānanda to answer his question, and the question is, 'How did you become interested in Buddhism?' In other words the Buddha recurs to fundamentals. He does not waste time asking Ānanda why he was late getting back from his errand, or why he did not keep his eyes firmly fixed on his almsbowl while begging for food at Mātaṅgī's house. Instead, like a thunderbolt out of a clear sky comes the question, 'How did you become interested in Buddhism?' As the import of the *sūtra* is universal and timeless, the question is addressed not only to Ānanda but to us, not only to the Ānanda on the stage of Buddhist history but to the Ānanda in our own minds, to that aspect of ourselves which, being unintegrated, is liable, as he was liable, to the attacks of the unconscious. We too need, periodically, to explore the nature of our own commitment, to examine our reasons for following the path to Enlightenment. Were we attracted to Buddhism by its art, or its ethics, or its metaphysics? Was it books that brought us to the feet of the Buddha or the living example of someone we know? Are we in search of psychological security? Has our Buddhist life become a matter of habit and routine? These are the sort of questions we should ask ourselves, and like Ānanda we should try to answer them spontaneously.

Well, how *did* Ānanda become interested in Buddhism? The answer that he gives to the Buddha's question is hardly one that it would be possible for anyone to give today. He became interested, he says, because he was impressed by the personal appearance of the Buddha, and because he was convinced that the aureole of transcendentally pure and golden brightness which he had seen emanating from his person could not originate in one who was not free from all sexual passion and desire. It was on account of this that he had admired the Buddha and it was this that had influenced him to become one of his true followers.

Approving this declaration, the Buddha then solemnly addresses the whole assembly. Sentient beings have been born and reborn since beginningless time, he tells them, because they have not realized the true Essence of Mind and its self-purifying brightness. On the contrary, they have been engrossed in deluding and transient thoughts which are nothing but falsehood and vanity, thus preparing for themselves the conditions for repeated rebirth. If Ānanda is desirous of more perfectly understanding supreme Enlightenment he must learn to answer questions spontaneously, without recourse to discriminative thinking, for it is by reliance on their intuitive minds that the Buddhas of the ten quarters of the universe have been delivered from the cycle of conditional existence. Having said this, the Buddha asks Ānanda a further question. When he saw him, and was impressed by his appearance, how did he perceive him?

Ānanda replies that he perceived the Buddha with his eyes and his mind.

And where are these located?

The eyes, like the other sense-organs, are located on the surface of the body, while the mind is hidden within the body.

This does not satisfy the Buddha. He points out that Ānanda is now sitting in the hall of the retreat. First he sees the people sitting in the hall, and other things in turn, only afterwards does he see the grove and park outside. Similarly, if Ānanda's mind were hidden within his body, in the sense of being spatially located there, he ought to be able to see his own internal organs first and external objects afterwards. Ānanda tries again. The mind may, after all, be located outside the body. It may be like a lamp which would illuminate the inside of the room first and then, shining through the doors and windows, illuminate the yard outside.

This, too, fails to satisfy the Buddha. One person's eating does not appease the hunger of all; in the same way, if Ānanda's perceiving, understanding mind is really outside his body, then what the mind perceives could not be felt by the body, and what the body feels could not be perceived by the mind. Mind and body are in mutual correspondence, as is proved by the fact that when Ānanda's eyes are looking at the Buddha's hand his mind makes discriminations about it. If mind and body are in mutual correspondence, it cannot possibly be said that the mind exists outside the body.

Ānanda still thinks the mind must be located somewhere. If it cannot exist either inside or outside the body it must be located somewhere in between. Indeed, it may be concealed within the sense-organ itself. Just as the eye may be covered with a crystal bowl, so the mind may be 'covered' by, or contained within, the eye. Being part of the eye it cannot see the inside of the body, but being concealed within the eye it can clearly perceive external objects.

To this explanation the Buddha objects that if the mind were, in fact, contained within the eye as the eye itself might be covered by a crystal bowl, then the mind ought to perceive the eye before perceiving external objects, just as the eye would see the bowl before seeing mountains and rivers.

In this way the dialogue proceeds. Ānanda and the other members of the great assembly eventually realize that the mind, not being a spatially conditioned phenomenon, cannot be located anywhere. There is no time to follow the argument in detail, as step by step the Buddha leads Ānanda to the highest realization, but it should already have become evident that the *Śūraṅgama Sūtra* is one of the most magnificent of all Buddhist dialogues. Rivalling even Plato in atmosphere and in beauty of setting, its content is even profounder, being nothing else than the progressive revelation of the Buddha's crowning experience, his experience of the highest *samādhi*.

Now the mind not only cannot be located anywhere, but it does not exist as a thing among things at all. Not being a thing, an object, it cannot really be perceived or seen. But the fourth line of our verse, the line with which we are at present dealing, speaks of seeing into one's own nature, that is to say, into one's mind. Obviously there is a contradiction here. How is it to be resolved?

This brings us to one of the profoundest and most important teachings of Mahāyāna Buddhism, to a teaching of which Zen, at its best, is simply a practical exemplification. *One sees the mind by not seeing*. Not being an object of perception but the principle of perception itself, the mind cannot ever be perceived. Whatever is perceived is not the mind. For the mind to try to perceive its own existence is therefore like the tip of the finger trying to touch itself. Whatever is touched is not the finger-tip. The only way in which the finger-tip can possibly 'touch' itself is by withdrawing from all contact with external objects and simply 'feeling' its own existence directly. Similarly with the mind. We can never know it by going after it – with the mind – as though it were an external object distinct from the mind. This is what Zen calls 'using the mind to seek for the mind' and it is quite useless. By following this procedure we may discover many 'minds', but we shall not be able to discover the true mind, the principle of perception itself. The true mind can be found only by not-finding, by realization, that is to say, of a pure non-dual awareness without distinction of subject and object.

What has been said about 'seeing one's own mind' applies with equal force to 'realizing Buddhahood', for, as we have already seen, the two are different aspects of the same process. 'Seeing' corresponds to 'realizing', 'mind' to 'Buddha'. Just as it is ridiculous for the mind to try to see the mind, so it is ridiculous for the mind to try to realize Buddhahood. Zen tells us: You are Buddha. All that we have to do, it declares, is to wake up to the significance of this supreme fact. Devotional practices, scriptural study, even meditation, are ultimately a waste of time. Engaging in them is 'using the Buddha to realize the Buddha', which is like a man's going in search of himself.

Of course it is not easy to wake up. In fact it requires a great deal of effort to do so. First of all we have to realize, however vaguely, that we are asleep. As you sit here listening to these words you are not awake, as perhaps you had imagined, but asleep, sound asleep. Zen is simply a voice crying 'Wake up! Wake up!' Loud and clear though it resounds in your ear, so deep are your slumbers that you hear it but faintly, and coming as it were from a great distance. For five weeks now I have been talking about Zen; yet no one seems to have woken up. Perhaps I have not yet woken up myself. Perhaps I have just been talking in my sleep all this while. However, it sometimes happens that by talking in his sleep one sleeping person may rouse another. Let us hope that as a result of these talks on the essence of Zen something of that nature may have occurred.

The FWBO and 'Protestant Buddhism'

Mañjuśrī, the bodhisattva who as the embodiment of wisdom presides over the propagation of the Dharma, is iconographically represented not only as bearing in his left hand a lotus blossom upon whose open petals rests a book, the scriptures of Perfect Wisdom, but also as wielding with his right hand a flaming sword. While the first symbolizes the establishment of Truth the second symbolizes the destruction of untruth, that is to say, of those doctrines which do not constitute a basis for the attainment of the transcendental path.

A Survey of Buddhism[164]

Writing is an excellent means of awakening in every man the system slumbering within him; and everyone who has ever written will have discovered that writing always awakens something which, though it lay within us, we failed clearly to recognize before.[165]

Georg Christoph Lichtenberg (1742–1799)

I
INTRODUCTION

In February 1986 I received a letter from a certain Philip Mellor.

> I am at the University of Manchester, where I am working on a Ph.D. on the cultural transference of Buddhism into the West in the Department of Comparative Religion, where my supervisor is Dr Alan Williams. I am concerned with the development of, and modifications to, Buddhism in this country. In the light of your personal commitment to Buddhism, your involvement with the English Sangha Trust in the 1960s, and the development of your own Friends of the Western Buddhist Order I consider it extremely important for my work to be able to talk to you. First of all I would like to hear your first-hand account of this period of Buddhism in this country, and second, I would appreciate your general thoughts on the wider topic of cultural transference or translation in terms of the Western context within which Buddhism has now to operate.

Naturally I agreed to Mr Mellor's request, and six or seven weeks later, on 16 April, we met at Padmaloka, my personal headquarters near Norwich. In the course of the interview, which lasted for about two hours and which he tape-recorded, Mr Mellor questioned me about the circumstances in which I returned to Britain in 1964, about why the English Sangha Trust refused, two years later, to renew their invitation to me to teach at the Hampstead Buddhist Vihara, about Christmas Humphreys' attitude to the FWBO, about the severing of the Buddhist Society's link with Theosophy after Humphreys' death, and about the relation between the Western Buddhist Order and the earlier, abortive organization of that name started by the venerable Robert Stuart Clifton.[166] Only towards the end of the interview did he ask me for my thoughts on 'the wider topic of cultural transference or translation in terms of the western context within which Buddhism has now to operate' and on what he saw as differences between the Friends of the Western Buddhist Order (FWBO) and the English Sangha, i.e. the Theravādin community closely related to the forest monasteries of Ajahn Chah in Thailand.

A year and two months after our meeting, Mr Mellor sent me a copy of the transcription of the interview, at the same time returning a copy of *The Thousand-Petalled Lotus*[167] that had been lent to him. That was four years ago. Thereafter I heard nothing from Mr Mellor and, occupied as I was with the actual task of the cultural transference of Buddhism into the West, thought no more of him and his Ph.D.

Early this year, however, there reached me reports to the effect that the FWBO was being held up, in certain academic circles in Britain, as an example of 'Protestant Buddhism'. These reports eventually came to centre on an article which, it was said, had appeared in the January 1991 issue of the journal *Religion* (not to be confused with *Religion Today*), published by the Department of Religious Studies, Lancaster University. With some difficulty I managed to obtain a copy. It was entitled 'Protestant Buddhism? The Cultural Translation of Buddhism in England' and was by Philip A. Mellor, the man who had interviewed me five years earlier. He had recently obtained his Ph.D. from the Faculty of Theology at the University of Manchester with a thesis dealing with problems of theory and method in the study of contemporary religion (so a note subjoined to the text informed the reader), and was now a lecturer in the Department of Theology and Religious Studies at the Liverpool Institute of Higher Education.

The article proved to be something of a disappointment. Not that I had expected the author to be particularly sympathetic to the FWBO or to agree with all my 'thoughts' on the cultural transference or translation of Buddhism. It was a disappointment because it contained a great deal of theory and methodology but very little in the way of actual information about the FWBO, even though the FWBO was one of the two 'English' Buddhist groups on which the author professed to concentrate in his discussion of the relationship of English Buddhism with Protestant Christian perspectives, the other group being the English Sangha. Worse still, such information as the article did provide was either so simplistic and selective as to give quite a misleading impression of the FWBO or simply erroneous. In some cases views were attributed to the FWBO which were the exact opposite of those it actually holds. What could be done to set the record straight? At my suggestion Dharmachari Kulananda drafted a reply to Philip Mellor's article for publication in *Religion*.[168] In this reply, which ran to 2,500 words, Kulananda confined himself to correcting some of the factual errors in Mellor's characterization of the FWBO – in itself a sufficiently extensive undertaking. This would suffice, I hoped, to set the record straight at least on matters of fact and at least so far as the (mainly academic) readership of the journal was concerned. But what of those larger theoretical and methodological questions in the context of which Mellor had made his mistakes about the FWBO and which were, perhaps, responsible for his Procrustean distortions of FWBO teaching and practice? Surely something should be done about them! In the end I decided to write a response of my own to Mellor's article. Not a reply but a response. I would look at some of the theoretical and methodological questions raised by his article, either explicitly or by implication. I would look at them in my own way, that is, I would look at them as a (western) Buddhist, without any pretence of adopting an 'objective' approach to Buddhism and without allowing myself to be restrained by considerations of academic propriety.

Mellor's article is divided into five sections. These are headed, respectively: 'The Burden of Self', 'Protestantism and Buddhism', 'Modernism and Buddhism', 'Culture and Buddhism', and 'The Cultural Translation of Buddhism'. My response will be similarly divided, though I shall not be looking at all the questions raised by the article, nor looking at them systematically; neither shall I be concerned to correct factual errors about the FWBO, except where these are particularly flagrant. At times I may permit myself to digress, or take advantage of an opportunity to clarify my position on certain topics beyond the immediate requirements of the discussion. But before the first section of Mellor's article there comes an introductory paragraph, the contents of which also need to be scrutinized. I give the paragraph in full.

> In the discussion that follows I suggest that the development of Buddhism in England is not necessarily an indicator of a complete disenchantment with western, Christian religious positions. I argue that this is a simplification of the real situation. Rather than understanding English Buddhism as a phenomenon completely at odds with western religious traditions, I consider a number of ways in which it participates in them. Religions are not free-floating, metaphysical phenomena impervious to all social, intellectual and political conditions. On the contrary, it is my contention that religions are always and everywhere embedded in social and cultural realities. The development of new forms of religious life in a particular culture is not necessarily a signifier of the collapse of the constraining forces of social structures and systems, but of these structures and systems enabling new developments to take place. As I shall note, there are many features in contemporary English Buddhism that indicate a complex relationship with Protestant Christian perspectives. I concentrate my discussion on the Friends of the Western Buddhist Order (FWBO), a consciously 'western' Buddhist group, and the English Sangha, a community closely related to the forest monasteries of Ajahn Chah in Thailand. The two groups are linked by the fact that neither are ethnic and that Sangharakshita, the founder and leader of the FWBO, also led the English Sangha for a brief period in the 1960s before founding the FWBO. Nevertheless, they demonstrate markedly different visions of how Buddhism should be understood and practised in the west. In the discussion of these two approaches I also intend to draw some general conclusions about the difficulties of translating an eastern religious tradition into a western cultural environment.

Here we are confronted by a number of ambiguities. The more serious of them relate to the expressions 'English Buddhism' and 'western religious traditions', to the relations between religions and social and cultural realities, and to the description of the FWBO as a consciously 'western' group.

I

At the very beginning of my interview with Philip Mellor (as by him transcribed) I spoke of my having had no intention of coming back to Britain. In this introductory paragraph, however, Mellor speaks of 'Buddhism in *England*' and '*English* Buddhism', as he in fact does throughout the article, in the body of which he also speaks, repeatedly, of *English* Buddhists. But 'England' is no more equivalent to 'Britain' than 'English' is to 'British'. Is Mellor so remote from social and cultural realities as to be unaware of this and unaware, therefore, that a discussion of the development of Buddhism in England is by no means the same thing as a discussion of the development of Buddhism in Britain? Apparently he is. At least he gives no indication of not being unaware. He is unaware that there are native-born Buddhists in Scotland, for example, who, while they might be happy for Buddhism in Scotland to be treated as part of Buddhism in Britain, and for themselves to be described as British Buddhists, would certainly object to Buddhism in Scotland being treated as part of Buddhism in *England* and themselves described as *English* Buddhists. The point is relevant to a discussion of the Friends of the Western Buddhist Order (FWBO) and cultural translation, the reason being that the FWBO has a presence not only in England but also in Scotland and Wales, as well as having a substantial number of Scots Order members and Mitras living and working in England. (I shall discuss the question of the extent to which the FWBO can be regarded as English later on.) It is also relevant in view of Mellor's contention that 'religions are always and everywhere embedded in social and cultural realities'. Scottish social and cultural realities are not the same as those in England (Scotland has its own educational system, for example). A discussion of the FWBO and cultural translation therefore needs to take into account the fact that the realities in which the FWBO are 'embedded' are not exclusively English, any more than the FWBO itself, even within the United Kingdom, is a purely English phenomenon.

II

'Buddhism in England' and 'Buddhism in Britain' are not the only expressions Mellor regards as synonymous. The same treatment is given to 'western, Christian religious positions' and 'western religious traditions'. Having in the first sentence of his introductory paragraph spoken of the development of Buddhism in England being not necessarily an indicator of complete disenchantment with western, Christian religious positions, in the next sentence but one he speaks of his refusal to understand English Buddhism as a phenomenon completely at odds with western religious traditions. But 'Christian religious positions' (apparently Mellor's euphemism for Christian dogmas) cannot really be equated with 'western religious traditions'. Besides the traditions of classical antiquity, such as Mithraism, Gnosticism, Hermeticism, and Neoplatonism in its more religious aspect, there are Alchemy, Theosophy, Rosicrucianism, and Freemasonry. There are, in fact, all the various alternative traditions of the West which, after surviving 'underground' in an attenuated form, or being reconstituted from the literary remains that became available at the time of the Renaissance, have come to constitute an increasingly serious challenge to Christianity. With these alternative traditions Buddhism in England is not necessarily 'disenchanted' in the way that it is with 'western, Christian religious positions'; nor is the phenomenon of English Buddhism by any means 'completely at odds' with them. In a paper on 'My Relation to the Order' I speak of Neoplatonism as being the major spiritual tradition of the West, just as Buddhism is the major spiritual tradition of the East, and make the point that Buddhists can no more afford to ignore Neoplatonism than Neoplatonists (should there be any left) can afford to ignore Buddhism.[169] I would go further than that. Having read, in the course of the last few years, all the major surviving texts of Neoplatonism, from Plotinus to Proclus, I have come to the conclusion that such affinities as exist between Buddhism and the religious traditions of the West are to be found in Neoplatonism rather than in Christianity, notwithstanding the fact that Christian theology and mysticism are both deeply indebted to Neoplatonism. This can, of course, be discounted as a minority view; but in point of fact there has been very little comparative study of Buddhism and Neoplatonism. We have a paper on 'Plotinus and Vijnañāvāda Buddhism' and a paper which, despite being headed 'Phraseology and Imagery in Plotinus and Indian Thought', is devoted mainly to Neoplatonic and Indian ideas on divine activity, in particular, the views of Plotinus and those expressed in the Mahāyāna Buddhist work *Uttaratantra* or *Ratnagotravibhāga* – and that is about all.[170] There can, however, be little doubt that westerners attracted to Buddhism are often sympathetically disposed, at the same time, to the alternative traditions of the West, especially as mediated by the writings of Carl Gustav Jung, Frances A. Yates, and Edgar Wind.[171]

Thus there is no question of English Buddhism being 'completely at odds' with western religious traditions, in the sense of being at odds with Christianity *and* the alternative traditions of the West. What English Buddhism is at odds with, whether completely or otherwise, is Christianity, or, in Mellor's euphemistic phrase, 'Christian religious positions'. English Buddhism denies what Christianity affirms, though that denial is incidental to its own spiritual affirmations and though individual English Buddhists may not be sufficiently informed about Christianity to be aware that they are, in effect, denying its fundamental teachings. But how strange it is that in speaking of the relation between the development of Buddhism in England/English Buddhism on the one hand and western, Christian religious positions/western religious traditions on the other, Mellor should make use of such expressions as 'at odds with' and 'disenchanted'! According to Collins Dictionary 'at odds' means 'on bad terms' (the Concise Oxford has 'variance, strife'). Surely to speak of serious religious and philosophical differences in this way is to reduce them to the level of a personal misunderstanding or even a personal quarrel. It is to trivialize the important issues involved. I am reminded of the line that well-meaning Christian friends used to take with me on learning that, though a Buddhist monk, I had been born into a (nominally) Christian family. 'Oh we *quite* understand!' they would exclaim sympathetically. 'You must have had a very bad experience of Christians (or of the Church). But you mustn't judge Christianity by Christians, you know. That wouldn't be fair.' But I didn't judge Christianity by Christians, I used to tell them. My experience of Christians had been quite positive. I judged Christianity by its teachings, and the reason I was a Buddhist and not a Christian (apart from the overwhelming appeal of Buddhism itself) was that I could not accept those teachings. Sometimes I added, for good measure, that my experience of Buddhists (I was then living in the East) had been much worse than my experience of Christians and that if my faith in Buddhism had depended on a positive experience of Buddhists I probably would have given up Buddhism long ago. What my well-meaning Christian friends were doing, and what Mellor in fact does, can be described as an attempt to 'personalize' matters of principle, and it is this tendency to personalization and subjectivization that is so prominent a feature of that very modernism of which, in the third section of his article, he is quick to accuse the FWBO.

It is the same with 'disenchant', defined by Collins as 'to free from or as if from enchantment; disillusion.' In speaking of 'disenchantment with western, Christian religious positions' Mellor is again personalizing matters of principle, thereby suggesting that to the extent that the development of Buddhism in England is due to such disenchantment it is due to a subjective, irrational disappointment with Christianity rather than being the result, as it is in the case of many English Buddhists, of a critical awareness of the inadequacies of that religion. Disenchantment in any case implies a previous state of enchantment. There are not a few English Buddhists who cannot be said to have been disenchanted with Christianity for the simple reason that they were never enchanted with it in the first place, either because they were brought up as Humanists, or Jews, or Theosophists, or Marxists, or because they were raised in an environment free from religious influences. I would also have thought that to speak of disengagement from Christianity in terms of disenchantment was rather unfortunate, at any rate from the Christian point of view, conjuring up as the expression does an image of Christianity as a Circean figure from whose spells the ex-Christian has succeeded in breaking free.

III

'Religions,' says Mellor, 'are not free-floating, metaphysical phenomena impervious to all social, intellectual and political conditions.' Of course they are not, and I very much doubt if there is anyone who really thinks they are. Mellor presumably states the rejected view in such extreme terms simply in order to make his own contrary – and no less extreme – view that 'religions are always and everywhere embedded in social and cultural realities' seem moderate and reasonable. But is it so reasonable – or so clear – as it appears? The word embedded means to be 'fixed firmly and deeply in the surrounding mass' or to be 'surrounded closely' (Collins), and it is therefore not the most appropriate term to use in connection with the kind of relation that obtains between religions and what Mellor calls social and cultural realities. An object may be fixed firmly and deeply in a surrounding mass in two ways. It may be fixed in it in such a way that only a part of it is enclosed by the surrounding mass (the relation of lotus plant to mud), or it may be fixed in it in such a way that it is completely enclosed by that mass (the relation of fossil to rock). If religions really are 'always and everywhere' embedded in social and cultural realities in the sense of being completely enclosed by those realities it follows that religions have only a social and cultural existence and that, earth-bound phenomena that they are, they possess no supra-social, supra-cultural, spiritual dimension. English Buddhism is not committed to such a view of religions, least of all to such a view of Buddhism itself. Whether it is Mellor's own view is not clear, but since in describing the relation between religions and social and cultural realities he makes use of a term which is, as we have seen, ambiguous, we cannot assume that it is not his own view.

There is a similar ambiguity in Mellor's description of the relation between new forms of religious life and the social structures and systems of the culture in which they arise. Having contended that, far from being free-floating metaphysical phenomena, religions are always and everywhere embedded in social and cultural realities, he goes on to say,

> The development of new forms of religious life in a particular culture in not necessarily a signifier of the collapse of the constraining forces of social structures and systems, but of these structures and systems enabling new developments to take place.

The ambiguity is in the word 'enabling'. In what sense do the social structures and systems of an existing culture positively 'enable' new developments to take place? Can it really be said that they 'provide [new forms of religious life] with adequate power, means, opportunity, or authority' to develop (Collins), or even that they make such developments 'possible or easy' (the secondary meaning of the word)? More often than not, the old structures and systems make the development of new forms of religious life possible – though not necessarily easy – only in the negative sense of not actually getting in the latter's way, and the reason they do not get in their way is that they no longer are in a position to do so. In the case of the new form of religious life that is English Buddhism, the 'constraining forces' of the structures and systems of the particular culture in which it has developed have been largely Christian, and it was only with the virtual 'collapse' of those forces that Buddhism could develop here. We all know what would have happened if a Sinhalese monk had tried to preach his non-theistic religion in fifteenth-century (Catholic) Oxford, or if a Tibetan lama had attempted to do the same thing in seventeenth-century (Puritan/Anglican) London. This is not to say that there are not in English culture structures which make the development of Buddhism in England easier, at least organizationally speaking. Christian and non-Christian bodies alike, for example, can be exempted from taxation. But what really enables new developments like English Buddhism to take place, in the sense of making them possible by default, is the virtual collapse of our largely Christian constraining forces – a collapse of which the existence of structures like the Charity Commission is itself a 'signifier'.

IV

According to Mellor, the FWBO is 'a consciously "western" Buddhist group' (it is not clear what the quotations marks are meant to convey). At the same time the FWBO is one of the two groups on which he concentrates his discussion of the 'complex relationship' between contemporary *English* Buddhism and Protestant Christian perspectives. Having treated 'English Buddhism' and 'English Buddhists' as equivalent to 'British Buddhism' and 'British Buddhists', he now proceeds to treat '"western" Buddhist group' as equivalent to 'English Buddhist group'. This is not only ambiguous but positively confusing. I shall therefore try to make it clear in what sense, and to what extent, the FWBO is western, with or without the mysterious quotation marks, and in what sense, and to what extent, it is English. This will enable us to see what Mellor is discussing – or ought to be discussing – when he discusses the FWBO.

In the latter part of my interview with Mellor I emphasized that, whether in India or elsewhere, I had been concerned only to teach the Dharma, so far as I understood it. There was no question of my teaching an eastern Buddhism in the East and a western Buddhism in the West, even though I found on my return to Britain that certain ways of presenting things were more effective or comprehensible in the West than others, or that certain practices and observances were not acceptable here.

> So I proceeded on a purely empirical, experimental basis [I explained], I was just concerned to teach the Dharma, not any western version of it – far from it. I was [and still am] very traditionally-minded. I'm not trying to 'adapt' the Dharma; I'm just trying to make it understandable.... If one can talk of a western Buddhism [at all] it is only in the sense of a form in which the Dharma can be understood and practised in modern western society. [So far as I am concerned] it is not an 'interpretation' of the Dharma.

Surprisingly, Mellor makes no reference to this passage from our interview, though he quotes the immediately following passage in which I distinguish between Tradition with a capital T and tradition with a small T – a passage which really needs to be read in the light of my previous remarks about my own teaching of the Dharma. He also seems to be unaware of my lecture 'The Individual and the World Today' (included in *New Currents in Western Buddhism*), in which, having characterized the modern world as a western world, a world which is either Westernized or in process of Westernization, I continue:

> When I say that the FWBO is western, I do not mean that it just happens to be geographically located in the west, or that it was started, geographically speaking, in the West; I mean that it has arisen under the conditions of secularized and industrialized western civilization. And it is with those conditions that the FWBO tries to cope. It tries to make the Buddhist way of life, the spiritual life ... possible, under these conditions. The FWBO is therefore western in the sense that it is concerned with the world of today, not with the world of yesterday, however bright that world may have been in some respects. Nor is it primarily concerned with the world of traditional religious culture.... That world has gone, it seems, for ever.[172]

Mellor appears not to understand this. Indeed, though the FWBO is, according to him, 'a consciously "western" Buddhist group' (by the time we get to the second section of his article it has become 'self-consciously western') he makes no attempt to ascertain in what sense it is western and no attempt, therefore, to ascertain whether '"western" Buddhist group' and 'English Buddhist group' can really be treated as equivalent and the bearing this has on the 'complex relationship' of either or both of them (as the case might be) with 'Protestant Christian perspectives'.

The extent to which the FWBO is western (in the non-geographical sense) varies from place to place. It is more western in urban Germany than in rural India, for example, because the conditions with which it has to cope in the former are more secularized and industrialized than those with which it has to cope in the latter. Though in his introductory paragraph, as throughout his article, Mellor speaks of the FWBO as if it were a single, monolithic body this is not really the case. What we in fact have is an Order, members of which conduct, with the help of Mitras and Friends (as they are called), the activities of some fifty different FWBOs and other legally and financially autonomous bodies in more than a dozen countries both West and East. Like the Order itself, these FWBOs are united by a common spirit – a spirit which, in the case of the Order in particular, is symbolized by the figure of the eleven-headed, thousand-armed Avalokiteśvara, the bodhisattva of universal compassion. At the same time, each autonomous FWBO possesses its own distinctive character, a character in part determined by the extent to which it is (non-geographically) western. In discussing the FWBO as 'a consciously "western" group' it is therefore not only necessary to understand in what sense it considers itself western; it is also necessary to realize that it is not equally western in all its parts.

But though the FWBO is not western in the geographical sense, it of course started in the West. It started in London, the first of the autonomous FWBOs being founded there in 1967 and the WBO a year later. Autonomous FWBOs have since been established throughout Britain and in eleven other countries in four continents. At present (September 1991) there are in the world 450 men and women Order members (the WBO is a unified order in the sense that it admits men and women on equal terms), approximately 1,000 Mitras, more than a third of whom are postulants, and at a conservative estimate 100,000 Friends. Nearly twenty per cent of all Order members are Indian, while there are twenty-one New Zealanders, thirteen Finns, and some two dozen representatives of fifteen or sixteen other nationalities. Among Mitras and Friends an even greater number of nationalities are represented, not to mention the imbalance created by the fact that the majority of Friends are Indian. Thus the FWBO is not English in the sense of having a purely English membership, and the extent to which it is English certainly varies from place to place. (Membership is by no means purely or uniformly English even in England.) The FWBO is English only in the sense that it started in England, and that the majority of Order members and Mitras are English – a state of affairs that on present form will not continue indefinitely.[173]

Mellor is unaware of all this, just as he is unaware of the sense in which, and the extent to which, the FWBO is western. For him the FWBO is simply a part of the English Buddhist scene and as such it is one of the two groups on which he proposes to concentrate his discussion of the relationship of contemporary English Buddhism with Protestant Christian perspectives, the other group being the English Sangha. The two groups are linked, he tells us,

> by the fact that neither are ethnic and that Sangharakshita, the founder and leader of the FWBO, also led the English Sangha for a brief period in the 1960s before founding the FWBO.

By saying neither are ethnic Mellor appears to mean that both the FWBO and the English Sangha consist not of immigrant 'born Buddhists' but of native converts, which is correct (except that in the case of the FWBO the converts are not all English). Nonetheless there is an important difference between the two groups. The FWBO has always been self-sufficient, in the sense of depending for financial support on its own members rather than on the non-Buddhist and non-FWBO general public. This is one of the reasons for the existence of the various FWBO right livelihood businesses, which besides providing for the material and spiritual needs of their workers (who normally are FWBO members) donate their profits to one or more of the autonomous FWBOs. The English Sangha, on the contrary, is not self-sufficient, indeed cannot be self-sufficient. As a Theravādin (as distinct from, say, a Chan or Zen) monastic community it depends for support not on its own members but on the Buddhist and non-Buddhist general public. In practice this means that it depends largely, if not predominantly, on the support of the immigrant 'born Buddhist' laity, particularly as represented by the Thais, the English Sangha being closely related to the forest monasteries of Ajahn Chah in Thailand, as Mellor notes. The immigrant Thai laity support the English Sangha for the same reason, presumably, that they support monks in their own country. They support it in order to acquire 'merit' and to be reborn in heaven after death. Thus the English Sangha is brought within the orbit, to some extent, of Thai ethnic Buddhism. Merit is acquired by supporting monks, but only if the monks are 'real' monks, and what is a 'real' monk, that is to say, a monk of a holiness sufficient to guarantee that offerings made to him really are productive of 'merit', is in practice determined by the supporting laity, who are quick to withdraw their support from any monk failing to conform to their ideas of how a 'real' monk should behave. (Revealing light is thrown on the 'merit-making' side of Thai Buddhism in Timothy Ward's *What the Buddha Never Taught*, described as 'an open-eyed, often humorous, personal account' of the author's sojourn at Wat Pah Nanachat in north-eastern Thailand, one of the forest monasteries to which the English Sangha is closely related.)[174] To the extent that it is dependent on the support of the immigrant Thais, and within the orbit of Thai ethnic Buddhism, the English Sangha is inevitably under a certain amount of pressure to conform to its Thai supporters' idea of how a 'real' monk should behave and what is and what is not 'real' Buddhism. Even apart from other considerations, it is therefore doubtful if the English Sangha can be regarded as an English Buddhist group, and part of English Buddhism, without serious qualification.

The FWBO and the English Sangha are not only linked by the fact that, according to Mellor, 'neither are ethnic'. They are also linked by the fact that 'Sangharakshita, the founder and leader of the FWBO, also led the English sangha for a brief period in the 1960s before founding the FWBO.' In fact I led it for two years, if indeed I can be said to have led a sangha which for the greater part of that time consisted of only myself (the English Sangha is, of course, a sangha of *monks*). These two years were among the most demanding and crucial – and the most spiritually rewarding – of my whole life, and I hope to be able to write an extended account of them one day.[175] In the 1980s, however, Ajahn Sumedho, the present (American) leader of the English Sangha, was also for five years president of the Buddhist Society, founded in 1924 by Christmas Humphreys as the Buddhist Lodge of the Theosophical Society and the longest-established Buddhist organization in Britain. The English Sangha and the Buddhist Society thus are more 'linked' than are the English Sangha and the FWBO. I therefore wonder why Mellor concentrates his discussion on the relationship between 'contemporary

English Buddhism' and 'Protestant Christian perspectives' on the FWBO and the English Sangha, rather than on the Buddhist Society and the English Sangha, especially as the Buddhist Society's activities are limited to England, not to say to the London area (except in the case of its journal *The Middle Way*, which circulates more widely). I also wonder why Mellor should be more concerned, apparently, with 'the markedly different visions of how Buddhism should be understood and practised in the west' demonstrated by the English Sangha and the FWBO than with whatever the two groups might have in common. In any case, if it is *differences* between English Buddhist groups which particularly interest him he ought to concentrate his discussion on the respective 'visions' of the English Sangha and the Buddhist Society, the 'vision' of the one being decidedly monastic in character and that of the other no less decidedly lay, as compared with the more unified 'vision' of the FWBO, which seeks to transcend the monk–lay dichotomy and to be simply and authentically Buddhist.

For reasons best known to himself, however, Mellor concentrates his discussion on the FWBO and the English Sangha, and it is in his discussion of the different approaches of these two groups that he draws his conclusions about 'the difficulties of translating an eastern religious tradition into a western cultural environment.' In responding to this discussion, and looking at the theoretical and methodological questions raised by Mellor's article, I shall not further concern myself with the ambiguities which, as I have shown, confront us in his introductory paragraph, even though the effect of these ambiguities is felt throughout much of the article. Nor shall I further concern myself with the English Sangha, except to the extent that misleading comparisons are made between it and the FWBO.

2
THE BURDEN OF SELF

This section of Mellor's article contains no direct reference to the FWBO or, for that matter, to any English Buddhist group. Its purpose seems to be to clear the ground prior to his engaging with the article's principal topic: the relationship between Protestantism, Modernism, and Culture, on the one hand, and Buddhism on the other. Mellor clears the ground by establishing, or seeking to establish, that in the contemporary West each person's self has become his principal burden; that this emphasis on self has diminished the significance of religious tradition; that one of the major defining characteristics of Buddhism is the rejection of self; and that the idea that a person's self is the principal burden has come to characterize certain areas of English Buddhism more than the traditional rejection of self. These positions have a definite bearing on what Mellor has to say about the FWBO in the discussion that follows, and I shall look at them carefully.

I

The idea that each person's self becomes his principal burden comes from Richard Sennett's *The Fall of Public Man*, an examination of the imbalance that exists between public and private life, its cause and significance. Mellor quotes the American sociologist as arguing that 'to know oneself has become an end, instead of a means through which one knows the world'.[176] This is corroborated, according to Mellor, by Edward Shils, who suggests that the attempt to discover oneself 'has come to be regarded as the first obligation of the individual',[177] an obligation that has meant that the significance of social ends has diminished and even called into question our ability to act, activity being only considered legitimate in as far as it takes place in an interpersonal context. Individuals withdraw into self, so Shils believes, 'to protect a precious psychic life which, it is understood, might wither if exposed to the harsh realities of the social world'.[178] Two causes which can be highlighted as being responsible for this emphasis on self are the Enlightenment (i.e. the eighteenth-century philosophical movement of that name) and Protestantism. Shils in this connection 'notes the immense significance of the Enlightenment's concern for self-regulation and expression and the vision of the individual as a self-contained and self-determining moral entity,'[179] while Louis Dumont 'has drawn attention to the radical shift in significance from the Church to the individual in the doctrines of Luther and Calvin'.[180] Both the Enlightenment and the Reformation, in Dumont's opinion, have contributed to the modern view of the individual as a 'quasi-sacred absolute', so that transpersonal social forms (such as the Church) and even society itself are seen as insignificant, or even tyrannical.[181]

With much of this the (western) Buddhist can agree, though the expression 'transpersonal' is ambiguous and needs to be examined. In the contemporary West there *is* an imbalance between public and private life, the attempt to discover oneself *has* come to be regarded as the first obligation of the individual, individuals *do* withdraw into self to protect a precious psychic life, and it is good that Sennett makes these things clear to us. *The Fall of Public Man* contains, in fact, a number of insights useful to anyone seeking to understand and practise Buddhism as this is understood and practised in the FWBO. Not that the idea of there being an imbalance between public and private life is really a new one, though Sennett certainly explores it more thoroughly than it has been explored before, or that the idea of one compensating for the other has not been expressed more clearly and more eloquently by earlier writers. In an article on 'The Isolation of Katherine Mansfield' John Middleton Murry comments on V. S. Pritchett's assumption that the cult of self-perfection is the natural compensation for the lack of a country in which one feels at home. 'Many have practised the cult of self-perfection, many indeed practise it today,' Murry writes, 'who have not been exiled from their native land. The natural consequence of living in exile from a familiar society is to seek compensation in a closer human relation. The friendliness, the ease of living, which is, as it were, diffused in one's manifold contacts with a familiar society, has to be recaptured in a more intense form in the ease and trust of more intimate and private relations. In a word, *the natural consequence of social insecurity is the search for security of love.*'[182]

This could hardly be better put. But the search for security of love (or the equivalent of love) is not confined to a single epoch or to any one quarter of the globe, any more than is the possibility of imbalance between public and private life. Even the idea of the self as a person's burden is to be found not only in the West but in the East, not only in twentieth-century sociology and literary criticism but in ancient Indian philosophy and religion. It may surprise Mellor to know that the *Saṃyutta Nikāya* or 'Book of the Kindred Sayings' contains a text called the *Bhāra Sutta* or 'Burden *Sutta*', in which the Buddha teaches the monks that the five *khandhas*, the five components of psychophysical existence, are the burden, while the burden-taker (or burden-taking – the prose and verse portions of the *sutta* differ here) is the *puggala*, the individual, or person, or man, as the term is variously translated:

The burden is indeed the fivefold mass:
The seizer of the burden, man:
Taking it up is sorrow in this world:
The laying of it down is bliss.

If a man lay this heavy burden down,
And take not any other burden up:
If he draw out that craving, root and all,
No more en-hungered, he is free.[183]

Since it is one or another of the five *khandhas*, or the five *khandhas* collectively, that is wrongly imagined to be the 'self' (*attan, ātman*), for a person to have his self for a burden amounts to much the same thing as his having the *khandhas* for burden. Whether there really is a person (*puggala*) distinct from the *khandhas* was a matter of vigorous and prolonged debate between the different Buddhist schools from very early times, a debate which some would say is unconcluded even today.

However that may be, the circumstance that for the Buddha the self, or what is wrongly imagined to be the self, is a burden, albeit an existential rather than a purely psychological one, should be sufficient to alert us to the fact that to experience the self as burdensome is not necessarily a bad thing. Such an experience need not be the result of an imbalance between public and private life in the sociological sense, nor does it always have to be dealt with by trying to correct that imbalance on its own level. Moreover, the 'radical shift in significance from the Church to the individual in the doctrines of Luther and Calvin' to which, Mellor tells us, Louis Dumont has drawn attention, is not really of the same order as Shils' 'emphasis on self' and does not, therefore, support Sennett's argument about each person's self being his principal burden in the way Mellor implies. Taking our own look at Dumont's essay 'A modified view of our origins: the Christian beginnings of modern individualism', we find that for Dumont Calvin (and Luther to the extent that Luther's views are presupposed by Calvin) represents '*inworldly* individualism' and that this is compared with the '*outworldly* individualism' which characterizes early Christianity and the Indian world-rejecting religions including Buddhism. The experience of the self as burdensome again is hardly seen as a bad thing.[184]

II

For Mellor, however, the experience of the self as burdensome is definitely a bad thing. It is a bad thing because it 'produces' the fragmentation of society and the fragmentation of society (Sennett's major concern, according to Mellor) means that the significance of religious tradition is diminished. The reason for this diminishment is that religious tradition 'is by its very nature something transpersonal' and what is transpersonal is, apparently, incompatible with modern individualism. At this point Mellor again refers to Shils, who 'notes the tension created between tradition and this emphasis on self' and whom he quotes as saying with regard to this emphasis:

> There is a belief, corresponding to a feeling, that within each human being there is an individuality, lying in potentiality, which seeks an occasion for realization but is held in the toils of the rules, beliefs and roles society imposes.[185]

Nor is that all. The acceptance of transpersonal norms is not only understood as unhelpful, Mellor explains, it is an encumbrance, for, according to Shils:

> To be 'true to oneself" means ... discovering what is contained in the uncontaminated self, the self which has been freed from the encumbrance of accumulated knowledge, norms, and ideals handed down by previous generations.[186]

To commit oneself to a tradition means, on the contrary, placing limits on one's individual potential, a belief that is not unrelated, so Mellor assures us, to Luther's position in the faith or works controversy, 'itself an indicator of the shift of significance attached to the individual which Dumont has referred to'.

Not for the first time in this section of Mellor's article I find myself wishing that he would state his views in a plain and straightforward manner, instead of presenting them by means of references to, and quotations from, his various sociologist mentors. It would then be easier for us to see what he is getting at. But no doubt this sheltering behind 'authorities' is an accepted part of what is known as methodology, and de rigueur for a young academic. I shall therefore have to disentangle Mellor's views on the significance of religious tradition, and its alleged diminishment by individualism, as best I can, separating what is true in them from what is false and, in the process, making clear my own position on certain issues. Let me take for my point of departure the notion, attributed by Shils to those whose emphasis is on self, of 'the uncontaminated self, the self which has been freed from the encumbrance of accumulated knowledge, norms, and ideals handed down by previous generations.'

To me the idea that there exists a self which is pure, that this self is enslaved by socially imposed beliefs and customs, and that all one has to do in order to 'be oneself' and realize one's potentiality is to break free from them, is simply false. It is what I sometimes call Rousseauism, or pseudo-Rousseauism, in the sense of a popular version of the French writer's belief in the natural goodness of man, who he felt was warped by society. Such Rousseauism, I hold, has done a great deal of harm. It has encouraged people whose self was far from pure to give untrammelled expression to that self, thereby damaging themselves, other people, and society at large. It has encouraged the mistaken idea that institutions and rules are bad per se. It has encouraged an attitude of soul-destroying bitterness and resentment on the part of those who, having been brought up to think that the world owed them not just a living but ideal happiness, find themselves far from happy. It has encouraged the shifting of moral responsibility for one's actions from self to society. It has encouraged talk of rights rather than duties. Above all, perhaps, it has encouraged people to believe that they do not need to *work on themselves* but have only to change the social, economic, and political conditions under which they live. Such Rousseauism has nothing in common with Buddhism.

Nonetheless, the fact that no pure self exists on the mundane level envisaged by profane sociology and psychology does not mean that at the very apex of his being man does not possess (or rather, is not possessed by) a transcendental element of which he is normally unconscious. It is with reference to this element that the Buddha declares, in the *Aṅguttara Nikāya* or 'Book of the Numerical Sayings', 'Luminous is this thought [or mind, or consciousness: *citta*], but it is defiled by adventitious defilements.'[187] Similarly, in the *Ratnagotravibhāga* it is said:

> The element of Tathāgatahood, as it is present in all, is immutable,
> and cannot be affected by either defilement or purification...
>
> Like the Buddha in a faded lotus flower, like honey covered
> by a swarm of bees,
> Like the kernel of a fruit in the husk, like gold within impurities,
> Like a treasure hidden in the soil, like fruit in a small seed,
> An image of the Jina in tattered garments,
>
> The universal monarch in the vile belly of a woman,
> And like a precious statue covered with dust,
> So is this element established in beings
> Who are covered with the stains of adventitious defilements.[188]

Here the thought is defiled by adventitious defilements, the element of Tathāgatahood covered by the stains of those defilements. In order to reveal the inherent luminosity of the thought, to uncover the element of Tathāgatahood, it is therefore necessary to get rid of the defilements, and it is with the getting rid of mental defilements that Buddhist praxis is, on its negative side, very largely concerned.

This does not mean that Buddhism is indifferent to social, economic, and political conditions, or that it disapproves on principle of trying to change them. There are some social, economic, and political conditions that are definitely unfavourable to the individual's efforts to rid himself of mental defilements, and it is entirely in keeping with the spirit of Buddhism that one should seek to replace these with conditions that are favourable to such efforts, though this must always be done by means that are in accordance with the spiritual end for the sake of which the change is made. Like those whose emphasis is on the self and who believe, according to Shils, 'that within each human being there is an individuality ... held in the toils of the rules, beliefs and roles society imposes',[189] Buddhism thus is prepared to countenance social reform, not to say social revolution, even at the risk of Sennett's 'fragmentation of society'. In the case of Buddhism, as represented for example by the ideal of the *dharmarāja*, the 'Righteous Monarch' or 'Religious King', social reform is not countenanced in the interests of modern individualism, much less still in the interests of what I have called Rousseauism.[190] It is countenanced in the interests of the individual-in-relation-to-Buddhahood (as we may describe him, adapting the terminology of Dumont's mentor Ernst Troeltsch), in order that his efforts to get rid of mental defilements may be facilitated and in order that, having rid himself of those defilements, he may reveal the inherent luminosity of thought, uncover the element of Tathāgatahood, and achieve liberation not just from society, good or bad, but from mundane existence itself.

Here I must make two points. Firstly, the idea that there exists, on the mundane level, a self that is pure or 'uncontaminated', is not simply an idea that happens to be false; it is also one of the mental defilements and, as such, to be got rid of by the Buddhist or individual-in-relation-to-Buddhahood as quickly as possible. Moreover, notwithstanding loose talk in pseudo-Zen circles about oneself being in reality Buddha and having 'only' to realize the fact, it should be understood that the luminous thought, or element of Tathāgatahood, is not to be regarded as lying as a potentiality within the mundane self in such a manner that the latter remains essentially unchanged even when that potentiality has been realized. In other words, realized or unrealized, the luminous thought, or element of Tathāgatahood, is not to be regarded as a predicate of which the mundane self – Shils' 'individual as a "quasi-sacred absolute"' – is the perduring subject. Secondly, the conditions that are unfavourable to the individual's efforts to rid himself of mental defilements, and that therefore have to be changed, are not always social, or economic, or political in the narrower sense. The creation of conditions more favourable to the eradication of mental defilements, as well as to the cultivation of the positive counterparts of those defilements, may involve the repudiation of 'transpersonal social forms (such as the Church)'. It may even involve the rejection of religious tradition. This brings me back to Mellor and to his contention that religious tradition 'is by its very nature something transpersonal', what is transpersonal being, apparently, incompatible with modern individualism.

The term 'transpersonal' is, however, an ambiguous one, and Mellor's use of it in this connection only serves to obscure a fundamental confusion in his thinking. That the term should be ambiguous is not surprising. It is not to be found either in *Collins* or the *Concise Oxford*, and seems to be a piece of undefined sociological jargon that Mellor has taken over from Dumont and Shils. The prefix 'trans-' has four or five different meanings, only two of which are relevant here: it can mean 'beyond' in the sense of 'on the other side', and it can mean 'surpassing, transcending'. Thus 'transpersonal' can mean 'beyond the person', in the sense of 'on the other side of the person', and it can also mean 'surpassing the person' or 'transcending the person' – two very different things. I therefore suggest that when speaking of something as transpersonal in the first sense we speak of it as *horizontally* transpersonal, in the sense of its being beyond the person on the same level, and that when speaking of something as transpersonal in the second sense we speak of it as *vertically* transpersonal, in the sense of its being on a higher level than the person or occupying a different dimension. The distinction is an important one. Neither social forms nor religious traditions are necessarily transpersonal in the vertical sense, and the fact that Mellor does not realize this means that he is unable to see that the repudiation of social norms, and the rejection of religious tradition, is not necessarily an expression of modern individualism. He is unable to see that social norms and religious traditions may be transpersonal only in the horizontal sense, and that to repudiate and reject them may, therefore, be the act of the individual-in-relation-to-Buddhahood.

We thus have three possible scenarios: (a) modern individualism versus the horizontally transpersonal, (b) modern individualism versus the vertically transpersonal, and (c) the individual-in-relation-to-Buddhahood – or, to speak in more general terms, the true individual[191] – versus the horizontally transpersonal. (A fourth scenario, that of the individual-in-relation-to-Buddhahood versus the vertically transpersonal, is only a formal possibility, not a real one, involving as it does a contradiction in terms.) What Mellor in effect does is to treat all cases of scenario (c) as cases of scenario (b), and he is able to do this because he assumes, as Dumont appears to assume, that 'transpersonal social forms (such as the Church)' are necessarily transpersonal in the vertical sense, as is religious tradition. To understand the acceptance of transpersonal norms as not only unhelpful but an encumbrance therefore cannot but be a bad thing. Not to commit oneself to a tradition because this means placing limits on one's individual potential cannot but be a bad thing. The diminishment of tradition cannot but be a bad thing. The fragmentation of society cannot but be a bad thing. The experience of the self as burdensome cannot but be a bad thing.

In all this I detect the presence of a hidden agenda, the heads of which seem to be that society, i.e. western society, must at all costs be held together, that it can be held together only by social forms (such as the Church) and (Catholic?) tradition, and that any attempt to undermine or diminish these must be discredited.

III

Though Mellor equates 'discovering what is contained in the uncontaminated self' with the diminishment of the significance of religious tradition, and this with the fragmentation of society which is produced by the modern burden of self, he is not afraid of a little inconsistency and is able to see self-discovery as not altogether a bad thing. Many notable religious figures, he tells us, have been sensitive to both the value and the dangers of self-discovery. St Teresa (of Ávila), for example, affirms the value of self-knowledge at all levels of spiritual development, though using the metaphor of the bee (which must leave the beehive in order to gather nectar) she cautions against excessive self-absorption.[192] 'The Buddha, however, is attributed with a far more severe rejection of self.' What St Teresa means by self-knowledge, and whether he considers her 'self-absorption' to pertain to the same order of experience as the 'self' rejected by the Buddha, Mellor does not say. Not that it really matters. St Teresa and her bee are introduced, apparently, simply as providing a means of transition to the Buddha and the 'far more severe rejection of self' with which he is attributed. 'He expressed the idea that it is because of the belief in self (*attan*) that people are vulnerable to the process of ageing, decay and dying, and therefore to suffering (*dukkha*).' This is all right so far as it goes, though it is by no means adequate as an account of the Buddha's teaching on the subject. Some Buddhists indeed would think it one-sided, especially as Mellor goes on to cite a contemporary Buddhist scholar's view that 'Buddhism aims at the salvation of the individual through the elimination of suffering, a process which necessitates the deconstruction of self, breaking down what appears to be "personal experience" into its constituent, *impersonal* elements.'[193]

This comes perilously close to saying that Buddhism seeks to save the individual by destroying him, a statement which though true in a certain paradoxical sense is not to be taken literally. Taken literally it amounts to the wrong, one-sided view of annihilationism (*ucchedadiṭṭhi*). What has to be destroyed is the wrong view that one or another of the five *khandhas*, or the five *khandhas* collectively, are the self or person, and whether after the destruction of that wrong view there was anything of the individual left was, like the larger question of whether there really is a person (*puggala*) distinct from the *khandhas*, a matter of debate. In the Buddha's case it was clear that, as he himself tells Anurādha in the *Saṃyutta Nikāya*, it is not proper to say of him that he exists after death, or does not exist after death, or both exists and does not exist after death, or neither exists nor does not exist after death. None of these alternatives applies to him because 'in this very life a Tathāgata is not to be regarded as existing in truth, in reality.'[194] Similarly, explaining to Ānanda why he had remained silent when asked by the wanderer Vacchagotta if the self exists, and again when asked if it does not exist, the Buddha says:

> If, when I was asked 'Does self exist?' I had answered 'Self exists,' that would have been the belief of those who hold the theory of eternalism. And if, when I was asked 'Does self not exist?' I had answered 'Self does not exist,' that would have been the belief of

> those who hold the theory of annihilationism. And if, when asked 'Does self exist?' I had answered 'Self exists,' would that have been in conformity with my knowledge that all things are not-self? And if, when asked 'Does self not exist?' I had answered 'Self does not exist,' then confused as he already is, Ānanda, the Wanderer Vacchagotta would have become still more confused, assuming 'Surely then I had a self before and now I have none.'[195]

The Buddha's attitude is pragmatic. It is better for Vacchagotta to go on believing he has a self, a belief which at least constitutes a basis for moral effort, than to believe that he has no self. Later it was sometimes said of the Buddha that he teaches annihilationists that the self exists, eternalists that it does not exist, and his own true followers that it neither exists nor does not exist.[196]

But there is no need for me to pursue the subject. Mellor is not interested in the Buddha's rejection of self for its own sake. He is interested in it, as he goes on to show, only as a means of establishing that in respect of what he describes, not incorrectly, as one of the major defining characteristics of Buddhism, 'certain areas of English Buddhism' are not so much traditional as untraditional. In other words Mellor is interested in the Buddha's rejection of self as a stick with which to beat the FWBO.

IV

He begins by blandly asserting that in view of the Buddha's rejection of self, the contemporary attachment to self which Sennett, Shils, and Dumont see as characteristic of the modern West ought to rule out the appeal of Buddhism in England (i.e. the appeal of Buddhism, in England, not the appeal of Buddhism-in-England). Previously he has quoted his sociologist mentors as speaking in terms of the *burden* of self, of the *discovery* of self, and of *emphasis* on self. He now represents them as all speaking in terms of *attachment* to self, which is not quite the same thing but which provides him with a sharper antithesis to that rejection of self which he has just described as one of the major defining characteristics of Buddhism. As I have shown, however, the experience of the self as burdensome is not necessarily a bad thing, so that the appeal of Buddhism in England need not be ruled out in view of the Buddha's rejection of self. Mellor switches to 'attachment' at this point simply as a means of emphasizing the unlikelihood of Buddhism appealing in England and to pave the way for his contention that some English Buddhists have adopted it for reasons connected with the un-Buddhistic idea that a person's self is their principal burden. Having asserted that the contemporary attachment to self ought to rule out the appeal of Buddhism in England, he therefore continues, with apparent candour:

> This is not so; neither is it generally the case that it has been adopted by a small group of people rebelling against this contemporary emphasis on self, though this is clearly true in some instances. Buddhism has had a much more sophisticated interaction with English culture.

What this more sophisticated interaction is we shall see shortly. Just now it is important for us to take a closer look at how people in Britain actually come to 'adopt' Buddhism. From the fact that for him the contemporary attachment to self ought to rule out the appeal of Buddhism in England, and that he would have expected it, apparently, to be adopted generally by people rebelling against the contemporary emphasis on self, it is clear that Mellor tends to see the appeal of Buddhism in predominantly intellectual terms. Academic that he is, he sees people as adopting Buddhism for a single clear-cut reason, whether because it rejects self or whether because, as mistakenly supposed by those for whom the self is their principal burden, it does not reject self. But this is not really the case. On the basis of more than a quarter of a century's continuous experience of British Buddhism, I can assert that people adopt Buddhism for many different reasons and in many different ways, not all of them rational, and not all of them very direct or very clear. Some adopt it for intellectual reasons, some for emotional reasons, and some for practical reasons. Some adopt it because they want to deepen their experience of meditation, others because they are attracted by the personality of a particular Buddhist teacher, and yet others because they like the atmosphere of a particular Buddhist centre or group. Some even adopt it as a result of reading a book by Lobsang Rampa, or after seeing a Bruce Lee film. There are even people who adopt Buddhism because they are drawn by the Buddha's rejection of self, like the young woman, a university student, who once came on an early FWBO retreat. Whether she was a rebel against the contemporary emphasis on self I cannot say, but in the course of the retreat she told me that she had always been attracted by the *anattā* doctrine and that she had just realized why she was attracted by it. She was attracted by it because she hated herself and liked to think that she did not really exist.

People in fact adopt Buddhism (which is not necessarily the same thing as Going for Refuge to the Three Jewels) for a hundred different reasons, from the sublime to the silly and from the simplest to the most complex. Perhaps the commonest reason for their adopting it is that they are dissatisfied with themselves, or with life, or even that, in Karl Jaspers's phrase, they 'feel ill and suffer from their psychic state'.[197] This does not mean that they are consciously 'attached' to self in Mellor's sense, that is, attached to it in a way that in view of the Buddha's rejection of self rules out the appeal of Buddhism. What it means is that they experience a sensation of lack, of there being something missing, and that out of this sensation they go searching, with varying degrees of determination and clarity, for that missing something, or at least are on the lookout for it from time to time. Not that they necessarily know what they are searching for, or have much idea where it is to be found; quite often they do not think of it as being 'religious' in nature at all, much less that it could possibly be connected with an 'eastern' religion like Buddhism. But sooner or later, in one way or other, such people come in contact with Buddhism, and having come in contact with it they feel, sometimes immediately, that the missing something has been found and that the sensation of lack is no longer there. This is, of course, only the beginning. Though what was missing has been found, the finders still have to take possession of it, or rather, have to allow it to take possession of them, a process which besides being a lengthy one entails painful conflicts between the mundane and the spiritual, attachment to self and rejection of self.

Mellor understands nothing of all this. Having singled out rejection of self as one of the major defining characteristics of Buddhism, he sees the religion as having been adopted, in England, by two different groups of people. There are those who are rebelling against the contemporary emphasis on self and there are those who are not rebelling against it, the latter apparently being very much in the majority. Thus it is that, according to Mellor, 'the idea that a person's self is their principal burden has come to characterize certain areas of English Buddhism more than the traditional rejection of self.' This is his 'more sophisticated' interaction of Buddhism with English culture, though presumably it is not so much the interaction itself which he regards as sophisticated as his own analysis of it. Not that he is unaware of the danger of overstating his case. 'While it would be an over-exaggeration to assert that Buddhism in England can be understood exclusively as a participant in this personalizing trend,' he continues smoothly, 'it would also be misleading to avoid confronting the continuities between English Buddhism and wider western trends, just because of our abstract perceptions of Buddhist doctrine.' Very true. But it would be no less misleading if on account of our abstract perceptions of Buddhist doctrine, and our ignorance of certain areas of English Buddhism, we were to imagine continuities where none really exist. Mellor concludes this section of his article with the statement: 'The religious and cultural context of English society must remain at the forefront of any study of the development of Buddhism in this country.' Indeed it must, except that one should not speak of the development of Buddhism in England as though it was synonymous with the development of Buddhism in Britain.

3
PROTESTANTISM AND BUDDHISM

Having established, to his own satisfaction, that the contemporary emphasis on self has diminished the significance of religious tradition, and that the idea that a person's self is his principal burden has come to characterize 'certain areas' of English Buddhism more than the traditional Buddhist rejection of self, Mellor is free to engage with his principal topic: the relationship between Protestantism, Modernism, and Culture, on the one hand, and Buddhism on the other. As we shall see, the Protestantism with which Mellor is concerned is, apparently, liberal Protestantism, and he approaches the relationship between Protestantism in this sense and English Buddhism via a brief consideration of the personalistic view of religion and the idea that there is a Buddhist 'essence' distinct from eastern cultures. From liberal Protestantism it is, of course, only a short step to English Buddhism and to the question of why English Buddhists, when they criticize Christianity, direct their criticisms against Roman Catholicism rather than against Protestantism, and this in turn leads Mellor to his first direct comparison between the English Sangha and the FWBO – a comparison which involves, unfortunately, a serious misrepresentation of the FWBO's views in respect of several important issues.

I

'In the light of the cultural and philosophical trends affecting religion today,' Mellor declares, 'an effort should be made to stand apart from the view which characterizes religion in exclusively personalistic terms. We might take the view that religion is not, primarily, a private and personal matter.' Indeed we might, though Mellor does not particularize the cultural and philosophical trends affecting religion today, nor explain why an effort should be made to stand apart from the view which characterizes religion in exclusively personalistic terms. I myself take the view that religion is an *individual* matter, though I would not care to say that it was primarily an individual matter without first of all going into the question of what 'primary' means. Religion is an individual matter that has a subjective aspect, represented for instance by faith, prayer, and meditation, and an objective aspect, represented for instance by ethics, ritual, and myth. In Buddhist terms, the individual-in-relation-to-Buddhahood *subjectively* goes for Refuge to the Three Jewels and *objectively* manifests the *bodhicitta* or (cosmic) will to Enlightenment, which latter is the other-regarding, altruistic dimension of the act of Going for Refuge and involves the practice of the six (or ten) *pāramitās* or 'perfections'. For me religion is both private and personal *and* objective and public because the individual himself is both subject and object, both soul and citizen, and I would not dream of characterizing it in purely personalistic terms. So much is this the case that normally I do not speak of the subjective aspect of religion as the private and personal aspect, and have done so on this occasion only because Mellor does. For me the word private, especially as occurring in the phrase 'private and personal', has connotations of exclusivity and self-indulgence which render its use in connection with religion quite unacceptable. (Within the FWBO it was debated, a few years ago, whether Order members were entitled to a private life in the sense of one exempt from ethical scrutiny by their peers. There was general agreement that they were not.)

Nonetheless, Mellor seems to think that the FWBO does not stand apart from the view which characterizes religion in exclusively personalistic terms and that it takes the view that religion *is*, primarily, a private and personal matter. This quite gratuitous assumption serves to introduce what is, in fact, an astonishing non sequitur.

> The FWBO, for example [*sic!*], might *believe* that a Buddhist 'essence' can be distilled from the eastern cultures and traditions in which it has been located until the recent past, but we cannot

> accept this idea uncritically. We should note that this position demonstrates certain continuities with Protestant perspectives.

The FWBO's *belief* that there is a Buddhist essence is thus contrasted with the inability of Mellor and his sociologist friends to accept this idea uncritically. No attempt is made to ascertain the grounds of the FWBO's 'belief'. The contrasting of the two in this invidious fashion smacks, in fact, more of rhetoric than philosophy, and need be taken no more seriously than Mellor's assertion that the belief or idea that there is a Buddhist 'essence' demonstrates continuities with his now familiar 'Protestant perspectives'. All the same, whether accepted critically or uncritically, the idea that there is a Buddhist 'essence' is a crucial one, and I would like to offer a few common-sense observations on it before dealing with Mellor's remaining comments on the view that religion is essentially a personal, private matter.

The idea that there is an 'essence of Buddhism' is not a new one. Books have been written with this title, including a small but seminal one by D. T. Suzuki.[198] The fact is, that however suspect it may be in the ultimate metaphysical sense, the idea that every existent thing has its own distinctive essence is a necessary presupposition of all discourse. Before we can discourse on a thing we must define it. Discourse *implies* definition. According to the dictionary, to define is to 'set forth [the] essence of' a thing (*Concise Oxford*), or '2. to describe the nature, properties, or essential qualities' of a thing (*Collins*). Thus when Mellor speaks of the rejection of self as 'one of the major defining characteristics of Buddhism,' he is in fact recognizing that Buddhism can be defined and, therefore, that it has an essence. Not that he is really disposed to question the idea that there is an 'essence of Buddhism'. All he wants to do, in this connection, is to make the point that unlike the credulous FWBO he is unable to accept the idea that Buddhism has an essence uncritically.

An essence is an essence of something. A Buddhist essence is the essence of 'Buddhist' culture and tradition, in which it is 'located'. Like the rejection of self, some elements in that culture and tradition may be major defining characteristics of Buddhism, and some may be minor defining characteristics. Other elements may not be *defining* characteristics at all, or may even be the contradictories of those characteristics. In other words, though a Buddhist essence is the essence of 'Buddhist' culture and tradition it is not necessarily present equally in all elements of that culture and tradition, and in the case of some elements may be entirely absent. The FWBO's belief that a Buddhist 'essence' can be distilled from the eastern cultures and traditions in which it has been located amounts to no more than the belief that it is possible to distinguish, within those cultures and traditions, between elements which are defining characteristics of Buddhism, whether major or minor, and those which are not. It amounts to the belief that it is possible to distinguish, within eastern 'Buddhist' cultures and traditions, between elements in which a Buddhist essence is present, to a greater or a lesser degree, and elements in which it is not present.

Mellor's inability to appreciate the grounds for the FWBO's 'belief' that there is an essence of Buddhism may not be unconnected with his failure to distinguish between Buddhism and the Dharma. He appears to be entirely unaware, throughout his article, that the modern western term 'Buddhism' is *not* interchangeable with the ancient Indian term Dharma or Dhamma and its Chinese and Tibetan equivalents, just as he appears to be unaware that the term 'religion' cannot be applied to Buddhism uncritically or without reflection. In order to show the difference between 'Buddhism' and 'the Dharma' one has only to ask a question like, 'Is the practice of drinking alcohol an element of the Dharma/Buddhism?' Drinking alcohol is not an element of the Dharma because mindfulness, or recollection, is one of the defining characteristics of the Dharma and drinking alcohol is not conducive to mindfulness. In the drinking of alcohol the Dharma is not present (though some Vajrayānists would argue that it is). On the other hand, drinking alcohol may be an element of Buddhism in the sense of being an element in a certain 'Buddhist' culture and tradition, though it would be an element in which a Buddhist essence cannot be located. Thus there is a difference between 'Buddhism' and 'the Dharma', though the *essence* of Buddhism and the Dharma may be regarded as identical, the *Dharma (-Vinaya)* itself being described by the Buddha in teachings such as that given to Mahāpajāpatī, the Gotamid, in the Vinaya Piṭaka or 'Book of the Discipline'.[199]

For Mellor Buddhism is, apparently, *all* the elements in 'Buddhist' cultures and traditions, whether a Buddhist essence is present in those elements or not. For him Buddhism is really no more than a culture. So successful is he in his own effort to stand apart from the view which characterizes religion in exclusively personalistic terms that, going to the other extreme, he ends up characterizing it in exclusively social terms. Having invited us to note that the FWBO's *belief* that a Buddhist 'essence' can be distilled from the eastern cultures and traditions in which it has been located, he therefore continues, invoking yet another of his mentors:

> As Jacob Neusner has pointed out, a major problem in the study of religion is that Protestant perspectives have combined with a post-Enlightenment scientific tradition to present religion as essentially a personal, private matter rather than an issue of culture.

From this he concludes:

> In studying contemporary religious change we are unlikely to be very sensitive to competing understandings of the nature of religion, or much else, if we share the same prejudices as one of our objects of study.

Which means, being interpreted, that the FWBO is prejudiced, because it takes the view that religion is, primarily, a private and personal matter! Mellor himself, of course, is free from prejudice.

II

A Christian scholar who has written extensively on Indian religions notes (as Mellor would say) that 'an elementary rule of methodology proscribes formulating a judgement on anything in categories foreign to it'.[200] The category Protestant is certainly foreign to Buddhism, yet despite having obtained his Ph.D. for a thesis dealing with problems of theory and method in the study of contemporary religion Mellor has no hesitation in describing certain characteristics that are significant factors in English Buddhism as Protestant characteristics:

> If we are to accept that certain Protestant characteristics are significant factors in English Buddhism, as I suggest we must, we are faced with the problem of knowing how to label this new religious form [i.e. English Buddhism] and the differentiations within it.

Not only does he formulate his judgement on English Buddhism in a category foreign to it; he 'suggests' that we *must* do this. True, he then asks: 'Is it legitimate to talk of Protestant Buddhism?' but like jesting Pilate he stays not for an answer, launching instead into a semi-critique of Ninian Smart's new 'pan-religious protestantism' to which I shall return. It would seem, however, that in some scholarly circles it *is* legitimate to talk of Protestant Buddhism. Chapter 6 of Gombrich and Obeyesekere's *Buddhism Transformed: Religious Change in Sri Lanka* is headed 'Protestant Buddhism',[201] though here the Buddhism so categorized is not English Buddhism but the 'modernist' Buddhism of Sri Lanka which Anagarika Dharmapala is regarded as exemplifying. It is also legitimate, it would seem, to talk of Puritan Buddhism, and even of a Puritan Buddha, as John Stevens does in *Lust for Enlightenment: Buddhism and Sex*.[202] Soon it will be legitimate to talk of Quaker Buddhism, Evangelical Buddhism, Anglican Buddhism, Primitive Methodist Buddhism, and Hard-Shell Baptist Buddhism. For all I know, some scholars are doing this already.

But to return to Smart's 'new pan-religious protestantism'. Mellor is not altogether happy with this. We should be very dubious, he thinks, about the evolutionary framework of Smart's position, and about that position's implicit approval of a trend which is envisaged as sweeping away all the 'external organisation and rituals of religion', as well as unpalatable dogmas and doctrines. Nevertheless Mellor finds Smart's analysis of religious history useful. Among other things, in such an analysis 'it is possible to elucidate the specific character of English Buddhism in the light of an awareness of this liberal Protestant trend'. Thus from categorizing English Buddhism as Protestant he passes, without comment, to categorizing it as liberal Protestant. He also passes from describing 'significant factors' in English Buddhism to elucidating its 'specific character'. But though he makes no attempt to define Protestantism, he does at least describe liberal Protestantism, and for this small mercy we must be thankful.

> Some major characteristics of liberal Protestantism, in a Christian context [he informs us] are an emphasis on faith above knowledge, on the individual person above the community, and on the rejection of doctrines such as the authority of the Church, the Virgin Birth, the Incarnation and even the existence of God.

Liberal Protestantism thus is undeniably liberal. Indeed, I must admit that despite occasionally reading the religious affairs section of a leading daily I had not realized how far, in the case of Protestant Christianity, the process of liberalization had gone and how many traditional doctrines had been rejected; but Mellor has a Ph.D. in Theology and I suppose I shall have to take his word for it. Having told us the worst about liberal Protestantism, of the Christian variety, he goes on to claim that 'pan-religious protestantism' is, as Smart suggests, the product of such rejections of traditional Christian doctrine,

> questionings and increased emphases on the individual reaching an extreme level where they exceed the boundaries of what can legitimately be called Christianity. At this point 'Buddhism' becomes a more attractive structure for individuals pursuing their spiritual goals.

Precisely as he had passed from Protestantism to liberal Protestantism, Mellor now passes from liberal Protestantism to pan-religious Protestantism, proposing in fact that *this* is the framework within which we might consider English Buddhism. Smart's analysis of the trend of religious history has a definite value for Mellor, even though he is critical of his demi-mentor's evolutionary narrative, but before we can see how that value becomes clear I want to refer back to his claim that it is at the point where the boundaries of what can legitimately be called Christianity are exceeded that 'Buddhism' becomes a more attractive structure for individuals pursuing their spiritual goals.

There is no doubt that there is such a thing as pan-religious Protestantism, and no doubt that it is at the point where the boundaries of traditional Christianity are exceeded that for some individuals in Britain 'Buddhism' becomes a more attractive structure. In the case of many of these individuals, however, Buddhism, or what they think of as Buddhism, is simply that: it is 'more attractive'. Though they might have rejected traditional Christian doctrines, or allowed them to slip away from them, they retain a sentimental attachment to Christianity which prevents them from committing themselves wholeheartedly to Buddhism or, in traditional Buddhist terms, from Going for Refuge to the Three Jewels. Thus they in fact remain within 'pan-religious Protestantism' or within what I sometimes call pseudo-universalism.

What proportion of the membership of Buddhist groups in Britain (other than the FWBO) such individuals make up today I do not know, but in 1964 they were very much in the majority and it was partly for this reason that I eventually decided that a new, more authentically Buddhist movement was needed in this country.

III

The value of Smart's analysis of the trend of religious history becomes clear, according to Mellor, when one considers the degree to which English Buddhists, when they criticize or attack Christianity, appear to be thinking mainly of Roman Catholicism. The principal 'problems' attributed to Christianity by English Buddhists are, in his view, authoritarianism, institutionalism, dogmatism, triumphalism, ritualism, and formalism, all of which are charges traditionally directed at Catholicism by Protestants, and it at first seems odd that English (or American) Buddhists, coming from a firmly Protestant culture, should direct their criticisms against a Catholic form of Christianity. 'Surely,' he objects, 'if western Buddhists were keen to differentiate themselves from their surrounding religious context, Protestantism should be the likely target?' It is only at first that it seems odd, however. Mellor is ready with an explanation. The fact that English (or American) Buddhists direct their criticisms against a Catholic form of Christianity, instead of at Protestantism, 'underlines the fact that western Buddhists and liberal Protestants have a great deal in common'. Not that he is suggesting that English Buddhism is not really Buddhism at all, Mellor hastens to assure us, but only that it is 'useful' to place it in a liberal Protestant trend, albeit one of a 'pan-religious' kind.

Whether the 'problems' attributed to Christianity by English Buddhists *are* all charges traditionally directed at Catholicism by Protestants it is not necessary to enquire. Nor is it necessary to enquire whether the culture from which such English (or American) Buddhists come is as 'firmly Protestant' as Mellor seems to think it is. The explanation of why the FWBO, at any rate, criticizes Roman Catholicism, and does not criticize Protestantism, is really quite simple, and has nothing to do with the 'fact' that western Buddhists and liberal Protestants have a great deal in common. But before giving that explanation I would like to express a wish.

In Parliament there is a practice known as 'declaring an interest'. If an honourable or right honourable member happens to have a connection, especially a prejudicial connection, with the matter under debate, he makes this known. I wish there was a similar practice within the academic community. I wish scholars would declare an interest when they have a personal connection, perhaps one that is of great emotional importance to them, with the subject that is being discussed, instead of writing or speaking as though their attitude was one of complete scientific objectivity and impartiality. Philip Mellor, I am told, is a Roman Catholic, in fact a convert to Roman Catholicism, and he as such has a personal connection with criticisms of Roman Catholicism on the part of English Buddhists. But he does not make this known, he does not declare an interest, with the result that his approach to such criticisms, like his approach to English Buddhism, in particular to the FWBO, perforce is oblique and tangential, not to say covert, tempting uncharitable English Buddhists who have not forgotten their Bible to exclaim, with the dying Isaac, 'The voice is Jacob's voice, but the hands are the hands of Esau.'[203] I therefore put it to Mellor that if he again writes on English Buddhism he should write as a believing and practising Roman Catholic rather than as an amateur sociologist. He has nothing to lose by so doing, at least in FWBO eyes. Personally, I would much rather he quoted Augustine and Aquinas at me than Sennett, Shils, and Co. It would be more of an honour to be proved wrong by him with *their* help than to prove him wrong despite the support given him by his sociologist mentors. But enough of quixotry! I have expressed my wish. Now let me give my explanation.

The reason the FWBO criticizes Roman Catholicism, and does not criticize Protestantism, is not only quite simple; it is one which reflects no discredit on Roman Catholicism. Since the tenth century, the time of the *filioque* dispute, Roman Catholicism, or Latin Christianity as we may also call it, has been the normative form of the Christian faith in Western Europe.[204] It is Roman Catholicism that for nearly a thousand years dominated our social, political, artistic, and intellectual life and even today, if we look at the west front of Chartres Cathedral, or read Dante, or visit the Arena Chapel, or listen to Palestrina or Monteverdi, it is Roman Catholicism that we encounter. When western Buddhists criticize or attack Christianity it is therefore of Roman Catholicism that they are mainly thinking, this being the form of Christianity with which they are, historically speaking, most familiar. They generally are not thinking of Protestantism, which may be described as Roman Catholicism in dilution. Protestantism may also be described, changing the metaphor, as the rebel child of Roman Catholicism, or rather as a whole tribe of rebel children (and grandchildren) who, as well as rebelling against their venerable Mother, until quite recently were often at loggerheads among themselves. Western Buddhists therefore usually do not care to criticize Anglicanism or Lutherism, Presbyterianism or Methodism, or any of the other forms of western Christianity, except perhaps on points wherein they differ from Roman Catholicism as well as from Buddhism itself. If they criticize Christianity at all they criticize Roman Catholicism, for in criticizing Roman Catholicism they are, in principle, criticizing them all.

But there is another reason why the FWBO, at least, does not criticize Protestantism. I have described Protestantism as Roman Catholicism in dilution, but what is the diluting element? The diluting element is secular humanism, by which I mean (a) the theory or doctrine that concerns itself with man rather than with something other than man, and concerns itself with him, moreover, as possessing no transcendental (*lokuttara*) dimension, as well as (b) the attitude and the practical consequences that go with such a theory or doctrine. Rousseauism, or pseudo-Rousseauism, with its belief in the natural goodness of man and the warping effect of society, is a form of secular humanism, and as I have already made clear it has nothing in common with Buddhism. Criticisms which Mellor seems to think should be directed against Protestantism are in effect directed, in the case of the FWBO, against the secular humanist element in Protestantism. They are not directed against Protestantism as such because there is, in a sense, no such thing as Protestantism. There is only Roman Catholicism and secular humanism: (Catholic) Christianity and materialism – both of which western Buddhists have, by definition, repudiated.

IV

Though for Mellor both the English Sangha and the FWBO have a relationship to liberal Protestantism there are, he believes, differences between them in terms of that relationship. In fact he is concerned to emphasize that this is the case. Unfortunately, his discussion of these differences, besides being bedevilled by his insistence on placing the

FWBO within a liberal Protestant trend, is confused by his penchant for labelling the English Sangha and the FWBO as more or less 'self-conscious', or more or less 'sophisticated', the one than the other, in this or that respect. Ignoring these irrelevancies, I shall concentrate on the way in which he compares the two groups with regard to selectivity in respect of Buddhist doctrine and practice, making Buddhism accord with Protestant sensibilities, the issue of morality, and the issue of ritual observances.

Whereas the FWBO, according to Mellor, is 'manifestly selective in which elements of Buddhist doctrine and practice it chooses to accept' the English Sangha 'locates itself in the Thai forest tradition'. This is rather disingenuous. One could just as easily say that the English Sangha is manifestly selective in which elements of Thai Buddhist doctrine and practice it chooses to accept and that the FWBO locates itself in the ecumenical Buddhist tradition as represented, for example, by the Chinese Tiantai school and the nineteenth-century Tibetan Rimé movement (to which several of my own teachers belonged). The fact is that western Buddhism, or western Buddhists, cannot but be selective, in that Buddhism is so vast in extent and so rich and varied in content that there can be no question of literally accepting it *in toto*. One is *forced* to choose. The only question is that of the basis on which the selection, or choice, is made. Broadly speaking, there are two possibilities: one can select an existing eastern Buddhist tradition, i.e. join it and follow it on its own terms, or one can select doctrinal and practical elements from one or more eastern Buddhist traditions and synthesize them in such a way as to create a 'new' Buddhist tradition. The English Sangha follows the first course. From among the different schools of Buddhism it has chosen the Theravāda (not the Tiantai, the Huayan, the Gelug, the Nyingma, the Zen, the Shin, etc.), from among the different forms of the Theravāda it has chosen the Thai (not the Sinhalese, the Burmese, the Cambodian, or the Laotian), and from among the different Thai traditions it has chosen the forest tradition (not the city tradition). The FWBO follows the second course. While in principle it accepts Buddhism *in toto*, practically speaking it selects doctrinal and practical elements mainly from the Theravāda, the Madhyamaka-Yogācāra, the Tiantai, the Nyingma, and the Chan/Zen schools.

In this connection there are two points to be borne in mind. Firstly, in selecting doctrinal and practical elements from one or more eastern Buddhist traditions the FWBO is doing no more, in principle, than individual eastern Buddhists, or groups of eastern Buddhists, do in the case of their own particular tradition. A Sinhalese Theravāda monk, for example, while in principle accepting the Theravāda tradition *in toto*, will not familiarize himself with *all* the doctrines, including those of the Abhidhamma, nor will he practise *all* the forty methods of meditation (*kammaṭṭhāna*) described in the *Visuddhimagga*.[205] He will select. He will study, perhaps, the *Dhammapada* and the *Sutta-Nipāta* and practise the mindfulness of in-and-out-breathing (*ānāpānasati*). Secondly, the FWBO has been in existence for nearly twenty-five years and there is now an FWBO tradition. Individuals in Britain (and elsewhere) for whom Buddhism has become, in Mellor's phrase, a more attractive structure, no longer have only eastern Buddhist traditions to choose from. They have the possibility of selecting a *western* Buddhist tradition – a tradition in which the Dharma is communicated in a way that directly addresses their own situation and their own spiritual needs.

V

Speaking of the English Sangha's relationship to liberal Protestantism, Mellor makes the point that Ajahn Sumedho has often referred to his own Protestant background, and has noted the suspicion among visitors and the ordained at Amaravati of things which are associated with Catholicism, such as rituals, incense, and chanting. Implicitly, according to Mellor, the Ajahn 'is aware that Buddhism in the west can, as he sees it, be deformed through the desire to make it accord with Protestant sensibilities. On the other hand, there is no evidence of any leading figure in the FWBO publicly worrying about Protestant characteristics which may exist in the FWBO, despite the extreme and open contempt persistently directed towards (Catholic) Christianity. This seems to signify a marked difference in the two forms of Buddhism.' Once again we have the 'Protestants under the bed' syndrome. There is no doubt that among visitors and Friends at FWBO centres in Britain, as among visitors and the ordained at Amaravati, there is suspicion of things Catholic; but this is at least as likely to be due, I have found, to a painful experience of Roman Catholicism as to a Protestant (actually secular humanist) cultural conditioning. Leading figures in the FWBO do not worry, publicly or otherwise, about Protestant characteristics which may exist in the FWBO because, as I have explained, there is in a sense no such thing as Protestantism and because Buddhism in the West can, as they see it, most easily be deformed through the desire to make it accord with Rousseauistic, secular humanist, or pseudo-liberal sensibilities.

Whether the English Sangha is quite so free from this latter desire as Mellor seems to think, I do not know. At any rate, I remember one of my Theravādin correspondents telling me, shortly before my return to Britain in 1964, that the Hampstead Buddhist Vihara was so located because Hampstead was where the left-wing intellectuals lived and these were the people who were most likely to be interested in Buddhism. I should add that during the two years that I led the English Sangha, and lived at the Hampstead Buddhist Vihara, I did not to my knowledge see there a single 'Hampstead intellectual'.

VI

Another difference between the English Sangha and the FWBO, according to Mellor, is in their approach to doctrine and traditional practices. The FWBO, he says, has a very liberal approach: 'whatever does not assist "individual development" must be discarded, as Subhuti asserts'. Once again Mellor is being disingenuous. Provided individual development is understood, as the FWBO understands it, as development in the direction of Enlightenment (*bodhi*), one could just as easily say that the FWBO has a very *traditional* approach to Buddhist doctrine and Buddhist traditional practices. After all, no Buddhist school would be prepared to maintain, as a matter of principle, that doctrines and traditional practices that did not assist individual development should *not* be discarded, though there might be disagreement as to whether certain doctrines and practices were unhelpful or not. Even the English Sangha would not be prepared to maintain *that*! The fact is, Mellor is far too ready to see differences between the English Sangha and the FWBO. Not that there are not differences: there are; but there are similarities too. After observing that the English Sangha, despite its strictness in following the doctrines and rituals of the Thai forest tradition, often talks of 'etiquette' rather than rules, and stresses the self-discovery of truth rather than the doctrinal definition of it, Mellor goes on to describe Ajahn Sumedho's problems with the issue of morality. When the Amaravati community was established in 1977, the Ajahn found that morality was associated with being narrow-minded, 'pre-modern', and that to talk about it was 'driving people away', so that he had to assert that 'Buddhist moral precepts are standards to be reflected on' rather than something imposed or used in a judgemental way.

> Hence, he modified his presentation of Buddhist morality but still asserted its significance although lay people did not want to hear about it at all: 'They wanted to hear about having more and more freedom to develop themselves.'

This was very much my own experience at the Hampstead Buddhist Vihara in 1964, as well as during the early years of the FWBO. I too found that for many people the word morality had a distinctively negative connotation, so that like Ajahn Sumedho thirteen years later I had to assert that Buddhist moral precepts were standards to be reflected on. In my case, however, this involved no modification of my presentation of Buddhist morality, since I had always presented it in this way and was to continue to do so. As I wrote in *The Ten Pillars of Buddhism*:

> What the ten precepts really represent are principles of ethics, or ethical principles. They are not rules, in the narrow, pettifogging sense of the term ... though rules may be founded on them, or derived from them. If we could think of the precepts as being what in fact they are, ethical principles in accordance with which, as a result of our commitment to the ideal of Enlightenment, we are doing our best to live, a good deal of this confusion would be avoided. We would also find the precepts themselves more inspiring.[206]

These words were originally addressed to members of the Western Buddhist Order, the work from which they are taken having first seen the light of day as a paper read to Order members in 1984, on the occasion of the Order's sixteenth anniversary. Ajahn Sumedho's words, taken from a public talk given at Amaravati two years later, were spoken with reference to lay people, as distinct from monks. It was lay people who did not want to hear about morality at all, lay people who wanted to hear about having more and more freedom to develop themselves, and lay people, presumably, for whose sake he was obliged to modify his presentation of Buddhist morality. In his case the difficulty may have been due partly to the nature of the Theravāda, for which there exists a world of difference between monks and lay people and for whom the monk is the real Buddhist. It is the monk who leads the spiritual life, the monk who practises meditation, the monk who observes the 227 precepts of the Vinaya or Monastic Code, the lay people being little more than his humble supporters. Hence Theravāda lay people, more often than not, do not feel themselves sufficiently Buddhist to take a serious interest in morality. In the West they may not even want to hear about it and may want, instead, to hear about having more and more freedom to develop themselves.

Interestingly enough, it is immediately after quoting Ajahn Sumedho's complaint about lay people wanting to hear about having more and more freedom to develop themselves that Mellor refers to the FWBO as having, 'on the other hand', a very liberal approach to doctrine and traditional practices: 'whatever does not assist "individual development" must be discarded, as Subhuti asserts.' The fact that the two quotations are juxtaposed in this way suggests that the 'freedom to develop themselves' of which Ajahn Sumedho complains and Subhuti's 'individual development' are more or less the same thing. But really they are very different things. The freedom about which Ajahn Sumedho's lay people want to hear is, presumably, the freedom of modern individualism, whereas the development of which Subhuti speaks is the development of the individual-in-relation-to-Buddhahood or true individual. Mellor has again confused two scenarios and, by seeking to equate something upheld by Subhuti with something complained of by Ajahn Sumedho, not only misrepresents the FWBO but exaggerates the differences between the FWBO and the English Sangha. Still more interestingly, perhaps, by one of those non sequiturs of which he is almost as fond as he is of the labels 'self-conscious' and 'sophisticated', Mellor jumps from his quotation from Subhuti straight to an assertion about the FWBO's approach to religious truth:

> The FWBO manifests an exclusivist approach to religious truth: not only are the theistic religions objects of harsh criticism, being associated with 'authoritarianism, dogmatism, fanaticism, inhumanity, weakness and guilt', but other forms of Buddhism are labelled 'middle-class', 'dilettante' exoticism.

Subhuti's reasoned criticism of the theistic religions (Mellor is again quoting from *Buddhism for Today*) though admittedly harsh[207] is fully in accordance with Buddhist tradition, as a glance at Helmuth von Glasenapp's *Buddhism – a Non-Theistic Religion*, for example, will amply demonstrate.[208] I shall therefore say no more of Mellor's assertion that the FWBO manifests an exclusivist approach to religious truth, especially as he follows it up with yet another non sequitur, to the effect that in relation to a general cultural 'concern for questions of selfhood' (Sennett), the FWBO does not find itself at odds with contemporary western culture but firmly in line with it.

I would, however, like to comment on two of his references to the English Sangha. Having pointed out that, for the English Sangha, the Thai forest tradition is an absolute standard by which the tradition in England must be judged, so that discipline, hierarchy, doctrine, and ritual observances are followed as strictly as possible in the West, Mellor observes, 'On the other hand, it often talks of "etiquette" rather than rules.' If it really does this the English Sangha is much more 'liberal' than the FWBO. There is, of course, a section of the Vinaya that is concerned with what are, in fact, only matters of etiquette (not that etiquette is unimportant),[209] but to talk of etiquette rather than rules is, in traditional Buddhist terms, to reduce *pakati-sīla* or natural morality to *paññati-sīla* or conventional morality and, in effect, to deny the significance of morality altogether.[210] Similarly, having described Ajahn Sumedho's discovery that morality was associated with being narrow-minded, and so on, Mellor observes, 'He had to assert that "Buddhist moral precepts are standards to be reflected on" rather than something imposed or used in a judgemental way.' The word judgemental is not in the *Concise Oxford Dictionary* (though it is in *Collins*), and I hope Ajahn Sumedho himself did not use it, since it is a piece of pseudo-liberal jargon the connotations of which are anything but Buddhistic. 'Oh, one mustn't be judgemental!' cry those of the pseudo-liberal persuasion whenever an attempt is made to apply ethical principles to specific instances of human behaviour. This amounts to denying that there is such a thing as ethics or any objective values.

VII

Yet another (alleged) difference between the English Sangha and the FWBO is in respect of ritual observances. According to Mellor, the issue of ritual observance is 'a major point of divergence' between the two forms of English Buddhism. The FWBO, he says, is highly suspicious of ritual and has shorn Buddhism of what it understands to be the unnecessary and cluttering baggage of eastern cultural accretions. Here a note refers us to *Buddhism for Today*, p. 6, but in fact there is *absolutely no mention* of ritual observances on this page and *absolutely no mention* of unnecessary and cluttering baggage, whether that of eastern cultural accretions or anything else.[211] But to proceed. Having declared the FWBO to be highly suspicious of ritual, and 'quoted' Subhuti in this connection, Mellor continues:

> It has developed certain rituals and ceremonies of its own, however, though form is understood to be strictly subordinate to a personalistic content, and practices such as making offerings to monks and prostrating oneself before them are firmly rejected.

Here a note refers us to *The History of My Going for Refuge*, pp. 74–5. But what do I actually say there? After referring to the fact that during my stay at the Hampstead Buddhist Vihara I had read a book on the Second Vatican Council in which the Roman Catholic Church was said to be characterized by triumphalism, I described how there suddenly struck me, with the force of a thunderbolt, the thought that the Theravāda monastic order, too, was characterized by triumphalism.

> I recalled occasions on which Sinhalese monks had arrogantly insisted on taking precedence over everyone else and on being treated, in effect, like VIPs, in the belief that they were thereby upholding the supremacy of the Dharma. Similarly, I recalled the way in which visiting Thai *bhikṣus* had confined themselves to teaching the newly converted ex-Untouchable Buddhists such things as how to prostrate themselves before members of the monastic order and how to make offerings to them, as though in so doing they were propagating Buddhism among the ex-Untouchables with a vengeance....
>
> Strange to say, at about the same time that I became aware that the Theravāda monastic order was characterized by triumphalism I became more aware of the fact that there was a good deal of triumphalism in my immediate surroundings, as well as a good

deal of formalism. Four or five Sinhalese and Thai monks were then staying with me at the Hampstead Buddhist Vihara, and all of them manifested a degree of triumphalism in their dealings with British Buddhists. So much was this the case, indeed, that I was reminded of the way in which the visiting Thai monks had taught the ex-Untouchable Buddhists, for though the monks who were staying with me at the Vihara certainly did not confine themselves to teaching their British disciples how to prostrate themselves before members of the monastic order and how to make offerings to them there was the same disproportionate emphasis on these things that I had witnessed in India.[212]

Thus there is no question of practices such as making offerings to monks and prostrating oneself before them being 'firmly rejected', as Mellor alleges. What I reject in this passage is the *disproportionate emphasis* on these things that is characteristic of south-east Asian *bhikkhus*. Nor is that all. Mellor speaks of the FWBO as 'firmly rejecting' (ritual) practices *such as* making offerings to monks and prostrating oneself before them, thereby clearly implying that there are (ritual) practices *other than* these that are rejected by the FWBO and of which I make mention in the passage in question, whereas this is not the case. In the same devious manner, immediately after asserting that the FWBO is 'highly suspicious of ritual', he observes, 'The English Sangha encourages ritual activity such as chanting, bowing, the use of candles and incense, and the offering of *dāna* gifts along with the all-embracing disciplinary structure legitimated with reference to tradition,' thus suggesting that these ritual activities are not encouraged by the FWBO.

It is difficult to know where Mellor got his impression, indeed his conviction, that the FWBO is 'highly suspicious of ritual', since he certainly did not get it from the sources to which he refers, and it is difficult to know just how to go about exposing the extent of his misrepresentation. Perhaps I had best begin by investigating whether the ritual activities encouraged by the English Sangha are encouraged by the FWBO or not, and then comment on Mellor's more general observations on the FWBO's attitude to ritual.

Chanting is practised throughout the FWBO, including FWBO centres and communities in Britain, and is an integral part of its religious life. In the case of the Refuges and Precepts chanting is in Pāli, in the case of mantras in Sanskrit. Sometimes devotional verses are chanted in Tibetan. Bowing is a hardly less popular ritual practice, the value of which is well understood. As Tejananda writes, after explaining the significance of the *anjali*-salutation or salutation with joined fingertips:

> Salutation, bowing, and prostration may be made at any appropriate moment when one feels moved to do so, but especially upon entering or leaving a shrine room, and when making a personal offering of flowers, lights, or incense at the shrine. Often, when making offerings, people make a more complete oblation to the Buddha by kneeling and lowering the forehead to the ground, at the Buddha's feet, so to speak. An even more complete salutation is the full prostration – throwing the entire length of one's body onto the ground in front of the shrine. These practices have a tremendous effect in reducing one's tendency to pride and egotism, as well as enhancing one's receptivity to the Ideal.[213]

In *Buddhism for Today* there is a chapter on 'Bowing Before the Buddha' which Mellor appears to have overlooked, and which contains, incidentally, a description of recitation and chanting as practised in the FWBO. It was on account of this and another chapter that Gerald du Pré, the chairperson of the Scientific Buddhist Association, on the appearance of Subhuti's book in 1983, criticized the FWBO for being under the necessity of emphasizing spiritual friendship and puja or ritual worship because it was not sufficiently scientific to be able to function without them. Prostration, in the sense of the Tibetan Buddhist Going for Refuge and Prostration practice, is the principal subject-matter of chapter 11 of *The History of My Going for Refuge*, entitled 'More Light from Tibetan Buddhism', in the course of which I refer to the fact that some members of the Western Buddhist Order had completed the 100,000 repetitions of the ('Tantric') Refuge-going formula and 100,000 prostrations of this particular *mūla yoga* or foundation yoga.[214] In this connection I recall an early convention of the Order on which I opened the shrine-room door one afternoon to be confronted by the inspiring spectacle of some three dozen perspiring men and women Order members totally absorbed in doing the very strenuous Going for Refuge and Prostration practice together. It is strange that a Buddhist group that is highly suspicious of ritual should encourage salutation, bowing, and prostration in this way, but Mellor says the FWBO is highly suspicious of ritual, and Mellor has a Ph.D. in the problems of theory and method in the study of contemporary religion.

Candles and incense are widely used in the FWBO.[215] Together with flowers, also widely used, these constitute the three basic ritual offerings made to the Buddha-image in all forms of Buddhism. As Subhuti puts it:

> They are expressions of the gratitude which it is natural to feel to those who have given the Dharma. When one receives something, one will feel grateful and want to give something oneself – not by way of exchange but spontaneously, in appreciation. Like bowing, the making of offerings in this way provides an opportunity to express gratitude and devotion and to cultivate these feelings if one does not readily experience them. During [FWBO] ceremonies there is often a point at which those principally concerned, for instance individuals being ordained, make offerings, and in daily devotional ceremonies everyone can go forward to light incense at the shrine. The consequence of such actions should be experienced in other aspects of life: one will feel more generous and thankful in all one's relationships, particularly with those who are, in any sense, one's teachers.[216]

Nor is it only candles, incense, and flowers that are used in the FWBO. Besides the seven 'external offerings' of Indo-Tibetan Buddhism, such things as mandala-type cosmographs, miniature Pure Lands, and models of the Seven Jewels of a World Conqueror may also be ritually offered to the Buddha-image. On the occasion of ordinations and Mitra ceremonies, new Order members or Mitras, as the case may be, offer gifts to their teachers and themselves receive gifts from friends and well-wishers. I particularly recall a women's ordination retreat some years ago on which, having conducted the ordinations and received my own offerings, I sat watching with great pleasure the pile of gifts in front of each new Dharmacharini steadily growing as, one by one, the seventy or eighty other women present on the occasion came forward and offered each Dharmacharini in turn a card, a bunch of flowers, a poem, or a book. Again it is strange that a Buddhist group that is highly suspicious of ritual should encourage the use of candles, incense, flowers, and other ritual items, as well as the offering of *dāna* gifts, in this way, but Mellor says the FWBO is highly suspicious of ritual, and Mellor has a Ph.D. in the problems of theory and method in the study of contemporary religion.

Mention could also be made of the fact that the FWBO's first publication was *The FWBO Puja Book*, which has now sold well over 15,000 copies.[217] In her introduction to the fifth edition Dhammadinna writes:

> Poetry, symbol, myth, and ritual carry us, as Shelley suggests in his *Defence of Poetry*, 'to regions of light and fire, where the winged faculty of calculation dare not ever soar'. We cannot live in the realm of rational thought alone. To feel fully and vibrantly alive, we must feel in touch with all the different aspects and levels of our being.
>
> Buddhism is a spiritual tradition, and as such speaks to us in our wholeness. Its various practices can help us to bring into being a harmony of body, speech, and mind. Throughout its history, therefore, many forms of ceremony and ritual have been developed.[218]

Whereas the *Puja Book* consists of texts for recitation and chanting, and as such is of a practical nature, another FWBO publication is concerned with the theory and rationale of ritual. This is *Puja and the Transformation of the Heart*, two essays by Tejananda and Vessantara which in their *Mitrata* and Windhorse editions have sold altogether 8,000 copies. Tejananda's essay, 'Faith, Devotion and Ritual', from which I have already quoted, not only explains the purpose of ritual and devotion in Buddhism, and specifically the purpose of practices of this sort used in the FWBO, but also surveys some of the reasons why westerners, in particular, so frequently experience adverse reactions to these practices.[219] Yet again it is strange that a Buddhist group that is highly suspicious of ritual should seek to promote recitation and chanting, and to explain the purpose of Buddhist ritual and devotion, in this way, but Mellor says the FWBO is highly suspicious of ritual, and Mellor has a Ph.D. in the problems of theory and method in the study of contemporary religion.

But the FWBO is not only highly suspicious of ritual, has not only shorn Buddhism of what it understands to be the unnecessary and cluttering baggage of eastern cultural accretions. As we have already seen, according to Mellor, 'It has developed certain rituals and ceremonies of its own, however, though form is understood to be strictly subordinate to a personalistic content, and practices such as making offerings to monks and prostrating oneself before them are firmly rejected,' – and it is to these more general observations and the FWBO's attitude to ritual that I must now go back. I have already pointed out that what I actually reject in the passage in *The History of My Going for Refuge* to which Mellor's note here refers us is the *disproportionate emphasis* on making offerings to monks and prostrating oneself before them that is characteristic of south-east Asian *bhikkhus*, indeed of south-east Asian Buddhism. Hence it will not be necessary for me to consider the question of making offerings to monks and prostrating oneself before them on its own merits, so to speak, though I would like to observe that monks who have become accustomed to the prostrations of 'lay people' can easily develop an inflated idea of their own spiritual attainments. The questions I shall consider relate to whether the FWBO has developed rituals and ceremonies 'of its own', and whether form is, in fact, understood to be 'strictly subordinate to a personalistic content'.

In conceding that the FWBO, despite its suspicion of ritual, has developed rituals and ceremonies 'of its own', Mellor seems to be conjuring up a picture of an essentially 'Protestant' Buddhist movement reluctantly devising observances that have no basis in tradition. This is far from being the case, as the merest glance at *Puja and the Transformation of the Heart* and *The FWBO Puja Book* would have sufficed to show him. The *Tiratana Vandanā* or 'Salutation to the Three Jewels', the Going for Refuge and taking of precepts, the short puja, and the Sevenfold Puja, all of which figure prominently in the devotional and ritual life of the FWBO, are thoroughly traditional in character. Even the dedication ceremony, which I composed for the opening of the Triratna Shrine and Meditation Centre in 1967, draws on traditional material.[220] Indeed, the production of liturgies for the use of one's disciples is a traditional Buddhist activity, as witness the enormous number of such liturgies in the canonical Buddhist languages – liturgies that were certainly not all produced by the Buddha in the fifth or sixth century BCE. During the last three or four years, moreover, a group of Order members has been engaged in trying out 'new' rituals and ceremonies with a view to their eventual introduction into the mainstream of the Movement. Like my own Dedication Ceremony, these rituals and ceremonies draw on traditional material and are as much, or as little, the FWBO's 'own' as the rituals and ceremonies of Sinhalese Theravāda, for example, or of Japanese Sōtō Zen, are their own.

Whatever the nature of the FWBO's rituals and ceremonies, it certainly is not true to say with regard to them that form is understood to be strictly subordinate to a personalistic content, and I am at a loss to know what could have led Mellor to make such a statement, especially as the reference he gives in this connection is to the passage in *The History of My Going for Refuge* in which I allegedly reject 'practices such as making offerings to monks and prostrating oneself before them' – a passage in which, moreover, there is no mention of 'form' and no mention of any 'personalistic content'. Not for the first time, Mellor attributes to the FWBO views that are the exact opposite of those it actually holds and has, in this case, always held. For the FWBO, form is not subordinate to a personalistic content. In my lecture 'The Psychology of Ritual', given in 1968 and the source of much of the FWBO's thinking on the subject, I speak of (rational, as distinct from neurotic) ritual in terms that are anything but personalistic. Following Erich Fromm, I define it as *shared* action, expressive of *common* strivings rooted in *common* values, the implication being that the performance of ritual is possible only within a spiritual community or, as one might also say, within *vertically* transpersonal social forms and religious traditions.[221]

But the question of form – or rather of rejection of form – is one that seems to bother Mellor. Having stressed the English Sangha's encouragement of chanting, bowing, and so on, and duly noted the tension introduced into these practices because of the association of ritual with Catholicism, he observes that owing to the religious background of England ritual is necessarily a more self-conscious form of activity, if not a problematic one, than it is in Thailand, and that this difficulty is increased when

> the Protestant suspicion of ritual becomes reinforced by a strong emphasis on the Buddhist rejection of form; that is, the distinction between two levels of truth, the provisional (or the conventional) and the ultimate, where it is understood that even 'Buddhism' as a form can be discarded.

This is perfectly true, and after commenting that caution about the use of ritual and form in the West can be inspired by factors other than the Buddhist doctrine of ultimate truth, and quoting Steven Collins to the effect that the Buddhist denial of self appears only in certain contexts, at a highly sophisticated level of doctrine, and that the use of the term 'self', or other categories of the person, appears throughout other levels of doctrine, Mellor rightly remarks:

> An awareness of such sophistication in traditional Buddhist discourse is important because it enables us to be cautious about a tendency in some areas of western Buddhism to forget about 'provisional' truth altogether.

Whether the FWBO is to be understood as being (wrongly) included in the areas of western Buddhism referred to is unclear, but presumably it is, especially as Mellor has somehow become convinced that the FWBO is highly suspicious of ritual and might, therefore, be expected to reject form and forget about provisional truth no less readily than it subordinates its 'own' rituals and ceremonies to a personalistic content. Be that as it may, his remark serves to bring Mellor back to the English Sangha and to Ajahn Sumedho's understanding of religious form. According to Mellor, though the Ajahn understands religious form as ultimately 'empty', and 'not an end in itself', he still asserts the value of secondary, conditioned forms, and Mellor goes on to quote him as saying:

> Some modern day religious leaders tend to say: 'Don't have anything to do with religious conventions. They're all like the walls of prison cells' – and they seem to think that maybe the way is to just get rid of the key. Now if you're already outside the cell of course you don't need the key. But if you're still inside then it does help a bit.

The religious leaders of whom Ajahn Sumedho is thinking are probably Krishnamurti and Rajneesh, latterly known as Osho. Mellor, in all likelihood, is also thinking of Sangharakshita – and of the FWBO. But if this is the case I shall have to disappoint him. As should be obvious from what I have already said about the FWBO's alleged suspicion of ritual, I am in complete agreement with Ajahn Sumedho on this point, though since he is so very much my junior it might be more in accordance with tradition to say that he is in agreement with me. I too, unlike some modern day religious leaders, assert the value of secondary, conditioned forms, and assert it strongly, even though understanding religious form to be ultimately empty and not an end in itself. For me, as for Ajahn Sumedho (according to Mellor), 'the Buddha did not make a distinction between provisional and ultimate truth in order to make provisional truth appear valueless'. The only respect in which I differ from Ajahn Sumedho is that for me the fact that one 'needs the key if one is still inside the cell' is *not* a basis from which I can 'stress the value of all religious form, both within Buddhism and without it'. For me there is some 'religious' form, both within and without 'Buddhism', that is definitely not of value, that is, not of value to the individual who is seeking to develop in the direction of Enlightenment. To assert otherwise is to come dangerously close to pseudo-universalism and pseudo-liberalism.

Thus the issue of ritual observance is not nearly so much a point of divergence between the English Sangha and the FWBO as Mellor asserts. In principle there is probably no divergence between them at all on this score. Any divergence in practice is due, I suspect, to the FWBO's having a wider range of ritual activities than the English Sangha and conducting them, moreover, on a grander scale and in a more colourful manner. If Mellor would do a little fieldwork, and attend (for instance) an FWBO Buddha Day celebration, he might be agreeably surprised. Admittedly he would not see much in the way of people making offerings to *monks* and prostrating themselves before them, but he would see Order members, Mitras, and Friends engaging in traditional Buddhist practices of many other kinds. So seeing, he might realize not only that the FWBO is *not* 'highly suspicious' of ritual but that he had, perhaps, thought this to be the case because he somehow had been led to believe that making offerings to monks and prostrating oneself before them was the Buddhist ritual activity par excellence and that, without it, a western Buddhist group could be safely assumed to reject ritual altogether.

But I am anticipating. Mellor is not quite finished with ritual and form. Having quoted Ajahn Sumedho to the effect that the Buddha did not make a distinction between provisional and ultimate truth in order to make provisional truth appear valueless, he concludes this section of his article by drawing attention – via a citation from R. J. Zwi Werblowsky, yet another of his sociologist mentors – to the fact that the form of Thai forest monasticism upon which the English Sangha is modelled is itself an extreme form which understands itself as a 'revival' of Buddhism, a response to the 'domesticated' sangha of Thailand.

> The syncretism characteristic of so much south-east Asian Buddhism is rejected in the teaching of Ajahn Chah, as is a great deal of ritual associated with the 'institutionalized' Sangha of the cities. The 'simplicity' of Ajahn Chah's teaching is persistently emphasized and seen as one of its most attractive characteristics, especially to westerners.

The significance and value of ritual is not something which would automatically be endorsed by Ajahn Chah, who in fact instructs lay visitors not to 'get caught up with outward form', while still asserting the value of monastic rules and discipline. All this makes the Thai forest tradition sound quite 'Protestant' in character. Not that the English Sangha is necessarily equally 'Protestant'. As Mellor points out, in a western context Ajahn Sumedho faces a very different problem, a major danger being not of people getting caught up in outward form, but of them rejecting form altogether. To the fear of many English Buddhists that they might 'cling' too much to tradition, Ajahn Sumedho responds that 'One can also cling to the idea that one does not need tradition.' Once again I am in agreement with Ajahn Sumedho – or he with me.

Mellor comments that Ajahn Sumedho has brought the Thai forest monastic tradition to England without 'adapting' it, but has recognized that context will have its effect, and that the tradition 'would take its own form accordingly'. Similarly, in a passage from my interview with Mellor – a passage that I have already quoted and to which, as I then said, Mellor makes no reference – I explain that on my return to Britain 'I was just concerned to teach the Dharma, not any western version of it.... I'm not trying to "adapt" the Dharma; I'm just trying to make it understandable. If one can talk of a western Buddhism [at all] it is only in the sense of a form in which the Dharma can be understood and practised in modern western society. [So far as I am concerned] it is not an "interpretation" of the Dharma.' In other words I, like Ajahn Sumedho, 'envisage a form [of Buddhism] that is traditional yet sensitive to its local context', though in my case that form is perhaps envisaged on a more generous scale and in relation to a broader context.

4
MODERNISM AND BUDDHISM

From Protestantism to modernism is but a small step. Another of Mellor's mentors, the Catholic theologian Hans Urs von Balthasar, 'has noted the genealogical link between liberal Protestantism and the phenomenon of modernism', and modernist narratives, so Mellor informs us, 'have been instrumental in the development of some contemporary, or recent, religious perspectives'. Since he views the FWBO as demonstrating 'continuities with Protestant perspectives' and as being, therefore, a form of 'Protestant Buddhism', it is not surprising that Mellor should view the FWBO as demonstrating continuities with modernist perspectives too. Halfway through his discussion of modernism and Buddhism he in fact throws his customary caution to the winds and roundly declares 'The FWBO is modernist.'

Modernism is (a) the comprehensive term for an international tendency arising in the poetry, fiction, drama, music, painting, architecture, and other arts of the West in the last years of the nineteenth century and subsequently affecting the character of most twentieth-century art; and (b) in theology, the movement to modernize doctrine by taking into account the results of higher criticism and scientific discovery, and the conditions of modern culture, but chiefly the term used as a label for the outlook of a group of Roman Catholic thinkers led by Alfred Loisy and George Tyrrell. But it is not modernism in the artistic sense, or even in the narrowly theological sense, that Mellor really has in mind in this section of his article, despite the fact that he speaks of (theological) modernism as having been condemned by the Roman Catholic Church. For him the modernist perspective, as he prefers to term it, 'is one which coerces historical phenomena into an evolutionary, singular narrative where the modern constantly supersedes, and therefore makes irrelevant, the traditional and the orthodox'. This perspective 'can happily co-exist with liberal Protestantism which also rejects the traditional and the orthodox, in terms of both dogma and religious practice, in favour of an increasingly personalist understanding of religion'. In other words, modernism is for Mellor the belief that the new is by definition better than the old, especially as that belief finds expression in the sphere of religion. Admittedly Mellor does not actually speak of the modern as being, for modernism, 'better' than the old. He speaks of it as *superseding* the traditional and the orthodox and making them *irrelevant* – fashionable, non-evaluative terms I would not have expected to find a man of his sympathies using. But from the whole trend of his discussion it is evident that for him modernism is, in fact, the (false) belief that the new is by definition better than the old, especially as that belief finds expression in the sphere of religion.

Now let me say at once that I do *not* believe that the new is by definition better than the old, whether in the arts or in religion, and at no time in my life have I been tempted to believe this to be the case. Thus I am not a modernist, at least not in the sense in which Mellor uses the term, and the FWBO is no more modernist than it is Protestant. For me Bertrand Russell is not necessarily a greater philosopher than Plato, nor Francis Bacon a finer painter than Botticelli. Priority and posteriority of achievement have nothing to do with relative merits. This is not to deny that *Hamlet* is superior to *Gorbuduc*; it is simply to affirm that *Hamlet* is superior *and* later, not superior *because* later. But not only do I not believe that the new is by definition better than the old. If I may be permitted to sound a confessional note, I actually love the old more than the new and have always done so. In literature, in the visual arts, and in architecture, as well as in philosophy and religion, I have always loved the pre-modern (classical, medieval, and Renaissance) much more than the modern, and have sometimes wished that I lived in an earlier period of history. Once I remarked, not altogether in jest, that I had a thoroughly medieval cast of mind, by which I meant that for me it was natural to think in terms of hierarchy and degree. (Nowadays, of course, 'medieval' is often assumed to be synonymous with 'primitive' and 'backward' and, therefore, with 'bad'. Prison conditions, for example, are said to be medieval.) Thinking in terms of hierarchy and degree as I do, it is not surprising that my views on many current social issues should not only be at variance with pseudo-liberalism but should be regarded, in some quarters, as positively reactionary.

That I love the old more than the new is not, of course, necessarily supportive of my belief that the new is *not* by definition better than the old. I mention my love for the old simply in order to show that I am not only not a modernist but have no disposition towards modernism. Mellor is able to label the FWBO as modernist simply because he has not bothered to find out what my views, or the views of the FWBO, really are, and he has not bothered to find out because, having proved to his own satisfaction that the FWBO is 'Protestant', he assumes that, there being a 'genealogical link between liberal Protestantism and the phenomenon of modernism', the FWBO is necessarily modernist. This specious logic enables him to misrepresent and misinterpret the FWBO's position on a variety of topics, from the relation between Buddhism and evolution to the necessity of ethics, and from the nature and value of tradition to the significance of 'charismatic authority', and to some of the more serious of these misrepresentations and misinterpretations I must now turn. Before turning to them, however, I would like to make some additional comments in connection with (a) (theological) modernism and (b) the new.

a. 'The Roman Catholic Church condemned modernism at the turn of the century,' Mellor informs us, 'but within certain Protestant groups it has flourished.' This is rather disingenuous, suggesting as it does that Pius X had the last word on the subject and that the phenomenon was thereafter unknown within the Petrine communion.[222] (Theological) modernism represented, among other things, an attempt to take into account the results of higher criticism[223] and scientific discovery, and while it would be an exaggeration to claim that modernism has ever flourished within the Catholic Church, even in the wake of Vatican II, there is no doubt that some of the results of higher criticism have been quietly appropriated by Catholic scholars and theologians. One of the consequences of this at a popular level has been the removal from the Calendar of Saints of the names of Catherine (of Alexandria), Christopher, and Ursula, on the grounds that they were probably non-existent, even though tradition had long held them to be historical personages. The same type of development is illustrated by an amusing episode in Giuseppe di Lampedusa's novel *The Leopard*, when a priest who had been a pupil at the Vatican School of Palaeography spends three hours examining the seventy-four holy relics which three aristocratic old spinster sisters have collected over the years and pronounces *five* of them authentic. All the other little bits of bone and gristle could be thrown on the rubbish heap; they had no value whatsoever.[224]

The fact is that all religions are having to take into account, and if possible come to terms with, the results of higher criticism and scientific discovery, and this inevitably sets up tensions and conflicts within their respective structures. Buddhism is no exception. I well remember the storm that, in the Ceylon of the 1950s, broke on the devoted head of the Director of Archaeology, himself a Theravāda Buddhist, when he suggested that the Buddha had *not* personally visited the island three times. That he should be dismissed from his post was the least of the punishments demanded by his 'orthodox' co-religionists. I myself, at about the same time, shocked a Sinhalese Buddhist woman who was on pilgrimage in India by appearing to doubt that the Buddha was eighteen feet tall. 'What sort of monk is *this*?' her expression very clearly conveyed. But things appear to be changing, both in Theravādin Sri Lanka and in other parts of the Buddhist world. The Dalai Lama, I hear, has recently written to Tibetan monks engaged in propagating Buddhism informing them that when in the West they did not have to teach that the Earth is flat, even though this is what Tibetan Buddhist tradition avers. Whether they were free to teach that the Earth is flat when in the East was not made clear. Like that of the Buddha's three visits to Sri Lanka, or that of his being eighteen feet tall, the example is an obvious and even a ludicrous one, but its very ludicrousness serves to underline the fact that we can ignore the results of higher criticism and scientific discovery only at the cost of our intellectual integrity – an integrity which is inseparable from moral and spiritual integrity. We can ignore them only by retreating into an attitude of obscurantism. Whether in Christianity or in Buddhism, (theological) modernism of a limited type would appear to be inescapable.

b. In 1969 I wrote a poem entitled 'New', in which I wished I might speak in a new voice, communicating new things and celebrating 'The new horizon, the new vision/ The new dawn, the new day.'[225] I quote this poem at the end of *My Relation to the Order*, the paper I produced for the twenty-second anniversary of the Western Buddhist Order. In case Mellor chances to see this paper and accuses me of expressing, in the poem, sentiments at variance with what I say above about my not believing the new to be by definition better than the old I should like to explain myself. 'New' is not necessarily the opposite of 'old'. It can also indicate that which does not really belong to the temporal order and which is, therefore, neither old nor new. Thus it is possible to distinguish between the vertically new and the horizontally new, as we may term them, the vertically new being that which has no connection with time but which irrupts into, or manifests within, the temporal process, from another dimension, while the horizontally new is simply that which is unprecedented in time. The vertically new may be signalized by an upper case initial letter, leaving the horizontally new unsignalized in this way. What is New may, of course, also be new, but it is not New because it is new. It is New because it is New. When I wish, in my poem, that I might speak in a new voice, communicating new things and celebrating 'The new horizon, the new vision/ The new dawn, the new day,' the new to which I refer is the New, not the new. Its affinities are not so much with the 'Make it new' of Ezra Pound as with the 'Behold, I make all things new' of the Apocalypse.[226]

I

For Mellor, as we have seen, 'a modernist perspective is one which coerces historical phenomena into an evolutionary, singular narrative where the modern constantly supersedes, and therefore makes irrelevant, the traditional and the orthodox'. Whether or not this is the case, Mellor certainly tries to force the FWBO into a modernist perspective, i.e. into the general framework of modernism.

> The FWBO uses what are recognizably modernist narratives and appears to embrace enthusiastically the personalist understanding of religious significance which developed in liberal Protestantism. In fact, these two perspectives come together in Sangharakshita's assertion that Buddhism affirms 'individual rather than collective values', corresponding to and coinciding with 'the upper reaches of the total evolutionary process'. Subhuti also talks of the 'suprahistorical', 'upward surge of the individual'.

That the FWBO does *not* embrace 'the personalist understanding of religious significance', whether enthusiastically or otherwise, has already been made clear (see above, pp. 399ff.), so that there is no question of its sharing the modernist perspectives that 'relegate religion from a socially significant, institutional level to a private, personal sphere' and no question of its being, like liberal Protestantism, 'happier to see it there'. Still less is there any question of the FWBO sharing the point of view of Wilfred Cantwell Smith who, according to Mellor, argues that there is no such thing as 'religion', only 'a vital personal faith'.[227]

Since the FWBO does not embrace liberal Protestantism's personalist understanding of religious significance it is difficult to see how the two perspectives, the personalist and the modernist, could

> come together in Sangharakshita's assertion that Buddhism affirms 'individual rather than collective values', corresponding to and coinciding with 'the upper reaches of the total evolutionary process'.

The individual values to which I refer are not private and personal values; they are the values proper to (true) individuals *and* the spiritual community (i.e. the community of [true] individuals) as distinct from the values of group members and the group. The nature of the difference between the spiritual community and the group, and between group members and those who are (true) individuals, as well as the nature of the consciousness or awareness that characterizes the spiritual community as such, is discussed in the very section of the *History* from which Mellor purports to quote, as are the social or communal, higher-evolutionary, and cosmic contexts in which the individual's Going for Refuge takes place.[228] This discussion Mellor completely ignores. He takes one phrase from the third page of this section, another from the fourth, reverses the order in which they occur in my text, and strings them together in a 'quotation' he then proceeds to treat as evidence of my holding views diametrically opposed to those I actually do hold. Thus he not only tries to force the FWBO into a modernist perspective; in order to accommodate my views within his own preconceived notions about the FWBO he goes so far as to truncate what I have written. Presumably this Procrustean procedure is what he understands by methodology.

Whether or not this is the case, Mellor's determination to see the FWBO as a form of 'Protestant Buddhism' and as demonstrating, therefore, continuities with both liberal Protestantism and modernism, is truly remarkable. What is the reason for this determination? Reluctant as I am to ascribe motives, in the absence of any objective grounds for his (distorted) perception of the FWBO I have no alternative but to assume that the grounds are subjective and that, whether he recognizes it or not, Mellor's attitude towards the FWBO is controlled by a hidden agenda of the type to which I referred in connection with his failure to distinguish between the horizontally transpersonal and the vertically transpersonal (see above, p. 391). That this may well be so is indicated by the fact that his 'quotations' from Subhuti and myself are immediately succeeded by the complaint that, in this 'evolutionary structure' of ours,

> Christianity has played its part in the development of the individual (from a lower level of consciousness) but has now been superseded by the higher path of Buddhism.

There's the rub, it would seem.

> Christianity is now a danger to the individual who wants to develop. To support this view, the FWBO can use both modernist secularization narratives and liberal Protestant Christian complaints about Roman Catholicism. Both support the idea that the world is evolving in a particular direction which leaves traditional Christianity behind.

Let us see to what extent Mellor's complaint is justified and whether the FWBO does, in fact, use modernist secularization narratives and liberal Protestant Christian complaints about Roman Catholicism to support its (alleged) view that Christianity is a danger to the individual who wants to develop. But first a few words about the total evolutionary process, i.e. about the other of the two perspectives that according to Mellor come together in my assertion that 'Buddhism affirms "individual rather than collective values", corresponding to and coinciding with "the upper reaches of the total evolutionary process".'

The concept of evolution is a comparatively recent one which, having been successfully employed as a principle of explanation in biology, has been extended to cover practically all other branches of knowledge. In speaking of Buddhism in evolutionary terms I am not, however, equating Buddhism with evolutionism of the Teilhardian type; much less still am I claiming that the Buddha anticipated Darwin (I shall have something to say about Scientific Buddhism later on in this section). I am simply using the concept of evolution as a medium for the exposition of Buddhism.[229] Such a procedure is, of course, double-edged. As Subhuti observes, the danger here is that old meanings may reassert themselves when an old language (in this case the language of biology) is made to express new (in this case Buddhist) understandings.

> Western Buddhists today often borrow the language of other systems – psychoanalysis, science, Christianity – but they underestimate the power which old meanings retain. Already some Buddhist groups seem more like psychotherapy gatherings, or those of humanists, or even of thinly disguised Christians. The importance of creating and safeguarding a new and diamond-clear vocabulary for the expression of the Dharma is obvious.[230]

The term 'evolution' can, I believe, be part of that vocabulary, the more especially since there is a degree of overlap between the principle of evolution and one of the fundamental principles of Buddhism, i.e. the principle of conditioned co-origination (*pratītya-samutpāda*). As I have explained elsewhere, Buddhism is a path (more correctly, the principial path).

> In one form or another, the concept of the Path has always been central to Buddhism. The Path consists of steps or stages. These steps or stages represent, essentially, states of consciousness, or of being, which are progressive, leading the individual from ignorance to Enlightenment, from the condition of *pṛthagjana* to that of *arhant* or Buddha. One could therefore say that the conception of spiritual development, or spiritual *evolution* (what I call the higher evolution of Man) is central to Buddhism.[231]

Higher implies lower. That there is a higher evolution of Man means there must also be a lower evolution. For many years I was concerned only with the higher evolution, because I was concerned only with

Buddhism, only with the Path taught by the Buddha. But eventually I came to realize that the principle of the higher evolution was reflected, in a distorted and fragmented manner, in the whole biological process from amoeba to man, and that this reflection was the lower evolution.

> Science revealed how far man had come. This was the lower evolution. Buddhism, as the Path, showed how far he still had to go. This was the higher evolution. Though not strictly continuous the two phases between them constituted the two halves of a single process.[232]

There was, in fact, a qualitative difference between the two halves, for though both were governed by the same universal principle, the principle of conditioned co-origination, they were governed by two different modes of it, the cyclical and the spiral. The difference was exemplified within the Path itself, in the broadest sense, only the upper reaches of which constituted the Path proper or transcendental Path, the lower reaches being spiritually positive but mundane. The crux of the difference between the two modes of conditionality was that in the former the reaction took place in a cyclical order between two opposites, such as pleasure and pain, virtue and vice, good and evil, while in the latter it took place in a progressive order between two counterparts or complements or between two things of the same genus, the succeeding factor augmenting the effect of the preceding one. Transition from the cyclical to the spiral mode of conditionality, from the lower reaches of the Path to the Path proper, constituted what was traditionally known as Stream Entry. It was also known as the Point of No Return. Once past that point, one was no longer governed by the cyclical mode of conditionality, and could not react to any opposite. One could only go forward.

Prior to that point, however, one *could* react to an opposite; one could suffer a relapse, could decline, could deteriorate. Thus the whole biological process up to and including pre-Stream-Entrant man and his social, economic, political, and cultural history was characterized not by continual progress but by progress interrupted by regress and regress by progress, with the ever present possibility of total relapse, total decline, and total deterioration. Continual progress was possible only on the transcendental Path. Only in the case of the steps or stages of the transcendental Path was the new invariably, and necessarily, better than the old. Only on the transcendental Path was the new always the New. If a modernist perspective is one which, in Mellor's words, 'coerces historical phenomena into an evolutionary, singular narrative where the modern constantly supersedes, and therefore makes irrelevant, the traditional and the orthodox,' then it follows that there can be no question of the FWBO using 'recognizably modernist narratives', and no question of modernist and personalist perspectives ever coming together in any statement of mine. For the FWBO, as for the rest of the Buddhist world, the evolutionary narrative is not singular but dual, the total 'evolutionary' process comprising as it does a higher evolution governed by the spiral trend of conditionality and a lower evolution governed by the cyclical trend. As for Subhuti's 'supra-historical' 'upward surge of the individual', this represents the emergence of the spiral process within the cyclical, the manifestation of the Transcendental within the mundane, and no more represents a 'recognizably modernist' narrative than do my own words.

II

In Sangharakshita's and Subhuti's evolutionary structure, Mellor complains, 'Christianity has played its part in the development of the individual (from a lower level of consciousness), but has now been superseded by the higher path of Buddhism. Christianity is now a danger to the individual who wants to develop.' Had the FWBO shared the modernist perspective, and had it really coerced historical phenomena into 'an evolutionary, singular narrative where the modern constantly supersedes, and therefore makes irrelevant, the traditional and the orthodox,' it would be obliged to see Buddhism as having been superseded by Christianity, Christianity itself by Islam, and Islam by Baha'ism, or Theosophy, or Christian Science. But obviously the FWBO does not see Buddhism as having been superseded by Christianity, merely because Christianity happens to be later. It does not even see Buddhism, in the West, superseding Christianity, and making it irrelevant, merely because it happens to have arrived later on the scene and is new within the western context. Personally, I do not use the fashionable language of supersession and irrelevance (or relevance) at all, and I doubt if anybody else in the FWBO does. I am a Buddhist, and not a Christian, not because

I think that Christianity has now been superseded by the higher path of Buddhism and is no longer relevant. I am a Buddhist because I think that Buddhism is (on the whole) true, and always has been true, and that Christianity is (on the whole) false, and always has been false.

By Christianity I do not mean the liberal Protestantism that, as I have learned from Mellor, rejects doctrines such as the authority of the Church, the Virgin Birth, the Incarnation, and even the existence of God. By Christianity I mean the Christianity of the Creeds and Councils, of the Popes, and of Augustine and Aquinas. In other words, by Christianity I mean traditional, orthodox Christianity, i.e. Roman Catholicism, since it is Roman Catholicism which, as I have already pointed out, has been the normative form of the Christian faith in Western Europe (see above, p. 406). *This* is the Christianity in which I do not believe and which I think false. I do *not* believe in God, the Father almighty, creator of heaven and earth. I do *not* believe in Jesus Christ, his only Son, our Lord. He was *not* conceived of the Virgin Mary, though he may have suffered under Pontius Pilate, may have been crucified, and certainly died and was buried (if he lived at all). He did *not* descend to the dead (*or*, into hell). On the third day he did *not* rise again. He did *not* ascend into heaven, and is *not* seated at the right hand of the Father. He will *not* come again to judge the living and the dead. I do *not* believe in the Holy Spirit, or in the holy catholic Church, or the communion of saints, or the forgiveness of sins (by God through Christ), or the resurrection of the body, or the life everlasting (in heaven). Amen. *Sadhu! Sadhu! Sadhu!*

This is not to say that there is no truth at all in the statements (of the Apostles' Creed) thus negatived. But such truth as they contain is of the symbolic rather than the literal order, especially in the case of such powerfully evocative symbols as the Virgin Birth, the Crucifixion, and the Descent into Hell, some of which have analogues in other religious traditions, including Buddhism. Traditional, orthodox Christianity is certainly aware that its dogmas have a symbolic dimension to them, but this does not prevent it from insisting, at the same time, on the literal and even the historical truth of those dogmas. That they are true means, in effect, that they are literally true.

According to Mellor, dogmatism is among the 'problems' attributed to Christianity by English Buddhists, the charge being one traditionally directed at (Roman) Catholicism by (liberal) Protestants. I have already explained why western Buddhists, when they criticize Christianity, criticize Roman Catholicism rather than any other form of western Christianity (see above, p. 406). Since the FWBO sees Christianity not as superseded or irrelevant but as false, there is no question of its being able to 'use both modernist secularization narratives and liberal Protestant Christian complaints about Roman Catholicism [to] support the idea that the world is evolving in a particular direction which leaves traditional Christianity behind,' as Mellor maintains. Nor can it use them to support the view that 'Christianity is now a danger to the individual who wants to develop.' Christianity, as a form of theism, has *always* been a danger to the individual who wants to develop. Any similarity between the FWBO's criticism of Roman Catholicism and liberal Protestant complaints about that form of Christianity are therefore entirely coincidental, and in no way underlines the (supposed) fact 'that western Buddhists and liberal Protestants have a great deal in common'. Starting from the *Brahmajāla Sutta* Buddhism has developed, over the centuries, its own critique of theism and other *diṭṭhis* or '(speculative) views', and those western Buddhists who criticize or attack Roman Catholicism have no need to take their weapons from the arsenal of liberal Protestantism.[233]

III

The FWBO having been convicted of using 'recognizably modernist narratives', Mellor turns to forest monasticism and to the English Sangha. 'The relation of forest monasticism to modernism is quite different,' he declares. 'The austere asceticism of Ajahn Chah's forest monasteries in Thailand is perhaps, to some degree, a reaction against the phenomenon of "Buddhist modernism".' At this point Mellor hastens to shelter himself beneath the authority of R. J. Z. Werblowsky who, so he assures us, is very critical of Buddhist modernism, and 'highlights its eclecticism, its emphasis on lay participation, and its "glib and naive" assertion that Buddhism is the most "scientific" and the most "modern" of religions.' However, although Werblowsky 'notes' that the origins of such perspectives are in the West (the 'Buddhist modernism' in question is a south-east Asian phenomenon), he does not develop this point in any detail, and Mellor himself goes on to explain that Buddhist modernism is, to some degree, a product of (or response to) Christian influence in Asia, and that it was argued that Buddhism was 'not only more modern than Christianity but more *western*, i.e. rational, scientific and relevant to the modern world'. Confirmation for this explanation is sought from one M. Southwold, who, according to Mellor, has 'noted' how widespread Buddhist modernism is in south-east Asia, and 'its propagation by a westernized middle class'.

Whether it is widespread in south-east Asia or not, I have no sympathy whatever with Buddhist modernism and never have had. Like Werblowsky I am critical of its eclecticism (in the sense of its attempting to combine elements from both Buddhism and science), its emphasis on lay participation, and its assertion that Buddhism is the most scientific and the most modern of religions. Its emphasis on lay participation is, I believe, mistaken, in that it is an emphasis that is given within the framework of the existing monk–lay dichotomy and does nothing to modify that framework. As for its emphasis on the 'scientific' character of Buddhism, I too would describe this as glib and naive, based as it is on a misunderstanding either of Buddhism or of science or of both. Nevertheless, according to Mellor the relation of forest monasticism to modernism is quite different, i.e. quite different from that of the FWBO. Since he goes on to observe that the austere asceticism of Ajahn Chah's forest monasteries in Thailand 'is, perhaps, to some degree, a reaction against the phenomenon of "Buddhist modernism",' he clearly is connecting the modernism of which he has convicted the FWBO with the Buddhist modernism against which Ajahn Chah's forest monasteries are a reaction and, consequently, connecting the FWBO with that emphasis on the scientific character of Buddhism which, according to Werblowsky, is a feature of Buddhist modernism. Before proceeding to consider the relation of forest monasticism to modernism I must therefore make plain my own and the FWBO's position with regard to the vexed question of the scientific character of Buddhism.

Perhaps I can best do this by adverting to an article I wrote in 1948, when I was still without external guidance and when mistakes in my interpretation of Buddhism might have been expected. This article was entitled 'Buddhism and Science' and was a review of the third edition of P. Lakshmi Narasu's *The Essence of Buddhism*. After commenting on the fact that many people felt a predilection for a work in which the Dharma was expounded in accordance with scientific terminology, I continued:

This method of exposition does, like every other, furnish certain advantages and entail certain dangers. Of the advantages it would be superfluous to speak, since the undiminished popularity of the book for more than four decades is sufficient testimony on their behalf; but with regard to the dangers a few words may be deemed not out of place.

The Buddha taught that the Dharma was only a raft to ferry his followers over to the other shore of Nirvāṇa. Japanese Buddhists believe that all teachings are as a finger pointing to the Full Moon of Enlightenment. The Blessed One ironically questioned his disciples whether, after safely reaching the farther bank of a river, they would take the raft on their shoulders and carry it with them out of gratitude to it for having brought them across.[234] Similarly, who will fix his eyes on the pointing finger thinking that it is the Full Moon? Yet the history of religion reveals that men have repeatedly committed exactly this mistake. They have invariably confused the spirit with the letter, have ever fed on the valueless husk rather than the precious kernel, have seen shadow for sunlight, have mistaken the means for the end, the local form for the universal truth, the manner in which a thing is expressed for the mode in which it exists. It is imperative that the truth which is the Buddhadharma should be presented to the men and women of this century not only in the verbal but also in the ideological language with which they are most familiar; but it is of the utmost importance that they should learn to discriminate between the letter that killeth and the spirit that giveth life.[235] The message is not the same as the vehicle by which it is conveyed. The truth of Buddhism as a whole does not coincide with the truth of science. This does not mean that Buddhism contradicts science; it simply affirms that the truth of Buddhism is propounded from the standpoint of that realization which is integral to all experiences whatsoever, whereas the truth of science is advanced from the standpoint of one phase only (the material) of the whole infinite range of experience integrated. Yet, inasmuch as every phase of experience is an integrated factor in the pure, harmonious wholeness of Integral Realization, the integral truth of that realization will be reflected in, and revealed by, the partial truth of the limited experience of every one of the integrated factors.

> Microcosm mirrors macrocosm. Every jewel in the jewel-net reflects the whole web. If experimental science is able to unearth within its own field of work the puissant presence of those very laws which Buddhism declares to be absolutely universal in scope and operation, then it will have testified to the very limit of its capacity to the truth of the Dharma.[236]

Thus the youthful Sangharakshita (then known as Anagarika Dharmapriya). Though I would put things differently now, and though I am less sure than I was then of the importance of expounding the Dharma in accordance with scientific terminology, even supposing it to be well understood that (*pace* Marshall McLuhan) the medium is *not* the message, fundamentally my views regarding the 'scientific' character of Buddhism remain unchanged. *The truth of Buddhism as a whole does not coincide with the truth of science.* Broadly speaking there are two levels of existence, that of the composite (*saṃskṛta*) or mundane and that of the incomposite (*asaṃskṛta*) or transcendental, and corresponding to these there are two degrees of knowledge: sense-based rational or scientific knowledge and supra-rational (though not irrational) 'intuitive' knowledge or gnosis (*prajñā*, i.e. *bhāvanā-mayī-prajñā*). While gnosis has access to both levels of existence (to that of the composite, in that it is capable of perceiving its true nature), rational or scientific knowledge has no access to the level of the incomposite or transcendental and is, in fact, completely blind to its existence. Hence there can be no question of equating the (mundane) truth of science with the (transcendental) truth of Buddhism, despite there being a degree of asymmetrical overlap, as we may term it, between them, and no question of identifying scientific knowledge with gnosis on account of similarities between their respective verbal expressions. Much less still can there be any question of proving the truth of Buddhism by appealing to alleged anticipations of modern scientific discoveries, as representatives of Buddhist modernism are wont to do, and neither I nor, so far as I am aware, any member of the FWBO has ever sought to demonstrate the truth of Buddhism in this way or even to recommend Buddhism on such grounds. So much has this been the case that, as I mentioned in connection with the FWBO's alleged suspicion of ritual (see above, p. 416), a leading exponent of Scientific Buddhism actually criticized the FWBO for being 'not related to scientific knowledge'. That the Christian academic should connect the FWBO with Buddhist modernism, while the exponent of Scientific Buddhism should accuse it of being unscientific, is an irony that tells us, perhaps, more about the FWBO's critics than it does about the FWBO.

IV

> Ajahn Chah, however, is not interested in being modern: for him, Buddhist truths and traditions are timeless and in no need of being up-dated.

The 'however' is meant to remind us that the relation of forest monasticism to modernism is quite different from the relation of the FWBO to modernism, the latter having been convicted of using 'recognizably modernist narratives' and shown to be connected with south-east Asian Buddhist modernism and its emphasis on the scientific character of Buddhism. Mellor continues:

> Although his [i.e. Ajahn Chah's] movement might also be a response to both external pressures on Buddhism, his approach to the renewal of Buddhism is not based on the desire to make it appear modern, but to *return* to a pristine model of what Buddhism should be. Ajahn Chah is using tradition to purify Buddhism.

This is exactly my own position and the position of the FWBO. One could even adapt Mellor's words, and say, 'Sangharakshita is not interested in being modern: for him, (transcendental) Buddhist truths and (truly Buddhist) traditions are timeless and in no need of being updated (though they may need to be restated in more understandable terms). Although his movement might also be a response to both Christian and pseudo-liberal pressures, his approach to the renewal of Buddhism is not based on the desire to make it appear modern, but to *return* to a pristine model of what Buddhism should be. Sangharakshita is using tradition to purify Buddhism.'

But it is well over a dozen lines since Mellor last appealed for support and confirmation to one of his sociologist mentors, and he now feels the need to do so.

> As Michael Hill has shown, 'tradition' often has this radical, creative role, establishing something which is often new, even revolutionary, through the appeal to a golden age, a pristine model, or to the purity of a tradition. Tradition is both a leverage for social change and the signifier of a particular approach to history; that is, history is a narrative of decay interrupted by periods of purification.

I could not agree more. This is exactly how the FWBO sees itself and how it sees (Buddhist) history. Not that the FWBO appeals to a literal 'golden age' of Buddhism, any more than I think Ajahn Chah does (disobedient disciples and disharmony in the sangha existed even in the Buddha's day);[237] but it certainly looks back to, and derives inspiration from, a time when what was of primary importance in the Buddha's teaching was actually treated as primary and what was of secondary importance as secondary. The FWBO's role, like that of tradition in Michael Hill's account, is radical, in the sense of being a return to the spiritual roots of Buddhism, and creative, in the sense of not allowing itself to be determined by the immediate past of British Buddhism or, for the matter of that, by the immediate past of the eastern Buddhist world. Thus the FWBO is engaged in establishing something which, within its immediate context, is new – and, it is hoped, New. It is also a leverage for social change, though this aspect is more apparent in India than in Britain (I shall have something to say about the FWBO's Indian dimension in the following section), and the signifier of a particular approach to history; that is, history as a narrative of decay interrupted by periods of purification, or, as one could equally well say, of purification interrupted by periods of decay.

> It is in this way [i.e. as representing a period of purification] that Ajahn Chah's teacher Ajahn Mun, and Ajahn Chah himself, can be understood as participating in the 'revival' of Buddhist meditation practice in the Thai forest monastic tradition.

As Mellor fails to see, it is also the way in which the FWBO can be understood as participating in the revival, in British Buddhist circles, of the practice of Going for Refuge as the central and definitive act of the Buddhist life.

Since the English Sangha has sprung from Ajahn Chah's movement, and Ajahn Chah is not interested in being modern, it follows that the English Sangha has a negative attitude to modernism. Not only that. Since the FWBO 'uses recognizably modernist narratives' it also follows that on the subject of modernism the English Sangha and the FWBO differ. The English Sangha, Mellor assures us,

> is totally opposed to the modernism which is so significant in the FWBO. For the English Sangha, the 'modern' is associated with decay rather than progress. Whatever characteristics the English Sangha and the FWBO share, they differ in their attitude to modernism. This has a number of repercussions.

What these repercussions are we shall have to see. They relate mainly to Christianity, to ethics, and to the significance of the individual. Since modernism is not significant in the FWBO, however, it may well be that the English Sangha and the FWBO differ less than Mellor supposes and that, where they do differ, it is not on account of the FWBO's (alleged) attitude to modernism.

V

Christianity is treated 'very differently' by the English Sangha and the FWBO. 'Instead of consigning Christianity to a lower stage of evolution,' Mellor informs us with some complacency, 'the English Sangha concentrates on its philosophical differences with Christianity, and often displays quite an appreciative attitude towards it (albeit to a Christianity interpreted firmly within Buddhist categories).' I have already explained that I do not consign Christianity to a lower stage of evolution in the sense of regarding it as having been superseded by Buddhism within an evolutionary, singular narrative where the modern constantly supersedes, and therefore makes irrelevant, the traditional and the orthodox (see above, pp. 425ff.). What the English Sangha's philosophical differences with Christianity are, and where and when it concentrates on them, I am at a loss to understand. Contrary to his usual practice, Mellor gives no references here, and in any case the English Sangha is not known for philosophical activity. Mellor also omits to cite any instance of the appreciative attitude towards Christianity which, according to him, the English Sangha 'often displays'. Not that this really matters. What is really astonishing in the comparison Mellor draws between the English Sangha's treatment of Christianity and that of the FWBO is the parenthesis. The English Sangha often displays an appreciative attitude towards Christianity, *albeit to a Christianity interpreted firmly within Buddhist categories*. Does Mellor realize what he is saying? Does he realize what these categories are, firmly within which Christianity is interpreted by the English Sangha? If the English Sangha is doctrinally orthodox, as I assume it is, then they will be categories deriving, ultimately, from the *Brahmajāla Sutta*, according to which belief in the existence of a Father Almighty, creator of heaven and earth, as asserted in the first clause of the Apostles' Creed, is one of the sixty-two *diṭṭhis* or '(speculative) views' that must be abandoned if gnosis is to be developed and deliverance from mundane existence achieved.[238] What difference there really is between relegating Christianity to a lower stage of evolution, as the FWBO (allegedly) does, and dismissing Christianity's central tenet as a '(speculative) view', as the English Sangha in effect does, I leave to students of comparative religion to determine.

VI

Mellor has rather more to say about differences relating to ethics, the second of the repercussions from the fact that the English Sangha and the FWBO differ in their attitude to modernism. According to him, this is the most important repercussion, the English Sangha being 'markedly separate from the FWBO in its strong emphasis on ethics'. This clearly implies that the FWBO's emphasis on ethics is either weak or non-existent. 'Strong' and 'weak' are, of course, relative terms, and Mellor does not tell us what standard of measurement it is that enables him to ascertain the strength (or weakness) of an ethical emphasis or whether such an emphasis is even present at all. There are two possibilities. Either Mellor is equating ethics with *monastic* ethics or he is equating it with *sexual* ethics. Since the English Sangha is a monastic order, whereas the FWBO (including the WBO) is neither monastic nor lay, it is to be expected that it should emphasize monastic ethics more strongly than does the FWBO; but it would be illogical to infer therefrom that the English Sangha emphasizes ethics *in general* more strongly, and I do not think this is what Mellor is doing. We thus are left with the other possibility: that in asserting that the English Sangha is 'markedly separate from the FWBO in its strong emphasis on ethics' Mellor is equating ethics with sexual ethics. That this is actually the case is borne out by the nature of the evidence he proceeds to produce in support of his thesis. The English Sangha, he assures us, understands contemporary sexual, familial, and social ethics as dangerously lax.

> In contrast, the FWBO encourages the exploration of different types of sexual relationships, sees marriage as a serious handicap to the development of the individual, attacks the 'shrill horror and raw vindictiveness' with which certain Christians attack pornography,[239] and always asserts the significance of the individual above the group.

All these are matters of *sexual* ethics, not excluding even the last, with which, as we shall see, Mellor is concerned only to the extent that it impinges on marriage and the family. Nor is that all. In Mellor's enumeration of the FWBO's sexual heresies do we not detect a note of that same shrill horror of which Subhuti speaks? Be that as it may, in connection with his allegation that the FWBO's emphasis on ethics is weak or non-existent there are a number of misunderstandings to be cleared up, as well as one misquotation to be corrected, and I shall therefore (a) refer briefly to my other writings on ethical subjects, (b) comment on the FWBO's sexual heresies as enumerated by Mellor, (c) give a few examples of the FWBO's position on sexual ethics, and (d) indicate the extent of the FWBO's ethical concerns.

a. Material on (Buddhist) ethics is to be found in all my writings, from *A Survey of Buddhism* (1957) to *A Guide to the Buddhist Path* (1990) and *The Buddha's Victory* (1991). It is even to be found in my writings on art. There are, however, three works which are entirely devoted to the subject. These works are *Aspects of Buddhist Morality*, *Vision and Transformation*, and *The Ten Pillars of Buddhism*.[240] In *Aspects of Buddhist Morality* (1978) I discuss the nature of morality, morality and the spiritual ideal, morality mundane and transcendental, patterns of morality, the benefits of morality, and determinants of morality. *Vision and Transformation* (1990, but based on lectures given in 1969) is devoted to the Buddha's Noble Eightfold Path, with Vision representing the first step or stage (*aṅga*, literally 'limb') and

Transformation the seven remaining steps or stages. *The Ten Pillars of Buddhism* (1984), a disquisition on the ten precepts, is divided into two parts. In part 1 I deal with the ten precepts collectively, under such headings as 'The Relation between the Refuges and Precepts', 'The Ten Precepts as Principles of Ethics', and 'The Ten Precepts as Rules of Training'; in part 2 I deal with them individually. Since ordination within the Western Buddhist Order consists in Going for Refuge to the Buddha, Dharma, and Sangha, *and* in undertaking to observe the ten precepts (as well as having the effectiveness of one's Going for Refuge 'witnessed' by experienced senior members of the Order), the ten precepts obviously occupy a position of central importance in the life of the FWBO, as indeed they (or the five or the eight precepts) do in the life of all genuinely Buddhist groups. It is therefore not surprising that I should speak of them as the Ten Pillars of Buddhism, or that I should eulogize them in the following terms:

> The ten precepts are, indeed, the massy supports of the entire majestic edifice of the Dharma. Without the ten precepts the Dharma could not, in fact, exist. Continuing the architectural metaphor, one might say that the Three Jewels are the three-stepped plinth and foundation of the Dharma, the ten precepts the double row of pillars supporting the spacious dome, meditation the dome itself, and wisdom the lofty spire that surmounts the dome. Elaborating, one might say that each of the ten pillars was made of a precious stone or precious metal, so that there was a pillar of diamond, a pillar of gold, a pillar of crystal, and so on. In this way we should be able to gain not only an understanding of the importance of the ten precepts but also, perhaps, an appreciation of their splendour and beauty.[241]

It is also not surprising that *The Ten Pillars of Buddhism* should be a prescribed text for postulants of the Western Buddhist Order (*Vision and Transformation* is included in the three-year Mitra study course). What *is* surprising is that Mellor, ignoring this work and my other writings on ethical subjects, should see the FWBO as not emphasizing ethics. If giving the ten precepts a position of central importance in one's life, and eulogizing them as necessary to the Dharma's very existence, does not constitute an emphasis on ethics it is difficult to know what would.

b. 'The FWBO encourages the exploration of different types of sexual relationships.' Here Mellor refers to *Buddhism for Today*, p. 167. On looking up the reference, however, we find that Subhuti is not speaking of sexual relationships, and that it is not the exploration of different types of *sexual* relationships that the FWBO encourages. What Subhuti actually says is: 'It should be possible for everyone to have a wide range of relationships of different kinds in which all his needs, biological, psychological, social, and spiritual can be met without conflict' – a very different thing. Mellor has not only attributed to Subhuti views he does not hold; he has also misinterpreted the FWBO. No doubt the reason for his so doing is that he equates ethics with sexual ethics and assumes, therefore, that 'relationships' means *sexual* relationships. Subhuti continues: 'Each person should be part of a network within which all these various needs can be met without overloading any one particular relationship.' We shall come back to this point when I give examples of the FWBO's position on sexual ethics.

'[The FWBO] sees marriage as a serious handicap to the development of the individual.' Here Mellor again refers us to *Buddhism for Today*, p. 166, but though he does not actually misquote Subhuti (apart from substituting his own 'serious handicap' for Subhuti's 'barrier') he is far from doing justice to the latter's temperate and balanced three-page discussion of the relation between the individual and the family.[242] In any case, it is surprising that for Mellor seeing marriage as a serious handicap to the development of the individual (i.e. the individual-in-relation-to-Buddhahood) should be one of the repercussions of *modernism*. As Subhuti reminds us, 'the young Buddha-to-be left behind his social position, his wealth, his parents, even his wife and son,' and as it should not be necessary for me to remind Mellor, Jesus never married and seems not to have considered the family to be an important or significant institution. Moreover, Mellor is contrasting the English Sangha's 'strong emphasis on ethics', i.e. sexual ethics, with the FWBO's weak or non-existent emphasis. But the English Sangha is a monastic order. Its members have renounced sex, marriage, and family life, at least for the time being (in Buddhism monastic vows are not taken for life). How is it, then, that Mellor sees the English Sangha and the FWBO as differing in their attitude to modernism, at least as regards (sexual) ethics? It is possible, of course, that the contradiction is not so much in Mellor himself as in the English Sangha, which although a celibate body seems to give guarded approval to legal marriage and the nuclear family – perhaps because it sees them as the only alternative to sexual anarchy. There is also the fact that a monastic order is economically dependent on the laity and cannot afford to depreciate the latter's chosen way of life beyond a certain point; but this is a consideration pertaining to an area of ethics with which we are not now concerned.

'[The FWBO] attacks the "shrill horror and raw vindictiveness" with which certain Christians attack pornography.' Once again we are referred to *Buddhism for Today*. Mellor also adds a note. 'Although Subhuti does not explicitly state that the FWBO approves of pornography, this passage [from *Buddhism for Today*] seems to imply that any limitations on an individual's *right* to experience different forms of sex-related activities (including the consumption or production of pornography) are to be opposed.' The passage implies no such thing. It implies no such thing because the FWBO does not discuss ethical questions in terms of rights. As long ago as 1951 I expressed the view that rights and duties are inseparable and that if all men did their duty to one another it would not be necessary even to speak of rights. Duties rather than rights were therefore to be emphasized.[243] Since then I have developed this line of thought further. I believe that 'rights' is not an ethical concept (though 'duties' is), but only a legal one. Ethically speaking, the individual has no rights. Hence there can be no question, from the FWBO's point of view, of an individual's right to experience different forms of sex-related activities (including the consumption or production of pornography) and no question, therefore, of Subhuti implying that any limitations on such a right are to be opposed. From the FWBO's point of view the real question is whether the consumption or production of pornography is conducive to the observance of the third precept, the precept of abstention from sexual misconduct (and cultivation of contentment). Order members and Mitras are, I think, generally agreed that it is not conducive. Whether the consumption or production of pornography should be illegal is a different matter altogether. It has not been discussed within the Order, so far as I know, and I personally do not hold definite views on either side of the question.

Mellor is therefore wrong in concluding, as he does in the last sentence of his note, that 'the FWBO approaches sex-related issues through liberationist discourse and favours leaving moral decisions to individuals.' The FWBO favours leaving moral decisions to individuals because it is only to individuals that, in the last resort, moral decisions *can* be left (even the decision to follow tradition, or the teaching of the Church, is a moral decision inasmuch as it is a decision to do what one believes is *right*). In practice this means, within the FWBO itself, that moral decisions are left to the individual-in-relation-to-Buddhahood, and that he makes his decision in the light of his commitment to the Three Jewels and in consultation with spiritual friends, both horizontal and vertical. As for Mellor's charge that the FWBO approaches sex-related issues through liberationist discourse, let me conclude my observations on his note with an extract from the 1951 essay (on 'Rights and Duties') to which I have already referred and which I probably wrote before Mellor was born and long before he immersed himself in the confusions of theory and methodology.

> The word for duty and the word for religion (which consists at bottom in the eradication of the ego-sense) are, in the languages of India, one word: Dharma. But the clamorous insistence upon our rights, upon what is legally, morally, or even spiritually due from others to us, only strengthens greed, strengthens desire, strengthens selfishness, strengthens egotism.
>
> The performance of one's duties results in the establishment of love and peace, the attempted extortion of one's rights in the outbreak of hatred and violence. Duties unite, rights divide. Duties are cooperative, rights competitive. The former depend upon our own selves, and are therefore swift and easy of accomplishment; the latter depend on others, and are therefore tardy and difficult, if not impossible, of achievement. Rights are wrested forcibly from other human beings outside, but duties are softly and sweetly laid upon us by the voice of the Divine – of our own potential Buddhahood – reverberating within.
>
> Buddhism, being based upon the realization of emptiness, upon egolessness, upon unselfishness, teaches the doctrine of the mutual interpenetration of all things, inculcates the practice of love and compassion, exhorts men and women to perform their duties in every walk of life, and therefore tends naturally towards the ultimate establishment of peace, both in the hearts

> and minds of men and in the world of events outside us. Western political systems, on the contrary, however different or even antagonistic they may outwardly seem, are all based upon the concept, ultimately of dogmatic Christian origin, of the existence of separate, mutually exclusive ego-entities which are socially, politically, and even spiritually valuable and significant in themselves. All such systems therefore justify hatred and excuse violence, all insist on the intrinsic reasonableness of clamorous agitation for rights, and all therefore, without exception – despite emphatic protestations to the contrary – result in the eventual outbreak of war, both in the individual psyche and in the life of societies and nations.[244]

If these words were true forty years ago, they are even truer today.

However, we must not forget that Mellor is citing the fact that the FWBO 'attacks the "shrill horror and raw vindictiveness" with which certain Christians attack pornography' as evidence in support of his thesis that, in contrast to the 'strong emphasis' of the English Sangha, the FWBO's emphasis on (sexual) ethics is weak or non-existent. But Subhuti is concerned with sexual ethics only indirectly. What he is doing is attacking the pseudo-ethical moralism of traditional, orthodox Christianity – a moralism by which, he believes, sexual morality has been made impossibly complex for most westerners. This is not evidence of a weak or non-existent emphasis on (sexual) ethics. If it is evidence of anything, it is evidence of a different kind of ethical emphasis, in the light of which the 'shrill horror and raw vindictiveness' with which certain Christians attack pornography is seen as being no more ethical than the pornography they attack.

Finally, '[the FWBO] always asserts the significance of the individual above the group'. Mellor apparently regards this as evidence of the weakness or non-existence of the FWBO's emphasis on (sexual) ethics because, as he goes on to explain, 'the FWBO seeks the destruction of traditional sexual and social structures, while the English Sangha would like to see them strengthened'. This enables him to conclude, 'The FWBO is modernist, while for the English Sangha what is modern is generally associated with decadence.' Leaving aside the question of whether the English Sangha would really like to see a strengthening of the banks, the public schools, and the trade unions, for example, as well as of legal marriage and the nuclear family, let us see in what manner the FWBO 'asserts the significance of the individual above the group'. But this is a question which chimes with the third of the repercussions from the fact that (according to Mellor) the English Sangha and the FWBO differ in their attitude to modernism, and I propose to deal with it when we come to that repercussion. Before proceeding to give a few examples of the FWBO's position on sexual ethics, however, I would like to make a comment on Mellor's statement, 'The FWBO is modernist, while for the English Sangha what is modern is generally associated with decadence.'

Writers on modernism generally distinguish between modernism and modernity. The fact that (according to Mellor) the English Sangha and the FWBO differ in their attitude to modernism does not necessarily mean that they differ in their attitude to modernity or that the English Sangha does, in fact, associate the modern (as distinct from modernism) with decadence. Indeed it would be strange if it did so, for though it belongs to the Thai forest tradition its members very sensibly live in houses, operate personal bank accounts, make use of gas and electricity, and rely on modern transport.

c. My examples of the FWBO's position on sexual ethics relate to (i) the sexual relationship, (ii) abortion, (iii) homosexuality, and (iv) celibacy or chastity.

i. The FWBO does not see the sexual relationship as being the principal relationship in human life. On the contrary, it believes that the true individual, or individual-in-relation-to-Buddhahood, will relegate his sexual relationships to a position nearer the periphery than the centre of his personal mandala (to use the FWBO idiom), the centre of the mandala being occupied, so far as human relationships are concerned, by spiritual friendships, both horizontal and vertical. This means that the FWBO does not subscribe to that idealization, romanticization, and, as we may say, pseudo-spiritualization, of the sexual relationship which is so marked a feature of modern western culture and which has even invaded the realm of serious religious thought. To take an example at random: commenting on Karl Barth's assertion that sexuality is 'the basic form of all association and fellowship, which is the essence of humanity', the philosopher and theologian John Macquarrie observes

> [sexuality is so interpreted] because the sexual relation is the most intimate act of mutual self-giving and communion possible for two human beings. Indeed, can we still speak of 'two'? Or have they become in a sense a new whole – 'one flesh' in the biblical language?[245]

It is partly because of its belief that the true individual relegates his sexual relationships to a position nearer the periphery of his personal mandala that the FWBO encourages the exploration of different types of relationships. These are not *sexual* relationships, as Mellor wrongly asserts, but a range of relationships of *different kinds* in which, in the words of Subhuti, everyone's needs, biological, psychological, social, and spiritual can be met without conflict (see above, p. 445). The scriptural basis for the FWBO's view that, as Subhuti goes on to say, each person should be part of a network within which all these various needs can be met without overloading any one particular relationship, is the *Sigālovāda Sutta*. In this *sutta*, which is widely studied in the FWBO, the Buddha teaches the young Brahmin Sigala the *right* way to worship the six quarters of earth and sky. He should revere his mother and father as the eastern quarter, his teacher as the southern quarter, his wife as the western quarter, his friends and counsellors as the northern quarter, his slaves and servants as the lower quarter, and ascetics and brahmins as the upper quarter, and he should revere each of them in five ways, all of which are explained in detail.[246] Here we truly have a network within which the individual's biological, psychological, social, and spiritual needs can be met without overloading any particular relationship.

In the modern West, however, we have no such network. As the quotation from John Macquarrie suggests, our reverence is directed too exclusively to the western quarter. We overload the sexual relationship, in the sense of making greater emotional demands on it than it is capable of meeting, with the result that other relationships are neglected and the sexual relation itself is put under severe strain. Besides encouraging the exploration of different types of relationships generally, the FWBO therefore recommends the cultivation of two other relationships in particular, partly for their own sakes and partly in order to take some of the strain off the sexual relationship. It encourages the individual to direct his reverence not only to the western quarter but also to the eastern and northern quarters. It encourages him to cultivate his relationship with his mother and father and his relationship with his friends and counsellors. (Reverence for the upper quarter, of cultivation of one's relationship with ascetics and brahmins, is encouraged only so far as it represents the cultivation of vertical spiritual friendship.)

The individual's relationship with his (or her) friends and counsellors in fact receives a good deal of attention in the FWBO. Texts on friendship from various traditions are studied, and there is a series of nine lectures on 'spiritual friendship' by Subhuti which cover virtually all aspects of the subject.[247] The individual's relationship to his (or her) parents receives rather less attention, though it is by no means neglected. As I have noticed since coming back to Britain, in the West children are often on bad terms with one parent or the other, or with both, sometimes even feeling anger and resentment towards them. The FWBO therefore emphasizes the importance of being on good terms with one's parents, for everybody's sake, and encourages its members to transform any negative feelings they may have towards their parents into positive ones. Some Order members and Mitras report a marked improvement in their relationship with their parents since they became involved with the FWBO, and I suspect that the relationship which FWBO members enjoy with their parents is on the whole more harmonious than that enjoyed by any comparable group of people in the wider community.

ii. Abortion or the deliberate termination of pregnancy before the foetus is viable constitutes an infraction of the first precept, that of abstention from taking life, and there can be no question of a female Order member (for example) undergoing an abortion or a male or female Order member or Mitra performing an abortion, or encouraging one, or even approving one. Women who have had an abortion prior to becoming involved with the FWBO will be asked to recognize that they have acted unskilfully, to confess their unskilfulness to their spiritual friends, and to resolve not to commit an unskilful action of this kind again. The FWBO does not agree that abortion is a woman's right. As already explained, I do not believe that 'rights' is an ethical concept, and in any case there cannot be an *ethical* right to perform an unethical action, though there may be a legal one.

iii. Traditional, orthodox Christianity has a horror of homosexuality, the vice 'not to be named among Christians',[248] and besides inflicting untold suffering on homosexuals has bequeathed a legacy of neurotic homophobia to practically the entire western world. The FWBO demonstrates no continuities with these perspectives, as Mellor would say. It does not discriminate against people on account of their sexual orientation, any more than it discriminates against them on account of their age, their class, their race, or their national origin. On the contrary, it welcomes all, would befriend all, and seeks to introduce all to the riches of the Dharma. It does this, in the case of homosexual men and women, as a matter of common justice to a beleaguered minority, and because conscious or unconscious fear of homosexuality is one of the factors preventing (heterosexual) men, in particular, from forming deep and emotionally satisfying friendships with members of their own sex. As Stuart Miller notes,

> The fear of homosexuality and how it affects the possibilities of male friendship in our times are topics that need contemplating.... The estate of male friendship – indeed, of nearly all human relationships – is sufficiently sunk that mere sex remains at the centre of people's imaginations. The only moving human relationships that people seem able to conjure up are the erotic ones.[249]

And again,

> Deep friendship between adult men is quite rare in our society.[250]

Thus the FWBO's position on homosexuality relates as much to the development of (non-sexual) male friendship as it does to homosexuality itself, and it relates to the development of male friendship because of the vital importance of spiritual friendship in the Buddhist life.

iv. The FWBO not only believes that the true individual will relegate his sexual relationships to the periphery of his personal mandala; it also believes that, regardless of sexual orientation, he will move in the direction of celibacy or chastity. Celibacy is the state or condition of being unmarried; chastity is abstention from sexual intercourse. Both words translate the Indo-Aryan term *brahmacarya*, which has connotations of celibate studenthood and religious chastity. Literally, the term means 'faring in the Divine' and is the archaic Buddhist expression for what nowadays we would call the spiritual life. Since members of the Western Buddhist Order are neither monks or nuns nor lay people the Order does not divide into those who practise, or try to practise, celibacy/chastity, and those who do not. All Order members move in the direction of *brahmacarya*, however slowly they do so and however distant the goal may be. *Brahmacarya* is not an absolute, particularly when it is seen as being verbal and mental as well as physical: it is a matter of degree, so that there is no question of passing from a state of complete non-*brahmacarya* to a state of complete *brahmacarya* at a single bound. Moving in the direction of *brahmacarya* means practising, or trying to practise, *brahmacarya* to a greater and ever greater degree. Moreover, the practice of *brahmacarya* is not only a matter of abstinence from sexual activity; it also involves the enjoyment of higher, progressively more 'divine' levels of consciousness wherein, as I explain in *The Ten Pillars of Buddhism*, one transcends the state of sexual dimorphism and lives an 'angelic' life of spiritual androgynousness.[251]

d. The extent of the FWBO's ethical concerns is indicated by the fact that Order members undertake to observe the ten precepts and that these 'ten pillars of Buddhism', as I call them, are the subject of intensive study within the Movement. It is also indicated by the fact that Order members and Mitras alike are encouraged to follow the Noble Eightfold Path, and thus gradually to transform each and every aspect of their lives in the light of right understanding or perfect vision (*samyag-dṛṣṭi*). Both these traditional formulations, that of the ten precepts and that of the Noble Eightfold Path, are quite comprehensive in scope, particularly the latter, the more especially since both cover social as well as personal ethics. They certainly do not equate ethics with sexual ethics, in the way Mellor does (see above, p. 443). Though sexual ethics are by no means neglected, these constitute only a small part of each formulation, being the subject-matter of the third precept, that of abstention from sexual misconduct (*kamesu-micchācāra*), and a portion of the third step or stage (*aṅga*, literally 'limb') of the Noble Eightfold Path, that of Right or Perfect Action (*samyak-karmānta*).

While in principle Order members observe abstention from killing, abstention from taking the not-given, and the rest of the ten precepts, equally, and while Order members and Mitras are encouraged to traverse all eight steps or stages of the Noble Eightfold Path, in practice certain precepts or certain steps or stages are emphasized more than others, at least in the sense of their being the objects of a greater amount of attention and discussion. One such emphasis is on the first precept, that of abstention from killing, as represented by the practice of excluding meat and fish from one's diet. The vast majority of Order members are vegetarians, and a few are vegans, and they find it difficult to understand why so many eastern Buddhists (including monks belonging to the Thai forest tradition), should be unable, apparently, to see any connection between eating meat and fish and the killing of living beings. In Britain, however, an increasingly large number of people do see a connection between them, and one of the ways in which the FWBO encourages vegetarianism, and thus the observance of the first precept, is by running vegetarian restaurants.[252] This does not mean that the FWBO regards vegetarianism and spiritual life as being virtually synonymous, as do certain orthodox Hindus. Much less still does it mean that the FWBO believes that absolute abstention from the killing of living beings (including microbes) is a real possibility, even for vegetarians and vegans. Health and economics apart, the FWBO encourages vegetarianism for two reasons. It encourages it in order to reduce the amount of animal suffering, and it encourages it as a means of affirming the principle of non-violence in today's increasingly violent society. Were the FWBO to equate ethics with non-violence in the way Mellor equates it with sexual ethics, one could reverse his pronouncement regarding the differences between the English Sangha and the FWBO relating to ethics (see above, p. 442–3), and say, 'The FWBO is markedly separate from the (non-vegetarian) English Sangha in its strong emphasis on ethics.'

Though the FWBO runs vegetarian restaurants, and runs them as a means of encouraging observance of the first precept, as represented by vegetarianism, it does not run them on the usual commercial lines. It runs them as what it terms team-based right livelihood businesses. As such they form part of the FWBO's emphasis on Right or Perfect Livelihood (*samyak-ājiva*), the fourth step or stage of the Noble Eightfold Path. Thus the FWBO's vegetarian restaurants embody a double ethical emphasis, on the first precept, that of abstention from killing, and also on right or perfect livelihood. Traditionally, right or perfect livelihood means gaining one's living by fair methods, without resorting to deceit, treachery, soothsaying, trickery, or usury. More specifically, it means not engaging in the five trades prohibited to all Buddhists: trading in arms, in living beings, in flesh, in intoxicating liquors, and in poison – military service, and the work of hunter, fisherman, etc. being understood as also included in the list.[253]

During the last ten or twelve years the FWBO has developed this basic concept in a number of ways, some of them with implications for other aspects of the ethical and spiritual life, with the result that right or perfect livelihood is now represented, for the FWBO, by its team-based right livelihood businesses. A team-based right livelihood business provides the Order member or Mitra who works in it with three things. (a) The means of meeting his material needs, including those of any dependants. (b) Work that does no harm, either physical or mental, to himself or to others, and which leaves him time for rest, meditation, and social and cultural activities. (c) An environment conducive to his development as a (true) individual, especially one that provides him with opportunities for living and working with other people and developing spiritual friendships. No less importantly, a team-based right livelihood business also applies its profits to the support of FWBO activities.

Besides vegetarian restaurants, the FWBO runs wholefood stores, gift shops, a publishing house, an export-import business, and a gardening service – all on the same team-based right livelihood principles.[254] That it runs so many businesses, of such widely different kinds, means that the FWBO is obliged to concern itself with all sorts of questions of business ethics. These questions are often the subject of intense discussion within the businesses immediately concerned, and if they are of sufficient general interest they may also be discussed within the wider Movement. Some of the questions with which the FWBO has to concern itself are questions of relevance to businesses in the outside world, and Order members with business backgrounds have begun investigating the whole subject of business ethics within this broader context. Following the recent crop of disclosures of unethical dealings on a grand scale in the upper echelons of business and finance, some British businessmen have become more alive to the importance of business ethics, and it may well be that the FWBO, with its emphasis on right or perfect livelihood, particularly as represented by its team-based right livelihood businesses, is in a position to contribute to the debate. Were the FWBO to equate ethics with business ethics in the way Mellor equates it with sexual ethics, one could again reverse his pronouncement regarding the differences between the English Sangha and the FWBO relating to ethics (see above, p. 443), this time saying, 'The FWBO is markedly separate from the (economically inactive) English Sangha in its strong ethical emphasis.'

The FWBO also emphasizes Right or Perfect Awareness (*samyak-smṛti*), the seventh step or stage of the Noble Eightfold Path, as represented by awareness of the natural environment, though it emphasizes it less strongly than vegetarianism or team-based right livelihood or, indeed, some of the other levels of awareness. Our attitude towards natural objects should be untainted by subjectivity. As I say elsewhere, 'We should learn to look, learn to see, learn to be aware, and in this way become supremely receptive.'[255] An aware attitude will also be a responsible one. That is, it will be an ethical attitude and, as such, one involving a serious grappling with environmental issues.

VII

Having contrasted the FWBO's weak or non-existent emphasis on ethics with the English Sangha's 'strong emphasis', Mellor goes on to point out that there is 'a marked divergence in the significance of the individual in each set of discourses'. This is the third repercussion from the fact that the English Sangha and the FWBO differ in their attitude to modernism, and echoes what Mellor has already said about the FWBO always asserting the significance of the individual above that of the group (see above, p. 448).

> For the FWBO the evolution of the individual is the 'point' of history, so that all that is perceived to inhibit individual development is regarded with hostility.

But who is this individual whose evolution is the 'point' of history and whose significance is above that of the group? He is not what I call the group member, or statistical individual, as Mellor seems to think. Rather is he the true individual, or the individual-in-relation-to-Buddhahood, and it is true individuals who constitute the spiritual community, just as it is statistical individuals who make up the group. Thus we have four categories: the group member or statistical individual, the group, the true individual, and the spiritual community. To these I sometimes add a fifth category, that of the positive group, which is not so much a separate and distinct kind of group as that aspect of the group which helps rather than hinders individual development, at least to the extent of not actively opposing it. Were the FWBO actually to speak of the evolution of the individual as being the 'point' of history (and neither I nor Subhuti speak of it in this way), it would be only in the sense that the true individual arises in dependence on the group member, just as the higher evolution arises in dependence on the lower evolution and the first stage of the transcendental path on the last stage of the mundane path.

Mellor seems unable to imagine a state of affairs in which group and (true) individual are in conflict. This is because he has only two categories, that of the group (as I term it)/society/tradition/Church and that of the individualist who, quite wrongly as he evidently thinks, rejects the authority of the group/society/tradition/Church and refuses to be bound by it. In other words, Mellor's categories are reductively sociological (quite early on in his article he uses language that suggests he views 'religions' as having only a social and cultural existence (see above, p. 372 and p. 376), and it is because his categories are reductively sociological and exclude the category of the true individual that he is unable to imagine Christianity and the nuclear family as inhibiting individual development, i.e. the development of the true individual, and unable to imagine them as being rightly attacked for so doing. When Subhuti criticizes Christianity and the nuclear family, therefore, as he does in *Buddhism for Today* (though not so one-sidedly as Mellor's rather selective quotations suggest), Mellor can see in this only a manifestation of antisocial, even antinomian, individualism. 'Hence, in spite of the Buddhist concept of non-self,' he concludes, after his final quotation from *Buddhism for Today*, 'the FWBO appears an exceptionally individualistic movement.'

The English Sangha presents a much brighter picture, even though one less bright than Mellor could have wished. But before we move on to this picture I must correct what seems to be an erroneous assumption on Mellor's part. Having noted that the nuclear family is an object of hostility to the FWBO 'because it is understood to put limits on individual development,' and having given instances of Subhuti's criticism of it on this score, he proceeds to quote Subhuti on the subject of the divorce rate. '"The mounting divorce rate",' Subhuti is represented as saying, 'is "to be rejoiced in as a sign of wholesale disaffection" from the unhealthy intensity of marriage and the nuclear family.' Leaving aside the circumstance that what Subhuti actually says is that the mounting divorce rate is to be rejoiced in 'from a certain point of view', the fact that Mellor should see such rejoicing as a manifestation of individualism, and therefore as being opposed to group/society/tradition/Church, shows he assumes that what is traditional in (Roman Catholic) Christianity is likewise traditional in Buddhism and that, conversely, what is untraditional in the one is also untraditional in the other. But this is by no means the case. Divorce is *not* untraditional in Buddhism, and the fact that Subhuti can rejoice in the mounting divorce rate is no more a signaller that the FWBO is individualistic than would be his rejoicing in an increase in polygyny and polyandry, neither of which is untraditional in Buddhism.[256]

The greater brightness of the picture presented by the English Sangha is owing to the fact that, according to Mellor, 'the concept of non-self occupies a prominent position in [its] discourse.' History is not an upward spiral but a downward one, he explains on the English Sangha's behalf, and therefore the individualism of western society needs eliminating not developing. The FWBO would certainly agree that the individualism of western society needs eliminating. All its activities, from the cultivation of spiritual friendship to the practice of the recollection of the six elements, are directed to this end. But it would not agree that history is a downward spiral. (Has humanity been only spiralling downwards since history began?) History consists of both upward and downward spirals, either one of which may predominate at any given time without ever gaining a permanent ascendancy, though the higher reaches of an upward spiral may at times support, in the person of the true individual, a supra-historical transcendental 'continuation'. However, the concept of history as a constant downward spiral would seem to represent Mellor's own reading of the English Sangha's position (he gives no reference here), and I would prefer to stay with the fact that for the English Sangha individualism is something to be eliminated, especially as Mellor goes on to observe that 'Ajahn Sumedho sees society as "a group of individual human beings" rather than as a genuinely collective, transpersonal reality.' It is as a group of individual human beings that the FWBO, too, sees society, though it also sees it as consisting of group members, or statistical individuals, who are in the majority, and true individuals, who are in the minority. The concept of society as a genuinely collective, transpersonal reality has been dealt with already. As I pointed out in connection with the individual's efforts to create conditions more favourable to the eradication of mental defilements, efforts which may involve the repudiation of 'transpersonal social forms (such as the Church)', it is necessary to distinguish between what is horizontally transpersonal and what is vertically transpersonal (see above, p. 391).

It is Ajahn Sumedho's failure to see society as being anything other than 'a group of individual human beings', so that for him (as for the FWBO) 'there is no "social world" in Richard Sennett's sense of the term', that detracts from the brightness of the picture presented by the English Sangha as compared with the individualistic FWBO. In respect of its concept of society, Mellor regretfully concludes, the English Sangha is in step with the general cultural orientation towards the individual in the contemporary West. However, he is able to console himself with the reflection that within this orientation 'Ajahn Sumedho demonstrates a very different approach to issues like the significance of the individual in relation to the family.' The nature of this approach is illustrated by a passage from one of Ajahn Sumedho's public talks, on 'The Family'. 'Rather than the family, we tend to think of ourselves,' declares the Ajahn, presumably in ringing tones.... 'We've been given free rein to develop our lives as much as we want to. Whether my family, my parents, like it or not doesn't matter. Whether it's disgracing the family name has never occurred to me. My background, my conditioning, has been one of "develop yourself", be a self-sufficient, independent person ... a *personality*.' A damning indictment indeed, and one can almost see the curl of Ajahn Sumedho's lip, and the condemnatory gleam in his eye, as he emphasizes the shocking word 'personality'. It is an indictment very much to Mellor's liking. It enables him to comment that, in this passage, 'western society is not a series of dangerous oppressions, but dangerous liberations,' and that, 'The apparent obsession with the individual makes contemporary life "a neurotic and meaningless existence".' It also enables him to conclude, no doubt to his own satisfaction, that the difference between the English Sangha and the FWBO in respect of the significance of the individual in relation to the family is rooted in competing understandings of history. 'The English Sangha sees itself as working against the grain of western culture, rather than as the pinnacle of a long evolutionary development.' Once again there are a number of misunderstandings to be cleared up. I shall consider them in relation to (a) the individual and the family, (b) the individual and liberation, and (c) the individual and evolution.

a. When Ajahn Sumedho declares, 'Rather than the family, we tend to think of ourselves,' it is presumably the individualist to whom he is referring. It is the individualist whom he sees as having been given freedom to develop, regardless of his family's wishes and regardless of whether it disgraces the family name. It is the individualist whose background and conditioning has been one of 'develop yourself, be a self-sufficient, independent person ... a *personality*.' As a critique of individualism this is unexceptionable, and the FWBO would endorse every word of it, though perhaps without giving the same pejorative emphasis to the word 'personality'. But what of the true individual, or individual-in-relation-to-Buddhahood? He, too, has been given the freedom to develop his life, and he, too, may choose to develop it in such a way as to bring disgrace, real or imagined, on the family name, even though in his case he will be aware of what he is doing. Ajahn Sumedho appears to believe that one who comes into conflict with his family cannot but be an individualist, and he appears to believe this because he fails to distinguish the individualist from the true individual, just as Mellor fails to do. It is almost as if he was arguing that since the individualist comes into conflict with his family one who comes into conflict with his family must be an individualist. But I do not want to make too much of this. Mellor may be quoting Ajahn Sumedho out of context, and the latter in any case is presumably speaking without reference to the FWBO. I shall therefore take the passage at its face value, so to speak, as though it had not been extracted from a talk by Ajahn Sumedho and as though Mellor had not produced it as evidence of the way in which the English Sangha's approach to the family differs from that of the individualistic FWBO.

Let me take for my starting point the notion of disgracing the family name. To disgrace means to bring shame and discredit upon, but whether the way in which one chooses to develop one's life disgraces the family name will depend upon the nature of the family and what it is that they consider to be shameful and discreditable. A philistine family will feel disgraced if one of its members becomes an artist, while a criminal family will feel disgraced if one of its members becomes a police officer. It could, of course, be argued that the artist and the police officer are being individualistic, and should *not* have disgraced their families in the way they did, but this would be straining logic. A family has not necessarily been disgraced, at least not in real ethical terms, because it feels shamed and discredited by the behaviour of one of its members. Indeed, it may feel disgraced when it is in fact being highly honoured.

The paradigmatic examples of individuals who have 'disgraced' their families in this way are the Buddha and Jesus. The Buddha disgraced his noble and wealthy family by begging in the streets of Kapilavastu, and was reproached by his father for so doing.[257] Jesus disgraced his family by preaching and healing, with the result that 'his relatives heard of this and set out to take charge of him, convinced that he was out of his mind.' (Thus *The Jerusalem Bible*. *The Unvarnished Gospels* has, 'He's gone mad!')[258] Unless one is prepared to argue that the Buddha and Jesus were individualists (as some modern defenders of the family no doubt would) one has to recognize that living in a way that disgraces the family name does not necessarily mean that 'Rather than the family, we tend to think of ourselves,' and therefore does not necessarily mean that we are individualists. The reason that the Buddha 'disgraced' his family by begging in the streets was that begging in this way was, as he explained to his irate father, the custom of his race, the race in question being not the mortal Śākyan lineage into which he had been born but the deathless Buddha-lineage into which he had been adopted by virtue of his own attainment of supreme Enlightenment. The customs of the group are superseded by the customs of the spiritual family, just as the group itself is superseded by the spiritual family or spiritual community.

But what does 'thinking of ourselves' mean? If living in a way that disgraces the family name does not necessarily mean that we are individualists, then, presumably, thinking of ourselves rather than of the family does not necessarily mean that we are individualists either. The truth is that the phrase is ambiguous. It is ambiguous because 'ourselves' is ambiguous. Is this self of ours of which we tend to think, rather than thinking of the family, the group-member self, or is it the true-individual self? If it is the group-member self, then 'thinking of myself' rather than of the family will represent a conflict between one part of the group and another, with the family thinking of itself, rather than of me, in much the same way that I think of myself rather than of the family. Here the conflict is horizontal. If on the other hand the self of which I tend to think is the true-individual self, then 'thinking of myself' rather than of the family will represent a conflict between the true individual and the group, with the family thinking of itself, rather than of me, but thinking of itself in a way very different from the way in which I think of myself. Here the conflict is vertical. If the self of which I am thinking when I think of myself rather than of the family is the true-individual self, I will use the free rein I've been given to develop my life 'as much as I want to' in a way that is not subjective and self-indulgent (i.e. indulgent of the group-member self or statistical individual) but which will help me to progress towards Enlightenment (*bodhi*). Whether my family, my parents, like it or not will certainly not be a matter of indifference to me. If they do not like the way in which I am using my free rein I will explain why I believe it is the best way for me to live. In any case, I will keep in touch with them and assist them in any way I can. Should they feel I am disgracing the family name I will explain in what real disgrace consists. If my background, my conditioning, has been one of 'develop yourself, be a self-sufficient, independent person ... a *personality*' in an individualistic sense, I will create a new background, a new, spiritually-positive conditioning, and do my best to be a true individual, an individual-in-relation-to-Buddhahood. I will be self-sufficient in the sense of taking from others as little as I can, and giving as much as I can, and independent in the sense of not allowing others to do for me what I can do for myself and doing for them what they are unable to do for themselves. I will try to be a person in the sense of a true individual, and a *personality* in the sense of a Selfless Person.

b. 'Licence they mean when they cry liberty,' exclaimed the indignant Milton, commenting on the uproar occasioned by the publication of his *Tetrachordon*.[259] Like 'liberty' itself, the word liberation is ambiguous, its meaning varying with the context within which it occurs and the kind of person to whom it refers. When we are told that 'western society is not a series of dangerous oppressions, but dangerous liberations,' we therefore have to ask what these liberations are, i.e. what they are liberations from, and what makes them dangerous. We also have to ask for whom they are liberations. (I leave aside the question of whether there in fact are no oppressions in western society, or at least no dangerous ones.) Just as the self of whom we are thinking when we 'think of ourselves' may be either the group-member self or the true-individual self, so it may be either the group-member self or the true-individual self for whom liberations are liberations, and for whom they are dangerous. In the passage quoted by Mellor from Ajahn Sumedho's talk the liberations are from the constraints of the family, and since the self for whom they are liberations is the group-member self they are dangerous because they are individualistic. But in the case of the true-individual self liberations, whether from the family or anything else of a collective or group nature, are not dangerous because they are not individualistic. The danger is in the individualism, for as Milton goes on to insist, 'Who loves [liberty], must first be wise and good,'[260] and wisdom and goodness are incompatible with individualism, whether in the seventeenth century or the twentieth. Hence although 'obsession with the individual' may indeed '[make] contemporary life "a neurotic and meaningless existence",' there is no doubt that a concern for true individuality, in oneself and in others, would transform contemporary or any other life into an existence that was psychologically healthy and spiritually meaningful.

For Mellor, if not for Ajahn Sumedho, liberty would appear to be a dirty word, possibly on account of its association with the French Revolution. But it is certainly not a dirty word for Buddhism. Principally in the form of *vimukti* it occurs throughout the Buddhist scriptures, *vimukti* or liberation from the fetters of mundane existence being one of the key concepts of the Buddha's teaching. In a famous passage in the *Udāna* the Buddha, describing the eight ways in which the *Dharma-Vinaya* resembles the mighty ocean, declares that as the mighty ocean has one taste, the taste of salt, just so the *Dharma-Vinaya* has one taste, the taste of freedom or liberation (*vimukti*).[261] Besides being one of the four *dharma-skandhas* or 'parts of righteous living', *vimukti* constitutes the penultimate *nidāna* or 'link' of the positive and progressive 'spiral' aspect of conditioned co-origination (*pratītya-samutpāda*).[262] It is also a synonym for Nirvāṇa. Hence it is not surprising that the concept of liberty, freedom, deliverance, or emancipation (as the word *vimukti* is variously translated) should feature prominently in the thinking of the FWBO or, for the matter of that, in the thinking of any Buddhist group, western or non-western. In my own expositions of the Dharma I usually connect *vimukti* with liberation from the first three fetters, as I do in *The Taste of Freedom*, with which Mellor appears not to be acquainted.[263] *Vimukti* being the fourth 'positive and progressive' *nidāna* on from the crucial fifth *nidāna*, or 'knowledge-and-vision-of-things-as-they-really-are' (*yathābhūta-jñānadarśana*), there is, I point out, no real liberation without (transcendental) insight or 'clear vision' (*vipaśyanā*), and since it is insight or clear vision that breaks the first three fetters (as it does the remaining fetters) this means, in effect, that there is no real liberation without liberation from those first three fetters, i.e. from the fetter of speculative views regarding the self, the fetter of pathological doubt, and the fetter of attachment to moral rules and formal religious observances. All three fetters are therefore dealt with at some length in my writings and lectures, and a good deal of FWBO teaching and practice centres upon them.

Not that it is easy to break the first three fetters. Not that it is easy to achieve real liberation, thus becoming what is traditionally known as a Stream Entrant. Before the first three fetters can be broken there are many minor liberations to be achieved, some of which Ajahn Sumedho and Mellor would doubtless regard as being no less dangerous, i.e. no less individualistic, than liberation from the constraints of the family. In the case of the true individual, however, such minor liberations are stepping-stones to the major liberations comprised in the breaking of the first three fetters or Stream Entry. Though minor liberations may indeed be the immediate concern of individual members of the FWBO, it nevertheless is the major liberations that are, short of Buddhahood, their ultimate concern. They are concerned with minor liberations, whether social, psychological, cultural, or even religious, *because* they are concerned with the major liberations. This is not to say that one may not sometimes be deceived and think that he is behaving like a true individual when in fact he is behaving individualistically. Between true individuality at one end of the spectrum and individualism at the other there is a whole range of attitudes and it is not always easy to know what one's own position in the spectrum really is, especially if one does not have the support of spiritual friends. But this is the only *real* danger. To escape from the dangers of the minor liberations by giving up the minor liberations is not only to escape from individualism but also, at the same time, to give up the possibility of real individuality and therewith the possibility of ethical and spiritual life.

c. The FWBO is an exceptionally individualistic movement. Because it is individualistic it is hostile to Christianity, which puts limits to individual development, and hostile to the family, because it does not allow the individual to think of himself. Moreover it is characterized by that obsession with the individual which according to Ajahn Sumedho makes contemporary life 'a neurotic and meaningless existence'. – Such is Mellor's estimate of the FWBO. Such is the estimate on which he bases his assertion that the difference between the English Sangha and the FWBO is rooted in competing understandings of history, with the English

Sangha seeing itself as 'working against the grain of western culture' and the FWBO seeing itself as 'the pinnacle of a long evolutionary development'. How the English Sangha is related to western culture, and how the FWBO is related to it, we shall see when we come to the next section of Mellor's article. Our present concern is with the question of whether the FWBO really does see itself as 'the pinnacle of a long evolutionary development'. Since the kind of context within which the FWBO views evolution has been touched on more than once already, in a general way, I can therefore be brief.

Real evolution is spiritual. Real evolution takes place when the group member or statistical individual becomes a true individual and when the true individual, upon the breaking of the first three fetters binding to mundane existence, becomes a Stream Entrant and starts ascending, without possibility of regress, the successive stages of the transcendental Path whose final stage conducts him or her into the presence of Nirvāṇa. Thus real evolution is not evolution in the usual collective, biological sense, and does not form part of human history, except to the extent that the true individual interacts with the group and affects its life in various ways. I therefore sometimes distinguish between evolution, progress, and development. Evolution, in this context, is a strictly biological process, and corresponds to what in other contexts I term the lower evolution. Progress has reference to complexity of social organization and extent of scientific knowledge and technology. In itself it has no ethical or spiritual value, though it may provide the material and cultural basis for that which does have ethical or spiritual value. Development appertains to the individual, especially the true individual, and corresponds to what I also term the higher evolution. Such development has two successive stages, that from individuality through true individuality to Stream Entry, and that from Stream Entry to Enlightenment (*bodhi*) or Nirvāṇa. If the FWBO was to see 'evolutionary development' as having a 'pinnacle' that pinnacle would not be the FWBO itself but the upper reaches of the higher evolutionary process, i.e. the purely transcendental second stage of development.

Within the confines of British Buddhism the FWBO sees itself as being a more adequate basis for the development of true individuality than were the Buddhist societies and eastern Buddhist groups by which it was preceded and which continue, in some cases, to exist alongside it. But it does not see itself as being a more adequate basis simply because it is subsequent to them in time (this would amount to linear evolutionism) but because it has, as it believes, brought out more clearly than they have done the fundamental character of Buddhism, especially as consisting, so far as the individual Buddhist is concerned, in the act of Going for Refuge to the Three Jewels. This is not to say that it is wrong to regard the FWBO as being an advance on previous British Buddhist groups, as Mellor seems to think. It is an advance on them in much the same way that the eastern Buddhist groups were an advance on the Buddhist societies, and the Buddhist societies themselves an advance on the scattering of scholarly knowledge about Buddhism by which *they* were preceded. If it is wrong to see in the FWBO an advance on the eastern Buddhist groups, then it is no less wrong to see in the Buddhist societies an advance on the scattering of scholarly knowledge about Buddhism and no less wrong to see in *this* an advance on the British people's former total ignorance of the subject. But I would characterize all these advances as *progress*, not as evolution and not as, necessarily, development. Though in theory all, from the scattering of scholarly knowledge about Buddhism to the FWBO itself, may be bases for the arising of true individuality (insight or clear vision may on occasion be sparked off by a single line of Buddhist text), in practice true individuality is much more likely to arise on the basis of a movement such as the FWBO than on the basis of a scattering of scholarly knowledge about Buddhism. If British Buddhism's one hundred year history is the 'long evolutionary development' to which Mellor refers, then it *may* be correct to see the FWBO as the pinnacle of that development. Personally, however, I see the FWBO not so much as a pinnacle as a foundation, even a part of a foundation.

VIII

Consideration of the repercussions from the FWBO's modernism has led Mellor to the subject of tradition. This he now considers on its own, which in turn leads him to a consideration of the subject of charisma. Having observed that 'tradition' is not a fashionable concept in contemporary society, he turns for support to Edward Shils, one of the sociologist mentors whom we encountered in the first section of his article. According to Shils, while people may use the term 'tradition' in a variety of senses, there is a widespread rejection of tradition as a normative power, traditions as normative models of action and belief being regarded as useless and burdensome.

> Those who are attached to institutions, practices and beliefs which are designated as traditional are called 'reactionaries' or rather 'conservatives'; they are placed on the 'right' on a line which runs from 'left' to 'right' and to be 'on the right' is to be in the wrong.

Shils traces the origin of such a perspective to the (eighteenth-century) Enlightenment which he sees as 'antithetical to tradition', a point which has been echoed, according to Mellor, by the ecclesiologist Joseph Ratzinger, in defence of the Catholic Church's tradition. 'Freedom emerges here [i.e. in the Enlightenment],' he quotes Ratzinger as saying, 'as liberation from the power of tradition to lay down norms.'

Unfortunately, though Shils can be relied on for support to a certain extent his position is not entirely satisfactory. He has, in fact, an ambivalent attitude to the Enlightenment. 'As a whole his book is in defence of the normative value of tradition,' Mellor complains, 'yet he applauds the Enlightenment for freeing the self from the "dark inheritance" of (Christian) tradition,' the ideal of the Enlightenment being (in Shils's words) 'to expunge from human beings all that came from the past and hindered their complete self-regulation and expression'. I am unable to refer to *Tradition* (it is out of print), but it is clear that for Shils belief, in principle, in the normative power of tradition is by no means incompatible with the rejection, in practice, of particular 'traditional' institutions, practices, or beliefs, which of course implies the existence of a criterion of what is really traditional and what is not.[264] Whether Shils has such a criterion I do not know. Mellor certainly does not have one. It is clear that for him the question of distinguishing between what is really traditional and what is not simply does not arise, the normative power of tradition being definitely incompatible with the rejection of particular traditional institutions, practices, or beliefs. For Mellor tradition is tradition is tradition just as for Gertrude Stein a rose is a rose is a rose.[265] Tradition is something unitary, monolithic, absolute. Tradition is, in short, God, and rejection of tradition is rebellion against God.

So far as Mellor's quarrel with the FWBO is concerned, however, the difference with Shils is immaterial. Shils traces the rejection of the normative power of tradition to the Enlightenment and in the present context this is what matters. The FWBO, being individualistic, rejects tradition, and since it rejects tradition its attitude to Christianity bears a close resemblance to the 'achievement' of the Enlightenment (the quotation marks are Mellor's), i.e. to the Enlightenment's freeing of self from the 'dark inheritance' of (Christian) tradition.

> Subhuti asserts that the idea of sin 'weakens the individual', disabling the attempt to regulate his own moral life or to develop spiritually. To fight these Christian 'dangers for the individual' Subhuti stresses the necessity and value of blaspheming, ridiculing and developing contempt for God.[266] The individual must be liberated from the past at all costs.

Needless to say, the individual who is weakened by the Christian idea of sin (very different from the Buddhist idea of *akuśala-karma* or 'unskilful action') is not the individualist but the true individual, or at least the nascent true individual. Again, Mellor is unable to imagine a state of affairs in which group and (true) individual are in conflict and unable, therefore, to understand that there are traditions which, since they weaken (true) individuality or even discourage its emergence altogether, have to be rejected if (true) individuality is to be developed. But there is no need for me to labour the point, as Mellor's confusion should by now be obvious. The nature of the 'therapeutic blasphemy' (as I term it) of which Subhuti speaks is explained in my *Buddhism and Blasphemy*, which Mellor appears not to have come across.[267] As for the individual having to be liberated from the past 'at all costs', does not the Buddha say, in the *Dhammapada*, 'Give up the future, *give up the past*, give up the present, and pass to the Farther Shore (i.e. Nirvāṇa)'?[268]

IX

But Mellor has not yet finished with the (eighteenth-century) Enlightenment. Continuity with Enlightenment discourse is of significance not only for the rejection (in the case of the FWBO) of the normative power of tradition but also for the legitimation of authority in 'English' Buddhism. Following, as he tells us, Max Weber's distinction between 'traditional authority' and 'charismatic authority', Mellor argues that the English Sangha conforms to a model of traditional authority in that it understands itself to be an organic development of Thai forest monasticism.

> Ajahn Sumedho trained with Ajahn Chah (who had himself trained with figures such as Ajahn Mun), giving the English Sangha an impeccable traditional pedigree, and therefore authority. The FWBO, on the other hand, is more akin to a model of charismatic authority, in that Sangharakshita distinguishes between what he regards as 'essentially' Buddhism and mere 'traditions', in the sense of cultural customs.

At this point Mellor quotes me as saying, in my 1986 interview with him:

> I distinguish between Tradition with a capital T and tradition with a small T. By tradition with a small T I mean those observances, customs, practices, which have become traditional in Buddhist countries but are quite peripheral in relation to the fundamental principles of Buddhist teachings.... I think that at present the Thai-trained Sangha Trust people [i.e. the English Sangha, the members of which are supported by the Sangha Trust] tend to look at tradition in that way, whereas I think of Tradition in the sense of the essential principles of Buddhism.

According to Mellor,

> This is a charismatic model of authority because Sangharakshita is understood to have the personal authority to be able to distinguish between what is, and is not, essential Buddhism.

Valid though Weber's distinction between traditional authority and charismatic authority may be, it is not so absolute as Mellor thinks, nor so applicable to contemporary 'English' Buddhism. What he says about the English Sangha and what he says about the FWBO could quite easily be transposed. 'The FWBO', it could be said, 'conforms to a model of traditional authority in that it understands itself to be an organic development of Indo-Tibetan *triyāna* Buddhism: Sangharakshita trained with Dhardo Rimpoche (who himself trained with such figures as Geshe Yeshe Lhundup), as well as with other Indian, Tibetan, and Chinese teachers, giving the FWBO an impeccable traditional pedigree, and therefore authority. The English Sangha, on the other hand, is more akin to a model of charismatic authority, in that Ajahn Chah, Ajahn Sumedho's teacher, distinguishes between what in Buddhism needs to be purified and what does not.' (Earlier in the section Mellor describes Ajahn Chah as 'using tradition to purify tradition'.) 'This is a charismatic model of authority because Ajahn Chah is understood to have the personal authority to be able to distinguish between what in Buddhism needs to be purified and what does not.' Thus whether one distinguishes between Tradition with a capital T and tradition with a small T, or between what in Buddhism needs to be purified and what does not, makes little difference. In either case, the fact that one distinguishes means that one has a criterion, a criterion implies a definition, whether of 'tradition' or of 'purity', and a definition implies essence (see above, pp. 400ff.). As Mellor perceives

> What the FWBO understands by 'Tradition' is *essence*; that is, the heart and core of Buddhism when shorn of all cultural accretions.

What he is unable to perceive is that the statement could be transposed, and that he could equally well say, 'What the Thai forest tradition understands by "Pure Buddhism" is *essence*; that is, the heart and core of Buddhism when shorn of all impure elements.' My 'Tradition' with a capital T thus corresponds in principle to Ajahn Chah's (and presumably the English Sangha's) 'Pure Buddhism' and my tradition with a small T or cultural accretions to Ajahn Chah's impure elements or what in Buddhism is in need of purification. It would therefore not be surprising if in applying our respective criteria to particular Buddhist customs and beliefs we should sometimes come to similar conclusions about them. An example will make this clear.

According to an article in the *Bangkok Post*, there are between 500,000 and 1,000,000 prostitutes in Thailand, a significant number of whom are 'eldest daughters who, according to tradition, are expected to sacrifice for the families' common welfare in time of need.' In many villages, monks are drawn into the procurement process. 'Procurers will come to the temples as hosts of the forest robe offering ceremony. The monks will recruit young girls to serve food and drinks during the event as part of the village's hospitality. The temple has become the ground to select girls for the next batch.' Moreover, monks often say that a woman becomes a prostitute because of bad deeds in past lives and that 'sins can be diluted by making merits by giving money to the temples,' with the result that, 'It is common to find temples in the home villages of prostitutes beautifully decorated from these girls' donations.'[269] Thailand is of course a Buddhist country, its monks are Buddhist monks, and the 500,000 to 1,000,000 prostitutes are Buddhist prostitutes. The tradition that eldest daughters become prostitutes in time of need, that monks take part in the procurement process, and that prostitutes dilute their sins by 'making merits' by giving money to the temples, are therefore *Buddhist* traditions and form part of Thai Buddhism. The FWBO would maintain, however, that they are traditions with a small T, not Tradition with a capital T, and that being in fact cultural accretions they are quite peripheral to the fundamental principles of Buddhism. In terms of my earlier analysis, a Buddhist essence is present in them only to a very limited degree, if at all (see above, p. 400). Ajahn Chah, I imagine, would be of a similar opinion, as would Ajahn Sumedho and the English Sangha. He would no doubt take the view that the traditions in question were, in his own terms, impure elements or part of what in Buddhism needs to be purified. What view Mellor would take I do not know. For him religions have only a social and cultural existence, and inasmuch as he does not distinguish between horizontally transpersonal and vertically transpersonal social forms there are, for him, no such things as cultural accretions or impure elements and there is nothing, therefore, that needs to be shorn away. Perhaps he would take the view that the prostitutes of Thailand should simply carry on 'making merits'. After all, to reject tradition would be individualistic.

Be that as it may, Mellor not only perceives that 'What the FWBO understands as "Tradition" is *essence*'; he also sees this as establishing a continuity with (eighteenth-century) Enlightenment discourse. That for the FWBO Tradition = essence is significant because 'it highlights how the FWBO shares in the Enlightenment's antipathy to tradition, even when it uses the word positively in its own discourse'. It highlights no such thing. Any 'antipathy' the FWBO may feel relates to such traditions as eldest daughters becoming prostitutes in time of need, monks taking part in the procurement process, and prostitutes diluting their sins by 'making merits' by giving money to the temples, and has a basis very different from the more individualistic basis of the Enlightenment's antipathy to tradition, the basis of the FWBO's antipathy being simply the obverse of its sympathy with and concern for the true individual or individual-in-relation-to-Buddhahood. As for the FWBO's positive use of the term 'tradition' in its own discourse, this is not inconsistent with its antipathy to tradition, as Mellor seems to think, since the tradition to which the FWBO is antipathetic is tradition with a small T, whereas the term it uses positively in its discourse is Tradition with a capital T. It is therefore not clear that 'To use Shils's terms ... the FWBO would place itself on the "left" of the line first drawn in the Enlightenment which runs from "left" to "right",' as Mellor goes on to assert. Far from this being clear, it should be evident from my previous explanations that the FWBO would no more place itself on the left of such a line than would the English Sangha. Indeed, it would not place itself in any relation to it at all, its preoccupations being of an entirely different order. Hence there can be no question of a reason for its so placing itself, and therefore no question of that reason being that 'they are not interested in the operation of traditions which they regard as "reactionary"'. Quite apart from the fact that the only traditions the FWBO regards as reactionary (a term it does not actually use) are traditions with a small T, it is certainly interested in the 'operation' of such (reactionary) traditions, if only because these are inimical to the development of (true) individuality and their influence has to be counteracted.

From the charismatic model of authority Mellor passes to the meaning of charisma in recent history. But before we follow him there I want to backtrack a little and (a) look at the notion of personal authority and (b) correct what may appear to be an inconsistency on my part with regard to the English Sangha.

a. According to Mellor, the FWBO is more akin to a model of charismatic authority because Sangharakshita is understood to have the personal authority to be able to distinguish between what is, and what is not, essential Buddhism. But what is this 'personal authority'? In what does it consist? Whence is it derived? I would say (and I think I have a voice in the matter) that it is not a question of first having the personal (i.e. charismatic) authority and then, because one has that authority, being somehow able to distinguish between what is, and what is not, essential Buddhism. Mellor puts the cart before the horse. It is really the other way round. First one becomes able, by virtue of study and meditation, to distinguish between what is essential Buddhism, and what is not, and then one is understood as having personal authority because, appealing to their reason and experience, one enables people to see the difference for themselves. The Buddha himself conforms to this 'charismatic' model of authority, as do all the great spiritual masters who were founders of schools. There is no question of their authority having its source in ecclesiastical position or political power, or in the supernatural in the Judaeo-Christian sense. There is not even any question of its having its source in tradition, in that tradition does not exist in the abstract, as it were, but only as embodied in individuals, so that even 'traditional' authority is *spiritually* efficacious only to the extent that it is mediated by 'charismatic' individuals.

b. I have shown that whatever Mellor says about the English Sangha and the FWBO, regarding their being authority models and regarding the matter of 'essence', can quite easily be transposed. I have also shown that *in principle* there is no difference between my rejection of cultural accretions to Buddhism and Ajahn Chah's purging tradition of impure elements. In the passage Mellor quotes from my interview with him, however, I describe the English Sangha as tending to see tradition as those observances, customs, and practices which, though they have become traditional in Buddhist countries, are quite peripheral in relation to the fundamental principles of Buddhism. The inconsistency is due to the fact that in order to show how Ajahn Chah and I, applying our respective criteria to particular Buddhist customs and beliefs, could come to similar conclusions about them, I deliberately chose an extreme example of such customs and beliefs, that of the Thai Buddhist prostitutes. The example had to be an extreme one so that there could be no doubt that Ajahn Chah and I *would* come to similar conclusions about it and no doubt, therefore, that we were *in principle* agreed that it was possible to reject cultural accretions, as I would say, or to purge impure elements, as he would say, even though these had become traditional in Buddhist countries – a possibility that for Mellor does not exist. That Ajahn Chah and I are agreed in principle does not necessarily mean that we always agree in practice, and indeed such is certainly not the case. Much that for me belongs to tradition with a small T for him is part of Tradition with a capital T, and probably this is the case to an even greater extent where the English Sangha is concerned. As Mellor observes in connection with the question of ritual,

> For the English Sangha, the Thai forest tradition is an absolute standard by which the tradition in England must be judged, so that discipline, hierarchy, doctrine and ritual observance are followed as strictly as possible in the west,

and it is for this reason that in the passage from my interview I describe the English Sangha as tending, at present, to see tradition in terms of observances, customs, and practices which, though peripheral to the fundamental principles of Buddhism, have become traditional in Buddhist countries. But even the English Sangha would, I am sure, agree in principle that it was possible to distinguish between Tradition with a capital T and tradition with a small T. If pressed, I suspect they would admit that the Thai forest tradition itself was not entirely free from cultural accretions, though it was not yet feasible to discard them.

That Ajahn Chah and I, while being agreed in principle, should differ considerably in practice, is hardly surprising. Differences with regard to tradition with a small T are to be found not only between different schools of Buddhism but also within the individual schools themselves. As I pointed out in my interview with Mellor, in the words represented in his quotation by a row of dots, some Theravāda monks consider it important to cover both shoulders with the upper robe when going for alms while others do not. The latter adhere to their own traditions (with a small T), regarding *them* as being of importance. I did not believe, I added, that it was important to maintain differences of this sort in the West, even if it was possible to decide which traditions with a small T one was going to perpetuate. Since then I have heard that there is a difference of opinion within the English Sangha with regard to the 'white cloth'. This is a piece of fabric on which the Theravāda monks of Thailand (though not those of Sri Lanka, Burma, Laos, and Cambodia) receive offerings from women, so as not to come into physical contact with them as they make their offerings. Some members of the English Sangha believe that it is important to perpetuate this tradition in the West, while others do not, though for the time being all continue to adhere to it.

x

The present section of Mellor's article is the longest, and my response to it has been long in proportion. He does not conclude it, however, without a parting shot at the FWBO's alleged antipathy to tradition. (He continues, of course, to ignore my distinction between Tradition with a capital T and tradition with a small T.) But if Mellor fires the shot, it is Sennett who loads the gun. Sennett draws attention, so Mellor tells us, to the modification of the meaning of charisma in recent history.

> He stresses that charisma in a Roman Catholic context has referred to something quite impersonal.... In contrast, the modern, secular understanding of charisma has come to refer to a forceful personality so that the public space, the trans-personal objectivity, of the Catholic doctrine has been lost.

For Mellor, Sennett's emphasis on the rational, personalistic character of this change recalls both Shils's and Ratzinger's understandings of the radical outlook of the (eighteenth-century) Enlightenment, secular charisma being, in Sennett's words,

> a rational way to think about politics in a culture ruled by belief in the immanent ... rejecting as hypothetical, mystical or 'pre-modern' belief in that which cannot be directly experienced. You can directly feel a politician's sentiments; you cannot directly feel the future consequences of his policies.

Presumably Sennett refers to the politician because he possesses 'secular charisma'. However that may be, Mellor hastens to assure us that 'Sangharakshita is not a politician so any parallel must be treated cautiously'. Having covered his back, so to speak, in this way, he proceeds to assert that the antipathy manifested in the appeal to a trans-historical essence (i.e. the FWBO's appeal), and the location of religious significance in the person (i.e. the FWBO's alleged location of it there) suggests a continuity with the sort of trend Sennett is describing. Thus a connection is established between secular charisma and the Enlightenment, and between the FWBO as represented by its founder and secular charisma, and Mellor is able to reiterate his charges that the FWBO is personalistic, liberationist, 'clearly modernistic' in its 'characterization of history', and individualistic. To crown all, the FWBO envisages tradition as 'a reactionary brake on the historical drive to liberation'. Since I have dealt with these misunderstandings and misrepresentations already I need say nothing about them now. There is, however, one new charge, to the effect that

> When the FWBO looks at the religious and cultural traditions of the west (and often of the east), they do not see Sennett's 'civilized' tolerance of 'human frailty', but enemies of the individual.

I shall take a look at this new charge. But first a few words about charisma. For Mellor I have charismatic authority, rather than traditional authority, in that I am understood to have the personal authority to be able to distinguish between what is, and what is not, essential to Buddhism. Since he regards me as having charismatic authority, and since that authority is personal, he obviously sees me as being possessed by charisma of some kind. But of *what* kind? Certainly not of the 'impersonal' Roman Catholic kind, in the sense of the 'gift of grace' which, according to Sennett (as quoted by Mellor), enters into the priest when he utters the holy words, so that the rituals he performs have meaning no matter what the (ethical and spiritual) state of his person. The other kind of charisma is that of the 'forceful personality' as exemplified by the politician, but Mellor is aware that I am not a politician and that any parallel between the politician's capacity to influence people and mine must be treated cautiously. Thus although he sees me as being possessed of charisma he is unable to say what kind of charisma I possess. This is not surprising. As I point out in connection with the charismatic model of authority (see above, p. 473), it is not a question of my having charismatic authority and then, because I have charismatic authority, being somehow able to distinguish between what is, and what is not, Buddhism. All I have is the ability to distinguish between what is, and what is not, Buddhism. Thus the fact that I have 'charismatic authority' does not mean that I have charisma. The truth of the matter is that I have never regarded myself as possessing charisma (in the popular sense), and have always been suspicious of it in others. Adapting the French poet's well known line, I once told a seminar, 'Take charisma and wring its neck.'[270] Charisma is to person what rhetoric is to speech, which is why I sometimes refer to charisma as 'the rhetoric of the person'. Rhetoric is the art of inducing people to accept what you say because they like the way you say it. Similarly, charisma is the trick of getting people to respond positively to what you stand for, or what you represent, simply because they respond positively to you, or what they think is you. Charisma thus tends to obliterate the vital distinction between reliance on a person (*pudgala-pratiśaraṇa*), as Buddhism terms it, and reliance on truth or reality (*dharma-pratiśaraṇa*),[271] and it is for this reason that communication of the Dharma by means of charisma is not encouraged in the FWBO. The only kind of 'charisma' that is encouraged is that of enabling people to understand and practise the Dharma by appealing to their reason and experience.

The notion of civilized tolerance of human frailty comes from Sennett's emphasis on the impersonality of the Roman Catholic doctrine of charisma, according to which the 'gift of grace' entered into the priest, when he uttered the holy words, so that the rituals he performed had meaning no matter what the state of his person. 'The doctrine of charisma was eminently civilized,' continues Sennett (as quoted by Mellor), 'it was tolerant of human frailty at the same time it proclaimed the supremacy of religious truth.' How Mellor can say, 'When the FWBO looks at the religious and cultural traditions of the west (and often of the east), they do not see Sennett's "civilized" tolerance of "human frailty", but enemies of the individual' is far from clear. The frailty of which the Roman Catholic doctrine of charisma is tolerant, in the passage quoted, is the frailty of the priest, whose person was so likely to be in a state of sin that, as the Church was quick to realize, unless the rituals he performed were meaningful (i.e. efficacious, in the sense of being channels of divine grace) independently of the state of his person there could be no meaningful rituals. What Subhuti attacks as enemies of the individual, in the passage of *Buddhism for Today* to which Mellor's note refers us, are the nuclear family, Christianity, and pseudo-liberalism.[272] Whether these really exhibit the same kind of 'frailty' as the priest and therefore whether 'tolerance' of that frailty is really a 'civilized' tolerance of *human* frailty is doubtful. Tolerance of human frailty is a very different thing from pandering to human weakness, and we pander to that weakness when we fail to attack religious and cultural traditions that are enemies of the individual in that they hinder the development of the (true) individual or individual-in-relation-to-Buddhahood. Such 'tolerance' is not tolerance but betrayal. True tolerance of human weakness is an expression of compassion, and I hope the FWBO hearkens to the voice of compassion. In what Sennett and Mellor have to say about the Roman Catholic doctrine of charisma, and about civilized tolerance of human frailty, I do not hear the voice of compassion. Rather do I hear the insidious accents of Dostoyevsky's Grand Inquisitor.[273]

5
CULTURE AND BUDDHISM

Mellor does not define culture, any more than he defines Protestantism, or modernism, or tradition, or any of the other key terms in his discourse (though he does list some of the major characteristics of *liberal* Protestantism), and it is therefore difficult to know the sort of idea of culture he has at the back of his mind when he considers the FWBO's and the English Sangha's particular understandings of the relationship between religion and culture. At the back of my own mind, as I protest some of Mellor's assertions about the FWBO and affirm its and my own attitudes, will be an idea of culture as discussed by Arnold, Eliot, and Steiner, as well as an awareness of the word's 'complexity of idea and reference', in Raymond Williams's phrase.[274] Not that I intend bringing that classic discussion of theirs, or any part of it, to bear on the questions ventilated by Mellor in this section of his article. Though I have long wanted to write systematically on the relationship between Buddhism and culture, a topic that has preoccupied me for almost as long as I have been a Buddhist, this is not the place for any move in that direction, the more especially since this 'response' of mine is already much longer than originally planned. Instead, I shall confine myself to commenting on Mellor's misunderstandings and misrepresentations of the FWBO's (and my own) position with regard to such issues as the separateness of Buddhism and culture, the idea of 'born Buddhists', and 'exoticism', without entering into issues of a more general nature, and without going over ground that has not been gone over already in connection with other issues.

I

'For both the FWBO and the English Sangha culture and religion are quite separate, although the ways in which this view is expressed vary considerably.' Having given us this information, which may well be true, Mellor proceeds, with the help of one of his sociologist mentors, to the most flagrant of his many misrepresentations of the FWBO. The mentor in question is Neusner, who argues, 'as noted earlier', that the Protestant location of religious significance in the individual makes religion a 'constituent of conscience' rather than a 'component of culture'. According to Mellor, 'The FWBO displays this understanding of religion and culture,' from which it follows that for the FWBO, 'one can be a Buddhist regardless of culture, adherence to traditional Buddhist disciplines and rituals, or even knowledge of Buddhist doctrine.' The first time I read this extraordinary statement it took my breath away. If from the FWBO's understanding of religion and culture it follows that one can be a Buddhist regardless of culture, adherence to traditional Buddhist disciplines and rituals, or even knowledge of Buddhist doctrine, then why is it that the FWBO's 450 Order members and 1,000 Mitras are found observing the precepts, meditating, performing pujas, studying Buddhist texts, both canonical and non-canonical, practising right or perfect livelihood, and celebrating Buddhist festivals? Why is it that I have been teaching meditation, leading pujas, and expounding Buddhist doctrine in the West for the last twenty-five years? Why is it that I am now concerning myself with misunderstandings and misrepresentations of the FWBO and, indeed, of the Dharma itself?

Mellor's present misrepresentation is based on his failure to understand the FWBO's (fully traditional) teaching on Going for Refuge. 'Sangharakshita rejects the idea of "born Buddhists", people who are "Buddhist" by virtue of being born into a Buddhist culture.' This is true, except that I would say, 'merely by virtue of being born into a Buddhist culture', and should be understood as saying this when we come to consider the idea of 'born Buddhists' later on. '[For Sangharakshita] becoming a Buddhist is a faith-decision, a "conversion", a personal decision to "go for refuge".' I have indeed spoken of becoming a Buddhist as a conversion, and once gave a series of four lectures on 'The Meaning of Conversion in Buddhism', but I have never spoken of becoming a Buddhist as a faith-decision.[275] Indeed, the term is quite new to me, and in applying it, without explanation, to the act of Going for Refuge, Mellor not only again violates an elementary rule of methodology but also compounds his failure to understand the FWBO's teaching on Going for Refuge by the introduction of an element of ambiguity. Is a faith-decision a decision *about* faith, in the sense of its being a decision as to the acceptance of a particular form of religious belief, or is it a decision that is the *result* of faith, in the sense of its being a decision made in consequence of adherence to a particular form of religious belief? Whichever it may be, Mellor evidently believes that 'a personal decision to "go for refuge",' on the one hand, and culture, adherence to traditional Buddhist disciplines, and knowledge of Buddhist doctrine, on the other, are incompatible, or at least distinct and separable. This implies a very superficial understanding of Going for Refuge. As explained in *The History of My Going for Refuge*, to which Mellor refers us at this point, but which he appears not to have actually read, there are four levels of Going for Refuge, broadly speaking: provisional, effective, real, and absolute. Provisional Going for Refuge (which includes cultural and ethnic, or merely formal, Going for Refuge) is that which is tentative and partial. In the FWBO this level is represented by the Mitra. Effective Going for Refuge is that which involves the individual's whole conscious being, and in which the Three Jewels are placed at the centre of the mandala of one's personal existence. This level is represented by the Order member, the 'effectiveness' of whose Going for Refuge receives formal (though not merely formal) recognition at the time of his or her ordination. Real Going for Refuge is that which takes place when one develops insight and wisdom, thereby entering upon the transcendental Path. This level is synonymous with Stream Entry and the opening of the Dharma Eye. Absolute Going for Refuge is that of the Buddha, who is his own refuge.[276] Far from Going for Refuge being incompatible with, or at least distinct and separable from, culture, adherence to traditional Buddhist disciplines, and knowledge of Buddhist doctrine, as Mellor believes, the latter are for the FWBO the very means by which Order members seek to transform their effective but still mundane Going for Refuge into real or transcendental Going for Refuge. Thus to assert that according to the FWBO 'one can be a Buddhist regardless of culture, adherence to traditional Buddhist disciplines and rituals, or even knowledge of Buddhist doctrine' is a misrepresentation of the most glaring kind.

Mellor is able to misrepresent the FWBO in this way, not just by ignoring facts, but also by means of the sleight of hand by which he links 'culture' with 'adherence to traditional Buddhist disciplines' and 'knowledge of Buddhist doctrine'. Since for the FWBO culture and religion are, according to Mellor, quite separate, it follows that for the FWBO adherence to traditional Buddhist disciplines and rituals and knowledge of Buddhist doctrine, on the one hand, and religion (i.e. religion as a 'constituent of conscience'), on the other, are quite separate too. For the FWBO, therefore, it is possible to be a Buddhist regardless of culture, adherence to traditional Buddhist disciplines and rituals, or even knowledge of Buddhist doctrine. Moreover, Sangharakshita's rejection of the idea of 'born Buddhists' means that 'becoming a Buddhist is a faith-decision, a "conversion", a personal decision to "go for refuge",' and a faith-decision, Mellor evidently thinks, is something that takes place in an ethical and intellectual vacuum. Nor is this all. Since for the FWBO culture and religion are 'quite separate', it also follows that for the FWBO culture is of very little significance and value. 'Even when the FWBO refers to culture in a positive sense,' Mellor charges, 'e.g. the creation of a new western Buddhist culture, it understands it as merely a beneficial offshoot of "spiritually-aware" individuals which, in turn, helps individuals to "grow".'

Though we are referred here to *Buddhism for Today*, p. 129, Mellor in fact is not even paraphrasing Subhuti who, despite the quotation marks, makes no mention of 'spiritually-aware' individuals, either on the page in question or in the rest of the chapter.[277] But we have grown accustomed to Mellor's rather cavalier treatment of his sources, and there is no need for me to dwell on the matter. Let us hear the rest of his charge against the FWBO's understanding of culture.

> Any possible autonomy of culture is severely restricted by the FWBO's hostility to the idea of the 'group': all collective, supra-individual structures are the objects of suspicion precisely because religious significance is located so exclusively within the individual. Even the idea of the Sangha is firmly differentiated from anything suggestive of a 'group'.

Here we are again referred to *Buddhism for Today*, this time to p. 131, and this time with some justification, and Mellor concludes his present charge against the FWBO by returning to a favourite theme. 'The FWBO's attitude to the relationship between religion and culture,' he declares, 'underlines its individualistic orientation.'

I have already shown that there is a difference between (true) individuality and individualism, and that the FWBO's emphasis on the development of the true individual, or individual-in-relation-to-Buddhahood, is *not* evidence of an individualistic orientation on its part. I have also shown that there is a difference between *horizontally* transpersonal social forms (or 'collective, supra-individual structures,' as Mellor now decides to call them) and *vertically* transpersonal forms, and a difference, therefore, between rejection of the one and rejection of the other. Finally (so far as Mellor's charge against the FWBO's understanding of culture is concerned), I have shown that for the FWBO religious significance is located not exclusively within the individual but within the (true) individual *and* the spiritual community, the individual himself being both subject and object, soul and citizen. These more basic misunderstandings and misrepresentations having been dealt with, it only remains for me to take Mellor up on his references to (a) culture as 'merely a beneficial offshoot', (b) the creation of a new western Buddhist culture, (c) the autonomy of culture, and (d) the idea of the sangha.

a. It is interesting that

> Even when the FWBO refers to culture in a positive sense ... it understands it as merely a beneficial offshoot of 'spiritually-aware' individuals which, in turn, helps individuals to 'grow'.

Merely? Ignoring the suggestion that for the FWBO 'culture' is usually a grubby word, what *more* (it might be asked) could be said of a phenomenon that for the FWBO is 'a beneficial offshoot' (in Mellor's minimizing phrase) than that, as the 'collective' creation of a community of spiritually-aware individuals, it performs the invaluable function of supporting the efforts of the individual-to-be, as Subhuti calls him, to develop into a true individual and eventually enter upon the transcendental Path? Short of the transcendental Path itself, one could hardly imagine anything greater or more glorious than such a culture. Yet for Mellor it is 'merely' a beneficial offshoot – presumably because it only 'helps individuals to "grow",' a process that for him has decidedly individualistic connotations. Individuals ought to be content just to follow tradition.

b. I am not being pedantic, I hope, in pointing out that when Mellor speaks of the FWBO as referring to 'the creation of a new western Buddhist culture' what he means to say is 'a new, western Buddhist culture'. There is no *old* western Buddhist culture for a new western Buddhist culture to supersede. At present western Buddhism has no culture of its own, though the FWBO has taken a few very tentative steps in this direction, as have other western Buddhist groups, particularly in the United States. Western Buddhism exists within a context of non-Buddhist culture. In this non-Buddhist and, in effect, often anti-Buddhist culture, it is possible to distinguish three strands or three components: folk culture, high culture, and mass culture. A distinctively western Buddhist culture, when it emerges, will probably have three main sources. It will be the product of (i) the interaction between western Buddhists and the traditional eastern Buddhist cultures, especially as represented by their literature and fine arts, (ii) the interaction between western Buddhists and elements of western folk and high culture (though not, I think, mass culture, now rapidly becoming world-wide), and (iii) the inspiration western Buddhists derive from their personal experience of the Dharma, especially their experience of meditation. Once this western Buddhist culture has come into existence, a process that will take centuries rather than decades, it will function as a support for the individual Buddhist's practice of the Dharma, instead of functioning, as so much of our culture does today, as an obstacle and a hindrance. Until then we have no alternative but to create, within western culture, pockets of more or less (western) Buddhist culture within which the individual Buddhist may find, to some extent at least, that support for his practice of the Dharma which is so lacking in the outside world. It is with such an end in view that the FWBO has established, and continues to expand, that network of centres, communities, and team-based right livelihood businesses which constitute the nucleus of what it calls the New Society or, in more traditional terms, the Kingdom of the Dharma.

c. 'Any possible autonomy of culture is severely restricted by the FWBO's hostility to the idea of the "group",' says Mellor, 'all collective, supra-individual structures [being] the objects of suspicion precisely because religious significance is located so exclusively within the individual.' We know that for the FWBO religious significance is *not* located exclusively within the individual, and we know that not all collective, supra-individual structures or transpersonal social forms are *vertically* transpersonal; but what is this 'autonomy of culture' which is said to be severely restricted by the FWBO's hostility to the idea of the 'group'? Mellor does not explain. Had one encountered the phrase in certain other contexts one would have assumed it referred to the idea that culture should be independent of religion, or even to the doctrine of 'art for art's sake', but in the present context such an assumption must be ruled out. Mellor would appear to believe that culture is identical with religion, just as society is identical with culture, the whole being, of course, 'transpersonal'. The only meaning I am therefore able to extract from his assertion that 'any possible autonomy of culture is severely restricted by the FWBO's hostility to the "group",' is to the effect that the FWBO is wrong in thinking that spiritually-aware individuals should exercise an influence on the group. For Mellor the individual, whether spiritually-aware or not, has no autonomy. Autonomy is the prerogative of the group, as represented by religion, or culture, or society, or tradition. Thus the individual is swallowed up in Leviathan. All else is individualism.

d. Just as the FWBO's attitude towards the group really is one of 'hostility' (though it is not a hostility that extends to the positive group), so its idea of the sangha really is 'firmly differentiated' from anything suggestive of a group. Speaking of the latter, however, Mellor says, 'Even the idea of the sangha' is differentiated in this way. *Even*? Again the adverb is significant, suggesting as it does, in this case, that for Mellor the sangha or spiritual community, the transcendental counterpart of which is the Āryasaṅgha, is in fact no more than the group par excellence. No wonder, then, that he should see the FWBO's attitude to the relationship between religion and culture as underlining its 'individualistic orientation'. So extreme is the FWBO's individualism, it would appear, that it is prepared to differentiate from anything suggestive of a 'group' even the idea of something as undeniably group-like in character as the sangha.

II

For Mellor it must be a relief to be able to turn from the FWBO's attitude to the relationship between religion and culture, underlined as this is by its 'individualistic orientation', to the English Sangha's 'more sophisticated' understanding of that relationship. 'Unlike Sangharakshita', he tells us, 'Ajahn Sumedho attributes some significance to traditionally Buddhist cultures, regardless of individual faith-decisions.' Whether Ajahn Sumedho himself, in the interview from which Mellor proceeds to quote, actually speaks of 'faith-decisions' is not clear (I am inclined to think he does not), but perhaps this is irrelevant, except as possibly furnishing us with yet another example of Mellor's propensity to violate the elementary rules of methodology. The Ajahn begins by making the point that Asian teachers have been raised in a society that thinks and lives Buddhism – a point with which it is possible to agree, provided one does not take too close a look at what 'thinks and lives Buddhism' actually means. 'Whether they are devout or not does not make any difference. Nevertheless, it affects their whole outlook on themselves and the world.' Whether 'they' refers to the society that thinks and lives Buddhism or to the Asian teachers who have been raised in the society is not clear. However, it is evident that Ajahn Sumedho does attribute 'some significance' to traditionally Buddhist cultures, and he concludes (at least so far as Mellor's quotation is concerned) by addressing his interviewer directly, and saying, 'Whereas you [unlike them] come from a culture which is materialistic, and where the values – based on greed and competition, and trust and faith in conceptual learning – have affected our mind.'

Mellor comments that as Ajahn Sumedho pictures things, 'the Buddhist has the support of culture in the east, but has to fight against it in the west'. This is broadly true, and I have no wish to underestimate the importance of the support a Buddhist culture is capable of giving to an individual's practice of the Dharma (it is because it does *not* underestimate the importance of such support that the FWBO seeks to create the nucleus of a New Society, or Kingdom of the Dharma). But Mellor's further comments on Ajahn Sumedho's 'more sophisticated' understanding of the relationship between religion and culture only serve to highlight the really dreadful confusion that lies at the heart of that understanding.

> In the east one can be a 'Buddhist' whether one is devout or not, whereas in the west there is, perhaps, more of a need to be devout, since being a Buddhist is not a natural option.

According to Mellor,

> This brings Ajahn Sumedho close to Sangharakshita's recognition of the significance of the faith-decision for the Buddhist. Such a faith-decision may be a significant factor in an English context because of the persistence of Protestant orientations, even when it is not formalized into a doctrinal position as in the case of the FWBO.

Whether Ajahn Sumedho has really been brought closer to Sangharakshita's 'recognition of the significance of the faith-decision for the Buddhist' it is difficult to say, the categories in which Mellor's comment is formulated probably being as foreign to the Ajahn as they are to me. For the same reason it is difficult to say whether such a faith-decision may be a significant factor in an English context and difficult, therefore, to say whether this is because of the persistence of Protestant orientations. In any case, I have shown that the FWBO, at least, is far from demonstrating what Mellor elsewhere calls 'continuities with Protestant perspectives' and therefore need not concern myself further with this particular misrepresentation. Let me proceed directly to the dreadful confusion, as I have termed it, that lies at the heart of Ajahn Sumedho's supposedly 'more sophisticated' understanding of the relationship between religion and culture. In so doing I shall, of course, be dealing with that confusion as represented by the quotation from Ajahn Sumedho's interview as utilized by Mellor for the purpose of comparing the English Sangha with the FWBO.

The confusion really is a dreadful one. Ajahn Sumedho appears to distinguish between 'thinking and living Buddhism', on the one hand, and 'being devout', on the other. But what does 'being devout' mean, especially as distinguished from 'thinking and living Buddhism'? In view of Mellor's comment that 'in the east one can be a "Buddhist" whether one is devout or not, whereas in the west there is, perhaps, more of a need to be devout' (a comment made, presumably, in the light of the interview as a whole), it would seem 'being devout' means actually practising Buddhism. Thus when Ajahn Sumedho distinguishes between 'thinking and living Buddhism' and 'being devout' he is in fact distinguishing between not practising Buddhism and practising it, which means that he identifies 'thinking and living Buddhism' with not practising Buddhism. No doubt this is why he goes on to say, 'Whether they [i.e. either the Asian teachers or the society in which they have been raised] are devout or not does not make any difference.' In other words, it does not make any difference whether one is devout or whether one thinks and lives Buddhism, that is, whether one practises Buddhism or does not practise it. 'Nevertheless,' the Ajahn adds, 'it affects their whole outlook on themselves and the world.' What affects it? Is it the fact that 'they' have been raised in a society that thinks and lives Buddhism (i.e. does not actually practise it), or is it the fact that it does not make any difference whether they are devout or not (i.e. practise Buddhism or do not practise it)? We are not told. Mellor's 'more sophisticated understanding' would appear to be indistinguishable from nonsense.

In order to extricate ourselves from the confusion we must go back to the statement, 'Whether they [i.e. either the Asian teachers or the society which they have been raised] are devout or not does not make any difference.' Does not make any difference to what? Obviously Ajahn Sumedho does not believe it makes no difference, ethically or spiritually, whether one practises Buddhism or not, since otherwise he would not have felt the need to 'be devout' and become a monk. What being or not being devout makes no difference to is the fact that, having been born in a Buddhist country, one is subject to the influence of Buddhist culture whether one practises Buddhism or does not practise it. As Mellor comments, 'in the east one can be a "Buddhist" whether one is devout or not,' the quotation marks indicating that it is Buddhist in the cultural sense that is meant. Unfortunately, Ajahn Sumedho speaks of a Buddhist society, i.e. a society with a traditionally Buddhist culture, and by implication the members of that society, as 'thinking and living Buddhism', not as being subject, simply, to the influence of traditional Buddhist culture. Though he distinguishes between 'thinking and living Buddhism' and 'being devout', and though 'being devout' means actually practising Buddhism, so that 'thinking and living Buddhism' means *not* practising it, as we have seen, it cannot be denied that the actual phrase 'thinking and living Buddhism' definitely does have a positive connotation suggestive of the practice of Buddhism rather than the contrary. Indeed, I suspect that the majority of people, confronted by the phrases 'thinking and living Buddhism' and 'being devout' (i.e. devoutly Buddhist) would find the former more appealing and more suggestive of the practice of Buddhism than the latter, 'being devout' being associated, in the popular mind, with conventional piety.

Ajahn Sumedho's confusion seems to stem from the fact that he is not sufficiently clear that there is no such thing as a 'born Buddhist', i.e. one who is a Buddhist, without quotation marks, simply by virtue of his having been born in a 'Buddhist' country. He is not sufficiently clear that one is a Buddhist not by birth but only by deeds, just as, in the Buddha's own terminology, one is a Brahmin not by birth but only by deeds.[278] 'Born Buddhist' is a contradiction in terms, and failure to realize this means falling into the 'Buddhist' equivalent of orthodox Brahmanism. Being brought up in a Buddhist society, i.e. in a society with a traditional Buddhist culture, is in many ways an inestimable blessing, but one brought up in such a society is himself a Buddhist only if he personally takes advantage of the opportunities for spiritual development that a traditional Buddhist culture provides. Had Ajahn Sumedho been clearer about this he probably would have said, in his interview, something like: 'One has to recognize that Asian teachers have been raised in a society with a traditionally Buddhist culture. Whether they actually practise the Dharma or not does not make any difference to this fact. Nevertheless, that they were raised in such a society affects their whole outlook on themselves and the world.' Had he said this there would be no confusion. But he said what he did say and having said it, and probably half-realized that he had got himself into a muddle, he follows it up with an attack on western culture, addressing his interviewer directly and saying, 'Whereas you [unlike those brought up in a Buddhist society] come from a culture which is materialistic, and where the values – based on greed and competition, and trust and faith in conceptual learning – have affected our mind.'

It is, of course, true that much of modern western culture is materialistic, and that many of its values are based on greed and competition, and trust and faith in conceptual learning, but we must not draw too sharp a contrast between materialistic West and idealistic, 'spiritual' East. The culture of a Buddhist country like Thailand, which has between 500,000 and 1,000,000 prostitutes, cannot be described as idealistic without some qualification. In the course of my lengthy sojourn in the Indian subcontinent I came to the conclusion that, although the spiritual traditions of the East are undoubtedly alive in a way that those of the West are not (Christianity having in any case killed off the non-Christian traditions and driven them underground), Asians are, in most cases, no less materialistic – no less greedy and competitive – than Europeans and Americans. The difference is that in the West people are enabled to fulfil their material ambitions by modern technology, whereas in the East they seek, traditionally, to fulfil them by occult or magical means. Since modern technology has increasingly shown itself to be more effective in this respect than rituals and spells, it is rapidly superseding these latter throughout the East – a fact that partly explains why practically the entire eastern world has either fallen prey to communism or is succumbing to the influence of capitalism.

III

Having commented on Ajahn Sumedho's more sophisticated understanding of the relationship between religion and culture, and having opined that a faith-decision may be a significant factor in an English context because of the persistence of Protestant orientations, even when it is not formalized into a doctrinal position as in the case of the FWBO, Mellor again represents the Ajahn as speaking of faith-decisions. 'In fact,' he says, 'the English Sangha is critical of the way Buddhist ex-Christians adopt a hostile attitude towards Christianity: one exclusivist faith-decision has been replaced by another one. Ajahn Sumedho rejects such attitudes, asserting that Buddhism is not about faith-decisions but about being able to "find out and know directly".' Whether members of the FWBO are among the Buddhist ex-Christians whom the English Sangha has in mind we need not enquire. Neither need we enquire whether a Buddhist ex-Christian's adoption of a hostile attitude towards Christianity can really be described as the replacement of one exclusivist faith-decision by another, quite apart from the methodological impropriety such an explanation involves. What concerns me is the fact that Mellor, having already represented me as seeing 'becoming a Buddhist' as a faith-decision and as equating this not only with conversion but also with 'a personal decision to "go for refuge"' (see above, p. 481), now cites Ajahn Sumedho as asserting that Buddhism is not about faith-decisions but about being able to 'find out and know directly'. Once again, it is not clear whether Ajahn Sumedho himself actually speaks of 'faith-decisions', but whether he uses the term or not Mellor evidently means to suggest that for me, as one for whom 'a personal decision to "go for refuge"' is a faith-decision, Going for Refuge is *not* about 'being able to "find out and know directly".'

Yet again we are confronted by a misrepresentation, and again that misrepresentation is based on Mellor's failure to understand the FWBO's (fully traditional) teaching on Going for Refuge. Broadly speaking, there are four levels of Going for Refuge (see above, p. 481), the third of which, real Going for Refuge, takes place when one develops insight and wisdom, thereby entering upon the transcendental Path. Ajahn Sumedho's 'being able to "find out and know directly"' is of the same order as this insight and wisdom, the development of which constitutes real Going for Refuge – assuming that his 'finding out and knowing directly' corresponds to *bhāvanā-mayī-prajñā* or wisdom based on meditation in the sense of the experience of the *dhyānas*, not to *cinta-mayī-prajñā* or wisdom based on reflection or to *śruta-mayī-prajñā* or wisdom based on learning.[279] Thus Going for Refuge and 'finding out and knowing directly' are not mutually exclusive, as Mellor suggests, and he is able to suggest that they are only because he has categorized Going for Refuge as a faith-decision. Since it is not clear whether Ajahn Sumedho himself actually speaks of 'faith-decisions' and not clear, therefore, whether he categorizes Going for Refuge as a faith-decision, it is also not clear whether, in asserting that Buddhism is about being able to 'find out and know directly', he too is suggesting that Going for Refuge and 'finding out and knowing directly' are mutually exclusive. In any case, the fact that for him Buddhism is about being able to find out and know directly, while for the FWBO (as for the whole Buddhist tradition) real Going for Refuge takes place when one develops insight and wisdom, means that the English Sangha and the FWBO differ less than Mellor thinks.

IV

As I have tried to show, Mellor misunderstands and misrepresents the FWBO on a number of issues. But it is not only the FWBO that he misrepresents. He misrepresents the English Sangha. He misrepresents Buddhism. Commenting on Ajahn Sumedho's assertion that Buddhism is 'about being able to find out and know directly', he says, 'This emphasis on knowing directly is indicative of what Sennett terms "a culture ruled by belief in the immediate". In other words, the rejection of one aspect of western culture (the exclusivism of faith-decisions) is balanced by the endorsement of another aspect – the contemporary stress on immediate experience rather than objective belief-systems or knowledges.' Since being able to find out and know directly is of the same order as insight and wisdom, the development of which constitutes real Going for Refuge, Mellor in effect criticizes not only the English Sangha but the FWBO, not to speak of Buddhism itself, and it is therefore not possible for me to ignore the criticism. An 'emphasis on knowing directly', whether that of Ajahn Sumedho or any other Buddhist, is *not* indicative of 'a culture ruled by belief in the immediate' (I overlook the fact that Mellor takes the phrase from Sennett's discussion of the rationality of secular charisma as a way to think about politics) and therefore does *not* amount to an endorsement of the contemporary stress on immediate experience, restricted as such experience is to the physical senses and the lower mind. Like insight and wisdom, direct knowledge is not mundane but transcendental in character, and far from being one-sidedly subjective in the contemporary manner, as Mellor believes, has for 'object' the various 'doors' to the Absolute (*asaṃskṛta-dhātu*) and, ultimately, the Absolute itself. Thus if an emphasis on knowing directly is indicative of anything, it is indicative of continuity with the central tradition of Buddhism, according to which the Dharma is 'to be understood individually, by the wise (*veditabba viññūhi*)'[280] and understood, moreover, by way of what the Buddha of the *Laṅkāvatāra* calls an inner realization (*pratyātma-gocara*).[281] That Mellor should equate Buddhist 'finding out and knowing directly' with the contemporary stress on immediate experience is reductionist in the extreme, and shows how far he is from understanding either the English Sangha or the FWBO or, for the matter of that, Buddhism itself.

V

From Ajahn Sumedho's endorsement of the contemporary stress on immediate experience Mellor passes to what he frankly admits is a contentious subject, albeit one to which the issue of culture and religion in relation to Buddhism is related. The subject is that of 'exoticism' (the quotation marks are his), which for him is 'the extent to which the appeal of Buddhism (or some forms of it) is in any way related to its cultural strangeness'. This is not quite the dictionary definition, but one cannot innocently use the term 'exotic' with reference to western Buddhism, so Mellor believes, 'merely to refer to something introduced from abroad'. The reason for this, according to him, is that the term has a long history of polemical usage, the perception of Buddhism as being 'exotic' being, in the early development of English Buddhism, both a factor which made it attractive to many westerners and a polemical tool in the arguments of those who wanted to develop western forms of it. To what remote period of British Buddhist history the expression 'early development' is meant to refer is not clear, but be that as it may, 'Of this latter tendency [i.e. the tendency to develop western forms of Buddhism] the FWBO is perhaps the historical fulfilment.' Nor is that all.

> In FWBO discourse the term 'exotic' is one of abuse: not only would it resent the use of the term in association with itself, it is actually a favoured term of its own which it uses to attack more (eastern) traditional forms of Buddhism.

At this point Mellor refers us to *Buddhism for Today*, p. 5. On looking up the reference, however, we find that Subhuti does not, in fact, use this term as one of abuse (members of the FWBO prefer, in any case, to avoid using abusive language) but in its primary sense of what is culturally strange. Speaking of the strictly limited appeal and significance of the successive waves of western interest in Buddhism, he says of these 'waves':

> For the most part, they have attracted the academic and the intellectual, the dilettante, and those who hunger for the exotic; few have been able to accept fully the unique challenge of establishing Buddhism as a living movement at the heart of Western culture.

If anything is being attacked here, it is *hunger* for the exotic, not the exotic itself, which in any case is never exotic per se but only in relation to its (foreign) surroundings or the (foreign) observer. I also wonder what makes Mellor so sure that 'the FWBO' (to him, apparently, a very monolithic body) would 'resent' the use of the term exotic in association with itself. It would depend who used the term. Eastern Buddhists visiting the FWBO have been known to describe it as exotic (i.e. to them culturally strange), and so far as I know this was not resented by anyone. But these are matters of detail. I have shown that Subhuti does *not* use the term exotic as one of abuse. Now let me offer a few comments of my own, both on the term 'exotic' and on the contentious subject of 'exoticism'.

As I have indicated, the primary sense of exotic is culturally strange or 'originating in a foreign country, especially one in the tropics; not native' (*Collins*). British Buddhism, whether as represented by the English Sangha or the FWBO, is exotic in this sense, Buddhism having originated in India 2,500 years ago and from there been introduced into Britain via Ceylon (Sri Lanka), China-Japan, Thailand, etc. British Christianity, too, is exotic in this sense, Christianity having originated in Israel 2,000 years ago and been introduced into Britain via Rome, Germany, Switzerland, etc. Christianity, however, has been established here for so many centuries that it does not *feel* exotic, especially since it has produced such distinctively British forms of Christianity as Anglicanism, Puritanism, Congregationalism, and Methodism; and there is little doubt that the same will be the case with Buddhism after it has been established here for a few hundred years. Meanwhile, British Buddhism is an exotic phenomenon (in the primary sense of the term) *and* is perceived to be such by the general public – a state of affairs that does not particularly trouble me. But the term also has a secondary sense; a sense which Mellor, in his haste to assert that in FWBO discourse the term 'exotic' is one of abuse, fails to notice. Exotic also means 'having a strange or bizarre allure, beauty, or quality' (*Collins*). This kind of allure, beauty, or quality is very much 'in the eye of the beholder', so that unlike the primary sense of the term, which has reference to an objective relation (to the foreign environment or foreign observer), this secondary sense of exotic has reference to a subjective impression or response. Thus whereas the primary sense of the term is *descriptive*, the secondary sense is *evaluative*. There is, of course, nothing wrong in seeing that which is exotic in the primary sense of the term, i.e. culturally strange, or 'originating in a foreign country, especially one in the tropics,' as exotic, also, in the secondary sense of the term, i.e. as 'having a strange or bizarre allure, beauty, or quality'. Why we should see what is merely culturally strange as having this kind of allure, beauty, or quality is a mystery not altogether dispelled by the invocation of that overworked psychological term 'projection'; but there is no doubt that we often do see what is merely culturally strange in this way, especially when we are very young, or when our immediate surroundings are dull and uninspiring. As a boy of thirteen or fourteen, I myself felt the allure and beauty of the South Seas and the Far East as depicted in the colourful pages of Pierre Loti and Lafcadio Hearn.[282]

That some westerners should find Buddhism exotic in the secondary sense of the term is not surprising. Buddhism is, after all, an exotic religion so far as the West is concerned, i.e. a religion originating in a foreign country. Nor is it surprising that some westerners should be strongly attracted to this 'exotic Buddhism' of theirs and become involved with it in this or that way. There is nothing actually wrong in seeing Buddhism as exotic in the secondary sense of the term, and nothing actually wrong in being attracted by such 'Buddhism'. What is wrong, or at least mistaken, is thinking (if one thinks about the matter at all) that what one sees is Buddhism itself, in the sense of those ethical and spiritual principles that comprise the Dharma, and that in being attracted to such 'Buddhism' one is aspiring to practise those principles or is even actually practising them already. It is this mistaking of what is, in fact, a Buddhism that is exotic in the (subjective) secondary sense for Buddhism itself that, for me, constitutes exoticism or, in Mellor's words, 'the extent to which the appeal of Buddhism (or some forms of it) is in any way related to its cultural strangeness'.

But while I certainly do regard as wrong, or at least mistaken, the idea that one's (subjectively) exotic Buddhism is Buddhism itself, it is incorrect to speak of me, as Mellor proceeds to do, as offering 'a vision of the English Buddhist as someone who despises the understanding of Buddhism as something exotic'. One does not necessarily despise what one considers mistaken. Having asserted that 'exotic' is a favoured term of the FWBO's own which it uses to attack more (eastern) traditional forms of Buddhism, Mellor continues:

> The rejection of such forms has long been the policy of Sangharakshita. In 1965, while still head of the English Sangha (and thus prior to the creation of the FWBO), Sangharakshita offered a vision of the English Buddhist as someone who despises the understanding of Buddhism as something exotic.

He then quotes from an article on 'Buddhism in England' that I wrote for *The Buddhist*, the journal of the English Sangha Association. By what means he managed to unearth this ancient article from the dusty files of a long defunct Buddhist monthly that never printed more than a few hundred copies is something of a mystery, the more especially since he shows a knowledge of only one of my two dozen published works and seems disinclined to do any research. Strange indeed are the ways of the methodologist![283] But let me reproduce the quotation. The omissions are Mellor's.

> The English Buddhist has, most often, been attracted to Buddhism on account of the spiritual principles of which it is the embodiment.... He is much less interested in the various national cultures wherein, throughout the traditionally Buddhist cultures of the east, these principles are embedded.... English Buddhism, he hopes, far from remaining a frail transplant carefully sheltered from the chill northern blast in some secluded pseudo-oriental hothouse, will in time develop into a sturdy and vigorous growth.

I trust Mellor is not suggesting that it is wrong for the English Buddhist to be attracted to Buddhism on account of its spiritual principles, or that he ought to be more, rather than less, interested in the traditionally Buddhist cultures than in these principles. Probably he is not suggesting any such thing, if for no other reason than that for him Buddhism and Buddhist culture are synonymous terms. I also trust he is not suggesting that it is wrong for the English Buddhist to hope that English Buddhism will in time develop into a sturdy and vigorous growth, though in view of Mellor's own religious sympathies one cannot be sure of this. Since my 'vision' of the English Buddhist does not really amount to a rejection of more (eastern) traditional forms of Buddhism (it would be more correct to say that I discriminate among them) I cannot help wondering why Mellor should quote from this article of mine at all, unless it is for the sake of my reference to the 'secluded pseudo-oriental hothouse'. In any case, he goes on to comment,

> It is clear that the FWBO must regard Amaravati, the English Sangha's centre, as one such 'pseudo-oriental hothouse': its strict adherence to a traditional Buddhist form of practice is a sharp contrast to what Sangharakshita feels is both desirable and necessary to the English Buddhist. As I noted earlier,

> Sangharakshita draws a clear distinction between the traditionalist approach of the English Sangha and the FWBO's emphasis on only the 'essential principles of Buddhism'.

I draw, in fact, no such distinction. The distinction I draw, in the interview to which Mellor's note here refers us, is between Tradition with a capital T and tradition with a small T, *not* between a traditionalist and a non-traditionalist approach. To the extent that the FWBO emphasizes 'the essential principles of Buddhism', and thus Tradition with a capital T, its approach could be said to be more truly traditionalist than that of the English Sangha. As for it being clear that the FWBO 'must' regard Amaravati as a pseudo-oriental hothouse, the necessity exists only in Mellor's own mind. I am, however, inclined to think that inasmuch as the English Sangha is culturally more 'eastern' than the FWBO it is more likely to be perceived as being exotic in the secondary sense of the term and more likely, therefore, to be of interest to those who are attracted by 'exotic Buddhism'.

Thus what the English Buddhist of my 'vision' is really saying, when he expresses the hope that English Buddhism will in time develop into a sturdy and vigorous growth, and not remain a frail transplant in some secluded pseudo-oriental hothouse, is not what Mellor supposes. Far from saying that the understanding of Buddhism as something exotic is to be despised, what he is saying, in effect, is that it is not enough simply to transplant Buddhism to this country. Buddhism must also become acclimatized here, and the Buddhism that will become acclimatized here is the Buddhism that is a matter of universally valid spiritual principles, not the 'exotic Buddhism' that is largely a matter of eastern 'Buddhist' culture and which attracts those who, in Subhuti's phrase, hunger for the exotic. The latter may be transplanted but it will not really acclimatize and become a sturdy and vigorous growth because it will be dependent for its survival on those special (exotic) cultural conditions which the English Buddhist of my vision characterizes as a hothouse, a hothouse which is pseudo-oriental in the sense of being an English imitation of an eastern 'Buddhist' original and secluded in the sense of being remote from English life and thought. If Amaravati is, in fact, a secluded pseudo-oriental hothouse, as Mellor thinks the FWBO must regard it as being, then surely one of the most exotic blooms in that hothouse is the 'white cloth', i.e. the piece of fabric used by monks to receive offerings from women without coming into physical contact with them. Being, as it is, a bloom that is unlikely to survive outside its 'Thai' hothouse, it is unlikely that it will ever form part of a sturdy and vigorous English (or British) Buddhism. Future women supporters of the English Sangha *may* embroider 'white cloths' for the monks in much the same way that Victorian spinsters embroidered hassocks and carpet slippers for the local curate, but I rather doubt it. The present women supporters of the Sangha are said to react to the 'white cloth' with either tolerant amusement or feminist outrage.

Having represented the distinction I draw between Tradition with a capital T and tradition with a small T, as a distinction between a traditionalist and a non-traditionalist approach, Mellor is able to repeat some of his old charges against the FWBO:

> Like Christianity, English Buddhism in an eastern, traditional form is given the status of a historically remote precedent to the FWBO. While Subhuti notes the appeal of such forms for 'those who hunger for the exotic', he sees the validity of them as lying only in the fact that they 'helped to prepare the ground' for the FWBO.

Since I have dealt with these misunderstandings (see above, pp. 406ff. and pp. 466ff.) I shall say nothing about them in this place, but will turn straight to Mellor's dig at the FWBO for using Sanskrit names.

VI

For Mellor 'exoticism' is the extent to which the appeal of Buddhism (or some forms of it) is in any way related to its cultural strangeness. Directly after referring to the fact that Subhuti notes the appeal of the eastern, traditional forms of Buddhism for 'those who hunger for the exotic' he is therefore able to say:

> Nevertheless, if by 'exotic' we refer to a cultural foreignness then it is ironic that the FWBO is hardly free of an overt exoticism either. Sangharakshita uses the full title of Ven. Maha Sthavira Sangharakshita rather than 'Dennis Lingwood', FWBO communities have names such as 'Padmaloka', and members use Sanskrit names prefaced by 'Dharmachari' or 'Dharmacharini'

(practitioners of the *Dharma*), though there is no traditional precedent for the use of Sanskrit names in this way.

It is not ironic at all. It is not ironic because I distinguish between that which is exotic in the primary sense of the term, i.e. which simply originates in a foreign country, and that which is exotic in the secondary sense, i.e. which in addition to originating in a foreign country has a strange or bizarre allure, beauty, or quality (see above, p. 494ff). Thus the FWBO's use of foreign (Indian) names does not mean that it is 'hardly free of an overt exoticism' but only that it is exotic inasmuch as Buddhism has its origin in a foreign country. We shall return to the subject of exotic nomenclature later. Meanwhile, let me make two points. Firstly, I stopped using the title 'Maha Sthavira' some years ago, as Mellor would have realized if he had looked at the title page of my more recent publications. I stopped using it mainly because an increasing number of Buddhist (and Hindu) teachers were awarding themselves such titles as 'His Holiness' and 'His Eminence' and I wanted to dissociate myself from a trend which, to me, smacked more of worldly ambition than of spiritual achievement. Friends and disciples of long standing, especially those in India, still address me as 'Maha Sthavira', whether from force of habit or out of respect. In recent years some of my western disciples have taken to addressing me as 'Urgyen Sangharakshita', Urgyen being the name I was given by my teacher Kachu Rimpoche in 1962 on the occasion of my receiving the Padmasambhava *abhiṣeka* or 'Tantric initiation'. Secondly, it is not clear what Mellor means when he claims that there is no traditional precedent for using Sanskrit names 'in this way', i.e. in the way they are used in the FWBO. In Indian Buddhism there are innumerable traditional precedents for the use of Sanskrit names, both for dwelling places and for persons, and innumerable precedents for the use of the literal translations of Sanskrit names in Chinese, Japanese, and Tibetan Buddhism. What Mellor means is therefore a mystery.

Mystery or no mystery, however, the question of the FWBO's use of Sanskrit names continues to bother him. Referring to my interview with him, he says,

Questioned about this adoption of Sanskrit names Sangharakshita rejected any charge of inconsistency, arguing that the maintenance of Christian names was inappropriate, that taking a new name had

> an important psychological effect, and that Sanskrit would provide a unifying characteristic of the FWBO across different cultures 'in the way that Latin used to in the Catholic Church'.

Since the subject of exotic nomenclature is being dealt with later, I shall take up first the question of Sanskrit as providing a unifying characteristic of the FWBO in the way that Latin used to in the Catholic Church, this being what Mellor himself takes up first. 'This latter comparison hardly seems justified,' he sneers. 'The FWBO's development outside Britain seems less successful than that of the English Sangha which now has branches in the USA, Australia, New Zealand and Switzerland.' Once again, Mellor has got his facts wrong. So very wrong, indeed, that his assertion would be truer if names were transposed and it read: 'The English Sangha's development outside Britain seems less successful than that of the FWBO which now has branches [i.e. autonomous centres run by teams of Order members] in the USA, Australia, New Zealand, India, Holland, Finland, Sweden, Germany, and Spain.' Since at least nine languages are involved here (India supplying three), the use of Sanskrit (and Pāli) for liturgical and other purposes does indeed provide a unifying characteristic for the FWBO across different cultures, as I can testify from repeated personal experience. Mellor's sneer about my comparison with the use of Latin by the Catholic Church being unjustified is therefore itself unjustified. But there is another sneer to come.

> The FWBO makes a great deal of its connection with Ambedkar's movement of 'ex-untouchables' in India, but there is little objective evidence for FWBO strength in a movement Trevor Ling has called only 'neo-Buddhist'. In fact, although Ling refers to Sangharakshita's writings on Ambedkar, and to a series of lectures he gave at one point, not once in a fairly detailed study of Ambedkar's movement does he mention the FWBO.

This is perfectly true. Trevor Ling does not once mention the FWBO in his *Buddhist Revival in India*. But had Mellor examined the book more carefully he would have noticed that it was published in 1980, after key chapters had appeared in academic journals and elsewhere as early as 1973. The FWBO, on the other hand, was not formally inaugurated in India (as the TBMSG or Trailokya Bauddha Mahasangha Sahayak

Gana) until 1979, when the first Indian Order members were ordained. Thus Mellor's information is at least twelve years out of date. If he is really interested in obtaining 'objective evidence' for the strength of the FWBO in Ambedkar's movement, rather than in sneering at its supposed lack of strength there, then I suggest he does a little research among the back issues of *Golden Drum* and the Karuna Trust *Newsletter*, or better still, does a little fieldwork and visits at least some of the FWBO's nine Dharma centres which, between them, conduct activities in more than one hundred places in India. It is also perfectly true that the FWBO 'makes a great deal of its connection with Ambedkar's movement of "ex-untouchables",' though not in the kind of way Mellor implies. We make much of it for a number of reasons, not least because the fact that our ex-Untouchable brothers and sisters tend to approach Buddhism from a social angle, whereas we in the West tend to approach it more psychologically, helps us to correct our one-sidedness and thus to create a more balanced attitude on the part of the FWBO as a whole.

From the FWBO's connection with Ambedkar's movement Mellor returns to the question of exotic nomenclature, and we must return with him. 'Sangharakshita's first reason for using Sanskrit names, that they did not want to use Christian ones,' he proceeds, 'is perhaps more significant. One of the major distinguishing features of the FWBO is its outright hostility to Christianity. Despite the insignificance the FWBO attaches to culture generally, western names and (Christian) religion *do* coincide in a way which is uncomfortable for the FWBO: because of this, Sanskrit names *are* appealing because they are exotic; that is, they are attractive because they are culturally alien.' Whether hostility to Christianity, outright or otherwise, is a 'major' distinguishing feature of the FWBO (part of its essence, as it were?) is debatable; but there is no doubt that in the last sentence quoted the number of misrepresentations is high even by Mellorian standards. I shall therefore have to deal with each of them separately. They relate to (a) the 'insignificance' the FWBO attaches to culture, (b) the 'uncomfortable' way in which, for the FWBO, western names and (Christian) religion coincide, and (c) the 'exotic' appeal of Sanskrit names.

a. Mellor does not define culture, of course, but if we take the word in its generally accepted sense, especially as relating to literature, the fine arts, drama, and music, then it is clear that he has not read, or not heeded, either chapter 10 of Subhuti's *Buddhism for Today*, entitled

'Beauty is Truth', or my own early essay 'The Religion of Art'. Having pointed out that 'Buddhist cultures flowered many times throughout the East,' Subhuti proceeds, a few pages later, to emphasize the importance of culture in a way that illustrates how little 'insignificance' the FWBO attaches to it.

> The appreciation of the arts and their value for the developing individual is strongly encouraged within the FWBO. Many Centres organise poetry readings, concerts, and other cultural activities, and lectures and study groups are often held on artists and their works. Many people find that, for the first time, they acquire an appreciation of such things as they deepen their experience of meditation. They are able to overcome the associations which art has for them of effete foppishness and boredom – the one the result of the prevailing directionlessness of much modern art, the other of the spiritless force-feeding of school. Many Order members and Friends find, now, a deep source of inspiration in some works of both western and eastern culture.[284]

The only way we can make sense of Mellor's belief that the FWBO attaches 'insignificance' to culture generally is by assuming that for him culture is an essentially group phenomenon and that he sees the FWBO, therefore, as regarding culture as being insignificant in comparison with the individual. But even so the FWBO cannot be described as attaching 'insignificance' to culture generally, especially inasmuch as the distinctively western Buddhist culture of its envisagement will be the product, in part, of interaction between western Buddhists and elements of both eastern (Buddhist) and western culture (see above, p. 484). Once again a little fieldwork on Mellor's part would not be out of place, particularly if this was to take him to FWBO centres in both East and West.

b. Western forenames and (Christian) religion obviously coincide, though with less inevitability now than they did in more God-fearing times. What Mellor means by saying that they coincide 'in a way that is uncomfortable for the FWBO' is less obvious. He seems to think he has scored a point, as though the fact of names and (Christian) religion coinciding in a way that is 'uncomfortable for the FWBO' somehow constitutes an argument against it or exposes a weakness in its understanding of the relationship between religion and culture. He also seems to regard the FWBO as a monolithic abstraction that is somehow susceptible to feelings of collective discomfort. The reality is far otherwise. The FWBO consists of individuals. Some of those individuals were brought up as Christians, and not a few who were brought up as Christians have been psychologically damaged by the experience, in some cases to such an extent that during the early years of their involvement with the FWBO they have to spend much of their time trying to repair the damage. For such ex-Christians, names and (Christian) religion coincide in a way that is not just uncomfortable but positively painful. One unfortunate woman, now an Order member, was christened Anne Maria Theresa Bernadette, and Mellor will perhaps understand the relief she felt when, on the occasion of her ordination, she was at last able to relinquish this blatantly Christian and Roman Catholic appellation, with all the unpleasant associations it had come to have for her, and receive in its place a name more in accordance with her spiritual aspirations.

c. Or perhaps he will not understand. We must not forget that Mellor is not only emphatic that 'despite the insignificance the FWBO attaches to culture generally, western names and (Christian) religion *do* coincide in a way that is uncomfortable for the FWBO.' He is also emphatic that 'because of this, Sanskrit names *are* appealing because they are exotic; that is, they are attractive because they are culturally alien.' This is certainly not the case, nor does it even follow that it is the case from Mellor's own (mistaken) premise. Whether as names of dwelling places or names of persons, Sanskrit names, i.e. Sanskrit (and Pāli) *Buddhist* names, do *not* appeal to members of the FWBO because they are exotic; they do *not* find them attractive because they are naturally alien. Sanskrit names appeal to members of the FWBO because they embody Buddhist principles or Buddhist precepts, or because they are the names of historical or mythical Buddhist personages, so that as often as we use those names we are reminded of those principles, precepts, or personages and of our own connection with them. Order members are always very much aware of the meaning of their 'Order names', the significance of which is explained to them at the time of their ordination and subsequently to the Movement at large.

The last paragraph of this section of Mellor's article is devoted to the role exoticism plays in the appeal or character of the English Sangha. Since Thai monasticism judges itself against a 'pristine model' that, in the case of the English Sangha, has been identified with Ajahn Chah's forest monasteries in Thailand, these monasteries, and indeed traditional Buddhism and traditionally Buddhist cultures, become immune from criticism. 'When Ajahn Sumedho draws a distinction between eastern and western culture,' Mellor reminds us, 'it is the *western* which is criticized. Unlike the FWBO, which only rejects those elements in western culture which it associates with hostility to the development of the individual, the English Sangha rejects western culture on a greater scale: since western culture is associated with "greed and competition", materialism, self-absorption and decadence, traditional Buddhist cultures bask in the reflected glow of the pristine Thai model. Thus,' he concludes, 'the foreignness of traditional Buddhist cultures does have an exotic appeal for Buddhists associated with the English Sangha.' This is very much in accordance with my own comment (see above, p. 497) that inasmuch as the English Sangha is culturally more 'eastern' than the FWBO it is more likely to be perceived as exotic in the secondary sense of the term and more likely, therefore, to be of interest to those who are attracted by 'exotic Buddhism'.

6

THE CULTURAL TRANSLATION OF BUDDHISM

Mellor appears to draw a distinction between cultural translation and cultural transferral, though it is only at the very end of the present section of his article, the fifth and last, that we are given an inkling of the nature of this distinction. Cultural transferral would seem to refer to Buddhism's bodily removal, so to speak, from Thailand or Tibet to Britain, much as the Virgin Mary's house was carried by angels lock stock and barrel from Nazareth to Loreto in central Italy.[285] Cultural translation, on the other hand, refers to the fact that in 'entering western culture' (whatever that may mean) Buddhism 'has become the focus for an interaction between eastern and western religious forms, creating discourses which are Buddhist but which have at the same time many of the features of Protestant Christian discourse.' Thus 'translation' does not mean quite what we may have thought it meant. It does not mean the expression of an identical meaning in a different medium, as when a sentence is rendered from one language into another, nor does it mean the expression of one mode or degree of knowledge in terms of another mode or degree of knowledge, as it does in my paper 'St Jerome Revisited' – St Jerome being the translator par excellence of western (i.e. Latin Christian) tradition.[286] For Mellor there does not exist a something that is translated as distinct from a something into which it is translated.

This is evident from the way his brief discussion of cultural translation opens. Any simple interpretation of the cultural translation of Buddhism into England is problematic, he declares. It is problematic because 'for the purposes of academic analysis it is difficult to isolate the "Buddhism" which is being "translated".' What Mellor means by *academic* analysis, and why it should be necessary to subject Buddhism to it, I do not know, though I cannot help feeling it has something to do with 'murdering to dissect'.[287] Probably he means analysing Buddhism in terms of sociological and methodological categories that are foreign to it. But be that as it may, the reason it is difficult to isolate the 'Buddhism' which is being 'translated' is that

> if we separate a Buddhist form from all its cultural 'expressions' and then consider how it is modified as it moves from one culture to another, then we are accepting the philosophical position of the FWBO as normative for academic analysis. We would also be basing our analysis on a signifier of perspectives critical to liberal Protestantism. If my discussion had proceeded on this basis then many of the major philosophical problems which have been considered would not only have been avoided, but may not even have been apparent.

This is a very curious argument indeed. It is rather like saying that we cannot base our astronomy on the Copernican system because if we did so base it many of the problems associated with the Ptolemaic theory of epicycles would not only be avoided, but may not even be apparent. Mellor is also guilty of arguing *ad hominem*. We cannot separate a Buddhist form from its cultural 'expressions' and then consider how it is modified as it moves from one country to another, because then we should be accepting the philosophical position of the FWBO. Why we should not accept the philosophical position of the FWBO, and why that position should not be normative for academic analysis, is not explained. Neither is there any explanation why we should not base our analysis on a signifier of perspectives critical to liberal Protestantism, the falsity of such perspectives apparently being regarded as self-evident. There is also the assumption that the philosophical position of the FWBO and the perspectives critical to liberal Protestantism are somehow bound up with each other; but as I have shown in my critique of the second section of Mellor's article, 'Protestantism and Buddhism', the FWBO cannot really be regarded as demonstrating continuities with these perspectives.

Despite his rejection of what he styles the FWBO's philosophical position, i.e. the position that a Buddhist form is separable from its cultural expressions, Mellor is aware that 'if we ... locate religion firmly within culture we are faced with another set of problems'. These problems are of a practical nature. 'In the final analysis,' he is forced to admit, 'it is difficult to see how such a model could cope with religious change at all, since all religion would be culture-bound, and therefore static. Even if a certain amount of dynamism was allowed into the model – religion is culture-bound but cultures can interact – it still could not deal with all the variables.' This is very true, and it is one of the reasons for my rejection of this particular model. Even if the FWBO's own model was found to be inadequate, there would still be a need for a model that could cope with religious change, which Mellor appears to think inevitable. The 'static' model of which Mellor speaks is, of course, the model with which the English Sangha seeks to align itself, and he therefore continues:

> For example, the English Sangha legitimates its adoption of eastern traditions and rituals on the grounds that religion cannot be so easily separated from culture: the English Sangha adopts the entire practice of Thai monasticism (as far as it can) because it is not confident about what can be discarded and what cannot.

As we have seen, it is not sure whether or not the 'white cloth' can be discarded.

> It does not seek to separate religion from culture. However, despite this orientation towards tradition the English Sangha does separate religion from culture as is shown by its very existence: rejecting its own (English) cultural models, it adopts a foreign (Thai) one.

The observation is just. The English Sangha adopts Buddhism *and* Thai culture because it regards religion and culture as inseparable. Yet in order to do this it has to reject its own (English) culture (the fact that Ajahn Sumedho is an American does not really affect the argument), which means it regards culture as separable. Thus according to Mellor the English Sangha's position is hopelessly self-contradictory. The

Sangha could, of course, rejoin (I do not know if it actually would) that not only does it regard Buddhism and Thai culture as inseparable; it also regards Christianity and western culture as inseparable, and that besides adopting Buddhism *and* Thai culture it rejects western culture *and* Christianity. But this would mean English (and American) Buddhists having to pretend to be Thai Buddhists, in which case they would either have to go and live permanently in Thailand (as some have done) or create a Little Thailand in Britain (as others are trying to do). In neither case would there be a western Buddhism, but at best only a 'cultural transferral' of Thai Buddhism to this country.

I

Now that he has come practically to the end of his article, Mellor would seem to want to strike a balance. His study, he tells us,

> has considered the relationship between religion and culture to be neither one of complete separation nor exclusive identity. Instead, this relationship has been understood as one of mutual definition and influence, though not without different sets of restrictions, on either side, according to context.

My own impression, throughout Mellor's article, has been that he considers religion and culture to be more or less identical and that his personal sympathies are, therefore, with the traditionalist English Sangha rather than the (supposedly) anti-traditionalist FWBO. But it could be that he has, all the time, been acting devil's advocate and criticizing the FWBO more strongly than he really thought was justified. In any case, he goes on to give what may be considered the rationale of his article.

> Because various discourses centred around Buddhism have been the object of study, rather than the translation of a predetermined intellectual formation the analyst labels 'Buddhism' (whether it is the doctrinal Buddhism of philosophy or the 'practical' Buddhism of anthropology), a range of relationships between English Buddhism and both western and eastern culture has been considered which might otherwise have been left unexplored.

The fallaciousness of such a position has already been exposed. Here I might only add that Mellor rejects the idea of studying 'the translation of a pre-determined intellectual formation the analyst labels "Buddhism"' only to embrace that of studying a no less pre-determined intellectual formation he labels 'English Buddhism' or 'English Buddhist group'. If Buddhism cannot be defined, because it has no 'essence', then 'Buddhist' cannot be defined either. Even discourses 'centred around Buddhism' cannot be studied or discussed, since they are the discourses of *Buddhists*, i.e. those who accept the predetermined intellectual formation 'Buddhism', whether as members of the English Sangha or members of the FWBO. Thus unless we accept a 'Buddhism' there can be no Buddhists and, therefore, no Buddhist discourses centred around Buddhism. As I commented in connection with the idea that there is an 'essence of Buddhism', discourse implies definition, and definition implies essence (see above, p. 400).

> Some of the major differences between the FWBO and the English Sangha are due not only to their different attitudes to eastern religious practices, but also to certain western discourses/practices, especially modernism which the FWBO embraces and the English Sangha despises.

This is hardly correct. Besides showing that there are fewer differences between the FWBO and the English Sangha than Mellor thinks, I have made it clear, in my comments on the third section of his article, entitled 'Modernism and Buddhism', that the FWBO is far from embracing modernism.

> In terms of such continuities, and disruptions, the whole issue of the influence of liberal Protestant perspectives cannot be addressed if the analysis is firmly anchored to the idea of an essential Buddhism which is being translated.

No doubt it cannot, from Mellor's point of view. But neither can it be addressed if we reject the idea of essence and, therewith, both definition and the possibility of discourse, including discourse on the influence of liberal Protestant perspectives.

Mellor would also seem to want to show his impartiality, as between the FWBO and the English Sangha. At any rate, he concludes his study with a parting shot at English Buddhism in general, for which he appears to feel a distaste amounting to positive dislike. But though Mellor fires the shot, this time it is Edward Conze who is (posthumously) conscripted into loading the gun. 'Finally,' he says, 'I suggest that this discussion has shown that "Buddhism" in England is a deeply problematic category.' The quotation marks are no doubt meant to emphasize just how deeply problematic that category is. 'It [i.e. "Buddhism" in England] is the focus for a number of different, sometimes competing, religious and cultural forces. While Buddhism is a religion of eastern origin, in England it has become part of a liberal Protestant trend, even though it still might manifest itself in an ostentatiously Asian mode.' Presumably it is *not* the FWBO that is under attack in the last part of this sentence, our 'mode' not being Asian in the West and not 'ostentatiously' Asian even in India. However, Mellor continues: 'One of the leading scholars of Buddhism this century, Edward Conze, has noted the Protestant character of Buddhism in the west: "Buddhist societies have sprung up for nearly eighty years, chiefly in Protestant countries. There they form one of the smaller Nonconformist sects".'[288] Dear old Edward Conze (whom I knew personally) was certainly one of the leading scholars of Buddhism this century, but his field of expertise was the Prajñāpāramitā or 'Perfection of Wisdom' literature, not the sociology of western Buddhism; moreover, he delighted in being deliberately provocative at the expense of the then British Buddhist establishment. His comment on the 'Protestant character of Buddhism in the west' cannot be regarded as being anything but a *jeu d'esprit*, the more especially since the work from which Mellor quotes was originally published (in Italian) in 1958. Mellor also overlooks the fact that Conze is speaking of Buddhist *societies*, the limitations of which are spelled out in Subhuti's *Buddhism for Today*.[289]

Conze's use of the term 'Nonconformist' is *not* overlooked, however. In fact Mellor seizes upon it. 'This reference to Nonconformism is pertinent,' he assures us. It is pertinent because 'there is an element of cultural rebellion in western people adopting Buddhism as a religion'. If there is an element of cultural rebellion in western people adopting Buddhism as a religion, there is an even greater element of *religious* rebellion – but Mellor does not mention this, presumably because he tends to think of religion and culture as being more or less identical. He continues: 'Buddhist groups emphasize the significance of this rebellion, suggesting that western culture generally is in a state of decay and needs a radical reorientation such as Buddhism can provide.' In the case of the FWBO, at least, this emphasis is selective: some areas of western culture are *not* in a state of decay and need a less radical reorientation than others. As Mellor himself recognizes, the FWBO does not reject all elements in western culture, but only those which it associates with hostility to the development of the individual (see above, p. 504). In fact it is not western culture that is in a state of decay so much as western religion. By this I do not mean that Christianity is in state of decay (though it may be, on its own terms), but rather that traditional Christianity is itself a state of decay. So much is this the case that for the last few hundred years it is secular literature, secular art, secular music, and secular philosophy that have been the principal bearers of spiritual values in the West, not religion, even though the old Christian forms and symbols have continued to be made use of to some extent. As Middleton Murry puts it in 'Romantics and Tradition', written in reply to T. S. Eliot,

> With the Renaissance the stream of religious tradition began to flow outside the Church. Science took upon itself the fulfilment of the outward exploration, literature the fulfilment of the inward exploration of life.[290]

Or as the same writer says, even more pithily, in 'The "Classical" Revival',

> England rejected Catholicism four centuries ago. And with the rejection of Catholicism English literature began.[291]

Literature being, for Murry, the principal bearer of spiritual values, at least in England.

Not only is there an element of cultural rebellion in western people adopting Buddhism as a religion, with Buddhist groups emphasizing the significance of this rebellion, thus suggesting that western culture generally is in a state of decay and in need of a radical reorientation such as Buddhism can provide. According to Mellor, Ling goes so far as to argue that western Buddhist groups may signify an important cultural development. This is a possibility Mellor himself does not contemplate with equanimity, and he moves to contain any such development within his own perspectives.

> However, as Conze indicates [he assures us] this desire for an 'alternative' type of society, takes place broadly within the established religious context of western culture. Buddhist groups in England are a 'significant new cultural development' not because they divert western culture into new religious channels, but because they explore the existing religious channels in new ways. Their significance rests in their ability to create new religious forms within liberal Protestant culture.

In the case of the FWBO, at least, this is not true. However much or however little it may 'divert' western culture into new religious channels, it certainly does not explore existing religious channels in new ways. Non-theism is not a new way of exploring theism; meditation is not a new way of exploring prayer. As for the FWBO's significance resting on its ability to create new religious forms within liberal Protestant culture, this present 'protest and affirmation' of mine has, I trust, shown the ludicrousness of any such assertion. Hence while agreeing with Mellor that 'Buddhism has not been "transferred" [bodily] into this culture, but has been "translated",' I cannot agree with him that such translation consists in the fact that 'in entering western culture it has become the focus for an interaction between eastern and western religious forms, creating discourses which are Buddhist but which have at the same time many of the features of Protestant Christian discourse'. So far as the FWBO is concerned, the cultural translation of Buddhism consists in the fact that on finding itself in a western environment it has become the focus for an interaction between the timeless truths of the Dharma and the language of the secular western culture through which it seeks to express those truths. Western Buddhism is/will be the creation of that interaction.

APPENDIX: A LETTER TO DR ZAEHNER

Dear Dr Zaehner,[292] having just read your *Evolution in Religion*, I am writing to say how greatly it has interested me and how much I find myself, as a Buddhist, in general agreement with the spirit of your approach. Interpretations of religion in 'evolutionary' terms nowadays seem to be rather 'in the air' and a comparative study such as yours, which compares two such prominent representatives of the evolutionary approach as the Hindu Aurobindo and the Catholic Teilhard, is undoubtedly to be welcomed. I would like, however, to make a few comments on your references to Buddhism, as well as to suggest that Buddhism, too, can be approached from the point of view of evolution.

In chapter 1, 'Religion and Religions', you point out that Teilhard and Aurobindo at least agree in thinking that Vedanta, Marxism, and Christianity are the only possible alternatives before mankind. You yourself, however, draw attention to the 'striking omission' of Islam, rightly questioning whether it can be written off quite so easily even from the 'integral' and 'convergent' point of view. For you, therefore, there are apparently four alternatives before mankind: Vedanta, Marxism, Christianity, and Islam. Having done justice to Islam, you recollect that besides the four 'alternatives' there are usually reckoned to be five other 'great' religions of the world. Zoroastrianism, Confucianism, and Taoism are rightly dismissed as virtually extinct, while Judaism, like Hinduism, remains the religion of a nation. Of its very nature it cannot become a world religion. As you say, there remains only Buddhism. Why, then, do neither Teilhard nor Aurobindo mention it? While agreeing with your explanation for their comparative silence, I wish to challenge the assumption upon which that silence is based – an assumption which you seem to share.

Briefly, the assumption seems to be that Buddhism can be reduced to its Theravāda form, or to Zen, or to a combination of the two. Surely this is like assuming that Christianity can be reduced to the Greek Orthodox Church, or to Methodism, or to a combination of both of these. In either case what may fairly be regarded as the central tradition of the religion concerned has been entirely omitted from consideration. The central tradition of Buddhism, broadly speaking, is that of the Mahāyāna, regarded as subsuming the Sarvāstivāda tradition, as consisting 'philosophically' of the Yogācāra-Madhyamaka schools, and as finding practical spiritual expression in terms of the bodhisattva ideal. This central tradition of Buddhism is/was the one dominant principally in China, Japan, Tibet, Korea, Mongolia, and Vietnam. Since Vedanta is really inseparable from Hinduism, for me the alternatives before mankind are: Marxism, Buddhism, Christianity, and Islam. Indeed, I would argue that Buddhism occupies, in a sense, a middle position between Marxism on the one hand and Christianity and Islam on the other. Like Marxism, Buddhism is non-theistic, and like Christianity and Islam it is a spiritual teaching as distinct from a form of materialism. It is this union of the non-theistic and the spiritual which, I believe, constitutes one of the great strengths of Buddhism, especially at the present time, giving it, for opposite reasons, a decided advantage over both the atheist-materialist and the theistic-spiritual alternatives.

Incidentally, Aurobindo seems to have been afflicted with as strange a blindness with regard to Buddhism as Teilhard with regard to eastern mysticism in general. Some twenty years ago, when I first read *The Life Divine*, I was astonished to find him again and again referring to the Buddhist Nirvāṇa as a purely negative state.[293] In so widely read a man as Sri Aurobindo this amounted to wilful ignorance: even in the Theravāda Nirvāṇa is not regarded as a state of pure negation of mundane existence.

Besides occupying a middle position between the atheist-materialist and the theistic-spiritual alternatives, Buddhism is more open to an approach in terms of evolution than either Christianity or Hinduism.

Teilhard's evolutionary interpretation of Catholicism strikes me, indeed, as something of a tour de force, and you are no doubt right in transferring to him the appellation of poet with which you were honoured in Delhi. In the case of Aurobindo, though his intentions are noble, even sublime, I do not think that much is likely to emerge from the cloud of words in which he has involved a few vague ideas. (Prompted by your quotations, I have just re-read *Thoughts and Aphorisms*, and am surprised how flat and essentially commonplace these sayings of his are. One has only to think of Blake's *Proverbs of Hell* to appreciate this.) Both Teilhard's and Aurobindo's spiritual evolutionism would seem, in fact, to go against the grain of their respective religions, and I am inclined to doubt if Christianity or Hinduism will be much affected by the thought of either of them. In the case of Buddhism, however, an approach from the point of view of evolution would seem to be very much in accordance with the genius of the tradition itself. Four considerations could be cited, among others, in support of this contention. You are, I am sure, familiar with them, though you may never have seen them quite in this light.

1. In one form or another, the concept of the Path has always been central to Buddhism. The Path consists of steps or stages. These steps or stages represent, essentially, states of consciousness, or of being, which are progressive, leading the individual from ignorance to Enlightenment, from the condition of *pṛthagjana* to that of *arhant* or Buddha. One could therefore say that the conception of spiritual development, or spiritual *evolution* (what I call the higher evolution of Man) is central to Buddhism.

2. It is well known that there grew up round the Buddha a sangha which continued after his death and still exists today. Ideally this sangha is a purely spiritual sodality, an 'assembly of the elect,' whether monk or lay, who have attained the higher spiritual stages of the Path, and who, being incapable of regression, are assured of Nirvāṇa. This sangha is the nucleus of an ideal community and it stands in the same relation to society at large as the individual *ārya* stands to the individual *pṛthagjana*. Thus spiritual evolution is clearly seen not only as individual but as collective.

3. As already stated, the central tradition of Buddhism, the Mahāyāna, finds practical expression in terms of the bodhisattva ideal. This represents much more than a personal ideal for ethical and spiritual

behaviour. The figure of the bodhisattva is the concrete embodiment of the principle of spiritual evolution, both individual and cosmic. The bodhisattva ideal being ubiquitous in the Mahāyāna, this principle is by implication ubiquitous too.

4. The Buddhist scriptures, especially those of the Mahāyāna, quite clearly envisage a universe (in the fullest sense of the term) in which, under the guidance of Buddhas and bodhisattvas innumerable, all sentient beings are ultimately destined to Enlightenment, even the Devadattas of the world not being excluded. In this sense one may therefore speak of Buddhism as the religion of evolution, of spiritual evolution, on a cosmic scale. Indeed, in texts such as the *Saddharma Puṇḍarīka* this is exactly how the Mahāyāna sees itself.[294] No tour de force of interpretation is necessary.

Though I have been preoccupied with Buddhism for thirty years, the fact that it was possible to approach Buddhism from the point of view of evolution – that Buddhism, more than any other religion, indeed was the leading historical embodiment of the principle of spiritual evolution – was far from being immediately apparent to me. For many years I was much more concerned with the practical problem of striving actually to follow the Path in the traditional manner than with any attempt to reinterpret it in contemporary terms. The realization that Buddhism was the higher evolution dawned on me only gradually, and my approach to it was oblique. Three main stages can perhaps be distinguished.

1. According to tradition, the Buddha's Enlightenment consisted in an insight into the truth of universal conditionality. This insight found conceptual expression in the fundamental teaching of the chain of 'dependent origination' (*pratītya-samutpāda*). With the help of Dr Beni Madhab Barua and Mrs C. A. F. Rhys Davids I discovered that this chain was not limited to an explanation of the process of repeated existence in the world, particularly of the phenomenon of human suffering, as was generally supposed, but also included the Path leading from the world to Nirvāṇa. In its entirety it in fact consisted not of one series of twelve links but of two, the first series being cyclical in character, the second progressive. This meant, in effect, that the Path to Enlightenment could not be reduced to the gradual cessation of the mundane but possessed a definite nature of its own. In other words, Buddhism was not just negative asceticism.

Nirvāṇa was not annihilation. All this I have explained in full detail in *A Survey of Buddhism*.[295]

2. Contemplating the twelve links that made up the missing half of the chain of dependent origination, the true nature of the Path became clear to me. It was not a thing of artificial steps and stages. Neither was it a succession of observances. Essentially, it consisted of a sequence of psychological and spiritual experiences. These experiences were not only progressive but cumulative. Between them they constituted a process of continuous growth and development by which the individual advanced from lower to higher states of being and consciousness. This process could well be termed not only a development but even an evolution. The twelve positive *nidānas*, as I term them, are explained at length in chapter 13, 'The Stages of the Path', of my book *The Three Jewels* (1967).[296]

3. So far my realization that Buddhism was the path of the higher evolution had remained within a strictly traditional framework. In 1964, however, having spent twenty years in the East, I returned to England, and soon felt the need, purely as a 'skilful means' (*upāya-kauśalya*), of a principle sufficiently familiar to the modern mind not to require much explanation and capable, at the same time, of being generalized in such a way as to provide a medium for the exposition of Buddhism. One day, while preparing a lecture, it flashed on me that the concept of evolution was such a principle. At once everything fell into place. Science revealed how far man had come. This was the lower evolution. Buddhism, as the Path, showed how far he still had to go. This was the higher evolution. Though not strictly continuous the two phases between them constituted the two halves of a single process. Science and religion, the lower and the higher evolution, were comprehended in one gigantic sweep. In the course of the last few years I have developed these ideas in detail, thus working out an approach to Buddhism in terms of evolution. So far I have not written any book on the subject, though I have dealt with it in several courses of lectures, the most important such course being the eight lectures on 'The Higher Evolution of Man' (autumn 1969).[297]

To what extent these words will be able to convey to you the nature of my evolutionary vision of Buddhism I do not know. They may well be too obscure to convey anything at all. Nevertheless, I venture to hope that they will at least serve to indicate the existence of an attempt to approach Buddhism, too, from the point of view of evolution, and that as such – as well as evidence of the interest your book has excited – you will welcome them.

Yours sincerely,

Sangharakshita
Muswell Hill
London N.10
9 August 1971

P.S. In case you would like to follow up the references I have given, I am asking the publishers to send you a copy of *A Survey of Buddhism* and of *The Three Jewels*.

From Genesis to the *Diamond Sūtra*

PREFACE

It was my intention some years ago to write a full-length comparative study of Buddhism and Christianity, but old age, and therewith the partial loss of my eyesight, have crept up on me and prevented me from carrying out this plan, which in any case was an ambitious one. I was unwilling, however, to give up the idea altogether, and it occurred to me that if I was unable to produce a full-length comparative study of the two religions I could at least write an account of my personal contact, over the years, with Christianity and Christians.

Thus the present work is largely autobiographical, though I have not hesitated to deviate, from time to time, from the autobiographical framework in order to explore an aspect of Christianity which was of special interest to me. I have written it for my own satisfaction. I wanted to take stock, as it were, of my attitude to Christianity as it had impinged on my life and thought in the course of the last eighty years. At the same time, I wanted to share my experience, and my reflections on my experience, with those western Buddhists who, like me, grew up within a Christian culture, as well as with students of comparative religion, and with Christians who might be interested to know how one modern Buddhist, at least, in retrospect views their religion.

After relating my early memories of Christianity and Christians in Chapter 1, I turn my attention, in Chapter 2, to the Bible, especially to the poetical books of the Old Testament, which I enjoyed as a boy and which I still enjoy. The fact that I am a Buddhist does not in the least detract from my enjoyment of them, for I read the Bible as literature, not as the Word of God. In Chapter 3, beginning with the Gunpowder Plot, the anniversary of which I celebrated as a small boy, and ending with the persecution of the Vietnamese Buddhists by the ruling Catholic oligarchy, I trace the way in which power has corrupted the Roman Catholic Church. I also relate my contact with Catholic priests, one of whom became a good friend.

In Chapter 4 I take a look at the Apostles' Creed, for it is this ancient formula which constitutes the basis of mainstream Christianity, whether Roman Catholic, Lutheran, Anglican, or Orthodox in its form. I wanted to make clear, to myself, and hopefully to others, the fundamental difference between Buddhism and Christianity. Even in the Creed there are elements I can accept, provided they are understood as myths and symbols, not as literal truth. The orthodox Christian believer regards the doctrine of the Virgin Birth as being a statement of historical fact. The Buddhist scriptures certainly contain myths and legends, but they form no part of Buddhist doctrine, and the individual Buddhist is free to accept or reject them as he or she pleases. Chapter 5 is devoted to what I call Christian mythology, which is for me, at least in the form it has assumed in the Western Church, the product of the Catholic collective imagination. In this chapter, as in several others, I give expression to my appreciation of, and delight in, some of the masterpieces of Christian art. I also critique, in connection with the figure of Satan, the twin notions of absolute evil and irremeable reprobation.

In Chapter 6, which deals with Christian ethics, I describe two incidents in my early childhood that were responsible for the awakening in me of a distinctly moral consciousness. This leads me to a consideration of violence, especially the violence that Christianity has regularly directed against heretics and homosexuals. I express myself strongly in this connection. It certainly was not my intention to offend any Christian, but there are elements in Christianity which I cannot but regard with horror, not just as a Buddhist but as a moral being. In the context of this chapter 'homosexuality' means male homosexuality, the Church for some reason being much less fierce against lesbianism, despite Leviticus and St Paul. The saints and mystics who are the subject of Chapter 7 were all remarkable personalities, and their lives are of great human interest. In their different ways they all made a strong impression on me, and it is for this reason that I have written about them.

After the saints and mystics comes Jesus, who figures in Chapter 8. In this chapter I tell how I oscillated, over the decades, between believing and not believing in his historical existence. These doubts did not prevent me from being deeply moved by paintings of his life, some of which I describe. I also discuss the Christology of Marcion, a 'heretical' teacher of the second century, and comment on a novelistic reconstruction of the gospel story by a great Irish writer – a reconstruction I found both plausible and appealing. Chapter 9 is devoted to the legend of Barlaam and Josaphat, which may be regarded as a sort of bridge between Buddhism and Christianity. In this chapter I trace the steps by which a traditional Indian biography of the Buddha was gradually transformed into the story of two Christian saints, one of whom – St Josaphat – is quite recognizably the Buddha. In the last chapter I ask myself what I have learned by immersing myself in Christianity for the nine months it took me to produce this book.

I would like to thank Jnanasiddhi for her helpful editorial suggestions, and Shantavira for his meticulous copy-editing, for which I have often had cause to be grateful. Above all, I would like to thank my friend Nityabandhu, to whom I dictated the whole book, and without whose cooperation it would not have seen the light.

Sangharakshita
Birmingham
26 April 2005

1
EARLY MEMORIES

I am a Buddhist. I have been a Buddhist for more than sixty years. But I was born to nominally Christian parents in a country where Protestantism in its Anglican form was the established religion, and in a part of the western world where Christianity had been for centuries the dominant religious and cultural influence.

My first contact with Christianity took place a few days after my birth on 26 August 1925, when I was baptized in St Nicholas Parish Church, Tooting Graveney, wearing the same christening veil in which my father had been baptized twenty-seven years before. What may have been my second contact with Christianity was also connected with my father. It was he who taught me at a very early age the prayer which his maternal grandmother had taught him when he himself was a child. The prayer ran:

When I lay me down to sleep
I pray the Lord my soul to keep.
If I should die before I wake
I pray the Lord my soul to take.

Why my father taught me this prayer I cannot say, but he told me I should repeat it every night before I went to sleep, probably because I slept alone and was subject to nightmares. The worst of these nightmares occurred only once. Towering above me I saw in the darkness an enormous black wooden cross. It rose up out of a kind of black wooden maze or labyrinth, and the atmosphere was one of indescribable gloom, horror, and dread.

My father was very fond of his old grandmother, having lived with her in her Norfolk village after the premature death of his father. It was she who had given him, apparently, what was known in the family as Grandmother's Bible. This was a massive volume with a tooled leather cover and a worn gilt clasp, and its richly coloured illustrations of such subjects as Daniel in the lions' den and Samson rending the lion must have been the first religious pictures I saw. In our home there were no religious pictures, though in the passage between my room and my parents' bedroom there were small reproductions of Rossetti's *Dante's Dream* and Holiday's *Dante and Beatrice*.[298] Ours was in fact not a religious family. My parents went to church only once every two or three years, nor did they ever discuss religion, and his teaching me his grandmother's prayer was the only religious instruction I ever received from my father.

I did of course have godparents, who by sponsoring me at the time of my baptism had made themselves responsible for my religious education. My godparents were my father's sister Helen and Thomas Whitehead, an old friend of the family, but though I saw both of them frequently (Uncle Tom, as I called him, lived across the road) neither of them ever gave me even as much religious instruction as I had received from my father when he asked me to repeat his grandmother's prayer every night. The only person on my father's side of the family who could be described as at all religious was his mother, widowed for the second time, who at least attended church regularly and who, when I reached the age of fourteen, was vaguely troubled that I was not being confirmed.

On my mother's side of the family things were hardly better. The only one who took religion seriously was Uncle Jack, her youngest brother but one, who lived in Tooting Bec and who, with his wife Hilda, was a fairly regular visitor to our house, as we were to theirs. A gentle, kindly man with a nervous manner and a fondness for lavatorial humour, he had been for many years a Sunday school teacher. It was he who presented my sister Joan and me with our first Bibles, for besides being our uncle he was her godfather. Later I gathered, from conversations I happened to overhear, that he had formerly been very religious indeed. He had been in the habit of falling on his knees in the High Street and calling upon people to pray. At family gatherings, moreover, he would hold forth on the subject of religion until told to shut up by his four unsympathetic sisters, who attributed his religious mania – as they saw it – to the fact of his having been shell-shocked while serving in the artillery during the Great War. Despite the fact that she was accustomed to join with her sisters in 'shutting up' poor Uncle Jack, Auntie Kate, my mother's eldest sister, who was a great favourite of mine, as I was of hers, was not wholly indifferent to religion. Unlike the rest of the family, she did not belong to the Church of England. She was a Roman Catholic, having married an Irishman at an early age, and a little of his ancestral faith seems to have rubbed off on her. Once she gave me a tiny medal that had been blessed by the pope, and on a later occasion, when my mother and I accompanied her to Westminster Cathedral, she lit a candle in front of one of the altars and knelt down and said a prayer.

Though they hardly ever set foot inside a church, my parents sent my sister and me to Sunday school every week. This was due partly, I imagine, to the fact that as children *they* had been sent to Sunday school, and partly in order that they might have an hour or two to themselves on Sunday afternoons. Joan and I went not to St Nicholas but to the octagonal Congregational Church, which was much nearer, where we sat on a hard bench against the wall, in the bottom class, feeling bored, and from which we returned clutching little coloured pictures illustrative of various Bible scenes. It was at this church that I attended my first service, at which I saw the Holy Ghost, as I told my astonished parents on returning home. They eventually came to the conclusion that what I must really have seen was the minister in his white surplice, but I have since wondered if that was the explanation. Perhaps I had had an experience similar to those that came upon me, six or seven years later, at Amen Corner, and as I was walking from Amen Corner in the direction of Tooting Broadway.[299] In any case, I'm not sure whether ministers of the Congregational Church do, in fact, wear surplices like their Anglican counterparts.

At the same time that I was attending Sunday school I was also attending the Selincourt Road Infant School, to which I started going – most reluctantly – when I was four. Besides the three Rs, the curriculum included Scripture, though lessons in this subject may not have begun for a year or two. 'Scripture' meant the Bible, particularly the parables of Jesus, which our teacher read to us from the New Testament or told us in her own words. We also repeated the Lord's Prayer at morning assembly and sang such hymns as 'All Things Bright and Beautiful' and 'Away in a Manger'. How deep an impression all this Religious Education, as it would now be called, made on me, I cannot tell. I absorbed words and phrases – even stories – but did not, I think, acquire any definite conceptions.

So far, there was little that was unusual about my story. Except for my 'seeing the Holy Ghost', it was the story of thousands of South London boys of my generation and class. But when I was eight, and had just started junior school, there took place in my life a sudden and violent change – a change that affected, directly and indirectly, the whole future course of my existence. I was diagnosed as having valvular disease of the heart and was confined to bed. There I spent two years or more, forbidden visitors, and unable to do anything except read.

Fortunately – for I soon worked my way through my father's small collection of books – a friendly neighbour gave me a complete set of Harmsworth's *Children's Encyclopedia*, which quickly became my constant and much-loved companion. As I wrote forty-five years ago:

> All sixty-one parts (including the Index) were at my bedside day and night, and rarely was I seen without one of them in my hand. Thanks to Mr Harmsworth I was no longer alone in my little room with the nasturtium-patterned wallpaper, the owl clock, the model yacht, and my one dozen oft-read volumes. I could now speak with the good and wise of all ages; I could follow Nature into her innermost recesses and explore all her secrets, from the constitution of the heavens to the structure of a crystal. The pageant of history from its first dawnings in Egypt, China, and Babylonia passed with all its kings and princes, its priests and nobles and common people, before my eyes. The buskined and unbuskined heroes of ancient and modern tragedy trod my bedside rug for their stage. Perseus slew Medusa the Gorgon, Hercules performed his Twelve Labours, and Jason went in search of the Golden Fleece in my sight. Shining presences of marble and bronze rose as though to music and stood before me in the naked glory of their perfectly proportioned Hellenic manhood; pensive Italian Madonnas smiled. The cross on which Christ was crucified, the tree beneath which the Buddha attained Enlightenment, had

> their roots in the floor of my room, wherein, as into a garner, the harvest of the ages was gathered unto me for the making of the bread that would keep my soul alive. The body was forgotten, and my imagination, now possessed of 'infinite riches in a little room',[300] rejoiced in the freedom of all the heavens of the spirit.[301]

The contact that I had with Christianity in the course of my immersion in the *Children's Encyclopedia* was largely mediated by the latter's numerous reproductions of Christian works of art or, at least, of paintings depicting scenes and personages from the Old and New Testaments, the lives and legends of saints, angels, and important events in ecclesiastical history. In later years I saw not a few of these paintings with my own eyes in Italy, Germany, and Spain, as well as in the museums and art galleries of my native land. There were also pictures of Gothic cathedrals, stained glass windows, and illuminated manuscripts. From the simply written articles I learned, moreover, about the Bible, about the Crusades and the Inquisition, about reformers like Luther and Calvin, and about such masterpieces of Christian literature as *The Pilgrim's Progress* and *Paradise Lost*. In one of the sections devoted to poetry I came across some excerpts from the latter. The reading of these sowed in me a lifelong admiration for Milton's poetic presentation of the great Christian myth, which begins with the Creation and Fall of Man, culminates in the Crucifixion, and concludes with the Last Judgement. What was more important still, I learned from the *Children's Encyclopedia* that Christianity was not the only religion in the world. There were Buddhism and Hinduism, Taoism and Confucianism, Zoroastrianism and Islam, all of which possessed thousands or even millions of adherents and had given rise to great civilizations and cultures.

When the days of my incarceration came to an end, my attention naturally was again directed to the outer world, from which I had so long been cut off. But this time it was not directed to that world more or less exclusively, as previously had been the case. The world of ideas and the imagination was now no less real to me than was the world of sights and sounds. In a way it was more real to me, for there were times when the people I saw from the wheelchair in which, for six or seven months, I was pushed around Tooting, were as phantoms compared with some of those I encountered in books. My two years in bed had brought about a permanent change in my character, outlook, and interests, a change that may not otherwise have taken place, at least not so early in my life. Henceforth I was to live in two worlds, one that I shared with others, one that was all my own. Inasmuch as they possess reflexive consciousness, all human beings live in two worlds, but whereas most people lived much more in the outer world of sights and sounds than in the inner world of ideas and the imagination, with me it was the precise opposite. With me, moreover, the imbalance between my two worlds was far greater than it generally is in the case of those who are labelled introverts, and so remained for some time.

On my being allowed to give up the wheelchair and walk, though not to run or play games, I not only went back to school but soon joined the Boys' Brigade. From then on, my contact with Christianity took place not just through the medium of books but through the connection I formed with its institutions and its official and unofficial representatives, for the Boys' Brigade was a Protestant organization, each of its companies being affiliated to the local Protestant church and having that church's minister as its colonel. I was a member of the Boys' Brigade for nearly four years, donning its uniform for the Friday evening parade, when our little company was drilled by its 'officers', taking part in the Wednesday evening prayer meeting and the Sunday morning Bible class, and, eventually, attending the Sunday morning and evening services at the Baptist church to which our company was affiliated. The pastor of the church was Mr Rudman, a sandy-haired man in his mid-thirties whose sermons, which were on the long side, were aimed at the heart rather than at the head, and generally left his congregation feeling deeply moved. The members of the church with whom I had greatest personal contact were short, sprightly Mr Ovey, the captain of our company, who liked to be addressed as 'Skipper', and elderly, grizzled Mr Young, one of the sidesmen, who plied me with little books of daily Bible readings and who once expressed his conviction that the Lord had chosen me for a great work. There was also the much younger Reg, the company's lieutenant, who drilled us in Mr Ovey's absence, and the still younger Ben, who after giving us tea at his house, two or three at a time, invited us to go down on our knees and offer up our souls to Jesus, which out of politeness we duly did.

They were all good people, and I liked and respected them, but I could not share their simple faith nor, so far as I remember, did the contact I had with them contribute to the development of my religious convictions. I might return home after a particularly moving sermon by Mr Rudman with my heart overflowing with love for the person of Christ, but at night, when I said my prayers, I did not say them only to him. As my habit was at this period, I said them to the Buddha, Christ, and Mohammed in turn, thus hedging my bets in a way that went one better than Pascal and his famous wager.[302] Membership of the Boys' Brigade satisfied my societal instinct, my need to belong to a group, but the church to which our company was affiliated could not meet my need for something more than a temporary emotional exaltation. Even at the weekly vestry prayer meeting, the sort of evangelical equivalent to the Anglican confirmation class, which after a couple of years I was invited to join, less emphasis was placed on doctrine than on devotion, though we did once study Bunyan's *The Holy War*[303] with a speaker from another church, and I did have one serious argument there. This argument was about salvation. Tommy, a boy of my own age, maintained that salvation was by faith alone, whereas I declared that salvation was by faith and works.

On 3 September 1939 I went to church as usual, having just attended Bible class in the adjacent hall. Only one hymn had been sung when there was a dramatic interruption to the proceedings. As I wrote twenty years later:

> A sidesman ascended the pulpit steps and handed the pastor a slip of paper. Slowly rising to his feet, the pastor announced, not the number of the next hymn, but the fact that our country was at war with Germany. Adding that members of the congregation would no doubt wish to return as quickly as possible to their homes, with a short prayer and a blessing he dismissed us. As we left the church the first air raid warning sounded.[304]

Less than a year later, the 'phoney war' having come to an end, with other boys from the Ensham Central School, which I had been attending for the last year or more, I was evacuated to Devon. This was a change which, even if it was not so sudden as the one that had occurred six years earlier, was hardly less violent. It was also of an exactly opposite nature. Instead of being confined to bed, seeing only my parents, the doctor, and the district nurse, I was sent to a distant, unfamiliar part of the country to live, at first as a not very welcome evacuee, among people who were not just strangers but strangers whose ways, in certain respects, including their habits of speech, were very different from those to which I was accustomed. The change also brought about an extension of my contact with Christianity. In Barnstaple, the North Devon town to which I was evacuated, I was billeted first with a grey-haired Anglican clergyman and his elderly aunt and uncle, then with a Church-hating Wesleyan Methodist and her two small sons, and on Sundays attended their respective places of worship. I was greatly struck by the difference – in furnishings, in atmosphere, and in the type of service – between the little parish church with its more traditional style of architecture, where my host conducted the service and preached, and the big barn-like Wesleyan chapel. One, I felt, was a sacred place, while the other was not.

In Torquay in South Devon, where I ceased to be an evacuee, and where I left school and started working, my contact with Christianity was further extended. To please my grandmother, then staying with Uncle Charles, my father's half-brother, who had been evacuated to Torquay with his firm, I sometimes accompanied her to the little corrugated-iron Anglican church she was attending at that time. One Sunday the dignified, ascetic-looking old priest who was in charge preached on the text 'And every several gate was of one pearl' from the Book of Revelation.[305] I do not remember what he said, but the image of gates that were 'one pearl' remained firmly lodged in my mind. Once I went to St Mary's, the local parish church, with Auntie Kath, Uncle Charles' lively and intelligent wife. Both Anglican churches were decidedly High Church, especially St Mary's, where there was incense and music, and where the service concluded with a grand procession round the church, complete with processional crosses and embroidered banners, surpliced choristers walking two and two, and priests in unusually colourful vestments. Auntie Kath loved all this, and I saw that ritual had a place in religion, especially popular religion. Auntie Kath also talked to me a lot about modern literature and about religion, and once I discussed religion with a Devonshire dairy farmer, my landlord at the time, who solemnly assured me that he believed in the historical existence of Adam and Eve and who was as astonished to find that I did not believe in it as I was to find that he did.

Even after my emancipation from the wheelchair I had continued to read voraciously, borrowing from the Tooting Public Library books on a variety of subjects including, especially, literature, history, and philosophy. My pocket money did not stretch to buying books except for half a dozen volumes in the Thinker's Library series, published by the Rationalist Press Association, which were remarkably cheap. The volumes I bought included Samuel Butler's *The Fair Haven*, the *Selected Works* of Voltaire, including his celebrated poem on the Lisbon earthquake and 'The Questions of Zapata', and *Gibbon on Christianity*, being chapters 15 and 16 of the great historian's *History of the Decline and Fall of the Roman Empire*. In Torquay, however, though I continued to borrow books from the public library, as I had done in Barnstaple, once I had started work I was able to buy them. Among the first books I bought were *Selections from St Thomas Aquinas* and *The Little Flowers*, and *The Life of St Francis*, both published in the Everyman's Library series.

The life of St Francis, as it emerges from the pages of *The Little Flowers* and St Bonaventura's short biography, must have affected me quite deeply. At this time of my life, and perhaps for a long time afterwards, I was of an extremely impressionable nature, and like the crystal in the traditional Indian simile, which takes on the colour of whatever object is placed next to it, I readily took on the mood, the emotional colouring as it were, of whatever book I happened to be reading. Thus it was that when, one morning on my way to work, I was accosted by a beggar, I saw standing before me not a beggar but Christ himself, just as St Francis might have done, and at once gave him all the money I had on me.

With this dramatic experience my contact with Christianity, as mediated by the written word, came to an end, for the time being. I had started borrowing from the Torquay Public Library, or buying, books on Hinduism, on Islam, and on Theosophy. Among the books I borrowed were the two stout volumes of H. P. Blavatsky's *Isis Unveiled*, one of the foundational documents of the Theosophical movement, both of which I read through twice, from cover to cover, within a fortnight. What I would make of it if I were to read the work now, I do not know, but its effect on me was far-reaching in its consequences. The emotion I felt at the time is evident from what I wrote two decades later:

> Impressed, bewildered, thrilled, excited, stimulated as I was by their staggeringly immense wealth – their 'inexhaustible truckloads', as Maeterlinck called them – of information on

> every conceivable aspect of philosophy, comparative religion, occultism, mysticism, science, and a hundred other subjects, the realization which dawned most clearly upon me, and which by the time I had finished stood out with blinding obviousness in the very forefront of my consciousness, was the fact that *I was not a Christian* – that I never had been, and never would be – and that the whole structure of Christian doctrine was from beginning to end thoroughly repugnant to me. This realization gave me a sense of relief, of liberation as from some oppressive burden, which was so great that I wanted to sing and dance for joy. What I was, what I believed, I knew not, but what I was not and what I did not believe, that I knew with utter certainty, and this knowledge, merely negative though it was as yet, gave me a foretaste of that freedom which comes when all obstacles are removed, all barriers broken down, all limitations transcended.[306]

I spent seven or eight months in Torquay. At the end of this period I returned to London, as I was feeling homesick. I had been away a year. For the next few months I did little except read books on my favourite subjects and write poetry, which I had been doing for some time. I borrowed books not only from the Tooting Public Library, as I had done before, but also from its counterpart in Streatham High Street, which had a better philosophy section. The only book on Christianity that I can recall reading at this time was Newman's *The Arians of the Fourth Century*, which I probably read as much for its literary style as for its contents.

This idyllic existence came to an end in November 1941, when I started working at County Hall. The fact that I now had a full-time job meant that I had less time for reading; but it also meant that since I was working I was earning, and since I was earning I had money with which to buy books. Soon I was spending much of my lunch hour, and most of Saturday afternoon, browsing in the bookshops of Charing Cross Road. In one of these I came across translations of the *Diamond Sūtra* and the *Sūtra of Wei Lang* (Huineng). These two books changed my life. Reading them I realized that I was a Buddhist, and always had been one.[307] Though I continued to have contact with Christianity, at least from time to time, henceforth I was in contact with it *as a Buddhist.*

2
THE BIBLE AS LITERATURE

For me, 'the Bible' means the English Bible. More specifically, it means the Authorized Version of 1611, so called on account of its having been 'newly translated out of the original tongues' by command of King James I. For me, therefore, the Bible is primarily a literary work, or rather, a collection of such works, and is as much a part of English literature as Dryden's *Virgil*, Pope's *Homer*, or FitzGerald's *Omar Khayyám*.

The fact that for me the Bible is a literary work means that, for me, it cannot be the Word of God. Quite apart from the circumstance that I am a Buddhist, and do not believe in the existence of a personal God, the creator and ruler of the universe, the fact that the Bible is clearly the work of a number of writers, living at widely separate periods, and that it contains as many factual errors, contradictions, and interpolations, as any other body of ancient writings, makes it impossible for me to regard it as the work of an omniscient author who at different times has dictated it, as it were, to various human amanuenses.

I have never read the Bible straight through, from the Book of Genesis to the Book of Revelation, as some pious Christians do every year, but in the course of my life I have read most of it, and some parts I have read a number of times. When I was in my teens my favourite books were the Book of Job and the Song of Solomon, especially the former, which I read over and over again. I had the good fortune to possess a separate edition of these works which besides printing the text as poetry, as the Authorized Version of 1611 had done, also contained

Blake's illustrations, which I have always admired no less than the Book of Job itself. According to modern scholarship the work was probably composed at the beginning of the fifth century BCE. The first two chapters are in prose, as is the last chapter. In between are fifty chapters of very fine, if sometimes repetitive, poetry. The poem revolves around a fundamental problem: why does the good man suffer? The ancient Jews believed that the good man did *not* suffer; only the wicked suffer. If a man fears God, and eschews evil, God will bless him with long life, offspring, and material wealth. Job is a good man, perfect and upright, and God had blessed him with seven sons and three daughters, and with seven thousand sheep, three thousand camels, five hundred yoke of oxen, five hundred she asses, and a very great household. But suppose God were to take all that away. Would Job not curse God?

The story begins in heaven. One day the sons of God come to present themselves before the Lord, and Satan also comes. He has been visiting the Earth, and the Lord asks him if he has observed Job, a perfect and upright man, who fears God and eschews evil. Satan replies that he has indeed observed him. But Job has good reason to fear God, he says, for has not God always protected him and all his possessions? If the Lord were to deprive him of his possessions Job would curse him to his face. The Lord thereupon delivers all Job's possessions into the power of Satan, but not Job himself. On one and the same day, the Sabeans fall upon his oxen and his asses and take them away, the fire of God falls from heaven and burns up his sheep, the Caldeans carry away his camels, and a great wind comes from the desert and blows down the house in which his sons and daughters are feasting, killing them all. Yet despite his misfortunes Job does not curse God. 'Naked came I out of my mother's womb,' he says, 'naked shall I return thither: the Lord gave, and the Lord hath taken away, blessed be the name of the Lord.' Satan therefore again presents himself before the Lord. This time the Lord delivers Job's body into his power, though not his life, whereupon Satan smites Job with boils, from the soles of his feet to the crown of his head. Taking a fragment of pottery with which to scrape himself, Job then sits down among ashes, where he is visited by his three friends, Eliphaz, Bildad, and Zophar, who have heard of his misfortunes and have come to comfort him. For seven days and seven nights they sit down with him on the ground, out of sympathy not saying a word. At last Job speaks, cursing the day he was born, and the poem proper begins:

Let the day perish, wherein I was born,
And the night in which it was said,
There is a man-child conceived.
Let that day be darkness,
Let not God regard it from above,
Neither let the light shine upon it.
Let darkness and the shadow of death stain it,
Let a cloud dwell upon it,
Let the blackness of the day terrify it.
As for that night, let darkness seize upon it,
Let it not be joined unto the days of the year,
Let it not come into the number of the months.
Lo, let that night be solitary,
Let no joyful voice come therein.
Let them curse it that curse the day,
Who are ready to raise up their mourning.
Let the stars of the twilight thereof be dark,
Let it look for light, but have none,
Neither let it see the dawning of the day:
Because it shut not up the doors of my mother's womb,
Nor hid sorrow from mine eyes.
Why died I not from the womb?
Why did I not give up the ghost when I came out of the belly?
Why did the knees prevent me?
Or why the breasts, that I should suck?
For now should I have lain still and been quiet,
I should have slept; then had I been at rest,
With Kings and counsellors of the earth,
Which built desolate places for themselves,
Or with Princes that had gold,
Who filled their houses with silver:
Or as an hidden untimely birth, I had not been;
As infants which never saw light.
There the wicked cease from troubling:
And there the weary be at rest.[308]

When Job has concluded his speech, of which I have quoted rather more than half, Eliphaz replies to him at even greater length. In the words of the translator's marginal note, he 'reproveth Job for want of religion'. No one who is innocent ever perishes, he declares, as Job himself has formerly taught many; but now when he is being afflicted himself, he complains and questions God's justice. Instead of complaining, he should reflect on the greatness of God and be glad that God is punishing him, for in the long run this will benefit him greatly.

Job will have none of this. He has cause for complaint, he exclaims, and after reproving his friend for his unkindness he proceeds to give eloquent expression to his desire for death, a desire which, he says, is quite justified. Bildad then speaks. How much longer will he go on repeating the same thing, he impatiently asks Job. God deals with men according to their works, as history abundantly shows. He punishes the wicked, and Job's present plight is simply an example of his justice. Job acknowledges God's justice, but goes on to argue that although God can destroy both the perfect and the wicked, if he so wills, the fact that he has afflicted him does not mean that he is not innocent. He then expostulates with God, asking why he has afflicted him. God knows he is not wicked. Why, then, should he afflict him, the work of his hands. He has suffered enough, he tells God. All he now wants is a little ease before death. Zophar then joins in the discussion, reproving Job for insisting on his innocence, and emphasizing that God's wisdom is unfathomable. To this Job replies in a long speech, occupying three chapters, in the course of which he acknowledges God's omnipotence, reproves his friends for their partiality, and affirms his confidence in God. 'Though he slay me, yet will I trust in him', he says. Eliphaz now speaks for the second time, again reproving Job for insisting on his innocence and describing at length the unhappiness of the wicked.

By this time Job has lost patience with his friends. 'Miserable comforters are ye all', he tells them. But the debate continues nevertheless for sixteen more chapters, after which Job's three 'comforters' fall silent, 'because he is righteous in his own eyes'. Elihu, who so far has not been mentioned, now speaks. (His speech may be an interpolation.) He is a much younger man, and has not spoken before out of respect for his elders. He is angry with Job because he 'justifies' himself, and with Job's three friends because they have not been able to convince him. He himself succeeds no better, however. Though he speaks at length, he is able to add little to what the friends had already said, and Job does not bother to answer him.

We are now nine tenths of our way through the work and have reached its climax – the Lord's speech. The Lord's speech covers four chapters, and is interrupted only by Job's brief acknowledgement of his vileness. He does not tell Job why he has been afflicted. Instead, speaking 'out of the whirlwind', he overwhelms him with a declaration of his greatness and power, as manifested by the whole of creation, saying:

Who is this that darkeneth counsel
By words without knowledge?
Gird up now thy loins like a man;
For I will demand of thee, and answer thou me.
Where wast thou when I laid the foundations of the earth?
Declare, if thou hast understanding.
Who hath laid the measures thereof, if thou knowest?
Or who hath stretched the line upon it?
Whereupon are the foundations thereof fastened?
Or who laid the corner stone thereof,
When the morning stars sang together,
And all the sons of God shouted for joy?
Or who shut up the sea with doors,
When it brake forth as if it had issued out of the womb?
When I made the cloud the garment thereof,
And thick darkness a swaddling band for it,
And brake up for it my decreed place,
And set bars and doors,
And said, Hitherto shalt thou come, but no further:
And here shall thy proud waves be stayed?[309]

He goes on in this vein, at one point asking Job, with heavy sarcasm, if he knows where light and darkness dwell because he was born then, or because the number of his days is great. More rhetorical questions follow:

Hast thou entered into the springs of the sea?
Or hast thou walked in the search of the depth?
Have the gates of death been opened unto thee?
Or hast thou seen the doors of the shadow of death?
Hast thou perceived the breadth of the earth?

Declare if thou knowest it all.
Where is the way where light dwelleth?
And as for darkness, where is the place thereof,
That thou shouldest take it to the bound thereof,
And that thou shouldest know the paths to the house thereof?
Knowest thou it, because thou wast then born?
Or because the number of thy days is great?
Hast thou entered into the treasures of the snow?
Or hast thou seen the treasures of the hail,
Which I have reserved against the time of trouble,
Against the day of battle and war?
By what way is the light parted,
Which scattereth the east wind upon the earth?
Who hath divided a water-course for the overflowing of waters?
Or a way for the lightning of thunder,
To cause it to rain on the earth, where no man is:
On the wilderness wherein there is no man;
To satisfy the desolate and waste ground,
And to cause the bud of the tender herb to spring forth?
Hath the rain a father?
Or who hath begotten the drops of dew?
Out of whose womb came the ice?
And the hoary frost of heaven, who hath gendered it?
The waters are hid as with a stone,
And the face of the deep is frozen.[310]

The Lord then directs Job's attention to the animal kingdom, asking him if he knows the ways of the hind, the wild asses, and the unicorn, and whether he is able to control them. Next, Job is asked about the horse, which the unknown author of the Book of Job describes in a manner that shows he had a painter's eye for the beauties and splendours of the natural world:

Hast thou given the horse strength?
Hast thou clothed his neck with thunder?
Canst thou make him afraid as a grasshopper?
The glory of his nostrils is terrible.
He paweth in the valley, and rejoiceth in his strength:

He goeth on to meet the armed men.
He mocketh at fear, and is not affrighted:
Neither turneth he back from the sword.
The quiver rattleth against him,
The glittering spear and the shield.
He swalloweth the ground with fierceness and rage:
Neither believeth he that it is the sound of the trumpet.
He saith among the trumpets, Ha, ha:
And he smelleth the battle afar off,
The thunder of the captains, and the shouting.[311]

Finally, after demanding of Job if he will disannul his judgement, or if he is in any way like him, he directs his attention first to Behemoth and then to Leviathan:

Behold now Behemoth which I made with thee,
He eateth grass as an ox.
Lo now, his strength is in his loins,
And his force is in the navel of his belly.
He moveth his tail like a Cedar:
The sinews of his stones are wrapt together.
His bones are as strong pieces of brass:
His bones are like bars of iron.
He is the chief of the ways of God:
He that made him, can make his sword to approach unto him.
Surely the mountains bring him forth food:
Where all the beasts of the field play.
He lieth under the shady trees,
In the covert of the reed, and fens.
The shady trees cover him with their shadow:
The willows of the brook compass him about.
Behold, he drinketh up a river, and hasteth not:
He trusteth that he can draw up Jordan into his mouth.
He taketh it with his eyes:
His nose pierceth through snares.[312]

The description of Leviathan is much longer, and no less magnificent, and concludes:

He maketh the deep to boil like a pot:
He maketh the sea like a pot of ointment.
He maketh a path to shine after him;
One would think the deep to be hoary.
Upon earth there is not his like:
Who is made without fear.
He beholdeth all high things:
He is a king over all the children of pride.[313]

The Lord's speech having come to an end, Job submits himself to God:

I have heard of thee by the hearing of the ear:
But now my eye seeth thee.
Wherefore I abhor myself, and repent
In dust and ashes.[314]

The story ends with the Lord telling Eliphaz, in the concluding prose chapter, that he is angry with him and his two friends for not having spoken rightly of God, as Job had done. They are to offer up seven bullocks and seven rams by way of penance and Job is to pray for them. Job himself is accepted by the Lord, who gives him three new daughters and seven new sons, and double the number of sheep, camels, and yoke of oxen than he had before. Moreover, Job lives a hundred and forty years and sees his sons' sons, even to four generations.

The Book of Job has been described as the masterpiece of Hebrew literature, a judgement from which it is difficult to dissent. It is not a theodicy. It does not attempt to 'justify God's ways to men'.[315] Indeed, it views any such attempt as presumptuous. Its God is not the God of love but the God of power – a power as manifest in the physical universe, from the starry heavens to the creatures of the earth, including man. As such he is well able to inflict suffering on man, but he cannot tell him why he does so. Though the Book of Job does not say so, man's questions must be answered by man himself.

The Song of Solomon is much shorter than the Book of Job, and is not nearly so great a work. But it contains some lovely poetry, the rhythms of which – in the Authorized Version – are much lighter than are those of the magnificent strophes of the Book of Job. Though the work is ascribed to King Solomon, it has no connection with him, and in its present form belongs to a much later period. It consists of a series of love poems – or wedding songs – which in one modern translation are distributed, quite plausibly, among the Bridegroom, the Bride, and the Chorus. I have always loved its celebration of the coming of spring, when the lover – or Bridegroom – shows himself through the lattice, and says:

Rise up, my Love, my fair one, and come away.
For lo, the winter is past,
The rain is over and gone.
The flowers appear on the earth,
The time of the singing of birds is come,
And the voice of the turtle is heard in our land.
The fig tree putteth forth her green figs,
And the vines with the tender grape
Give a good smell.
Arise, my Love, my fair one, and come away.[316]

There is also a passage which itemizes the charms of the loved one in terms that modern taste is likely to find odd, even grotesque; such descriptions are not unusual in Elizabethan and Jacobean poetry:

How beautiful are thy feet with shoes, O prince's daughter!
The joints of thy thighs are like jewels,
The work of the hands of a cunning workman.
Thy navel is like a round goblet,
Which wanteth not liquor:
Thy belly is like an heap of wheat,
Set about with lilies.
Thy two breasts are like two young roes
That are twins.
Thy neck is as a tower of ivory:
Thine eyes like the fish pools in Heshbon, by the gate of Bathrabbim:
Thy nose is as the tower of Lebanon,
Which looketh toward Damascus.
Thine head upon thee is like Carmel,
And the hair of thine head like purple,
The king is held in the galleries.

How fair, and how pleasant art thou,
O Love, for delights!
This thy stature is like to a palm tree,
And thy breasts to clusters of grapes.[317]

A more solemn note is struck in a short passage near the end of the work, where the lover says:

Set me as a seal upon thine heart, as a seal upon thine arm:
For love is strong as death,
Jealousy is cruel as the grave:
The coals thereof are coals of fire,
Which hath a most vehement flame.
Many waters cannot quench love,
Neither can the floods drown it.[318]

The Song of Solomon was accepted into the Jewish canon of scriptures only after its contents had been interpreted as an elaborate allegory of God's love for his chosen people, the Jews. When the books of the Old Testament became part of the Christian Bible, the Song of Solomon continued to be treated as an allegory, this time as an allegory of Christ's love for the Church and the Church's love for Christ. Some of the Christian mystics, especially those of a more devotional type, continued this tradition of allegorical interpretation of the work, in whose erotic imagery they found a language for the expression of their devotional longings and spiritual experiences. St Bernard once delivered a series of impassioned sermons on the work, while its imagery informs some of the most beautiful poetry of St John of the Cross.[319]

The Book of Job and the Song of Solomon both belong to a group of works known as the 'wisdom writings', as do the Book of Psalms, the Proverbs, and Ecclesiastes or the Preacher. They are called wisdom writings because Jewish tradition ascribes most of them to the proverbially wise King Solomon, and the wisdom of which they treat is of a worldly, prudential kind that does not exclude an element of theistic piety. The Psalms have never appealed to me, but I have dipped into Proverbs from time to time and have come across such maxims as 'whoso loveth instruction, loveth knowledge; But he that hateth reproof, is brutish', and 'A soft answer turneth away wrath; but grievous words stir up anger', both of which have their parallels in the much more ancient wisdom literature of Babylon and Egypt.[320] I have also enjoyed, in the admonition to the sluggard, the delightful vignette of the busy ant:

> Go to the Ant, thou sluggard,
> Consider her ways, and be wise.
> Which have no guide,
> Overseer, or ruler,
> Provideth her meat in the Summer,
> And gathereth her food in the harvest.
> How long wilt thou sleep, O sluggard?
> When wilt thou arise out of thy sleep?
> Yet a little sleep, a little slumber,
> A little folding of the hands to sleep.
> So shall thy poverty come as one that travaileth,
> And thy want as an armed man.[321]

I have also appreciated the realistic description, from the unknown author's personal observation, of what the marginal note bluntly calls 'the cunning of a whore':[322]

> For at the window of my house
> I looked through my casement,
> And beheld among the simple ones,
> I discerned among the youths,
> A young man void of understanding,
> Passing through the street near her corner,
> And he went the way to her house,
> In the twilight in the evening,
> In the black and dark night:
> And behold, there met him a woman,
> With the attire of an harlot, and subtle of heart.
> (She is loud and stubborn,
> Her feet abide not in her house:
> Now is she without, now in the streets,
> And lieth in wait at every corner.)
> So she caught him, and kissed him,

> And with an impudent face said unto him,
> I have peace offerings with me:
> This day have I paid my vows.
> Therefore came I forth to meet thee,
> Diligently to seek thy face, and I have found thee.
> I have decked my bed with coverings of tapestry,
> With carved works, with fine linen of Egypt.
> I have perfumed my bed
> With myrrh, aloes, and cinnamon.
> Come, let us take our fill of love until the morning,
> Let us solace our selves with loves.
> For the good-man is not at home,
> He is gone a long journey.
> He hath taken a bag of money with him,
> And will come home at the day appointed.
> With her much fair speech she caused him to yield,
> With the flattering of her lips she forced him.
> He goeth after her straightway,
> As an ox goeth to the slaughter,
> Or as a fool to the correction of the stocks,
> Till a dart strike through his liver,
> As a bird hasteth to the snare,
> And knoweth not that it is for his life.

My least favourite books of the Bible are the so-called historical books of the Old Testament, such as the Book of Judges, and 1 and 2 Samuel, which are not genuine histories but a mixture of history, folklore, legend, and myth. They contain some good stories, some of which are as familiar to me from certain Renaissance paintings as they are from the pages of the Bible. But the historical books also contain much that I find abhorrent, so that I can well understand why Aldous Huxley should have referred to the Old Testament as 'this savage Bronze Age literature'.[323] For example, in 1 Samuel the Lord commands King Saul, through the prophet Samuel, to destroy the Amalekites, saying:

> Now go and smite Amalek, and utterly destroy all that they have, and spare them not; but slay both man and woman, infant and suckling, ox and sheep, camel and ass.[324]

Since for orthodox Christians the Bible, including the historical books, is the Word of God, passages like this one have enabled them to conduct crusades and pogroms with a clear conscience.

For me, then, the Bible is literature, and it is as literature that I enjoy it. That it is not the Word of God does not mean that, for me, it is not inspired. Some parts of it, at least, are inspired in much the same way that some of my favourite poets are inspired, and in my book that is no small praise.

3
THE CHURCH

When I was a small boy, growing up in South London, I was reminded, every year, of the Catholic conspiracy to blow up James I and his parliament on 5 November 1605. 'Please to remember the fifth of November, gunpowder, treason, and plot', we chanted at school on the anniversary of that day; and in the evening, as soon as it was dark, we burnt an effigy – a 'guy' – of Guy Fawkes on a bonfire in our back yards and let off fireworks.

The Gunpowder Plot must have left deep traces in the English folk memory for us to be still celebrating Guy Fawkes Day or Bonfire Night, as it was also called, more than three hundred years after the event. It was as though we had always known about the Plot and about how Guy Fawkes was surprised, in the vaults below the Palace of Westminster, with barrels of gunpowder and a lighted torch. There were other traces, left by earlier events in English history in which Catholics, or the Roman Catholic Church, had played a sinister part. There was the Spanish Armada of 1588, which Philip II of Spain had launched with the object of dethroning Queen Elizabeth, installing her Catholic cousin Mary, Queen of Scots in her place, and with the help of the Inquisition returning England to the Catholic fold. We knew about the great Armada, and about how it had been defeated by Drake and the elements, not so much from our history lessons as from stories in the various boys' papers that were set in that period.

Later, I learned about the Ridolfi Plot, the aim of which was to assassinate Elizabeth, place Mary on the throne, bring about a general uprising of Catholics against the government, and restore Catholicism as the religion of the land. The plot had been sanctioned, in effect, by Pope Pius V's bull of 1570, in which he denounced Elizabeth as a heretic, excommunicated her, and absolved her subjects from all obedience to her. A subsequent directive from the papal Secretary of State decreed that if any English gentleman were to undertake the 'glorious work' of assassinating Queen Elizabeth it would not be regarded as a sin.

In the previous reign, that of Elizabeth's Catholic half-sister Queen Mary I, there had taken place an event that probably left even deeper traces in the English folk memory than the Gunpowder Plot. This was the burning at the stake, as heretics, of nearly three hundred Protestants of both sexes and all ages. Among the victims were Bishops Ridley and Latimer, and Archbishop Cranmer, who met their deaths in Oxford in 1555 and 1556, near the spot on which a memorial to them, erected in 1839, now stands. Latimer's last words to his colleague Ridley were, 'Be of good cheer, Master Ridley, for I trust that this day we will light such a candle in England as by God's grace shall never be put out.'

I do not remember when I first read about the Ridolfi Plot or about the burning of Protestants in the reign of Mary I – 'Bloody Mary', as she came to be called – but I retain a distinct visual impression of two illustrations I saw, illustrations connected with two of the most horrifying episodes in European religious history. I came upon the first of these while still confined to bed, and I came upon it in the *Children's Encyclopedia*. It depicted a scene in the English embassy in Paris at the time of the Massacre of St Bartholomew's Eve, when in 1572, in the course of a single week, 25,000 Huguenots – French Protestants – were slaughtered in Paris and elsewhere in the country on the orders of the French king, Charles IX. In the illustration seven or eight men are gathered in front of a large window, their backs to the viewer. They are observing the carnage going on outside. To the right, an older man stands with hands clasped behind his back and head bowed, deep in thought. In the foreground, one woman bends solicitously over another, whose head is buried in the lap of a third woman.[325]

The second illustration occupied the front cover of a booklet I bought in Westminster Cathedral, on the occasion when my mother and I visited it with my Auntie Kate. The booklet was about the Spanish Inquisition, and the illustration depicted a single figure. He is carrying a lighted taper, and on his head there is a kind of dunce's cap inscribed with various symbols. His posture is extremely dejected. Apparently he is a reclaimed heretic doing public penance for his sins.

The two illustrations must have affected me deeply for me to have retained visual images of them for so long. I must have felt the horror, the grief, and the distress of those people in the English embassy and have shared the dejection of the penitent. I certainly have a clear recollection of what I thought and felt when I read the booklet I had bought. The author did not seek to deny that the Inquisition had burnt people at the stake, which he could hardly have done without blushing, but he sought to excuse the Inquisition, to an extent, by maintaining that the total number of persons burnt had been greatly exaggerated by Protestant historians. It was not true, as they alleged, that altogether 80,000 persons had been burnt. It was only 30,000. To me this quibbling over numbers was shockingly beside the point. It was horrible that *anyone* should be burnt at the stake. It was horrible that Catholics should kill Protestants and that such killing should have the sanction, even the blessing, of the pope, the head of the Roman Catholic Church. Later I discovered that the reigning pope had struck a medal commemorating the Massacre of St Bartholomew's Eve, and that it was one of his predecessors who, in 1231, had established the Inquisition, or Holy Office, as it was later styled, to suppress heresy.

My feelings in this connection led me, in the next few years, to take an interest in the history of the Church. For me, 'the Church' means the Roman Catholic Church. This is not because I believe the Roman Catholic Church to have a monopoly of Christian faith or Christian virtue, but because I am a European, and from 313, when Constantine formally recognized Christianity as one of the religions legally permitted within the Roman Empire, to 31 October 1517, when Martin Luther nailed his ninety-five theses to the door of a church in Wittenberg, the history of Europe and the history of the Roman Catholic Church have been virtually inseparable. I did not study the subject systematically, but picked up knowledge about it in the course of my general reading, which at this time included John Addington Symonds' *The Renaissance in Italy*, Mandell Creighton's *History of the Papacy*, and biographies of Elizabeth I and Savonarola (all borrowed from the Tooting Public

Library). I also learned something of the reign of Henry VIII, father of Mary I and Elizabeth I, in which reign there took place the greatest upheaval in the religio-political history of England since the arrival of St Augustine on these shores in 597.

Between 1532 and 1539, exasperated by the continued reluctance of Clement VII to grant him a divorce from Catherine of Aragon, who had failed to produce a male heir to the throne, Henry rejected the authority of the pope, abolished annates to Rome, dissolved the monasteries, declared himself Head of the Church in England, and married Anne Boleyn, the mother of the future Queen Elizabeth. This did not mean that from being Roman Catholic England became Protestant all at once. Henry himself was theologically conservative, and more than one 'heretic' was burnt at the stake in his reign. Mary's four-year reign saw a violent swing from the Protestantism of her brother Edward VI, Henry's immediate successor, back to the Roman Catholic Church, the pope's supremacy being restored and Protestants persecuted. It was only during the long reign of Elizabeth, with her decided preference for the *via media*, that Protestantism in its moderate Anglican form became the predominant – and official – religion of the English people.

But why was it necessary for Henry VIII to ask the pope, more than a thousand miles away in Rome, to grant him a divorce from Catherine of Aragon? And why was the pope so reluctant to accede to his request? The short answer to the first question, I discovered, was that marriage and divorce, like so much else at the time, were matters that came within the jurisdiction of the Church, the supreme head of which was the pope; to the second, that as ruler of the States of the Church – the vast stretch of territory that occupied much of central Italy – the pope was subject to political and military pressure from other European rulers, especially, at that time, from the Holy Roman emperor, Charles V, whose troops had sacked Rome in 1527 and who for reasons both personal and political did not want Henry to get his divorce. But how had the pope – how had the papacy – come to possess so much power, both spiritual and temporal? *That* was the question that now confronted me.

But by the time I reached this point Buddhism had begun to occupy the forefront of my consciousness, so that it was only much later, after my return to England after spending twenty years in the East that, conscious I was teaching the Dharma in a country still predominantly Christian, I picked up the threads of my old studies and gave some attention to Christianity, including the Church. Meanwhile, popes had come and popes had gone, and John XXIII and his Vatican Council had done their work. Much that hitherto had been deemed an essential part of the building had been dismantled, so that the nature of the Church's structure could now be more clearly discerned. Basically, the Roman Catholic Church was – or at least had been, until recently – a spiritual-cum-temporal kingdom – Christendom – of which the pope was king, possessing both spiritual and temporal power.

It was not always so. Believing that Christ would soon return and establish his kingdom, the little Christian church in Rome, with its bishop, refused to take part in the civil and military life of the Roman state. Its members were accordingly proscribed and persecuted by the authorities and regarded as criminals by the rest of society. Being a Christian meant being ready to face death at any time. In 313 all this changed. Constantine, the first Christian emperor of Rome, in that year recognized Christianity as one of the religions permitted within the Roman empire. Nor was this all. The following year he gave the then bishop of the Christian church in Rome, Silvester I, one of the imperial palaces to live in, an enormous amount of money, and much real estate, this becoming the occasion, a thousand years later, of Dante's sorrowful reproach, as translated by Milton:

> Ah Constantine, of how much ill was cause,
> Not thy conversion, but those rich domains
> That the first wealthy pope received of thee![326]

The 'ill' consisted in the fact that the patronage of Constantine transformed the bishop of the Christian church in Rome into 'the pope', a temporal as well as a spiritual ruler, and his church into the Roman Catholic Church. Before long the Church had its own government (the hierarchy), its own legal system (canon law), its own court (the hated 'ecclesiastical court' of English history), its own fortresses and prisons, and eventually its own army.

Silvester's spiritual power was not bestowed on him by Constantine. It resided in the fact that as Bishop of Rome he was the successor of the Apostle Peter, the first bishop, to whom Christ had said,

> Thou art Peter, and on this rock I will build my church; and the gates of hell shall not prevail against it. And I will give unto thee

> the keys of the kingdom of heaven; and whatsoever thou shalt bind on earth shall be bound in heaven: and whatsoever thou shalt loose on earth shall be loosed in heaven.[327]

It was by virtue of the spiritual power entrusted by Christ to St Peter, and possessed by all Peter's successors as Bishop of Rome, that the pope could excommunicate individuals and communities, and place whole kingdoms under an interdict. Innocent III excommunicated King John and placed England under an interdict (1208 CE) when John resisted his attempts to encroach upon the traditional right of the English crown in episcopal elections. Excommunication not only meant being expelled from the visible Church on earth; by virtue of Christ's promise to Peter it also meant being excluded from heaven. Under an interdict the clergy were prohibited from administering the sacraments and the dead could not be buried in consecrated ground. In the Ages of Faith, when men believed that 'outside the Church there is no salvation', excommunication and interdict were formidable weapons, and the popes did not hesitate to employ them in support of their increasingly grandiose claims, whether spiritual or temporal. They were the means by which recalcitrant princes could be brought to heel, as King John eventually was.

In Shakespeare's *King John* there is a scene in which the king surrenders his crown to Cardinal Pandulph, 'the holy legate of the pope', who hands it back to him in token of the fact that, as the legate says, John now holds his royal authority 'of the pope', meaning that John is now the pope's vassal.[328] A few years ago I attended a performance of *King John* at Stratford-upon-Avon, Shakespeare's birthplace, and was greatly struck by the way in which this scene was presented.[329] Only Pandulph and the king were on stage. Pandulph, in his scarlet robes, was enthroned aloft, his head almost touching the ceiling, while John crouched below him in a posture of abject surrender. At this point in the production I thought I felt a kind of frisson run through the audience, as if some members of it had been put in mind of the fact that, eight hundred years after King John, the country might again have to give up its sovereignty, this time not to Rome but to Brussels. When *King John* was first performed, sometime between 1591 and 1598, much more than a frisson must have passed through the audience. They must have remembered, with a surge of patriotic pride, the defeat of the Spanish Armada and the failure of Philip II's attempt to bring England back into the Roman Catholic Church by force of arms.

Be that as it may, the scene from *King John*, as I saw it acted that evening, was a perfect representation of the blatant triumphalism of the medieval papacy, whose spiritual-cum-temporal power was at its height during the reign of Innocent III, before it was weakened by the Great Schism, when two, or even three, rival popes cursed and excommunicated each other. Innocent III (1198–1216) is in the line of Leo I, Gregory I, and Nicolas I, all of whom are styled 'the Great' because they had a 'high' conception of the pope's prerogatives and sought – with varying degrees of success – to act in accordance with it. Leo I (440–461) laid down the doctrine that the bishops depended for the exercise of their jurisdiction on the pope, who alone possessed the plenitude of power. Gregory I (590–604) decreed that the pope alone had the right to depose emperors and kings; that the pope could absolve subjects from their oaths of loyalty; and that the pope could be judged by no one. Nicolas I (858–867) claimed the right to legislate for the whole of Christendom. In his view the pope was the supreme judge, by whom all major disputes were to be judged, and who could accept appeals from lesser courts.

These popes, more than any of the others, determined the basic mindset of the Roman Catholic Church for centuries to come. It was a mindset that was legalistic, intolerant, and authoritarian, and one that above all was bent on its own aggrandisement in the name of Christ. As late as 1864, when the papacy was about to lose what was left of the papal states, the then pope, Pius IX, condemned as erroneous the opinion that 'the Church has not the power of using force, nor has she any temporal power, direct or indirect'.

When the Devil tempted him in the wilderness, offering to give him 'all the kingdoms of the world, and the glory of them', if he would fall down and worship him, Jesus had said 'Get thee hence, Satan'.[330] Three hundred years later, when the Devil appeared again, in the benign form of the emperor Constantine, Silvester I did not treat him so rudely. He accepted the palace, the money, and the civil jurisdiction that were offered him, thus in effect falling down and worshipping the Devil.

The pope, now a ruler among rulers, used his temporal power as ruler of the papal states in the interests of his spiritual authority, and his spiritual power as Bishop of Rome, the successor of St Peter, in the interests of his – and the Church's – worldly power and prestige.

Before long the two powers, and the two sets of interests, were virtually indistinguishable, and the Church became a spiritual-cum-temporal kingdom ruled by a pope-king who for a time was the most important ruler in Europe. 'Power tends to corrupt', wrote Lord Acton, historian and Roman Catholic, 'and absolute power corrupts absolutely.'[331] The papacy never quite possessed absolute power, though it strove to achieve it, but the corruption nevertheless was spectacular. I was therefore not surprised, especially after I had read about the Renaissance popes, to learn that there were Protestants who identified the papacy with the Great Whore seen by St John the Divine in the Book of Revelation:

> And I saw a woman sit upon a scarlet coloured beast, full of names of blasphemy, having seven heads and ten horns. And the woman was arrayed in purple and scarlet colour, and decked with gold and precious stones and pearls, having a golden cup in her hand full of abominations and filthiness of her fornication: And on her forehead was a name written, MYSTERY, BABYLON THE GREAT, THE MOTHER OF HARLOTS AND ABOMINATIONS OF THE EARTH. And I saw the woman drunken with the blood of the saints, and with the blood of the martyrs of Jesus.[332]

For those who saw the papacy as the Great Whore, the blood with which the woman was drunk was the blood of the Protestant martyrs, like those who had been burnt at the stake in the reign of Mary I, or who had died in the Massacre of St Bartholomew's Eve.

That the Church was corrupt, inasmuch as it was based on power, did not mean that something of its original spirit did not survive within its massive structures. I am well aware that in every generation there were Catholics who led honourable and blameless lives, though the fact that they were members of the Church meant that they helped support, even if they did not directly contribute to, the general corruption. In recent times this has been much less the case than it was formerly, there now being much less of the Church to support, so to speak, even in countries where the population is largely Catholic. Since 1870, when the papacy was shorn of its temporal power, and especially since Vatican II, papal authority has weighed less heavily on clergy and laity alike than at any time in the Church's history. Interdicts are unknown, while the formal excommunication of Marcel Lefebvre in 1988 for the unauthorized ordination of priests – the first excommunication within the Church for more than a hundred years – was so exceptional as to be front page news.[333]

One of the consequences of the Church's updating, as it has been called, is that Catholics are now free to enter into dialogue with the followers of other faiths, and even to learn about those faiths. In the course of the last fifty years, therefore, I have been able not only to read about the Church but also to have personal contact, as a Buddhist, with some of its more open-minded members. During my time in India most of the Christians I got to know were missionaries. Kalimpong, a hill station in the foothills of the eastern Himalayas, where I lived for fourteen years, was particularly rich in missionaries. There were the Scottish Presbyterians, who did their best to ignore me, the friendly American Seventh Day Adventists who invited me to lunch, and the two 'missionary girls' fresh from Bible college in England, who after their failure to convert me regarded me, with evident horror, as one of the irretrievably lost. There were also the loners, such as the saintly American member of the Cowley Fathers, an Anglican religious order, who loved lepers and scandalized his fellow missionaries by refusing to convert anyone, and the bumptious, red-bearded Scottish evangelist who belonged to no Christian body and who 'took his orders direct from God'. And there were the Roman Catholics.[334]

The Catholics were the mainly Swiss priests and brothers at St Augustine's Priory and the nuns, some of them Indian, at St Philomena's Convent nearby. The former conducted a boarding school for boys, the latter a boarding school for girls. Each had built their own church. The priests and brothers had constructed theirs on the model of a Tibetan *gompa*, while the nuns had opted for something vaguely Gothic, with stained glass windows. Some of the brothers got into the habit of visiting me, as the rented building in which I was then living was situated halfway between the priory and the bazaar, and it was easy for them to drop in on their way to market. I returned their visits, and in this way got to know some of them quite well. I lent them books on Buddhism and borrowed Christian classics from the Priory library, and we had long and interesting discussions on Buddhism, comparative religion, and mysticism. This friendly contact, which took place in the early 1950s, did not continue for more than two or three months. The brothers suddenly stopped coming to see me, and when I happened to meet them on the road they seemed embarrassed. Much later I learned that someone in authority had forbidden them to have anything more to do with me.

A year or two later I met a Roman Catholic of a very different kind from whoever it was had told the Augustinian brothers that they were to stop seeing me. This was a little gnome-like, bright-eyed French priest called Father Monchanin, one of the founders of the first 'Christian ashrams' in India, and thus a forerunner of the better known Father Bede Griffiths, whose autobiography, *The Golden String*, I read some years later. I met Father Monchanin not in Kalimpong but in Bangalore, at the Indian Institute of Culture, where for two hours or more we discussed Buddhism, especially the Mādhyamikavāda, Vedanta, and comparative mysticism. I would have liked to see more of Father Monchanin, but our paths did not cross again, though we exchanged a few letters, and not many years after our meeting he died.

At about the same time I made the acquaintance of two other Catholic priests, with one of whom I was to be in fairly regular contact for the rest of my time in India. I met both of them in Bombay, at the home of my Parsee friend Dinshaw Mehta, founder of the Society of Servants of God, with whom I often stayed when I was lecturing in that cosmopolitan city. Father Mascarhenas, a Goanese by birth, was a large, cheerful, communicative man in his mid-fifties with an enormous paunch that threatened to burst the buttons on his tightly stretched white soutane. A very learned man, the master of many languages, his views on Indian Catholicism, or rather, on Catholicism in India, were very much in accord with Father Monchanin's. He believed that the Church had to become culturally much more Indian. In particular, he believed that just as, in Europe, Catholic theology, in the person of St Thomas Aquinas, had absorbed and Christianized the philosophy of Aristotle, so in India it had to absorb and Christianize the philosophy of Śaṅkara, and since I had studied the works of the great exponent of Advaita Vedanta we had some interesting discussions. Father Mascarhenas also believed that the Three Magi who, in the Gospel According to St Matthew, present the infant Jesus with gold, frankincense, and myrrh, all came from western India, possibly from Goa.

Not surprisingly, he was often in trouble with his ecclesiastical superiors for his views on the Indianization of the Church, and more than once had to appear before the Archbishop to receive a warning or a reprimand. For a period he had even been suspended from the exercise of his priestly functions, though for precisely what offence he did not say. All this was as water off a duck's back, however, and among his non-Christian friends, at least, he continued to air his unorthodox views, as well as to denounce what he called 'the Roman racket' in unsparing terms. Once he told me that he hated Christmas. He hated it because it was in the week before Christmas Day that many Bombay Catholics made their annual confession, and he was obliged to sit for hours on end listening to the same dreary catalogue of petty sins until he felt thoroughly nauseated. Later on, Father Mascarhenas may have had sins of his own to confess. The last time I had news of him, on a return visit to India, he had moved to Poona and was living with a woman.

The other priest I met only once. I do not remember his name, but I well remember his story. We met at the suggestion of my Theosophist friend Sophia Wadia, editor of the *Aryan Path*, who told me that the priest was in a state of great mental distress and might, she thought, find it helpful to talk to me. He came accompanied by an armed bodyguard in the form of two senior police officers, who stationed themselves in the hallway while we talked privately in my room. He was an ex-Jesuit, he explained, and until recently he had been professor of philosophy at a Catholic college near Bangalore. In his classes he had made it clear that certain truths the Church regarded as beyond doubt were, in fact, open to question, at least from the standpoint of philosophy, and could be freely discussed. For this he had got into serious trouble, both with the college authorities and with his Jesuit superiors, and in the end he had decided to leave both the Jesuit order and the Church. At one point he had had an interview with the head of the order in India, who told him that if he agreed to stay in the order and in the Church and to keep his ideas to himself he could have unlimited credit at his wine merchant and unlimited credit with his tailor. (I noticed that my visitor was elegantly dressed in sober black.) He had not agreed. Instead, he had resigned from the Jesuit order and made it known that he no longer considered himself a member of the Catholic Church. During the next few weeks he received more than 1,800 abusive and threatening letters (he told me the exact figure), many of them obscene, and some of them from distant parts of India. One night a group of men, in order to discredit him, had tried to introduce a prostitute into the cottage in which he had taken refuge. In desperation he had fled to Bombay, where Sophia Wadia and other influential friends had secured for him the protection of the police. He was evidently a refined, cultured, and sensitive person and I could see that the experiences he had undergone had left him badly shaken. What I said to him I do not remember. Perhaps all he needed at that time was a sympathetic ear. Nor do I know what happened to him afterwards, though on subsequent visits to Bombay I enquired after him.

'So the Church has been up to its old tricks,' I reflected after my visitor and his bodyguard had left. The Church had been up to its old tricks elsewhere in India too, as I was well aware. Recently one of the Jesuit fathers of North Point, the Catholic boys' college in Darjeeling, had gone to the Deputy Commissioner, the seniormost government officer in that part of West Bengal, and reported that I was a communist spy, at the same time suggesting that in the interest of national security I should be expelled from the Darjeeling district in which Kalimpong was located. Fortunately I knew the Deputy Commissioner and his wife and the next time we happened to meet he told me about the incident. 'I know very well why he reported you,' he added, 'you have nothing to worry about.'

The Church was up to its old tricks not only in India but also in South Vietnam. Like its immediate neighbours, Laos and Cambodia, Vietnam was a Buddhist country, though it did not, as they did, follow the Theravāda, but the Mahāyāna in its Chinese form, with a mixture of Chan and Pure Land Buddhism predominating. In the seventeenth century French Catholics started missions, and it was not long before the Flag followed the Cross. Between 1858 and 1884 France conquered Vietnam, and with Cambodia and Laos it became part of the French colonial possession of Indo-China. After the Second World War, when Vietnam was occupied by the Japanese, France tried to regain control of the territory, being finally defeated at Dien Bien Phu only after eight years of bitter fighting. At the 1954 Geneva Conference the country was divided into communist North Vietnam, led by Ho Chi Minh, with its capital at Hanoi, and pro-western South Vietnam, led by Ngo Dinh Diem, with its capital at Saigon.

President Diem was a Roman Catholic, as was his younger brother Ngo Dinh Nhu, whom he made his personal adviser and put in charge of Intelligence and the Secret Police. His elder brother Ngo Dinh Thuc was Roman Catholic Archbishop of Hue, while his sister-in-law Mme

Nhu, described by her American admirer Clare Booth Luce as 'a militant Catholic', led the paramilitary women's organization. It was therefore not surprising that under the Diem regime, as under French colonial rule, the Catholic minority should have been supported and encouraged while the less organized Buddhist majority should have been discriminated against, suppressed, and finally systematically persecuted.

Things came to a head when on 6 May 1963 the President issued an order prohibiting the Buddhists of Hue from flying the Buddhist flag on the Buddha's birthday two days later, even though a few days earlier, on the occasion of a Catholic festival, the Vatican flag had been flown all over the city. On 8 May, their leaders having failed to get the order rescinded, the Buddhists of Hue protested against the ban by going in procession from Tu Dam Pagoda to the Hue Radio Station. There government troops broke up the procession with tear gas, then fired on the crowd. Twelve people were killed and more than fifty wounded. The Buddhist clergy and laity of South Vietnam then presented the Government with five requests, namely: (1) that the Government rescind the order prohibiting the flying of the Buddhist flag; (2) that Buddhism benefit from the same special treatment granted to the Roman Catholic missions; (3) that the Government stop arresting and terrorizing the Buddhists; (4) that the Buddhist clergy and laymen be free to practise their faith and to spread it; and (5) that the Government pay equitable compensation for the people killed and punish those responsible in a fitting manner.

These requests formed part of a manifesto, the concluding sentence of which read, 'We all are ready to sacrifice ourselves until these reasonable requests are granted.' Events soon showed Diem and the other members of the Catholic oligarchy that the Buddhists meant what they said. On 11 June a 67-year-old monk burnt himself to death in a crowded Saigon thoroughfare in protest against the government's persecution of the Buddhists. The monk, Thích Quảng Đức, struck a match after his saffron robes were drenched with petrol, and sat motionless in the meditation posture while the flames enveloped him. Several hundred monks and nuns sat in a circle round the blazing body, chanting and weeping.

I was still living in India at the time and well remember the shock waves that went round the Buddhist world, as well as round India and the West, as reports of the self-immolation – and pictures of the burning monk – appeared in the newspapers. Only Vietnam's Roman Catholic oligarchy remained unmoved. 'If any more monks want to barbecue themselves,' Mme Nhu told reporters, 'I'll be happy to provide the petrol and a match.' More monks did want to 'barbecue' themselves, and in the course of the next few months, as the Diem government declared martial law and a state of siege, desecrated and destroyed major pagodas throughout South Vietnam, arrested and imprisoned thousands of monks and nuns, and held demonstrating students in concentration camps, eight more monks and one nun followed Thích Quảng Đức's heroic example.

On 1 November the Diem government was overthrown by a long-expected *coup d'état* in which both the president and his younger brother were killed. Mme Nhu was then on a lecture tour in the United States, where she assured university audiences that there was no religious persecution in South Vietnam and that Vietnamese Buddhist monks were Communists in disguise. On being told of the *coup d'état* she angrily accused the United States government and the CIA of being behind it. This was in fact quite true, for Washington had become convinced that by persecuting the Buddhists Diem was undermining South Vietnam's – and the United States' – fight against Communism.

After my return to England in 1964 I was too busy teaching Buddhism and, eventually, starting a new Buddhist movement, to have much time for personal contact with Christians, whether Catholic or Protestant. I did, however, find time to read about Christianity. Besides taking up the thread of my old studies, as I have already related, I read several scholarly volumes on the Eastern Orthodox Church as well as a few works of popular theology. The most interesting of the latter was the best-selling *Honest to God* by John A. T. Robinson, then Bishop of Woolwich. It was of interest to me principally on account of the Bishop's apparent belief that theism was finished, a view that to my mind pointed in the direction of non-theistic religion, even in the direction of non-theistic Christianity, and thus to a possible overlap between Christianity and Buddhism, of which the Bishop seemed not to have heard. I therefore gave my usual Buddhist and quasi-Buddhist audience a lecture on 'Buddhism and the Bishop of Woolwich'.[335] A member of the audience sent a tape-recording of the lecture to the Bishop, who eventually expressed a desire to meet me. We met at his house (bishops no longer lived in palaces), where we had a long and interesting, though not very deep, discussion in which, Dr Robinson being an Anglican bishop, his wife also joined.

For many years after this encounter I had no contact with Christians, so far as I remember, other than at the rather unexciting interfaith gatherings that I was occasionally prevailed upon to attend. After handing on my responsibilities as founder of the new Buddhist movement, which I did in the year 2000, at the age of 75, it occurred to me that I now had time to revisit the interfaith scene. I did this in Birmingham, where I was then living. At meetings of the Birmingham Council of Faiths I met Hindus, Muslims, Sikhs, Parsees, followers of the Bahá'í faith, Roman Catholics, Protestants, and Jews, as well as fellow Buddhists following traditions other than my own.

Strange to relate, it was the Roman Catholics who seemed most interested in following up the contacts we had made. Thus I was invited to Oscott College, where I gave a talk on the Buddhist scriptures, was shown Cardinal Newman's rooms at the Birmingham Oratory, which he had founded, attended a mass celebrated by the new Archbishop of Birmingham, whom afterwards I met several times, and attended a reception given by the archdiocese to the Cardinal Archbishop of Westminster, whom I also met. I even started receiving each year, on the anniversary of the Buddha's attainment of supreme Enlightenment, a friendly message from the Vatican.

What had happened? Had the Roman Catholic Church experienced a change of heart? Did Roman Catholics no longer have to believe that there was no salvation outside the Church? And what of the past? Did the Church realize that it had been morally wrong for it to preach crusades and condemn heretics to death, and was it now trying to make amends? Or was the Catholic Church's present friendly attitude towards non-Catholics due to the fact that it no longer had any temporal power and that, in Britain at least, Catholics had been in a minority for several centuries, and therefore were more or less obliged to be friendly?

These were the sort of questions I wanted to ask my new friends, but before I knew them well enough to be able to ask them without giving offence I was struck down by chronic illness and the questions have remained, for the time being at least, unanswered.

4
THE APOSTLES' CREED

Though I was born into a Church of England family and baptized in the parish church, I did not attend another Anglican service until I was fourteen. This was when, as an evacuee in Torquay, I attended, for a few Sundays, the church at which the clergyman with whom I had been billeted officiated. It must have been the morning service that I attended, for at one point I found myself reciting, with the rest of the congregation, 'I believe in God, the Father Almighty, Maker of heaven and earth: And in Jesus Christ his only Son our Lord' – and so on through the other clauses of what I subsequently learned was the Apostles' Creed. I did not give much thought to what I was reciting but I remember that when we came to the words 'he descended into hell' the organ, which had been accompanying our recitation, sounded a particularly deep and solemn note that vibrated through the little church.

A creed has been defined as 'a form of words in which the articles of faith are comprised' and the Apostles' Creed was the oldest of the three creeds officially authorized by the Western Church, the two others being the Nicene Creed and the Athanasian Creed. It was used in the daily offices of the Roman Catholic and Anglican churches, and in the services of several leading Protestant churches. The Eastern Orthodox Church had its own versions of the Apostles' Creed, and it did not regard the Athanasian Creed as authoritative. Besides featuring in the Church of England's morning service the Apostles' Creed also featured in its baptismal service, and must have been recited by the congregation at my own baptism as an infant.

Although infant baptism was practised in the Early Church, in the case of adults the candidate was interrogated before the ceremony, being asked 'Do you believe in God, the Father Almighty, Maker of heaven and earth?' and so on, and having to answer 'I do' as each clause was put to him in this manner in order to be accepted. In the Roman Catholic and Anglican churches the Apostles' Creed therefore has come to be known as 'the baptismal creed'. It is belief in the articles of faith comprised in this particular form of words that made one, in the Western Church at least, a Christian in the traditional sense. Hence if I want to know what Christians traditionally believe, and if, moreover, I want to find out to what extent my own beliefs, as a Buddhist, are in agreement with theirs, I will have to take a look at the Apostles' Creed.

Before I can take that look, however, I must clear up a possible confusion. It is a confusion of the kind that is likely to arise when the Inquisition, for example, is discussed. 'The inquisitors were not true Christians,' one will be told, 'and Christianity should not be blamed for the terrible things they did in its name.' But can it really be said that the inquisitors were not true Christians? For my part, I feel it is not for me, as a Buddhist, to say who is a Christian, true or otherwise, and who is not. The inquisitors, like the crusaders and the bad popes, claimed to be Christians, and I feel I have to take the claim at its face value. Similarly, it is not for me to say what Christians really believe. They say it clearly enough when they recite the Apostles' Creed, and I have to take it that they mean what they say. If I want to find out the extent to which my own beliefs, as a Buddhist, are in agreement with those held by Christians, I shall therefore have to take a look, not at some selective, sanitized version of Christianity that exists only in someone's imagination, but at the Christianity that dominated the life and thought of Europe for more than a thousand years, and which faith finds definitive expression in the certain form of words. I shall have to take a look, in other words, at the Apostles' Creed.

As I found when I recited the Apostles' Creed for the first – and last – time, the Christian begins by affirming his belief in the existence of God.

I believe in God, the Father Almighty, Maker of heaven and earth:

The Nicene Creed, common to the Eastern and Western Churches, not only substitutes 'one God' for 'God' but adds on 'and of all things visible and invisible' – presumably in the interest of greater clarity. I do not wish to offend or shock my Christian friends, but I have to admit that to me this article of the Christian faith is meaningless. Though I understand the meaning of the words *as words*, I am unable to connect them with any intelligible idea. I think I must never have believed in God, even as a child. In my early teen years I responded emotionally to the white-robed, compassionate figure of Jesus as evoked in the moving sermons of the minister of the Baptist church I attended, but talk of God left me completely cold. When I first encountered the Buddha's teaching I therefore was not dismayed to find that there was no place in it for an almighty Creator. For the same reason, unlike many Victorians, eminent and otherwise, and not a few western Buddhists, I never had to go through the painful process of losing my faith in God, and with it my faith in Christianity.

Christians and other believers in God have sometimes asked me what proof I had that God does not exist. I have usually replied that it was not for me to prove to their satisfaction that God does not exist but for them to prove to mine that he does, and so far none of them have succeeded in doing this. None of the arguments I have heard or read, whether the argument from the necessity of there being an uncaused first cause, or the argument from design, or the intellectually more sophisticated argument that the idea of God necessarily involves that of his existence, have been able to convince me that such a being as God does indeed exist.

Some Christians think that one who does not believe in the existence of God, and who cannot be convinced by any of the traditional arguments, is somehow deficient in the religious sense, but this is to identify the religious sense with the theistic sense, as it may be called, which is merely one of its numerous forms. Not only are there primitive societies in which the idea of an almighty Creator is unknown; there are, also, advanced cultures that have no word for such an idea. A Thai Buddhist once told me that when the early Christian missionaries started translating the Bible into the Thai language they were astonished to find it had no word for God. They therefore coined the term 'the Buddha who created the universe'.

The term obviously implies that there is a Buddha who has not created the universe and indeed, such a Buddha – the Buddha of the

Buddhist scriptures and of Buddhist tradition – does exist. This Buddha, who is the supreme object of Buddhist faith and devotion, and going for Refuge to whom makes one a member of the Buddhist community, possesses various attributes. He is boundlessly compassionate, in that he feels love for all suffering sentient beings, perfectly pure, in that he is free from all mental defilements, and infinitely wise, in that he knows what leads, and what does not lead, to the state of complete freedom from suffering, or Nirvāṇa; but unlike the God of Christian belief he is neither omniscient nor omnipotent. Nor is that all. The state or condition of ultimate reality, by virtue of his transcendental knowledge of which the man Gautama became the Buddha, the Enlightened One, boundlessly compassionate, perfectly pure, and infinitely wise, does not stand in the relation of cause, creator, or source to the universe or, in the words of the Nicene Creed, all things visible and invisible.

But if the Buddha did not create the universe, then who did create it? Someone must have created it. And anyway, why is there no place in Buddhism for an almighty Creator? Such are the questions one is sure to be asked should one try to explain Buddhism to those who are new to its teachings, as I have often found, both in India and the West. But Buddhism has a question of its own to ask in return, one might say, a question of a more fundamental nature than these in as much as it challenges the assumptions on which they rest. It asks whether it is really necessary to believe in an almighty Creator and whether, in any case, we really need to know how the universe came into being. In what are probably the oldest Buddhist scriptures the Buddha is emphatic that his teaching has only one aim. That aim, he declares, is to point out the way that leads to the attainment of Enlightenment or Nirvāṇa and make clear what beliefs and practices will help, and what not help, those who seek to follow that way to the end.[336] Beliefs and speculations regarding the origin of the universe are irrelevant so far as that aim is concerned, and it is principally for this reason that belief in the existence of an almighty Creator has no place in Buddhism. Some misguided western Buddhists would like to fill what they see as a God-shaped hole in the Buddha's teaching with a sanitized version of the traditional Christian idea of God, just as some Hindus would like to fill it with the Vedantic notion of Brahman. I have generally referred such persons, when I encountered them, to Helmuth von Glasenapp's excellent study *Buddhism – a Non-Theistic Religion*.[337]

The Buddha also declares, in the same scriptures, that the origin of the universe or 'world' cannot be perceived.[338] It cannot be perceived because perceiving mind and perceived object are correlative, so that however far back in time the mind travels it can never reach a point where there is no object to be perceived, that is, where there is no universe or world. Hence the Buddha also declares that within this six-foot body of ours is the origin and cessation of the world.[339] In other words, the world 'ceases' when the subject–object duality is transcended and there is no world to be experienced by the defiled-mind consciousness, as it was later termed. Paradoxically, the beginning of the world is 'perceived' when there is no one to perceive it.

In view of these facts I have to recognize that at least so far as the first article of the Apostles' Creed is concerned there is no agreement between my own beliefs, as a Buddhist, and the beliefs held by Christians.

And in Jesus Christ his only Son our Lord,

The Nicene Creed's version of this article of the Christian faith is much longer and more elaborate, as though to preclude all possibility of misunderstanding. It runs, 'And in one Lord Jesus Christ, the Son of God, begotten of the Father, only-begotten, God of God, Light of Light, God of very God, begotten not made, of one substance with the Father, by whom all things were made, both those in heaven and those on earth.' The principal point to emerge from this welter of words is that Jesus is not merely the 'anointed one' (*christos*) or Messiah, as in the synoptic gospels, i.e. the gospels according to Sts Matthew, Mark, and Luke; he is also God, as in the fourth Gospel, the Gospel According to St John. Since I do not, as a Buddhist, believe in the existence of God it follows that I cannot see Jesus as God incarnate, especially as identified, in the famous prologue to the fourth Gospel, with the *logos* or Word that was in the beginning, that was with God, and was God, by whom all things were made, and without whom nothing was made that was made.[340] I can, perhaps, see Jesus as a Jewish religious teacher, but that is quite another matter. Christians see him as God, and since I cannot see him in this way my beliefs, as a Buddhist, are again not in agreement with those held by Christians.

Who was conceived by the Holy Ghost, Born of the Virgin Mary,

With this article of faith we come to the Holy Ghost or Holy Spirit, the third member of the divine Trinity, the two other members, God the Father and God the Son being the subjects, respectively, of the first and second articles of the Apostles' Creed. So far as I have been able to make out, the Holy Ghost is a person, not an impersonal influence, in the sense in which the Father and the Son are persons, though 'orthodox' Christian theologians are careful to warn us that in this context the word 'person' is to be understood in an analogical, not a univocal, sense. Yet although the Holy Ghost is a person and not an impersonal influence, in the art of the Western Church, at least, he is not represented in the same kind of way that the Father and the Son are represented. Whereas the latter are boldly anthropomorphized, the Holy Ghost is depicted in the form of a white dove. It is as a white dove that he appears in depictions of the Trinity, balancing on outstretched wings between the Father and the crucified Son; it is as a white dove that John the Baptist sees him descending on Jesus after he has baptized the latter in the River Jordan; and it is as a white dove that he hovers over the meekly bowed head of the Virgin Mary as she receives from the angel Gabriel the news that she is to be the mother of Jesus.

Sceptics have questioned whether Jesus really was born of a virgin, on the grounds that parthenogenesis is unknown among vertebrates, being confined to such lowly life forms as plant lice and water flies. The Christian Church seems to have believed in the Virgin Birth from very early, even apostolic times, though there was also a tradition current among the Jews – attributed by the Christians to malice – that Jesus was the illegitimate son of a Roman soldier named Panthera – a view that has been adopted by some modern writers.[341] The Church naturally regards the Virgin Birth as a miracle, though according to at least some theologians it is not so much that a miracle took place as that it had to take place. It had to take place because the pre-existing Word taking human flesh was an event unique in history, and as such it demanded a unique beginning, just as it was to have a unique consummation on earth in the Resurrection. Thus the Virgin Birth is implied by the Incarnation, and since, as a non-theistic Buddhist, I do not see Jesus as God I am unable to share the Christian belief in the Virgin Birth, even if I were to be convinced that parthenogenesis was possible in the case of the human female.

The Nicene Creed does not add anything to the above two articles of the Apostles' Creed, on the Holy Ghost and the Virgin Birth. It has in their stead a quite different article, which runs, 'Who for us men and for our salvation came down and was made flesh and lived as Man among men'. The idea of the descent of the Divine to earth in order to help and save humanity is by no means peculiar to Christianity. In some of the best-known verses of the *Bhagavad Gītā*, perhaps the most popular of all Hindu scriptures, Sri Krishna tells Arjuna:

> Though I am unborn, of imperishable nature, and though I am the Lord of all beings, yet ruling over my own nature I am born by my own delusive power (*maya*). Whenever there is a decline in religion (*dharma*), O scion of Bharata, a predominance of irreligion (*adharma*), then do I manifest myself. For the protection of the good, and the destruction of the wicked, and for the firm establishment of religion, I am born age after age.[342]

Thus whereas in Christianity the Divine descends only once, in Hinduism there are many such descents or *avatāras*, to use the Sanskrit term, which in fact literally means 'descents'. There is a standard list of the ten *avatāras* of Vishnu from the Meena or Fish *avatāra* to Kalki, the *avatāra* who is yet to come and who will destroy the *mlecchas*, the foreigners, barbarians, or non-Aryans. Sri Krishna, who in the course of the eighteen chapters of the *Bhagavad Gītā* gives Arjuna a complete course in Hindu religion and philosophy, is eighth in the series, coming between the hero-king Rama and the Buddha, whom Hindus recognize as an *avatāra* of Vishnu and Buddhists do not. It should be noted, incidentally, that the *dharma* of which Sri Krishna speaks is not *dharma* in the Buddhist sense. According to the commentary of Śaṅkara, the founder of Advaita Vedanta, the *dharma* of which Sri Krishna speaks is *dharma* as embodied in the institution of the four castes (*varṇa*) and four stages of life (*āśramas*), 'which are the means of attaining prosperity and salvation'.

The idea of descent or *avatāra* is not unknown in Buddhism. The Buddha – or rather the Buddha-to-be – also descends; but he descends not from the Absolute or Unconditioned but from a heavenly realm. According to Buddhist tradition, the Buddha-to-be prepared himself for the attainment of supreme Enlightenment by practising the virtues of transcendental generosity, morality, patient endurance, energy, meditation, and wisdom for many hundreds of lifetimes. He is eventually reborn in the Tuṣita heaven. There he stays until it is time for him to descend. He descends in the form of a white elephant and is born as a son to Suddhodana, a Śākyan nobleman, and his wife Māyādevī, the Śākyans being a people living on the southern flank of the Himalayas, within the borders of the kingdom of Kosala. Thus unlike Sri Krishna, whose historicity is highly problematic, the Buddha is an historical figure, who lived and taught within a definite historical context. Christians believe that the founder of their religion, too, was an historical figure, a figure who, in the words of the next two articles of the Apostles' Creed,

> Suffered under Pontius Pilate,
> Was crucified, dead, and buried.

Pontius Pilate was Procurator of Judea in the reign of the Roman emperor Tiberius, so that when the Christian asserts that Jesus suffered 'under Pontius Pilate' he is affirming his belief in the historicity of the founder of his religion and, at the same time, affirming his belief in the reality of the Incarnation. For the Christian the question of whether Jesus actually did live 'as Man among men' is not one that is open to discussion. It is an article of faith, the truth of which may be supported by, but is in no way dependent on, empirical evidence. Thus it is not so much that the Christian does not doubt the historicity of Jesus as that he cannot doubt it, for to doubt it would be to undermine the entire Christian scheme of redemption, in which God descends to earth in order to save mankind.

For me the question of whether Jesus actually did live is very much one that is open to discussion. As a Buddhist, I have no emotional vested interest in its being decided either way, or in its being decided at all. Were it to be proved 'beyond reasonable doubt' that Jesus actually did live, I would not find it difficult to believe, given the fact of his existence, that he really was 'crucified, dead, and buried', crucifixion being the common mode of execution for criminals in the Roman empire at the time. What I cannot believe is that the Jewish religious teacher who was crucified was in fact no other than God, the Almighty Creator.

But what of the historicity of the Buddha? And even if the founder of the Buddhist religion actually did live, as seems to be beyond reasonable doubt, could it not be argued that for the Buddhist it is as much an article of faith that Gautama was the Buddha, the Enlightened One, as it is for the Christian that Jesus was God Incarnate? Buddhists certainly do believe that Gautama was the Buddha, the *arhant* free from greed, hatred, and delusion, but their faith is of a fundamentally different kind from the faith Christians have in God, the Incarnation, the Virgin Birth, and so on. And it is a pity we have to use the same word for both kinds. The difference consists in the fact that the faith of the Buddhist is capable of verification. It is verified when, through practice of the traditional spiritual disciplines, faith is gradually transformed into transcendental knowledge. The disciple no longer needs to believe, for having attained Enlightenment as the Buddha did, he now is himself the embodiment of that which formerly was the object of his faith. The faith of the Christian is capable of no such verification. He can never become God, an idea he would regard as blasphemy. He can only believe, and trust that his belief will be suitably rewarded.

It is possible for one to have an intellectual grasp of the Buddha's teaching, up to a point, without believing the truth of that teaching. But one cannot practise it without faith – faith that Gautama was indeed the Enlightened One, the Buddha, and that his teaching, the Dharma, indeed leads to the attainment of Enlightenment or Nirvāṇa by the disciple. 'Faith is the seed' the Buddha therefore declares in the *Sutta-Nipāta*.[343] Unfortunately, that seed seems not to have found lodgement in the hearts of some western Buddhists. Although the Buddha made it perfectly clear that attainment of Enlightenment is inseparable from the entire cessation of greed, hatred, and delusion, such Buddhists maintain that this is not in fact the case. They believe it is possible to attain Enlightenment and yet to go on giving way to anger, for example, just as one did before, a view which leaves me wondering what kind of enlightenment they could possibly have in mind. They appear even to believe that the complete eradication of greed, hatred, and delusion is beyond human capacity, thereby implying that Gautama was not what he claimed to be, the Buddha or Enlightened One, and that it is therefore not possible for us to have faith in him as such, or in his Dharma as leading to Enlightenment. I am therefore also left wondering what kind of Buddhists they are. The Buddha would no doubt have regarded such views as wrong views, and warned those holding them that they were heading in a downward direction.

Which serves to bring us to the next article of the Apostles' Creed, which is:

He descended into hell;

The Nicene Creed has nothing to say about this, but I have seen a number of Russian icons in which the event is depicted, so I assume that the descent into hell is an article of faith within the Eastern as well as within the Western Church. In these icons a white-robed Christ breaks down the doors of hell, despite Satan's protests, and releases from limbo the souls of Adam and Eve, the patriarchs and prophets, and the just who died before his birth. I also remember reading, in my early teens, a mystery play known as the *Harrowing of Hell*,[344] the existence of which suggests that in the English Middle Ages the idea of Christ's descent into hell occupied a place in the popular religious consciousness, along with the Creation and Fall of Man and the Deluge, on which there are also mystery plays. So far as I am aware, the Buddha never visited the hells (plural in Buddhism), though his disciple Maudgalyāyana is said to have visited the realm of the *pretas* or hungry ghosts.[345] There is, however, in the Mahāyāna, the figure of the great 'mythical' bodhisattva Kṣitigarbha, represented in Chinese and Japanese Buddhist art as a monk bearing a beringed monastic staff, who out of compassion visits the various hells in order to bring to their denizens the light of the Buddha's teaching.

Thus both Buddhists and Christians believe in the existence of a post-mortem state or place of suffering in which souls or beings experience the consequences of the evil they have done while on Earth, consequences determined by the law of karma, according to Buddhism, or decreed by the Divine Justice, according to Christianity. There is another difference between Buddhist and Christian beliefs regarding the existence of such a state or place, a difference which is, if anything, of an even more fundamental character. In Buddhism, the being who is reborn in hell suffers there only for so long as the force of the karma – his own karma – which has resulted in his being there is not exhausted. Once it is exhausted, he is reborn into a different state or place, perhaps into the human world. In Christianity, the soul that is sent to hell stays there for ever. 'All hope abandon, ye who enter here' are the dreadful words inscribed above the entrance to Dante's Inferno.

The idea of eternal punishment in hell is surely one of the most horrible ideas ever to have entered into the mind of man, yet belief in its truth seems to have been an article of faith within what was to become mainstream Christianity from the beginning, and to have scriptural authority behind it. In the Gospel According to St Mark Jesus speaks repeatedly of hell and of 'the fire that never shall be quenched',[346] while at the end of the 'Little Apocalypse' in the Gospel According to St Matthew he says with regard to the Last Judgement, 'Then shall he say also unto them on the left hand, Depart from me, ye cursed, into everlasting fire, prepared for the devil and his angels.... And these shall go away into everlasting punishment; but the righteous into life eternal.'[347] Few people who have seen Michelangelo's 'Last Judgement' in the Sistine Chapel can forget the giant, almost Herculean figure of Christ the Judge and the terrible finality of the tremendous gesture of dismissal with which he sends those on his left plunging headlong into hell with expressions of horror and terror.

In the 'Little Apocalypse' it is those who have offended against charity who are sent to hell, but in his First Letter to the Corinthians St Paul greatly extends the list of offences for which one can be so condemned. 'Be not deceived:' he writes, 'neither fornicators, nor idolaters, nor adulterers, nor effeminate, nor abusers of themselves with mankind, nor thieves, nor covetous, nor drunkards, nor revilers, nor extortioners, shall inherit the kingdom of God'.[348] Not to inherit the kingdom of God means, presumably, to be sent to hell. It is clear in any case that St Paul believes in hell, for in his First Letter to the Thessalonians he speaks of the Last Judgement in much the same way that Jesus does, assuring his correspondents that God will 'Recompense tribulation to them that trouble you: And to you who are troubled rest with us, when the Lord Jesus shall be revealed from heaven with his mighty angels, In flaming fire taking vengeance on them that know not God, and that obey not the gospel of our Lord Jesus Christ: Who shall be punished with everlasting destruction from the presence of the Lord, and from the glory of his power'.[349]

All this was understood quite literally by the early Christian writers. They believed that hell was eternal, that the suffering of the damned was without end, and that the flames with which they were punished were of material fire. It was only with the appearance of Origen, the great Alexandrian philosopher and theologian, in the third century, that some rays of light were thrown into this dismal scene. Origen, one of the most attractive figures in the history of Christianity, taught that hell was not eternal and that the souls of the wicked were not punished for ever. Indeed, he believed that their punishment was remedial; it was a purifying power, the sole purpose of which was to purify them and prepare them for eventual admittance to heaven. Origen's hell is therefore really a purgatory, like its Buddhist equivalent. He also believed in the pre-existence of the soul and in world cycles, so that it is not surprising that his Christian contemporaries should have regarded him with mixed feelings or that his subsequent influence should have been negligible. Mainstream Christianity went on its way without him, so that, to this day, most Christians believe that the punishment of the souls in hell is without end.

An idea as horrible as this naturally gave rise to some horrible emotions. In some parts of the Christian world it was considered a refinement of revenge if one could not only kill one's enemy but kill him when he was in a state of mortal sin, so that his soul would go straight to hell. Thus when the eponymous hero of *Hamlet* finds the king at prayer he decides not to kill him just then. For, he reflects,

> A villain kills my father, and for that
> I, his sole son, do this same villain send
> To heaven.
> O, this is hire and salary, not revenge.
> He took my father grossly, full of bread,
> With all his crimes broad blown, as flush as May;
> And how his audit stands who knows save heaven?
> But in our circumstance and course of thought
> 'Tis heavy with him: And am I then reveng'd,
> To take him in the purging of his soul,
> When he is fit and season'd for his passage?
> No!
> Up, sword; and know thou a more horrid hent:
> When he is drunk asleep, or in his rage,
> Or in th'incestuous pleasure of his bed,
> At gaming, swearing, or about some act
> That has no relish of salvation in't,
> Then trip him, that his heels may kick at heaven
> And that his soul may be as damn'd and black
> As hell, whereto it goes.[350]

Here we see, in the cultivated Renaissance prince, primitive desire for revenge coexisting with Christian belief in heaven and hell, the latter providing him, perhaps, with a rationalization for his inaction over his father's death.

But Hamlet's mention of heaven brings us back to the Apostles' Creed, and to the Christian's belief that

> The third day he rose again from the dead, ascended into heaven, and sitteth on the right hand of God the Father Almighty; From thence he shall come to judge the quick and the dead.

So far as I know, it has never been shown that it is possible for a human being to come back to life after being really dead, and to come back, moreover, of their own accord. It is therefore difficult for me to believe that Jesus, having been 'crucified, dead, and buried', could have risen from the dead, whether on the third day or any other day. For me to believe that he really did rise from the dead I would have to be convinced (1) that it was possible for human beings to come back to life of their own accord and (2) that there was reliable empirical evidence that Jesus had done just that. Christians believe in the Resurrection not so much because they believe in the credibility of the rather contradictory gospel accounts of the event, as because they believe, as I as a Buddhist do not believe, that Jesus was God, and that, being God, he had power over death, as he had shown when he raised Lazarus from the dead, saying, 'Lazarus, come forth.'[351] As for the Ascension, this article of faith presents difficulties even for some Christians. Given that it was the physical body of Jesus that rose from the dead, was it this same body that ascended into heaven? If it was, heaven must be located somewhere within the material universe. But if, on the other hand, he ascended in a spiritual body, then at what point was his physical body transformed into the spiritual body that ascended into heaven? For my part, I see both the Resurrection and the Ascension as belonging to mythology rather than to history, though this is not say that as myths they may not have their own spiritual significance and value, a significance perhaps better communicated by art than by the bald affirmations of an official creed.

The Apostles' Creed concludes with a series of articles not found in the Nicene Creed, except for the first of them, in which the believer affirms his faith in the Holy Ghost, the third member of the Trinity.

> I believe in the Holy Ghost; the Holy Catholic Church; The communion of Saints; The Forgiveness of Sins; The Resurrection of the body, and the life everlasting. Amen.

Since the Holy Ghost is God, as are the Father and the Son, it follows that I can no more believe in his existence than I can in theirs. Similarly, I cannot believe in the Holy Catholic Church, though this is not merely on account of the Church's moral record, bad as that record has frequently been, but on account of its claim that it was founded by Christ himself, God incarnate, when he told St Peter, the first pope, that he was the rock on which he would build his church and that he would give him the keys of the kingdom of heaven.[352] The fact that I cannot share the Christian's belief either in the Holy Ghost or the Holy Catholic Church does not, however, mean that I cannot share, to a limited extent, his belief in two other articles in the series, namely the ones relating to the forgiveness of sins and the life everlasting. But before I take a look at them I want to take a closer look at the workings of the Holy Ghost.

It was the Holy Ghost that descended upon the apostles at Pentecost, causing them 'to speak with other tongues, as the Spirit gave them utterance',[353] just as it causes Pentecostalist Christians to speak with tongues today. It was the Holy Ghost who, according to the Creed of Epiphanius, 'spake by the prophets', as when the prophet Isaiah, for example, prophesies that 'a Virgin shall conceive, and bear a son',[354] or when Job testifies to his faith in the resurrection of the body, saying that at the latter day 'within my flesh shall I see God'.[355] Both 'prophecies' are based on a misunderstanding, even on a mistranslation. What Isaiah actually wrote was that 'a young woman (*almah* in the original Hebrew) would conceive, and bear a son', apparently referring to a happy event shortly expected to take place within the royal household; while Job says exactly the opposite of what his translators, from St Jerome onwards, make him say, his words actually being either 'out of my flesh' or 'without my flesh', as Froude pointed out more than a hundred and fifty years ago.[356] Christians traditionally set great store by such prophesies and revelations, believing that the fact that they predicted events in the life of Jesus and anticipated articles of Christian faith proves that their authors were divinely inspired and that God does indeed intervene in human history.

Belief in the forgiveness of sins is not one of the articles of the Nicene Creed, though the doctrine appears to be universal in Christianity, whether eastern or western, Roman Catholic or Protestant. But what is sin, who is it that forgives, and in what does forgiveness consist? The short answer to these questions, so far as I have been able to make out, is that sin is transgression of the known will of God as embodied in, for example, the Ten Commandments; that it is God who forgives, as well as men; and that forgiveness consists in the remission, on repentance, of the penalty which otherwise would have been incurred. There is very little in all this with which I, as a Buddhist, can agree. To begin with, there is the idea of sin as the transgression of the known will of God, a being who for Buddhism does not exist. If there is in Buddhism a concept corresponding, roughly, to the idea of sin, it is *akusala-kamma* or 'unskilful action' of body, speech, and mind, action which has as its natural consequence unpleasant or painful experience in this life, in a future life or lives, or in both. According to Buddhism unskilful action is rooted in greed, hatred, and delusion, the threefold hub on which revolves the wheel of life, and these may be seen as corresponding, collectively, to the Christian idea of original sin, a state of sin innate in mankind as descendants of Adam. Christians believe that they are redeemed from sin by the sacrificial death of Jesus on the Cross, Buddhists that they can overcome greed, hatred, and delusion, and attain Enlightenment or Nirvāṇa, by following the Noble Eightfold Path. In the fourth Gospel John the Baptist says, as Jesus comes towards him, 'Behold the Lamb of God, which taketh away the sin of world'.[357] In the *Dhammapada* the Buddha says, 'By you must the zealous effort be made. The Buddhas are only proclaimers of the Way.'[358]

It is only with regard to the forgiveness of one man by another that there is any agreement between Christianity and Buddhism. In the Lord's Prayer, which I learned as a small child and can still repeat, Christians ask God to forgive them their trespasses 'as we forgive them that trespass against us'. As a Buddhist, I forgive someone when I feel no hatred for him on account of the injury he has done me and have no desire for retaliation or revenge. The Buddha indeed goes so far as to tell his renunciant disciples, 'Bhikkhus, even if bandits were to sever you savagely limb by limb with a two-handled saw, he who gave rise to a mind of hate towards them would not be carrying out my teaching.' Nor is it enough that this should not give rise to a mind of hate. The Buddha continues:

> Herein, bhikkhus, you should train yourself thus: 'Our minds will remain unaffected, and we shall utter no evil word; we shall abide compassionate for their welfare, with a mind of loving-kindness, without inner hate.'[359]

The fact that I forgive someone does not, however, mean that by virtue of my forgiveness they will escape the karmic consequences of their unskilful action. The Buddha also says, 'Not in the sky, nor in the midst of the sea, nor yet in the clefts of mountains, nowhere in the world, in fact, is there any place to be found where, having entered, one can abide free from the consequences of one's evil deeds.'[360] The law of karma does not forgive.

Since Christians believe in eternal punishment in hell for the wicked it is natural that they should also believe in 'life everlasting' in heaven for the righteous. As a Buddhist I can believe in neither. According to Buddhism, sentient beings are born in heaven or hell according to the nature of their previous karma, whether predominantly skilful or predominantly unskilful, and when the force of that karma is exhausted they are reborn in other realms of conditioned existence. No life in any such realm lasts for ever.

Now that I have taken my look at the Apostles' Creed it is clear to me that hardly any of my beliefs, as a Buddhist, are in agreement with the fundamental beliefs of mainstream Christianity. Only in connection with the existence of post-mortem states of happiness and suffering, and the need for men to forgive, is there agreement even to a limited extent. I was also greatly struck by the fact that in the Apostles' Creed the Christian affirms his belief in certain theological doctrines, as well as in the historicity of certain events, not in any ethical principles. It could, of course, be argued that the ethical principles derive from, and are dependent on, theological doctrines, and Christianity is not lacking in ethical teachings, such as those given in the Sermon on the Mount,[361] but in the Apostles' Creed, as in all the other ancient creeds, it is the theological doctrines that are highlighted.

Such highlighting is symptomatic of the Christian Church's preoccupation, during the first four or five hundred years of its existence, with giving precise theological expression to its fundamental beliefs. All the creeds, in fact, are intensely theological, and none more so than the latest of them, the Athanasian (probably late fifth century CE), the forty or more clauses of which are devoted mainly to expounding the exact nature of the relation between the three persons of the Trinity, 'neither confounding the persons nor dividing the substance', and with asserting that Jesus Christ, while indissolubly one in person, was simultaneously fully divine and fully human.

The Athanasian Creed also contains a stern warning, a warning that in the version included in the Church of England's Book of Common Prayer reads, 'Whosoever will be saved: before all things it is necessary that he hold the Catholic Faith. Which Faith except every one do keep whole and undefiled: without doubt he shall perish everlastingly.' The literal meaning of the word *catholic* is 'universal; relating to all men; all-inclusive', so that the 'Catholic Faith' is the universal faith, the faith held by all Christians; but this is just what the Athanasian Creed is not. Like the Apostles' Creed and the Nicene Creed, it represents the faith only of some Christians. It represents the faith of Christians belonging to the Western Church, its doctrine of the double procession of the Holy Ghost – from the Father *and* the Son – making it unacceptable to the Eastern Church. In the case of the Nicene Creed it did not represent the faith of all Christians living at the time of the First Council of Nicea (325 CE), at which the creed was formally adopted. What it represented was the faith of the party within the Christian Church that was favoured by the emperor Constantine – the party that was to become the Roman Catholic Church. That the Nicene Creed was the creed of a party, albeit a large and influential one, is shown by the fact that the Council condemned Arius and his teaching, a teaching according to which the Son was not of one substance with the Father, as the Nicene Creed maintained, but was a created being subordinate to the Father.

Thus the Nicene Creed defined not only what for its supporters was the true Christian faith but also, conversely, what for them was not the true faith. Henceforth Christians who did not keep that faith 'whole and undefiled', as the Athanasian Creed puts it, were not true Christians, not members of the Catholic Church, and would perish everlastingly. Nor was this all. The very existence of such 'heretical' Christians threatened the unity of the Holy Catholic Church, and if they could not be persuaded to submit to the authority of that church and to accept the Nicene Creed they were to be excommunicated, persecuted, and even killed, while their books were to be burnt wherever found. Among the thousands of books thus destroyed there were not only original writings by 'heretical' theologians of various persuasions but also a number of 'heretical' gospels, accounts of the life and teaching of Jesus other than the four recognized by the Church and included in the New Testament. Yet try as the Church might, it could never entirely extirpate heresy. In every generation new heresies would arise, and old ones be revived, as men insisted on thinking for themselves about the nature of the Christian faith. The list of those holding views opposed to the views of the Church was therefore a long one and included Montanists, Arians, Donatists, Priscillians, Pelagians, Nestorians, Adoptionists, Cathars or Albigensians, Anabaptists, Lollards, Hussites, and Waldensians.

Over the years I have come to know something about all these alternative Christianities, as they should rightly be called, and especially about the Cathars or Albigensians, whose story so moved me that in 1981 I visited Carcassonne, and had circumstances permitted would also have visited their mountain fortress of Montsegur, which was sacked in 1244 by the combined forces of the Church and the French crown and more than two hundred *perfecti* burnt. It was only the Waldensians who were no more than a name to me. As I have recently learned, their Church was founded in 1170 by Peter Waldo, a merchant of Lyons. They lived in voluntary poverty, refused to take oaths or shed blood, and later rejected certain Roman Catholic doctrines, including transubstantiation. Though often persecuted, they spread to many parts of Europe, and in the seventeenth century were still to be found inhabiting the Luserna and Angrogna Valleys on the Italian side of the Cottian Alps. In 1655 an army of 15,000 men invaded the valleys, sent by the 'Council for the Propagation of the Faith' in Turin, consisting of the chief councillors of State and Church dignitaries, the Waldensians having refused to abjure their ancestral faith and become Roman Catholics. Altogether 1,712 Waldensians were slaughtered, including women and children, thus occasioning Milton's famous sonnet 'On the late Massacre in Piedmont', with which I had long been familiar without knowing just who the innocent victims were.

Avenge, O Lord, thy slaughter'd Saints, whose bones
Lie scatter'd on the Alpine mountains cold,
Ev'n them who kept thy truth so pure of old
When all our Fathers worship't Stocks and Stones,
Forget not: in thy book record their groans
Who were thy Sheep and in their ancient Fold
Slain by the bloody *Piemontese* that roll'd
Mother with Infant down the Rocks. Their moans
The Vales redoubl'd to the Hills, and they
To Heaven. Their martyr'd blood and ashes sow

O'er all th'*Italian* fields where still doth sway
The triple Tyrant: that from these may grow
A hundredfold, who having learnt thy way
Early may fly the *Babylonian* woe.[362]

The 'triple Tyrant' is the pope, who wears a three-tiered crown, as God the Father does in some medieval altarpieces. At the time of the massacre the reigning pontiff was Alexander VII, but responsibility for the holocaust cannot be ascribed to any one person, however eminent. It must be ascribed, ultimately, to the fundamental character of the Catholic Church, with its conviction that the Christian faith can be permanently enclosed within a particular form of words, its horror of heresy, and its readiness in the past to have recourse to violence and bloodshed in support of its claims.

5
CHRISTIAN MYTHOLOGY

When I was twelve my parents gave me a copy of Milton's *Paradise Lost* for Christmas, thus giving me what I have elsewhere described as 'the greatest poetic experience of my life'.[363] Since then I have read the poem repeatedly, not often reading it straight through, but dipping into it here and there, revisiting favourite passages and discovering new beauties in familiar lines.

Looking back on my initial experience of the poem, I see that I read it – as I have continued to read it – in the same spirit that I would later read a play by Shakespeare or a novel by Dickens. While I was engaged in reading the work the characters represented in the one or described in the other would be very real to me, and I would respond emotionally to what they said or did, or what befell them, as though they actually existed. At the same time I would be quite aware that those characters existed only in the fertile imagination of their creator, as that imagination was bodied forth in the play or novel, or in my own imagination to the extent that it was able to participate in the imagination of Shakespeare or Dickens through the enjoyment of their work. There could be no question of my being able to experience the presence of Ariel independently of *The Tempest* or that of Mrs Gamp independently of *Martin Chuzzlewit*. Outside those works they did not exist. Like Isaac Watts' rose in winter, they had essence but not existence.[364] Similarly, for me the principal characters in *Paradise Lost* existed only in Milton's imagination, and in my own imagination to the extent that I was able, through my enjoyment of the poem, to participate in his. For me, outside the poem they did not exist.

There is a great difference, however, between a play like *The Tempest* or a novel like *Martin Chuzzlewit* on one hand, and mythology on the other. Both the play and the novel are the work of an individual of genius, but a mythology is the product of the collective imagination of a whole people. An individual cannot create a mythology single-handed, as Blake tried to do in *The Four Zoas*, though a poet may make use of images drawn from a particular mythology, as Goethe made use of Christian images in the closing scenes of the second part of Faust. Every people has, or has had, a mythology of its own creation. Thus there are the mythologies of the Sumerians and the Egyptians, the Greeks and the Romans, the Indians and the Chinese, the Celts and the Teutons, the Aztecs and the Incas, and so on. Probably there is no people, however few in number, without a mythology. A people without a mythology is a people without a soul.

Religions also have their mythologies, which in some cases are simply one of its parts, along with ritual, doctrine, and a code of ethics, and in others virtually identical with it. *Paradise Lost* is Milton's poetic version of Christian mythology, just as the *Divine Comedy* is Dante's poetic version of the same mythology. Milton's version is a Protestant version, Dante's a Roman Catholic one, the principal difference between the two versions being that in Paradise Lost there is no place for Purgatory and no place for the glorified Madonna of the Roman Catholic collective imagination.

A mythology has been defined as 'a set of stories about gods and other supernatural beings, with whom humans may have relationships'. In *Paradise Lost* the principal supernatural beings are the Eternal Father, the Son, various angels and archangels, such as Michael, 'of celestial armies prince', Raphael, the 'affable archangel', and Uriel, 'regent of the sun', together with Satan, 'the infernal serpent', leader of the rebel angels, now become devils, among whom are Moloch, Belial, and Mammon. The humans are Adam, the first man, and Eve, the first woman, though many others are briefly mentioned in the course of Raphael's rapid survey of human history from the fallen Adam and Eve down to the Deluge, and from the Deluge down to the Crucifixion.

Milton certainly believed in the objective existence of the Eternal Father, the Son, and all the other supernatural beings of his poem, though it is unlikely that he believed they existed exactly as he had described them. For me, however, they exist only for as long as I am reading the poem. They have no existence outside it. I am therefore able to read *Paradise Lost* in the same way that I read the *Iliad* and the *Odyssey*, the only difference being that whereas it is at least 1,500 years since anyone believed in the existence of Homer's gods and goddesses, millions of people still believe in the supernatural personages of Christian mythology. Perhaps in 1,500 years' time people will be reading *Paradise Lost* as they now read the *Iliad* and the *Odyssey* and as I and other lovers of English literature already read Milton's great poem. Perhaps its mythology will prove to be the most enduring part of Christianity.

Because I read *Paradise Lost* as I read the *Iliad* and the *Odyssey*, I am free to respond to the Eternal Father and the rest of Milton's supernatural beings, as I am free to respond to Homer's gods and goddesses, without being constrained by theological considerations. The Eternal Father is not a very attractive character. No doubt Milton believed in him, even worshipped him, and no doubt he lavished on him all the resources of his art; but the Judeo-Christian conception of God was a datum beyond which he could not or would not go. His angels are a very different matter. They are among Milton's most beautiful creations, especially Raphael, 'the sociable archangel', whom the Eternal Father sends to earth to converse with Adam 'as friend with friend' and warn him that Satan is plotting his and Eve's downfall. Having traversed the vast distance between heaven and earth,

> At once on th' eastern cliff of Paradise
> He lights, and to his proper shape returns,
> A Seraph winged. Six wings he wore, to shade
> His lineaments divine: the pair that clad
> Each shoulder broad came mantling o'er his breast
> With regal ornament; the middle pair
> Girt like a starry zone his waist, and round
> Skirted his loins and thighs with downy gold
> And colours dipped in Heaven; the third his feet
> Shadowed from either heel with feathered mail,
> Sky-tinctured grain. Like Maia's son he stood,
> And shook his plumes, that heavenly fragrance filled
> The circuit wide.[365]

Milton's angels were probably the first with which I became acquainted. They must have made a strong impression on me, for I started drawing pictures of individual angels, notably the archangel Michael, whom I depicted hovering with outstretched wings and brandishing a sword. Angels with swords and lances also appeared in the background of a very large drawing I made of Thomas Becket receiving the archiepiscopal ring from Pope Alexander III, which astonished my teachers not so much on account of its angels as because of my knowledge of the word 'archiepiscopal'. These angels were all Miltonic angels, as was the angel who, in the opening lines of the epic poem I was writing, appeared in my bedroom, though by this time I was also acquainted, thanks to the Tooting Public Library – with Fra Angelico's very different angels, with their high-waisted pink, blue, or green gowns, their gold aureoles, and gold or multicoloured wings. The next angelic encounter took place in Barnstaple, at the vicarage where, as a fourteen-year-old evacuee from London, I was billeted for a while. Above my bed there hung a large monochrome reproduction of a painting depicting not one but four angels. As I discovered later, the original was the work of Sir Joshua Reynolds, and had been very popular in the Victorian period, when reproductions of it were to be seen on the walls of many a pious home. It depicted four very beautiful children's heads, all clustered together, each head being equipped with a pair of little wings.[366]

Why I should have been so fascinated by angels I do not know. Perhaps it was because of all the supernatural beings of Christian mythology they are the ones nearest to us (apart from the devils, of course), occupying as they do a realm intermediate between the human world and the Divine. Or perhaps the bright, beautiful winged forms fascinated me because they corresponded to something deep in my own nature, something as yet hidden and undeveloped. I was therefore on the lookout for books about angels as well as for pictures of them, but the only book I came across at this period was the *Celestial Hierarchies* of Dionysius the Areopagite, which I read, in a translation by the Editors of the Shrine of Wisdom, at about the same time that I realized I was a Buddhist. Dionysius the Areopagite, whom Christian tradition identified with St Paul's Athenean convert, an identification that served to confer immense authority on his works, was in fact a Christian Neoplatonist, probably a Syrian, writing under the influence of Proclus (412–487 CE), the great pagan Neoplatonist, or one of his successors. In the *Celestial Hierarchies*, Dionysius describes the angels as being divided into three groups, each with three subdivisions (Seraphim, Cherubim, and Thrones; Dominions, Virtues, and Powers; Principalities, Archangels, and Angels), each group being nearer to the Divine than the group below, the Seraphim being nearest of all, with the Angels having below them in the chain only mankind. Milton does not make use of this scheme in *Paradise Lost* but he adopts Dionysius's nomenclature, using it rather loosely, as when he refers to Raphael, who is a Seraph, as 'the affable archangel'.

That I had realized I was a Buddhist, and was reading as much Buddhist literature as I could lay my hands on, meant that it was not long before I encountered the *devas*, the Indian equivalents of the angels of Christian mythology. In the Buddhist scriptures, *devas* often visit the Buddha, usually at night. The introduction to the *Maṅgala Sutta*, for example, tells us that once, when the Blessed One was dwelling near Sāvatthi, at Jeta Grove, in Anāthapiṇḍika's Park, 'a certain deva of wondrous beauty lit up the Jeta Grove, and coming to the Blessed One saluted him and stood to one side'.[367] During my long stay in India, deepening my understanding of the Buddha's teaching, I discovered that the *devas* were not the equivalents of the angels in all respects. Whereas the angels were created by God out of nothing, the *devas* were human beings born into this or that heavenly world as a result of the good deeds they had performed while on earth. According to Buddhist tradition there are altogether twenty-two classes of *devas*, from those known as the four great kings up to the *devas* who are beyond both perception and non-perception, and including the *devas* of limited radiance, of unlimited radiance, and of splendid radiance, who between them make up the 'celestial hierarchy' of Buddhism. Only two of these *devas* are commonly represented in Buddhist art, one being Indra, the other Mahābrahma, who are often seen escorting the Buddha as he descends to earth down a stairway of gold, silver, and crystal after instructing his deceased mother in the Abhidhamma in the heavenly realm into which she had been reborn.[368]

But perhaps the true Buddhist equivalents of the angels, at least of Dionysius's angels, are the bodhisattvas of the Mahāyāna. Dionysius says nothing about the angels having been created *ex nihilo*. In a sense they were not created at all. Though his language is obscure, it would seem that for Dionysius the different orders of angels are so many manifestations of various attributes of the Divine, each order transmitting to the one below it what he calls the Providential Stream. This downward-flowing Life has a threefold operation. It is perfective in the first group of angels, illuminating in the second, and purifying in the third. Moreover, each order of angels has an inner connection with every human soul, by virtue of which each soul is able, with their help, to purify, illumine, and perfect itself. Similarly, what I have elsewhere termed the bodhisattva hierarchy, and described at some length, consists of five 'orders', the first being the nearest to the *dharmakāya* or absolute *bodhicitta*, the fifth the farthest from it.[369] The first order is that of the bodhisattvas who are direct emanations of the *dharmakāya*; the second, that of the Buddhas who after attaining Enlightenment retain their bodhisattva form; the third, that of the irreversible bodhisattvas, who have reached the higher stages of the bodhisattva path and cannot resile from it; the fourth, that of the bodhisattvas of the path, who have reached the lower stages of that path and can resile from it; and the fifth, that of the novice bodhisattvas who in principle accept the bodhisattva ideal but who have not reached the first stage of that path. Through these orders there runs the golden thread of the *bodhicitta* or will to Enlightenment, absolute in the first two orders, real in the third, effective in the fourth, and preparatory in the fifth. In 1958, inspired by the beauty of the bodhisattva ideal, I wrote a poem entitled 'The Guardian Wall', of which the first verse was

> With sweet compassionate faces,
> Hands outstretched, humanity's friends,
> Up to the golden Zenith
> The Hierarchy ascends.[370]

In 1962, two years before my return to England, I received from one of my Tibetan teachers, himself widely revered as a living bodhisattva, the eighteen major and forty-six minor bodhisattva precepts.[371]

Once back in England, and again having access to public libraries and art galleries, it was not long before I resumed my acquaintance with the angels and other supernatural beings of Christian mythology. I soon noticed that there were as many kinds of angels as there were artists who painted them. Fra Angelico's angels were very different from Raphael's, Botticelli's from Leonardo da Vinci's, El Greco's from

Delacroix's, William Blake's from Cecil Collins'. They all had wings, golden, white, or multicoloured, most had haloes or aureoles, and they were generally depicted as beautiful youths or boys with long, curling hair, some of whom played on musical instruments, some sang, some fluttered aloft in the air, while others were of those concerning whom the murmuring poet was admonished that 'They also serve who only stand and wait'.[372] But perhaps the greatest and most significant difference I saw as I turned the pages of an art book or visited, over the years, the churches and art galleries not only of my native land but also of Italy and Germany, France and Spain, was in the expressions of their faces. Some were serene, some joyful, some pensive almost to the point of melancholy. There were looks of ineffable sweetness, looks of calm, majestic dignity, and looks of tender compassion. It was as though when the artist painted the face of an angel he was painting his own soul, or at least what his soul aspired to be. In the case of those angels – and there were not a few of them – whose expressions were vacant, or coarse, or sentimental, and who therefore were not really angels at all, despite their wings and haloes, it was as though the soul of the artist was spiritually underdeveloped, however excellent his technique might be.

No angel is solitary. Except when sent on an errand to earth, they live in companies or orders, and it is as companies that I have sometimes seen them. Their natural place is in heaven, where they sing the praises of the Almighty, as in Milton's great poem, or, as in Fra Angelico's vision of paradise, where they dance upon flowering turf, among fruit-bearing trees, dancing circle-wise with graceful movements and holding each other's hands.[373] They also assemble in large numbers on special occasions, as when the Virgin Mary is assumed bodily into heaven, or when, on another red-letter day in the celestial calendar, she is crowned Queen of Heaven, and Queen of the Angels by the Trinity, a white-robed Father and a red-robed son doing the crowning together, when the Holy Ghost in the form of a white dove hovers above their heads and a blue-mantled Virgin, her hands clasped in prayer, gazes up at the light streaming down from above, as in El Greco's painting of the event in Toledo.[374]

But I have most often seen individual angels in contact with certain favoured persons, for Christian mythology, like all the other mythologies of the world, is 'a set of stories about gods and other supernatural beings, with whom humans may have relationships'.

Raphael and Gabriel are particularly prominent in this respect. In the Book of Tobit, one of the apocryphal books of the Old Testament, Raphael, the 'affable archangel', assumes the name and appearance of Azarias and accompanies Tobias, Tobit's son, from his home in Nineveh to the city of Rages, whither his strangely blinded father has sent him to collect some money. In Rages Tobias marries Sarah, and with Raphael's help overcomes the demon who has killed Sarah's seven previous husbands on their wedding night, and returns home with Raphael, Sarah, the money, and his faithful dog, who has accompanied him throughout his journey. Raphael then rewards Tobit for all his good deeds by restoring his sight, reveals his true identity, and returns to heaven.

I have seen many paintings of *Tobias and the Angel*. My favourite is the one by Verrocchio in London's National Gallery, which I have seen a number of times. A curly-headed young Tobias strides along arm in arm with Raphael, who is half a head taller, the fingers of his right hand resting lightly on the angel's left wrist. He is stylishly clad in a dark-blue pleated jerkin, tightly belted at the waist, with scarlet sleeves and scarlet stockings; his dark-blue cloak billows out behind him. The artist has depicted Raphael not as Azarias but in his true angelic form, complete with multicoloured wings and gold halo. Over a white gown he wears a plum-coloured cloak, one corner of which he holds in his left hand. Tobias looks up at him with a bright, trusting expression, while his little woolly dog keeps close to the angel's feet. Some western Buddhists see the painting as an image of *kalyāṇa mitratā* or 'spiritual friendship', a relationship in which the older acts as a mentor to the younger man, and which the Buddha once declared to be not the half but the whole of the spiritual life.[375]

Tobias and Raphael are not always depicted walking arm in arm along the road to Rages, the river Tigris winding its way in the distance. In 1984 I saw at the Royal Academy's 'Genius of Venice' exhibition a very different painting of the two travellers. It was by Savoldo,[376] and I wrote a poem on it:

> He sits at ease upon the rocks,
> The Angel with the outspread wings;
> Loosely to limbs of noblest mould
> His rose and silver vesture clings.

Watchful he sits, right arm half raised
In monitory gesture sweet,
While travel-worn the small grey dog
Sleeps darkling near his naked feet.

Caught by that gesture as he kneels
Tobias turns, as in a dream;
Knowing his destined hour is come
The great fish gapes from out the stream.[377]

The 'stream' is the Tigris, and the 'great fish' the one that Tobias catches on Raphael's instructions (in Verrocchio's painting the fish is quite small, and dangles from a string held in Tobias's left hand). With the smoke of the fish's heart Tobias will exorcise the demon who had killed Sarah's previous husband, while its gall will be used to cure Tobit's blindness.

In this very popular religious short story, as it has been called, Raphael acts as the guardian angel of Tobias. Belief in the guardian angels is common to Christianity and Judaism and, within its own theological parameters, to Islam as well. All human beings have guardian angels of their own, who watch over them, protect them from harm, and encourage them to do what is good. Nations and cities also have their guardian angels. Indeed, in some esoteric and magical systems the planets, the seasons, the months, the days of the week, the hours of the day, as well as hills, mountains, and herbs, all have their guardian angels, which perhaps suggests that everything in Nature has a subtle and invisible – even a spiritual – side to its existence. In Christian mythology, the guardian angel watches over a human being from the time of his birth, a belief that Jesus himself appears to endorse when he warns the disciples, 'Take heed that ye despise not one of these little ones; for I say unto you, that in heaven their angels do always behold the face of my Father which is in heaven'.[378] The image of angels that behold the face of the Father puts me in mind of the passage in *Paradise Lost* in which Milton says of God as he sits 'High Thron'd above all highth' in the pure Empyrean:

About him all the Sanctities of Heaven
Stood thick as starrs, and from his sight received
Beatitude past utterance.[379]

For Milton, as no doubt for Jesus too, angels had, as we would say, an objective existence. They were not products of the human imagination. But the guardian angel, at least, can be viewed as the better, or higher, self of the individual – the self that it is possible for one to become and which, 'in heaven', one already is.

I have never actually seen an angel (though I have seen other supernatural beings), but I did once hear what I described to myself at the time as an angelic voice. Nearly forty years ago I was on the point of committing a certain act when a voice said in my ear, clearly and distinctly, 'Don't.' The voice was indescribably soft and gentle, without the least emphasis or insistence. It did not order a command. Yet it was impossible not to obey it, and I at once refrained. A few days later I learned that by refraining, and not doing what I had intended to do, I had saved myself from suffering some very unpleasant consequences. I was convinced at the time, and remain convinced, that the angelic voice I heard came from without, not from within; it was not the product of my imagination. What, then, could it have been? Was it akin to the daimon of Socrates, which on occasion told him what he was not to do, but never what he was to do?[380] Or was it the Buddhist equivalent of the guardian angel – a *deva* or a bodhisattva – watching over me and preventing me from harming myself?

The guardian angels belong to the ranks of the good angels. In fact 'good angel' sometimes means guardian angel. But there are also bad angels. There are devils. There is Satan. There is hell. According to Christian tradition the devils, including Satan, were originally angels. They are those angels who, having rebelled against God, were by him cast down into hell, there to suffer eternally. Some theologians believe that the angels who rebelled – a third part of the entire angelic host – rebelled at the very instant of their creation; others, that they rebelled subsequently, as in the version of the myth followed by Milton in *Paradise Lost*. Milton, like Blake, did not forget that Satan, the leader of the rebellion against God, was a *fallen angel*, one who in heaven had been known as Lucifer, the Light Bearer, who even in his fallen state retained some vestige of his original glory. As Milton finely says of him, as he is about to address his followers after their catastrophic defeat:

> he above the rest
> In shape and gesture proudly eminent

Stood like a Towr; his form had yet not lost
All her Original brightness, nor appear'd
Less than Arch Angel ruind, and th' excess
Of Glory obscur'd: As when the Sun new ris'n
Looks through the Horizontal misty Air
Shorn of his beams, or from behind the Moon
In dim Eclips disastrous twilight sheds
On half the Nations, and with fear of change
Perplexes Monarchs.[381]

One of Blake's illustrations to *Paradise Lost* depicts Lucifer in the glorious, six-winged seraphic form in which he was created and which he enjoyed until his rebellion and fall.[382] So far as I know, only Blake has ventured to depict Satan in his unfallen state, though other illustrators of *Paradise Lost* may possibly have done so too.

That Milton did not forget that Satan was a fallen angel is interesting, even significant. It may be that he describes him in Book I of *Paradise Lost* as not appearing 'less than Arch Angel ruind' for reasons of poetic propriety. *Paradise Lost* is an epic poem, and an epic has to have a hero, as the *Iliad* has Achilles, the *Odyssey* Odysseus, and the *Aeneid* Aeneas. God could hardly be that hero, nor could Messiah, despite his victory over the rebel angels, and Adam certainly could not. That left Satan. Milton therefore endows him with courage, fortitude, endurance, and resourcefulness, all of which are heroic qualities. He may also have felt, in the depths of his poetic soul (though probably not as a theologian) that Satan, having been created good, could never become wholly evil or utterly lost. And it could have been on this account that Blake famously declared Milton to have been 'of the Devil's party without knowing it'.[383] Be that as it may, there is little doubt that Milton's portrayal of Satan carries conviction, as does the way in which he portrays Moloch, Belial, and Mammon, his principal associates in the great rebellion, to each of which he assigns, in Book II of his poem, the speech appropriate to his particular character and temperament.

Mainstream Christianity does exactly the opposite. In keeping with its strongly held belief that Satan and his fellow devils are utterly evil, it consistently portrays them in the darkest colours. They are horrible, disgusting, and repulsive in the highest degree. In Dante's *Divine Comedy*, Dante and Virgil, his guide, having visited eight previous circles of Hell, come to the fourth round of the ninth circle, where they see Satan. Of enormous size from mid-breast he stands fixed in ice, the torment here being that of freezing cold.

> Oh, what a sight!
> How passing strange it seem'd, when I did spy
> Upon his head three faces: one in front
> Of hue vermilion, the other two with this
> Midway each shoulder join'd and at the crest;
> The right 'twixt wan and yellow seem'd; the left
> To look on, such as come from whence old Nile
> Stoops to the lowlands. Under each shot forth
> Two mighty wings, enormous as became
> A bird so vast. Sails never such I saw
> Outstretched on the wide sea. No plumes had they,
> But were in texture like a bat.[384]

At every mouth his teeth chew and rend a sinner. The three sinners being thus tormented, Virgil tells Dante, are Judas, Brutus, and Cassius, for in this circle are punished the souls of those who betrayed their masters and benefactors. In Gustave Doré's black-and-white – mostly black – illustration of the dreadful scene, Satan has the horns, ears, and beard of a goat, long teeth, and a look of baffled rage.[385] Even more horrible, to my mind, is the expression on Satan's half-animal face in the war-damaged fresco of the Last Judgement in the Campo Santo in Pisa, which I have seen more than once. It is an expression not just of frustrated rage, but also of horror at his own situation, and a dull despair bordering on insanity.

In the Christian art of the Middle Ages and the Renaissance Satan is often seen seated in hell surrounded by his devils, just as God is seen enthroned in heaven surrounded by his angels. In Giotto's fresco of the Last Judgement in the Arena Chapel in Padua an enormous grey Satan, his arms half raised and hands each grasping a sinner, sits surrounded by his very much smaller devils, who are all of human size, though not human form or feature. They are covered in black, red, or grey hair, have half-simian faces, and they set upon the naked sinners like a pack of wild dogs, chasing them, biting and clawing them, throwing them down, and torturing them in various ways. But the devils are not confined to

Hell, nor is Satan. It is Satan himself who, according to the Synoptic Gospels, tempted Jesus in the wilderness, challenging him first to show that he was the Son of God by changing stones to bread, then by casting himself down from the pinnacle of the Temple, whither the Tempter had transported him, and finally offering to give him all the kingdoms of the world and the glory of them if he would fall down and worship him.[386] It was Satan, too, who entered into Judas Iscariot, one of the twelve disciples, whereupon he 'communed with the chief priests and captains, how he might betray [Jesus] unto them. And they were glad, and covenanted to give him money'.[387] One of Giotto's frescoes in the Arena Chapel depicts the episode. A black, semi-bestial figure stands immediately behind Judas, its black clawed hand on his shoulder, as he receives the money from a red-robed high priest.

Devils are in fact very much in evidence in the New Testament. Five or six years ago, having not read any of the Gospels for several decades, I read the Gospel According to St Mark straight through, and was struck by the extent to which devils and demoniacal possession entered into the story. In the very first chapter of this gospel, the earliest of the four recognized as authentic by the Church, we see Jesus ordering an unclean spirit to leave the man who was possessed, 'And when the unclean spirit had torn him [i.e. thrown him into convulsions], and cried with a loud voice, he came out of him.'[388] News of what Jesus had done soon spread throughout the region, so that people brought Jesus all that were diseased, 'And he healed many that were sick of divers diseases, and cast out many devils.'[389] Later on we find scribes from Jerusalem, the headquarters of Jewish orthodoxy, alleging that Jesus himself is possessed by Beelzebub, the prince of the devils, and casts out devils through him. Jesus reacts strongly to the allegation, declaring that he who says of him 'He hath an unclean spirit [i.e. is possessed] sins against the Holy Ghost; he shall not be forgiven but shall be in danger of eternal damnation.'[390] Then there is the bizarre episode of the demoniac who lived among the tombs, howling and gashing himself with stones night and day, and whom no one had the strength to control. When Jesus commands the evil spirit to leave the man, and asked his name, 'he answered, saying, my name is Legion: for we are many. And he besought him much that he would not send them away out of the country.' Jesus therefore permits the devils to enter into a herd of pigs, whereupon the pigs – about two thousand in number – charge down the cliff and are drowned in the lake below.[391]

As I read on, and got further into the story, I found Jesus causing an unclean spirit to leave the daughter of a Greek woman without his actually seeing the girl,[392] commanding a deaf and dumb spirit to come out of an epileptic boy and not enter him again,[393] and telling the disciples not to forbid those who cast out devils in his name, 'for there is no man which shall do a miracle in my name, that can lightly speak evil of me'.[394]

By the time I finished reading Mark's gospel I had a mental picture of Jesus moving through a surreal landscape inhabited mainly by the sick, the diseased, and the insane, and swarming with devils of every kind. Satan and his devils were also to be met with in the two other synoptic gospels, in the Gospel According to St John, in the Acts of the Apostles, in the Epistles of St Paul, and in the Book of Revelation. The world of the New Testament is a world in which devils are everywhere, all of them on the lookout for opportunities for possessing, deceiving, and misleading human beings. St Paul therefore exhorts the Ephesians:

> Put on the whole armour of God, that ye may be able to stand against the wiles of the devil. For we wrestle not against flesh and blood, but against principalities, against powers, against the rulers of the darkness of this world, against spiritual wickedness in high places.[395]

With such words ringing in their ears, and as Christianity spread throughout the Roman Empire, it was not difficult for Christians to see the gods and goddesses of paganism as devils who had taken on those forms in order to lure men into committing the sin of idolatry. This was in fact an article of belief with Christians for centuries. Milton makes extensive use of the belief in *Paradise Lost*, some of the loveliest passages in the poem being those in which, having had occasion to refer to a particular devil, he proceeds not only to tell us by what name the devil was known in ancient times but also to relate a myth or legend in which he features under that name. Thus he says of the devil who is the architect of Pandemonium, the infernal capital,

> ... and in Ausonian land
> Men called him Mulciber; and how he fell
> From Heaven they fabled, thrown by angry Jove

Sheer o'er the crystal battlements: from morn
To noon he fell, from noon to dewy Eve,
A summer's day; and with the setting sun
Dropped from the zenith like a falling star,
On Lemnos th' Aegean isle.[396]

But, Milton the poet having dwelt lovingly on the old myth, Milton the theologian does not omit to add:

Thus they relate,
Erring.

Even when describing the Archangel Raphael Milton cannot help concluding the description with a comparison drawn from classical mythology:

Like Maia's son he stood
And shook his plumes, that heavenly fragrance filled
The circuit wide.[397]

From believing that the gods and goddesses of paganism were devils it was but a step to believing that their worshippers, if not devils themselves, at least were very much under their influence. Eventually, mainstream Christianity came to think that whoever was opposed to the Holy Catholic Church, or differed from it in doctrine, was an agent of Satan. Here St Paul had undoubtedly led the way. In his Second Letter to the Corinthians he denounced certain rival Christian teachers as 'false apostles, deceitful workers, transforming themselves into the apostles of Christ', adding caustically, 'And no marvel; for Satan himself is transformed into an angel of light. Therefore it is no great thing if his ministers also be transformed as the ministers of righteousness.'[398] Not many generations later, therefore, Irenaeus, author of the encyclopedic *Against Heresies*, was able to denounce the followers of Valentinius, the great Gnostic Christian teacher, in similar terms. Their theology was the devious result of Satan's own inspiration, he declares, and God will punish them: they will be consumed by fire from heaven.[399] Fire seems to have been very much in the mind of orthodox Christians in those days, and it was not long before they were burning 'heretical' Christians alive, thus setting a precedent that would be followed for the next fifteen hundred years.

Besides dictating misleading theologies to heretical teachers, Satan and his devils busied themselves tempting ascetics like St Anthony, assuming for the purpose all kinds of horrible, menacing, or seductive shapes; invading the bodies of epileptics and madmen; causing churches to collapse or their steeples to lean awry; and entering into compacts with sorcerers and witches. Medieval artists liked to depict devils as tiny black figures with horns, hoofs, and tails, and it is in such a form that one of them pops out of the mouth of a demoniac who is being exorcised by St Benedict, the father of western monasticism, in one of Spinello Aretino's frescoes in the church of San Miniato in Florence, which I saw when I visited the church many years ago. But devils may also take on the appearance of human beings, as in a painting I saw once in which devil's hoofs peep out from beneath his garments, thus revealing his real identity to an evidently suspicious hermit. Whether all such appearances belong simply to the feverish, frightened imagination of the Middle Ages, or whether there may not be discarnate 'evil' entities capable of harming human beings, are questions which are open to discussion. Whatever the truth of the matter may be, I had in 1970 or thereabouts an experience about which I still sometimes think.

The experience took place in the prosaic surroundings of the London Underground. I was travelling on the Northern Line, heading for home after taking a meditation class in town. Happening to look along the carriage, I saw a man standing in the doorway, his back towards me. Evidently he intended to get out at the next stop. The instant I set eyes on him I knew, intuitively, 'That's not a human being. That's a little devil.' I therefore kept an eye on him. He was of medium height, of slightly stocky build, and wore a dark suit. As soon as the train halted and the doors opened, the man turned round and very deliberately thumbed his nose at me, then skipped out onto the platform and ran away laughing. It was as if he was saying, 'I know you've spotted me, but you haven't caught me yet.' Later I wondered why I had spontaneously described him to myself as a little *devil*. As a Buddhist I do not believe in devils in the Christian sense of the word. I do not believe that there exist discarnate diabolical entities who are so irremeably evil as to be forever incapable of becoming good and who are, therefore, beyond all hope of redemption. A class of non-human beings called *māras* do, however, feature in the lives of the Buddha and his disciples, according to the Pāli scriptures. They are wicked rather than evil, troublesome rather than really dangerous, and generally run away when recognized – just like my man on the Underground. Perhaps I described him as a *little* devil because he was more like a *māra* than a real Christian devil. I certainly did not see the tail protruding from his trouser leg.

The devils of medieval Christianity kept their horns, hoofs, and tails for quite a long time, until the painters of the Italian Renaissance, in particular, found it difficult to incorporate such grotesque figures into their sublime and beautiful art. Sometimes, however, they can be seen perched on the top of columns normally occupied by the statues of pagan deities, spectators rather than participants, in paintings in which an episode from the New Testament, or from the life of a saint, takes place against a background of imposing classical architecture. Thus devils never entirely disappear from the scene. Some devils, indeed, assume an aesthetically more pleasing outward form, and appear in certain Renaissance and Baroque paintings with magnificently proportioned human bodies, miniature horns, and an enormous reptilian tail. More often than not they are being pursued downwards by the Archangel Michael, who is ready to plunge his spear into the hindmost.

From devils to the Virgin Mary is both a short step and a long one. It is a short one in that she sometimes appears with Satan, in the form of a dragon, beneath her feet. It is a long – a very long – step from the devils to the Virgin Mary in that on account of her spotless purity – her complete freedom from sin, both actual and original – she is for Catholics the highest of all created beings.

I was attracted to the figure of the Virgin Mary even as a child. It must have been in the *Children's Encyclopedia* that I first saw a picture of her. Probably it was Murillo's *The Immaculate Conception*,[400] for when, a few years later, I painted a picture of her, it was this famous painting that I had in mind. There was the same blue outer robe, the same long dark hair, the same hands crossed on the breast. I cannot remember if I gave her a crescent moon beneath her feet, but in place of the twelve stars that often surround her head, as in Velázquez's hardly less famous version of the same subject,[401] I gave her three red roses – one above her head and one on either side. A few years later, not long before my departure for India, I happened to hear on the radio, quite unexpectedly, the words 'Blessed be the great Mother of God

Mary Most Holy' intoned by a priest, as I imagined, in the course of a Roman Catholic service. They made a strange impression on me. I had not known that for many Christians Mary was not just the mother of Jesus but the Mother of God, and it was not until some years after my return to England that I came to understand the theological implications of the belief. Meanwhile, I had at least one contact with her during my years in India. This was when, in the summer of 1947, I took up the serious practice of Buddhist meditation. A few days into the practice, I saw the Virgin Mary – just as I had once painted her. This was not a true vision but an eidetic image of my painting, released from my subconscious mind by the pressure of the meditation.

Considering how prominent a place Mary occupies in Catholic faith, worship, and private devotion, it is astonishing how infrequently she appears in the Gospel narrative. Her most important appearances on the scene are at the Annunciation, when she receives from Gabriel the angelic salutation, and is told she is to conceive by the Holy Ghost and bear a son,[402] and at the Crucifixion, when with St John, the beloved disciple, she stands beside the Cross.[403] To depict the first of these events has been the delight of Christian artists through the ages, from Duccio and Cimabue to Rossetti and the Nazarenes. My two favourite paintings of the scene are the one by Simone Martini in the Uffizi and the one by Fra Angelico in the Prado. In Martini's painting, against a gold background, and beneath three Gothic arches, a white-robed angel, colourfully winged, holding an olive branch and wreathed with olive leaves, kneels with a friendly, eager expression before the blue-clad, seated Virgin, who shrinks back in dismay at his message, seeming to avert her face. Fra Angelico's painting is all cool blues and greys and warm pinks, except on the extreme left of the picture where Adam and Eve are being driven from a very green Garden of Eden by an angel. Framed by two slender columns and a round arch, Gabriel, in a pink robe and with gold wings, bows before a blue-manteled Virgin similarly framed, his hands crossed on his breast. She bows her head in complete acceptance of the Divine Will; her hands, too, are crossed on her breast, and a shaft of light from the top left-hand corner of the painting gently strikes her. Though depicting the same event, that of the Annunciation, the two artists have chosen to depict different moments in the event as described by St Luke. Simone Martini depicts Mary's initial shock and astonishment at the news that she is to be the mother of the Messiah; Fra Angelico, her eventual submission and acceptance of the role. 'Behold the handmaid of the Lord', she says to Gabriel, 'Be it unto me according to thy word.'[404]

There is no mention of Mary's death in the New Testament, much less any mention of her being received body and soul into heaven, yet both events – the Dormition and the Assumption, as Catholics call them – have inspired countless paintings. The most impressive representation of the Dormition or Falling Asleep (i.e. death) of the Virgin Mary I have seen was not a painting but a kind of tableau. I saw it in Valencia Cathedral, some three or four years ago. In front of the high altar, on a catafalque draped in white satin, lay the white-robed figure of the Virgin, her crown on her head. Above her was suspended a canopy of white silk, while all around her were huge vases of white lilies. The place was very silent. It was as though a living person was lying there. Very likely I had chanced to visit the cathedral on the day, or perhaps in the week, of the Feast of the Dormition. But it was strange there were so few people about, though votive candles were burning at some of the side altars.

All too many paintings of the Assumption are unconvincing. In some, angels appear to be lifting the Virgin Mary up bodily into heaven; in others, she ascends with melodramatic gestures. Titian's *Assumption* in the Franciscan Frari in Venice is a glorious exception. It occupies a place above the high altar in the main chapel of the huge, grandly simple, Gothic structure, and is better seen than described. I saw it in 1983, and was amazed by the way in which the figure of the red-robed Virgin, her dark cloak swirling about her, soars out of reach of the disciples, soaring with outstretched arms and upturned face, a soft golden haze behind her, up to the eternal Father – soars from earth to heaven, from history into the realm of legend and myth.

Though she is Queen of Heaven and Queen of Angels, Mary likes to descend from time to time, with or without the Child, and show herself on earth. It seems she is particularly fond of the saints. Indeed, she has her favourites among them, as befits a great queen – favourites to whom she pays little visits and whom she graciously honours with gifts. Thus we again and again see her in paintings either giving a rosary to St Dominic, or a chasuble to St Ildefonso, or even squirting a stream of milk from her breast into the mouth of St Bernard, who was particularly devoted to her and who sings her praises in the third part of Dante's

Divine Comedy, the *Paradiso*.[405] That Mary has a particular fondness for the saints, and even has her favourites among them, does not mean that she is not interested in Christians who lead less exemplary lives. Once she took the place of an absconding nun, so that her absence from the convent was not noticed by the other nuns; and once she stepped down from her altar to wipe the sweat from the brow of a poor juggler who had been juggling to please her – the only way of showing his devotion that he knew. There was even an occasion when she secretly opened the back door of hell, allowing some damned souls to escape, much to the annoyance of Satan, who complained bitterly to the Holy Trinity that the Virgin had infringed his ancient rights. In more recent times she has appeared to a number of people including children. A hundred and fifty years ago she appeared at Lourdes, in France, to Marie Bernadette Soubirous, a French peasant girl, to whom she revealed her identity with the words, 'I am the Immaculate Conception.'

She is the Immaculate Conception because, in the words of the papal pronouncement of 1854, she was 'at the first moment of her conception preserved immaculate from all stain of original sin'. As the Immaculate Conception she appears alone, without the Child, robed in white and blue, and with the crescent moon beneath her feet, and it is in this form that Velázquez, Murillo, Zurbaran, and other artists, mostly Spanish, often depict her. In this form she floats free from her role as the Mother of God; she is no longer defined by her relationship to the Incarnate Word. She is Queen of Heaven in her own right, so to speak. Though orthodox theologians warn that Mary is not to be regarded as a fourth member of the Trinity, this is what she seems to have become in the Roman Catholic collective imagination. Indeed, she seems to have become rather more than that in some quarters. I remember seeing in a German museum a little figure of the Virgin, apparently a reliquary, with a door in the belly, a door that could be opened to reveal the Father, Son, and Holy Ghost within. Whether this is theologically correct or not I do not know, but there is little doubt that Mary came to acquire, especially in the form of the Immaculate Conception, some of the attributes of the pagan Great Mother of the lands surrounding the Mediterranean, thus becoming the object of the devotion formerly directed to Rhea and Cybele, Ishtar and Astarte, Isis and Artemis. No wonder, then, that during the Middle Ages churches dedicated to her should have risen all over Western Europe, even as they had risen to her non-Christian predecessors all over the ancient world. The Cathedral of Notre Dame at Chartres parallels the great temple of Diana at Ephesus, the citizens of which protested against St Paul's disparagement of their goddess with repeated cries of 'Great is Diana of the Ephesians!'[406]

The Immaculate Conception made her appearance in the New World not long after the conquest of Mexico by the Spanish. In 1531 she appeared to Juan Diego, a Roman Catholic convert, on the hill of Tepeyac, a site sacred to the Aztec mother goddess Tonantzin in Guadalupe (now part of Mexico city). The Virgin instructed him to tell the archbishop to build a church in her honour on that very site. The archbishop proved sceptical, and she had to work a miracle to convince him of the truth of Juan Diego's story. She caused flowers to appear on the hill, and ordered Juan Diego to take them to the archbishop in his cloak. But when he opened the cloak the flowers spilled out revealing the image of the Immaculate Conception on the cloth. The sceptical archbishop was convinced, the church – later a basilica – was built, and the cult of the dark-skinned Virgin of Guadalupe came to occupy a central place in the religious life of the Mexican people.

Brought up as I was in England, most of my contacts with the supernatural beings of Christian mythology have been mediated by the art and literature of the Christian West. Only occasionally have they been mediated by the art and literature of the Christian East. In more recent years I have seen two important collections of icons, one in England and one in Germany, and I have also seen the 'Art of Holy Russia' exhibition held in London and elsewhere in the late 1980s. This was a very different kind of religious art. There was no saccharine sweetness, no overt sensuous appeal (though colours were sometimes very rich), no idealization of the human form. Its Virgins were sad-eyed, its bearded Christs stern, its saints severe, its angels distant and rather forbidding. What was more, it had no time for naturalistic detail, and monocular perspective seemed to be unknown to it. Yet despite its limitations, if indeed limitations they are, the supernatural beings depicted in this strange Russian art were really not of this world. They existed in another dimension, outside time and space, a dimension of which the symbol was the gold or black background against which they were often portrayed.

But it was not in any collection of icons, or at any exhibition, that I made contact with the being who, of all the supernatural beings of the Russian Orthodox version of Christian mythology, fascinated and intrigued me most. I first came across her in the poems of Vladimir Solovyov, the Russian philosopher, theologian, and mystic, into whose writings I have dipped from time to time.[407] This being was Sophia, the Divine Wisdom, in whose honour the great church of Hagia Sophia in Constantinople (Istanbul) was built by the emperor Justinian, and to whom many churches in Russia are dedicated. In icons she is shown seated on a throne, her feet resting on a terrestrial globe. She is red in colour, with red wings, is clad in royal vestments, wears a crown, and carries a sceptre. Some icons show her flanked by a dark-robed Virgin Mary, who holds a disc with the image of Christ, and a dark-robed John the Baptist. Thus she is not to be identified with Mary or with the second member of the Trinity. Similarly she is not to be identified with the Holy Ghost, who in other icons appears above her head in the form of a white dove. She is distinct from all three of them. Moreover, she is a person, just as the Holy Ghost, for example, is a person, not a mere personification of a virtue, like Justice or Fortitude.

Although the concept of Sophia, the Divine Wisdom, occupies with the concept of Godmanhood a central place in Solovyov's religious philosophy, it was as a person that he experienced her, and as a person that he describes her, and speaks to her, in his poetry. In his long poem 'Three Meetings' he describes his three encounters with Sophia, who for Solovyov is not only Divine Wisdom but also the World Soul and the Eternal Feminine.[408] The first encounter took place in Moscow when he was nine, during a church service, after a girl of his own age had rejected his love; the second in London, in the Reading Room of the British Museum, where he was studying the history of mysticism; the third in Egypt, in the desert near Cairo. The last two encounters seem to have been visionary experiences, in which he saw the face of Sophia 'in heavenly radiance'.

Sophia, the Divine Wisdom, has been compared with the Prajñāpāramitā, or Perfect Wisdom, of Mahāyāna Buddhist thought and Tantric Buddhist spiritual practice. Both can be seen as beings as well as concepts, and as beings both are feminine in form. To what extent the Divine Wisdom of which Sophia is the embodiment resembles the Perfect Wisdom of which Prajñāpāramitā is the embodiment is a topic that would repay scholarly investigation, provided the approach was not merely academic. Whether or not it is ever investigated, the

Sophia of the Russian Orthodox Church, especially as she appears in the life and thought of Vladimir Solovyov, remains for one western Buddhist, at least, one of the most interesting of the supernatural beings of Christian mythology.

6
CHRISTIAN ETHICS

I suspect that had I been able to write the full-length comparative study of Buddhism and Christianity that I planned to write many years ago I would have found the chapter on the ethics of the two religions the most difficult to write. Buddhist ethics is comparatively simple, straightforward, and clear, standing in little need of interpretation. It is an ethics of intention, according to which the moral status of an act is determined by the nature of the volitional state with which it is performed, and it is for this reason that the ethics of Buddhism has been termed a psychological ethics. That it is an ethics of intention does not mean that it is a matter of those 'good intentions' with which the path to hell is said to be paved, for the kind of volitional state that renders an act moral (*kuśala*) necessarily includes an element of non-delusion (*amoha*) with regard to the true nature of things.

The ideal of Buddhism is the attainment of Enlightenment or Buddhahood. That state is attained by insight into, or realization of, the nature of ultimate reality, whether conceived as emptiness (*śūnyatā*), or as non-dual awareness (*advayacitta*). This insight, or realization, arises on the basis of an integrated, inspired, transformed, and radiant consciousness (the state of *samādhi*), and this in turn on the basis of a life purified by moral actions (*śīla*), i.e. actions expressive of volitional states of kindness, generosity, contentment, authenticity, and awareness. Reversing the order of these three levels of Buddhist experience, we have *śīla*, *samādhi*, and insight (*prajñā*, *vipaśyanā*), the three great stages of the spiritual path. All three stages have been divided and subdivided in various ways by Buddhist teachers of various schools. Nonetheless, the broad outline of the path – its architectonic, as it were – remains quite clear. The intentional ethics of Buddhism thus does not stand alone. It forms an integral part of the Buddhist spiritual path. Indeed, it is the foundation of that path.

Christian ethics is a much more complex thing, at least in the eyes of the Buddhist observer. It is complex because it has more than one source. Although its principal source is the New Testament, in particular the ethical teachings of Jesus in the four Gospels and of St Paul in his Epistles, it also draws upon the laws of the Old Testament, in particular the Ten Commandments, and upon the ideas and terminology of Hellenism, as well as being influenced by the theologies of St Augustine and the medieval schoolmen, most of whom were themselves influenced, directly or indirectly, by the ethical theories of Plato and Aristotle. The ethics of Protestantism, unlike those of Roman Catholicism and Orthodoxy, have been influenced by the main currents of modern western thought from the eighteenth-century Rationalist Enlightenment to twentieth-century Existentialism.

The moral atmosphere by which I was surrounded as I grew up was that of Protestantism in its Anglican and Baptist forms. I was affected by it through my parents, through my teachers at school, through my membership of the Boys' Brigade from the age of twelve to the age of fourteen, and through my contact with certain elders of the Baptist church to which my company of the BB was affiliated. I breathed that atmosphere much as I breathed the air, without knowing of what elements it was composed, and without being aware how it was affecting me or even that it was affecting me at all. It was only later, after my realization that I was a Buddhist, that, comparing Buddhist ethical values with those of Christianity, I could begin to see the extent to which the latter had influenced me and were, perhaps, influencing me still.

Though my father taught me at an early age to repeat a short prayer each night before I slept, I cannot remember ever receiving any explicit moral instruction either from him or my mother. Instruction, if instruction there was, was entirely by example. My parents both had a strong sense of duty, and both were hard working, though without being driven by the Protestant work ethic. They worked cheerfully, and could thoroughly enjoy whatever pleasures their modest means permitted. My mother's principal pleasures, apart from those of home, were seeing those of her nine brothers and sisters who still lived in London, going to the local cinema once a week with her best friend, and occasionally, with the same friend, eating out at a restaurant or attending a matinee in town. My father went to the cinema only when a nature film was being shown, or a film of historical interest, in which case he took me with him, and he hated eating out at restaurants and having to 'dress up' for the occasion. His principal pleasures were working in his garden (an extremely small one for the first eleven years of my life, until we moved), spending time with his friends, reading tales of travel and adventure, and taking the family to Wimbledon Common on Sundays and to the seaside for our annual holiday. My father was very much a countryman at heart, whereas my mother was city born and bred, and preferred the bright lights of the West End to a prospect of green fields and trees. I suspect she did not really enjoy our holidays at the seaside, except as they afforded her a week's respite from shopping, cooking, and cleaning. She never went in the sea, as she was too prudish to wear a bathing costume, an inhibition my father certainly did not share. Both my parents drank and smoked only in moderation, especially my mother, and I never heard from either of them any but the mildest of expletives. I was all the more shocked, therefore, when at the house of a friend of my own age, with whom I was accustomed to share the boys' papers I was still reading, I heard his rather notorious mother give vent to a four letter word I had not heard before but which I instinctively knew was a taboo word. I was shocked not so much by the word itself as by the ugly, vicious mood of which it was the expression.

At infant school I learned about Jesus, heard some of the parables, but none of this had the effect of imparting to me a moral impulse, and when I rejoined junior school, after being confined to bed for two years or more, I found myself in the same position. There must have been Scripture lessons, but I have no recollection of them, which suggests they made no impression on me, ethically or otherwise. This does not mean that a distinct moral consciousness had not yet arisen in me. It had arisen while I was still attending infant school, and its arising was connected with two incidents, both of which I clearly remember. The first incident took place when I was four or five, and it took place in the infant school playground. I deliberately hit a smaller boy, who ran away crying. I think I hit him because I did not like his jersey, with its alternate bands of white and orange. I instantly knew that I had *done wrong*, and this knowledge made me feel *guilty*.

But how was it that I *knew* I had done wrong, and why should that knowledge have made me feel guilty? I knew I had done wrong by virtue of the fact that the other boy was a human being like me, so that in hitting him I was to an extent disrupting the natural solidarity which exists, fundamentally, between one human being and another. The guilt I felt was the affective concomitant of my awareness that it was *I*, and no other, who was *responsible* for the wrong I had done the other boy. I had inflicted a wound on the body of our common humanity, and my feeling of guilt was the *pain* of that wound. No doubt I did not understand all this at the time, but the fact that I could know I had done wrong, that I could know that it was I who was responsible for what I had done, and that I could feel guilt on its account, certainly constituted, so far as I can remember, the first arising of a distinct moral consciousness in me.

I have heard it said, even by some who should have known better, that guilt is an entirely negative emotion and that one should neither feel guilt oneself nor make others feel it. This is to confuse rational guilt with irrational guilt. One experiences rational guilt when one offends against what Buddhist ethics terms natural morality (*pakati-sīla*), and irrational guilt when one fails to observe what it terms conventional morality (*paññatti-sīla*).[409] Natural morality is based on the fundamental difference that exists between those actions that are expressions of volitional states of greed, hatred, and delusion, such as killing and stealing, and those that are expressions of the opposite volitional states, such as deeds of kindness and generosity. Conventional morality is not so based. As the term suggests, it is simply a matter of social custom and observance, and is in itself morally neutral. Offences against natural morality are not only accompanied by the feeling of rational guilt; sooner or later they are followed, under the law of karma, by suffering. The most serious offence against natural morality that one can commit is the deliberate killing of another human being, an offence which brings upon the offender the most serious consequences, both social and karmic. This does not mean that the deliberate killing of animals, especially for pleasure, is not also an offence against natural morality, for it disrupts our sense of kinship, as human beings, with other forms of life, especially the higher forms. It is for this reason that abstention from killing (Pāli: *pāṇātipātā veramaṇī*) is the first of both the five and the ten moral precepts of Buddhism. One who habitually breaks this precept, and who moreover experiences no feeling of guilt on that account, has sunk below the truly human level, or at least has regressed to the pre-moral condition of infancy and early childhood.

The second incident with which the arising in me of a distinct moral consciousness was connected, took place when I was six. It took place at the South London Hospital for Children, to which I had been admitted for the then routine tonsillectomy. I stayed there for two or three days, and during that time I was kept in bed, as were the other children in the ward. It once so happened that I urgently needed a bedpan, and as the nurse passed by my bed I called out to her to bring me one. But she ignored my call. In the course of the next few minutes she passed by several times, and each time I called out to her for the bedpan, but she continued to ignore my appeals, even though I called more and more loudly and insistently. Eventually, as was inevitable, I fouled the bed, whereupon the same nurse at once came over to me and scolded me vigorously for what had happened, as though it was my fault. I keenly felt the injustice of the scolding. When I hit the boy in the playground I knew I had done wrong, and I felt guilty. Now, when the nurse scolded me, I knew *she* was doing what was wrong, and I felt indignant. She had committed an offence against natural morality, for in scolding me for what had happened as though it was my fault, when it was hers for repeatedly ignoring me when I called out for the bedpan, she was acting a lie. She was refusing to accept responsibility for her action, or rather for her inaction, and 'inaction in a deed of mercy becomes an action in a deadly sin'.[410] I did not think all this at the time, but the incident burned into my young being the consciousness that injustice is morally wrong.

My membership of the Boys' Brigade, and my contact with the church to which our company was affiliated, afforded me no such incidents as the two I have described. The pastor's moving sermons served merely to inflame my religious emotions. Specifically moral instruction came only at the BB's Sunday morning Bible class and after the Friday evening drill. The instructor was our brisk, cheery little captain, who also led the prayers and the hymn-singing. The principal sins, I gathered, were smoking, drinking, and swearing. The three went together, so that if you fell victim to one sin you would almost certainly fall victim, sooner or later, to the two others. There were also exhortations to lead 'a clean life', though just what this meant was not spelled out. Sex was in fact never mentioned, either at the BB itself, at school, or within the family circle, and it was only when I was transferred to a 'better' school, at the age of thirteen or fourteen, that I heard the subject discussed – smuttily and surreptitiously – by some of the older boys. It must have been at about this time that I received the only sex education I ever had. One Sunday afternoon my father handed me his copy of Health and Strength magazine, and pointing to one of the articles said 'I think you should read this.' The article was about masturbation. I read it with interest, but I did not need its advice as much as my father may have thought, for I was leading as 'clean' a life as the BB could have desired. My father never asked if I had read the article, nor did I tell him I had done so. He probably thought that in drawing my attention to the article he had done his parental duty so far as that department of my education was concerned.

It must have been at about this time, too, that I became aware that I was physically and emotionally attracted to members of my own sex. Indeed, though I read the article on masturbation with genuine interest, I looked with much greater interest at the photos of well-built young men, naked except for a posing pouch, that were a leading feature of the magazine. Some of them reminded me of sculptures of the Greek gods – Apollo, Hermes, and the rest – pictures of which I had seen in the *Children's Encyclopedia*. That I was attracted to older boys, and to young men, in this way, did not make me feel guilty; nor did I feel guilt when the attraction started to assume a definitely sexual character, as it did a year or two later. It was a feeling that had arisen in me quite naturally; it was part of me, and I did not question its rightness. At the same time I instinctively knew, even at that early age, that it was something of which society disapproved and that I should not talk about it to anyone.

Since I could not talk about my feeling to anyone it was several years before I discovered that there were others who were attracted to members of their own sex and that there was a name for this attraction. Enlightenment eventually came when I was about seventeen, and it came from Edward Carpenter's *The Intermediate Sex* and from the chapter on homosexuality in Havelock Ellis's *The Psychology of Sex*, a work that has been described as sympathetic and scientific.[411] In the meantime, a lot had been happening in my life. I had left school and started work, I had realized I was not a Christian, and in the moral writings of the Roman Stoic philosopher Seneca I had breathed a cleaner, fresher moral atmosphere than that of Christianity. Above all, I had realized on reading the *Diamond Sūtra* and the *Sūtra of Wei Lang* that I was a Buddhist, and that in the depths of my being I had always been one. I also became increasingly aware, during the period of these developments, of the way in which society regarded sexual feelings such as mine. It did not merely disapprove of them. It regarded them with the utmost abhorrence, and in some countries to act upon them was a criminal offence. In 1895, only thirty years before I was born, the poet and playwright Oscar Wilde, then at the height of his career, was sentenced to two years' imprisonment with hard labour for breaking the law prohibiting sexual relations between men, and that law was still on the statute book.

How had such a state of affairs come about? Why did society regard with such hostility, and punish so harshly, an inclination which, if my own experience was anything to go by, arose quite naturally, and which, as I now understood from my reading of *The Psychology of Sex*, was found in all periods of history, and in all walks of life, and not least among some of the most gifted writers, artists, and musicians. It was Havelock Ellis who provided me with a clue. Only with the coming of Christianity had homosexuality fallen into disrepute, it having been idealized by the ancient Greeks in association with intellectual, aesthetic, and ethical qualities. After the time of the Byzantine emperor Justinian (483–565 CE) it was regarded as 'a vulgar vice, or rather as a crime, deserving of the most severe secular and ecclesiastical penalties, even burning at the stake'.[412]

What had led the Christian Church to devalue, even to demonize, homosexual relations in this way? The answer was to be found, I discovered, in the Bible. Both the Book of Leviticus in the Old Testament and St Paul's Epistle to the Romans in the New contain a passage dealing with the subject. Leviticus is short and to the point. God tells the Israelites, through Moses, 'Thou shalt not lie with mankind, as with womankind: it is abomination.'[413] St Paul is more prolix, and seems almost to foam at the mouth as he delivers his diatribe against the pagans and denounces homosexuality as one of the degrading passions to which God, in his anger, has abandoned them for worshipping not him, the immortal God, but images made with their own hands, thus giving up divine truth for a lie. The key verses are,

> For this cause God gave them up unto vile affections: for even their women did change the natural use into that which is against nature: And likewise also the men, leaving the natural use of the woman, burned in their lust one toward another; men with men working that which is unseemly, and receiving in themselves that recompense of their error which was meet.[414]

Probably few passages in the Bible have been responsible for as much human misery as these from Leviticus and the Epistle to the Romans.

But although I had been provided with a clue to the mystery of society's hostility to homosexuality, twenty years were to pass before I was in a position to follow that clue through the labyrinth of Christian ethics. During this time I did at least read one book that had some bearing on the subject. This was André Gide's *Corydon*, a cautious but courageous defence of homosexuality in Socratic dialogue form, which I came across in a Calcutta bookshop. I also discovered that homosexuality was not unknown in the *gompas* of Tibet or the viharas of South-East Asia. Though the Vinaya or Code of Monastic Discipline prohibits monks (and nuns) from engaging in sexual activities of any kind, I gathered from conversations with some of my brother monks that pederasty, at least, was generally regarded as a peccadillo rather than as a serious offence. There was also an unheralded visit from the American Beat poet Allen Ginsberg, who did not hide the fact that he had a male lover and that he was interested in exploring the possibility of practising Tantric sex 'with a boy'.[415]

By the time I returned to England the moral climate had changed a little, at least in some quarters and in some respects. Sex was now being talked about more openly, books previously banned for their 'obscenity', like Radclyffe Hall's lesbian novel *The Well of Loneliness*, had been republished, and the newly elected Labour government was about to repeal the law under which Oscar Wilde had been convicted and replace it with one permitting homosexual acts between consenting adults in private. The Roman Catholic Church, together with the Anglican Church and other Protestant bodies, strongly opposed this more liberal attitude to homosexuality, though within each communion a few brave souls refused to toe the official line, maintaining that it was possible to be actively homosexual *and* a practising Christian. Over the years, however, even the Roman Catholic Church shifted its position slightly. It was not a sin to be a homosexual, in the sense of having homosexual feelings, but it was a sin to act in accordance with those feelings. God thus was credited with endowing some human beings with certain very powerful desires and then, for his own mysterious reasons, forbidding them to fulfil those desires on pain of damnation. The absurdity of such a position had already been the subject of an untitled, bitterly satirical poem by A. E. Housman, written around the time of the trial of Oscar Wilde but published only after the author's death in 1936.

> Oh who is that young sinner with the handcuffs on his wrists?
> And what has he been after that they groan and shake their fists?
> And wherefore is he wearing such a conscience-stricken air?
> Oh they're taking him to prison for the colour of his hair.
>
> 'Tis a shame to human nature, such a head of hair as his;
> In the good old time 'twas hanging for the colour that it is;
> Though hanging isn't bad enough and flaying would be fair
> For the nameless and abominable colour of his hair.
>
> Oh a deal of pains he's taken and a pretty price he's paid
> To hide his poll or dye it of a mentionable shade;
> But they've pulled the beggar's hat off for the world to see
>   and stare,
> And they're haling him to justice for the colour of his hair.
>
> Now 'tis oakum for his fingers and the treadmill for his feet,
> And the quarry-gang on Portland in the cold and in the heat,
> And between his spells of labour in the time he has to spare
> He can curse the God that made him for the colour of his hair.

Obviously, it is not easy for Christians to be more sympathetic to homosexuality, for the Bible evinces no such sympathy for it whatever. Leviticus categorically forbids sexual relations between men and the Epistle to the Romans represents homosexuality as the object of God's anger and classes it with all manner of wickedness, including murder. Since for Christians the Bible is divinely inspired, it follows that it is possible for them to accept homosexuality, whether in others or in themselves, only if they understand that inspiration to be of a general nature, not as extending to every sentence of every author contributing to its formation. Judging by their attitude to homosexuality, practically all the churches believe every sentence of the Bible to be divinely inspired, not culturally conditioned, and applicable to all human beings at all periods of history. The non-Christian is therefore entitled to ask the leaders of those churches about their attitude to witches, witches having been persecuted by the Church between the fifteenth and seventeenth centuries, hundreds of thousands of them having been put to death during those years. After all, the Book of Exodus's 'Thou shalt not suffer a witch to live'[416] is no less categorical than the Book of Leviticus's 'Thou shalt not lie with mankind as with womankind'. Witchcraft is no longer a criminal offence in Europe, though self-styled witches still exist among us, but so far as I am aware neither the Roman Catholic Church nor any of the Protestant churches advocate the revival of the old laws against witchcraft or believe that in an ideal Christian society witches would again be put to death. Exodus 22:18 has been allowed to become a dead letter, along with many other of the Old Testament's prohibitions and injunctions. Why cannot Leviticus 18:22 be allowed to become a dead letter, too?

The Jesus of the four Gospels does not say anything about homosexuality, but he has quite a lot to say about how people should behave towards one another. In the course of his Sermon on the Mount (actually a later compilation of the Master's sayings) Jesus tells the disciples that their virtue should go beyond that of the Scribes and Pharisees. Not only should they not kill, they should not even get angry; not only should they not commit adultery, they should not even look at a woman lustfully; and so on. Moreover, they are to love their enemies, pray for those who persecute them, forgive others their failings, and are not to judge anyone. Above all, 'Whatsoever ye would that men should do to you, do ye even so to them: for this is the law and the prophets'.[417] Here Jesus emphasizes the spirit rather than the letter of morality, and the eponymous author of the Gospel reports that the people were deeply impressed by his teaching, accustomed as no doubt they were to the more legalistic moral teaching of the religious authorities. Jesus in fact is appealing to the natural sense of solidarity that exists between one human being and another, any breach of which is the real immorality. This sense of human solidarity is the basis of what Buddhism terms natural morality, which in turn constitutes the ultimate basis of social morality and of law.

Christians therefore have a choice with regard to their attitude to homosexuals. They can treat them either in accordance with the letter of the Old Testament or in accordance with the spirit of the New. They can treat them with hostility, as breakers of what they believe to be a divinely revealed commandment binding on all men for all time, or they can treat them with sympathy and respect as fellow human beings. They can denounce them, and class them with criminals, as St Paul does (despite his singing the praises of love in 1 Corinthians 13), or they can behave towards homosexuals in the way in which Jesus, in the Sermon on the Mount, tells the disciples they are to behave towards their fellow men. For Jesus the golden rule, in its positive form, was 'the law and the prophets', and the golden rule by its very nature excludes no one – not even homosexuals. Unfortunately, Christians on the whole have chosen to treat homosexuals with hostility, the Church having decided early in its history, on the basis of Leviticus 18:22 and Romans 1:26–7, that sexual relations between men were a grave sin and to be punished accordingly.

Even in the Middle Ages, however, there were men who, while not questioning the Church's teaching on the sinfulness of homosexuality, were nonetheless able to feel affection and respect for individual homosexuals. Dante was such a man. In the *Divine Comedy* he represents himself and his guide, the poet Virgil, as meeting in the seventh Circle of Hell a troop of spirits. They are running along beside a river of blood, on a margin of burning sand, and are tormented by a shower of fiery rain. They are being punished for 'violence against Nature'. One of the spirits is the Florentine scholar Brunetto Latini, Dante's old preceptor. He and Dante recognize each other and a touching conversation ensues. Dante expresses his deep gratitude to Latini, who predicts a glorious future for him if he follows his star but warns him to have no truck with the ungrateful and malignant Florentines. The other members of his troop, Latini tells Dante, were all clerics and scholars of great fame who on earth were guilty of the same crime as himself. There were so many of them that there was not time for him to relate all their histories, but he would mention three of them individually; Priscian (the Roman grammarian), Francesco, son of Accorso (an eminent lawyer), and the notorious bishop whom the pope was obliged to transfer to another see. Continuing on their way, Dante and his guide see another troop of spirits running along. Three of them run on ahead and circle round Dante, naked, and bleeding from the fiery rain. They were citizens of Florence distinguished in war and council, and Virgil tells Dante they deserve to be treated with courtesy. Two of them were noblemen, the third a rich man of humble birth who abandoned his savage-tempered wife for what one of Dante's Victorian translators calls 'wicked ways'. Dante tells the three that he feels not contempt but sorrow at their plight and that he has always honoured them for their patriotism. One of the spirits then inquires if courage and courtesy still abide within their native city; but Dante is unable to give them a positive reply, and the three resume their running along the burning sand.[418]

Dante's attitude to Brunetto Latini, his old preceptor, and the rest of those who were being punished for 'violence against Nature', stands in luminous contrast to the attitude of the vast majority of Christians to homosexuals, both before and after his time. So different is his attitude that I cannot but wonder if Dante was privately of the opinion that homosexuality was not so great a sin as the Church thought, or perhaps not a sin at all. This seems all the more likely in view of his attitude to those who were being punished for usury, another form of 'violence against Nature', whom he sees at the limit of the seventh Circle. They are seated on the burning sand, vainly trying to ward off with their hands the fiery rain that falls upon them. Dante does not recognize any of them. One of them speaks to him, but he does not reply. The very least one can conclude is that Dante probably had more sympathy for homosexuals than for moneylenders. The Roman Catholic Church, of course, has long since ceased to regard usury as a sin, but homosexuality is as much a sin as ever. The same may be said of the Anglican and other major Protestant churches. They, too, have quietly dropped usury from the catalogue of sins, while continuing to regard homosexuality as one of the worst sins a human being can commit. On this subject Rome, Canterbury, Geneva, and Wittenberg all speak with one voice.

That they should do so is not astonishing, given that the attitude to homosexuality of all of them is predicated on Leviticus 18:22 and Romans 1:26–7. What is really astonishing is that Christianity should have been able, during the period of its ascendency in Europe, to implant its abhorrence of homosexuality so deeply in the western psyche that it continued to be felt not only by Christians but even by some of those who had abandoned Christianity. It was surely one of the most successful exercises in mass indoctrination that the world has ever seen. Just how successful it was is illustrated by what happened to Oscar Wilde after his release from prison. Since it was impossible for him to live in England he went to stay in France. There, as Hesketh Pearson relates, he was treated as a moral leper to the end of his days.

> At a word from some American or Englishman, barmen would refuse to serve him drinks, restaurant proprietors would ask him to leave, hotel managers would turn him out, barbers would decline to shave him, respectable fathers would clutch their children to their sides as he passed by. Many men who had known all about his sexual oddity in the days of his success, and had been proud of his acquaintance then, now disowned him and either cut or avoided him. The English and Americans were his chief traducers and tormentors, but every self-important French writer kept out of his way, vicious little paragraphs about him appeared at regular intervals in the French press, and only the younger and more rebellious spirits were to be seen in his company.[419]

Oscar Wilde died in 1900. Since then, and especially since the 1960s, 'the love that dare not speak its name' has increasingly found a voice; more and more people are prepared to tolerate, even if not to accept, homosexuality, and homosexuals are better able to lead free and open lives. At the same time, the picture is a mixed one. The churches, led by the Roman Catholic Church, remain implacably hostile to homosexual behaviour, which they continue to regard as a grave sin, the President of an African state has publicly denounced homosexuals as 'worse than animals', and in some parts of the world, including England, it is still possible for homosexuals to be attacked and killed on account of their sexuality. It is no accident that in the twentieth century the word 'homophobia' should have entered the language and found a place in English dictionaries, where it is defined as 'intense hatred or fear of homosexuals or homosexuality'. That hatred or fear is in part due, in the Anglo-Saxon world at least, to one-sided ideas, on the part of the heterosexual majority, of what it means to be a man; but it is also due, to a great extent, to the continued influence of the 'theological homophobia' of Christianity.

'The priest lays his curse on the fairest joys,' wrote William Blake.[420] Friendship is one of the fairest and truest joys of life, and the Roman Catholic Church, in particular, has laid its curse on it by its stern warning against the moral dangers of what it calls 'particular friendships', that is to say, friendships between men (and between women) that are more intimate, more emotionally intense, and even more passionate, than is customary in our culture between members of the same sex. Though the warning was addressed primarily to those living in single-sex, celibate religious communities it also had a much wider application. Particular friendships were morally dangerous not only for monks and nuns but also for lay persons, especially the young and impressionable. They were dangerous not merely because they could lead, in religious communities, to exclusivity and factionalism; they were dangerous because sexual feelings might be aroused in the parties to the friendship and this might lead to their having (homo)sexual relations. This linkage of particular friendships with the 'danger' of homosexuality has had unfortunate consequences. It has made many men in the West, especially those brought up as Roman Catholics or under the influence of Catholicism, fearful of entering into any friendship with another man that goes deeper than casual acquaintanceship or superficial camaraderie. The result is that they are emotionally impoverished.

Some years ago I came across Aelred of Rievaulx's *Spiritual Friendship* and was so pleased with the little work that I recommended it to a number of Buddhist friends. Aelred was a twelfth-century English monk who spent the latter part of his life as abbot of the Cistercian monastery of Rievaulx in Yorkshire, the extensive ruins of which I once visited on a misty, melancholy autumn afternoon. One of the reasons I was pleased with *Spiritual Friendship* was that Aelred, unlike other abbots of his own and later times, did not allow himself or his monks to be prevented from enjoying emotional, even physically demonstrative, friendships by the bogey of homosexuality. He rates friendship very highly; he is an enthusiastic advocate of its value and importance. It is part of the moral life, and in his eyes those who seek to live without it are more beasts than men. It is also part of the spiritual life, and Aelred goes so far as to assert that

'God is friendship'.[421] This striking assertion cannot but remind me, as a Buddhist, of the Buddha's emphatic declaration that spiritual friendship (*kalyāṇa mitratā*) was not half the holy life (*brahmacarya*), as Ānanda had supposed; it was the whole of it.[422]

Today, after centuries of neglect, Aelred of Rievaulx's *Spiritual Friendship* is again being studied, and Catholics interested in the social implications of the Christian life are taking seriously his assertion that 'God is friendship'. Similarly, certain western Buddhists have begun to take seriously the Buddha's declaration that spiritual friendship is the whole of the holy life, an insight which for more than two millennia had lain hidden in the depths of the Pāli Buddhist scriptures, apparently unnoticed by the official custodians of those scriptures. Such western Buddhists see the Buddhist spiritual community (sangha) as a network of spiritual friendships, the strength of that community being dependent on the strength of the multitudinous friendships of which the network is composed.

Just as Christians have a choice with regard to their attitude to homosexuals, so do they have a choice with regard to their attitude to non-Christians. They can behave towards them in accordance with the letter of the Old Testament, where God commands the Israelites to destroy the Amalekites[423] and other unclean and idolatrous people (e.g. Numbers 31) or in accordance with the spirit of the New Testament as represented by the Sermon on the Mount and the golden rule. History shows that they have harkened more often to the commands of Jehovah than to the counsels of Jesus and that, given the power and the opportunity, they could treat non-Christians no better than they treated heretics and homosexuals. In every generation there were, of course, Christians who took the Sermon on the Mount and the example of Jesus seriously, some of them being persecuted for so doing, as the Spiritual Franciscans were by the Roman Catholic Church and the early Quakers by the Church of England.

Much of the violence of which Christians have been guilty, whether towards Muslims, Jews, South American Indians, or Vietnamese Buddhists, can no doubt be ascribed to the ignoble passions that they share with the rest of unregenerate humanity. Hence it would be not right for me, as a Buddhist, to criticize Christians for being subject to passions to which Buddhists are also subject and to which they, too, despite the Buddha's teaching, may sometimes give hurtful and destructive expression. But there is in the historical violence of Christians towards non-Christians, as well as towards heretics and homosexuals, an element that is not to be found in the violence of backsliding Buddhists, however reprehensible. It is an element that is not peculiar to Christianity but which characterizes other divinely revealed monotheistic religions. I do not find it easy to define this element, the horrifying nature of which is illustrated by a Spanish short story I once read, a story of which the following is a bald summary.

In the days of Philip II there lived in Spain a nobleman of ancient lineage who had two beautiful unmarried daughters. He was a widower, and resided with them in his ancestral mansion on the outskirts of the town. Since he possessed properties in different parts of the country, he was often away from home for weeks at a time, so that the two young women were left very much to their own devices. Visitors were of course forbidden, and since both daughters were of a serious turn of mind they spent much of their time discussing religious matters. One day the father returned home unexpectedly and on going to his daughters' room caught them studying the New Testament. When he demanded to know what this meant, for the New Testament was virtually a banned book in Catholic Spain, they confessed that as a result of reading the Gospels they had become Lutherans. Now the nobleman was a devout, even fanatical, son of the Church, and he had no words to express his horror, astonishment, and grief that they should have disgraced him in this terrible way. As was his duty, he at once reported his daughters to the Holy Office of the Inquisition. They were arrested, imprisoned, and tried for heresy, and since they steadfastly refused to renounce their new faith they were sentenced to be burnt at the stake as heretics. On the eve of the execution the father went to the Inquisitors and asked, as a particular favour, to be allowed to provide the firewood with which his heretical daughters would be burnt and to pile it up round them with his own hands. This pious request was readily granted. Two days later, after the young women had met their terrible end, the mansion in which they had lived caught fire and was burned to the ground. Their father perished in the flames, and it was rumoured that he had set fire to the building with his own hand.

I do not know whether the story is based on an historical incident or whether it is the product of the author's imagination. In any case, it was powerfully written and made a strong and lasting impression on my mind. It perfectly illustrates the nature of the horrifying element within Christian violence with which I am concerned. Morality is born from a sense of the natural solidarity of human beings with one another and, ultimately, with all forms of life. That sense is strongest in relation to those with whom we are connected by ties of blood, which is why patricide and matricide have always been considered such dreadful crimes, even when committed unknowingly, as when Oedipus killed Laius without being aware of his real identity.[424] In actively bringing about (with the Inquisition) the horrible death of his two daughters the nobleman in the story disrupts the natural solidarity that exists between parent and child. He thus is guilty of committing an act of the blackest immorality, and he commits it on account of his religion and with the full approval of its highest authorities. It is his religion that makes him immoral, as it has made immoral the countless Christians who, through the centuries, have persecuted and killed fellow human beings who thought, believed, or behaved differently from themselves. Why was this? What is there in Christianity that has caused Christians to behave in this heartless and inhuman fashion?

Eventually I realized that the answer to these questions lay a long way back in the history of Christianity and in the history of its predecessor, Judaism. During the two centuries following the death of Jesus there was not one Christianity but many. In the countries surrounding the Mediterranean there were scores, even hundreds, of little groups or 'churches' of believers, all having their own leaders, their own doctrines, and their own scriptures, and all competing with one another as well as with the various pagan cults. Irenaeus, the influential second-century Bishop of Lyon, in effect divided Christians into two great categories, the orthodox and the heterodox, the latter and their heretical writings being the subject of his encyclopedic *Against the Heresies*. Orthodox Christians were those who belonged to his own church, the church of which the Bishop of Rome (later to become 'the pope') was the head and St Peter, the Prince of the Apostles, the founder. Irenaeus moreover championed the Gospel According to St John, adding it to the three Synoptic Gospels to make the 'four formed gospel', the only complete and reliable record of the life and ministry of Jesus. It is this gospel that portrays Jesus as God Incarnate, not simply as the Messiah, and represents him as saying, 'I am the way, the truth, and the life: no man cometh unto the Father, but by me,'[425] – words which have enabled Christians to insist that only through faith in Jesus Christ can anyone be saved.

By the beginning of the third century, thanks to Irenaeus, the 'orthodox' church headed by the Bishop of Rome was a well organized, centralized international body. It had a corpus of 'reliable' scriptures, a 'high' conception of the nature of Jesus, and an unswerving conviction that it alone was in possession of the fullness of Christian truth. When the emperor Constantine became a Christian it was this orthodox Catholic church that he patronized to the exclusion of all others, endowing it and its head with property, money, and civil power, thereby enabling it to persecute heretics and destroy their heretical books. There thus came into existence the Holy Catholic Church, doctrinaire, authoritarian, intolerant, and not averse to the use of violence in pursuit of its aims. In the twelfth century, after a long period of estrangement between Latins and Greeks, the Catholic Christian Church split into two great halves: the Roman Catholic Church and the Eastern Orthodox Church, a schism that was confirmed by the sacking and looting of Constantinople in 1202 by the Frankish Crusaders during the Fourth Crusade. In the middle of the sixteenth century the Western Church itself split in two, one half consisting of the rump Roman Catholic Church, the other of the Lutheran, Calvinist, and Anglican churches, together with their respective offshoots. All these churches have inherited, to a greater or a lesser extent, the mindset of their remote ancestor the Constantinian Holy Catholic Church of the fourth century. It is this mindset which is responsible for that element within Christian violence which my Spanish short story illustrates. It is on account of this mindset that Christians have only too often been prepared to disrupt, in the supposed interests of their faith, the natural solidarity which exists between one human being and another, disrupting it even in those cases where it normally is strongest.

The historical violence of Christianity towards non-Christians is also due, in part, to the example of ancient Judaism. The Old Testament notoriously sanctions violence against the worshippers of other gods, and the books of the Old Testament form part of the Christian Bible. There were, however, some early Christians who believed that there was so great a discrepancy between the religious and moral teaching of the Old Testament and that of the New that they could not have issued from the same divine source. One such Christian was Marcion, the founder of Marcionism, who lived and taught in Rome in the middle of the second century and whose teachings spread to many parts of the

Roman empire. According to Marcion there were two Gods, the just God of the Law and the Prophets, and of the Old Testament generally, and the benevolent God, the heavenly Father of whom Jesus had spoken. Jesus was not of human birth. He was a purely spiritual being who, descending from heaven into the world created by the just God, had suddenly appeared in Galilee (apparently as a full-grown man) in the fifteenth year of the reign of Tiberius; and he had only appeared to suffer on the Cross. Marcion regarded the Third Gospel, which he did not attribute to St Luke, as containing a reliable account of the life and ministry of Jesus, at least in part; the three other gospels he rejected out of hand for what he saw as their Judaizing tendency. In the rest of the New Testament he accepted only the Pauline Epistles.

Had other Christians cut themselves loose from the Old Testament, as Marcion and his followers did, or had Constantine patronized the Marcionites instead of the Catholics (an unlikely event in view of the kind of church for which he was looking) the history of Christianity, and with it the history of Europe, may well have been different. As it was, the Old Testament was accepted along with the New, and its sanctioning of violence in the interests of religion helped reinforce Christianity's intolerance of religious difference. This has led me, as a Buddhist, to reflect that the history of Buddhism, and with it the history of Asia, would have been very different had the Vedic literature been bound up in a single volume, so to speak, with the Dialogues of the Buddha, so that Buddhists had a choice between performing animal sacrifices, as enjoined by the Vedas, and developing goodwill (*maitrī*) towards all living beings, as taught by the Buddha. Fortunately, this never happened, and rarely in the history of Buddhism has theology been allowed to subvert ethics or dogma to disrupt the natural solidarity between one human being and another.

7
SAINTS AND MYSTICS

Biography has always been one of my favourite forms of literature. It was therefore to be expected that I should have read, in the course of a long life, not only the lives of poets, painters, and philosophers, but also those of Christian saints, mystics, visionaries, and prophets. I did not read the biographies of these Christian worthies for the sake of spiritual uplift and illumination, although this did sometimes come, just as it sometimes came when I read the lives of great poets, painters, and philosophers. I read their biographies because they were remarkable men and women whose lives were of intense human interest.

In my teens I encountered, thanks to their biographers, a saint, a mystic, and a prophet. The saint was St Francis of Assisi, the mystic was Mme Guyon, and the prophet was Savonarola. I have related elsewhere how affected I was by *The Little Flowers* and *The Life of St Francis*, and how when I saw a beggar standing before me I gave him all my money, just as St Francis might have done – except that St Francis probably would not have possessed any money.[426] As so many have done, I delighted in his preaching to the birds, whom he called his little sisters, and his conversion of the fierce wolf of Gubbio. But Francis was no sentimental romantic. Poverty and humility were his two ideals, and he practised both to the utmost extent. He spoke of himself as wedded to Lady Poverty, and the closeness of that union can be seen from his worn, patched tunic, of the coarsest sackcloth, still preserved as a holy relic in an Italian church. At the same time he was no sour ascetic.

Until the end, when the order he had founded started to depart from his teaching, his life was one of joy.

The nature of that joy is well illustrated by an episode in *The Little Flowers*. It was a winter's day, and Francis was going from Perugia with Friar Leo to St Mary of the Angels suffering sorely from the bitter cold. As they went, he called out to Friar Leo, who was walking before him, that even if the friars minor in every land were to give good example of holiness and edification, nevertheless he should write and note down diligently that perfect joy was not to be found therein. In the same way he called out to Friar Leo that perfect joy was not to be found in the friar minor's miracles of healing, nor in his knowing all the sciences and all the Scriptures, nor in his speaking with the tongues of angels, nor in his preaching so well that he converted all the infidels to the faith of Christ, each time telling him to write down and note this diligently. When they had gone on for two good miles in this fashion Friar Leo, in great wonder, prayed Francis in God's name to tell him where perfect joy *was* to be found. Francis answered him thus:

> When we are come to St Mary of the Angels, wet through with rain, frozen with cold, and foul with mire and tormented with hunger; and when we knock at the door, the doorkeeper cometh in rage and saith, 'Who are ye?' and we say, 'We are two of your friars,' and he answers, 'Ye tell not true; ye are rather two knaves that go deceiving the world and stealing the alms of the poor; begone!' and he openeth not to us, and maketh us stay outside hungry and cold all night in the rain and snow; then if we endure patiently such cruelty, such abuse, and such insolent dismissal without complaint or murmuring, and believe humbly and charitably that that doorkeeper truly knows us, and that God maketh him to rail against us; O Friar Leo, write – there is perfect joy.[427]

In other words, true joy did not depend on external conditions; it was even heightened when they were adverse. Reading this episode from *The Little Flowers* again many years later, I was at once reminded of Tibet's great yogi Milarepa, who also was wedded to Lady Poverty and who, wearing only a thin cotton robe and sometimes not even that, sang songs of joy as he dwelt in the snowy mountains of his native land.

Mme Jeanne Marie Bouvier de la Motte Guyon lived in the France of Louis XIV, and as an advocate of quietism played a prominent if controversial part in the spiritual life of her country. The dictionary defines quietism as a form of religious mysticism requiring withdrawal of the spirit from all human effort and complete passivity to God's will, but for its opponents it is the exaggeration and perversion of the mystical doctrine of interior quiet. I do not remember much of Upham's biography of Mme Guyon, which I have not seen since my impressionable teens, but I do remember at least one thing clearly. This was Mme Guyon's doctrine of pure or disinterested love, according to which one should love God purely, without hope for heaven or fear of hell[428] – which was also the doctrine of certain Sufi mystics. As I subsequently learned from other sources, Mme Guyon suffered for her views. Despite the championship of Fénelon, the saintly Archbishop of Cambrai, she spent many years in prison, and eventually quietist teaching received papal condemnation. Like other forms of mysticism, quietism was perceived as dangerous by the religious authorities, for it made a spiritual life independent of the institutional church and its sacraments.

Girolamo Savonarola was a Dominican friar, preacher, and prophet who fell foul of the religious authorities in another way. Though the contemporary of Mantegna and Piero della Francesca, Botticelli and Leonardo da Vinci, he was no 'Renaissance man' but a throwback to the Middle Ages. Shocked by the corruption he saw in Florence, where he was prior of the monastery of San Marco, a corruption he believed was due to the city's wealth and to the discovery of the pagan classics, he delivered a series of passionate sermons in which he so terrified the people with predictions of the judgement to come if they did not mend their ways that they drove out their cultivated Medici ruling family and established a Christian republic with Savonarola himself as spiritual dictator. During the carnival season of 1497 a great 'bonfire of vanities' was held, in which personal ornaments, lewd pictures, and cards and gambling tables were consigned to the flames. Botticelli, who had been deeply affected by the friar's preaching, is said to have contributed some of his own works to the fire. But soon a reaction set in. People grew tired of having to be virtuous. Moreover, Savonarola had made political enemies, both at home and abroad. These enemies joined forces with the pope, the infamous Alexander VI, whom Savonarola had attacked in his sermons. In the end the populace turned against him. Savonarola was arrested, tortured, and condemned (he can hardly be said to have been tried). One year after the 'bonfire of vanities' he was publicly hanged, with his two close companions, and his body burned.

My second encounter with a saint (an uncanonized one) took place a few years later, when I was in Singapore, and it took place through the medium of the little book of his sayings and letters that was put together after his death. The saint was Brother Lawrence of the Resurrection, a French Carmelite friar who was an older contemporary of Mme Guyon, and author of the book *The Practice of the Presence of God*.[429] Brother Lawrence was a simple man of humble birth who had been a soldier, a manservant, and a hermit before entering the Carmelite monastery in Paris, where he was employed as cook. He was not a visionary, and perhaps not even a mystic, if to be a mystic is to experience ecstasies like those of St Teresa. His spiritual practice was to remain constantly aware of the presence of God, whatever he was doing. Though I did not make the comparison at the time, Brother Lawrence's practice of the presence of God was perhaps not dissimilar to the Buddhist practice of *buddhānusati*, (Pāli, Sanskrit *buddhānusmṛti*) the constant recollection of the Buddha, with or without the repetition of his attributes or of a mantra.[430] I did, however, write an article comparing certain aspects of Brother Lawrence's teaching with the yogas of the *Bhagavad Gītā*, and the article was published, in two instalments, in a Hindu religious magazine. I must have been quite touched by his sincerity and directness.[431]

But touched though I was by Brother Lawrence's little book it had no practical consequences for my own spiritual life as a Buddhist. Such was not the case with the book I was given by a Roman Catholic priest four or five years later. The book was *Seeds of Contemplation* by the Irish-American Trappist monk Thomas Merton. At the time I was in India. I had recently become a Buddhist monk, and with my teacher, the venerable Jagdish Kashyap, I was on pilgrimage to the Buddhist holy places of Bihar. One of them was Rajgir. There, besides visiting the site of the Bamboo Grove, where the Buddha had often stayed, we called at the Roman Catholic mission and had a friendly talk with the priest. When we left he presented me with two books. One of them was *Seeds of Contemplation*. The rest of the story is best told in the words of my first volume of memoirs.

> For some time past I had been greatly preoccupied with the question of ego, not only with the theoretical question of what it was, or was not, but with the more practical one of how to get round it, or get rid of it, or get beyond it. Meditation did not seem enough. Something more drastic and more down-to-earth was needed, something that could be practised every hour of the day, something that would provide a constant check to the unruly motions of the egoistic *will*. In *Seeds of Contemplation* I found what I wanted, or at least a clear enough indication of it. The disciple should surrender his will absolutely to the will of his spiritual superior. In small matters as in great he should have no will of his own, not even any personal wishes or preferences. This was the secret. This was the way to subjugate the ego, if not to destroy it completely. Though the idea was certainly not unfamiliar to me, it had never struck me so forcibly before, and I resolved to apply it forthwith to my relations with Kashyap-ji. In future his wishes would be my law. I would have no wishes of my own. Whenever he asked me if I would like to do something, as in the goodness of his heart he often did, I would reply that I had no preference in that matter, and that we would do just as he wished. For the remainder of the time that we were together I faithfully adhered to this resolution. As a result, I had no troubles, and experienced a great peace of mind.[432]

The result was that when, our pilgrimage over, Kashyap-ji took me up to Kalimpong, in the foothills of the eastern Himalayas, and instructed me to stay there and work for the good of Buddhism, I did just that. For the next fourteen years, with Kalimpong as my headquarters, I worked for Buddhism – writing, teaching, and lecturing – in Kalimpong and the surrounding area as well as in other parts of India. Only in 1964, with the blessing of Kashyap-ji and my other teachers, did I return to England, where I seemed to be more needed.

I had not been long in England when I was introduced by Walter Nigg's *Warriors of God*[433] to eleven more saints, all of them founders of religious orders, and all canonized. It was a thoughtful, well-written book, and although the author, a Swiss Protestant clergyman, treated the founders sympathetically, and tried to understand them, he could also be critical. They were very different from one another, and though all were officially saints some were not very attractive characters. St Pachomius, the fourth-century founder of the first Christian monastery, spoke contemptously of Origen, the great Alexandrian theologian and philosopher, dismissing his writings as 'foolish chatter' and declaring that anyone who read his works and accepted his ideas would be consigned to the depths of hell. According to Pachomius's biographer, Pachomius could tell by a stranger's smell whether he was infected with Origen's 'heretical' ideas, which makes him seem more like an African witch doctor than a Christian monk. St Bernard of Clairvaux, the founder of the Cistercian order, who dominated the religious and political life of Western Europe for much of the twelfth century, had an even keener nose for heresy than St Pachomius. Heresy was everywhere, he complained bitterly towards the end of his life. No sooner was it stamped out in one place than it sprang up in another. He seems not to have understood that orthodoxy and heterodoxy were the obverse and reverse of the same coin, and that if there was orthodoxy, and if men had minds and could think, there would inevitably be heresy. Though Nigg has much to say about St Bernard's mysticism and his intense devotion to the person of Christ, as exemplified by his eloquent sermons on the Song of Solomon, he says little about his involvement in the Second Crusade. At the joint entreaty of the pope and the king of France he travelled through France and Germany whipping up popular support for the enterprise with his oratory. Like his contemporaries, St Bernard believed that fighting the infidel was an activity highly pleasing to God. In the event, the Second Crusade was a disaster. The crusaders achieved nothing, and nine-tenths of them lost their lives.

For me, the most impressive of Nigg's 'warriors' was St Bruno of Cologne, and the Carthusian order the most remarkable of the orders they had founded. A bitter experience of the simony[434] that was endemic in the eleventh-century Church convinced him of the vanity of the world, and he decided to become a monk. He seems also to have had a profound experience of the inevitability of death and the Last Judgement and the certainty, if one had led only a nominally Christian life, of eternal damnation. The Benedictine monastery of Molesne proving not strict enough for him, he settled with six companions in the wilds of the Dauphine mountains. There they built the first Carthusian monastery. Unlike the monks of other orders, they did not live conventually. Each monk had his own separate cell, where he worked, prayed, and studied, and they met together only on Sunday. They rarely spoke. These verses from Ernest Dowson's poem 'Carthusians' well captures the spirit of Carthusian monastic life:

Within their austere walls no voices penetrate;
  A sacred silence only, as of death, obtains;
Nothing finds entry here of loud or passionate;
  This quiet is the exceeding profit of their pains.

From many lands they came, in divers fiery ways;
  Each knew at last the vanity of earthly joys;
And one was crowned with thorns, and one was crowned with
  bays,
And each was tired at last of the world's foolish noise.

It was not theirs with Dominic to preach God's holy wrath,
  They were too stern to bear sweet Francis' gentle sway;
Theirs was a higher calling and a steeper path,
  To dwell alone with Christ, to meditate and pray.

A cloistered company, they are companionless,
  None knoweth here the secret of his brother's heart:
They are but come together for more loneliness,
  Whose bond is solitude and silence all their part.[435]

The Carthusian order was remarkable for its never having been reformed. It had never been reformed because it had never become corrupted. In the case of other religious orders a short initial period of rapid growth was usually followed by a much longer period of slow decline, after which it had to be revived or reformed. The Carthusians started modestly and continued steadily, and it was not until two hundred years after St Bruno's death that the order he had founded was really under way. After that, even the Great Schism could not halt it. According to Walter Nigg, the secret of Carthusian stability lay in the order's stern adherence to its ancient discipline. Connected with this was a concern for the quality rather than the quantity of its membership.

In England the Carthusians lasted until the dissolution of the monasteries under Henry VIII. Four monks of the London Charterhouse, including the prior, were executed in 1553 for treason on account of their refusal to repudiate the supremacy of the pope and recognize the king as head of the Church in England. They died nobly, but I, for one, wish they could have died for a nobler cause than that of papal supremacy. The Roman Catholic Church naturally regards them as martyrs. In 1989 I was in Spain, and happening to visit the grand Cartuja on the outskirts of Granada I saw, hanging in the monastery's refectory, several large paintings depicting the arrest, trial, and execution of the unfortunate monks. As I wrote at the time, 'the paintings were quite well executed, and it was in any case interesting to see an episode from the history of Protestant England through Spanish Catholic eyes.'[436]

Over the years I became acquainted with many more saints or 'warriors of God', not all of them the founders of religious orders. I came to know them not through the biographies of disciples and latter-day admirers, or through their own writings, but more often through the paintings I saw in churches and art galleries. I did not always meet them under the best conditions. St John the Baptist was being beheaded, as were St Maurice and his ten thousand companions; St Lawrence was being roasted on a gridiron; St Agatha was having her breasts cut off (sometimes I saw her holding them on a little dish); St Sebastian, tied naked to a tree, was being shot at with arrows; and St Erasmus was having his intestines drawn out with the help of a windlass. All this I found quite distasteful, especially when there was a lot of blood around. Christians seemed to be rather fond of blood. Of course, St John the Baptist and the rest had all been executed under the pagan Roman emperors, when executions were cruel and bloody affairs, so that if these martyrdoms were to be depicted at all there would have to be at least a little blood. What was more, Jesus himself had been crucified, so that if the Crucifixion, too, had to be depicted, it would have to be depicted similarly, with blood trickling from the hands and feet of the Saviour and from the wound in his side.

However, as I moved from room to room of the art galleries, and from period to period of European art, I noticed that as religious art became more realistic it also tended to be more sanguinary. In early Christian art there was no blood at all to be seen. Jesus hangs on the Cross without a single drop of blood falling from his hands or feet or from the wound in his side. Sometimes he seems not to hang from the Cross at all but rather to be laid flat on the wood, without there being any tension. Sometimes he looks straight ahead. Even in the Middle Ages, when the emaciated body of Jesus twists in agony, and his head slumps to one side, the artists of the time were not preoccupied with the gory concomitants of the Crucifixion. That preoccupation came later, reaching its apogee in some of the life-size polychrome figures of Spanish religious art. I once saw in a church in southern Spain a particularly gruesome example of the genre. Jesus has just been flogged, prior to being crucified; he is naked except for a loincloth, and his body is streaming with blood. In the interest of greater verisimilitude his loincloth is made of real cloth and his hair and beard of real hair. Crudely realistic representations of the sufferings of Jesus such as this are meant to evoke a strong emotional response on the part of the spectator, whether one of horror, or pity, or indignation, or devotion. They are also meant to make him feel guilty, for it is on account of *his* sins, together with those of the rest of mankind, that Jesus suffers.

St Jerome was not a martyr, for he was born when Catholic or 'orthodox' Christianity had just become the official religion of the Roman empire; neither was he the founder of a religious order, though one was founded in his name many centuries after his death. We often met, especially in the course of my various Italian journeys of the 1980s, when I spent as much time as I could visiting the churches and art galleries of Florence and Siena, of Venice, Rome, and Naples. Sometimes he appeared wearing – anachronistically – the broad-brimmed red hat and red robes of a cardinal, either alone or in the company of other saints. At other times he could be seen on his knees in the desert, performing penance for his sins, or seated in his peaceful study, or secluded cell, translating the scriptures. He performed his penance beneath blue skies, amidst magnificent mountain scenery, and in the shadow of fantastic rock formations. Besides the huge volumes from which he was translating, his study contained little more than a human skull and an hourglass, one reminding him of the inevitability of death, the other that time was passing and that not a moment should be wasted. Sometimes his cardinal's hat hangs on the wall. Whether outside or inside, he is attended by his faithful lion.

I particularly liked seeing St Jerome when he was translating. There were times when he worked in almost total darkness, the page over which his bald head was bent illumined by a single candle. There were times, also, when sunlight came streaming in through the window, lighting up every detail of the place. The more I saw of St Jerome in his study, translating, the more I felt drawn to him. I was drawn to him not just as an interesting historical personality who, after a varied career as teacher, traveller, hermit, pilgrim, and secretary to the reigning pope, had left Rome out of disgust at the corruption of the Roman clergy and made his way to the Holy Land, there to spend the rest of his life in literary activity. Rather was I drawn to him on account of what he represented, or embodied. With his long white beard, and venerable appearance, for me he was the embodiment of the Wise Old Man, one of Jung's archetypes of the collective unconscious. That he was engaged in the work of translating, especially that of rendering the Word of God, as contained in the Hebrew of the Old Testament and the Greek of the New, into Latin, the lingua franca of the Roman world, meant that something hidden in the depths was being brought to the surface and the light of day. A sonnet I wrote on St Jerome in 1967, a year after my first Italian journey, concludes with the following lines:

> In a world of sin
> The Empire changes hands, the Churches fight
> Factious as dogs. By day the old man, stung,
> Magnificently answers Augustine,
> Then, dredging from the deep, night after night
> Translates THE WORD into the vulgar tongue.[437]

Because St Jerome was 'dredging from the deep' he was the Alchemist, another embodiment of the Wise Old Man, and his study was the Alchemist's laboratory, where lead was transmuted into gold.

No doubt I was drawn to St Jerome partly because of my personal situation at the time. As I explain in a paper written in the course of my 1984 Italian journey,

> I was living in the desert. I had left the 'Rome' of collective, official, even establishment, Buddhism, and was seeking to return to the origins of Buddhism in the actual life and experience of the Buddha and his immediate disciples. Not only that. I was trying to teach Buddhism in the West, which meant I was trying to communicate the spirit of the Dharma in terms of western rather than in terms of eastern culture. I was thus a translator, with all

> that that implies in the way of seeking to fathom the uttermost depths of what one is trying to translate so that one may translate it faithfully, i.e. bring its meaning to the surface, or from darkness into light. Thus I was drawn to the image of St Jerome, and was able to see that image as an embodiment of the archetype of the Wise Old Man as 'Translator' and Alchemist, because I had a personal affinity with that image, or because there was something in me that corresponded to that image.[438]

Although St Jerome is regarded as a saint, in certain respects he was not a very saintlike person. A Christian scholar says of him, 'He was passionate and sensuous, yet he was the champion of the most rigid asceticism. Full of petty vanity and learned rivalry, he was self-assertive and unjust to his opponents; and though destitute of the creative theologian's gift, he liked to pose as a pillar of orthodoxy.' Nonetheless, St Jerome's historical importance cannot be denied, and the same authority therefore continues, 'By his translation of the Bible he exercised an immense influence upon the succeeding centuries, and in that work he produced what must be numbered among the supreme achievements of the Christian mind in any age.' Despite his being the champion of rigid asceticism, St Jerome seems to have been more scholar and litterateur than saint.

There could be no doubting the saintliness of St Catherine of Siena, who impressed me as much as St Jerome, though not as the embodiment of an archetype but as a remarkable human being. She was born in Siena, the city of the *palia* or 'banner', in 1347. On account of its romantic hilltop situation, and the fact that within its walls it remained essentially a medieval town, it was my favourite Italian city, and I visited it a number of times. I loved the Tuscan Gothic cathedral with its colourful, ornate façade, its bands of black and white marble on walls and pillars, its unique marble mosaic floor, and its many art treasures including Duccio's *Maestà*. I loved the shell-shaped main piazza with its fountain by Jacopo della Quercia, the lofty bell-tower of the flanking city hall, and the gentle, almond-eyed saints and virgins who thronged the churches and the city art gallery. I also loved the grass-grown city walls, the cavernous shops (open-fronted like those in India), and the steep, cobbled streets, in one of which I found, on my first visit to Siena, the house in which St Catherine had been born to a prosperous dyer and his wife as the last but one of their twenty-five children. Every room in the house had been turned into a chapel or oratory, with coffered ceilings and frescoed walls, and on what once had been the family's kitchen garden there stood a baroque church.

As a small child, Catherine was of a lively, affectionate disposition, but when she was seven or eight she had her first vision, and a change took place. She became silent and withdrawn, and devoted herself to prayer and penance. This displeased her parents, who sought by various means, both gentle and harsh, to induce her to give up her austerities. They desisted only when her father, entering her room one day when she was kneeling in prayer, saw a pure white dove on her head – an incident depicted in one of the frescoes, along with others relating to her early life. When Catherine was sixteen she was received as a Penitent of the Third Order of St Dominic, and henceforth wore the black and white habit of the Order. She continued to live at home, occupying the tiny room that had become her cell, and giving herself up to a life of extreme austerity, not to say self-mortification.

On leaving the House and Sanctuary of St Catherine, as the complex was called, I made my way up the steep acclivity that led to the tall, brick-built Dominican church that occupied the top of the hill, dominating the narrow streets below. The first thing I saw on entering the building was the preserved head of the saint, behind glass, high up on the wall, it having been separated from her body shortly after her death and sent to Siena from Rome, where she had died and where her body was still preserved. In the gloom of the church it was just possible to make out the features. More appealing than this grisly relic was the portrait by Andrea Vanni, a friend and admirer of the saint, that hung in a little chapel to which the saint had often come to pray, and where she had been received as a Penitent. She wore the white robe and black mantle of the Order, the white symbolizing innocence and the black humility. In her left hand she held a lily, while her right hand was presented to a female votary kneeling at her feet, who seemed about to kiss her fingers. The expression with which the saint looked down at the votary was calm and thoughtful. There were other paintings in the chapel, all of them depicting scenes from Catherine's life, and all by Bazzi, also known as Sodoma. The most beautiful of them depicted the saint being supported by two nuns as she swoons in ecstasy, overcome by some mystical experience. It seemed incredible that this slight, delicate young woman, with what the Victorian author of a sketch taken from

Vanni's portrait described as a 'spare, worn, but elegant face, with small, regular features', should not only have engaged in the most fearsome austerities, in the midst of which she experienced both spiritual raptures and terrible diabolical temptations, but should also have played, for eight years of her short life, a central, even pivotal, part in the religious and political life of Italy.

In the middle of the fourteenth century much of Italy was in turmoil. There were wars between rival city states, as well as bitter, bloody internecine strife in the case of some of them, including Siena. Roving bands of mercenaries plundered and looted, and there was the arrival from the East of the Black Death, with its appalling economic and social consequences. The turmoil extended to the Church. Morals were lax, not least among the higher clergy, and simony and nepotism were rife. Worst of all, in 1308 the reigning pope had moved from Rome to Avignon in France, and at the time of Catherine's birth the papacy had been based there for forty years, with the result that Rome, no longer the capital of Christendom, had become a city of ruins haunted by thieves and murderers. It was into this turmoil that Catherine threw herself when, at the age of twenty-five, she began what she called her 'mission to the world'. By this time a small band of disciples had formed around her and she had gained a widespread reputation for sanctity. Her mission began with an impassioned letter to a leading cardinal, the pope's representative in Italy, in which she sang the praises of charity, in the sense of selfless love of others, as the true foundation of social harmony and political stability. That Italy should be at peace was her greatest earthly desire. When Gregory XI called for a Crusade against the Muslims she therefore gave the idea her enthusiastic support, apparently seeing it as a means of ridding Italy of the marauding mercenary bands, and wrote to princes and prelates all over Europe urging them to take up the Cross. Neither princes nor prelates wanted to take part in the Crusade, however, and preparations for the enterprise never got off the ground. Catherine realized that peace would come to Italy only if the pope returned to Rome, and in the course of a visit to Avignon she was able to persuade him, despite strong opposition from the French cardinals, to take this momentous step.

In 1377, amid general rejoicing, Gregory entered the eternal city and took up residence in the Vatican, thus bringing to an end the papacy's 'Babylonian Captivity' in Avignon. A year later he died, to be succeeded by Urban VI. The new pope had been elected under duress, the Romans having threatened to kill the cardinals if they did not give them a Roman or at least an Italian pope, and it was not long before a group of cardinals met at nearby Fondi and elected another pope, Clement VII. Christendom now had two popes, and later would have three, each anathematizing and excommunicating the two others and their adherents. Catherine regarded Urban as the true pope, and did her utmost to persuade the adherents of Clement to accept him as such. Amid these stirring events she reconciled deadly enemies, comforted the sick and bereaved, and consoled the dying, as she had done ever since leaving her cell for the world. In this connection there occurred, towards the end of the saint's life, an incident which strikingly illustrates her character. Niccola di Tondo, a young Perugian noble, had been unjustly sentenced to death by the government of Siena for uttering some rash words against the state. Mad with despair, he refused to make his confession or to listen to a word about the salvation of his soul. But when Catherine visited him in his cell and spoke to him he calmed down and accepted his fate. She was with him to the last, as she had promised him she would be, and received his severed head into her hands as it fell from the block. Then to her ecstatic gaze the heavens seemed to open and she saw the Saviour, in likeness like the sun, receive the victim's blood into his own open wounds.

In 1378, having finished dictating her *Dialogue*, a mystical treatise, the saint left Siena for Rome, where she was received with great honour by Urban, and where she helped reorganize the Church. Two years later, still living in Rome, she died, worn out by her austerities and her labours in the cause of peace. She was thirty-three. In 1461 she was canonized by Pius II, a fellow Sienese. The event is commemorated in one of the brilliant frescoes with which Pinturicchio, with the assistance of the young Raphael, decorated the walls of the Piccolomini Library in Siena Cathedral. Wearing the papal tiara, his right hand raised, Pius sits enthroned aloft, beneath a canopy, flanked by his red-robed cardinals. The body of Catherine, habited in the Penitent's white and black, lies stretched out on a catafalque at his feet, her head slightly raised. Below, in the foreground, monks, nuns, and lay people stand holding lighted tapers.

Today St Catherine of Siena's body lies, behind glass, beneath the high altar of Santa Maria sopra Minerva, one of the finest of the old basilica churches of Rome. I have twice seen her there, and it seemed to me that there emanated from her, in death as in life, that same 'fragrant purity' of which one of her disciples spoke.

St Bridget of Sweden died in Rome seven years before St Catherine did, having lived there for twenty-three years. Unlike St Catherine she had been married and had children before becoming a nun, and unlike the Italian saint she had founded a religious order, that of the Sisters of the Most Holy Saviour or Brigittines. In other respects these two saints were very much alike. St Bridget, too, had practised severe austerities, had seen visions and received revelations. Many of the revelations related to the corruption of the times, especially the corruption of the Church, and called for reform. Some called for the return of the pope from Avignon to Rome, a cause for which St Bridget worked as enthusiastically as St Catherine did after her, if with less success. Her visionary experiences included a vision of the crucified Saviour which influenced her whole life and outlook. She seems to have been more visionary than mystic and more prophetess than visionary, receiving from God messages in which princes and prelates were threatened with dire consequences if they did not mend their ways. As a visionary she cannot be compared with a fellow countryman of hers who lived five hundred years later, in whose name there was founded, after his death, not a religious order but a new church, the Church of the New Jerusalem.

Swedenborg was born in Stockholm in 1688 and died in London in 1772. He had a distinguished career as scientist, philosopher, and civil servant in the course of which he published a number of works of a philosophical or scientific nature, some of them quite substantial. But in 1744, when he was 55, a dramatic change took place. One night God appeared to him in his room, in the form of a man. He had chosen him to declare to men the spiritual contents of Scripture, he told Swedenborg, and he himself would tell him what he should write on the subject. Then, that same night, Swedenborg's spiritual eyes were opened and he was enabled to have conscious perception of the spiritual world and its inhabitants. Thereafter Swedenborg gave up all worldly pursuits and devoted himself entirely to writing about his travels in the spiritual world, where he met, and conversed with, angels, deceased human beings, and devils, and to explaining the true, spiritual meaning of the Bible in the light of the principle of correspondences, according to which everything in the material world has its counterpart in the spiritual world. Probably the best known of Swedenborg's theological writings is *Heaven and its Wonders and Hell: From Things Heard and Seen*, which I read when I was fifteen in a Penguin paperback edition. I cannot remember what I made of it then. I think I read it in the same spirit in which I read *Paradise Lost* and *The Divine Comedy*, both of which had much to say about the inhabitants of the spiritual world, both celestial and infernal. Swedenborg was buried in the Swedish Church in London, but in 1908 the Swedish government had his remains removed to Uppsala Cathedral, where they were deposited in a magnificent sarcophagus of Swedish red granite. The last time I was in Sweden I visited Uppsala, and in the gloom of the cathedral had a glimpse of the dull red bulk of the sarcophagus behind its protecting iron grille.

The lives of Swedenborg and Blake overlapped by thirty-five years. William Blake was born in 1757, and it was in this year, according to Swedenborg, that the Last Judgement took place. It took place not on Earth but in the spiritual world, when all who had lived from the beginning of creation were gathered together and judged and when a New Church was instituted in the heavens. Blake was familiar with Swedenborg's writings, and annotated his own copies of several of them. Though he spoke highly of Swedenborg, calling him a 'divine teacher', and though he adopted, or adapted, many of Swedenborg's ideas, he did not hesitate to criticize him drastically or even to parody him in one of his own works. Both Blake and Swedenborg were visionaries, with this difference: that Blake not only communicated his visions in words but could also draw and paint them. Blake cannot be described as a saint or a mystic in the Christian sense of those terms, nor was he a Christian in any sense other than that which he himself attached to the word. With Blake, as with Swedenborg to a lesser degree, we pass from the Christian to the post-Christian era of European history. In the sixties and seventies I found in his poetry and his art, as well as in his life, a source of great inspiration, as did many others in those heady days. As I wrote at the time:

> A whole century before Buddhism was really known in the West, Blake offers us the unique example of a non-theistic imaginative vision of rare intensity and integrity. That he could do this was

due in the first place to his own extraordinary creative powers – powers which manifested early, and of which he remained in unimpaired possession to the end of his days, he being faithful to them, and they being faithful to him.[439]

8
JESUS

The first thought that occurs to me as I start thinking about Jesus is that I don't have any strong feelings about him, whether positive or negative. I would not go so far as to say he leaves me cold; but he certainly leaves me feeling rather lukewarm. In my early teen years a particularly moving sermon by the pastor of the Baptist church I was attending could leave me with a heart overflowing with love for Jesus, but by the time I reached home the emotion would usually have evaporated and I was never anywhere near 'accepting Jesus as my personal saviour', as it was called, and never even thought seriously about doing such a thing.

One of the reasons why I don't have any strong feelings about Jesus is that I have never been able finally to convince myself that such a person as Jesus of Nazareth did once live as a man among men, whatever myths and legends may later have gathered around his name. At one time I would be convinced that Jesus was an historical figure; at another, that he was not. It depended on which of the many books on the subject I happened to be reading just then. Thus over the years my mind swung back and forth between the two alternatives at least four or five times, though without my ever having an emotional investment in either of them. Eventually I decided that it was more likely that Jesus had not lived than that he had, and this remained my position until fairly recently, when I happened to read about Marcion, the founder of Marcionism, who was active as a teacher in Rome between the years 150 and 160 (his date of birth is unknown). According to Marcion,

Jesus was a purely spiritual being who, descending from heaven, had suddenly appeared in Galilee in the fifteenth year of the reign of the Roman emperor Tiberius.

I was at once reminded of the beginning of the Gospel According to St Mark. This gospel, the oldest of the four gospels that were to be recognized as authentic by the Catholic Church, begins by relating how Jesus came from Nazareth in Galilee to the river Jordan, there to be baptized by John the Baptist.[440] It makes no mention of the antecedents of Jesus, or of what he was doing before he 'came from Nazareth of Galilee'. There is nothing about his miraculous conception, as there is in two of the other gospels, nothing about the visit of the Magi, nothing about the flight into Egypt, nothing about the massacre of the Innocents. For the author of Mark's gospel, as more explicitly for Marcion, the life of Jesus began when he suddenly appeared, not necessarily from heaven, in the Galilean town of Nazareth (thus Mark) or Capernaum (thus Marcion). Mark's gospel does, of course, refer briefly to the mother and brothers of Jesus; but Marcion would have regarded this as an example of the false Judaic traditions that had grown up around the Apostles, on account of which he had been obliged to reject *in toto* the gospels of Matthew, Mark, and John, regarding as authentic only certain parts of the gospel ascribed to Luke.

All this suggests to me that Jesus may in fact have 'appeared' from somewhere outside Palestine, perhaps even from India or Central Asia. This is no more than a hypothesis, and Christians no doubt will reject it out of hand, but I, for one, find it easier to believe that Jesus may have come from somewhere outside Palestine than that he was born of a virgin and was God incarnate. Indeed, the possibility of his having come from somewhere outside Palestine makes it more likely, in my view, that Jesus lived than that he did not.

Some Christians will tell me that the truth about Jesus has been handed down within the Church, in an unbroken tradition, since the days of the Apostles, and that I ought therefore simply to accept its testimony that he was a historical figure. As a Buddhist, or even as a thinking human being, I cannot do this. Christians of another kind will tell me that if I were to study the four Gospels intensively I would be convinced, in the end, that Jesus really had lived. For this I have never had either the time or the interest. Or rather, I would have found the time had the interest been sufficiently strong. But for me the question of whether Jesus had or had not lived was not a pressing one, for it had no bearing on my own spiritual life as a Buddhist. Nonetheless I did once read Albert Schweitzer's *The Quest of the Historical Jesus*, a history of the critical study of the life of Jesus by a succession of nineteenth-century German scholars, for whom the existence of Jesus was a matter of religious as well as scholarly concern. Some had discovered a rational Jesus behind the gospel narratives, others a 'liberal' Jesus, and so on. Schweitzer himself opted for an eschatological Jesus, a Jesus who believed he was the Messiah and that the world would come to an end within the lifetime of the disciples; he opts for a Jesus who escapes from history, a Jesus who cannot be known historically but only as a spirit within men. For Schweitzer, the quest for the historical Jesus had ended in failure; but that did not mean that it was devoid of value, for it had shown where Jesus was *not* to be found. Indeed, Schweitzer insists that it is impossible to overestimate the value of what German research upon the life of Jesus had accomplished. He goes so far as to call it 'a uniquely great expression of sincerity, one of the most significant events in the whole mental and spiritual life of humanity'.[441] This is a large claim and one which to some people will seem a little Eurocentric, not to say Germanocentric.

The quest for the historical Jesus did not cease with the publication of Schweitzer's famous book. Though it seems not to have continued in Germany, it certainly continued elsewhere, if in academically less reputable quarters. In the course of the last forty years I have come across Jesus the Great Initiate, Jesus the leader of an uprising against the power of Rome, Jesus the Magician, Jesus the Socialist, the Aryan Jesus, the New Age Jesus, Jesus the Archetype of the Self, and the extraterrestrial Jesus who came from another planet and who returned there, thus explaining the Ascension. The list is far from complete, and I am sure that as time goes on other Jesuses will be discovered, whether in the scriptures or in the depths of someone's imagination.

Although I have never made an intensive study of the four Gospels it was inevitable that in the course of my life I should have acquired some knowledge of them, either directly or through references to them in my general reading. One does not have to read the Gospels in order to know the parables. The literature of Europe is full of allusions to them. I cannot remember when I first read, or heard, such parables as those of the good Samaritan, the prodigal son, and the mustard seed. It is as though I had drawn them in with my earliest breath. Some parables I came to know through paintings that illustrated them. I cannot even think of the parables as being essentially Christian. Many of them give expression to universal human values, and are independent of their immediate context in this or that Gospel. A few parables, such as that of the sower, have parallels in the Buddhist scriptures, the genre being one that was widespread in the ancient world.[442] I regard the parables as part of my cultural heritage as a European, and I do not hesitate to make use of them in writing for, or speaking to, a western audience about Buddhism.

Just as one doesn't have to read the Gospels in order to know the parables, so one does not need to read them in order to familiarize oneself with the sayings of Jesus. These pithy utterances, too, are part of European literature. Such sayings as 'No man can serve two masters,' 'Judge not that ye be not judged,' and 'By their fruits ye shall know them,' stuck in my mind, though I do not know when I first heard them or read them, and could not say offhand just where in the Gospels they are to be found. They stuck in my mind partly because they reached me in the language of the Authorized Version, which is more forceful, direct, and concise than that of more recent translations of the Bible. As the Buddha's poet-disciple Vaṅgīsa chanted in the Master's presence, 'Truth verily is immortal speech' – which I take to mean that truth is made memorable when it finds poetic expression.[443] In the case of some of the sayings I felt there was a living individual behind them, giving emphatic utterance to his thoughts and feelings. But whether that same individual was also behind all the other sayings, discourses, diatribes, and prophecies ascribed to Jesus by the authors of the four Gospels was quite another matter.

Besides telling us what Jesus said, the Gospels also tell us what he did. One of the things he did was perform miracles, a miracle being defined, in this connection, as 'an effect above human or natural power, performed in attestation of some truth' (Johnson). The truth to which the miracles of the Gospels attest is that Jesus possesses divine authority. Most of the miracles are miracles of healing, the healing sometimes involving the casting out of a demon who has taken possession of the sick person. There were also cases of what we would call faith healing, as when a woman who had suffered from a haemorrhage for twelve years came up behind Jesus in the crowd and touched his garment, thinking that could she but touch his clothes she would be cured. She was instantly cured, and Jesus told her, 'Daughter, thy faith hath made thee whole.'[444] There is also the curious episode in which Jesus, on a visit to Nazareth, his home town, was unable to work any miracle there, though he cured a few sick people by laying his hands on them. The author of the Gospel comments that Jesus 'marvelled because of their unbelief', or as a modern translation has it, 'was amazed at their lack of faith'.[445] Another class of miracles demonstrates that Jesus has power over the elements. He calms a storm, feeds five thousand people with five loaves and two fish, turns water into wine, and raises Lazarus from the dead.[446]

How do I, as a Buddhist, view these miracles? I certainly believe there is such a thing as faith healing, a form of treatment not, however, to be confused with spiritual healing, which takes place *without* the need for faith on the part of the patient. I therefore see no reason why Jesus, had such a person existed, could not have performed miracles of this kind. Unlike the authors of the Gospels, and unlike Christians down to our own times, I do not regard them as miracles in the sense defined above and not, therefore, as attesting to the possession by Jesus, or any other faith healer, of Divine authority. Similarly, I see no reason why Jesus could not have calmed a storm. The art of weather-making is still known to certain Tibetan lamas, one of whom, a friend of mine, once said that it was relatively easy to stop rain from falling on a particular spot but quite difficult to conjure it from a clear blue sky. On the turning of water into wine I have an open mind. There could be a natural explanation (Schweitzer gives one),[447] or, alternatively, it could have involved the use of psychic powers not unknown to the yogis of India and Tibet. The raising of Lazarus from the dead is a miracle of a radically different kind. So far as I know, it is beyond human power to bring back to life a man who is really dead, especially when he has been dead four days, as Lazarus had, and 'stinketh'.[448] It is possible for one to believe that Jesus literally raised Lazarus from the dead only if one believes that Jesus was God Incarnate, and as such had power over death. Since I cannot believe, as the Christian does, that Jesus was God Incarnate (for as a Buddhist I do not believe in the existence of God), I cannot believe, either, that Jesus once brought a dead man back to life. The author of John's gospel evidently included this miracle in his narrative in attestation of the Divine status and authority of Jesus, and it is significant that he chose to locate it shortly before Jesus's own death and resurrection.

From debates about whether or not Jesus had really lived, and about the reliability or otherwise of the Gospel narratives, I have at times turned with relief to Jesus as depicted in Christian art. The Christian artist believed in the existence of Jesus, just as he believed, *as an artist*, in the existence of the gods and goddesses of pagan antiquity when, with the dawn of the Renaissance, he came to depict them, too. He did not know what Jesus had looked like any more than he knew how Mars and Venus looked. In the Christian art of the fourth to the twelfth centuries there is in any case little attempt at realism. Attitudes tend to be stiff and hieratic, as they still are in Orthodox religious art, and Jesus is sometimes depicted as a beardless youth, as in the mosaics at Ravenna, sometimes as a bearded man of mature years, as in the mosaics of certain basilica churches in Rome. As art became more realistic, the artists attempted to give Jesus a consistent, recognizable individual character, as Duccio does in the panels illustrating the life of the Saviour in his *Maestà* in the cathedral museum of Siena, and as Giotto does to an even greater degree in his frescoes in the Arena Chapel in Padua. In the latter series it is very much the same Jesus who attends the marriage at Cana in one fresco, and who in others raises Lazarus from the dead, enters Jerusalem riding on a donkey, and expels the merchants from the temple. He is a handsome, dignified man in the prime of life, with brown hair and beard. His expression is calm, his gesture hieratic. Even when being crowned with thorns, in another fresco, he remains impassive, simply half-closing his eyes. It is only in the fresco of the Crucifixion that, with eyes now closed, and head fallen to one side, that he shows any sign of suffering – a suffering Giotto has the good taste not to exploit in the way some later artists were to do.

With Masaccio, a hundred years after Giotto, Jesus becomes more statuesque, occupying not two-dimensional but three-dimensional space, as do the disciples. He is depicted with them in Masaccio's finest work, his fresco in the Brancacci Chapel, Florence, illustrating the miracle of the tax money, part of which I saw when the chapel was undergoing restoration. The circumstances of the miracle are described in the Gospel According to St Matthew, and only there, and were as follows. Jesus and his disciples were staying at Capernaum. There the collector of the temple tax asked St Peter if his master paid the tax. When St Peter told

Jesus this the latter directed him to cast a hook in the lake, take the first fish that bit, and open its mouth. There he would find a piece of money, which he was to give to the tax collector for the two of them.[449] In the fresco Jesus occupies the centre of the composition. The disciples stand in a semicircle round him, and he is flanked by St Peter on the left and by the tax collector on the right. Jesus, his right arm extended, points to St Peter, who, extending *his* right arm in a vigorous gesture which continues that of the Master, points to a small, crouching figure at the extreme left of the fresco who is taking something from the mouth of a fish. The small figure is St Peter himself, for Masaccio has united the three parts of the episode in a single scene, the third part being that in which, at the extreme right of the fresco, St Peter gives the money into the hand of the tax collector. The weakest part of the fresco, unfortunately, is the head of Jesus, now widely attributed to Masolino. One critic goes so far as to describe it as doll-like and lifeless compared to the heads of the disciples. He finds it difficult, he says, to imagine Masaccio conceiving Divinity in terms so mild and dreamy.

But why did Masaccio not paint the head of Jesus himself, thus putting the finishing touch to his masterpiece? This was the question that puzzled me as I studied a small reproduction of the fresco. Did Masaccio die before he was able to complete his fresco by painting the head of Jesus? Or did Masolino insist that he, as the older and more experienced artist, ought to do the work? So far as I am aware, there is no evidence to support either of these theories, though it is known that Masaccio died young, at the age of twenty-six, not in Florence but in Rome, allegedly by poisoning. My own explanation of the mystery is not circumstantial but psychological. According to the critic to whom I have referred above, the head of Jesus in the fresco is doll-like and lifeless *compared to the heads of the disciples*. The latter are, in fact, very finely portrayed. This is particularly true of the head of St Peter. His hair and beard are grizzled, the corners of his mouth are turned down, and he glares rather than looks at Jesus. He is evidently an irascible old man, and one possessed of great force of character. Masaccio seems to have seen into St Peter's soul. He must have asked himself what sort of man St Peter was. He must have pondered deeply on those passages in the Gospels and in the Acts of the Apostles where the saint plays a part and then have portrayed him in accordance with the impression he received. Why, then, did he not do the same in the case of Jesus? My belief is that he wanted to do so but found he was unable to see into the soul of Jesus as he had seen into St Peter's. The four Gospels do not give, between them, a very consistent picture of the character of Jesus, and Masaccio must have found it no less difficult to make up his mind what sort of man Jesus was than have many others since his time. The question was complicated by the fact that Jesus was not just a man. For Masaccio, as a Christian, Jesus was God Incarnate, the Word that had been made flesh and had dwelt among us. How could such a being be portrayed? An artist of Masaccio's genius could not be content simply to portray Jesus as other artists had portrayed him. He must therefore have thrown down his brushes in despair and left the work of painting the head of Jesus to Masolino.

There is, perhaps, a more prosaic explanation of the mystery. It may be that Masaccio was accustomed to paint from the live model. With the growth of realism in art the practice must have been fairly widespread by this time. Perhaps Masaccio painted his portraits of the disciples from beggars he brought in from the street, just as El Greco, two centuries later, painted *his* portraits of the disciples from the inmates of the local lunatic asylum, and perhaps he had been unable to find anyone from whom he could paint the portrait of Jesus.

Though the artists of the Renaissance and the Baroque period might idealize the features of the models from whom they painted their biblical personages, the latter often show traces of the national or regional provenance of their real-life originals. Thus we have Virgins who are really Italian peasant women holding a fat Italian baby and Jesuses who are really Spanish patricians in oriental costume. Nowadays we also have the blond, blue-eyed Nordic Jesus, and the almond-eyed Chinese Jesus who, as I recently saw, rides into Jerusalem on a donkey to be welcomed by the city's almond-eyed inhabitants. There are also those artists who sought – with or without the help of a model – to penetrate into the character of Jesus, as I believe Masaccio had wanted to do. Leonardo da Vinci was such an artist, his genius being one that delighted in exploring what was mysterious and unfathomable. Though it seems he hardly ever drew or painted the adult Jesus, it is the figure of Jesus that occupies the central position in what is probably his greatest work, the wall-painting of the Last Supper in the refectory of Santa Maria delle Grazie, Milan. Jesus has just told the disciples that one of them will betray him,[450] and Leonardo shows them reacting in their different ways, each in accordance with his individual character. He sits with arms spread wide, hands resting palms uppermost on the table. His head is turned a little to one side and his eyes are half closed. There is no halo, but his head, with its long hair, is framed by the rectangular window immediately behind him. Time has not dealt kindly with the painting, and it is not easy to see what Leonardo made of the character of Jesus. Moreover, according to Vasari Leonardo did not 'perfect' the head of Jesus as he could not find a model that could express 'that beauty and celestial grace'.[451] However, there exists, in Milan, a pastel head of Jesus that appears to be a study for the Last Supper. So expressive is it of that 'beauty and celestial grace' for which Leonardo sought that I find it difficult to believe that Leonardo drew the head from a model, however much he might have idealized the features. Leonardo must have sought – and found – that beauty and celestial grace in the depths of his own soul.

There are those artists, again, who were concerned not so much to penetrate into the character of Jesus as to depict the main incidents of his life in as dramatic a manner as possible. One of the most eminent of these was Tintoretto. The paintings in which he tells the gospel story from the Annunciation to the Ascension are the glory of the Scuola di San Rocco in Venice and the fullest expression of Tintoretto's extraordinary genius. Some paintings contain dozens of figures, and much movement, and Tintoretto breaks many compositional rules, so that at first glance it is difficult to make out what is happening, as I found when I visited the Scuola twenty or more years ago. I nonetheless have the distinct recollection of two of the paintings, one depicting the Temptation, the other Jesus before Pilate. In the first painting there are only two figures. Jesus is seated at the top right under the dark, unevenly projecting beams of what appears to be a roof; his head is surrounded by a mild luminescence, against which his features show in profile. From the bottom left springs a young, epicene Satan, mockingly holding up two stones, one in each hand, tempting Jesus to turn them into bread. The other painting contains a number of figures, but it is the slim, silent figure of Jesus that dominates the scene. Wrapped in a white mantle that trails down the steps, he stands like a column of light against a dark architectural background, his head bowed. A red-robed Pilate, seated in the shadows a step or two higher than Jesus, washes his hands of responsibility for the prisoner's death, which has been loudly demanded by the assembled Jews with shouts of 'Crucify him!'[452]

Several films of the life of Jesus have been made, but I have seen only one of them. This was Pasolini's *The Gospel According to St Matthew*, with background music from Bach's *St Matthew Passion*, which I saw shortly after its London release. Pasolini was said to be a devout Roman Catholic, but I could more easily have believed him to be a militant atheist. As I commented afterwards to the friend with whom I saw the film, it was as though Pasolini was saying, 'Look, I've told the story of Jesus as convincingly as I could, sticking close to the gospel narrative – but how can anyone believe it?'

Besides encountering Jesus in churches and art galleries, and at the cinema, I also encountered him in literature. When I was sixteen or seventeen I read Sholem Asch's *The Nazarene*, a novelistic version of the life of Jesus written from a Jewish point of view. It is a substantial work, but all I can remember of it is the passage in which Jesus, on a visit to a cosmopolitan coastal city, is shocked by the nudity he sees there – an illustration of the difference between Hellenic and Hebraic culture.[453] Much more recently I read George Moore's *The Brook Kerith*, which likewise is a novelistic version of the life of Jesus. Beautifully written, from the standpoint of a non-believer with a sympathetic interest in modernist theology, it is one of the Irish author's finest works. The Jesus of *The Brook Kerith* is an Essene, a member of a Jewish sect or brotherhood that lived in the region of the Dead Sea, practising asceticism and awaiting the coming of the Messiah. Next to Jesus, the most important character in the novel is Joseph of Arimathea, with an account of whose early history the story begins. Though strongly attracted to the miracle-working preacher who claimed to be the Messiah, about whom he has heard from the fisherman who worked for his father, a pious Jew in the fish-salting trade, he does not become a disciple as he is reluctant to sell all that he has and give the proceeds to the poor as Jesus demands. Instead, he carries on his father's fish-salting business and becomes friends with the cultivated ruler of Roman Palestine, Pontius Pilate. Thus he is in a position, a few years later, to rescue the body of Jesus from the cross for burial.

Late that night, to Joseph's astonishment, the body shows signs of life. Jesus has not died on the cross, but he is severely traumatized, and it is many months before the careful nursing of Joseph and his woman-servant restores him to health. Moore's lengthy description of Jesus's gradual recovery is not only very convincing but extremely moving. From Joseph's house the erstwhile Messiah returns to the Essene monastery beside the Brook Kerith from whence he originally came, and shortly afterwards Joseph himself is murdered by a Zealot, a fanatical anti-Roman Jewish nationalist. But though physically healed, mentally Jesus is in a state of shock. He remains in that state for fifteen years, saying little, and living mainly by himself as an Essene shepherd in the hills. When he finally emerges from his silence it is with the realization that his Messiahship was a delusion and his former teaching harsh and cruel.

At this point, some twenty years after the Crucifixion, Paul appears on the scene. He is on his way to Rome, having been arrested for causing a riot in Jerusalem, and having appealed, as a Roman citizen, from Jewish law to the law of Rome. His guard has granted him leave from prison while he is waiting for the ship that will take him to Rome for his trial, but he and his companion are pursued by a band of Zealots and Paul, separated from his companion in the night, finds refuge in a cliff-side cave with the very sect of Essenes that has for shepherd Jesus of Nazareth. There he harangues the Essenes at great length, telling them how he was a Jew of scrupulous orthodoxy, how he cruelly persecuted the Christians, as the followers of Jesus of Nazareth were called, how that same Jesus appeared to him in a vision, and how, since then, he has travelled the world proclaiming the joyful tidings that Jesus Christ, who was crucified under Pontius Pilate, was raised by God from the dead, and that only through faith in him could anyone be saved. When Jesus arrives later and assures Paul that he did not die on the cross, Paul does not believe him. His Jesus and the shepherd Jesus are not the same man, he thinks, though both come from Nazareth, and in any case Jesus is a common enough name.

The following day, when Jesus guides Paul through the desert to a point from where he can see the port which is his destination, he again tries to convince him that there is only one Jesus of Nazareth, that he is that Jesus, and that he did not perish on the cross; but this time Paul thinks he must be out of his wits or that he is a demon come to tempt him. However, he asks Jesus what thoughts came to him in the hills, and Jesus tells him. Shortly after they part Paul sees people in a strange garb going towards the hillside on which he has left Jesus. They are monks from India, a shepherd informs him. Paul sees the likeness between the thoughts Jesus has confided to him and the shepherd's account of the doctrines that were being preached by the monks from India. The monks will meet Jesus in the valley, Paul muses, 'and if they speak to him they will soon gather from him that he divined much of their philosophy by watching his flock, and finding him of their mind they may ask him to return to India with them and he will preach there'.

9

BARLAAM AND JOSAPHAT

There is a scene in Shakespeare's *The Merchant of Venice* in which the suitors of Portia, a spirited young heiress, are shown three caskets, one of gold, one of silver, and one of lead. One of them contains Portia's portrait, and according to her father's will the suitor who chooses the right casket, the one containing the portrait, will be able to marry Portia. The Prince of Morocco chooses the gold casket, but on opening it he finds only a skeleton and some verses beginning

> All that glitters is not gold;
> Often have you heard that told.

Similarly the Prince of Aragon, on being shown the caskets, chooses the silver one and to his chagrin finds the portrait of a 'blinking idiot' and some sardonic verses. The third suitor is Bassanio, a young Venetian with whom Portia herself is secretly in love. He chooses the lead casket, where he finds Portia's portrait and verses inviting him to claim the lady 'with a loving kiss'. Few of those who have seen the play will have known that Shakespeare took the theme of the three caskets from the romance of Barlaam and Josaphat, a Christianized version of episodes from the life of the Buddha, which he found in *The Golden Legend* (1483), Caxton's version of a French translation of the *Legenda Aurea*, a work compiled in Latin by the thirteenth-century Dominican friar Jacobus de Voragine who became Archbishop of Geneva.[454]

The story of the monk Barlaam and prince Josaphat underwent many changes before eventually passing from Voragine to Caxton and from Caxton to Shakespeare, but in Caxton's English version, still very readable, incidents which are parts of the Buddha's biography as handed down in Buddhist tradition can nevertheless still be discerned. The story begins in a legendary India, which is represented as being 'full of Christians and of monks'. At this time there arose a powerful king named Avennir who persecuted the Christians, and especially the monks. Nonetheless, a friend of the king who was also his chief minister was inspired to leave the palace and become a monk. When the king heard of this he was beside himself with rage and ordered a search to be made for the monk, who was eventually found and brought before the king. On seeing his former minister 'in a vile coat and much lean for hunger' Avennir called him fool and madman and wanted to know why he had changed his honour into disgrace and made himself a mockery. If he was willing to listen to reason, the monk replied, then he should put from him his enemies. The king naturally wanted to know who his enemies were. They were anger and greed, the monk explained, for they obscured and hindered the mind, so that the truth might not be seen. 'The fools despise the things that be', the monk continued, 'like as they were not, and he that hath not the taste of the things that be, he shall not use the sweetness of them, and may not learn the truth of them that be not.'

I was greatly struck by these words. Behind them, beneath all the layers of adaptation and modification, I could see an important teaching of the Buddha that must have come from one of the traditional Indian biographies. The spiritually immature despise the real because they see it as unreal; and he that has no experience of the real will not benefit from the happiness it brings, nor, since he sees the real as unreal, will he see the unreal as unreal. This is reminiscent of a verse in one of the best-known Buddhist scriptures: 'Those who, having known the real (*sāra*) as the real, and the unreal (*asāra*) as the unreal, they, moving in the sphere of right thought, will attain the real'.[455] Whoever was originally responsible for this version of the story of Barlaam and Josaphat must have felt that the monk's teaching to the king was not particularly Christian, as indeed it is not, for he credits the monk with having gone on to 'show many things of mystery of the incarnation', which is obviously out of place and very likely was added at some stage. Be that as it may, Avennir was not impressed by the monk's teaching. Had he not promised to put away anger, he tells him, he would have burned him alive. Let him go now, lest he should do him some harm.

Meanwhile, it so happened that a son was born to the king, who hitherto had been childless. The boy was called Josaphat, which is not really a proper name but the form assumed by the Sanskrit word 'bodhisattva' after it had been transcribed from the alphabet of one language into that of another, and from that into yet another, thus becoming a little further removed from its original spelling and pronunciation each time. In the traditional biographies the term 'Bodhisattva' refers to the Buddha in the pre-Enlightenment phase of his career, the word meaning 'Enlightenment-being' or 'one bent on Enlightenment'. On the birth of Josaphat 'the king assembled a right great company of people for to sacrifice to his gods for the nativity of his son, and also assembled fifty-five astronomers, of whom he enquired what should befall of his son.' In the *Abhiniṣkramaṇa Sūtra* or '*Sūtra* of the Great Renunciation', one of the canonical biographies of the Buddha, the astrologers assembled by King Suddhodana, the Bodhisattva's father, predicts that his son will become either a universal monarch or a Buddha, an Enlightened One. A sage who has arrived from the Himalayas, however, predicts that he will definitely become a Buddha.[456] King Avennir's astronomers tell him that Josaphat will be 'great in power and in riches'; but one of them, wiser than the others, predicts that the child will be a Christian, a member of the religion that the king persecutes. Disturbed by the prediction, Avennir took measures to ensure that Josaphat does not hear about Jesus Christ. They are the same measures taken by Suddhodana, in the traditional biographies of the Buddha, to ensure that Siddhārtha does not learn about the realities of human existence. In Caxton's words:

> And when the king heard that, he doubted much, and did do make without the city a right noble palace, and therein set he his son for to dwell and abide, and set there right fair younglings, and commanded them that they should not speak to him of death ne of old age, ne of sickness, ne of poverty, ne of no thing that may give him cause of heaviness, but say to him all things that be joyous, so that his mind may be esprised with gladness, and that he think

> on nothing to come. And anon as any of his servants were sick the king commanded for to take them away, and set another, whole, in his stead, and commanded that no mention should be made to him of Jesus Christ.[457]

Except for the reference to Jesus, the Buddhist will find himself on familiar ground here. He will also know what follows. But at this point the story of Barlaam and Josaphat, as translated by Caxton, is interrupted by a tale of palace intrigue, in which King Avennir tries to trick his chief noble into admitting that he was a Christian by telling him that he has decided to become a monk, and in which the noble tricks the king, and saves his own life, by becoming a monk in order, as he says, to accompany the king into the desert and serve him there. The story is then resumed, and the Buddhist again finds himself on familiar ground. When Josaphat grew up he wondered why his father had so enclosed him, and became greatly depressed that he could not go out. On hearing this the king made arrangements for 'horses and joyful fellowship' to accompany him, but in such a way that he should see no distressing sight.

> And on a time thus as the king's son went, he met a mesel [leper] and a blind man, and when he saw them he was abashed, and enquired what them ailed, and his servants said: These be passions [sufferings] that come to men. And he demanded if those passions come to all men, and they said: Nay. Then said he: Be they known which men shall suffer these passions without definition? And they answered: Who is he that may know the adventures of men? And he began to be much anguishous for the incustomable thing thereof. And another time he found a man much aged which had his cheer [face] frounced [wrinkled], his teeth fallen, and was all crooked for age. Whereof he was abashed, and he desired to know the miracle of this vision. And when he knew that this was because he had lived many years, then he demanded what should be the end, and they said: Death; and he said: Is then death the end of all men or of some? And they said for certain that all men must die. And when he knew that all should die, he demanded them in how many years that should happen, and they said: In old age or four score years or a hundred, and after that age the death followeth. And this young

> man remembered oft in his heart these things, and was in great discomfort, but he showed him much glad tofore his father, and he desired much to be informed and taught in these things.[458]

Josaphat has now seen the first two, and heard about the third, of the four sights that are described at length, and with a wealth of detail, in the traditional biographies of the Buddha; but he has yet to see the fourth sight, that of a monk. In the story of Barlaam and Josaphat it is naturally a Christian monk that he meets. The monk's name is Barlaam. The derivation of the name is uncertain: it may be a corrupt form of the Sanskrit word *bhagavan*, meaning 'lord'. Barlaam is described as 'a monk of perfect life and good opinion that dwelled in the desert of the land of Senaar'. Coming to know about Josaphat by divine inspiration, he disguised himself as a merchant and gained access to him by telling 'the greatest governor of the king's son' that he had a miraculous precious stone to sell and wished to offer it to the prince. The governor wanted to see the precious stone, but on hearing that it could be safely seen only by one who was wholly chaste he changed his mind and brought him to Josaphat, who received him honourably. Barlaam told him he did well in taking no heed of his 'littleness that appeareth withoutforth'. He was like the king whose barons were displeased with him for getting down from his chariot and humbly saluting to poor men, thus compromising his royal dignity. In order to teach them a lesson the king ordered four chests to be made. Two of the chests he covered with gold and jewels and filled with dead men's bones and filth. The other two he covered with pitch and filled with precious jewels and rich gems. Here we obviously have the originals of the three caskets in *The Merchant of Venice*, where despite his more romantic handling of the theme Shakespeare draws much the same moral as Barlaam, who continues:

> And after this the king do call his great barons … and did do set these four chests tofore them, and demanded of them which were most precious, and they said that the two that were gilt were most of value. Then the king commanded that they should be opened, and anon a great stench issued out of them. And the king said: They are like them that be clothed with precious vestments and be full withinforth of ordure and of sin. And after he made open the other and there issued a marvellous sweet odour. And after,

the king said: These be semblable to the poor men that I met and honoured, for though they be clad in foul vestments, yet shine they withinforth with good odour of good virtues, and ye take none heed but to that withoutforth, and consider not what is within.[459]

Having related this apologue, Barlaam preached Josaphat a long sermon about the creation of the world, about the day of judgement, and about the reward of good and evil. This he followed up with a series of apologues, some of them quite amusing, on the foolishness of idol worship, the fallaciousness of worldly pleasure, the difference between true and false friendship, and the inevitability of death. Several of the apologues have, to me, a familiar, almost Buddhistic ring to them, especially the one on true and false friendship. There was a man who had three friends. He loved the first friend as much as himself, the second less than himself, the third little or naught. It so happened that this man was in danger of his life, and was summoned before the king. He ran for help to his first friend, reminding him how much he had always loved him. But the friend refused to help, saying he had to spend the day with other friends, and in any case he did not know him. The man went sadly to his second friend, who excused himself from accompanying him to the king, saying he had many responsibilities; but he would accompany him as far as the palace gate. At last the man went to his third friend. 'I have no reason to speak to thee,' he admitted, 'ne I have not loved thee as I ought, but I am in tribulation and without friends, and pray thee that thou help me.' The third friend readily agreed to the man's request, saying, 'I confess to be thy dear friend and have not forgotten the little benefit thou hast done to me, and I shall go right gladly with thee tofore the king, for to see what shall be demanded of thee, and I shall pray the king for thee.' The first friend, Barlaam explained, was possession of riches, for the sake of which man puts himself in many dangers, and of which he can take with him, when death comes, only the winding sheet in which he will be buried. The second friend was his sons, his wife, and his kin, who can go with him only as far as his grave, after which they will return home and get on with their own lives. The third friend was faith, hope, and charity, and other good works we have done, which when we leave our bodies may go before us and pray for us to God, and may deliver us from our enemies the devils.

The first time I read this apologue, in Caxton's English version, it at once put me in mind of the old morality play of *Everyman*, which

I saw in the form of a ballet at a London theatre during the War. This ballet moved me more deeply than had the play on which it was based, with which I was already familiar. On the drop curtain Blake's 'Ancient of Days', enormously enlarged, bent over the Deep with his compasses creating the world. Then, out of the darkness, came a tremendous voice, declaring:

I behold here in my majesty
How that all beings be to me unkind,
Living without fear in worldly prosperity,
On earthly treasure is all their mind.[460]

God therefore sends a messenger to Everyman, requiring him to appear before him. The 'mighty messenger' is Death. On receiving the message Everyman runs in turn to his friends Fellowship, Kindred, Cousin, and Goods, but none is willing to go with him on his journey. At length he calls out to his Good Deeds, asking her where she is. But she is 'called in ground', his sins having bound her so tightly that she is unable to move. He releases her, and she goes with him on his journey, as does Knowledge, to whom the play's unknown author gives the memorable lines:

Everyman, I will go with thee and be thy guide,
In thy most need to go by thy side.[461]

The play may be derived from a Dutch close counterpart, as one scholar believes; or, alternatively, it may be based on Barlaam's apologue on true and false friendship, publication of *The Golden Legend* having preceded the composition of *Everyman* by about twenty-five years. In any case, the play is a work of something like genius and must have touched the hearts of the audience for which it was written, including as it does a universal truth – the truth that 'you can't take it with you'.

When he had been fully instructed by Barlaam, Josaphat wanted to leave his father and follow the monk. Barlaam approved his resolution, and to illustrate it he related another apologue; but he did not agree that Josaphat should follow him into the desert. Instead, he should wait until it was the right time for them to meet. He then baptized Josaphat and 'returned into his cell'. Shortly afterwards Avennir heard that his son had become a Christian. On the advice of his friend Arachis he sought out an old pagan hermit who resembled Barlaam and instructed him to engage in public debate with the pagan masters. First he should defend the Christian faith, then allow himself to be defeated by the arguments of the pagans and revert to paganism. In this way Josaphat would lose faith in Christianity and follow suit. But Josaphat was not deceived. He told the false Barlaam, whose name was Nachor, that if he was defeated by the pagan masters he would, when he became king, tear out his tongue with his own hands for having dared to teach a king's son a false religion. Judging that he had more to fear from the son than from the father, who had promised him immunity whatever the result of the debate, he attacked the gods of paganism with great vigour. The Chaldees worshipped the elements, the Greeks worshipped gods and goddesses who were guilty of the grossest immorality, and the Egyptians worshipped animals, whereas Christians worshipped 'the son of the right high king that descended from heaven and took nature human'. He then defended Christianity so clearly and convincingly that the pagan masters were discomfited and did not know what to say. Josaphat was overjoyed at the false Barlaam's victory. He told him privately that he knew who he really was, converted him to Christianity, and sent him into the desert, where he was baptized and led the life of a hermit.

On coming to hear of these things an enchanter named Theodosius approached the king and advised him to take away his son's present attendants and replace them with beautiful, well-adorned women who should be instructed never to leave the prince, for 'there is nothing that may so soon deceive the young man as the beauty of women'. He would then send to the prince an evil spirit who would inflame his mind with lust. The king did what the enchanter advised, but when Josaphat felt himself to be inwardly burning with lust he prayed to God for help, whereupon all temptation left him. The king then sent to him a beautiful young princess who was fatherless. Josaphat preached to her and she promised to become a Christian if he would marry her. When he refused she promised that if he would lie with her for only that night she would become a Christian in the morning, arguing that according to his own religion 'the angels have more joy in heaven of one sinner doing penance than on many others'. Seeing how strongly the woman was assailing Josaphat the devils came to her aid, so that the prince's fleshly craving incited him to sin at the same time that he desired the woman's salvation. Weeping, he betook himself to prayer, fell asleep, and

> saw by a vision that he was brought into a meadow arrayed with fair flowers, there where the leaves of the trees demened a sweet sound which came by a wind agreeable, and thereout issued a marvellous odour, and the fruit was right fair to see, and right delectable of taste, and there were seats of gold and silver and precious stones, and the beds were noble and preciously adorned, and right clear water ran thereby.

He then entered into a city the walls of which were of fine gold, and where he saw in the air 'some that sang a song that never ear of mortal man heard like'. This, he was told, was the abode of the blessed saints. He then was shown a horrible place full of filth and stench, and told this was the abode of the wicked. When Josaphat awoke, it seemed to him that 'the beauty of the damosel was more foul and stinking than all other ordure'.

Despairing of ever being able to persuade his son to abjure Christianity, King Avennir made over to him half his kingdom, though Josaphat desired with all his heart to go and live in the desert. For the sake of spreading his faith, however, he consented to rule for a while, and built churches, and raised crosses, and converted many people to Christianity, including his own father, who after leaving the whole kingdom to his son engaged in works of penance. Josaphat himself, after ruling for much longer than he wanted, at last fled away into the desert, 'and as he went in a desert he gave to a poor man his habit royal and abode in a right poor gown', just as the Bodhisattva, in one of the traditional biographies of the Buddha, exchanges his princely robes for the saffron-coloured dress of a huntsman.[462] What directly follows is reminiscent of the Bodhisattva's defeat of Māra, prior to his attaining Enlightenment, except that Josaphat prays to God whereas the Bodhisattva relies on his own inner resources.[463]

> And the devil made to him many assaults, for sometimes he ran upon him with a sword drawn and menaced to smite if he left not the desert; and another time he appeared to him in the form of a wild beast and foamed and ran on him as he would have devoured him, and then Josaphat said: Our Lord is mine helper. I doubt no thing that man may do to me.[464]

Josaphat then spent two years wandering in the desert looking for Barlaam. At last he found a cave in the earth, knocked at the door, and said, 'Father, bless me.'

> And anon Barlaam heard the voice of him, and rose up and went out, and then each kissed other and embraced straitly and were glad of their assembling.[465]

Afterwards Josaphat told Barlaam all that had happened to him since they parted. Barlaam died in the year 408, the story goes on to relate. As for Josaphat, he left his kingdom in his twenty-fifth year, and lived the life of a hermit for thirty-five years, and was buried by the body of Barlaam. On hearing of this, King Barachius, who it seems had been left in charge of the kingdom, removed the bodies of the two saints to his city, where their tomb was the scene of many miracles.

Just as Caxton translated the story of Barlaam and Josaphat from Voragine's Latin version, via the French, Voragine himself drew his material from an earlier source, that drew from one still earlier, and so on through layer upon layer of different languages and cultures back to the Sanskrit text with which the whole process began. Scholars have not been able to identify this urtext, as it may be called, but it must have been related to such works as the *Lalitavistara* and the *Buddhacarita*.[466] In any case, it was freely translated or adapted into Pehlevi in central Asia under Manichaean auspices, the prophet Mani, the third-century founder of Manichaeism, having regarded the Buddha as God's messenger to India, just as Zarathustra was his messenger to Persia, Jesus his messenger to the West, and Mani himself his messenger to Babylonia. This Pehlevi version, which appears to be no longer extant, was translated into Arabic probably in the eighth century by an unknown author and still survives. Under the title of *The Book of Balawha and Budasf* the Arabic version became popular in the Islamic world, and gave rise to numerous abridgements and adaptations in the same language. It also was the basis of the various Greek, Christianized versions of the story, the last and most highly embellished recension of which appeared in the ninth century and was later attributed to St John of Damascus, the last of the Greek Fathers.[467] Versions of the Arabic work appeared not only in Greek but also in Hebrew, Persian, and Georgian.

So far as Western Europe is concerned, the most important of the versions deriving from *The Book of Balawha and Budasf* is the one attributed to St John of Damascus, for it was from this version that the Latin translations of the Middle Ages were all made. The first of the extant translations appears to have been made in the twelfth century. Other translations followed, including that of Jacobus de Voragine, which was the source not only of Caxton's English version of the story of Barlaam and Josaphat but also of versions in French, German, Italian, Spanish, Portuguese, Swedish, Icelandic, Irish, and a number of other languages. The abundance of these versions testifies to the popularity of the story through the Middle Ages and well into the Renaissance period. Caxton's version of the *Legenda Aurea*, of which the story of Barlaam and Josaphat forms a part, was his most popular publication. It was often reprinted, and a copy of the work must have fallen into Shakespeare's hands before he came to write *The Merchant of Venice*, which he did between 1596 and 1598.

There were two main reasons for the widespread popularity of the romantic story of the young prince who, having lived a life of enforced seclusion, was suddenly confronted by the facts of human existence and became a monk. In the first place, the story of Barlaam and Josaphat as it stands now is a good read. It has been described as 'a strange mixture of parable and fable, of folklore and history, and romance, in which shrewd worldly wisdom is mingled with the highest and greatest religious truths in such a way that the perusal thereof will increase the piety of the godly, the wisdom of the wise, and the pleasure of those who seek amusement and instruction in the writings of teachers of olden times'.[468] Secondly, the story was set in the distant, mysterious, almost mythical land of India, about whose geographical location most people in the Middle Ages had only the vaguest of ideas. According to Christian tradition St Thomas, one of the twelve apostles, travelled to India not long after the death of Jesus and converted the whole country to Christianity. In the course of time it slipped back into paganism and it was Barlaam and Josaphat who, between them, reconverted the land to the true faith. For this pious work, as well as for the holiness of their lives, the two saints were greatly honoured by both the Eastern Orthodox Church and the Western Church, Barlaam and Josaphat being commemorated by the Roman Catholic Church on 27 November, while the Greek Church commemorates Josaphat by himself on 26 August and the Georgian

Church Barlaam by himself on 19 May. In the Russian Church Barlaam and Josaphat, together with the latter's father King Avennir, are all commemorated on 19 November, though this day properly belongs to St Barlaam of Antioch, an early Christian martyr.

To the best of my knowledge, no churches were dedicated to Barlaam and Josaphat, nor do they feature in the religious art of the Middle Ages and the Renaissance, though it may well be that paintings illustrating their story are hidden away in remote churches and obscure provincial art galleries. Despite this apparent neglect, there are probably churches where their feast days are still celebrated, and where neither priest nor people realize that in venerating Barlaam and Josaphat they are in fact honouring the Buddha and the unknown Indian ascetic who, as the last of the four sights, had inspired the young Siddhārtha to go forth from home in quest of Enlightenment.

10
BUDDHISM AND CHRISTIANITY

For the last nine months I have spent much of my time thinking and writing about the contact I have had with Christianity and Christians in the course of the last eighty years. This is the longest time I have ever spent immersed in the religion into which I was born (or at least baptized), and to which I never really belonged, and those who have followed me thus far may want to know what I have learnt from the experience. Have I changed my ideas about Christianity, or about Buddhism, or about the relation between the two religions? Have I learned anything about myself? I do not think I have learned from my immersion in Christianity anything that I did not know before, but it certainly helped me to see more clearly, and feel more deeply, some of the things I already knew, and for this reason I believe the experience to have been worthwhile. Though I was not in a position to embark on a systematic comparative study of Buddhism and Christianity, which in any case would have been an immense undertaking, such limited comparisons as I was able to make were sufficient to highlight the fundamental differences that exist between the two religions.

The fact that there are such differences, not only between Buddhism and Christianity but also between them and other religions, and between the other religions themselves, at once gives rise to certain questions. How, for instance, can people of different religious beliefs live together in peace and harmony, or at least without overt conflict? One answer is that this happy state of affairs would be achieved if everybody were to believe that religions were in essence the same, or that they all lead ultimately to the same goal. Neither orthodox Buddhists nor orthodox Christians would agree that religions are, in fact, the same in essence, or that they all lead ultimately to the same goal, and this has been my position, too, ever since I started thinking seriously about the Buddha's teaching. But at this point Buddhists and Christians part company. According to Buddhism, it is possible for one to be convinced of the truth of one's own faith and yet, at the same time, to feel no hatred for those who think differently. Indeed, for one who is a Buddhist it is desirable, even imperative, that he should have towards those of other faiths an attitude not of hatred but of positive goodwill, for hatred is an obstacle on the path to Enlightenment, besides being disruptive of that sense of natural solidarity with other human beings on which ethics is based. Judging by the way the Church has treated heretics and non-believers when it was in a position of power, Christians believe that conviction of the truth of one's own faith is not incompatible with hatred for those who think differently. Indeed, many Christians seem to have believed that it was good and right, and pleasing to God, that they should, as a natural expression of their faith, hate and persecute pagans and heretics.

I have always been aware of the Christian record in this respect, but as a result of my recent immersion in Christianity, especially in its Roman Catholic form, I have become more aware of what that record tells us about the nature of Christianity. Like most other people, I tended to regard such phenomena as the Inquisition and the Crusades as unfortunate episodes in European history, regrettable mainly on account of the tens of thousands of human lives they had brought to an untimely end. The officers of the Inquisition, in conjunction with the secular authorities, sent men and women to the stake because they refused to believe as the Church believed. The Crusaders slew Muslims because they were followers of a different religion. As I reflected on these things, I felt more deeply than ever the enormity of religious intolerance, springing as it does from an unholy alliance of ignorance, hatred, and fear. I thought of the lonely death of the Bohemian reformer Jan Hus, sent to the stake by the Council of Constance in 1415 as a heretic for attacking the ecclesiastical abuses and rejecting the pope's authority. I recalled seeing, in the Prado, Berruguete's famous painting of St Dominic presiding over the burning of heretics, in the bottom right hand corner of which two naked, anonymous victims of the Inquisition are seen fastened to posts, ready for burning, while St Dominic, seated aloft beneath a huge canopy, his throne surrounded by clerical and lay dignitaries, calmly presides over the proceedings. I also bethought me of the two hundred and more *perfecti* who, after the surrender of the great Cathar fortress of Montsegur in 1244, were thrust into a wooded palisade with combustible material and burnt.

Jan Hus, the anonymous victims of the Inquisition, and the two hundred and more Cathar *perfecti*, as well as tens of thousands of other heretics, were all *burnt alive*, thus suffering one of the most horrible of deaths. These burnings took place under the auspices of the highest religious and secular authorities; they were justified by theologians, approved by saints and mystics, and applauded by ordinary people. Apologists for Christianity have naturally sought to minimize the significance of the burnings, arguing that the number of victims has been exaggerated, or that Christianity has done more good in the world than harm, or that what men did in the Middle Ages is not to be judged by modern standards. I find none of these arguments convincing. Nothing can minimize the horror of a man or woman being burnt alive for believing differently from the rest of the community. It was not that the officers of the Inquisition, for example, necessarily enjoyed their work, or that they became Inquisitors because it put them in the position of being able to inflict pain and suffering on others. For the most part they seem to have been learned and pious men who were determined to stamp out heresy and who believed that in burning heretics they were doing their duty by God and man. If they ever felt pity for the sufferings of their victims they would probably have stifled the feeling, regarding it as being inspired by the Devil. There would seem to be in the very nature of Christianity a strand of intolerance that is capable of overriding all considerations of common humanity. In the course of recent months I have become more aware of this deadly strand, and more aware of the difference, in this and other respects, between Buddhism and Christianity.

Though I have spoken of my being immersed in *Christianity*, I have in fact often been immersed in Roman Catholicism, this being the form of Christianity that has played a dominant part in the political and economic life of Western Europe, as well as in its religious and cultural life. It is no accident that Roman Catholicism is so called. It is the

Roman Catholic Church itself that is the true legatee of the Roman Empire, not the so-called Holy Roman Empire, for it was the Roman Church which for a thousand years – from the sack of Rome by the Goths to the Reformation – provided the iron framework that helped to hold the peoples of Western Europe together as the religio-political entity known as Christendom, of which the pope was the supreme head and ultimate authority. This iron framework prevented Western Europe from falling into chaos, and to this extent it was a good thing, as I saw more clearly as I renewed my acquaintance with the history of Western Europe during the period of papal ascendancy. But although that iron framework helped to ensure a degree of social and political stability and cohesion, intellectually and spiritually it was often constrictive, and to this extent it was a bad thing. At its most constrictive, intellectually and spiritually speaking, it could be destructive not only of independent thought but of life as in its treatment of heresy and heretics.

In every generation there were, however, men and women who, while the rest were content to live out their lives within the framework, contrived to find, or make, little openings in it, through which they could get a glimpse of the wider world outside. There were others who made use of it for their own purposes, whether noble or ignoble, creative or exploitive. Among these were the poets and artists, especially the artists. The framework consisted not only of dogmas and laws; myths, symbols, and sacred history were also part of it. Provided he respected certain conventions, the artist was free to depict a subject taken from the Bible, or the legends of the saints, or ecclesiastical history, in accordance with the dictates of his own genius. If he painted a picture of St Jerome in his study, for example, he would almost certainly have included the saint's broad-brimmed cardinal's hat, and the hat would have been red, not any other colour; but such details as the dimensions of the study, the nature of its furniture, how it was lighted, and whether or not St Jerome was half naked, or had a long white beard, were all left to the discretion and taste of the artist – unless the individual or community commissioning the painting had some wishes in this connection, in which case he would have respected them just as he respected the conventions laid down by the Church. Altogether there must be scores, even hundreds, of such paintings of St Jerome, all making use of at least some of the traditional iconographic elements but all differing in style and treatment. From the best of these we learn less about St Jerome than about the character, temperament, and depth of insight of the artist himself. A painting of St Jerome in his study may be not so much a Christian work of art as a manifestation of human creativity, as may a painting of a subject taken from the Bible, or the lives of the saints, or ecclesiastical tradition.

This is why I am able, though a Buddhist, to appreciate and enjoy, even to be deeply moved by, what is best and greatest in Christian art, as well as what is best and greatest in Christian poetry and music. In this I am not alone among western Buddhists, some of whom would say that it was only after becoming Buddhists that they learned to appreciate Christian art. A Christian painting contains no overt doctrinal element, which would be repugnant to me; for viewed simply as a painting it does not contain, and cannot contain, any conceptual element. On the other hand, a Christian musical composition, such as Bach's *Mass in B Minor* or Handel's *Messiah*, does contain a doctrinal element, inasmuch as it is a setting to music of the words of a certain religious text, in which case I can either ignore the words (this is easier if they are in a language I do not understand) or mentally give them a Buddhist application. A Christian poem consists of words, as does any poem, and some of these words will be expressive of concepts, including doctrinal concepts. If the poem happens to be a narrative one, like *Paradise Lost* or the *Divine Comedy*, the doctrinal concepts will be part of the story, like Homer's assertions about his gods and goddesses in the *Iliad* and the *Odyssey*, and their presence therefore does not obstruct my enjoyment of the poem.

It is because I distinguish between Christianity and Christian culture, and see the latter as owing far more to human genius than to the teaching of the Church, that I am able, though a Buddhist, to appreciate and enjoy the 'Christian' art, music, and poetry of the West. I am thus in a paradoxical position. As a Buddhist, I reject Christian doctrine, but as a westerner I am able to appreciate and enjoy 'Christian' culture. But I am a *western* Buddhist. Though I accept the Buddha's teaching, which comes to me from the East, as a westerner I do not feel as much 'at home' with eastern Buddhist culture, whether Sinhalese, Thai, or Tibetan, as one brought up within it. Moreover, although there is western Buddhism, in the sense that there are tens of thousands of Europeans and Americans who regard themselves as Buddhists, there is no such thing as a western Buddhist culture. I can therefore well understand the feelings of the English academic who, having converted back to Catholicism after twenty-five years as a member of a Tibetan Buddhist group, was delighted to find himself surrounded, in his native land, by the cathedrals, pilgrimage sites, and other holy places of his religion.[469] As a western Buddhist, I am not similarly situated. The English landscape is not dotted with stupas and *maṇi* walls and other reminders of the Dharma. My practice of the Dharma does not have the support of an indigenous Buddhist culture.

But things will change. I am confident that the next hundred years will see the beginnings of an indigenous western Buddhist culture. A few green shoots have already appeared here and there. But even when we have our own western Buddhist culture many western Buddhists will continue to enjoy the poetry, music, and art of the old 'Christian' culture. Meanwhile, now that I have finished recalling, and reflecting upon, my personal contact with Christianity and Christians, I cannot but feel that it is infinitely better for me to be a western Buddhist without a culture of his own than a Christian with one.

SOURCES

Tibetan Buddhism: an Introduction began life as a lecture series at the Hampstead Buddhist Vihara in London in 1966 (though it was not prepared for publication until 1996, when it was published by Windhorse Publications).

Creative Symbols of Tantric Buddhism is based on talks given by Sangharakshita in London in 1972. They were published in a series of the periodical *Mitrata* under the title 'Creative Symbols of the Tantric Path to Enlightenment' in 1988–1990, and then published by Windhorse Publications in book form, with some additional material gleaned from seminars, in 2002, under the title *Creative Symbols of Tantric Buddhism.*

The illustrations in this *Complete Works* edition were originally commissioned for *Mitrata* and created by Dharmachari Aloka, who has created many images of Buddhas and Bodhisattvas, notably the paintings in the shrine room at Padmaloka men's retreat centre in Norfolk. Many thanks to Aloka for his permission to include his work in this volume.

The Essence of Zen is an edited version of a series of five lectures given at the Hampstead Buddhist Vihara in London in 1965.

The FWBO and 'Protestant Buddhism': an Affirmation and a Protest, was written in 1992 in response to an English academic's critique of the FWBO which had been published in the journal *Religion.*

From Genesis to the Diamond Sūtra was dictated, due to Sangharakshita's failing eyesight, in 2005.

NOTES AND REFERENCES

TIBETAN BUDDHISM

1 The Samye Debate described from the Tibetan point of view is recorded in the *History of Buddhism in India and Tibet* by Butön Rinchen Drub (1290–1364). A contrasting Chinese account of the debate, the *Verification of the Greater Vehicle of Sudden Awakening*, was discovered in the caves of Dunhuang and translated into English by Paul Demieville in 1952. Kamalaśīla himself wrote three treatises summarizing the themes of the debate, the *Bhāvanākrama*, which are now available in English translation.

2 The glossary commissioned by Ralpacan is called in Sanskrit the *Mahāvyutpatti*. Its Tibetan name translates as '*The Great Work Made by Many Lotsawas and Pandits that Brings Comprehension of Particulars*'. It was first translated into English by Alexander Csoma de Körös, and parts 1, 2, and 3 were published in 1834, 1910, and 1944.

3 Sangharakshita describes his connection with Kachu Rimpoche in *Precious Teachers*, Windhorse Publications, Birmingham 2007, chapter 8 (*Complete Works*, vol. 22). The story of the banner of victory on the vihara roof is told in that chapter; also Sangharakshita, *In the Realm of the Lotus*, Windhorse Publications, Birmingham 1995, p. 27 (*Complete Works*, vol. 26).

4 For more about Dudjom Rimpoche, see Sangharakshita, *Precious Teachers*, Windhorse Publications, Birmingham 2007, chapter 11 (*Complete Works*, vol. 22).

5 For this episode, see Milarepa's biography, for example,

Tsangnyön Heruka, *The Life of Milarepa*, trans. Andrew Quintman, Penguin Books, London 2010, pp. 150–1.

6 Ibid., p. 139.

7 One well known English translation of Milarepa's songs and stories is Garma C. C. Chang (trans.), *The Hundred Thousand Songs of Milarepa*, Shambhala Publications, Boston 1999; and the translation by Christopher Stagg published in 2017, also by Shambhala, has the same title. See also *Complete Works*, vols. 18 and 19, *Milarepa and the Art of Discipleship* I and II.

8 See, for example, Tsongkhapa Lobzang Drakpa, *Tsongkhapa's Six Yogas of Naropa*, trans. Glenn H. Mullin, Snow Lion Publications, Ithaca 1996.

9 The *History of Buddhism in India and Tibet* by Butön Rinchen Drub, said to be 'pseudo-historical', was written in 1322 and translated into English by Eugene Obermiller in 1931. See Butön, *The History of Buddhism in India and Tibet: The Jewellery of Scripture*, trans. E. Obermiller, Indian Book Centre, New Delhi 1998.

10 This is the *Rājataraṅginī*, 'River of Kings', a history of Kashmir and the neighbouring lands written in the twelfth century CE by Kalhaṇa.

11 Vinaya Piṭaka i.79. See I. B. Horner (trans.), *The Book of the Discipline*, part 4, Pali Text Society, Oxford 1996, p. 99.

12 Thomas Traherne was a seventeenth-century Herefordshire priest who wrote ecstatic mystical prose and verse. His literary work was obscure until discovered (some of it quite by chance, one book being on the point of being burned on a bonfire, not having been recognized for what it was) in the twentieth century. This phrase comes from his *Centuries of Meditation*, towards the end of the famous passage which begins, 'The corn was orient and immortal wheat, which never should be reaped, nor was ever sown.' He goes on to say, 'So that with much ado I was corrupted, and made to learn the dirty devices of this world. Which now I unlearn, and become, as it were, a little child again that I may enter into the Kingdom of God.' *Centuries of Meditation*, iii.3.

13 The *Lamrim Chenmo* has been published in English as Je Tsong-kha-pa, *The Great Treatise on the Stages of the Path to Enlightenment*, vols. 1, 2, and 3, Snow Lion Publications, Ithaca 2015. The *Ngakrim Chenmo* appears not to be available in English translation.

14 After the death of the tenth Panchen Lama in 1989, a controversy arose over the identification of his successor. In 1995 the Dalai Lama named one boy as the eleventh

Panchen Lama, but the Chinese government named a different successor. For one account of the story, see Melvyn C. Goldstein, *The Snow Lion and the Dragon: China, Tibet, and the Dalai Lama*, University of California Press, Berkeley 1997.

15 See chapter 1, 'The Tibetan Wheel of Life' in Sangharakshita, *Creative Symbols of the Tantric Path*, pp. 125–41, in this volume.

16 'The Tibetan Tradition: Its Presiding Idea' is chapter 9 of Marco Pallis, *The Way and the Mountain*, Peter Owen Limited, London 1961.

17 The 'Younghusband expedition', which some historians say was tantamount to invasion, was a British military force led by Colonel Francis Younghusband which entered Tibet and reached Lhasa in August 1904, having provoked the Tibetans into an attempt to defend their country with arms, resulting in armed conflict in the course of which many Tibetans were killed due to the much heavier weaponry deployed by the British. By the time the British arrived in Lhasa, the Thirteenth Dalai Lama had fled to Mongolia.

18 For more about the eighteen schools, see Sangharakshita, *A Survey of Buddhism* chapter 1, section 19, 'The Foundations of Buddhism: Early Schools, *Complete Works*, vol. 1, pp. 182–90.

19 The twelfth Dorje Phagmo, born in 1938 (or perhaps 1942), left Tibet for Bhutan in 1959 and eventually returned to Chinese-occupied Tibet, where she accepted various Chinese government posts.

20 The eighteen major and forty-six minor precepts are sometimes called vows and sometimes the eighteen root downfalls and the forty-six secondary downfalls. The eighteen 'root downfalls' range from 'praising oneself and belittling others' to 'giving up the pledge of altruistic aspiration', and the forty-six 'secondary downfalls' range from 'not making offerings every day to the Three Jewels' to 'not using miraculous powers, if one possesses this ability, in order to stop others from doing unwholesome actions'.

21 Part of the Gesar epic is now available in English translation: Robin Kornman and Lama Chonam (trans.), *The Epic of Gesar of Ling: Gesar's Magical Birth, Early Years, and Coronation as King*, Shambhala Publications, Boulder 2015:

> The epic of Gesar is the longest single piece of literature in the world canon, encompassing some 120 volumes; here the first three volumes are translated, telling of Gesar's birth, his mischievous childhood and

> his youth spent in exile, and his rivalry for the throne with his treacherous uncle.

The love songs attributed to the Sixth Dalai Lama, Tsangyang Gyatso, have been translated by Geoffrey Waters, who explains that, the Fifth Dalai Lama having died in 1682, at a time when Tibet was threatened by neighbouring powers, the existence of the Sixth Dalai Lama was kept secret, and he was not ordained as a monk until the deception was uncovered in the mid-1690s.

> By then his personality had developed outside the monastic tradition. For the rest of his short life, he preferred drinking and lovemaking to his tedious official duties as Tibet's God-king.

See Geoffrey Waters, *White Crane: Love Songs of the Sixth Dalai Lama*, White Pine Press, Buffalo NY 2007.

22 In the sixth book of *The Republic* (507b–509c), Plato records a dialogue between Glaucon (Plato's elder brother) and Socrates. Glaucon asks Socrates to define goodness, but Socrates says he cannot. Instead he offers to talk about 'the child of goodness', and reveals this to be the sun:

> As goodness stands in the intelligible realm to intelligence and the things we know, so in the visible realm the sun stands to sight and the things we see.

23 See Lama Anagarika Govinda, *Bilder aus Indien und Tibet*, Irisiana Verlag, Haldenwang 1978, in which a number of Lama Govinda's paintings are reproduced in colour. Many of his paintings can also be seen, albeit in black and white, in R. C. Tandan, *The Art of the Anagarika Govinda*, Kitablstan, Allahabad and London 1940.

24 For more information, see chapter 6, 'Five Element Symbolism and the Stupa', in Sangharakshita, *The Drama of Cosmic Enlightenment* (*Complete Works*, vol. 16, pp. 139 ff.).

25 Sangharakshita describes the six element practice in, for example, *What is the Dharma?* (*Complete Works*, vol. 3, pp. 346–8). A canonical reference to the practice is found in the *Mahārāhulovāda Sutta*, *Majjhima Nikāya* 62 (i.421–4). See Bhikkhu Ñāṇamoli and Bhikkhu Bodhi (trans.), *The Middle Length Discourses of the Buddha*, Wisdom Publications, Boston 1995, pp. 528–30; or I. B. Horner (trans.), *The Collection of the Middle Length Sayings*, vol. ii, Pali Text Society, Oxford 1994, pp. 92–5.

26 L. Austine Waddell, *The Buddhism of Tibet, or Lamaism: with its mystic cults,*

symbolism and mythology, and in its relation to Indian Buddhism, W. H. Allen, London 1895, e.g. p. 99.

27 The five hindrances are listed in many places in the Pāli canon; for example, the *Mahāvagga* of the *Saṃyutta Nikāya* (v.91–8) has a whole section on them; see Bhikkhu Bodhi (trans.), *The Connected Discourses of the Buddha*, Wisdom Publications, Somerville 2000, pp. 1591–4; also F. L. Woodward (trans.), *The Book of the Kindred Sayings*, part 5, Pali Text Society, London 1979, pp. 76–81. They are described (in Woodward's translation, p. 81) as

> the five hindrances which cause blindness, loss of sight and ignorance, which obstruct insight, consort with pain and conduce not to Nibbāna.

28 Samuel Taylor Coleridge, Table Talk, 27 April 1823, in *Table Talk*, Routledge, New York 1884, p. 38.

29 Gandhi often reflected on ends and means and the connection between them; for example, he once wrote (in *Hind Swaraj*, 1952),

> The means may be likened to a seed, the end to a tree, and there is just the same inviolable connection between the means and the end as there is between the seed and the tree.

30 For a brief account of Sangharakshita's connection with Tomo Geshe Rimpoche, see Sangharakshita, *Moving Against the Stream*, Windhorse Publications, Birmingham 2003, p. 349 (*Complete Works*, vol. 23).

31 The Buddha is recorded as describing the four *brahma vihāras* in the *Tevijja Sutta*, *Dīgha Nikāya* 13 (i.251). See M. Walshe (trans.), *The Long Discourses of the Buddha*, Wisdom Publications, Boston 1995, p. 194; or T. W. Rhys Davids (trans.), *Dialogues of the Buddha*, part 1, Pali Text Society, London 1973, pp. 317– 8. Buddhaghosa describes in detail how to practise the *brahma vihāras* at *Visuddhimagga* 317–25; see Pe Maung Tin (trans.), *The Path of Purity*, Pali Text Society, London 1975, chapter 9, pp. 365–75. For Sangharakshita's advice on the practices, see section 3, 'The Development of Positive Emotion' in *The Purpose and Practice of Buddhist Meditation*, *Complete Works*, vol. 5; also *Living with Kindness*, in *Complete Works*, vol. 15.

32 In *In Praise of Tara: Songs of the Saviouress* (Wisdom Publications, London 1986, pp. 17–8) Martin Willson says that Tārā

> dwells in wild places such as ... the Khadira Forest. As Khadiravaṇī-Tārā, She wears flowers in Her hair and even Her body is green in colour.

For verses in praise of Khadiravaṇī-Tārā, see ibid., pp. 282–5.

33 For more about this story, see *Facing Mount Kanchenjunga*, *Complete Works*, vol. 21, p. 331.

34 The Parsi community of India and elsewhere is in decline, mainly due to the tradition forbidding marriage outside the community. In 2016 the BBC reported that Parsi numbers in India were declining by 12 percent each census decade (whereas the population of India as a whole was increasing by 23 percent each decade).

35 The Sudhamma Council was first convened in 1784 by King Bodawpaya to resolve the 'two-shoulder' controversy, which had already been dividing the monastic community for a hundred years (Helen James, *Governance and Civil Society in Myanmar: Education, Health and Environment*, Routledge, London 2005, p. 81). Evidently Bodawpaya resolved the matter, deciding in favour of orthodoxy and decreeing that all *bhikkhus* had to cover both shoulders on their daily almsround.

> This ruling created one unified sect throughout Myanmar under the leadership of a council of senior bhikkhus appointed by the king. These were called the Thudhamma Sayadaws and the Thudhamma sect has survived in Myanmar down to the present day.

Collected Wheel Publications, vol. xxvi, Buddhist Publication Society, Kandy 2014, p. 161.

36 See David Snellgrove, *The Hevajra Tantra: a Critical Study*, Orchid Press, Bangkok 2010; and Geshe Sonam Rinchen, *Atīśa's 'Lamp of the Way to Enlightenment'*, trans. Ruth Sonam, Snow Lion Publications, Ithaca 1997. The *Lamrim Chenmo* has been published in English as Je Tsong-kha-pa, *The Great Treatise on the Stages of the Path to Enlightenment* volumes 1, 2 and 3, Snow Lion Publications, Ithaca 2015.

37 For Sangharakshita's commentary on some of the Perfection of Wisdom *sūtras* see Sangharkashita, *Wisdom Beyond Words*, Windhorse Publications, Birmingham 1993 (*Complete Works*, vol. 14).

38 Sangharakshita says more about Jamyang Khyentse in *Precious Teachers*, Windhorse Publications, Birmingham 2007, pp. 12ff. (*Complete Works*, vol. 22).

CREATIVE SYMBOLS OF TANTRIC BUDDHISM

39 A significant point in the history of Tantric Buddhism occurs, probably sometime during the late seventh century, with the appearance of the term Vajrayāna, 'The Diamond Way'. This expression, which was to become one of the standard self-descriptions of Tantric Buddhism, emerged at a time when the word vajra, meaning equally 'diamond' and 'thunderbolt', had assumed a major symbolic role in certain texts, standing for the indestructibility and power of the awakened, enlightened, state (bodhi). It is worth stressing that the term 'Vajrayāna' was not employed before this period, and that, therefore, the expressions 'Vajrayāna Buddhism' and 'Tantric Buddhism' are not synonymous. What is true of Vajrayāna Buddhism is not necessarily true of Tantric Buddhism as a whole.

Anthony Tribe, 'Mantranaya/ Vajrayāna – Tantric Buddhism in India', in *Buddhist Thought: A complete introduction to the Indian tradition*, by Paul Williams with Anthony Tribe, Routledge, London and New York, 2000, pp.196ff.

40 This is familiar from the *Heart Sūtra*: 'form is no other than emptiness, emptiness no other than form'. For Sangharakshita's commentary on this line of the *sūtra*, see Sangharakshita, *Wisdom Beyond Words*, Birmingham 2000, pp. 27–8 (*Complete Works*, vol. 14).

41 This is the sixth line of John Keats' sonnet, 'When I have fears that I may cease to be', written in 1818.

42 See chapter 7, 'The Bodhisattva Hierarchy', in Sangharakshita, *The Bodhisattva Ideal* (*Complete Works*, vol. 4).

43 What has become known as the Tibetan wheel of life is said to have originated among the followers of the Sarvastivāda school of Indian Buddhism, which formed around the third century BCE. In the *Divyāvadāna*, or 'Divine Heroic Feats [of the Buddha and his disciples]', there is a story about how the Buddha described how the wheel of life should be painted over the gateway of the Veḷuvana Vihāra at Rājagṛha:

> 'The Elder Moggallāna or a bhikkhu like him cannot be at many places (at the same time for teaching people). Therefore, in the (monastery) gateways a wheel having five sections should be made.' Thus the Lord laid down that a wheel with five sections should be made (whereupon it was remarked:) 'But the bhikkhus do not know what

sort of wheel should be made.'

The Lord explained: 'The five bourns should be represented – the hellish bourn, that of the animal kingdom, of ghosts, of men, and the bourn of the gods. In the lower portion (of the wheel), the hells are to be shown, together with the animal-kingdom and the realm of the ghosts, while in the upper portion gods and men should be represented. The four continents should also be depicted, namely, Pubbavideha, Aparagoyāna, Uttarakuru and Jambudīpa. In the middle, greed, aversion and delusion must be shown, a dove symbolizing greed, a snake symbolizing aversion, and a hog, delusion. Furthermore, the Buddhas are to be painted (surrounded by their) halos pointing out (the way to) Nibbāna. Ordinary beings should be shown as by the contrivance of a water-wheel they sink (to lower states) and rise up again. The space around the rim should be filled with (scenes teaching) the twelve links of Dependent Arising in the forward and reversed order. (The picture of the Wheel) must show clearly that everything, all the time, is swallowed by impermanence and the following two verses should be added as an inscription:

Make a start, leave behind
(the wandering-on)
firmly concentrate upon the
Buddha's Teaching.

As He, Leader like an
elephant, did Nālāgiri rout,
so should you rout and
defeat the hosts of Death.

Whoever in this Dhamma-
Vinaya will go his way
ever vigilant and always
striving hard,
Can make an end of dukkha
here
and leave behind Saṃsāra's
wheel of birth and death.

Thus, at the instance of the bhikkhus, it was laid down by the Lord that the Wheel of Wandering-on (in birth and death) with five sections should be made in the gateways (of monasteries).

Translation by Ven. Pasadiko from the opening paragraphs of the *Sahasodgata Avadāna*, *Divyāvadāna* 21, Mithila Edition, pp. 185ff.

Later, in the *Visuddhimagga*, written in Sri Lanka in the fifth century CE, Buddhaghosa describes the wheel of life thus:

It is the beginningless round of rebirths that is called the 'Wheel of the round of rebirths' (saṃsāracakka).

> Ignorance (avijjā) is its hub because it is its root. Ageing-and-death (jarā-maraṇa) is its rim because it terminates it. The remaining ten links (of the dependent origination) are its spokes because ignorance is their root and ageing-and-death their termination.

Visuddhimagga 198 in Buddhaghosa, *The Path of Purification*, Bhikkhu Ñāṇamoli (trans.), Buddhist Publication Society, Kandy 1991, p. 193.

44 *The Awakening of Faith in the Mahāyāna* is a fifth-century Chinese Yogācāra work, a systemization of the teachings of the *Laṅkāvatāra Sūtra* which was traditionally said to have been translated from a Sanskrit original by the great Indian *ācārya* Aśvaghoṣa, but has more recently been shown to be the work of a Chinese author.

45 This essay appears in Edward Conze, *Thirty Years of Buddhist Studies*, Cassirer, London 1967, pp. 185–90.

46 See ibid., p. 185.

47
> As on the unwholesome plane hatred does not cling, does not stick to its object, so wisdom on the wholesome plane. As hate seeks for faults, even though they do not exist, so wisdom seeks for the faults that do exist. As hate leads to the rejection of beings, so wisdom to that of all conditioned things.

Buddhaghosa, *Visuddhimagga* 102, quoted in Edward Conze (trans.), *Buddhist Scriptures*, Penguin Books, London 1959, pp. 116–7; also Edward Conze, *Thirty Years of Buddhist Studies*, Cassirer, London 1967, pp. 186–7.

48 *Amṛta* does mean nectar or ambrosia, a meaning that goes back to the *Rigveda*, but the word also means 'deathless', the Pāli equivalent, *amata*, often being used in the Pāli canon to describe *nibbāna*. For example, in the *Ariyapariyesanā Sutta*, *Majjhima Nikāya* 26 (i.167), the Buddha explains how he managed to attain the deathless (*amata*) supreme security from bondage, *nibbāna*. See Bhikkhu Ñāṇamoli and Bhikkhu Bodhi (trans.), *The Middle Length Discourses of the Buddha*, Wisdom Publications, Boston 1995, p. 260; or I. B. Horner (trans.), *The Collection of the Middle Length Sayings*, vol. i, Pali Text Society, London 1976, p. 212.

49 See the *Dhammacakkappavattana Sutta*, *Saṃyutta Nikāya* v.421; Bhikkhu Bodhi (trans.), *The Connected Discourses of the Buddha*, Wisdom Publications, Boston 2000, p. 1844; or F. L. Woodward (trans.), *Book of the Kindred Sayings*, part 5, Pali Text Society, London 1979, p. 357; also I. B. Horner (trans.), *The Book of the Discipline*, part 4,

Pali Text Society, Oxford 1996, p. 15.

50 sGam.po.pa (Gampopa), *The Jewel Ornament of Liberation*, trans. H. V. Guenther, Rider, London 1970, p. 41.

51 This is from William Blake's 'Auguries of Innocence', a 132-line poem probably composed in the early years of the nineteenth century and found in what is called the Pickering Manuscript; the poem was not published until 1863.

> Joy & Woe are woven fine
> A Clothing for the soul divine
> Under every grief & pine
> Runs a joy with silken twine.

52 Sangharakshita (trans.), *Dhammapada*, Windhorse Publications, Birmingham 2001, verse 182 (*Complete Works*, Vol. 15).

53 See *Saṃyutta Nikāya* v.455–6 (56.47); Bhikkhu Bodhi (trans.), *Connected Discourses of the Buddha*, Wisdom Publications, Boston 2000, pp. 1871–2; or F. L. Woodward (trans.), *The Book of the Kindred Sayings*, part 5, Pali Text Society, London 1979, pp. 383–4. The Buddha uses the same metaphor in the *Bālapaṇḍita Sutta*, *Majjhima Nikāya* 129 (iii.170), though there it is to illustrate the amount of time it would take a 'fool' who had been born in a hell realm to regain the human state; see Bhikkhu Ñāṇamoli and Bhikkhu Bodhi (trans.), *The Middle Length Discourses of the Buddha*, Wisdom Publications, Boston 1995, pp. 1020–1; or I. B. Horner (trans.), *The Collection of the Middle Length Sayings*, Oxford 1993, vol. iii, pp. 214–5.

54 The teaching of the twelve cyclical *nidānas* has its origin in the Pāli canon; for example, sections 17–21 of the *Mahātaṇhāsaṅkhaya Sutta*, *Majjhima Nikāya* 38 (i.261–4). See Bhikkhu Ñāṇamoli and Bhikkhu Bodhi (trans.), *The Middle Length Discourses of the Buddha*, Wisdom Publications, Boston 1995, pp. 353–7; or I. B. Horner (trans.), *The Collection of the Middle Length Sayings*, vol. i, Pali Text Society, London 1976, pp. 318–9. Alternatively, the *Mahānidāna Sutta*, *Dīgha Nikāya* 15 (ii.55–9); see M. Walshe (trans.), *The Long Discourses of the Buddha*, Wisdom Publications, Boston 1995, pp. 223–4; or T. W. Rhys Davids (trans.), *Dialogues of the Buddha*, part 2, Pali Text Society, London 1971, pp. 50–5. For Sangharakshita's commentary, see chapter 2, 'The Dynamics of Being', in *What is the Dharma?*, *Complete Works*, vol. 3, pp. 192–204.

55 The distinction between the reactive and the creative process is considered in detail in Sangharakshita's lecture 'Mind – Reactive and Creative', in Sangharakshita, *Buddha*

Mind, Windhorse Publications, Birmingham 2001, pp. 35–66 (*Complete Works*, vol. 11).

56 See H. T. Francis and R. A. Neil (trans.), *The Jātaka*, vol. iii, Allen & Unwin, London 1973, no. 316, pp. 34–7.

57 An example of someone who was full of joy at the very idea that there was a Buddha in the world is Anāthapiṇḍika, who (according to the Pāli canon) lay awake all night in his excitement that the next day he might meet the Buddha. See Vinaya Piṭaka ii.154–7 (*Cullavagga* 6.4); I. B. Horner (trans.), *The Book of the Discipline*, part 5, Pali Text Society, London 1975, pp. 216–20. On the other hand, according to tradition, the first person whom the Buddha met on the road after his Enlightenment – his name was Upaka – despite being impressed by the Buddha's appearance, having questioned him and been told that he was indeed Enlightened, simply said, 'May it be so, friend,' and walked away. See *Ariyapariyesanā Sutta*, *Majjhima Nikāya* 26 (i.172); Bhikkhu Ñāṇamoli and Bhikkhu Bodhi (trans.), *The Middle Length Discourses of the Buddha*, Wisdom Publications, Boston 1995, pp. 263–4; or I. B. Horner (trans.), *The Collection of the Middle Length Sayings*, vol. i, Pali Text Society, London 1976, pp. 214–5. Another example of a less favourable response is that of Saccaka, a 'debater and clever speaker' who started out determined to get the better of the Buddha in argument, and had a very insolent style of questioning. At the end of the *sutta* he remarks how, 'assaulted by discourteous courses of speech', the colour of the Buddha's skin 'brightens, and the colour of his face clears, as is to be expected of one who is fully enlightened'. Then he announces, 'And now, Master Gotama, we depart. We are busy and have much to do.' See the *Mahāsaccaka Sutta*, *Majjhima Nikāya* 36 (i.238–51); see Bhikkhu Ñāṇamoli and Bhikkhu Bodhi (trans.), *The Middle Length Discourses of the Buddha*, Wisdom Publications, Boston 1995, pp. 332–43; or I. B. Horner (trans.), *The Collection of the Middle Length Sayings*, vol. i, Pali Text Society, London 1976, pp. 291–305.

58 The *Mahāparinibbāna Sutta* (Pāli) is the only detailed account we have of the last months of the Buddha's life. See *Dīgha Nikāya* 16 (ii.72–168); Maurice Walshe (trans.), *Long Discourses of the Buddha*, pp. 231–77; or T. W. Rhys Davids (trans.), *Dialogues of the Buddha*, part 2, Pali Text Society, London 1971, pp. 78–189. The *Mahāparinirvāṇa Sūtra* (Sanskrit) does not describe the Buddha's death at all, being mainly devoted to

lengthy doctrinal expositions. See Sangharakshita, *The Eternal Legacy*, Windhorse Publications, Birmingham 2006, pp. 218–29 (*Complete Works*, vol. 14).

59 *Mahāparinibbāna Sutta, Dīgha Nikāya* 16 (ii.134). See M. Walshe (trans.), *The Long Discourses of the Buddha*, Wisdom Publications, Boston 1995, p. 260; or T. W. Rhys Davids (trans.), *Dialogues of the Buddha*, part 2, Pali Text Society, London 1971, pp. 145–6.

60 The whole story is told in the *Mahāparinibbāna Sutta, Dīgha Nikāya* 16 (ii.99–168). See M. Walshe (trans.), *The Long Discourses of the Buddha*, Wisdom Publications, Boston 1995, pp. 244–77; or T. W. Rhys Davids (trans.), *Dialogues of the Buddha*, part 2, Pali Text Society, London 1971, pp. 106–91.

61 The fourteen 'inexpressibles' are listed in various locations in the Pāli canon – for example in the *Aggivacchagotta Sutta, Majjhima Nikāya* 72 (i.484–5), in which the Buddha is asked a whole range of speculative questions of this kind by the wanderer Vacchagotta. The question of the Buddha's nature after death crops up in the seventh, eighth, and ninth inexpressibles; see Bhikkhu Ñāṇamoli and Bhikkhu Bodhi (trans.), *The Middle Length Discourses of the Buddha*, Wisdom Publications, Boston 1995, pp. 591; or I. B. Horner (trans.), *The Collection of the Middle Length Sayings*, vol. ii, Pali Text Society, Oxford 1994, pp. 164–5.

62 For details of the source of this tradition, see Reginald Ray, *Buddhist Saints in India*, Oxford University Press, Oxford 1994, p. 326.

63 H. V. Guenther, *Philosophy and Psychology in the Abhidhamma*, Shambhala Publications, Berkeley and London 1976, p. 146.

64 Lama Govinda discusses the 'unfoldment of inner space' in *Foundations of Tibetan Mysticism*, Rider, London 1969, p. 117.

65 This was the occasion when Sangharakshita received the Vajrasattva *abhiṣeka* from Dudjom Rimpoche; see Sangharakshita, *Precious Teachers*, Windhorse Publications, Birmingham 2007, p. 114 (*Complete Works*, vol. 22).

66 Frances Fremantle and Chögyam Trungpa (trans.), *The Tibetan Book of the Dead*, Shambhala Publications, Berkeley and London 1975, p. 17.

67 There are various traditional Buddhist accounts of the evolution of the universe; for example, the Pāli canon's *Aggañña Sutta*: 'On the Knowledge of Beginnings', *Dīgha Nikāya* 27; M. Walshe (trans.), *The Long Discourses of the Buddha*, Wisdom Publications, Boston 1995,

pp. 407–15; or T. W. Rhys Davids (trans.), *Dialogues of the Buddha*, part 3, Pali Text Society, London 1971, pp. 77–94; and a dramatically told account of the 'Genesis of the World' in J. J. Jones (trans.), *Mahāvastu*, vol. i, Pali Text Society, London 1987, pp. 285–301. Elements of this account of the 'fire-mist' are given in Evans-Wentz's introduction to his edition of *The Tibetan Book of the Dead*; see Kazi Dawa-Samdup (trans.), *The Tibetan Book of the Dead*, Munshiram Manoharlal Publishers, New Delhi 2000, p. 8.

68 This is the *Diamond Sūtra*, one of the two Buddhist texts Sangharakshita first came across and which convinced him he was a Buddhist. (See Sangharakshita, *The Rainbow Road*, Windhorse Publications, Birmingham 1997, p. 80 (*Complete Works*, vol. 20.) For Sangharakshita's commentary on the text see *Wisdom Beyond Words*, Windhorse Publications, Birmingham 1993, pp. 37–180 (*Complete Works*, vol. 14).

69 This is a reference to two lines in the second verse of Rudyard Kipling's 1910 poem 'If':

> If you can meet with
> Triumph and Disaster
> And treat those two
> impostors just the same,...

70 The methods of overcoming the hindrances, including 'cultivating the opposite', are described, with similes, in the *Vitakkasaṇṭhāna Sutta*, *Majjhima Nikāya* 20 (i.119–22); I. B. Horner (trans.), *The Collection of the Middle Length Sayings*, vol. i, Pali Text Society, London 1976, pp. 152–6; or Bhikkhu Ñāṇamoli and Bhikkhu Bodhi (trans.), *The Middle Length Discourses of the Buddha*, Wisdom Publications, Boston 1995, pp. 211–14.

71 Garma C. C. Chang (trans.), *The Hundred Thousand Songs of Milarepa*, Shambhala Publications, Boulder and London 1999, p. 455. For Sangharakshita's commentary on the verse, see *Milarepa and the Art of Discipleship II*, *Complete Works*, vol. 19, pp. 160–5.

72 This was Kachu Rimpoche. The story of the banner of victory on the vihara roof is told in this volume pp. 24–5 and in *Precious Teachers*, Windhorse Publications, Birmingham 2007, chapter 8 (*Complete Works*, vol. 22); also Sangharakshita, *In the Realm of the Lotus*, Windhorse Publications, Birmingham 1995, p. 27 (*Complete Works*, vol. 26).

73 For a little more about this lama, see *Milarepa and the Art of Discipleship II*, *Complete Works*, vol. 19, pp. 160–1.

74 This was the 'Chini Lama'; for more about this incident,

see *Milarepa and the Art of Discipleship* II, *Complete Works*, vol. 19, p. 163.

75 A collection of these 'breathed-out' utterances is part of the *Khuddaka Nikāya* of the Sutta Piṭaka, and several English translations are available, for example John D. Ireland (trans.), *The Udāna and the Itivuttaka*, Buddhist Publication Society, Kandy 2007.

76 David Snellgrove's translation of Sarahapāda's *Dohākośa, The Treasury of Songs*, can be found in Edward Conze et al. (trans.), *Buddhist Texts Through the Ages*, Oneworld Publications, Oxford 1993, pp. 224–39. *The Hundred Thousand Songs of Milarepa* is available in English translation, most recently translated by Christopher Stagg (Shambhala Publications, Boulder 2017); for Sangharakshita's commentary on some of the songs, see *Complete Works*, vols. 18 and 19.

77 The early Buddhist tradition identified three 'unwholesome roots' (Pāli *akusala-mūla*): greed, hatred, and delusion or ignorance. For example, in the *Itivuttaka* (section 50, in the Chapter of the Threes), the Buddha is represented as saying, 'Bhikkhus, there are these three unwholesome roots. What three? The unwholesome root greed, the unwholesome root hate, and the unwholesome root delusion.' John D. Ireland (trans.), The *Udāna and Itivuttaka*, Buddhist Publication Society, Kandy 1997, p. 186. It was the Mahāyāna tradition that began to call them the 'three poisons' (Sanskrit *triviṣa*), and to these three it added two more, pride and jealousy, arriving at the list of five poisons (*pañca kleśaviṣa*).

78 See, for example, *Saṃyutta Nikāya* iii.48 (22.49), where the Buddha is represented as asking Soṇa whether 'any ascetics and brahmins' can consider themselves as superior, inferior, or equal on the basis of any of the five *skandhas* (Pāli *khandas*):

> Soṇa, when any ascetics or brahmins, on the basis of form – which is impermanent, suffering, and subject to change – regard themselves thus: 'I am superior,' or 'I am equal,' or 'I am inferior,' what is that due to apart from not seeing things as they really are?

See Bhikkhu Bodhi (trans.), *The Connected Discourses of the Buddha*, Wisdom Publications, Boston 2000, p. 887; or F. L. Woodward (trans.), *The Book of the Kindred Sayings*, vol. iii, Pali Text Society, London 1975, p. 42. In a note in the *Connected Discourses* (p. 355), Bhikkhu Bodhi gives some other sources and also explains how it is shown that the three become ninefold, because each triad may be entertained by one who is truly better, truly equal, or truly worse. See also *Aṅguttara Nikāya* vi.49; Bhikkhu Bodhi (trans.), *Numerical Discourses of the Buddha*, Wisdom Publications, Boston 2012, p. 985; or E. M. Hare, *The Book of the Gradual Sayings*, vol. iii, Pali Text Society, Oxford 1995, p. 255.

79 See Lama Govinda, *Foundations of Tibetan Mysticism*, Rider, London 1969, p. 120.

80 See *Mahā-assapura Sutta*, *Majjhima Nikāya* 39 (i.276–9); Bhikkhu Ñāṇamoli and Bhikkhu Bodhi (trans.), *The Middle Length Discourses of the Buddha*, Wisdom Publications, Boston 1995, pp. 366–7; or I. B. Horner (trans.), *The Collection of the Middle Length Sayings*, vol. i, Pali Text Society, London 1976, pp. 329–30.

81 *Udāna* 8.3. Peter Masefield (trans.), *The Udāna*, Pāli Text Society, Oxford 1994, p. 166.

82 *Dhammapada* 189–92, trans. Sangharakshita.

83 For original texts, see the *Larger Sukhāvatī-vyūha*, *Smaller Sukhāvatī-vyūha*, and the *Amitāyur-dhyāna Sūtra* in *Buddhist Mahāyāna Texts*, ed. E. B. Powell, Dover Publications, New York 1969; and for text and commentary, see Ratnaguna and Śraddhāpa, *Great Faith, Great Wisdom*, Windhorse Publications, Cambridge 2016.

84 This well-known story is also told in, for example, Edward Conze, *Buddhism: Its Essence and Development*, Windhorse Publications, Birmingham 2001, p. 63.

85 Sangharakshita first spoke on the topic of the higher evolution in his 1966 lecture 'Evolution: Lower and Higher'. Many of his subsequent talks about evolution are to be found in *Complete Works*, vol. 3.

86 In Tantric yoga, the thousand-petalled lotus is said to represent the crown chakra, and in Buddhism the flowering of that lotus is seen as synonymous with Enlightenment.

87 It was Dhardo Rimpoche who helped with the translation, as mentioned in section 11 of Sangharakshita, *The History of My Going for Refuge*, Windhorse Publications, Cambridge 2010, p. 63 (*Complete Works*, vol. 2, pp. 443ff).

88 See Yeshe Tsogyal, *The Life and Liberation of Padmasambhava*, Dharma Publishing, Emeryville 1978; or Yeshe Tsogyal, *The Lotus-Born: The Life Story of Padmasambhava*, Rangjung Yeshe Publications, Boulder 2004.

89 Sangharakshita describes various forms of this meditation in chapter 11, 'The

Threefold Path: Meditation', in *What is the Dharma?* (*Complete Works*, vol. 3, pp. 344–6). For traditional descriptions, see, for example, sections 7–10 of the *Mahāsatipaṭṭhāna Sutta*, *Dīgha Nikāya* 22 (ii.295–7); see M. Walshe (trans.), *The Long Discourses of the Buddha*, Wisdom Publications, Boston 1995, pp. 338–9; or T. W. Rhys Davids (trans.), *Dialogues of the Buddha*, part 2, Pali Text Society, London 1971, p. 332; also Buddhaghosa, *Visuddhimagga* 178–96 in Bhikkhu Ñāṇamoli (trans.), *The Path of Purification*, Buddhist Publication Society, Kandy 1991, pp. 173–90.

90 Hans Holbein the Younger's sequence of woodcuts of the Dance of Death were made in the 1520s and first published in book form in 1538. See Hans Holbein, *The Dance of Death*, Penguin Books, 2016.

91 For more on the eight consciousnesses, see Sangharakshita, *The Meaning of Conversion in Buddhism*, Windhorse Publications, Birmingham 1994, pp. 66–9 (*Complete Works*, vol. 2, pp. 278–83).

92 See, for example, canto 22 of Yeshe Tsogyal, *The Life and Liberation of Padmasambhava*, Dharma Publishing, Emeryville 1978, pp. 142–3.

93 Carl Jung's writings on the anima and animus are to be found in C. G. Jung, *Collected Works*, volume 9, part 2, chapter 3.

94 The story of this event (which took place in Los Angeles) is told in Michael Schumacher, *Dharma Lion: a critical biography of Allen Ginsberg*, St Martin's Press, London 1992, p. 242. For a little about Sangharakshita's connection with Ginsberg, see 'With Allen Ginsberg in Kalimpong', in Sangharakshita, *The Priceless Jewel*, Windhorse Publications, Glasgow 1993, pp. 215–8 (*Complete Works*, vol. 22); and Sangharakshita's poem, 'In Memory of Allen Ginsberg', in *The Call of the Forest*, Windhorse Publications, Birmingham 2000, pp. 14–15 (*Complete Works*, vol. 25).

95 To take one of very many examples, see the *Tevijja Sutta*, *Dīgha Nikāya* 13; Maurice Walshe, *The Long Discourses of the Buddha*, Wisdom, Boston 1995, p. 195:

> Excellent, Reverend Gotama, excellent! It is as if someone were to set up what had been knocked down, or to point out the way to one who had got lost, or to bring an oil-lamp into a dark place, so that those with eyes could see what was there. Just so the Reverend Gotama has expounded the Dhamma in various ways.

See also T. W. Rhys Davids (trans.), *Dialogues of the*

Buddha, part 1, Pali Text Society, London 1973, p. 332.

96 A parure is a set of jewellery intended to be worn together. The story of Visākha and her 'parure' is told in the *Dhammapada* commentary; see Eugene Watson Burlingame (trans.), *Buddhist Legends*, part 3, Pali Text Society, Luzac and Co., London 1969, pp. 59–84. See p. 66 for the account of the making of the 'great-creeper-parure' (which required four pint-pots of diamonds, eleven pint-pots of pearls, etc.). In fact we *are* told what happened to Visākha's donation; p. 79 describes how she gave its value to found a monastery.

97 For example, the *Mahāvastu Āvadāna*, describing stupa worship, says,

> Whoever shall there place garlands or perfumes or paint, or make salutation there or become in its presence calm in heart, that shall long be to them for a profit and a joy.

Quoted in Sangharakshita, *The Three Jewels*, Windhorse Publications, Birmingham 1998, p. 247 (*Complete Works*, vol. 2, p. 221).

98 The thirty-seven *bodhipakkhiyadhammas* ('wings of Enlightenment' or 'requisites of Enlightenment') are listed by the Buddha in, for example, the *Mahāparinibbāna Sutta*, *Dīgha Nikāya* 16 (ii.120). See M. Walshe (trans.), *The Long Discourses of the Buddha*, Wisdom Publications, Boston 1995, p. 253; or T. W. Rhys Davids (trans.), *Dialogues of the Buddha*, part 2, Pali Text Society, London 1971, p. 128. For Sangharakshita's comments on this passage, see his talk 'The Five Pillars of the FWBO', in *Complete Works*, vol. 12.

99 For more about the link between the senses and Amoghasiddhi, see Sangharakshita, *The Meaning of Conversion in Buddhism*, Windhorse Publications, Birmingham 1994, p. 70 (*Complete Works*, vol. 2, p. 280).

100 The chewing of betel nuts and leaves bound together with lime paste (paan) is an ancient custom throughout Asia; it is traditionally offered to the honoured guest, although its benefits have been questioned in more recent times: it is said to be addictive, and it also has the effect of staining the teeth red.

101 For more details, see chapter 6 of *Tibetan Buddhism*, pp. 85ff. above.

102 This is in the story called 'Rechungpa's Repentance'; see Garma C. C. Chang (trans.), *The Hundred Thousand Songs of Milarepa*, Shambhala Publications, Boston and London 1999, p. 450. For Sangharakshita's commentary, see *Milarepa and the Art of*

Discipleship II, *Complete Works*, vol. 19, p. 105.

103 Machig Labdrön (1055–1153) was a Tibetan woman who, in her youth, supported herself by reading the Perfection of Wisdom volumes. Patrons would employ her to read the texts aloud to gain merit, and she excelled at reading.... Reading these scriptures, she herself began to gain insight into the Perfection of Wisdom. Later she met an Indian teacher called Phadampa Sangye who taught her a form of the extraordinary meditation known as the Chöd rite.

Vessantara, *Female Deities in Buddhism*, Windhorse Publications, Birmingham 2003, p. 81.

104 See Nāgārjuna, *The Precious Garland and the Song of the Four Mindfulnesses*, trans. Jeffrey Hopkins and Lati Rimpoche with Anne Klein, Harper & Row, New York 1975, p. 18:

> Not drinking intoxicants, a good livelihood,
> Non-harming, considerate giving, honouring
> The honourable, and love –
> Practice in brief is that.

105 sGam.po.pa (Gampopa), *The Jewel Ornament of Liberation*, trans. H. V. Guenther, Rider, London 1970, pp. 94–5.

106 The *Ratana Sutta* is found at *Sutta-Nipāta* 2.1. This translation is by Sangharakshita, published in *Complete Poems 1941–1994*, Windhorse Publications, Birmingham 1995 (*Complete Works*, vol. 15).

107 This is from 'The Tale of Red Rock Jewel Valley' in Garma C. C. Chang (trans.), *The Hundred Thousand Songs of Milarepa*, Shambhala Publications, Boston and London 1999, p. 5. For Sangharakshita's commentary, see *Milarepa and the Art of Discipleship I*, *Complete Works*, vol. 18, p. 26.

108 *Sutta-Nipāta* 7.2:

> Easily known is the progressive one, easily known the one who declines. He who loves Dhamma progresses; he who hates it declines.

H. Saddhatissa (trans.), *Sutta-Nipāta*, Curzon Press, London 1985, p. 12.

109 For more about 'the release called the beautiful', see the Buddha's words in the *Pāṭika Sutta*, *Digha Nikāya* 24 (iii.34); M. Walshe (trans.), *The Long Discourses of the Buddha*, Wisdom Publications, Boston 1995, pp. 382–3; or T. W. Rhys Davids (trans.), *Dialogues of the Buddha*, part 3, Pali Text Society, London 1971, pp. 31–2. See also Sangharakshita, *The Three Jewels*, Windhorse

Publications, Birmingham 1998, p. 76 (*Complete Works*, vol. 2, p. 84). For a description of the eight *vimokṣas*, see Sangharakshita, *The Three Jewels*, Windhorse Publications, Birmingham 1998, pp. 135ff (*Complete Works*, vol. 2, pp. 143ff).

110 The description of the ascending scale of beauty in the *Symposium* (sections 210–2) was actually related (according to the *Symposium* itself) by a woman called Diotima of Mantinea, who is said by Socrates to have taught him the philosophy of love.

111 Vinaya Piṭaka ii.193–5 (*Cullavagga* 7.3); see I. B. Horner (trans.), *The Book of the Discipline*, part 5, Pali Text Society, London 1975, pp. 273–4. The mad elephant let loose by Devadatta (the elephant's name was Nālāgiri) was pacified by the Buddha.

112 Edmund Spenser, *The Faerie Queene* (1590): book 1, canto 9, stanza 41.

113 Philippians 4:7.

114 See Lama Anagarika Govinda, *Foundations of Tibetan Mysticism*, Rider, London 1969, p. 27.

115 Donald Lopez, *Prisoners of Shangri-la*, University of Chicago Press, 1998. Chapter 4 is devoted to a full examination of the ways in which this mantra has been misconstrued by westerners.

116 Doṇa was a Brahmin teacher who met the Buddha while he was travelling between Ukkaṭṭhā and Setavyā. Amazed by the superhuman signs evident in the Buddha's footprints, he followed them until he found the Buddha seated beneath a tree, whereupon he questioned him as to his true nature. This story is found in the *Doṇa Sutta*, *Aṅguttara Nikāya* iii.223; see Bhikkhu Bodhi (trans.), *The Numerical Discourses of the Buddha*, Wisdom Publications 2012, pp. 425–6; or F. L. Woodward (trans.), *The Book of the Gradual Sayings*, vol. ii, Pali Text Society, Oxford 1995, pp. 43–4.

117 For example, see the *Sāmaññaphala Sutta*, *Dīgha Nikāya* 2 (i.77); M. Walshe (trans.), *The Long Discourses of the Buddha*, Wisdom Publications, Boston 1995, p. 104; or T. W. Rhys Davids (trans.), *Dialogues of the Buddha*, part 1, Pali Text Society, London 1973, pp. 87–8. For another example, see the *Mahāsakuludāyi Sutta*, *Majjhima Nikāya* 39 (ii.17); Bhikkhu Ñāṇamoli and Bhikkhu Bodhi (trans.), *The Middle Length Discourses of the Buddha*, Wisdom Publications, Boston 1995, p. 643; or I. B. Horner (trans.), *The Collection of the Middle Length Sayings*, vol. ii, Pali

Text Society, Oxford 1994, pp. 217–8.

118 'Docetic' (from the Greek verb *dokein*, 'to seem') is a term used in Christian theology to describe those Christians who denied the reality of Christ's physical incarnation as a human being and claimed that his birth, life, death, and suffering were impossible for a divine being, and therefore only apparent and not real. About one hundred years after the death of the Buddha a major schism occurred within the sangha between the *sthaviras* (Pāli *theras*), or 'elders', and the *Mahāsaṅgha*, or 'great community'. After this time the latter, known as the Mahāsāṃghikas, produced several sub-sects, of which the Lokottaravāda was one. The main characteristic of Lokottaravādin thought was the view that all worldly (*laukika*) *dharmas*, or phenomena, are unreal, and only supramundane or transcendental (*lokottara*) *dharmas* are real; furthermore that the Buddha's body was entirely supramundane. See Sangharakshita, *A Survey of Buddhism*, Windhorse Publications, Birmingham 2001, p. 216 (*Complete Works*, vol. 1, pp. 189–90).

119 But see Paul Williams with Anthony Tribe, *Buddhist Thought: A complete introduction to the Indian tradition*, Routledge, London and New York, 2000, p. 129.

120 For example, at Vinaya Piṭaka i.21 (*Mahāvagga* 1.10) the Buddha is reported as saying, 'O monks, I am freed from all bonds, human and divine. You also are freed from all bonds, human and divine', which suggests that he saw their attainment as equal to his. The only difference was that the Buddha realized the truth first and the disciples realized it afterwards by following the Buddha's teaching (so that their Enlightenment was termed *anubodhi*, 'subsequent Enlightenment'). I. B. Horner (trans.), *The Book of the Discipline*, part 4, Pali Text Society, Oxford 1996, p. 28.

121 The *Lalitavistara Sūtra* is published as Gwendolyn Bays (trans.), *The Voice of the Buddha*, Dharma Publishing, Berkeley 1983.

122 To get a sense of Śākyamuni as the ideal Buddha in the *Lotus Sūtra*, see *The Drama of Cosmic Enlightenment*, chapter 2, Sangharakshita's commentary on the *White Lotus Sūtra*, in *Complete Works*, vol. 16, pp. 32ff.

123 The nineteenth-century writer was Brian Houghton Hodgson (1801–1894), the British Resident in Kathmandu from 1833, who became deeply interested in Himalayan culture and proficient in Pāli and Sanskrit. He collected the first Sanskrit text of the

Lotus Sūtra and acquired many Tibetan works; his collection of writings and drawings is now held by the Royal Asiatic Society in London. The Theosophist Madame Blavatsky picked up on his coinage 'Dhyani-Buddha' in, for example, *The Secret Doctrine*, in which she wrote 'Dhyani-Buddha is a Sanskrit compound term from *dhyāni* ('contemplative, one who meditates') and *buddha* (an 'awakened one' or 'the enlightened one'), which could be translated as 'Buddha of Contemplation'. Helena Petrovna Blavatsky, *The Secret Doctrine*, vol. i, Theosophical Publishing House, Wheaton 1993, p. 109.

124 *Aṅguttara Nikāya* v.33:

> The Lion: This, monks, is a name for the Tathāgata, the Arahant, the Fully Enlightened One. When, monks, the Tathāgata expounds the Dhamma in an assembly, that is his lion's roar.

See Bhikkhu Bodhi (trans.), *The Numerical Discourses of the Buddha*, Wisdom Publications, Boston 2012, p. 1362; or F. L. Woodward (trans.), *The Book of the Gradual Sayings*, vol. v, Pali Text Society, Oxford 1996, pp. 23–4. But would the Buddha ever literally have heard a lion roar? Quite possibly. The Asiatic lion formerly occurred in south-eastern Europe, the Black Sea basin, Caucasus, Mesopotamia, and much of India. Lions are depicted on top of some Aśoka pillars, for example the one at Sarnath.

125 The story of the Buddha, Māra, and the earth goddess seems first to have been introduced to the accounts of the Buddha's journey to Enlightenment in the Mahāyāna tradition's *Lalitavistara Sūtra*. For a translation, see Gwendolyn Bays (trans.), *The Voice of the Buddha*, vol. ii, Dharma Publishing, Berkeley 1983, pp. 481–2.

126 A stirring account of Siddhārtha leaving the palace is given in the *Mahāvastu*; see J. J. Jones (trans.), *Mahāvastu*, vol. ii, Pali Text Society, London 1987, pp. 155–6.

127 This is the windhorse. For another description, see *Milarepa and the Art of Discipleship* II, *Complete Works*, vol. 19, pp. 438–9.

128 See Ratnaguna and Śraddhāpa, *Great Faith, Great Wisdom*, Windhorse Publications, Cambridge 2016, which includes translations of Sanskrit versions of both *Larger* and *Shorter Sukhāvatī-vyūha Sūtras* which describe Sukhāvatī in lavish detail. For a survey of the Pure Land literature see Sangharakshita, *The Eternal Legacy*,

Windhorse Publications, Birmingham 2006, chapter 11 (*Complete Works*, vol. 14).

129 Clothes in the world certainly have no scent in themselves, but if a man permeates them with perfumes, then they come to have a scent. It is just the same with the case we are speaking of. The pure state of Suchness certainly has no defilement, but if it is permeated by ignorance, then the marks of defilement appear on it. The defiled state of ignorance is indeed devoid of any purifying force, but if it is permeated by Suchness, then it will come to have a purifying influence.

Aśvaghoṣa, *The Awakening of Faith in the Mahāyāna*, trans. Yoshiko S. Hakeda, Columbia University Press, New York 1967, p. 56.

130 For a canonical reference see *Mahā-assapura Sutta*, *Majjhima Nikāya* 39 (i.279); Bhikkhu Ñāṇamoli and Bhikkhu Bodhi (trans.), *The Middle Length Discourses of the Buddha*, Wisdom Publications, Boston 1995, p. 369; or I. B. Horner (trans.), *The Collection of the Middle Length Sayings*, vol. i, Pali Text Society, London 1976, p. 332. See also the *Mahāsakuludāyi Sutta*, *Majjhima Nikāya* 77 (ii.17); Bhikkhu Ñāṇamoli and Bhikkhu Bodhi (trans.), *The Middle Length Discourses of the Buddha*, Wisdom Publications, Boston 1995, pp. 642; or I. B. Horner (trans.), *The Collection of the Middle Length Sayings*, vol. ii, Pali Text Society, Oxford 1994, p. 217.

131 See sections 13 and 14 of the *Alagaddūpama Sutta*, *Majjhima Nikāya* 22 (i.134–5); Bhikkhu Ñāṇamoli and Bhikkhu Bodhi (trans.), *The Middle Length Discourses of the Buddha*, Wisdom Publications, Boston 1995, pp. 228–9; or I. B. Horner (trans.), *The Collection of the Middle Length Sayings*, vol. i, Pali Text Society, London 1976, pp. 173–4.

THE ESSENCE OF ZEN

132 This event is described in Sangharakshita, *The Rainbow Road from Tooting Broadway to Kalimpong*, *Complete Works*, vol. 20, p. 85.

133 This was Yogi C. M. Chen. Sangharakshita describes their relationship in *Precious Teachers*, Windhorse Publications, Birmingham 2007, pp. 142–51 (*Complete Works*, vol. 22).

134 In this context 'synoptic' could be said to mean broad, general, or comprehensive.

135 This is from Ralph Waldo Emerson's 1841 essay, 'Self-Reliance':

> A foolish consistency is the hobgoblin of little minds, adored by little statesmen and philosophers and divines.

136 Among many canonical references to the five *indriyas*, the *Indriyasaṃyutta* (*Saṃyutta Nikāya* v.193–243) describes them in various ways in a section on the faculties; see Bhikkhu Bodhi (trans.), *The Connected Discourses of the Buddha*, Wisdom Publications, Somerville 2000, pp. 1668–708, also F. L. Woodward (trans.), *The Book of the Kindred Sayings*, part 5, Pali Text Society, London 1979, pp. 169ff. See also 'The Five Spiritual Faculties', section 2 of chapter 3 in Sangharakshita, *A Survey of Buddhism*, Windhorse Publications, Birmingham 2001, pp. 315–30 (*Complete Works*, vol. 1, pp. 279–94).

137 *Saṃyutta Nikāya* v.115 (46.53); see Bhikkhu Bodhi (trans.), *The Connected Discourses of the Buddha*, Wisdom Publications, Somerville 2000, p. 1607; or F. L. Woodward (trans.), *The Book of the Kindred Sayings*, part 5, Pali Text Society, London 1979, p. 98.

138 See Sangharakshita, *A Survey of Buddhism*, chapter 3, sections 2 and 3, *Complete Works*, vol. 1, pp. 277–99.

139 See chapter 6, 'The Buddhism of Faith and Devotion', in Edward Conze, *Buddhism: Its Essence and Development*, Windhorse Publications, Birmingham 2001, pp. 120–34.

140 Wong Mou-lam and A. F. Price (trans.), *The Diamond Sūtra and the Sūtra of Hui-neng*, Shambhala Publications, Boston 2005, p. 94.

141 The threefold way – ethics, meditation, and wisdom – is the threefold division of the Noble Eightfold Path, sometimes called the threefold training. The Buddha is said to have expounded the threefold way many times during his last teaching tour; see, for example, the *Mahāparinibbāna Sutta*, *Dīgha Nikāya* 16 (ii.81): M. Walshe (trans.), *The Long Discourses of the Buddha*, Wisdom Publications, Boston 1995, p. 234; or T. W. Rhys Davids (trans.), *Dialogues of the Buddha*, part 2, Pali Text Society, London 1971, pp. 85–6.

142 In his *Buddhist Dictionary* (Buddhist Publication Society, Kandy 1980), Nyanatiloka translates *cetovimutti* (Pāli) as deliverance of mind, and *paññāvimutti* as deliverance through wisdom, saying that deliverance of mind, in the highest sense, is that kind of concentration (*samādhi*) which is bound up with the path of arhantship; and deliverance through wisdom is the knowledge (*ñāṇa*) bound up with the fruition of arhantship. These two deliverances are often paired – as in, for example, the *Mahāsīhanāda Sutta*, *Majjhima Nikāya* 12 (i.71), in which they are jointly described as the tenth of the ten powers of a Tathāgata:

> Realizing for himself with direct knowledge the Tathāgata here and now enters upon and abides in the deliverance of mind and deliverance by wisdom that are taintless with the destruction of the taints.

See Bhikkhu Ñāṇamoli and Bhikkhu Bodhi (trans.), *The Middle Length Discourses of the Buddha*, Wisdom Publications, Boston 1995, p. 166; or I. B. Horner (trans.), *The Collection of the Middle Length Sayings*, vol. i, Pali Text Society London 1976, p. 95.

143 Since these talks were given in 1966 very many more books on Zen have been published. For the works mentioned here see Charles Luk, *Ch'an and Zen Teaching* (vols. 1 to 3), Rider and Company, London 1960, 1961, 1962; Trevor Leggett, *First Zen Reader*, Charles E. Tuttle, Rutland, Vermont and Tokyo 1960; and Trevor Leggett, *The Tiger's Cave*, Routledge & Kegan Paul, London 1964.

144 The tradition of 'thirty blows' evidently originated with Zen master Tokusan (819–914), who gave the koan, 'Even though you can say something about it, I will give you thirty blows of the stick. And even if you can't say anything about it, I will also give you thirty blows of the stick.' See Philip Kapleau, *The Three Pillars of Zen*, Knopf Doubleday, New York 2013, p. 208.

145 In chapter 3 of *The Eternal Legacy*, Windhorse Publications, Birmingham 2006, p. 18 (*Complete Works*, vol. 14), Sangharakshita makes the point that

> the separation in respect of the two older Piṭakas, of Sūtra from Vinaya, corresponds to the even older distinction, in the Buddha's teaching itself, between Dharma, in the sense of a coherent body of spiritual teachings, and Vinaya, or those teachings practically applied, especially their ideal exemplification in the Buddha's own life.

Aspects of the Buddha's life story are told in the Vinaya Piṭaka; see I. B. Horner (trans.), *The Book of the Discipline*, part 4, Pali Text Society, Oxford 1996, especially *Mahāvagga* 1, which begins with the Buddha's Enlightenment and proceeds to describe many well-known incidents in the life of the Buddha (pp. 1–129), and *Mahāvagga* 10, which includes the story of the harmonious life of the Anuruddhas (pp. 501–3), the quarrel at Kosambi (pp. 503–5), and the Buddha's advice to Mahāpajāpatī (pp. 507–8).

146 Since this book was first published, many more translations of Mahāyāna

texts have become available, including *The Threefold Lotus Sutra* (Kosei Publishing, Tokyo, 1975), Schiffer and Tamura's revision of Soothill and Katō's translation of the *Saddharma Puṇḍarīka Sūtra*; Robert Thurman's translation of the *Vimalakīrti-nirdeśa* (*The Holy Teaching of Vimalakīrti*, Pennsylvania State University Press, University Park and London 1976); Emmerick's translation of the *Suvarṇabhāsottamasūtra* (*The Sūtra of Golden Light*, Pali Text Society, third edition, Oxford 2001); Thomas Cleary's translation of the *Avataṃsaka Sūtra* (*Flower Ornament Sūtra*, Shambhala Publications, Boston 1993); and Gwendolyn Bays' translation of the *Lalitavistara* (*The Voice of the Buddha*, Dharma Publishing, Berkeley 1983).

147 Both before and after this talk was given, Sangharakshita spoke and wrote a great deal about the tradition of ordination and the question of 'transmission', offering a substantial critique of the conventions; and when the Western Buddhist Order (later the Triratna Buddhist Order) was founded, one of its features was that it was 'neither monastic nor lay'. See, in particular, *The History of My Going for Refuge*, *Was the Buddha a Bhikkhu?*, and *Forty-Three Years Ago*, all in *Complete Works*, vol. 2.

148 Different sources give slightly different versions of this list.

149 The two names are simply different ways of transliterating the Patriarch's Chinese name into English. Huineng is now the standard spelling.

150 Phrases of this kind are usually associated with Socrates. For example, in Plato's *Apology* (21d), Socrates is quoted as saying (after a discussion with someone):

> I am wiser than this man, for neither of us appears to know anything great and good; but he fancies he knows something, although he knows nothing; whereas, as I do not know anything, I do not fancy I do. In this trifling particular, then, I appear to be wiser than he, because I do not fancy I know what I do not know.

151 See D. T. Suzuki (trans.), *The Laṅkāvatāra Sūtra*, George Routledge, London 1932, pp. 124–5.

152 This translation of the line from *The Awakening of Faith in the Mahāyāna* is taken from Dwight Goddard, *A Buddhist Bible*, Beacon Press, Boston 1966, p. 363.

153 See R. A. F. Thurman (trans.), *The Holy Teaching of Vimalakīrti*, Pennsylvania State University Press, University Park and London 1976, p. 77.

See also Sangharakshita, *The Inconceivable Emancipation*, *Complete Works*, vol. 16, pp. 548–9.

154 See C. M. Chen, *Buddhist Meditation, Systematic and Practical*, published by Dr Yutang Lin, El Cerrito 1989, pp. 27–8.

155 See, for example, D. T. Suzuki, *Outlines of Mahāyāna Buddhism*, Schocken Books, New York 1970, pp. 157–63, 'Ānanda's attempts to locate the soul'. Suzuki explains his use of the term 'soul' in a footnote on p. 53 of *Açvaghosha's Discourse on the Awakening of Faith in the Mahāyāna*, Open Court Publishing Company, Chicago 1900.

156
> Though one should conquer in battle thousands upon thousands of men, yet he who conquers himself is (truly) the greatest in battle.

Dhammapada 103.

> One is oneself one's own saviour (or: protector). What other saviour should there be? With oneself well-controlled, one finds a saviour (who is) hard to find.

Dhammapada 160.

> A man besmirches himself by the evil he personally commits. (Similarly) he purifies himself by personally abstaining from evil. Purity and impurity are matters of personal experience: one man cannot purify another.

Dhammapada 165.
All translations by Sangharakshita; see *Complete Works*, vol. 15.

157 This translation of the verse from the *Dao De Jing* is from Ch'u Ta-kao (trans.), *Tao Tê Ching*, Unwin Paperbacks, London 1985, p. 55.

158 These five factors are enumerated by the Buddha in the *Anupada Sutta*, *Majjhima Nikāya* (i.25–9); see Bhikkhu Ñāṇamoli and Bhikkhu Bodhi (trans.), *The Middle Length Discourses of the Buddha*, Wisdom Publications, Boston 1995, p. 899; or I. B. Horner (trans.), *The Collection of the Middle Length Sayings*, vol. iii, Pali Text Society, Oxford 1993, p. 78. See also Sangharakshita, *The Purpose and Practice of Buddhist Meditation*, Ibis Publications, Ledbury 2012, e.g. pp. 242–5 (*Complete Works*, vol. 5).

159 The Buddha refers to these four 'formless spheres' as 'liberations that are peaceful and immaterial, transcending forms' in the *Ākaṅkheyya Sutta*, *Majjhima Nikāya* 6 (i.33); see Bhikkhu Ñāṇamoli and Bhikkhu Bodhi (trans.), *The Middle Length Discourses of the Buddha*, Wisdom Publications, Boston 1995, p. 116; or I. B. Horner (trans.), *The Collection of the Middle Length Sayings*, vol. i,

Pali Text Society, London 1976, p. 42. The development of these highly refined levels of consciousness is explained in detail by Buddhaghosa at *Visuddhimagga* 326–40. See Bhikkhu Ñāṇamoli (trans.), *The Path of Purification*, Buddhist Publication Society, Kandy 1991, chapter 10 'The Immaterial States' pp. 320–36. For Sangharakshita's commentary on the *arūpa dhyānas*, see various passages in *The Purpose and Practice of Buddhist Meditation* (*Complete Works*, vol. 5).

160 Hampstead and Highgate are neighbouring districts of London.

161 'Has a dog Buddha-nature?' is the basis of the first koan in the collection *The Gateless Gate*: Case 1, 'Jōshū's Dog': 'A monk asked Jōshū in all earnestness, "Has a dog Buddha nature or not?" Jōshū said, "Mu!"' See, for example, Kōun Yamada, *Gateless Gate*, Center Publications, Los Angeles 1979, p. 13.

The koan 'Why did Bodhidharma come from the West?' occurs twice in *The Blue Cliff Record* (Cases 17 and 20) and in many other contexts in the Zen tradition. See Thomas and J. C. Cleary (trans.), *The Blue Cliff Record 1*, Shambhala Publications, Boulder and London, pp. 110–4 and pp. 129–38.

162 See Dwight Goddard (ed.), *A Buddhist Bible*, Beacon Press, Boston 1970, pp. 108–276.

163 This is a metaphor, not in any sense a statement about those 'at the very bottom of the Indian social system'. The Buddha was completely opposed to the caste system, despite the use of this symbol in Tantric Buddhism. In the *Vasala Sutta*, *Sutta-Nipāta* 1.7, the Buddha makes it clear that one's status in life is not to be decided by the caste assigned to one at birth but by one's virtuous deeds. See H. Saddhatissa (trans.), *The Sutta-Nipāta*, Curzon Press, London 1995, pp. 13–15. Elsewhere he affirms that he does not recognize himself as belonging to any caste: see the *Pūralāsa Sutta*, *Sutta-Nipāta* 3.4, in Saddhatissa's translation ibid., p. 51.

The order of *bhikkhus* and the order of *bhikkhunīs* ('monks' and 'nuns') which the Buddha founded admitted people from all four castes, as well as those regarded as outcastes, all of whom he taught equally, and all of whom were considered able to progress on the path to Enlightenment.

THE FWBO AND 'PROTESTANT BUDDHISM'

164 In chapter 3, section 4 of *A Survey of Buddhism*, *Complete Works*, vol. 1, p. 432.

165 Georg Christoph Lichtenberg, from 'Notebook J' (1789–93), in *Aphorisms*, Penguin Books, Harmondsworth 1990, p. 119.

166 Robert Stuart Clifton (1903–63), born in Birmingham, Alabama, went to the Far East to pursue his interest in Buddhism and was ordained in the Theravādin tradition, being given the name Sumangalo. He briefly established a Western Buddhist Order, as Sangharakshita explains in his memoir *Facing Mount Kanchenjunga*, Windhorse Publications, Glasgow 1991, pp. 366–70 (*Complete Works*, vol. 21, pp. 339–43).

167 *The Thousand-Petalled Lotus* was the original title of Sangharakshita's first volume of memoirs, published by Heinemann, London, in 1976. The publisher decided to drop the first part of the book, about Sangharakshita's childhood, and this part was later published (as *Learning to Walk*) by Windhorse Publications in 1990. The whole work was finally published in one volume, and this now appears as volume 20 of the *Complete Works*, *The Rainbow Road from Tooting Broadway to Kalimpong*.

168 Dharmachari Kulananda, 'Protestant Buddhism', *Religion*, vol. 22, January 1992, pp. 101–3.

169 Sangharakshita, *My Relation to the Order*, Windhorse Publications, Glasgow 1990, p. 35 (*Complete Works*, vol. 2, p. 537).

170 Thomas McEvilley, 'Plotinus and Vijnañāvāda Buddhism', in *Philosophy East & West* 30, no. 2, University Press of Hawaii, April 1980, pp. 181–94; Richard T. Wallis, 'Phraseology and Imagery in Plotinus and Indian Thought', in R. Baine Harris (ed.), *Neoplatonism and Indian Thought*, State University of New York Press, Albany 1990, pp. 101–20.

171 Carl Gustav Jung (1875–1961) was the Swiss founder of analytical psychology, initially working with Freud but then finding that his ideas and insights diverged from those of his teacher; his work includes many influential ideas: archetypes, the collective unconscious, animus and anima, individuation, synchronicity, the shadow, and many others. Frances A. Yates (1899–1981) was an English historian and writer of works on Neoplatonism, the Hermetic tradition, and other esoteric subjects. Edgar Wind (1900–70) was born in Germany but settled in England, where he became a professor of art history; he is best known for his work on allegory and pagan mythology.

172 Sangharakshita, *New Currents in Western Buddhism*, Windhorse Publications,

Glasgow 1990, pp. 18–19 (*Complete Works*, vol. 11).

173 The number of centres (now Triratna rather than FWBO) has grown over time; the current figure and a list of centres, groups, and retreat centres in various countries throughout the world can (at the time of writing, 2018) be found on the website www.thebuddhistcentre.com

174 Timothy Ward, *What the Buddha Never Taught*, Element Books, Shaftesbury 1990.

175 That account was eventually written and published as Sangharakshita, *Moving Against the Stream*, Windhorse Publications, Birmingham 2003 (*Complete Works*, vol. 23).

176 R. Sennett, *The Fall of Public Man*, Cambridge University Press, 1974, p. 4.

177 E. Shils, *Tradition*, Faber and Faber, London 1981, p. 11.

178 Ibid., p. 4.

179 Ibid., p. 43.

180 L. Dumont, 'A modified view of our origins: The Christian beginnings of modern individualism', in M. Carrithers, S. Collins, and S. Luke (eds.), *The Category of the Person*, Cambridge University Press, 1986, pp. 117–8.

181 L. Dumont, *Homo Hierarchicus*, Paladin, London 1962, p. 39.

182 Malcolm Woodfield (ed.), *Defending Romanticism: Selected Essays of John Middleton Murry*, Bristol Press, 1991 (paperback edition), p. 131.

183 *Saṃyutta Nikāya* iii.25 (22.22); for this translation see F. L. Woodward (trans.), *The Book of the Kindred Sayings*, part 3, Pali Text Society, London 1975, pp. 24–5; see also Bhikkhu Bodhi (trans.), *The Connected Discourses of the Buddha*, Wisdom Publications, Boston 2000, p. 871.

184 L. Dumont, 'A modified view of our origins: The Christian beginnings of modern individualism', in M. Carrithers, S. Collins, and S. Luke (eds.), *The Category of the Person*, Cambridge University Press, 1986, p. 95.

185 E. Shils, *Tradition*, Faber and Faber, London 1981, p. 11.

186 Ibid.

187 *Aṅguttara Nikāya* i.10: see Bhikkhu Bodhi (trans.), *The Numerical Discourses of the Buddha*, Wisdom Publications 2012, p. 97; or F. L. Woodward (trans.), *The Book of the Gradual Sayings*, vol. i, Pali Text Society, Oxford 2000, p. 8.

188 Edward Conze (trans.), *Buddhist Texts Through the Ages*, Oneworld Publications, Oxford 1993, p. 182.

189 E. Shils, *Tradition*, Faber and Faber, London 1981, p. 11.

190 For a discussion of the role of kingship in the Mahāyāna, see chapter 7, 'The Moral Order and its Upholders', in Sangharakshita,

Transforming Self and World, *Complete Works*, vol. 16, pp. 414–35. For Sangharakshita on 'Rousseauism', see, for example, *Ritual and Devotion in Buddhism*, Windhorse Publications, Birmingham 1995, pp. 15–16 (*Complete Works*, vol. 11):

> We must beware of a generalized romantic Rousseauism or old-fashioned communism: the notion that people would be really good and happy and healthy and positive and friendly, if you only removed the social restrictions; if you only changed the political system; if you only took them out of the big evil cities and settled them down in some Utopia or some Eden. This view is simply not justified. Although Buddhism suggests that the right conditions will help people develop in a positive way, changes in external conditions are not always enough.

191 For Sangharakshita's usage of the term 'true individual', see *What is the Sangha?* part 2, in *Complete Works*, vol. 3, pp. 467–517.

192

> The bee is constantly flying about from flower to flower, and in the same way, believe me, the soul must sometimes emerge from self-knowledge and soar aloft in meditation upon the greatness and the majesty of its God.

Teresa of Ávila, *The Interior Castle* (1577), 'The First Mansions', chapter 2 section 9.

193 S. Collins, *Selfless Persons*, Cambridge University Press, Cambridge 1982, p. 192.

194 *Anurādha Sutta*, *Saṃyutta Nikāya* iii.118; see Bhikkhu Bodhi (trans.), *The Connected Discourses of the Buddha*, Wisdom Publications, Boston 2000, p. 937; or F. L. Woodward (trans.), *The Book of the Kindred Sayings*, part 3, Pali Text Society, London 1975, p. 101.

195 *Saṃyutta Nikāya* iv.400–1 (44.10); see Bhikkhu Bodhi (trans.), *The Connected Discourses of the Buddha*, Wisdom Publications, Somerville 2000, pp. 1393–4; or F. L. Woodward (trans.), *Kindred Sayings*, part 4, Pali Text Society, London 1980, pp. 278–9.

196 For example, Nāgārjuna in the *Mūlamadhyamakakārikā* (section 18.6) says that

> 'The self" is conveyed and 'non self' is taught by buddhas; it is taught as well that neither self nor non self is the case.

Mark Siderits and Shōryū Katsura (trans.), *Nāgārjuna's Middle Way*, Wisdom

Publications, Somerville 2013, p. 198.

197 Karl Jaspers, *The Nature of Psychotherapy: a critical appraisal*, Manchester University Press, 1965, p. 1.

198 Daisetz Teitaro Suzuki, *The Essence of Buddhism*, The Buddhist Society, London 1946.

199 Vinaya Piṭaka ii.258–9 (*Cullavagga* 10.5). See I. B. Horner (trans.), *The Book of the Discipline*, part 5, Pali Text Society, London 1975, p. 359. See also *Aṅguttara Nikāya* iv.280, in Bhikkhu Bodhi (trans.), *The Numerical Discourses of the Buddha*, Wisdom Publications, Boston 2012, p. 1193; or E. M. Hare (trans.), *Gradual Sayings*, vol. iv, Pali Text Society, Oxford 1995, pp. 186–7.

200 Raimondo Pannikar, *The Silence of God: The Answer of the Buddha*, Orbis, New York 1989, p. 3.

201 Richard Gombrich and Gananath Obeyesekere, *Buddhism Transformed: Religious Change in Sri Lanka*, Motilal Banarsidass, Delhi 1988.

202 John Stevens, *Lust for Enlightenment: Buddhism and Sex*, Shambhala Publications, Boulder 1990.

203 Genesis 27:22.

204 The *filioque* dispute, which came to create a great conflict between Western Christianity and Eastern Christianity, centred on the question of whether or not the Latin word *filioque* (literally 'and from the son') should be included in the Creed, its inclusion or exclusion having implications for how the Holy Trinity was viewed. It was included in the original Niceno-Constantinopolitan Creed, and hence appears in the Nicene Creed of the Western Church, but was rejected by the Eastern Orthodox Church, which said that the Holy Spirit proceeded 'from the Father' and that there was no need for the addition of 'and from the Son'.

205 *Visuddhimagga* 110–17; see Bhikkhu Ñāṇamoli (trans.), *The Path of Purification*, Buddhist Publication Society, Kandy 1991, pp. 109–17; or Pe Maung Tin (trans.), *The Path of Purity*, Pali Text Society, London 1975, pp. 129–37.

206 Sangharakshita, *The Ten Pillars of Buddhism*, Windhorse Publications, Cambridge 2010, pp. 41–2 (*Complete Works*, vol. 2, p. 341).

207 Dharmachari Subhuti, *Buddhism For Today*, Windhorse Publications, Glasgow 1988, pp. 177–80.

208 Helmuth von Glasenapp, *Buddhism – a Non-Theistic Religion*, Allen & Unwin, London 1970.

209 Vinaya Piṭaka ii.207–35 (*Cullavagga* 8); see I. B. Horner (trans.), *The Book*

of the Discipline, part 5, Pali Text Society, London 1975, pp. 291ff.

210 This distinction between 'natural morality' (Pāli: *pakati-sīla*) and 'conventional morality' (*paññatti-sīla*) is found in the Theravādin commentarial tradition; for more about it, see Sangharakshita, *A Survey of Buddhism*, Windhorse Publications, Birmingham 2001, p. 170 (*Complete Works*, vol. 1, p. 145).

211 The reference is perhaps to Subhuti's statement that

> the Western Buddhist must ... look with a respectful but discriminating eye at the mass of tradition. He must be careful not to be seduced by the glittering but, to him, irrelevant cultural accretions; he must seek the genuine treasures which are present in all forms of Buddhism.

Dharmachari Subhuti, *Buddhism for Today*, Windhorse Publications, Glasgow 1998, p. 23.

212 See 'Light from Vatican II', in Sangharakshita, *The History of My Going for Refuge*, Windhorse Publications, Cambridge 2010, p. 86 (*Complete Works*, vol. 2, pp. 458–9).

213 Dharmachari Tejananda, 'Faith, Devotion and Ritual', in *Puja and the Transformation of the Heart*, Windhorse Publications, Glasgow 1987, p. 20.

214 Sangharakshita, *The History of My Going for Refuge*, Windhorse Publications, Cambridge 2010, pp. 63–6. See also chapter 6, 'The Four Foundation Yogas', in Sangharakshita, Tibetan Buddhism, this volume pp. 76ff; and chapter 4, 'The Cosmic Refuge Tree and the Archetypal Guru', in Sangharakshita, *Creative Symbols of Tantric Buddhism*, in this volume, pp. 191ff.

215 In more recent years, incense has tended not to be used in collective devotional practice – not for any ideological reason, but simply because some people find the smoke makes them cough.

216 Dharmachari Subhuti, *Buddhism For Today*, Windhorse Publications, Glasgow 1988, p. 60.

217 In 2018 the text of Triratna's main devotional ceremonies is available in twenty-eight languages, including Afrikaans, Welsh, Hungarian, Turkish, Chinese, and Hebrew; see Lokabandhu (ed.), *Buddhist ceremonies in several languages, as used in the Triratna Community*, Lulu 2014.

218 Sangharakshita (ed.), *Puja: The Triratna Book of Buddhist Devotional Texts*, Windhorse Publications, Cambridge 2012, p. 1.

219 Tejananda's essay, 'Faith, Devotion and Ritual', was published (along with an essay by Vessantara) in *Puja and the Transformation of the Heart*, Windhorse Publications, Glasgow 1987. Sangharakshita's own book, *Ritual and Devotion in Buddhism*, which is based on lecture and seminar material, was published by Windhorse Publications (Birmingham) in 1995, and is found in *Complete Works*, vol. 11.

220 The text of the *Tiratana Vandanā* is found in several places in the Pāli canon, notably in the *Mahāparinibbāna Sutta*, *Dīgha Nikāya* 16 (ii.93). See M. Walshe (trans.), *The Long Discourses of the Buddha*, Wisdom Publications, Boston 1995, p. 241; or T. W. Rhys Davids (trans.), *Dialogues of the Buddha*, part 2, Pali Text Society, London 1971, pp. 99–100.

The Sevenfold Puja used in the Triratna Buddhist Community is composed of verses from chapters 2 and 3 of Śāntideva's *Bodhicaryāvatāra*, as translated by Mrs Adrienne Bennett. For Sangharakshita's account of how this puja came to be composed, see Sangharakshita, *Ritual and Devotion in Buddhism*, Windhorse Publications, Birmingham 1995, pp. 39–40 (*Complete Works*, vol. 11). A shorter threefold puja, which reverences the Three Jewels and describes the traditional offerings of flowers, candles, and incense, was composed by Sangharakshita in the 1970s for the Finnish sangha, who found the Sevenfold Puja too elaborate. Sangharakshita remarked that 'Vajrabodhi, I remembered, had once told me about Finnish Friends who were not happy reciting the Sevenfold Puja because they were not actually offering mandarava flowers, lamps encrusted with jewels, etc.' (*Travel Letters*, Windhorse Publications, Glasgow 1985, p. 45; *Complete Works*, vol. 24.)

The dedication ceremony (which is still used for the dedication of new Triratna centres and at the start of retreats) was composed on the day of the ceremony for the opening on 6 April 1967 of the 'new Triratna Meditation and Shrine Room' which was the movement's first centre, in Monmouth Street, central London. See Sangharakshita, *Moving Against the Stream*, Windhorse Publications, Birmingham 2003, pp. 377–8 (*Complete Works*, vol. 23). The dedication ceremony is based on the Tibetan image of the mandala, with its surrounding circles of lotuses, *vajras*, and flames.

221 The lecture 'The Psychology of Ritual' appeared in print in Sangharakshita, *Ritual*

and Devotion in Buddhism, Windhorse Publications, Birmingham 1995, pp. 26–36 (*Complete Works*, vol. 11).

222 The 'Petrine communion' is the church founded by St Peter – that is, the Roman Catholic Church.

223 'Higher criticism' is a branch of literary analysis that investigates the origins of a text. Higher criticism, whether biblical, classical, Byzantine, or medieval, focuses on the sources of a document to determine who wrote it, when it was written, and where.

224 Chapter 8, 'Relics', in Giuseppe Tomasi di Lampedusa, *The Leopard*, first published in 1958.

225 See Sangharakshita, *Complete Poems 1941–1994*, Windhorse Publications, Birmingham 1995, pp. 272–3 (*Complete Works*, vol. 25).

226 The phrase 'make it new', discovered by Modernist poet Ezra Pound in a Chinese history (the phrase was said to have been the slogan of a Chinese ruler) is found in Pound's 'Canto 53' (first published in 1940), and became a kind of rallying cry for the Modernist movement. 'Behold, I make all things new' is the King James Bible's translation of Revelation 21:5.

227 Wilfred Cantwell Smith (1916–2000) was a Canadian professor of comparative religion. In his influential book *The Meaning and End of Religion* (Fortress Press, 1964, p. 50), he wrote:

> I have become strongly convinced that the vitality of personal faith, on the one hand, and, on the other hand (quite separately), progress in understanding – even at the academic level – of the traditions of other people throughout history and throughout the world, are both seriously blocked by our attempt to conceptualize what is involved in each case in terms of (a) religion.

228 What Sangharakshita means by the spiritual community, the group, and the true individual is explained in parts 1 and 2 of *What is the Sangha?* (*Complete Works*, vol. 3).

229 The higher evolution is one of the ways Sangharakshita has chosen to frame the process of spiritual development. For an outline, see Sangharakshita, *What is the Sangha?*, Windhorse Publications, Birmingham 2000, chapter 9, 'The Evolution of the Individual' (*Complete Works*, vol. 3, pp. 475ff).

230 Dharmachari Subhuti, *Buddhism For Today*, Windhorse Publications, Glasgow 1988, p. 108.

231 From 'Letter to Dr Zaehner', printed as an appendix to *The FWBO and 'Protestant Buddhism'* in this volume, p. 515.

232 Ibid., p. 517.

233 For a list of the sixty-two wrong views identified by the Buddha, see the *Brahmajāla Sutta*, *Dīgha Nikāya* 1 (i.12–38); M. Walshe (trans.), *The Long Discourses of the Buddha*, Wisdom Publications, Boston 1995, pp. 73–86; or T. W. Rhys Davids (trans.), *Dialogues of the Buddha*, part 1, Pali Text Society, London 1971, pp. 30–52.

234 See the *Alagaddūpama Sutta*, *Majjhima Nikāya* 22 (i.134–5); Bhikkhu Ñāṇamoli and Bhikkhu Bodhi (trans.), *The Middle Length Discourses of the Buddha*, Wisdom Publications, Boston 1995, pp. 228–9; or I. B. Horner (trans.), *The Collection of the Middle Length Sayings*, vol. i, Pali Text Society, London 1976, pp. 173–4.

235 2 Corinthians 3:6

236 Sangharakshita's 1948 essay 'Buddhism in Science' has now been published in *Early Writings 1944–1954*, Ibis Publications, Ledbury 2014; for this extract, see pp. 178–9 (*Complete Works*, vol. 7).

237 For example, there was Meghiya, who would not listen to the Buddha's advice; see *Meghiya Sutta*, *Udāna* 4.1 in John D. Ireland (trans.), *The Udāna and the Itivuttaka*, Buddhist Publication Society, Kandy 1997, pp. 50–4. There was the quarrel at Kosambi, where an intemperate dispute broke out among the Buddha's disciples: *Kosambiya Sutta*, *Majjhima Nikāya* 48 (i.320–5); see Bhikkhu Ñāṇamoli and Bhikkhu Bodhi (trans.), *The Middle Length Discourses of the Buddha*, Wisdom Publications, Boston 1995, pp. 419–23; or I. B. Horner (trans.), *The Collection of the Middle Length Sayings*, vol. i, Pali Text Society, London 1976, pp. 383–8. The most serious incidents occurred at the instigation of the Buddha's cousin Devadatta, whose actions were calculated to cause a schism in the sangha, as described at *Itivuttaka* 18 and elsewhere; see, for example, John D. Ireland (trans.), *The Udāna and the Itivuttaka*, Buddhist Publication Society, Kandy 1997, pp. 162–3; see also Vinaya Piṭaka ii.188 (*Cullavagga* 7.3) in I. B. Horner (trans.), *The Book of the Discipline*, part 5, Pali Text Society, London 1975, p. 264.

238 *Brahmajāla Sutta*, *Dīgha Nikāya* 1 (i.19):

> And then, monks, that being who first arose there thinks: 'I am Brahma, the Great Brahma, the Conqueror, the Unconquered, the All-Seeing, the All-Powerful, the Lord, the Maker and Creator, Ruler, Appointer and Orderer, Father of All That Have Been and Shall Be. These beings were created

> by me. How so? Because I first had this thought: "Oh, if only some other beings would come here!" That was my wish, and then these beings came into existence!'

This translation is from M. Walshe (trans.), *The Long Discourses of the Buddha*, Wisdom Publications, Boston 1995, p. 76; see also T. W. Rhys Davids (trans.), *Dialogues of the Buddha*, part 1, Pali Text Society, London 1973, p. 32.

239 Dharmachari Subhuti, *Buddhism For Today*, Windhorse Publications, Glasgow 1988, p. 77.

240 *Aspects of Buddhist Morality* is included in *Complete Works*, vol. 11; *Vision and Transformation* (later retitled *The Buddha's Noble Eightfold Path*) in vol. 1; and *The Ten Pillars of Buddhism* in vol. 2. To these three works completely devoted to ethics can be added *Living Ethically*, Windhorse Publications, Cambridge 2009 (*Complete Works*, vol. 17), which is Sangharakshita's commentary on Nāgārjuna's *Precious Garland*.

241 Sangharakshita, *The Ten Pillars of Buddhism*, Windhorse Publications, Cambridge 2010, p. 7 (*Complete Works*, vol. 2, pp. 318–9).

242 Dharmachari Subhuti, *Buddhism For Today*, Windhorse Publications, Glasgow 1988, pp. 165–7.

243 See 'Rights and Duties' in Sangharakshita, *Crossing the Stream*, Windhorse Publications, Birmingham 1996, pp. 35–40 (*Complete Works*, vol. 7).

244 Ibid., pp. 37–8.

245 John Macquarrie, *Mary for all Christians*, Collins, London 1990, p. 19.

246 See the *Sigālaka Sutta* (also known as the *Sigālovāda Sutta*), *Dīgha Nikāya* 31 (iii.180–93); M. Walshe (trans.), *The Long Discourses of the Buddha*, Wisdom Publications, Boston 1995, pp. 461–9; or T. W. Rhys Davids (trans.), *Dialogues of the Buddha*, part 3, Pali Text Society, London 1971, pp. 173–84. For Sangharakshita's commentary on the text, see *What is the Sangha?* part 3, 'The Network of Human Relationships', *Complete Works*, vol. 3, pp. 521ff.

247 Subhuti's talks on friendship were edited and published as Dharmachari Subhuti, *Buddhism and Friendship*, Windhorse Publications, Birmingham 2004.

248 Ephesians 5:3:

> But fornication and all uncleanness or covetousness, let them not once be named among you, as becometh saints.

King James Bible.

249 Stuart Miller, *Men and Friendship*, Gateway Books, London 1983, p. 3.

250 Ibid., p. 4.

251 See the discussion of the third precept in Sangharakshita, *The Ten Pillars of Buddhism*, Windhorse Publications, Cambridge 2010, pp. 87–92 (*Complete Works*, vol. 2, pp. 370–3).

252 Vegetarian restaurants have come and gone throughout Triratna's history. At the time of writing (2018), there are vegetarian cafés run by Sheffield and Manchester Buddhist centres and various Buddhafield teams who cater for festivals throughout the summer. Vegetarianism – and veganism – is still very much an expression of the Triratna Community's commitment to the first precept; for an overview, see Bodhipaksa, *Vegetarianism: a Buddhist View*, Windhorse Publications, Cambridge 2009.

253 For this list of kinds of wrong livelihood, see, for example, *Aṅguttara Nikāya* iii.208; Bhikkhu Bodhi (trans.), *The Numerical Discourses of the Buddha*, Wisdom Publications, Boston 2012, p. 790; or E. M. Hare (trans.), *The Book of the Gradual Sayings*, vol. iii, Pali Text Society, Oxford 1995, p. 153.

254 Triratna right livelihood businesses have appeared and disappeared over the years, and at the time of writing (2018), most of the businesses mentioned here are no more – the publishing house being a notable and obvious exception! At present, right livelihood businesses around Triratna include Evolution Arts in Brighton, the Earth Cafe in Manchester, the Dāna Cafe in Sheffield, and New View Residential, an ethical letting agency in Cambridge, Lama's Pyjamas in East London, and an arts centre as well as outreach in the form of Breathworks, Wildmind, freebuddhistaudio, and the running of websites, urban Buddhist centres and retreat centres.

255 See the introduction to chapter 7, 'Perfect Awareness: the Levels of Awareness', in Sangharakshita, *The Buddha's Noble Eightfold Path*, *Complete Works*, vol. 1, p. 572.

256 Dharmachari Subhuti, *Buddhism For Today*, Windhorse Publications, Glasgow 1988, p. 176.

257 See Eugene Watson Burlingame (trans.), *Buddhist Legends*, part 3, Pali Text Society, Luzac and Co., London 1969, pp. 2–4. See also Sir Edwin Arnold, *The Light of Asia*, Book the Seventh, for a poetic version of this episode.

258 Mark 3:21 in Andy Gaus (trans.), *The Unvarnished Gospels*, Putney, Vermont 1988, p. 76.

259 This is a line from John Milton's Sonnet 12, which, along with Sonnet 11, was probably written early in 1646, as a satirical response to the widely negative reception enjoyed by his divorce tracts, *The Doctrine and Discipline of Divorce*, *Tetrachordon*, and *The Judgement of Martin Bucer*. In what scans like a Petrarchan love sonnet, Milton responds with ridicule and acid sarcasm to those who attacked his treatises from the pulpit. He pokes fun at the ignorance of those who cannot even pronounce the title, let alone follow the arguments.

260 John Milton, Sonnet 12.

261

> Just as in the great ocean there is but one taste – the taste of salt – so in this Doctrine and Discipline (dhammavinaya) there is but one taste – the taste of freedom.

This is the sixth of the eight qualities of the great ocean described by the Buddha in the *Uposatha Sutta*, *Udāna* 5.5; see John D. Ireland (trans.), *The Udāna and the Itivuttaka*, Buddhist Publication Society, Kandy 2007, p. 68. See also Sangharakshita's talk 'The Taste of Freedom' in the book of that title (*Complete Works*, vol. 11).

262 A detailed description of the spiral path is included in chapter 7, 'The Spiral Path', in Sangharakshita, *What is the Dharma?* (*Complete Works*, vol. 3); also Sangharakshita, *The Three Jewels*, Windhorse Publications, Birmingham 1998, chapter 13 (*Complete Works*, vol. 2, pp. 101ff). A canonical reference to the twelve positive *nidānas* occurs in the *Upanisa Sutta*, *Saṃyutta Nikāya* ii.29–31 (12.23); see Bhikkhu Bodhi (trans.), *The Connected Discourses of the Buddha*, Wisdom Publications, Boston 2000, p. 554; or C. A. F. Rhys Davids (trans.), *The Book of the Kindred Sayings*, part 2, Pali Text Society, Oxford 1997, pp. 25–7.

263 See Sangharakshita, *The Taste of Freedom*, chapter 1 (*Complete Works*, vol. 11) in which these three fetters, traditionally identified as fixed self-view, doubt, and dependence on rules and rituals as ends in themselves, are described as habit, vagueness, and superficiality. These are the first three of ten fetters identified by the Buddha; for a canonical reference, see, for example, *Saṃyutta Nikāya* v.61 (45.179–80); Bhikkhu Bodhi (trans.), *The Connected Discourses of the Buddha*, Wisdom Publications, Boston 2000, pp. 1565–6; or F. L. Woodward (trans.), *Kindred Sayings*, part 5, Pali Text Society, London 1979, p. 224.

264 Edward Shils, *Tradition*, The University of Chicago Press, 1981, p. 43.

265 The writer Gertrude Stein (1874–1946) came up with

various meanings for this phrase of hers, which has been quoted and parodied by many writers, poets, and songwriters.

266 Dharmachari Subhuti, *Buddhism For Today*, Windhorse Publications, Glasgow 1988, p. 180.

267 Sangharakshita's *Buddhism and Blasphemy* was written in response to the prosecution of the magazine *Gay News* in 1977. Published as a booklet in 1978 it now appears in *Complete Works*, vol. 11.

268 *Dhammapada* 348.

269 Reported by Sanit Ekachai, 'Buddhism and Prostitution', Bangkok Post, 11 February 1991. Reprinted in *NIBWA Newsletter on International Buddhist Women's Activities*, no. 27, April–June 1991.

270 The French poet in question was Paul Verlaine, the sixth verse of whose 1884 poem 'L'Art Poétique' is 'Prends l'éloquence et tords-lui son cou!' – 'Take rhetoric and wring its neck!' Sangharakshita's aphorism is quoted in the collection *A Stream of Stars*, Windhorse Publications, Birmingham 1998, p. 91 (*Complete Works*, vol. 26) and adds: 'Charisma, one might add, is the psychological equivalent of rhetoric.'

271 This is one of the 'four great reliances' listed in the *Vimalakīrti-nirdeśa*. See R. A. F. Thurman (trans.), *The Holy Teaching of Vimalakīrti*, Pennsylvania State University Press, University Park and London 1976, p. 99. For Sangharakshita's commentary on the first great reliance – 'one should rely on the Dharma, not on any person' – see chapter 8, 'The Four Great Reliances: Criteria for the Spiritual Life', in Sangharakshita, *The Inconceivable Emancipation*, *Complete Works*, vol. 16, pp. 576–8.

272 Dharmachari Subhuti, *Buddhism For Today*, Windhorse Publications, Glasgow 1988, pp. 176–82.

273 'The Grand Inquisitor' is a poem or parable recited by the character Ivan in Fyodor Dostoyevsky's 1880 novel *The Brothers Karamazov*.

274 Raymond Williams, *Culture and Society 1780–1950*, Penguin Books, Harmondsworth 1979, p. 17.

275 These four lectures, 'Going for Refuge', 'Entering the Stream', 'The Arising of the Bodhicitta' and 'The Turning About in the Deepest Seat of Consciousness', were published in Sangharakshita, *The Meaning of Conversion in Buddhism*, Windhorse Publications, Birmingham 1994 (*Complete Works*, vol. 2, pp. 233–85).

276 See section 18, 'Levels of Going for Refuge', in Sangharakshita, *The History of My Going for Refuge*, Windhorse Publications, Cambridge 2010, pp. 119–26

(*Complete Works*, Vol. 2, pp. 479–83).

277 The reference to *Buddhism for Today*, p. 129, is a mystery, but it is possible that the phrase meant here is not 'spiritually-aware individual' but 'self-aware individual', as described by Subhuti earlier in the book; see Dharmachari Subhuti, *Buddhism for Today*, Windhorse Publications, Glasgow 1998, pp. 10–11.

278 This is the theme of *Dhammapada* chapter 26; for example: 'I call him a brāhmaṇa by whom no evil is done by the body, by speech, (or) by the mind, and who with regard to these three is restrained.... One is not a brāhmaṇa on account of matted hair, or (one's) clan, or birth. He in whom there exists both truth and principle (*dhamma*), *he* is pure, *he* is a brāhmaṇa.' Sangharakshita (trans.), *Dhammapada* 191 and 193, Windhorse Publications, Birmingham 2001 (*Complete Works*, vol. 15).

279 *Prajñā* is the direct intuitive apprehension of the real nature of things. This can be brought about, according to Buddhist tradition, in three stages: (1) listening to the Buddha's teachings, (2) reflecting upon them, (3) meditating upon them. For an account of these three stages see Sangharakshita, *What is the Dharma?*, Windhorse Publications, 1998, pp. 148–50 (*Complete Works*, vol. 3, pp. 301–4). The three levels of wisdom are enumerated in, for example, the *Saṅgīti Sutta*, *Dīgha Nikāya* 33 (iii.219); see M. Walshe (trans.), *The Long Discourses of the Buddha*, Wisdom Publications, Boston 1995, p. 486; or T. W. Rhys Davids (trans.), *Dialogues of the Buddha*, part 3, Pali Text Society, London 1971, p. 212.

280 This is the last line of the description of the Dharma in the *Tiratana Vandanā*. For Sangharakshita's commentary, see the introduction to *What is the Dharma?*, *Complete Works*, vol. 3, p. 263.

281 See Daisetz Teitero Suzuki, *Studies in the Laṅkāvatāra Sūtra*, Routledge & Kegan Paul, London 1972, pp. 104, 340, and 397–8.

282 This would have been the period in which the young Dennis Lingwood was 'becoming more attracted to the exotic in literature', as described in *The Rainbow Road from Tooting Broadway to Kalimpong*, *Complete Works*, vol. 20, p. 61. Pierre Loti (1850–1923) was a French naval officer and novelist whose works include novels set in Turkey, Israel, India, China, and Japan. Lafcadio Hearn (1850–1904) was of Irish and Greek descent and eventually settled in Japan. His literary works include *Gleanings in Buddha-fields*.

283 This article was reprinted in the 'Newsletter of the Friends of the Western Buddhist Order', number 62, published in Summer 1984, in an issue on the theme 'Sangharakshita: Twenty Years in the West', so that is probably where Philip Mellor found it.

284 Dharmachari Subhuti, *Buddhism For Today*, Windhorse Publications, Glasgow 1988, p. 99.

285 The Basilica della Santa Casa is now a place of pilgrimage in Loreto. Folklore relates how the house, in which Mary grew up in Nazareth, was miraculously carried to Italy (by way of Croatia) by four angels, towards the end of the Crusades.

286 See 'St Jerome Revisited' in Sangharakshita, *The Priceless Jewel*, Windhorse Publications, Glasgow 1993, pp. 86–8 (*Complete Works*, vol. 26).

287 This line comes from William Wordsworth's poem 'Tables Turned', whose seventh stanza is:

> Sweet is the lore which
> Nature brings;
> Our meddling intellect
> Mis-shapes the beauteous
> forms of things: –
> We murder to dissect.

288 See Edward Conze, *A Short History of Buddhism*, George Allen & Unwin, London 1980, p. 131.

289 Dharmachari Subhuti, *Buddhism For Today*, Windhorse Publications, Glasgow 1988, p. 25.

290 Malcolm Woodfield (ed.), *Defending Romanticism: Selected Essays of John Middleton Murry*, Bristol Press, Bristol 1991, p. 145.

291 Ibid., p. 183.

292 Robert Charles Zaehner (1913–1974), was a British scholar of Eastern religions. The book that prompted Sangharakshita's letter to him was his *Evolution in Religion: Study in Sri Aurobindo and Pierre Teilhard De Chardin*, Oxford University Press, Oxford 1971.

293 Sri Aurobindo, *The Life Divine*, first published in 1939.

294 For example, in chapter 12 of the *Saddharma Puṇḍarīka*, 'Devadatta', the Buddha says that in a former life, 'through the good friendship of Devadatta I was enabled to become perfect in the Six Pāramitās' and foretells that Devadatta will become a Buddha called Devarāja, 'King of the Gods'. See Bunnō Katō et al. (trans.), *The Threefold Lotus Sūtra*, Weatherhill, New York & Tokyo 1978, p. 209; or Leon Hurvitz (trans.), *Scripture of the Lotus Blossom of the Fine Dharma*, Columbia University Press, New York 1976, p. 196.

295 Sangharakshita, *A Survey of Buddhism*, chapter 1, section 14; see *Complete Works*, vol. 1, pp. 114–9.

296 The sequence of the positive *nidānas*, also sometimes

called the spiral path, begins when in dependence upon unsatisfactoriness (*duḥkha*) arises not craving (*tṛṣṇā*) but faith (*śraddhā*). A detailed description of this process is to be found in Sangharakshita, *The Three Jewels*, Windhorse Publications, Birmingham 1998, chapter 13, 'The Stages of the Path' (*Complete Works*, vol. 2, pp. 101–19); and chapter 7, 'The Spiral Path', in Sangharakshita, *What is the Dharma?* (*Complete Works*, vol. 3, pp. 258–79). A canonical reference to the twelve positive *nidānas* occurs in the *Upanisa Sutta*, *Saṃyutta Nikāya* ii.29–31 (12.23). See Bhikkhu Bodhi (trans.), *The Connected Discourses of the Buddha*, Wisdom Publications, Boston 2000, p. 554; or C. A. F. Rhys Davids (trans.), *The Book of the Kindred Sayings*, part 2, Pali Text Society, Oxford 1997, pp. 25–7.

297 Sangharakshita first spoke on the topic of evolution in his 1966 lecture 'Evolution: Lower and Higher'. Most of Sangharakshita's 1969 lecture series on 'The Higher Evolution of Man' now appear (in edited form) in *Complete Works*, vol. 3: see *Who is the Buddha?*, chapter 1, 'The Evolution of a Buddha' (pp. 3–17); *What is the Dharma?*, chapter 6, 'The Gravitational Pull and the Point of No Return' (pp. 241–57); chapter 7, 'The Spiral Path' (pp. 258–79); chapter 9, 'The Pattern of Buddhist Life and Work' (pp. 296–314); and chapter 11, 'The Cosmic Significance of the Bodhisattva Ideal' (pp. 363–84); and *What is the Sangha?*, chapter 8, 'The Path of Dissatisfaction' (pp. 459–64): the introduction to part 2 (pp. 467–74); chapter 9, 'The Evolution of the Individual'; chapter 11, 'Overcoming the Self' (pp. 493–504); and chapter 12, 'The Artist as the True Individual' (pp. 506–17). Volume 3 also contains some of the lectures in the 1970 series 'Aspects of the Higher Evolution of the Individual': the introduction to part 1 of *What is the Sangha?* (pp. 389–93); and also chapter 5, 'The Group and the Spiritual Community'; chapter 9, 'The Evolution of the Individual'; chapter 10, 'The Integrated Individual' (pp. 486–92): the introduction to part 3 (pp. 521–9); and chapter 14, 'Is a Guru Necessary?' (pp. 545–62). For the lecture titles, see the list of sources in vol. 3, pp. 695–7. The other (previously unpublished) lectures in the series appear in *Complete Works*, vol. 12. For full lists of the lectures in these series, and to listen to/read the text, go to www.freebuddhistaudio.com.

FROM GENESIS TO THE DIAMOND SŪTRA

298 *Dante's Dream* by the Pre-Raphaelite painter Dante Gabriel Rossetti was painted c.1869–71 and Henry Holiday's *Dante and Beatrice* is dated 1883. Both paintings are now in the collection of the Walker Art Gallery, Liverpool.

299 See Sangharakshita, *The Rainbow Road from Tooting Broadway to Kalimpong*, *Complete Works*, vol. 20, p. 73.

300 The line 'Infinite riches in a little room' comes from Act 1 of Christopher Marlowe's 1590 play *The Jew of Malta*.

301 Sangharakshita, *The Rainbow Road from Tooting Broadway to Kalimpong*, *Complete Works*, vol. 20, pp. 20–2.

302 In his *Pensées* (published posthumously in 1670) the French philosopher Blaise Pascal outlined his 'wager', arguing (to put it very briefly) that it is better to believe in the existence of God than not to do so, because if you are right, heaven is the reward for your faith, and if you are wrong, the mistake has cost you nothing. If, on the other hand, you stake your life on the non-existence of God and you are wrong, you are destined for hell.

303 John Bunyan's *The Holy War*, published in 1682, is an allegory which sets out to recall the fall and redemption of mankind under the guise of a besieged city.

304 Sangharakshita, *The Rainbow Road from Tooting Broadway to Kalimpong*, *Complete Works*, vol. 20, p. 45.

305 Revelation 21:21 (King James Bible).

306 Sangharakshita, *The Rainbow Road from Tooting Broadway to Kalimpong*, *Complete Works*, vol. 20, pp. 63–4.

307 See Sangharakshita, *The Rainbow Road from Tooting Broadway to Kalimpong*, *Complete Works*, vol. 20, p. 85.

308 Job 3:3–17, King James Bible.

309 Job 38:1–11.

310 Job 38:16–30.

311 Job 39:19–25.

312 Job 40:15–24.

313 Job 39:19–25.

314 Job 42:5–6.

315 A reference to the beginning of John Milton's *Paradise Lost*, in which the poet invokes the Heavenly Muse to help him 'assert Eternal Providence/ And justify the ways of God to men.' (*Paradise Lost*, book 1, lines 25–6.)

316 Song of Solomon 2:10.

317 Song of Solomon 7:1–7.

318 Song of Solomon 8:6–7.

319 The sermons on the Song of Songs (Song of Solomon) given by St Bernard of Clairvaux (named after the Cistercian monastery he founded in 1115) are available in various published forms. In *Spectrum* magazine (9 June 2011) Rachel Davies says of him,

> Bernard of Clairvaux was one of the most influential

religious and political voices of twelfth-century Western Europe, and as a result, his eighty-six sermons on the Song of Songs had a significant impact on future generations of Christian thinkers and mystics. Like Origen before him, Bernard viewed the Song of Songs as spiritual allegory rather than as a record of physical passion shared between two created beings. Its intimacy reveals the soul in love with a most lovely Divine lover.

The *Spiritual Canticle* of St John of the Cross is an eclogue in which the bride (representing the soul searches for the bridegroom (representing Jesus Christ) and is anxious at having lost him; both are filled with joy upon reuniting. It can be seen as a free-form Spanish version of the Song of Songs at a time when translations of the Bible into the vernacular were forbidden.

St John of the Cross, a Spanish Carmelite friar and priest during the Counter-Reformation, was jailed in 1577 at the Carmelite Monastery of Toledo because of his close association with St Teresa of Ávila in the Discalced Carmelite reforms. He remained imprisoned for nine months in a cell, in bad conditions that caused him much suffering. He memorized, in the absence of the means to write it down, a thirty-one-stanza version of the *Canticle*.

320 Proverbs 12:1 and 15:1.

321 Proverbs 6:6–11.

322 The marginal note is in the King James Bible, and reads more fully: 'Solomon persuadeth to a sincere and kind familiarity with wisdom. In an example of his own experience, he sheweth the cunning of a whore and the desperate simplicity of a young wanton.' Proverbs 7: 6–23.

323 Aldous Huxley, *Ends and Means: An Enquiry into the Nature of Ideals*, Chatto and Windus, London 1946, p. 93.

324 1 Samuel 15:3.

325 Illustration by P. H. Calderon (Philip Hermogenes) for Cassell's *Illustrated History of England* (1861).

326 John Milton, *Poetical Works*, Baynes and Son, London 1825, p. 435.

327 Matthew 16:18–19.

328 William Shakespeare, *King John*, Act III, Scene i.

329 To judge from photographs, this would probably have been the RSC production directed by Barry Kyle in 1974.

330 Matthew 4:8–10.

331 Lord Acton wrote, 'Power tends to corrupt, and absolute power corrupts absolutely. Great men are almost always bad men….' in a letter to Bishop Mandell Creighton, 5 April 1887, published in

J. N. Figgis and R. V. Laurence (eds.), *Historical Essays and Studies*, Macmillan, London 1907.

332 Revelation 17:3–6.

333 Marcel Lefebvre was a French Roman Catholic archbishop (1905–1991) who played a controversial role in the preparations for the Second Vatican Council in 1962. In 1970, he founded the Switzerland-based Society of Saint Pius x. He was ordered by the Holy See to disband the organization, but refused, and went so far as to consecrate four bishops to continue his work with it. This was the reason for his excommunication in 1988.

334 For more about these encounters, see chapter 17, 'The Enemy of the Church', in Sangharakshita, *Facing Mount Kanchenjunga*, Windhorse Publications, Glasgow 1991 (*Complete Works*, vol. 21, pp. 345–66).

335 The lecture on 'Buddhism and the Bishop of Woolwich', given in 1965, was published as a booklet and now appears in *Complete Works*, vol. 11.

336 See, for example, the *Alagaddūpama Sutta*, *Majjhima Nikāya* 22 (i.140); Bhikkhu Ñāṇamoli and Bhikkhu Bodhi (trans.), *The Middle Length Discourses of the Buddha*, Wisdom Publications, Boston 1995, p. 234; or I. B. Horner (trans.), *The Collection of the Middle Length Sayings*, vol. i, Pali Text Society, London 1976, p. 180.

337 Helmuth von Glasenapp, *Buddhism – a Non-Theistic Religion*, Allen & Unwin, London 1970.

338 See the *Rohitassa Sutta*, *Aṅguttara Nikāya* ii.47; Bhikkhu Bodhi (trans.), *Numerical Discourses of the Buddha*, Wisdom Publications, Boston 2012, p. 434; or E. M. Hare, *The Book of the Gradual Sayings*, vol. ii, Pali Text Society, Oxford 1995, p. 58.

339 The Buddha's declaration that the whole world is contained in 'this six-foot long' (or sometimes 'fathom-long') body appears in the *Rohitassa Sutta* at *Aṅguttara Nikāya* ii.47; see Bhikkhu Bodhi (trans.), *Numerical Discourses of the Buddha*, Wisdom Publications, Boston 2012, pp. 434–5; or E. M. Hare, *The Book of the Gradual Sayings*, vol. ii, Pali Text Society, Oxford 1995, p. 58. See also *Saṃyutta Nikāya* i.62 (2.26); Bhikkhu Bodhi (trans.), *The Connected Discourses of the Buddha*, Wisdom Publications, Boston 2000, p. 158; or Mrs C. A. F. Rhys Davids (trans.), *Kindred Sayings*, part 1, Pali Text Society, London 1979, pp. 86–7.

340 John 1:1–3.

341 This hypothesis was apparently based on a work by the ancient Greek philosopher Celsus, mentioned by the

Christian writer Origen in his work *Contra Celsum*. The story was told in the Jewish tradition in the *Talmud* and also in the medieval *Toledot Yeshu*. Recent scholarly opinion is divided, some giving credence to the story and others repudiating it.

342 *Bhagavad Gītā* iv.6–8.

343 *Kasibhāradvāja Sutta*, *Sutta-Nipāta* 1.4, verse 2.

344 The medieval mystery plays of England represented Bible stories in the form of tableaux with accompanying songs, which were performed by the craft guilds. ('Mystery' here means 'miracle', but is sometimes said to be derived from *ministerium* or craft, underlining the association with the guilds.) The 'Harrowing of Hell' is an episode in the cycle of mystery plays associated with York and Wakefield. The story of Christ's descent into hell and liberation of the Old Testament beings imprisoned there derives not from the orthodox Bible but from an apocryphal work, the Gospel of Nicodemus or Acts of Pilate.

345 A book in the *Khuddaka Nikāya* of the Pāli canon called the *Petavatthu* ('Hungry Ghost Stories'; the Pāli *peta* is equivalent to the Sanskrit *preta*) describes, in fifty-one stories, how their actions led these beings to be born as hungry ghosts in this unhappy realm, and also how those at present living in the human realm can help to alleviate the misery of the hungry ghosts. Some sections describe the visits of Moggallāna (Sanskrit Maudgalyāyana) to the realms of the hungry ghosts and his conversations with them there. Book 2, chapter 2 tells the story of how Sāriputta's mother came to be reborn among the hungry ghosts, and how he rescued her from that plight. This story later became a favourite in China, where it came to be about Maudgalyāyana's mother and is called 'Mulian saves his mother from hell'. See H. S. Gehman (trans.), *Minor Anthologies of the Pali Canon*, part 4, Pali Text Society, London 1974, *Petavatthu* pp. 29–32.

346 Mark 9:43–8.

347 Matthew 25:41,46.

348 1 Corinthians 6:9–10.

349 2 Thessalonians 1:6–9.

350 *Hamlet*, Act III, Scene iii.

351 John 11:43.

352 Matthew 16:18–19.

353 Acts 2:4.

354 Isaiah 7:14.

355 Job 19:26.

356 See 'The Book of Job', in James Anthony Froude, *Essays in Literature and History*, Everyman edition, J. M. Dent & Sons, London 1911, p. 83.

357 John 1:29.

358 *Dhammapada* 276.

359 See section 20 of the *Kakacūpama Sutta*, *Majjhima Nikāya* 21 (i.129); Bhikkhu

Ñāṇamoli and Bhikkhu Bodhi (trans.), *The Middle Length Discourses of the Buddha*, Wisdom Publications, Boston 1995, pp. 223; or I. B. Horner (trans.), *The Collection of the Middle Length Sayings*, vol. i, Pali Text Society, London 1976, p. 166.

360 *Dhammapada* 127.

361 Matthew 5–7.

362 John Milton's Sonnet 18, published in 1673.

363 Sangharakshita, *The Rainbow Road from Tooting Broadway to Kalimpong*, *Complete Works*, vol. 20, p. 36.

364 Ariel is an airy spirit in Shakespeare's *The Tempest* and Mrs Gamp is a disreputable 'nurse' in Charles Dickens' novel *Martin Chuzzlewit*. In chapter 2, section 1 of his book *Logic*, Isaac Watts says:

> Essence therefore is but the very nature of any being whether it be actually existing or no. A rose in winter has an essence, in summer it has existence also.

Isaac Watts, *The Works of the Rev. Isaac Watts*, Edward Baines, Leeds 1813, vol. 7, p. 318.

365 *Paradise Lost*, book 5, lines 275–87.

366 Sir Joshua Reynolds' *A Child's Portrait in Different Views: Angels' Heads*, on display at Tate Britain in London, consists of five different portraits of the head of the five-year-old Lady Frances Gordon.

367 *Mahāmaṅgala Sutta*, *Sutta-Nipāta* 3.4, in H. Saddhatissa (trans.), *Sutta-Nipāta*, Curzon Press, London 1985, p. 29.

368 This scene is depicted, for example, in a carved stone panel, *Descent of Buddha from Trayastriṃśa Heaven*, made in the second or third century CE and now in the collection of the Victoria and Albert Museum in London.

369 See chapter 7, 'The Bodhisattva Hierarchy', of Sangharakshita, *The Bodhisattva Ideal* (*Complete Works*, vol. 4).

370 See Sangharakshita, *Complete Poems 1941–1994*, Windhorse Publications, Birmingham 1995, p. 239 (*Complete Works*, vol. 25).

371 This was Dhardo Rimpoche, an eminent Tibetan lama of the Gelugpa tradition. Sangharakshita, who met him in Kalimpong in 1953, described him (in *The History of My Going For Refuge*, Windhorse Publications, 2010, p. 105; *Complete Works*, vol. 2, p. 471) as 'perhaps embodying the bodhisattva ideal to a greater extent than any other person I had known'. See also 'Bodhisattva Ordination' in chapter 13 of *The History of My Going for Refuge*, and Sangharakshita, *Precious Teachers*, Windhorse Publications, Birmingham

2007, pp. 151–4 (*Complete Works*, vol. 22). For more about Dhardo Rimpoche see Suvajra, *The Wheel and the Diamond: The Life of Dhardo Tulku*, Windhorse Publications, Glasgow 1991; and Sara Hagel (ed.), *Dhardo Rimpoche: A Celebration*, Windhorse Publications, Birmingham 2000; The Dhardo Rimpoche whom Sangharakshita knew in Kalimpong was the thirteenth of that name and died in 1990; the fourteenth Dhardo Rimpoche was born in 1991 and received his monastic education in South India.

372 'They also serve who only stand and wait' is the last line of John Milton's sonnet 'On his blindness', which begins 'When I consider how my light is spent' and was published in 1673 but probably written in the 1650s, when Milton became completely blind.

373 This is part of Fra Angelico's painting *The Last Judgement*, painted c.1431 and on display in the Museo Nazionale di San Marco, Florence.

374 Domenikos Theotocopoulos, called El Greco, painted *The Assumption of the Virgin* in the church of Santa Domingo el Antigo in Toledo c.1577.

375 *Upaḍḍha Sutta, Saṃyutta Nikāya* v.2 (45.2); see Bhikkhu Bodhi (trans.), *The Connected Discourses of the Buddha*, Wisdom Publications, Boston 2000, pp. 1524–5; or F. L. Woodward (trans.), *Kindred Sayings*, part 5, Pali Text Society, London 1979, p. 2.

376 Giovanni Girolamo Savoldo's painting *Tobias and the Angel*, painted between 1522 and 1525, is in the Galleria Borghese, Rome.

377 The poem, called 'Tobias and the Angel: After the painting by Savoldo', is the second in a sequence of six 'Poems on Paintings from the "Genius of Venice" exhibition at the Royal Academy', written in 1984. See Sangharakshita, *Complete Poems 1941–1994*, Windhorse Publications, Birmingham 1995, p. 353 (*Complete Works*, vol. 25).

378 Matthew 18:10.

379 *Paradise Lost*, book 3, lines 60–2.

380 Socrates referred to this in the *Apologia*, which followed his being sentenced to death in the Athenian court in 399 BCE:

> Hitherto the familiar oracle (daimon) within me has constantly been in the habit of opposing me even about trifles, if I was going to make a slip or error about anything; and now as you see there has come upon me that which may be thought, and is generally believed to be, the last and worst evil. But the oracle made no sign of opposition, either as I was leaving my house and

> going out in the morning, or when I was going up into this court, or while I was speaking, at anything which I was going to say; and yet I have often been stopped in the middle of a speech; but now in nothing I either said or did touching this matter has the oracle opposed me. What do I take to be the explanation of this? I will tell you. I regard this as a proof that what has happened to me is a good, and that those of us who think that death is an evil are in error. This is a great proof to me of what I am saying, for the customary sign would surely have opposed me had I been going to evil and not to good.

Apologia 40a–c, trans. Benjamin Jowett.

381 *Paradise Lost*, book 1, lines 589–99.

382 William Blake's 1805 watercolour *Satan in his original glory: 'Thou wast Perfect until Iniquity was Found in Thee'* is now in the Tate Gallery, London.

383 In his 1790 work *The Marriage of Heaven and Hell*, William Blake wrote that

> the reason Milton wrote in fetters when he wrote of Angels & God, and at liberty when of Devils & Hell, is because he was a true Poet and of the Devils party without knowing it.

384 Dante, *Inferno*, canto 34, trans. Revd H. F. Cary, Cassell and Company, London 1892.

385 Gustave Doré's engraving (created between 1861 and 1868) illustrating canto 34 of Dante's *Inferno* has the caption: 'Lucifer, King of Hell'. See ibid.

386 Matthew 4:1–11.

387 Luke 22:3–5.

388 Mark 1:26.

389 Mark 1:34.

390 Mark 3:29–30.

391 Mark 5:2–13.

392 Mark 7:26–30.

393 Mark 9:17–26.

394 Mark 9:39.

395 Ephesians 6:11–12.

396 *Paradise Lost*, book 1, lines 739–46.

397 *Paradise Lost,* book 5, lines 285–7.

398 2 Corinthians 11:13–15.

399 Elaine Pagels, *The Origin of Satan: How Christians Demonized Jews, Pagans, and Heretics,* Vintage, London 1996, p. 177.

400 The seventeenth-century Spanish painter Bartolomé Estaban Murillo of Seville produced a number of paintings of this subject. One, *The Immaculate Conception of the Virgin*, is held by the National Gallery in London, and several more can be seen in the Prado, Madrid.

401 *The Immaculate Conception* by Diego Velázquez, painted in 1618, can be seen in the National Gallery in London.

402 Luke 1:26–38.

403 John 19:25–7.

404 Luke 1:38.

405 Dante Alighieri, *La Divina Commedia*, *Paradiso*, canto 31, lines 100–2: 'The Queen of Heaven, for whom I wholly burn with love, will grant us every grace, since I am her faithful Bernard.'

406 Acts 19:34.

407 See Vladimir Sergeyevich Solovyov, *Divine Sophia: The Wisdom Writings of Vladimir Solovyov*, Cornell University Press, Ithaca 2009.

408 Solovyov had this mysterious encounter with Sophia in Egypt in 1875. See *The Religious Poetry of Vladimir Solovyov*, Semantron Press 2014.

409 This distinction is found in the Theravādin commentarial tradition; for more about it, see Sangharakshita, *A Survey of Buddhism*, Windhorse Publications, Birmingham 2001, p. 170 (*Complete Works*, vol. 1, p. 145).

410 See 'The Two Paths', in H. P. Blavatsky, *The Voice of The Silence*, Theosophy Trust 2006, p. 14.

411 Edward Carpenter's *The Intermediate Sex* was first published in 1908 and is now published by Echo Library, Fairford 2007. See also chapter 5 in Havelock Ellis, *The Psychology of Sex*, William Heinemann, London 1933, pp. 188–219.

412 Havelock Ellis, *The Psychology of Sex*, William Heinemann, London 1933, p. 189.

413 Leviticus 18:22.

414 Romans 1:26–7.

415 See 'With Allen Ginsberg in Kalimpong', in Sangharakshita, *The Priceless Jewel*, Windhorse Publications, Glasgow 1993, pp. 215–8 (*Complete Works*, vol. 22).

416 Exodus 22:18.

417 Matthew 7:12.

418 Dante Alghieri, *Inferno*, canto 15.

419 Hesketh Pearson, *The Life of Oscar Wilde*, Methuen, London 1954, pp. 358–9.

420 'As the caterpillar chooses
the fairest leaves to lay her eggs
on, so the priest lays
his curse on the fairest joys.'
This is proverb 55 of the 'Proverbs of Hell' in William Blake's *The Marriage of Heaven and Hell*, published in the author's own illustrated edition in 1793.

421 Aelred of Rievaulx, *Spiritual Friendship*, trans. Lawrence C. Braceland, Cistercian Publications, Collegeville, Minnesota, 2010, p. 69:

> IVO. To what does this lead? Should I say of friendship what John, the friend of Jesus, said of charity, 'God is friendship'?
>
> AELRED. This is novel indeed and lacks the authority of the Scriptures. The rest of that verse about charity, however, I surely do not hesitate

to attribute to friendship, because the one who remains in friendship remains in God, and God in him.

422 *Upaḍḍha Sutta, Saṃyutta Nikāya* v.2 (45.2); see Bhikkhu Bodhi (trans.), *The Connected Discourses of the Buddha*, Wisdom Publications, Boston 2000, pp. 1524–5; also F. L. Woodward (trans.), *The Book of the Kindred Sayings*, part 5, Pali Text Society, London 1979, p. 2.

423 1 Samuel 15:3.

424 In Greek mythology, Oedipus, told by the oracle at Delphi that he was destined to kill his father, Laius, and marry his mother, Jocasta, fled Thebes to avoid that fate; or another version of the story has it that it was Laius who heard this prophecy and cast his infant son out of the kingdom. Later in life, on a journey back to Thebes, Oedipus got involved in an altercation at a crossroads and killed his father Laius, not knowing who he was, and then went on to Thebes, where he met and married Jocasta. The legend is told by many Greek writers, including Homer, and is the subject of Sophocles' tragedy *Oedipus the King*.

425 John 14:6.

426 See chapter 1, 'Early Memories', in *From Genesis to the Diamond Sūtra*, in this volume, p. 533.

427 See chapter 8, 'How St Francis, walking one day with Brother Leo, explained to him what things are perfect joy', in *Little Flowers of St Francis*, which was composed at the end of the fourteenth century.

428 Thomas Cogswell Upham, *Life, religious opinions, and experience of Madame Guyon: including an account of the personal history and religious opinions of Fénelon, Archbishop of Cambray*, first published in America in 1847.

429 *The Practice of the Presence of God* is a book of collected teachings of Brother Lawrence (born Nicholas Herman), a seventeenth-century Carmelite monk, compiled by Father Joseph de Beaufort. The compilation includes letters, as well as records of his conversations kept by Brother Lawrence's interlocutors. The basic theme of the book is the development of an awareness of the presence of God.

430 Recollection of the Buddha or, in Sanskrit, *buddhānusmṛti* (Pāli *buddhānusati)*, has often been taught as a contemplation of the qualities of the Buddha, familiar to many Buddhists from the *Tiratana Vandanā* or Praises to the Three Jewels. Buddhaghosa wrote extensively on the practice at *Visuddhimagga* 198–213: 'Recollection of the Enlightened One'. See Bhikkhu Ñāṇamoli (trans.), *The Path of Purification*, Buddhist Publication Society, Kandy 1991, pp. 192–209.

431 This article, 'Brother Lawrence: A Study in Mysticism, Eastern and Western', now appears in Sangharakshita, *Early Writings 1944–1954*, Ibis Publications, Ledbury 2014 (*Complete Works*, vol. 7).

432 See Sangharakshita, *The Rainbow Road from Tooting Broadway to Kalimpong*, *Complete Works*, vol. 20, pp. 463–4.

433 Walter Nigg, *Warriors of God: The Great Religious Orders and their Founders*, Secker & Warburg, London 1959.

434 Simony, as defined by the *Encyclopedia Britannica*, is

> the buying or selling of something spiritual or closely connected with the spiritual. More widely, it is any contract of this kind forbidden by divine or ecclesiastical law. The name is taken from Simon Magus (Acts 8:18), who endeavoured to buy from the Apostles the power of conferring the gifts of the Holy Spirit.

It often refers to the sale of church offices and roles. Simony was outlawed in Britain by the Simony Act of 1588, which still has legal force.

435 These are stanzas 2 to 5 of Ernest Dowson's 'Carthusians', written in 1891 after a visit to a Carthusian monastery in Cowfold, Sussex.

436 Sangharakshita, *Through Buddhist Eyes*, Windhorse Publications, Birmingham 2000, p. 225 (*Complete Works*, vol. 24).

437 The sonnet's title is 'St Jerome in the Desert'; see Sangharakshita, *Complete Poems 1941–1994*, Windhorse Publications, Birmingham 1995, p. 269 (*Complete Works*, vol. 25).

438 From 'The Journey to Il Convento', in Sangharakshita, *The Priceless Jewel*, Windhorse Publications, Glasgow 1993, pp. 53–4 (*Complete Works*, vol. 26).

439 For Sangharakshita's essay 'Buddhism and Blake', see Sangharakshita, *Alternative Traditions*, Windhorse Publications, Glasgow 1986, pp. 185–97 (*Complete Works*, vol. 26).

440 Mark 1:9–11.

441 Albert Schweitzer, *The Quest of the Historical Jesus*, Adam and Charles Black, London 1911, chapter 10, 'Results', p. 556.

442 The Christian parable of the sower is similar to one found in the *Dhammapada* commentary; see Eugene Watson Burlingame, *Buddhist Parables*, Pilgrim Books, Delhi 1999, pp. 180–1. A version of the parable is also to be found as part of the story of Barlaam and Josaphat. See *The Balavariani (Barlaam and Josaphat): a tale from the Christian East*, translated from

the old Georgian by David Marshall Lang, George Allen and Unwin, London 1966, pp. 76–7. It also appears in an Arabic version of the life of the Buddha:

> The sower went out to sow with his good seed. When he had filled his hand with some and he had dispersed it, part fell on the edge of the road. There the birds were quick to peck it. Part fell on rock, where there were water, moisture, and mud. It sprang up, but when it grew, its roots reached the dry layer of rock, and it died. Part fell on land covered with thorns. When it had grown up and was about to bear fruit, thorns choked it and made it die. Finally, a small part fell into good, well-hoed soil. It remained intact, grew, matured and prospered.

This is Douglas Galbi's translation from modern French into English. The parable of the sower in the original Arabic and in modern French translation is given in Gimaret, Daniel, 'Traces et parallèles du Kitab Bilawhar wa-Budasaf dans la tradition Arabe' (*Bulletin d'études orientales*. 24:97–133, 1971, pp. 111–2). Another parable with obvious similarities is the parable of the prodigal son, told in Luke 15:11–32 and also in the *Lotus Sūtra*. For Sangharakshita's commentary on this parable, see chapter 4, 'The Myth of the Return Journey', in Sangharakshita, *The Drama of Cosmic Enlightenment*, *Complete Works*, vol. 16, pp. 85–115.

443 *Theragāthā* 1229; see K. R. Norman (trans.), The *Elders' Verses I*, Pali Text Society, Oxford 1995, p.112. The Buddha also describes truth as immortal at *Udāna* 3.3; see John B. Ireland (trans.), *The Udāna and the Itivuttaka*, Buddhist Publication Society, Kandy 1997, p. 50.

444 Mark 5:34.

445 Mark 6:6.

446 Mark 4:39–40; Matthew 14:19–20; John 2:1–11; John 11:11–44.

447
> Nothing could be simpler than the explanation of the miracle at Cana. Jesus had brought with Him as a wedding-gift some jars of good wine and had put them aside in another room. When the wine was finished and His mother became anxious, He still allowed the guests to wait a little, as the stone vessels for purification had not yet been filled with water. When that had been done He ordered the servants to pour out some of his wine, but to tell no one whence it came. When John, as an old man, wrote his Gospel, he got all this rather mixed up—

had not indeed observed it very closely at the time, 'had perhaps been the least thing merry himself,' says Venturini, and had believed in the miracle with the rest. Perhaps, too, he had not ventured to ask Jesus for an explanation, for he had only become His disciple a few days before.

Albert Schweitzer, *The Quest of the Historical Jesus*, chapter 4, 'The Earliest Fictitious Lives of Jesus', Adam and Charles Black, London 1911, pp. 67–8.

448 John 11:39.

449 Matthew 17:24–7.

450 Luke 22:21–3.

451 In his *Lives of the Painters* (first published in 1550), Giorgio Vasari wrote that Leonardo da Vinci, giving a progress report to his patron, the Duke of Milan, explained that he had not finished two heads, one of which was the head of Christ: 'which he would not seek for in the world, and which he could not hope that his imagination would be able to conceive of such beauty and celestial grace as was fit for the incarnate divinity'.

452 Mark 15:12–14.

453 Sholem Asch, *The Nazarene*, Carroll & Graf, New York 1996.

454 The William Caxton translation of *The Golden Legend* has been published in many editions, including one by William Morris and the Kelmscott Press, and there are various other more recent translations. The excerpts that follow are from the seventh (and final) volume of the Temple Classics edition of the Caxton version, edited by F. S. Ellis and published as Jacobus de Voragine, *The Golden Legend; or, Lives of the Saints, as Englished by William Caxton*, London, J. M. Dent and Co., 1900. This edition has been republished as Jacobus de Voragine, *The Golden Legend: Lives of the Saints*, Aeterna Press 2015.

455 *Dhammapada* 12.

456 *Abhiniṣkramaṇa Sūtra*, published as Samuel Beal (trans.), *The Romantic Legend of Śākya Buddha*, Motilal Banarsidass, Delhi 1985 (first published 1875), p. 104.

457 Jacobus de Voragine, *The Golden Legend: Lives of the Saints*, vol. 7, J. M. Dent & Co., London 1900, p. 86.

458 Ibid., p. 88.

459 Ibid., p. 91.

460 This is from God's first speech of the fifteenth-century morality play *The Summoning of Everyman*.

461 The character Knowledge makes this promise to comfort Everyman as he sets out on his journey in *The Summoning of Everyman*. The lines will be familiar to anyone who has read any of the volumes of Everyman's Library, as they

are found at the front of each book. Everyman's Library is an extensive set of literary works the first of which were brought out by the English publisher (and autodidact) J. M. Dent in 1906, to make literature accessible to everyone: 'for a few shillings the reader may have a whole bookshelf of the immortals; for five pounds (which will procure him a hundred volumes) a man may be intellectually rich for life'.

462 The detail from the story of Barlaam and Josaphat is told in Jacobus de Voragine, *The Golden Legend: Lives of the Saints*, vol. 7, J. M. Dent & Co., London 1900, p. 105. In most legendary accounts Siddhārtha gives his clothes to his charioteer, Channa, but in Aśvaghoṣa's version, the clothes are swapped with those of a hunter who serendipitously appears. See E. H. Johnston (trans.), *Buddhacarita* (iii.34), Motilal Banarsidass, Delhi 1984, pp. 89–90.

463 Jacobus de Voragine, *The Golden Legend: Lives of the Saints*, vol. 7, J. M. Dent & Co., London 1900, p. 105.

464 Ibid.

465 Ibid.

466 The *Lalitavistara Sūtra* is a Mahāyāna text that tells the life story of the Buddha; *Lalitavistara* means 'extended play', referring to the Mahāyāna view that the Buddha's last incarnation was a 'display' or 'performance' given for the benefit of the beings in this world. It has been published in two volumes as Gwendolyn Bays (trans.), *The Voice of the Buddha*, Dharma Publishing, Berkeley 1983. Aśvaghoṣa's *Buddhacarita* or *Acts of the Buddha*, is a long poem written in the second century CE, which gives a legendary account of the Buddha's life; see Aśvaghoṣa, *The Buddhacarita*, trans. E. H. Johnston, Motilal Banarsidass, Delhi 1984.

467 The story attributed to the seventh-century Syrian monk St John of Damascus (known as St John Damascene) is told in George Ratcliffe Woodward and Harold Mattingly, *St John Damascene: Barlaam and Ioasaph*, Loeb Classical Library 34, 1914.

468 E. A. Wallis Budge, *Baralam and Yewasef: The Ethiopic Version of a Christianized Recension of the Buddhist Legend of the Buddha and the Bodhisattva*, Routledge, London 2011, p. xii.

469 This is Paul Williams, author of *Mahāyāna Buddhism: The Doctrinal Foundations*, among other works. He has written about his experience of converting back to Catholicism in Paul Williams, *The Unexpected Way: On Converting from Buddhism to Catholicism*, T. & T. Clark, London 2002.

INDEX

Page numbers for illustrations are in italics.

A GUIDE TO THE COMPLETE WORKS OF SANGHARAKSHITA

Gathered together in these twenty-seven volumes are talks and stories, commentaries on the Buddhist scriptures, poems, memoirs, reviews, and other writings. The genres are many, and the subject matter covered is wide, but it all has – its whole purpose is to convey – that taste of freedom which the Buddha declared to be the hallmark of his Dharma. Another traditional description of the Buddha's Dharma is that it is *ehipassiko*, 'come and see'. Sangharakshita calls to us, his readers, to come and see how the Dharma can fundamentally change the way we see things, change the way we live for the better, and change the society we belong to, wherever in the world we live.

Sangharakshita's very first published piece, *The Unity of Buddhism* (found in volume 7 of this collection), appeared in 1944 when he was eighteen years old, and it introduced themes that continued to resound throughout his work: the basis of Buddhist ethics, the compassion of the bodhisattva, and the transcendental unity of Buddhism. Over the course of the following seven decades not only did numerous other works flow from his pen; he gave hundreds of talks (some now lost). In gathering all we could find of this vast output, we have sought to arrange it in a way that brings a sense of coherence, communicating something essential about Sangharakshita, his life and teaching. Recalling the three 'baskets' among which an early tradition divided the Buddha's teachings, we have divided Sangharakshita's creative output into six 'baskets' or groups: foundation texts; works originating in India; teachings originally given in the West; commentaries on the Buddhist scriptures; personal writings; and poetry, aphorisms, and works on the arts. The 27th volume, a concordance, brings together all the terms and themes of the whole collection. If you want to find a particular story or teaching, look at a traditional term from different points of view or in different contexts, or track down one of the thousands of canonical references to be found in these volumes, the concordance will be your guide.

1. FOUNDATION

What is the foundation of a Buddhist life? How do we understand and then follow the Buddha's path of Ethics, Meditation, and Wisdom? What is really meant by 'Going for Refuge to the Three Jewels', described by Sangharakshita as the essential act of a Buddhist life? And what is the bodhisattva ideal, which he has called 'one of the sublimest ideals mankind has ever seen'? In the 'Foundation' group you will find teachings on all these themes. It includes the author's *magnum opus, A Survey of Buddhism*, a collection of teachings on *The Purpose and Practice of Buddhist Meditation*, and the anthology, *The Essential Sangharakshita*, an eminently helpful distillation of the entire corpus.

2. INDIA

From 1950 to 1964 Sangharakshita, based in Kalimpong in the eastern Himalayas, poured his energy into trying to revive Buddhism in the land of its birth and to revitalize and bring reform to the existing Asian Buddhist world. The articles and book reviews from this period are gathered in volumes 7 and 8, as well as his biographical sketch of the great Sinhalese Dharmaduta, Anagārika Dharmapala. In 1954 Sangharakshita took on the editing of the *Maha Bodhi*, a journal for which he wrote a monthly editorial, and which, under his editorship, published the work of many of the leading Buddhist writers of the time. It was also during these years in India that a vital connection was forged with Dr B. R. Ambedkar, renowned Indian statesman and leader of the Buddhist mass conversion of 1956. Sangharakshita became closely involved with the new Buddhists and, after Dr Ambedkar's untimely death, visited them regularly on extensive teaching tours.

From 1979, when an Indian wing of the Triratna Buddhist Community was founded (then known as TBMSG), Sangharakshita returned several times to undertake further teaching tours. The talks from these tours are collected in volumes 9 and 10 along with a unique work on Ambedkar and his life which draws out the significance of his conversion to Buddhism.

3. THE WEST

Sangharakshita founded the Triratna Buddhist Community (then called the Friends of the Western Buddhist Order) on 6 April 1967. On 7 April the following year he performed the first ordinations of men and women within the Triratna Buddhist Order (then the Western Buddhist Order). At that time Buddhism was not widely known in the West and for the following two decades or so he taught intensively, finding new ways to communicate the ancient truths of Buddhism, drawing on the whole Buddhist tradition to do so, as well as making connections with what was best in existing Western culture. Sometimes his sword flashed as he critiqued ideas and views inimical to the Dharma. It is these teachings and writings that are gathered together in this third group.

4. COMMENTARY

Throughout Sangharakshita's works are threaded references to the Buddhist canon of literature – Pāli, Mahāyāna, and Vajrayāna – from which he drew his inspiration. In the early days of the new movement he often taught by means of seminars in which, prompted by the questions of his students, he sought to pass on the inspiration and wisdom of the Buddhist tradition. Each seminar was based around a different text, the seminars were recorded and transcribed, and in due course many of the transcriptions were edited and turned into books, all carefully checked by Sangharakshita. The commentaries compiled in this way constitute the fourth group. In some ways this is the heart of the collection. Sangharakshita often told the story of how it was that, reading two *sūtras* at the age of sixteen or seventeen, he realized that he was a Buddhist, and he has never tired of showing others how they too could see and realize the value of the '*sūtra*-treasure'.

5. MEMOIRS

Who is Sangharakshita? What sort of life did he live? Whom did he meet? What did he feel? Why did he found a new Buddhist movement? In these volumes of memoirs and letters Sangharakshita shares with his readers much about himself and his life as he himself has experienced it, giving us a sense of its breadth and depth, humour and pathos.

6. POETRY, APHORISMS, AND THE ARTS

Sangharakshita describes reading *Paradise Lost* at the age of twelve as one of the greatest poetic experiences of his life. His realization of the value of the higher arts to spiritual development is one of his distinctive contributions to our understanding of what Buddhist life is, and he has expressed it in a number of essays and articles. Throughout his life he has written poetry which he says can be regarded as a kind of spiritual autobiography. It is here, perhaps, that we come closest to the heart of Sangharakshita. He has also written a few short stories and composed some startling aphorisms. Through book reviews he has engaged with the experiences, ideas, and opinions of modern writers. All these are collected in this sixth group.

In the preface to *A Survey of Buddhism* (volume 1 in this collection), Sangharakshita wrote of his approach to the Buddha's teachings:

> Why did the Buddha (or Nāgārjuna, or Buddhaghosa) teach this particular doctrine? What bearing does it have on the spiritual life? How does it help the individual Buddhist actually to follow the spiritual path?... I found myself asking such questions again and again, for only in this way, I found, could I make sense – spiritual sense – of Buddhism.

Although this collection contains so many words, they are all intent, directly or indirectly, on these same questions. And all these words are not in the end about their writer, but about his great subject, the Buddha and his teaching, and about you, the reader, for whose benefit they are solely intended. These pages are full of the reverence that Sangharakshita has always felt, which is expressed in an early poem, 'Taking Refuge in the Buddha', whose refrain is 'My place is at thy feet'. He has devoted his life to communicating the Buddha's Dharma in its depth and in its breadth, to men and women from all backgrounds and walks of life, from all countries, of all races, of all ages. These collected works are the fruit of that devotion.

We are very pleased to be able to include some previously unpublished work in this collection, but most of what appears in these volumes has been published before. We have made very few changes, though we have added extra notes where we thought they would be useful. We have had the pleasure of researching the notes in the Sangharakshita Library at 'Adhisthana', Triratna's centre in Herefordshire, UK, which houses his own collection of books. It has been of great value to be able to search among the very copies of the *suttas*, *sūtras* and commentaries that have provided the basis of his teachings over the last seventy years.

The publication of these volumes owes much to the work of transcribers, editors, indexers, designers, and publishers over many years – those who brought out the original editions of many of the works included here, and those who have contributed in all sorts of ways to this *Complete Works* project, including all those who contributed to funds given in celebration of Sangharakshita's ninetieth birthday in August 2015, and to a further outpouring of generosity after Sangharakshita's death in October 2018. All these donors have made the publication of this series possible, and we are very grateful. Many thanks to everyone who has helped; may the merit gained in our acting thus go to the alleviation of the suffering of all beings.

Vidyadevi and Kalyanaprabha
Editors

THE COMPLETE WORKS OF SANGHARAKSHITA

I FOUNDATION

VOLUME 1 A SURVEY OF BUDDHISM / THE BUDDHA'S NOBLE EIGHTFOLD PATH
A Survey of Buddhism
The Buddha's Noble Eightfold Path

2 THE THREE JEWELS I
The Three Jewels
The Meaning of Conversion in Buddhism
Going for Refuge
The Ten Pillars of Buddhism
The History of My Going for Refuge
My Relation to the Order
Extending the Hand of Fellowship
Forty-Three Years Ago
Was the Buddha a Bhikkhu?

3 THE THREE JEWELS II
Who is the Buddha?
What is the Dharma?
What is the Sangha?

4 THE BODHISATTVA IDEAL
The Bodhisattva Ideal
The Endlessly Fascinating Cry (seminar)
The Bodhisattva Principle

5 THE PURPOSE AND PRACTICE OF BUDDHIST MEDITATION
The Purpose and Practice of Buddhist Meditation

6 THE ESSENTIAL SANGHARAKSHITA
The Essential Sangharakshita

II INDIA

7 CROSSING THE STREAM: INDIA WRITINGS I
Early Writings 1944–1954
Crossing the Stream
Buddhism in the Modern World: Cultural and Political Implications
The Meaning of Orthodoxy in Buddhism
Buddhism in India Today
Ordination and Initiation in the Three Yānas
A Bird's Eye View of Indian Buddhism

VOLUME 8 BEATING THE DHARMA DRUM: INDIA WRITINGS II

Anagarika Dharmapala and Other 'Maha Bodhi' Writings
Dharmapala: The Spiritual Dimension
Beating the Drum: 'Maha Bodhi' Editorials

9 DR AMBEDKAR AND THE REVIVAL OF BUDDHISM I

Ambedkar and Buddhism
Lecture Tour in India, December 1981–March 1982

10 DR AMBEDKAR AND THE REVIVAL OF BUDDHISM II

Lecture Tours in India 1979 & 1983–1992
Other Edited Lectures and Seminar Material

III THE WEST

11 A NEW BUDDHIST MOVEMENT I

Ritual and Devotion in Buddhism
The Buddha's Victory
The Taste of Freedom
Buddha Mind
Human Enlightenment
New Currents in Western Buddhism
Buddhism for Today – and Tomorrow
Buddhism and the West
Aspects of Buddhist Morality
Buddhism, World Peace, and Nuclear War
Dialogue between Buddhism and Christianity
Buddhism and Blasphemy
Buddhism and the Bishop of Woolwich
Buddhism and the New Reformation
Great Buddhists of the Twentieth Century
Articles and Interviews

12 A NEW BUDDHIST MOVEMENT II

Previously unpublished talks

13 EASTERN AND WESTERN TRADITIONS

Tibetan Buddhism
Creative Symbols of Tantric Buddhism
The Essence of Zen
The FWBO and 'Protestant Buddhism'
From Genesis to the Diamond Sūtra

WINDHORSE PUBLICATIONS

Windhorse Publications is a Buddhist charitable company based in the UK. We produce books of high quality that are accessible and relevant to all those interested in Buddhism, at whatever level of interest and commitment. We are the main publisher of Sangharakshita, the founder of the Triratna Buddhist Order and Community. Our books draw on the whole range of the Buddhist tradition, including translations of traditional texts, commentaries, books that make links with contemporary culture and ways of life, biographies of Buddhists, and works on meditation.

To subscribe to the *Complete Works of Sangharakshita,* please go to: windhorsepublications.com/sangharakshita-complete-works/

THE TRIRATNA BUDDHIST COMMUNITY

Windhorse Publications is a part of the Triratna Buddhist Community, an international movement with centres in Europe, India, North and South America and Australasia. At these centres, members of the Triratna Buddhist Order offer classes in meditation and Buddhism. Activities of the Triratna Community also include retreat centres, residential spiritual communities, ethical Right Livelihood businesses, and the Karuna Trust, a UK fundraising charity that supports social welfare projects in the slums and villages of India.

Through these and other activities, Triratna is developing a unique approach to Buddhism, not simply as a philosophy and a set of techniques, but as a creatively directed way of life for all people living in the conditions of the modern world.

For more information please visit thebuddhistcentre.com